Collections for Young Scholars

FRAMEWORK FOR EFFECTIVE TEACHING™

GRADE 6 BOOK 2

PROGRAM AUTHORS
Carl Bereiter
Valerie Anderson
Ann Brown
Marlene Scardamalia
Joe Campione

CONSULTING AUTHORS
Michael Pressley
Iva Carruthers
Bill Pinkney

OPEN COURT PUBLISHING COMPANY
Chicago and Peru, Illinois

TERC
PE

CHAIRMAN
M. Blouke Carus

PRESIDENT
André W. Carus

EDUCATION DIRECTOR
Carl Bereiter

CONCEPT
Barbara Conteh

SENIOR EXECUTIVE EDITOR
Sheelagh McGurn

EXECUTIVE EDITOR
Shirley Graudin

SENIOR PROJECT EDITORS
Wiley Blevins
Linda Cave
Theresa Kryst Fertig
Nancy H. Johnson

PROJECT EDITORS
Joseph Barron
Nita Garvin
Jennifer Johnson
Janette McKenna
Karen Sapp
Ana Tiesman

ASSESSMENT PLANNING
Karen Herzoff

ASSESSMENT DEVELOPMENT
Bernard Fletcher

SUPERVISOR, EDITORIAL SERVICES
Janice Bryant

SENIOR COPYEDITOR
Lucille Alaka

ART DIRECTOR
John Grandits

DESIGN
Diane Hutchinson

**VICE-PRESIDENT, PRODUCTION
AND MANUFACTURING**
Chris Vancalbergh

COVER ARTIST
Beth Peck

Acknowledgments can be found
on page 527 of this book and
are hereby incorporated as part
of this copyright page.

OPEN COURT and ✳ are registered
trademarks of Open Court Publishing Company.

COLLECTIONS FOR YOUNG SCHOLARS and
FRAMEWORK FOR EFFECTIVE TEACHING
are trademarks of Open Court Publishing Company.

Copyright © 1995 Open Court Publishing Company

All rights reserved for all countries.
No part of this work may be reproduced or utilized in
any form or by any means, electronic or mechanical, including
photocopying, recording, or by any information storage or
retrieval system, without the written permission of Open Court
Publishing Company unless such copying is expressly permitted
by federal copyright law. Address requests for permission to
reproduce Open Court material to Permissions Coordinator, Open
Court Publishing Company, 315 Fifth Street, Peru, IL 61354.

Printed in the United States of America

ISBN 0-8126-6200-8

1 2 3 4 5 6 7 8 9 10

CONTENTS

● Award-winning author and/or illustrator
▲ Full-length trade book
■ Dramatized on audiocassette

UNIT 5: ECOLOGY SCIENCE UNIT

●   Award-winning author and/or illustrator

▲   Full-length trade book

■   Dramatized on audiocassette

● Award-winning author and/or illustrator
▲ Full-length trade book
■ Dramatized on audiocassette

Using Open Court's Framework for Effective Teaching™

Contents
for Using
Framework
for Effective
Teaching™

You never get closer to the end of learning; you only get further away from where you began.

—Carl Bereiter

A Program for the 21st Century

Getting Acquainted

Rapid increases in knowledge and technology are making the concept of literacy more and more complex. Basic reading and calculating skills are no longer adequate. Educated graduates will need to evaluate critically what they read; express themselves clearly, in speaking and in writing; understand scientific and mathematical reasoning; keep abreast of increasingly complex technological advances; and work effectively in groups. To meet these needs, our educational system must change.

Collections for Young Scholars™ represents a profound departure from mainstream basal programs. This completely new approach to the teaching of reading focuses on preparing independent, self-motivated critical thinkers who take responsibility for their own learning. Reading, writing, and responding form the basis of an integrated learning environment in which the students interact with and respond to text in purposeful, real-life situations.

Student Outcomes Focus on Intentional Learning

Students who experience *Collections for Young Scholars™*
- Learn how to access information
- Learn how to communicate effectively and share information
- Learn how to work and learn in collaborative groups
- Become independent, self-directed, engaged learners
- Develop high self-esteem
- Learn to value diversity in themselves and others
- Give sustained effort to thinking and learning
- Learn to recognize commonalities among all peoples and cultures

Senior Author Team

If schools are going to change in any direction that's relevant to the future, it has to be in helping students work toward deeper knowledge in whatever they are studying. That's why I'm excited about the research component of this reading series. It's unique in that it does move the students toward deeper and deeper knowledge in some area that they're working on.—Carl Bereiter

Carl Bereiter is Professor at the Centre for Applied Cognitive Science at the Ontario Institute for Studies in Education in Toronto and a member of the National Academy of Education. He has co-authored many curriculum projects, including Open Court's reading and mathematics programs. He is coauthor with Marlene Scardamalia of *The Psychology of Written Composition* (1987) and *Surpassing Ourselves: The Nature and Implications of Expertise* (1993); and he has published extensively on the nature of teaching and learning. Computer-supported intentional learning environments and collaborative knowledge building have been the subjects of his most recent classroom investigations and publications.

Valerie Anderson is Research Associate at the Centre for Applied Cognitive Science at the Ontario Institute for Studies in Education and has had extensive experience both in designing curriculum and in training teachers. Her most recent work with children has centered on helping them learn to use thinking strategies to become independent readers.

Throughout this program, not only does the teacher provide and model strategies . . . , he or she encourages children to bring out their own strategies and to apply them to reading. This is unusual in strategy instruction.—Valerie Anderson

Ann Brown is Professor of Math, Science, and Technology in the Graduate School of Education at the University of California at Berkeley. She was previously associated with the Center for the Study of Reading at the University of Illinois. Dr. Brown, 1993–94 President of the American Educational Research Association (AERA), is an internationally recognized expert in cognitive science. She has published extensively on such topics as memory strategies, reading comprehension, analogical thinking, self-regulated reading, metacognition, and reciprocal teaching. Ann Brown and her colleague Joe Campione are focusing their current research on students as researchers and teachers, a significant aspect of their study of distributed expertise in the classroom.

Students in the research classroom, because they are doing their own research, are free to become expert in something that interests them. Our deliberate intent is that everyone is responsible for some part of the curriculum.—Ann Brown

The notion of bringing the students up to fine literature, to history, to sociology, to astronomy instead of bringing the content down to them is critical both to the program and to the spirit students can develop. It's a real "I can do it" spirit, and indeed they can. And we believe they will with this program.—Marlene Scardamalia

Marlene Scardamalia is Professor and Head of the Centre for Applied Cognitive Science at the Ontario Institute for Studies in Education in Toronto. She is currently a Fellow in the Center for Advanced Study in the Behavioral Sciences at Stanford. Her extensive list of publications includes books, journal articles, and papers focusing on cognitive, developmental, and instructional psychology. She is presently engaged in studies of text-based questioning by children; computer technology for collaborative processes; and collaborative, knowledge-building environments for tomorrow's schools.

Joe Campione is Professor in the School of Education at the University of California at Berkeley. He is also Director of the Berkeley component of the Joint Doctoral Program in Special Education between UC Berkeley and San Francisco State University. Campione has long been known for his work in cognitive development, transfer of learning, individual differences, and assessment. He is working with Ann Brown to discover ways to restructure elementary-school learning environments to take advantage of distributed expertise in the classroom and to use interactive learning to promote scientific literacy within communities of learners.

People aren't happy with the way schools have been run in very traditional ways. We really see a lot of agreement that people want students working on longer-term projects, thinking in depth about things, working collaboratively, and taking responsibility for their own learning. I think that's true of parents, it's true of teachers, and it's true of administrators.—Joe Campione

Consulting Authors

Intentional learning, what's that? Well, it's sort of going around the world as kind of an active, problem-solving thinker. We have become incredibly aware that the best readers, when they're reading, are very active. They're very planful. They're very reactive. They're filtering what they read through prior knowledge. They're thinking about what they're going to do with what they read. The same goes for when they're composing or writing.—Michael Pressley

I think that what we want to always ensure is that there is cultural integrity in the materials that we put before children. It's not having to elevate one's culture over another but affirming that all culture is correct.—Iva Carruthers

You've got to have a dream. And when you have a dream, you've got to find out what it takes to make that dream come true. Everything takes something. There's no free lunch. It's not just going to happen. You're going to have to do something. And, if you're willing to pay that price, you can make the dream a reality.—Bill Pinkney

Michael Pressley is Professor of Educational Psychology and Statistics at the State University of New York at Albany, as well as Principal Investigator for the National Reading Research Center, centralized at the Universities of Maryland and Georgia. He does both basic laboratory research on cognition and learning and applied work in educational settings. Memory development and reading comprehension strategies have received much of his attention.

Iva Carruthers is Professor and former Chairperson of the Sociology Department of Northeastern Illinois University. She is also President of Nexus Unlimited, Inc., a human resources development and computer services consulting firm, and of Ed Tech, a computer software development company. In addition to developing educational software aids for teaching history and interdisciplinary subjects, she has produced fourteen study guides on African-American and African history for students to use in preparing for "Know Your Heritage," a television quiz program she coproduces.

Bill Pinkney is the first African American to sail solo around the world, traveling around the five great capes in his sailboat named *Commitment*. Only forty-one individuals have accomplished this feat. More than 30,000 students across the United States were able to share in his legendary voyage thanks to advanced satellite and computer technologies. Not only did he give these students lessons in math, science, geography, and social studies, but Captain Pinkney also modeled for them the courage, perseverance, skill, and commitment required to realize one's dreams. He has been recognized by the President of the United States and by the governors and legislatures of several states. The story of his exploits has been read into the *Congressional Record* and has been featured in several award-winning television documentaries.

Charles Abate, Ed.D.
Elementary Principal
Orchard Elementary School
Ridgewood, New Jersey

Doris B. Ash, M.S.
Assistant Director
Fostering a Community of Learners Research Project
University of California, Berkeley

Mary Lamon, Ph.D.
Project Director
Middle School Curriculum Development Project
St. Louis Science Center, St. Louis, Missouri

Martha E. Rutherford, M.A.
Assistant Director
Fostering a Community of Learners Research Project
University of California, Berkeley

Barbara Appleberry, *Grade 1*
Mollison Elementary School
Chicago, Illinois

Marie Beacham, *Grade 1*
Ephraim Elementary School
Ephraim, Utah

Joyce Bell, *Grade 1*
Brown School
Newburyport, Massachusetts

Kim Carey, *Grade 6*
Crestmont Elementary School
Northport, Alabama

Peggy Clelland, *Grade 1*
Washington Terrace Elementary
    School
Ogden, Utah

Emmy Daniel, *Grade 1*
South Shores School
Decatur, Illinois

Tony Dillon, *Grade 1*
John Foster Dulles School
Chicago, Illinois

Dorothy Dorsey, *Grade 4*
Glenmount Elementary School
Baltimore, Maryland

Kay Ericksen, *Grade 5*
Ephraim Elementary School
Ephraim, Utah

Debra Evans, *Grade 3*
Goldblatt Elementary School
Chicago, Illinois

Margaret Ewing, *Grade 3*
Abraham Lincoln Elementary
    School
Palm Desert, California

Sr. Susan Faist, *Grade 2*
Christ the King School
Toledo, Ohio

Mary Fatsi, *Grade 1*
Brooklyn Elementary School
Brooklyn, Connecticut

Susan Fowler, *Grade 2*
Yaquina View Elementary School
Newport, Oregon

Bonnie French, *Grade 6*
Carl Sundahl Elementary School
Folsom, California

Lena Gates, *Grade 1*
Crispus Attucks School, P. S. 21
Brooklyn, New York

Lila Gilchrist, *Grade 3*
The Orchard School
Ridgewood, New Jersey

Leticia Gonzalez, *Grade 4*
Saenz Elementary School
Alice, Texas

Lora Gordy, *Grade 5*
Buckingham Elementary School
Berlin, Maryland

Janice Green, *Grade 1*
Francis T. Bresnahan School
Newburyport, Massachusetts

Joyce Haffey, *Grade 4*
St. Therese School
Kansas City, Missouri

Jackie Herath, *Grade 3*
Sunderland Elementary School
Sunderland, Maryland

Dorothy Hines, *Grade 2*
Benefield Elementary School
Lawrenceville, Georgia

Karen Horace, *Grade 6*
Goldblatt Elementary School
Chicago, Illinois

Patricia Horst, *Grade 5*
Harding Elementary School
Clinton, Ohio

Hurtice Howard, *Grade 1*
Julia L. Armstrong Elementary
    School
Greenville, Mississippi

Nancy Hughes, *Grade 2*
Eleanor Roosevelt School
Vancouver, Washington

Celeste James, *Grade 1*
John Foster Dulles School
Chicago, Illinois

Christine Johnson, *Grade 1*
Kelley School
Newburyport, Massachusetts

Patricia Johnson, *Grade 3*
Crispus Attucks School, P. S. 21
Brooklyn, New York

Laurie Jones, *Grade 4*
Grantswood Community School
Birmingham, Alabama

Lisa Kane, *Grade 5*
Disney Magnet Elementary School
Chicago, Illinois

Charlotte Lewis, *Grade 1*
L. B. Weemes Elementary School
Los Angeles, California

Rhet Lickliter, *Grade 6*
Park Tudor School
Indianapolis, Indiana

Sandra Loose, *Grade 1*
Indian Lane Elementary School
Media, Pennsylvania

Frank Lopez, *Grade 5*
Parker Elementary School
Panama City, Florida

Kathryn Lopez, *Grade 1*
Millville Elementary School
Panama City, Florida

Mary Ann Luebbert, *Grade 6*
Russell Elementary School
Hazelwood, Missouri

Ruth MacGregor, *Grade 3*
Mildred M. Fox School
South Paris, Maine

Lynne Malone, *Grade 3*
Carver Elementary School
Dawson, Georgia

Pam Martin, *Grade 1*
L. B. Weemes Elementary School
Los Angeles, California

Melony Maughan, *Grade 1*
Grantswood Community School
Birmingham, Alabama

Ursula McClendon, *Grade 3*
George West Primary School
George West, Texas

Phyllis Miles, *Grade 4*
Our Lady of Mount Carmel
Carmel, Indiana

Sue Miller, *Grade 1*
The Valwood School
Valdosta, Georgia

Nancy Mitchell, *Grade 2*
Pleasant Ridge School
Grass Valley, California

Trudy Mockert, *Grade 1*
Nicolaus Copernicus School, P. S. 25
Jersey City, New Jersey

Anna Molina, *Grade 1*
Ezra Nolan School, P. S. 40
Jersey City, New Jersey

Roberta Montoya, *Grade 3*
Alamosa Elementary School
Albuquerque, New Mexico

Carol Neyman, *Grade 5*
Cotton Boll Elementary School
Peoria, Arizona

Margaret Nichols, *Grade 1*
Brown School
Newburyport, Massachusetts

Cindy Noland, *Grade 2*
Jefferson Elementary School
Parkersburg, West Virginia

Bettye Nunnery, *Grade 2*
Otken Primary School
McComb, Mississippi

Jane Offineer, *Grade 5*
Belden Elementary School
Canton, Ohio

Sara Oliveira, *Grade 5*
Portsmouth Elementary School
Portsmouth, Rhode Island

Kathleen Pabst, *Grade 3*
Charles Drew Elementary School
San Francisco, California

Judith Palermo, *Grade 1*
St. Helen's School
Chicago, Illinois

Terri Patterson, *Grade 4*
Paradise Elementary School
Las Vegas, Nevada

Becky Philips, *Grade 2*
Sunderland Elementary School
Sunderland, Maryland

Donna Powell, *Grade 2*
Melville School
Portsmouth, Rhode Island

Barbara Purcell, *Grade 3*
Education Service Center
Corpus Christi, Texas

Caron Reasor, *Grade 6*
La Quinta Middle School
La Quinta, California

Sharon Robinson, *Grade 2*
Flournoy Elementary School
Los Angeles, California

Kathy Rodger-Sachs, *Grade 4*
The Orchard School
Ridgewood, New Jersey

Judith Roy, *Grade 1*
Grantswood Community School
Birmingham, Alabama

Maxine Rushing, *Grade 4*
Plymouth Day School
Detroit, Michigan

Agnes Schutz, *Grade 1*
Alamosa Elementary School
Albuquerque, New Mexico

Donna Sedlacek, *Grade 3*
Bear Creek Elementary School
Lakewood, Colorado

Ruth Seiger, *Grade 1*
Francis T. Bresnahan School
Newburyport, Massachusetts

Cheryl Sheehan, *Grade 1*
Nicolaus Copernicus School,
   P. S. 25
Jersey City, New Jersey

Margaret Simmons, *Grade 6*
Corpus Christi Elementary School
San Francisco, California

Renee Singer, *Grade 1*
Grantswood Community School
Birmingham, Alabama

Jacqueline Smith, *Grade 1*
John Foster Dulles School
Chicago, Illinois

Patricia Terrell, *Grade 4*
Gatewood Elementary School
Oklahoma City, Oklahoma

Barbara Uhrin, *Grade 2*
Amos Hutchinson Elementary
   School
Greensburg, Pennsylvania

Celia Waddell, *Grade 5*
Grantswood Elementary School
Birmingham, Alabama

Laurie Walters, *Grade 1*
L. B. Weemes Elementary School
Los Angeles, California

Robin Wexler, *Grade 5*
Roosevelt Elementary School
River Edge, New Jersey

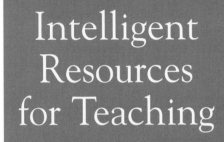

All components of *Collections for Young Scholars*™ are carefully focused on developing self-motivated students who take primary responsibility for their own learning.

Core Teacher Materials

Framework for Effective Teaching™

More and more often, schools are being told that students need to develop skills and strategies that they can use in the real world. They need to work cooperatively. They need to be self-motivated. They need to be responsible for their own learning.

The *Collections for Young Scholars*™ teacher's guide is truly a framework that

- Provides instructional support
- Helps you effectively guide your students toward becoming stategic, independent readers who construct meaning by interacting with and responding to text
- Helps create an integrated learning environment in which students can explore concepts that are relevant to their lives
- Guides you and the students in learning to work cooperatively and efficiently in knowledge-building groups
- Presents models that demonstrate how to turn responsibility for learning over to the students

Creating a Community of Scholars:
An Educator's Handbook for Change

Schools today are charged with educating students for life in the twenty-first century. Research has shown that the most effective learning takes place when the students are engaged in intentional, self-directed learning in an integrated learning environment. *Creating a Community of Scholars: An Educator's Handbook for Change* presents clear guidelines for restructuring the classroom to create a community of scholars in which the students and the teacher are collaborative members. This handbook

- Offers practical guidelines for encouraging students to assume responsibility for their learning
- Outlines the crucial role the teacher plays as both leader and member of this community
- Gives teachers the research base of *Collections for Young Scholars*™
- Serves as an instructional guide for the teaching of *Collections for Young Scholars*™

The Teacher Toolbox

Learning Framework Cards

Many classroom techniques are repeated throughout the program. These learning frameworks provide predictable approaches to instruction that enable students to focus on actual learning without wasting time getting organized for learning. These clear and simple frameworks offer the students invaluable tools that they can easily apply to all new learning.

Outlined on convenient cards stored in the Teacher Toolbox, these learning frameworks include the following:

1. Cognitive and Responsive Reading
   1A. Setting Reading Goals and Expectations
   1B. Responding to Text
   1C. Checking Understanding
   1D. Clarifying Unfamiliar Words and Passages
2. Exploring Through Discussion
3. Exploring Through Reflective Activities
4. Exploring Through Research
   4A. Problem Phase 1 and 2
   4B. Conjecture Phase
   4C. Needs and Plans Phase 1 and 2
5. Independent Workshop
6. Reading Roundtable
7. Writing Process
   7A. Prewriting
   7B. Drafting
   7C. Revising
   7D. Proofreading
   7E. Publishing
8. Writing Seminar

Each Learning Framework Card contains
- A statement of the purpose of the classroom technique
- An explanation of the recommended procedure
- Ways to utilize the technique
- Suggestions for applying each framework in other content areas
- Suggestions for assisting students who are not proficient in English

Teacher Tool Cards

The set of Teacher Tool Cards is an easy-to-use, practical resource designed to support opportunity-driven instruction. These cards
- Provide basic lessons that can be used to *meet the needs of your students at any time, not just during language arts class*
- Provide on-the-spot instruction in skills and conventions that are applicable across the curriculum
- Help you meet students' needs during tutorial sessions
- Contain lessons in Writer's Craft/Reading; Grammar, Mechanics, and Usage; Spelling and Vocabulary; Study and Research; and Phonics at second and third grade
- Provide Classroom Supports to help you encourage essential behaviors in the classroom

Home/School Connection

The stronger the connection between the home and the school, the stronger the student's total educational environment will be. The Home/School Connection is designed to help the students communicate to their families what they are learning and to encourage those at home to become actively involved in exploring the concepts of each unit. The Home/School Connection includes

- Letters written in both English and Spanish explaining the unit concepts
- Activities on which the students and their families can work cooperatively
- Activities that enhance the students' understanding of the concepts
- Bibliographies that lead the students and their families to resources that can help them explore concepts together

Reproducible Masters

The Reproducible Masters allow teachers and students to make choices. You can select the pages that will provide additional practice for students based on their individual needs. The students can select the pages they need for their Writer's Notebook, customizing the notebook to be of the most use. The Reproducible Masters include

- Pages, such as the Vocabulary Exploration form, that can be made available to the students in quantity
- A table of contents and dividers for organizing each student's Writer's Notebook
- Informational pages to be inserted in the Writer's Notebook for future reference in independent writing
- Extensive bibliographies the students can use in their exploration of the concepts
- Extension pages to be used in conjunction with lessons from the Teacher Tool Cards
- Stories for use with the second-grade phonics review

Assessment

The assessment component provides options that let you choose how you want to evaluate your students' progress. Ongoing assessment is accomplished through teacher observation, portfolios, and student self-evaluation. Unique end-of-unit assessments provide cumulative evaluations of the students' progress as well. A special assessment manual, *Formative Assessment: A Teacher's Guide,* is provided in the Teacher Toolbox to explain how to use the various assessment components. These components include

- Teacher's Observation Log
- Self-Assessment Questionnaire
- Portfolio system
- Student anthology unit assessment
- Comprehension Assessment
- Essay and Writing Assessment
- Research Assessment

Core Student Materials

Student Anthologies with Learning Units Designed Around Explorable Concepts

In *Collections for Young Scholars*™, volume 6, book 1, and volume 6, book 2, the students will experience literature that includes time-honored and contemporary classics, as well as award-winning fiction and nonfiction. The reading selections are organized into powerful learning units focused on important, engaging, and complex Explorable Concepts that are designed to encourage the students to think, raise questions, and learn. Each level includes units about topics that are worth exploring. There are three types of learning units:

• Units dealing with social studies

• Units dealing with science

• Units of universal interest

Explorer's Notebook

The focus of *Collections for Young Scholars*™ is on helping students become independent, intentional learners. Each student, individually and as part of a community of learners, works to build a useful body of knowledge as he or she works through the program.

The Explorer's Notebook is designed to help students develop this body of knowledge. Notebook pages are revisited throughout the unit as knowledge is added or expanded. Most pages are designed to be used in

small-group situations in which the students cooperate in recording information. The Explorer's Notebook provides opportunities for students to

- Access their prior knowledge
- Respond to the text
- Record questions they have
- Make connections between and across selections and units
- Plan and organize their research
- Keep a record of and assess their learning throughout the year

Reading/Writing Connection

It is the goal of our program to have students approach all reading with a writer's eye, noting the techniques used to communicate ideas clearly and transferring this insight to their own writing. Each lesson of *Collections for Young Scholars*™ encourages the development of effective writing techniques by having the students examine the methods used by exemplary authors in the selections. The Reading/Writing Connection

- Helps students connect what they read to their own writing
- Provides opportunities for them to note, examine, and comment on examples of good writing techniques

Writer's Notebook

Reading is often treated as wholly separate from writing. An essential aspect of *Collections for Young Scholars*™ is helping students grasp and implement the connection between what they read and what they write. To help solidify this connection, every student is encouraged to keep a Writer's Notebook. The Writer's Notebook becomes an invaluable personalized writing tool for the students in which they

- Record their personal responses to the selections they read
- Compile writing reference materials based on classroom lessons
- Compile their own personal word list from their readings in *Collections for Young Scholars*™ and their outside reading
- Record meaningful examples of writing styles that they would like to incorporate in their own writing
- Record their own writing ideas

Student Toolbox

This component offers students a wide variety of opportunities to take responsibility for their own reading and learning. This invaluable resource, designed for use in a learning center in your classroom, can add immeasurably to the students' independence and motivation.

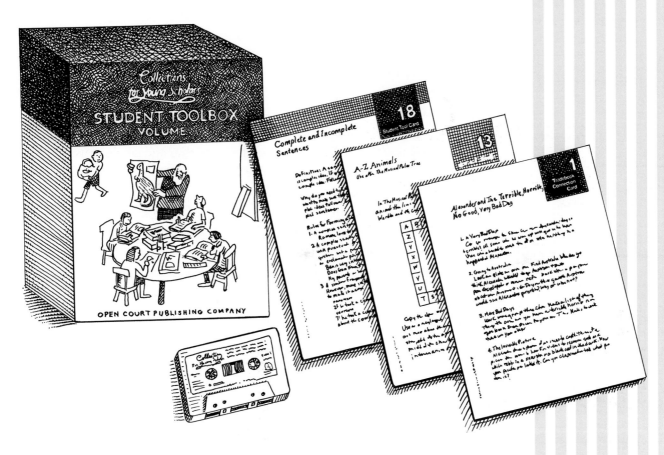

Student Tool Cards

The Student Tool Cards help the students become intentional learners by encouraging them to determine for themselves what they need to know and when they need to know it. These cards

- Are written in appropriate language for students' independent use
- Provide independent instruction and rules for literary techniques, language conventions, spelling and vocabulary, and study and research that students can access as needed
- Guide students in classroom participation
- Can be used individually or in small groups

Cross-curricular Activity Cards

One of the goals of *Collections for Young Scholars* is to help students understand that all learning is interconnected. The Cross-curricular Activity Cards in the Student Toolbox present engaging activities that help students make connections between the selections, the concepts they are exploring, and other areas of the curriculum. There are approximately sixteen included for each unit. Cross-curricular Activity Cards

- Offer independent activities in curricular areas such as art, drama, mathematics, music, science, and social studies
- Are selection related
- Are varied enough to provide interesting activities for all students

- Can be used by individuals or small groups
- Always include a statement of purpose to let students know what they are learning by doing the activity

Tradebook Connection Cards

Adult readers select their own reading material. They interact with text as they read, and they discuss and share passages and whole texts they find particularly interesting. The twelve Tradebook Connection Cards in the Student Toolbox

- Encourage students to become self-directed, interactive readers
- Provide engaging activities to accompany popular tradebooks that your students may choose to read
- Can be used as the basis of the Reading Roundtable discussions that are suggested in *Framework for Effective Teaching*™

Student Support Materials

Writer's Handbook

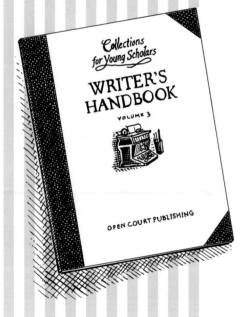

Collections for Young Scholars emphasizes clear, effective communicating through writing. The optional *Writer's Handbook* is designed as an easily accessible writing reference tool for students to keep and use independently. Students are encouraged to look for good examples as they review their own writing and also to look for examples where improvement can be made.

The *Writer's Handbook* contains three sections:

- Write It Well offers pointers for developing a clear and appealing style
- Write It Right explains correct usage
- Writer's Quick Reference provides proofreading checklists, common abbreviations, commonly confused words, commonly misspelled words, spelling generalities, and synonyms

What Can You and Your Students Expect?

Explorable Concepts

In each level of *Collections for Young Scholars*, learning revolves around compelling Explorable Concepts that lead students to pursue personal and collaborative inquiry, to identify and access the information they need, and to communicate their findings to their peers. All students are challenged to stretch and to grow, each at her or his own level.

Two kinds of explorations are included in the program: Exploration Through Research and Exploration Through Reflective Activities. Research units focus on content in areas such as science and social studies. Units of Exploration Through Reflective Activities encourage students to bring their own experiences to familiar themes and, through exploration, to gain a deeper perspective. All units are organized so that each selection adds more information or a different perspective to the students' growing body of knowledge. The students' job is to learn more and to help their peers learn more about the unit concepts.

Exploration Through Research

As they progress through Research units, such as Ecology, the students carry out the phases of the Research Cycle—Problem Phase 1 and 2, the Conjecture Phase, and the Needs and Plans Phase 1 and 2—culminating in their presenting a project that showcases what they have learned. The Explorer's Notebook systematically guides the students through this process, and the Research Cycle poster is provided to remind them of the phases. First, the students determine a **problem** and generate **questions**. They then **conjecture**, or pose their own explanations and theories about the problem. Next, they **determine what they need to know** and what sources of information might be helpful. Finally, individually or in groups, the students plan a project to present what they have learned. For each Research unit, the Explorer's Notebook contains a calendar that the students can fill out to help them pace their work. Together, you and the students can use the calendar to keep track of progress and to remind students of what is yet to be done. The Independent Workshop time is used by the students for their ongoing research, either individually or in collaborative groups.

Exploration Through Reflective Activities

The units for Exploration Through Reflective Activities, such as Music and Musicians, are organized to help students expand their perspectives in familiar areas. As they explore unit concepts, students are involved in activities that extend their experiences and offer opportunities for reflection. Such activities include writing, drama, art, interviews, debates, and panel discussions. Throughout the unit students can be involved in a single project or they can participate in a number of activities. The Independent Workshop time again is used by the students to work on their projects individually or in collaborative groups.

Preparing to Use Collections for Young Scholars™

1 Check Your Materials

You will need the following program materials for each student:

- *Collections for Young Scholars™:* Volume 6, Book 1
- *Collections for Young Scholars™:* Volume 6, Book 2
- Explorer's Notebook, Volume 6
- Reading/Writing Connection, Volume 6
- Writer's Notebook (Each child should keep his or her own Writer's Notebook in a binder or a folder, supplied by either the student or by the school. See the directions for the Writer's Notebook in the Organize Student Materials section that follows.)

In addition, you should have the following:

- *Framework for Effective Teaching™:* Grade 6, Book 1
- *Framework for Effective Teaching™:* Grade 6, Book 2
- *Creating a Community of Scholars: An Educator's Handbook for Change*
- Teacher Toolbox
- Student Toolbox (one per classroom)
- Classroom Instructional Posters (one set)

You will find it helpful to have the following optional component:

- Writer's Handbook (one per student)

2 Become Acquainted with the Instructional Goals

Before you begin *Collections for Young Scholars,* read *Creating a Community of Scholars: An Educator's Handbook for Change.* This resource offers a comprehensive overview of the research, the goals, and the principles that have determined the instructional design of the program.

Clarity and concrete support for helping students become intentional, self-directed learners were primary goals in the writing of the lessons contained in *Framework for Effective Teaching.* In addition, all lessons were thoroughly reviewed by panels of teachers actively involved in the classroom. Both the **Scope and Sequence Chart, pages 502–507,** and the **Index, pages 528–532,** can give a **quick overview** of the lessons covered in *Framework for Effective Teaching.* These can help you in meeting the needs of your students.

Pages 32F–49F contain an annotated unit overview and an annotated lesson to help you organize your daily plans.

3 Organize Your Teaching Materials

Teacher Toolbox   The Teacher Toolbox serves as easily accessible storage for your instructional materials. In it you will find Teacher Tool Cards, Learning Framework Cards, assessment materials, the Home/School Connection, Reproducible Masters, and a set of dividers. Unpack the materials and use the dividers to organize the box. See pages 20F–22F for descriptions of these materials. To help you familiarize yourself with the contents, each section divider contains a list of the cards that can be found in that section.

4 Set Up Your Classroom

Concept Board and Question Board   One of the primary goals of *Collections for Young Scholars* is to help you and your students form a community of scholars. In order to do this, communicating and sharing questions and knowledge is essential. The Concept Board and the Question Board can facilitate this communication and publicize what is learned.

Plan to set aside two areas where the students can post information. If you don't have bulletin board space, two large charts can be posted where they are accessible to students. One of these boards should be designated the Concept Board and the other the Question Board. It is also a good idea to have on hand a large supply of self-stick notepads for use with these boards.

The students should share their growing knowledge about unit concepts on the Concept Board. Here they can post relevant news clippings, magazine articles, or ideas that help expand the growing body of knowledge about the unit concepts. As they progress through the unit, this board also serves as a place where common interests become evident. The students can use these interests to form collaborative groups to explore their ideas.

Throughout this program, the students are encouraged to take responsibility for their own learning. The Concept Board is one of the vehicles used to promote individual responsibility. The Question Board is another. As the students read selections in the unit or materials they find on their own, they post questions they have about their reading or the concepts in general. In this way, questions are no longer considered problems. They now become opportunities to grow and learn. All class members will know the questions interesting their peers. Questions become the springboard to further exploration and learning.

The students can write their questions directly on the board, pin them to the board, or use self-stick notes to present them. It is recommended that the students sign or initial their questions. In this way, students can see who is interested in the same questions they are. Collaborative groups can easily be formed around the categorizing of identical or related questions.

As the students progress with their exploration, questions should be reevaluated. Perhaps they will be answered. Perhaps they won't. Often these initial queries will lead the students to further questions. Sometimes they will become irrelevant to the larger issues involved with the concepts.

Both the Concept Board and the Question Board are focal to the explorations taking place in each unit. The boards are dynamic; they change constantly. They serve both as a reference point and as a repository for individual and group questions. They become the public declaration of the work and growing knowledge of the group.

Posters   Learning should never be a secret process. We strive at all times to let the students know what they are learning and why they are learning it. The more public we make tools for learning, the more likely the students will become adept at using them.

Collections for Young Scholars™ offers a set of posters that help to make public those strategies and processes that will help the students become effective readers, writers, and learners. These posters include
- Reading strategies
- Writing strategies
- The phases of the writing process
- The phases of the research cycle
- A menu of projects and activities that can help in exploring and sharing ideas in units on universal topics
- Discussion starters

Display the posters where they can be clearly seen by the students so they can use this information independently as they need it. The posters are reproduced in the Explorer's Notebook or in the Reading/Writing Connection. As poster content is introduced in the lessons, there will be a reminder to review the poster with the students. The posters then remain as a constant aid to the students as they read, write, research, and learn in all areas of the curriculum.

5 Organize Student Materials

Writer's Notebook   Reproducible Master 6 contains this Table of Contents for the Writer's Notebook:

- Writing Ideas
- Personal Dictionary
- Author's Style
- Story Elements
- Genres
- Checking My Work
- My Response Journal

Reproducible Masters 7–13 contain section dividers that can be copied for each student. These dividers list the sections that are suggested for the notebook. The sections entitled Writing Ideas and My Response Journal can contain blank notebook paper. The students may add more pages as needed. Keep a supply of copies of the Vocabulary Exploration form, Reproducible Master 15, for the students to use to add words to the Personal Dictionary section. The Teacher's Guide contains instructions for other Reproducible Masters that can be added to the remaining sections of the Writer's Notebook.

The students will need a three-ring binder and a set of dividers. If the student or the school is unable to provide the binder and dividers, the students can use a folder with brass clasps.

Student Toolbox   The Student Toolbox contains Cross-curricular Activity Cards, Tradebook Connection Cards, Student Tool Cards, a Listening Library Audiocassette, and a set of dividers. Unpack the cards and use the dividers to organize the box.

Place the Student Toolbox in an area where the students will have access to it during Independent Workshop and other times when they can choose their own activities. Explain the kinds of cards available in the box.

Each section divider contains a list of all the cards in that section. The divider for the Tradebook Connection section lists all the books included on the Tradebook Connection Cards. You may want to locate copies of these books in your school or local library and make them available to the students.

Annotated Lesson

Presented here is an annotated lesson, designed to help you use this guide as efficiently and effectively as possible. This version of lesson 3, "Linnea's Almanac: January," in grade 3, unit 5, takes you point-by-point through a typical lesson, showing you where to locate all the information you'll need for planning and conducting lessons and assessing the progress of your students. The annotations also explain how to find and interpret important author, illustrator, and selection information that you may want to share with your students and their families.

1 Each **selection** in the unit is listed along with its **genre**, **author**, and **illustrator**.

2 Each selection has been chosen to add another perspective or to contribute new information that can be explored about the concepts.

3 A bullet (•) indicates an **award-winning** author and/or illustrator.

4 A triangle (▲) indicates the reproduction of a **full-length trade book**.

5 Each unit contains one selection that is designated especially for **independent reading**. During this lesson, the students demonstrate their ability to use strategies independently and to conduct discussions and skills lessons.

6 Every unit contains reproductions of **fine-art** pieces that add a further dimension to the unit concepts.

7 A square (■) indicates that a selection is dramatized on the **Listening Library Audiocassette**.

8 One selection in each unit is designed to be used for **assessment** of the students' growing knowledge of the concepts. The focus of these assessments is on connecting new knowledge to existing knowledge.

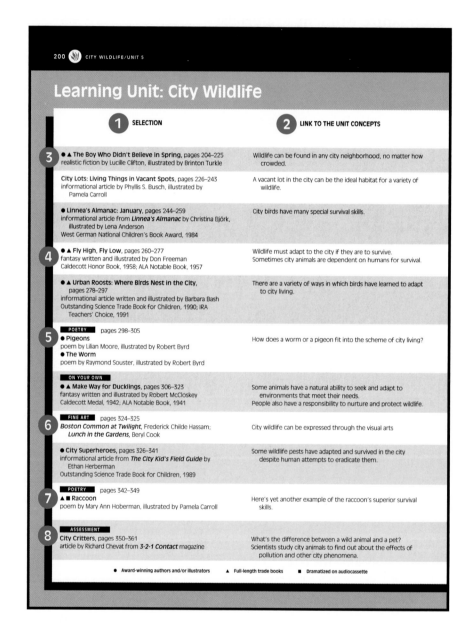

200   CITY WILDLIFE/UNIT 5

Learning Unit: City Wildlife

1 SELECTION	**2** LINK TO THE UNIT CONCEPTS
3 • ▲ The Boy Who Didn't Believe in Spring, pages 204–225 realistic fiction by Lucille Clifton, illustrated by Brinton Turkle	Wildlife can be found in any city neighborhood, no matter how crowded.
City Lots: Living Things in Vacant Spots, pages 226–243 informational article by Phyllis S. Busch, illustrated by Pamela Carroll	A vacant lot in the city can be the ideal habitat for a variety of wildlife.
• Linnea's Almanac: January, pages 244–259 informational article from *Linnea's Almanac* by Christina Björk, illustrated by Lena Anderson West German National Children's Book Award, 1984	City birds have many special survival skills.
4 • ▲ Fly High, Fly Low, pages 260–277 fantasy written and illustrated by Don Freeman Caldecott Honor Book, 1958; ALA Notable Book, 1957	Wildlife must adapt to the city if they are to survive. Sometimes city animals are dependent on humans for survival.
• ▲ Urban Roosts: Where Birds Nest in the City, pages 278–297 informational article written and illustrated by Barbara Bash Outstanding Science Trade Book for Children, 1990; IRA Teachers' Choice, 1991	There are a variety of ways in which birds have learned to adapt to city living.
5 POETRY pages 298–305 • Pigeons poem by Lilian Moore, illustrated by Robert Byrd • The Worm poem by Raymond Souster, illustrated by Robert Byrd	How does a worm or a pigeon fit into the scheme of city living?
ON YOUR OWN • ▲ Make Way for Ducklings, pages 306–323 fantasy written and illustrated by Robert McCloskey Caldecott Medal, 1942; ALA Notable Book, 1941	Some animals have a natural ability to seek and adapt to environments that meet their needs. People also have a responsibility to nurture and protect wildlife.
6 FINE ART pages 324–325 *Boston Common at Twilight*, Frederick Childe Hassam; *Lunch in the Gardens*, Beryl Cook	City wildlife can be expressed through the visual arts
• City Superheroes, pages 326–341 informational article from *The City Kid's Field Guide* by Ethan Herberman Outstanding Science Trade Book for Children, 1989	Some wildlife pests have adapted and survived in the city despite human attempts to eradicate them.
7 POETRY pages 342–349 ▲ ■ Raccoon poem by Mary Ann Hoberman, illustrated by Pamela Carroll	Here's yet another example of the raccoon's superior survival skills.
8 ASSESSMENT City Critters, pages 350–361 article by Richard Chevat from *3-2-1 Contact* magazine	What's the difference between a wild animal and a pet? Scientists study city animals to find out about the effects of pollution and other city phenomena.

● Award-winning authors and/or illustrators   ▲ Full-length trade books   ■ Dramatized on audiocassette

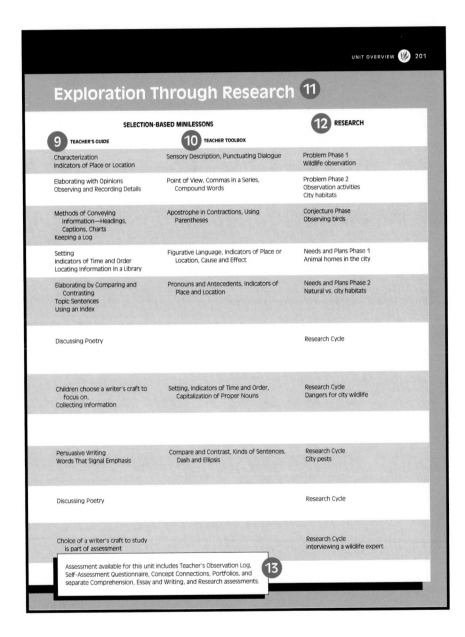

Exploration Through Research ⑪

SELECTION-BASED MINILESSONS   ⑫ **RESEARCH**

⑨ TEACHER'S GUIDE	⑩ TEACHER TOOLBOX	RESEARCH
Characterization Indicators of Place or Location	Sensory Description, Punctuating Dialogue	Problem Phase 1 Wildlife observation
Elaborating with Opinions Observing and Recording Details	Point of View, Commas in a Series, Compound Words	Problem Phase 2 Observation activities City habitats
Methods of Conveying Information—Headings, Captions, Charts Keeping a Log	Apostrophe in Contractions, Using Parentheses	Conjecture Phase Observing birds
Setting Indicators of Time and Order Locating Information in a Library	Figurative Language, Indicators of Place or Location, Cause and Effect	Needs and Plans Phase 1 Animal homes in the city
Elaborating by Comparing and Contrasting Topic Sentences Using an Index	Pronouns and Antecedents, Indicators of Place and Location	Needs and Plans Phase 2 Natural vs. city habitats
Discussing Poetry		Research Cycle
Children choose a writer's craft to focus on. Collecting Information	Setting, Indicators of Time and Order, Capitalization of Proper Nouns	Research Cycle Dangers for city wildlife
Persuasive Writing Words That Signal Emphasis	Compare and Contrast, Kinds of Sentences, Dash and Ellipsis	Research Cycle City pests
Discussing Poetry		Research Cycle
Choice of a writer's craft to study is part of assessment		Research Cycle interviewing a wildlife expert

Assessment available for this unit includes Teacher's Observation Log, Self-Assessment Questionnaire, Concept Connections, Portfolios, and separate Comprehension, Essay and Writing, and Research assessments. ⑬

---

⑨ **Selection-Based Instruction** is included within the Reading with a Writer's Eye portion of every lesson in the Teacher's Guide. You may use this instruction, or select from the Options for Instruction.

⑩ The contents of the Teacher Toolbox provide support for opportunity-driven instruction. Choose those lessons you believe are the most valuable. The **Options for Instruction** are based on selection text; however, you may choose any minilessons you wish based on your students' needs and/or district requirements. These lessons appear on **Teacher Tool Cards** in the **Teacher Toolbox** for your use whenever the need arises.

⑪ Each grade presents two ways of exploring the unit concepts: through **research** and through **reflective activities.** The kind of exploration expected from the students differs for each type of unit.

⑫ In research units involving science and social studies content, students progress through the **Research Cycle.**

⑬ A number of **assessment options** for each unit are available in the Assessment Module of the Teacher Toolbox. They are designed to actively involve both students and teachers in creating an atmosphere conducive to authentic assessment of the students' growing ability.

1 **Link to the Unit Concepts** explains the connections between this selection and the concepts discussed in the unit introduction. Each selection has been carefully chosen to add to the students' increasing understanding and knowledge of the unit topic and unit concepts.

Linnea's Almanac: January

1 READING THE SELECTION
INFORMATION FOR THE TEACHER

About the Selection

This entry from a fictional almanac is an excellent format for exploring ways to help birds through the winter. Young Linnea, the narrator, offers suggestions for opening a "bird restaurant." She writes about the proper food for various species and gives "fun facts" about bird habits and needs. The friendly, informal tone makes this informational selection engaging and easy to follow.

1 Link to the Unit Concepts

"Linnea's Almanac: January," pages 120–123, tells about the special survival skills of city birds. These include getting a helping hand from human city dwellers in the winter. It also illustrates how a nature-lover can find plenty of nature to love in an urban environment. After reading this selection, the children may wonder why birds are so successful at city living and whether they could survive in the city without people.

About the Author

Christina Björk, born and raised in Stockholm, Sweden, is a writer and journalist who is best known for her three books about a girl named Linnea. In the first Linnea book, *Linnea in Monet's Garden,* the girl develops a love of gardening as she finds out about the famous French painter. The next in the series, *Linnea's Windowsill Garden,* was an ALA Notable Book. *Linnea's Almanac,* from which this selection is taken, won the West German National Children's Book Award in 1984.

Björk designed the Linnea books to give young readers a knowledge of plants and animals. As A. R. Williams writes in the February 1990 issue of *Junior Bookshelf,* Björk's young heroine is "a city girl who brings the countryside into her home and heart." Björk has written numerous books for children, including *Fiffi and Birger and Left and Right* and *Elliot's Extraordinary Cookbook.* She also writes for Swedish television and contributes to various Swedish magazines.

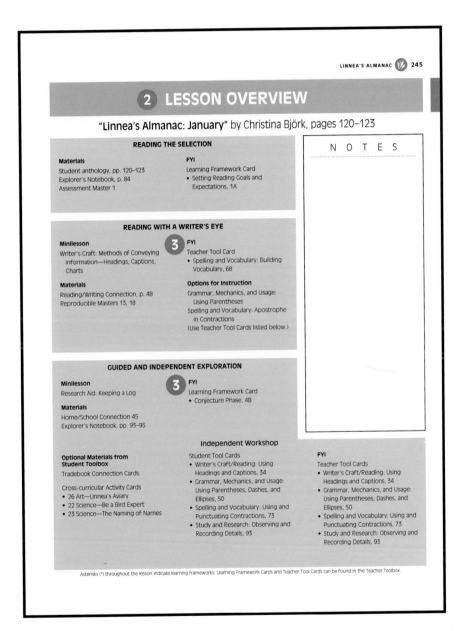

2 LESSON OVERVIEW

"Linnea's Almanac: January" by Christina Björk, pages 120–123

READING THE SELECTION

Materials
Student anthology, pp. 120–123
Explorer's Notebook, p. 84
Assessment Master 1

FYI
Learning Framework Card
• Setting Reading Goals and
  Expectations, 1A

NOTES

READING WITH A WRITER'S EYE

Minilesson
Writer's Craft: Methods of Conveying
  Information—Headings, Captions,
  Charts

Materials
Reading/Writing Connection, p. 48
Reproducible Masters 13, 18

3 FYI
Teacher Tool Card
• Spelling and Vocabulary: Building
  Vocabulary, 68

Options for Instruction
Grammar, Mechanics, and Usage:
  Using Parentheses
Spelling and Vocabulary: Apostrophe
  in Contractions
(Use Teacher Tool Cards listed below.)

GUIDED AND INDEPENDENT EXPLORATION

Minilesson
Research Aid: Keeping a Log

Materials
Home/School Connection 45
Explorer's Notebook, pp. 93–95

3 FYI
Learning Framework Card
• Conjecture Phase, 4B

Independent Workshop

**Optional Materials from
Student Toolbox**

Tradebook Connection Cards

Cross-curricular Activity Cards
• 26 Art—Linnea's Aviary
• 22 Science—Be a Bird Expert
• 23 Science—The Naming of Names

Student Tool Cards
• Writer's Craft/Reading: Using
  Headings and Captions, 34
• Grammar, Mechanics, and Usage:
  Using Parentheses, Dashes, and
  Ellipses, 50
• Spelling and Vocabulary: Using and
  Punctuating Contractions, 73
• Study and Research: Observing and
  Recording Details, 93

FYI
Teacher Tool Cards
• Writer's Craft/Reading: Using
  Headings and Captions, 34
• Grammar, Mechanics, and Usage:
  Using Parentheses, Dashes, and
  Ellipses, 50
• Spelling and Vocabulary: Using and
  Punctuating Contractions, 73
• Study and Research: Observing and
  Recording Details, 93

Asterisks (*) throughout the lesson indicate learning frameworks. Learning Framework Cards and Teacher Tool Cards can be found in the Teacher Toolbox.

---

2 Each **Lesson Overview** provides a quick look at what you can expect while working with the unit. The Lesson Overview is organized to reflect the three standard parts of each lesson.

• **Reading the Selection** indicates student anthology pages and Explorer's Notebook pages used in the lesson.

• **Reading with a Writer's Eye** indicates minilessons included in the lesson and the materials needed for working on those minilessons. **Options for Instruction** are also offered to help you tailor your curriculum planning to your individual classes.

• **Guided and Independent Exploration** contains information about minilessons presented in this section of the lesson, along with materials references and Student Toolbox materials appropriate to the lesson.

3 FYI (For Your Information) indicates relevant Teacher Tool Cards and Learning Framework Cards that might be helpful in teaching the lesson.

1 Information that is pertinent to the understanding of a selection or that would enhance the students' enjoyment of the selection is provided before the students begin reading.

2 **Learning Frameworks** such as Cognitive and Responsive Reading are indicated with an asterisk (*). Additional information for each learning framework can be found on the Learning Framework Cards stored in the Teacher Toolbox.

3 The **students** are encouraged to **make choices** about how to read the selections. The recommendations found here can help you help the students make that decision.

4 As the year progresses, students should be taking more and more responsibility for their own learning. **Steps Toward Independence** help you gauge the students' independence.

About the Illustrator

Lena Anderson frequently collaborates with Christina Björk, with whom she shares a studio in downtown Stockholm. Anderson began her career as an art director, producing both books and magazines. After writing and illustrating her first children's book in 1971, she has gone on to win many prestigious European children's book prizes.

1 INFORMATION FOR THE STUDENT

Tell the children that "Linnea's Almanac: January" was written by Christina Björk and illustrated by Lena Anderson. You might want to share with the children A. R. Williams's comment about the character of Linnea, and have them discuss what he may have meant. As appropriate, share other information about the author and illustrator.

As they prepare to read the selection, you may want to alert the children to the unusual nature of the text. "Linnea's Almanac: January" does not fit into conventional genre categories. Since the character of Linnea is fictional, the selection might be categorized as fiction. However, its purpose is to convey information about wildlife, and it has several features found in expository texts (section headings, captions, a chart). In this sense, "Linnea's Almanac: January" is nonfiction.

Note: When discussing or reading it with the children, treat the selection as an informational text and avoid using the terms *fiction* and *nonfiction*.

2 * COGNITIVE AND RESPONSIVE READING

Activating Prior Knowledge

Ask the children what they know about almanacs. Allow volunteers to share experiences they have had in reading or using an almanac. If possible, have an almanac available so that the children can see what kind of information it contains and how it is organized.

Setting Reading Goals and Expectations

Have the children **browse the selection** and use the clues/problems/wondering procedure. They will return to these observations after reading. For a review of **browsing**, see **Learning Framework Card 1A, Setting Reading Goals and Expectations.**

3 **Recommendations for Reading the Selection**

Allow the children to decide how they wish to read this selection. Because of its informal tone and informational purpose, paired oral readings are suggested. Partners can take turns "giving" each other Linnea's advice. When they come to the chart, they can pause to examine it together.

During oral reading, use and encourage think-alouds. During silent reading, allow discussion as needed. Discuss problems, strategies, and reactions after reading.

This would also be a good selection for **responding to text by wondering** while reading aloud. Model this response, and then invite the children to do the same.

STEPS TOWARD INDEPEDENCE By this time in the year, the children should be able to make wise decisions about the most appropriate way to read the selection.

4

---

5 About the Reading Strategies

The children will soon discover that Linnea herself wonders about things ("I wonder who will come to my restaurant"). As they get to know this character and find out what she has to say about city birds, the children may find themselves **wondering** how Linnea learned about birds, for example, or how birds keep warm in winter. Since the selection includes section headings and a chart that conveys important information, the children may also find it useful to **sum up** what they learn in each section or from the chart.

Remind the children to work together to clear up anything in the text that confuses or puzzles them and to refer to the **reading strategy posters** if they need help.

7 **TEACHING TIP** Model various strategies for working out reading problems, and invite the children to apply them.

6 Think-Aloud Prompts for Use in Oral Reading

The think-aloud prompts with the page miniatures are merely suggestions of ways to deal with the text and help the children use the strategies. Remind the children to use whatever strategies they need to help them understand the selection. Refer them to the reading strategy posters if necessary. Encourage them to share the strategies they use as they read.

5 Helping students become mature strategic readers is one of the goals of this program. The different reading strategies are introduced and discussed in **About the Reading Strategies**.

6 **Think-Aloud Prompts** are included with the selection page miniatures. These prompts are placed where the students may need to use the reading strategies. The prompts are only suggestions for handling these text situations. The response of your class should always determine when and why the strategies are used.

7 **Teaching Tips** give you reminders and special teaching hints as you progress through each lesson.

1 **Think-Aloud Prompts** are included to help you encourage the students to think strategically as they read. As you and the students model this thinking, students learn to use this process independently.

2 For your convenience, prompt references are clearly marked on miniature pages of the student text.

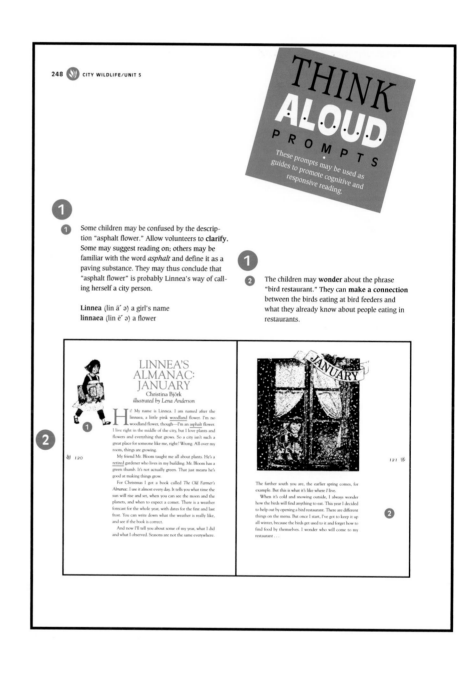

3 Making thinking public can help the students understand how to use the strategies as they read. After reading the selections, the students are encouraged to discuss and share their **strategy use.** They are also encouraged to develop their own strategies and to share them with their classmates.

THE ART OF FEEDING WINTER BIRDS

3 Remember: Never stop feeding the birds until winter is over. But don't start too early either, because then you might fool some migratory birds into staying, and they can't stand the cold. I usually start around Christmastime (a little earlier if it's really cold). In the city, you can't put out food for the birds on the ground (then the rats come), so I feed them from my window.

Birdhouses aren't as good as bird feeders, where the birds can sit around the edge without getting their droppings into the food. Bird droppings can spread diseases, such as salmonellosis (food poisoning), that birds most often die of.

Seeds for a feeder are sold at plant nurseries, pet stores, or supermarkets. Feeders have to be refilled every now and then.

Pigeons, crows, magpies, and gulls eat everything they're offered.

Other bird goodies: unshelled peanuts, apple cores, coconut halves, or nuts (in a plastic net) on a string.

Dangerous for birds: moldy, spicy or salty foods!

THIS IS HOW CITY BIRDS LIVE

If you think how warm a down jacket is, then you'll understand how warmly "dressed" birds are with all their down and feathers. But the smaller a bird is, the more it has to eat to survive the winter. A little bird has to eat twice its weight every day. That much "fuel" is needed to keep its tiny body warm.

5 In the winter, food is hard to find. There are no insects (they're sleeping), no seeds (they're buried under the snow), and no water (it's turned to ice). That's why many birds fly to warmer places for the winter. But some stay, in spite of everything. They've learned survival tricks, such as moving into the city and getting on "bird welfare" in the parks and by the water, where they are fed.

I usually go to one place where the water never freezes. Seven sacks of food are put out for the birds there every day during the colder months. But the sacks are not filled just with bread crumbs—that would make the birds sick. Birdseed, suet, and lime are added, so the birds will get their vitamins.

I usually bring my own bag with fresh bread, boiled potatoes, chopped white cabbage or lettuce, and birdseed.

Some birds are marked with a numbered band on one leg. That way you can see if the same bird returns year after year. One swan came back every year for twenty years! But that was a record for swans.

Feed water birds in the water! Don't try to get them to come up on land, where they can be run over.

---

3 If they are confused by the section heading, the children may need to **clarify** the word *art*. It is used here to mean "skill," something a person learns how to do. Encourage the children to use the headings in informational text to check their understanding.

4 The children may need to clarify that in this section head, *live* means to "survive," which is the focus of this selection.

5 Some children, especially those whose first language is not English, may be confused by the quotation marks around words that are being used in a metaphorical sense—such as "dressed" and "fuel." They may ask for **clarification.** If necessary, allow volunteers to **interpret** the meanings of these words and then to suggest how the words might be applied to birds—in this case, to their feathers and to the food they eat to keep alive.

Discussing Strategy Use

Invite the children to share and discuss the reading strategies that they used. For example, those who used headings and chart information to sum up may share how doing this helped them grasp the information presented in the selection. **3**

1 Students **explore** selections **through** a framework of **discussion** that includes a general response to the text; a return to the clues, problems, and wonderings recorded as part of browsing before reading; and making connections between the selection and the unit concepts.

2 As a group, **students reflect** on the selection and return to the clues, problems, and wonderings recorded before reading. They raise any additional questions and discuss wonderings that they want to pursue.

3 **Discussion ideas** are presented to help you assess the students general understanding of the selection.

4 Students are encouraged to always record their impressions of the selection in their **Response Journals.**

5 When students have discussed the selection and their reaction to it, they form **small groups** and **discuss connections** between the selection and the unit concepts.

6 Small groups share their **discussion of the connections** with one another. Similarities and differences of opinion are discussed and the **links** between the selection and unit concepts take shape.

7 For your convenience, possible links to the explorable concepts are noted.

8 The students record their ideas and questions on the **Concept Board** and the **Question Board.**

9 The students are encouraged to make connections between the selection and the works of art illustrated in the **fine-art feature** included in every unit.

10 The students point out and discuss how each selection fits into the unit as a whole and what each selection adds to the understanding of unit concepts.

11 For your convenience, possible connections to other selections in the unit are noted. Students are also encouraged to make connections across units.

12 As a conclusion to each discussion, the students **evaluate the discussion** and comment on its value to their exploration of the unit concepts.

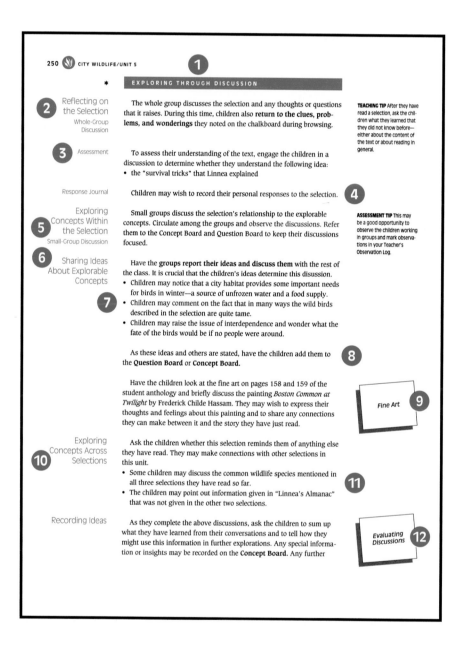

250 CITY WILDLIFE/UNIT 5 **1**

EXPLORING THROUGH DISCUSSION

2 Reflecting on the Selection
Whole-Group Discussion

The whole group discusses the selection and any thoughts or questions that it raises. During this time, children also **return to the clues, problems, and wonderings** they noted on the chalkboard during browsing.

TEACHING TIP After they have read a selection, ask the children what they learned that they did not know before—either about the content of the text or about reading in general.

3 Assessment

To assess their understanding of the text, engage the children in a discussion to determine whether they understand the following idea:
• the "survival tricks" that Linnea explained

Response Journal

Children may wish to record their personal responses to the selection. **4**

5 Exploring Concepts Within the Selection
Small-Group Discussion

Small groups discuss the selection's relationship to the explorable concepts. Circulate among the groups and observe the discussions. Refer them to the Concept Board and Question Board to keep their discussions focused.

ASSESSMENT TIP This may be a good opportunity to observe the children working in groups and mark observations in your Teacher's Observation Log.

6 Sharing Ideas About Explorable Concepts

7

Have the **groups report their ideas and discuss them** with the rest of the class. It is crucial that the children's ideas determine this disussion.
• Children may notice that a city habitat provides some important needs for birds in winter—a source of unfrozen water and a food supply.
• Children may comment on the fact that in many ways the wild birds described in the selection are quite tame.
• Children may raise the issue of interdependence and wonder what the fate of the birds would be if no people were around.

As these ideas and others are stated, have the children add them to the **Question Board** or **Concept Board.** **8**

Have the children look at the fine art on pages 158 and 159 of the student anthology and briefly discuss the painting *Boston Common at Twilight* by Frederick Childe Hassam. They may wish to express their thoughts and feelings about this painting and to share any connections they can make between it and the story they have just read.

Fine Art **9**

10 Exploring Concepts Across Selections

Ask the children whether this selection reminds them of anything else they have read. They may make connections with other selections in this unit.
• Some children may discuss the common wildlife species mentioned in all three selections they have read so far.
• The children may point out information given in "Linnea's Almanac" that was not given in the other two selections.

11

Recording Ideas

As they complete the above discussions, ask the children to sum up what they have learned from their conversations and to tell how they might use this information in further explorations. Any special information or insights may be recorded on the **Concept Board.** Any further

Evaluating Discussions **12**

Recording Concept Information continued

"Linnea's Almanac: January" by Christina Björk

_____
_____
_____
_____
_____

Fly High, Fly Low by Don Freeman

_____
_____
_____
_____
_____

Urban Roosts: Where Birds Nest in the City by Barbara Bash

_____
_____
_____
_____
_____

84 EN   City Wildlife/Unit 5

Explorer's Notebook, page 84

questions that they would like to think about, pursue, or investigate may be recorded on the **Question Board.** They may want to discuss the progress that has been made on their questions. They may also want to cross out any questions that no longer warrant consideration.

❯ The children should record their ideas and impressions about the selection on page 84 of their Explorer's Notebook.

2 READING WITH A WRITER'S EYE
MINILESSON

16 Writer's Craft: Methods of Conveying Information— Headings, Captions, Charts

Ask the children to talk about ways in which authors convey information and to give any examples they can from their reading or writing. Mention to the children that author Christina Björk uses several common devices to convey important points. These devices are often used in expository, or informational, texts.

Explain that **an author can convey information to the reader in different ways.** The main one, of course, is in paragraphs of text. Another is through the use of **headings, captions,** and **charts.** Have the children mention examples of the latter from their readings in other subject areas.

---

13 As they proceed through the lessons, the students are constantly updating the **Concept Board** and the **Question Board.**

14 Miniature pages of the student ancillaries provide you with the convenience of seeing what the students will be working on in conjunction with the various parts of the lesson.

The **Explorer's Notebook** helps the students to progress through their exploration and research.

15 Students are encouraged to always look for examples of writing techniques in their reading and to use these techniques in their own writing.

16 All **Writer's Craft** and writing minilessons depend entirely on selection content, thus providing your students with a wealth of examples to reinforce the lesson content.

Each lesson overview lists Teacher Tool Cards, stored in the Teacher Toolbox, that contain alternate lessons. The needs of your class should determine the lessons you choose to teach.

1 As a group, the students find and **discuss** the selection author's use of **writing techniques and conventions.** Not until these techniques and conventions are thoroughly discussed are students asked to work independently.

2 Students use their **Reading/Writing Connection** books to continue their study of the author's use of writing techniques. In continuing their study and discussions, the students may choose to work alone or in small groups.

3 **The Reading/Writing Connection** gives students the opportunity to identify, analyze, and discuss examples of writing techniques found not only in the student anthology but also in their other reading.

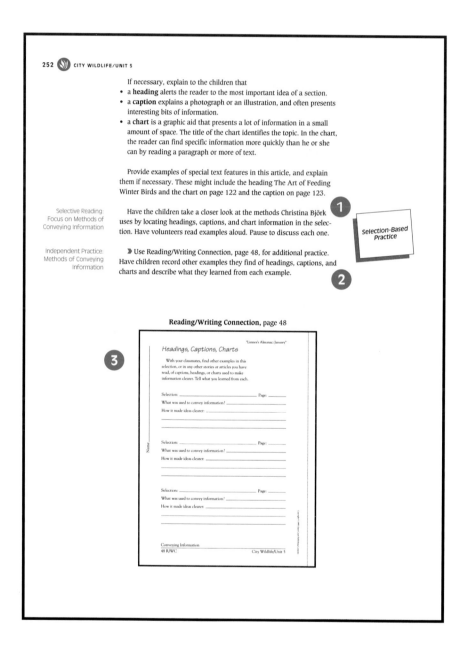

If necessary, explain to the children that
- a **heading** alerts the reader to the most important idea of a section.
- a **caption** explains a photograph or an illustration, and often presents interesting bits of information.
- a **chart** is a graphic aid that presents a lot of information in a small amount of space. The title of the chart identifies the topic. In the chart, the reader can find specific information more quickly than he or she can by reading a paragraph or more of text.

Provide examples of special text features in this article, and explain them if necessary. These might include the heading The Art of Feeding Winter Birds and the chart on page 122 and the caption on page 123.

Selective Reading: Focus on Methods of Conveying Information

Have the children take a closer look at the methods Christina Björk uses by locating headings, captions, and chart information in the selection. Have volunteers read examples aloud. Pause to discuss each one.

Independent Practice: Methods of Conveying Information

➤ Use Reading/Writing Connection, page 48, for additional practice. Have children record other examples they find of headings, captions, and charts and describe what they learned from each example.

Selection-Based Practice

Reading/Writing Connection, page 48

"Linnea's Almanac: January"

Headings, Captions, Charts

With your classmates, find other examples in this selection, or in any other stories or articles you have read, of captions, headings, or charts used to make information clearer. Tell what you learned from each.

Selection: _____ Page: _____
What was used to convey information? _____
How it made ideas clearer: _____
_____

Selection: _____ Page: _____
What was used to convey information? _____
How it made ideas clearer: _____
_____

Selection: _____ Page: _____
What was used to convey information? _____
How it made ideas clearer: _____
_____

Conveying Information
48 R/WC   City Wildlife/Unit 5

WRITING

④ Linking Reading to Writing

Continue discussing ways of conveying information by having the children think about their own writing. Ask them how they might use each of these devices in putting together a report on city wildlife.

❯ Suggest that they add these ideas to their copy of Reproducible Master 18, Writing Ideas, in the Writing Ideas section of their **Writer's Notebook.** Have available additional copies of Reproducible Master 18 if necessary.

Then encourage the children to do any or all of the following:
- Look through their informational writing (including reports or displays) for good examples of the use of headings, captions, or charts and add them to their Writer's Notebook.
- See if there are places in their writing where the information might be clearer if headings were added, a chart were used, and/or captions were included.
- Revise an existing informational piece from their writing folder or begin a new piece, using headings, captions, and charts.

⑤ * Writing Process

Suggest to the children that they try writing a new informational piece that describes a time of year. Encourage them to use headings, captions, and/or charts in their writing. Remind them to use the writing process as they develop this new piece.

Reproducible Master 18

Writing Ideas

Ideas for _____

	Idea	Check if used
1.		
2.		
3.		
4.		
5.		
6.		
7.		
8.		
9.		
10.		

RM 18 — Writer's Notebook: Writing Ideas

④ Students are always asked to link to their writing what they learned from the minilessons. By applying what they have learned to their own writing, the students are given the opportunity to immediately reinforce this new learning.

⑤ The students are introduced to and encouraged to use the **phases of the writing process** as they produce their own pieces of writing.

⑥ The students are often presented with copies of **Reproducible Masters** as reference materials or as a means of keeping notes about their writing. They store these pages in their **Writer's Notebook.**

1 The students are asked to view new vocabulary in two distinct ways. First, since unit concepts are critical to all of the work done in *Collections for Young Scholars*™, words that are important to understanding these concepts are pointed out and discussed. Then the students are asked to identify and discuss words from the selection that they think will be useful in their writing.

Students are always encouraged to use **Vocabulary Exploration** forms to record and study words they choose and to place these forms in the Personal Dictionary section of their Writer's Notebook.

2 Convenient **Vocabulary Tips** help guide you in working with students in developing vocabulary.

3 **Exploration** forms the heart of the program. Each lesson guides you and the students in exploring unit concepts and learning how to become a community of scholars.

4 The students have explored and discussed unit concepts as they apply to the lesson text; the students have also connected the new text to selections they have read previously. Now they take their **exploration beyond the student text** and out into the larger world. Learning doesn't just take place in the classroom.

5 Suggestions and guidance are supplied to help you and the students at each step of their explorations. Students know what your expectations of them are and why their explorations are important.

6 In science and social studies units, the **Research Cycle** helps guide students through in-depth exploration on questions related to the unit topic.

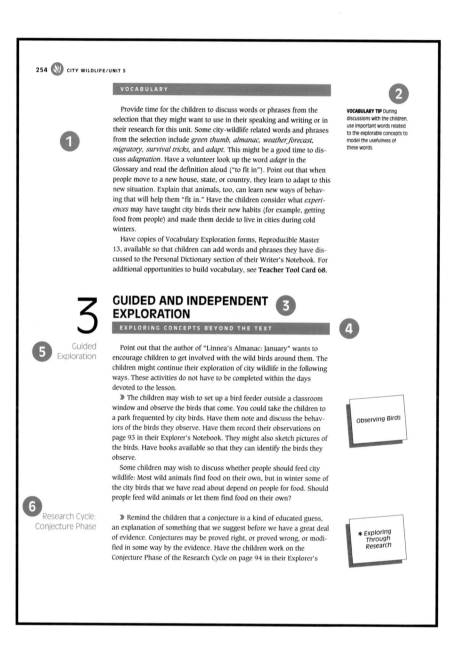

VOCABULARY

1 Provide time for the children to discuss words or phrases from the selection that they might want to use in their speaking and writing or in their research for this unit. Some city-wildlife related words and phrases from the selection include *green thumb, almanac, weather forecast, migratory, survival tricks,* and *adapt.* This might be a good time to discuss *adaptation.* Have a volunteer look up the word *adapt* in the Glossary and read the definition aloud ("to fit in"). Point out that when people move to a new house, state, or country, they learn to adapt to this new situation. Explain that animals, too, can learn new ways of behaving that will help them "fit in." Have the children consider what *experiences* may have taught city birds their new habits (for example, getting food from people) and made them decide to live in cities during cold winters.

Have copies of Vocabulary Exploration forms, Reproducible Master 13, available so that children can add words and phrases they have discussed to the Personal Dictionary section of their Writer's Notebook. For additional opportunities to build vocabulary, see **Teacher Tool Card 68.**

2 VOCABULARY TIP During discussions with the children, use important words related to the explorable concepts to model the usefulness of these words.

3
3 GUIDED AND INDEPENDENT EXPLORATION
EXPLORING CONCEPTS BEYOND THE TEXT

5 Guided Exploration

4 Point out that the author of "Linnea's Almanac: January" wants to encourage children to get involved with the wild birds around them. The children might continue their exploration of city wildlife in the following ways. These activities do not have to be completed within the days devoted to the lesson.

➤ The children may wish to set up a bird feeder outside a classroom window and observe the birds that come. You could take the children to a park frequented by city birds. Have them note and discuss the behaviors of the birds they observe. Have them record their observations on page 93 in their Explorer's Notebook. They might also sketch pictures of the birds. Have books available so that they can identify the birds they observe.

Some children may wish to discuss whether people should feed city wildlife: Most wild animals find food on their own, but in winter some of the city birds that we have read about depend on people for food. Should people feed wild animals or let them find food on their own?

Observing Birds

6 Research Cycle: Conjecture Phase

➤ Remind the children that a conjecture is a kind of educated guess, an explanation of something that we suggest before we have a great deal of evidence. Conjectures may be proved right, or proved wrong, or modified in some way by the evidence. Have the children work on the Conjecture Phase of the Research Cycle on page 94 in their Explorer's

✳ *Exploring Through Research*

Observing Birds

As you observe birds or as you research city wildlife, record on this chart what you find out about birds. Add to the chart whenever you can.

Bird	Description	Food	Behavior

Unit 5/City Wildlife   EN 93

Research Cycle: Conjecture Phase

Our problem:

_____

_____

_____

Conjecture (my first theory or explanation):

_____

_____

_____

_____

_____

_____

_____

_____

_____

_____

_____

_____

As you collect information, your conjectures will change. Return to this page to record your new theories or explanations about your research problem.

94 EN   City Wildlife/Unit 5

Explorer's Notebook, page 93

Explorer's Notebook, page 94   **7**

Notebook. Prior to this, it will be helpful to have a group discussion and for you to model a conjecture. To model a conjecture, you might choose a problem that has already been suggested for research but that has not been chosen by any group. In that way, the whole class can engage in conjecturing without taking anything away from an individual group's work on a problem. You may wish to record the conjectures, since they will be useful in a later lesson. As the children share their conjectures, record them on the chalkboard. Explain that it is not necessary to come to a consensus at this point. As they begin their research, they will revisit their conjectures and revise them based on new information. If necessary, explain to the children that the phases in the Research Cycle are recursive, therefore children will continually return to the previous phases of the cycle and assess how the problem and the conjectures have changed and what new information is necessary.

If the children are comfortable with the conjecture phase of the Research Cycle, they can go directly to work on their research problem in Independent Workshop. However, if the children are having difficulty with forming conjectures, refer to **Learning Framework Card 4B** for ideas. Encourage them to record their own ideas, even if these are vague or limited. The important thing is that they progress toward more sophisticated conjectures in subsequent cycles.

7 **Explorer's Notebook** pages help guide the students through the research process.

45F

1 **Research** minilessons provide an opportunity for you to help students with specific study and research skills.

2 The students use their **Explorer's Notebook** as a basis for discussion and practice of study and research skills.

MINILESSON

1 Research Aid: Keeping a Log

Read this sentence from "Linnea's Almanac: January" aloud to the children: "And now I'll tell you about some of my year, what I did and what I observed." Point out that a person can keep notes on what he or she has seen, done, or thought about. Some people keep a diary of daily events and thoughts; some keep ideas about what they have read and written in a journal.

Explain that Linnea's actions and observations are focused on a scientific question: How do wild birds live in the city during the winter? Tell the children that **a record of scientific data** is often called a **log**. (The children may or may not be familiar with a ship's log, which contains notations on the weather, the ship's course and speed, and shipboard events during a voyage.)

2 Guided Practice: Keeping a Log

➤ Use Explorer's Notebook, page 95 and discuss with the children some reasons for keeping a log and some guidelines for entering information.

Independent Practice: Keeping a Log

To give the children practice in keeping a log, have them experiment with keeping a log of their research of city wildlife. They should record their progress, including the date and what they accomplished. Consider keeping a log yourself, in an abbreviated form perhaps, to provide a model for the children.

➤ Distribute Home/School Connection 45, in which the children are asked to keep logs over a two-day period—preferably the weekend—of either the weather or their eating habits.

Have the children return their logs to school. Conduct a follow-up session. Begin by sharing some of your log entries. Then encourage the children to share some of theirs. Draw attention to particularly good entries the children have made—ones in which they stick to facts, include important details, and give precise times.

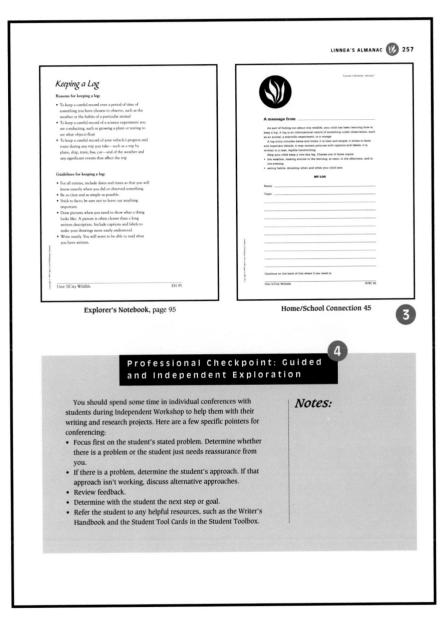

Explorer's Notebook, page 95

Home/School Connection 45

Professional Checkpoint: Guided and Independent Exploration

You should spend some time in individual conferences with students during Independent Workshop to help them with their writing and research projects. Here are a few specific pointers for conferencing:

- Focus first on the student's stated problem. Determine whether there is a problem or the student just needs reassurance from you.
- If there is a problem, determine the student's approach. If that approach isn't working, discuss alternative approaches.
- Review feedback.
- Determine with the student the next step or goal.
- Refer the student to any helpful resources, such as the Writer's Handbook and the Student Tool Cards in the Student Toolbox.

Notes:

3 Through the **Home/School Connection,** adults at home are not only kept informed of what their children are studying, they are also shown how to take active roles in the unit explorations.

4 **Professional Checkpoints,** found at the end of one of the major sections of each lesson, offer valuable advice in helping you and the students create an energized learning environment.

1 **Independent Workshop** gives students the time they need to pursue their explorations. Students may work individually, in pairs, or in small groups to read, discuss, research, write about, and present ideas pertaining to their exploration and research.

2 The students are always encouraged to take responsibility for their own learning. Part of this growing responsibility is learning to budget and organize time and energy. **Students** are encouraged to **make choices** about their use of Independent Workshop time. Although most of the time will be spent exploring unit concepts, other options are available as time permits.

3 Adult readers enjoy sharing with friends what they are reading. They discuss their reading, give opinions on it, and recommend books to each other. The students are encouraged at all times to cultivate the habits and behaviors of mature readers. **Reading Roundtable** offers students this opportunity. Tradebook Connection Cards, available in the Student Toolbox, can be used to give students ideas about activities and discussions related to popular trade books and familiar classics.

✤ I N D E P E N D E N T   W O R K S H O P **1**
Building a Community of Scholars

2 Student-Directed Reading, Writing, and Discussion

Research Cycle: Conjecture Phase Each child should develop his or her own conjectures regarding the research problem of his or her group and enter them in the Explorer's Notebook, page 94. Then groups should meet to discuss their conjectures.

As you observe the groups discussing their conjectures, encourage them to record the ideas of everyone in the group. Tell them that they can refine their conjectures as they collect information. Rephrasing the children's conjectures will help you elicit additional information from them and will help them clarify and refine their ideas. Remind the children that they will return to this page later in their research.

4 The students may decide to use some of this time to work on writing projects they started earlier in this lesson or in previous ones. During a **Writing Seminar,** students may choose to conference with their peers to gain feedback about their writing. This is also a good time for you to conference with the students about their writing. Guidance is also offered here on using the writing process.

Student Tool Cards contain lessons that the students can use independently to help them in their writing, revising, and proofreading.

5 Both you and the students will be choosing representative work to place in their **portfolios.** Independent Workshop provides the time necessary to carefully consider additions to the portfolio.

6 **Cross-curricular Activity Cards** highlight for the students cross-curricular applications of what they are learning in *Collections for Young Scholars.* Students are given the opportunity to participate in activities related to the selections and the explorable concepts that have broad applications in science, mathematics, social studies, art, drama, and music.

7 Independent Workshop affords you an additional **opportunity to observe the students as they interact in their research groups, discuss literature, and work on their writing.** The Teacher Tool Cards give you the freedom to address the students' individual needs during this time. Tool Cards that work particularly well with the lesson text are listed here. These cards, however, are just suggestions; you and your students will be the best judges of what they need to focus on.

The students should be encouraged to use the Student Tool Card lessons stored in the Student Toolbox to help them in their study.

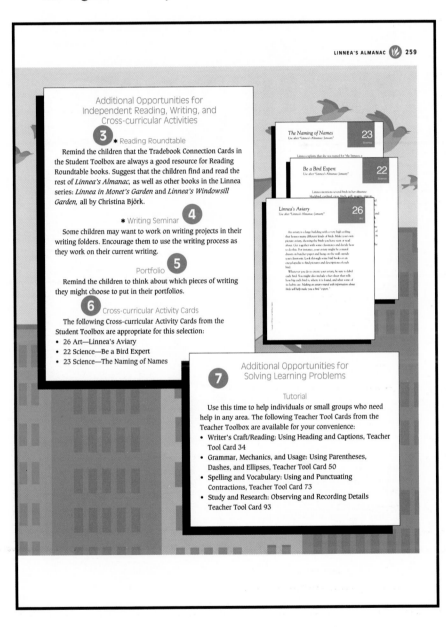

Additional Opportunities for Independent Reading, Writing, and Cross-curricular Activities

3 ✷ Reading Roundtable
Remind the children that the Tradebook Connection Cards in the Student Toolbox are always a good resource for Reading Roundtable books. Suggest that the children find and read the rest of *Linnea's Almanac,* as well as other books in the Linnea series: *Linnea in Monet's Garden* and *Linnea's Windowsill Garden,* all by Christina Björk.

4 ✷ Writing Seminar
Some children may want to work on writing projects in their writing folders. Encourage them to use the writing process as they work on their current writing.

5 Portfolio
Remind the children to think about which pieces of writing they might choose to put in their portfolios.

6 Cross-curricular Activity Cards
The following Cross-curricular Activity Cards from the Student Toolbox are appropriate for this selection:
• 26 Art—Linnea's Aviary
• 22 Science—Be a Bird Expert
• 23 Science—The Naming of Names

7 Additional Opportunities for Solving Learning Problems

Tutorial
Use this time to help individuals or small groups who need help in any area. The following Teacher Tool Cards from the Teacher Toolbox are available for your convenience:
• Writer's Craft/Reading: Using Heading and Captions, Teacher Tool Card 34
• Grammar, Mechanics, and Usage: Using Parentheses, Dashes, and Ellipses, Teacher Tool Card 50
• Spelling and Vocabulary: Using and Punctuating Contractions, Teacher Tool Card 73
• Study and Research: Observing and Recording Details Teacher Tool Card 93

Volume 6

Framework for Effective Teaching™

Introducing *Collections for Young Scholars*™

Preview by the Students

Activating Prior Knowledge

Ask the children whether they are familiar with any kinds of book collections. They may mention some popular series like Little House, Encyclopedia Brown, or a set of encyclopedias. If they are unsure about the meaning of *collection,* explain that a collection is a group of books created to be read, studied, or kept together and that each book is called a volume. Have children who are familiar with collections explain why the different volumes go together.

Setting Reading Goals and Expectations

Ask the children to tell how they choose a book at the library. Emphasize the aspects of **browsing** mentioned by the children—reading the title, looking at the illustrations, flipping through a few pages to find out what the book is about. Then point out that before they start reading, **good readers** spend some time **setting reading goals** and **deciding what they expect from a text**. A good reader often begins setting reading goals and expectations by looking at and thinking about the **title** of the book or story. Have a volunteer read aloud the title of this book, *Collections for Young Scholars*.

Invite the children to give their definitions or impressions of the word *scholar.* Be sure to allow sufficient time for the children to discuss any ideas they have about scholars. At the conclusion of this discussion, you may want to ask the children whether they consider themselves scholars and why.

Read the following definition to the class:

> Scholars are people who study subjects that are important to them. They interpret, analyze, communicate, reason, and solve problems because these are ways to gain knowledge and understanding.

Have volunteers **paraphrase** this **definition**. Then ask how the definition affects their past ideas about scholars. Tell the children that whether or not they have previously considered themselves scholars, they will be expected to grow as scholars as the year progresses.

Cover Illustration

Invite volunteers to share their impressions of the **illustration** on the **cover of the book**. Tell the students that the cover illustration on volume 6, book 2 of *Collections for Young Scholars*™ was done by **Beth Peck** and share with them the following information about Peck and the illustration:

> Illustrator Beth Peck wanted her illustration on the cover of *Collections for Young Scholars*™ to suggest an urban setting as a background for contemporary young people who enjoy reading. The children lean on a brick wall that reminds the viewer of the brick stoops found around New York City and other large cities.
>
> Peck, who grew up in New York state, is now a resident of Wisconsin. To capture the look of the children lounging against a brick wall, she posed models against the wooden railing in front of her house. The illustration is done in oils.
>
> Peck graduated from the Rhode Island School of Design and has been an illustrator for ten years. She is married and has a young daughter.

Browsing *Collections for Young Scholars*™

The **purpose** of this initial browsing is to **help** the **children think** about what they will be reading and to **build** a sense of **anticipation** for the reading they will be doing.

Have the children spend a few minutes browsing *Collections for Young Scholars*™, volume 6, book 2. Tell the children that when they browse, they should **quickly go through** the book to

- Get an idea of what the book is about
- Think about what they may learn from it
- See what looks interesting
- Notice things that may raise questions or cause problems

When the children have had ample time to browse the entire book, invite volunteers to point out things that they noticed. The children may have noticed particular illustrations, familiar story titles, or familiar unit topics. They may also point out titles that they have never encountered before or topics that they are not accustomed to seeing in a book such as this. As many **children** as possible should be given the opportunity to **comment on what they found** in their browsing.

You may want to **record comments** that have to do with the children's expectations. It will be interesting for the children to go back later to see whether their expectations were fulfilled.

Parts of the Book

Ask the children to look briefly at the **title page** and to tell what information they find there. Do the same for the **copyright page**. Review the meaning of the information given on the copyright page, including the copyright date.

When they have finished looking at these first few pages, have the children look at the table of contents. Ask them to share what they already know about a **table of contents** and its use. They should mention that a table of contents lists the **title of each selection,** the **author of each selection** (and the source of each selection if it is an excerpt), and the **page** on which **each selection begins.** This particular table of contents also lists for each selection the **genre,** the **illustrator,** and some of the **awards** it has won; and for some selections, special **author/illustrator information.** This table of contents also lists the pages on which the **unit opener, bibliography,** and **fine art** can be found. Give the children time to browse the table of contents and pick out titles or information that particularly interests them. Encourage them to share their impressions of the table of contents and the information contained in it.

When they have completed their discussions of the front of the book, ask the children to turn to the **glossary,** page 371, and spend a few minutes browsing through it. Then ask them to share what they know about glossaries in general and what they noticed about this glossary in particular. If necessary, explain that the words in the glossary are words the children may need help with as they read the selections throughout the year.

Finally, encourage the children to think about the **whole book** and to tell what some of the subjects were and what they noticed that looked particularly interesting. As they respond, **write the titles of specific selections that they mention.** In each case, ask what it was about the selection that caught their attention. It will be interesting for the children to return to this list after they have read the selections.

Other Program Materials

In addition to the anthologies, each child will need one **Explorer's Notebook** and one **Reading/Writing Connection.** This may be a good time to **distribute** these books and have the children spend some time **browsing** them. Encourage the children to share what they notice.

Introduce the **Student Toolbox** to the children, and tell them where it will be permanently located. You may at this time want to tell the children about the **materials** that they will find in the Student Toolbox:
- **Student Tool Cards,** containing lessons in grammar, mechanics, and usage; reading and writing; spelling and vocabulary; study and

research; and information about classroom participation that the children can access at any time
- **Cross-curricular Activity Cards,** containing activities that apply information from the selections across the curriculum
- **Tradebook Connection Cards,** containing activities to accompany trade books that can be found in the library
- **Listening Library Audiocassette,** containing selected readings from anthology selections

To avoid confusion and ensure that everyone has an opportunity to look through the box, you may want to suggest that the children not all try to go through the box at the same time. If possible, allow **small groups** of four or five children each to go through the **Student Toolbox.**

Allow time for **discussion** and **questions** concerning the **contents** of the **Student Toolbox,** and assure the children that they will become very familiar with all of these materials as the year progresses.

At this point, you and your children may want to spend additional time to look over and to discuss *Collections for Young Scholars*™, volume 6, book 2; or you may go directly to unit 4, Perseverance, and begin your explorations.

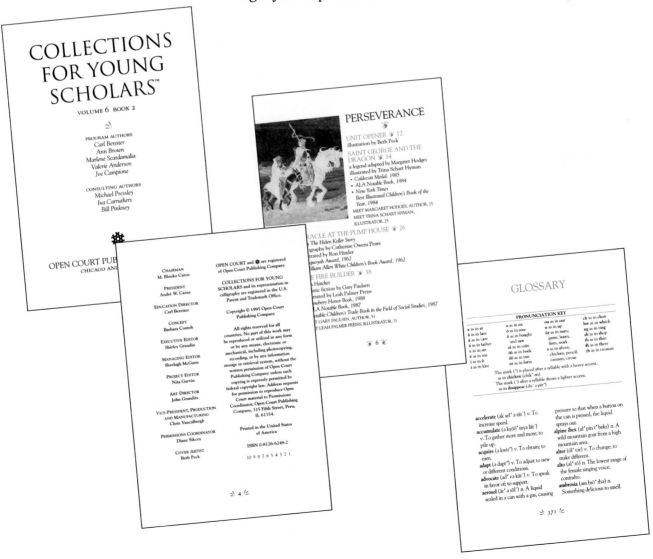

Perseverance

UNIT INTRODUCTION

BACKGROUND INFORMATION FOR THE TEACHER

Explorable
Concepts

Writers on leadership have always stressed the importance of sticking to what one believes in, persisting in one's purpose, staying the course. Ray Kroc, the president of McDonald's Hamburgers who built that company into a worldwide empire, made this quotation from Calvin Coolidge his motto:

Nothing in the world can take the place of persistence.
Talent will not; nothing is more common than unsuccessful men with
    talent.
Genius will not; unrewarded genius is almost a proverb.
Education will not; the world is full of educated derelicts.
Persistence, determination alone are omnipotent.

And Thomas Edison said that "Genius is one percent inspiration and ninety-nine percent perspiration." This unit is intended to help students explore this idea, and enable them to see it from inside—to see it as more than a pious exhortation or moralistic imposition.

The mere desire to persist is nothing in and of itself—we persist with something if we regard it as being of supreme importance. Perseverance is the determination to implement some goal or dream, no matter how much energy or patience or time it may take. Sometimes the goal is forced upon one—like the sheer need to survive in a dangerous situation. But

PERSEVERANCE

mostly, the goal is chosen freely, and the persistence one shows in pursuing it is a direct measure of how strongly one believes in it.

Inquiry, in this unit, will probably not take the form of research. Students can deepen their understanding of the concepts, however, through the exploration of fictional stories and writing of their own. Historical instances of spectacular perseverance (or business stories, such as the one in this unit) can also provide a focus for inquiry and exploration. The problem of what caused particular people to persist in an outlandish quest—Charles Goodyear or the Wright Brothers, in this unit, but there are many other examples students may prefer to explore—can lead to many interesting reflections on the nature of human ideals and motivation. No particular outcome to these discussions is prescribed; however, the important thing is that students are left with a deeper and more differentiated idea of the importance of perseverance than when they began.

Perseverance raises a wide variety of questions. To stimulate your own thinking, you might ask yourself questions like the following:

- Is it better to persevere in an evil goal or be lackadaisical about a good one?
- Is perseverance necessarily a force for good, or can it also be a force for something that is harmful?
- Is it possible to do anything well without perseverance? Why or why not?

- Why is perseverance often difficult?
- Does persevering in a goal guarantee you will accomplish it? Why or why not?
- Is it possible to persevere in a goal without risk?
- Can there be perseverance without choice?
- What is the difference between stubbornness and perseverance?
- How does perseverance depend on time and opportunity?

Resources

Among the following resources are **professional reference books, read-alouds, audiovisual materials, and community/school resources.** The reference books are intended to help you develop the concepts and organize information to share with the students in whatever way you choose. The read-alouds are books that may be too difficult for most students of this age to read independently, but fit the concepts well and are quality literature. Among the audiovisual materials are some that your students may not be able to obtain and others that will be available to both you and your students. For a complete list of audiovisual sources, see page 000. The community/school resources include people, agencies, and institutions that may be helpful in your exploration.

In addition to the resources listed here, **bibliographies for the students** appear on pages 132–133 in the student anthology, on **Reproducible Masters 41–44,** and on **Home/School Connection 27–28.** Encourage the students to use these bibliographies as they explore the concepts in this unit.

You should also read books from the students' bibliographies. Reading stories about perseverance written for students will help you understand the nature of the information the students are learning.

Professional Reference Books

Mithaug, Dennis E. *Self-Determined Kids.* Lexington Books, 1991. Written as a guide for parents and teachers, this book examines the essential principles of success—competence, intelligence, and persistence—and shows concerned adults how to guide children toward the goals of self-determination and achievement. There is an entire chapter on persistence.

Montessori, Maria. *The Absorbent Mind.* Delta Books, 1969 (paperback). Learn this innovative educator's thoughts on the development of perseverance in chapter 21 of her book.

Powledge, Fred. *You'll Survive!* Charles Scribner's Sons, 1986. Advice on surviving adolescence, whether it's late-blooming, early-blooming, klutzy, or lonely, is given by adults and young people who have just completed their teens. This book serves as a good reminder for adults working with this age group.

Roberts, Wess. *Straight A's Never Made Anybody Rich: Lessons in Personal Achievement.* HarperCollins Publishers, Inc., 1991. Chapter 7,

"Guts and Grit Never Hurt Anyone," gives two examples of perseverance—one from Greek mythology and one from real life.

Sullivan, Mary Beth; Brightman, Alan J.; and Blatt, Joseph. *Feeling Free.* Addison-Wesley Publishing Co., Inc., 1979. Five children with disabilities including deafness, dwarfism, blindness, cerebral palsy, and dyslexia share their experiences along with their need to persist to develop skills, maintain relationships, and overcome discouragement. These comments are interspersed with cartoons, fiction, and handicapped awareness exercises. Some of these would be useful to read aloud to the students.

Waite, Helen E. *Valiant Companions.* Macrae Smith Company, 1959. This very readable, complete story of Helen Keller and her teacher, Anne Sullivan, include events both before and after the episode detailed in this unit.

Read-Alouds

Bennett, William J., ed. *The Book of Virtues: A Treasury of Great Moral Stories.* Simon & Schuster, 1993. Chapter 7 of this book contains seventy-two pages of short stories, poetry, fables, folk tales, Bible stories, and speeches on perseverance. The editor is a former Secretary of Education of the United States.

Blackwood, Gary L. *Wild Timothy.* Atheneum Children's Books, 1987. Timothy is a reader, not a can-do outdoorsman like his father. When he gets lost in the woods, his persistence in his trial-and-error attempts at survival brings him to a new realization of his own competence.

Cousins, Margaret. *The Story of Thomas Alva Edison.* Random House, Inc., 1965. Thomas Alva Edison's single-minded tenaciousness in solving the problems he encountered while inventing is particularly featured in chapter 6, "Lighter of the Lamp." The rest of this biography is also worth reading as it continues to provide a real understanding of the life of a creative genius.

George, Jean. *My Side of the Mountain.* E. P. Dutton, 1959. This novel, a Newbery Honor Book, is written as a first-person account of thirteen-year-old Sam Gribley's year spent living off the land after being inspired by the writings of Thoreau.

Pfeffer, Susan Beth. *What Do You Do When Your Mouth Won't Open?* Yearling Books, 1981 (paperback). Reesa has just won an essay contest, but her phobia about speaking in public has her consulting a psychologist for a cure. She only has two weeks before she has to read her essay to an audience of hundreds of people. Relaxation techniques, imaging, and her own persistence and determination help to defeat her fear for the first time.

Audiovisual Materials

Experimental by Robin Lehman. Phoenix Films, Inc., 1974. The excitement, humor, and perseverance underlying man's attempts to fly are displayed in this film. 13 minutes; film or videocassette.

Helen Keller in Her Story by Nancy Hamilton. Phoenix Films, Inc., 1973. Helen Keller tells her unique and dramatic story of courage, faith, perseverance, and hope in this black-and-white film of the deaf-blind woman's life. 45 minutes; film or videocassette.

Jack London's To Build A Fire. BFA Educational Media, 1975. This adaptation of a classic story dramatizes the conflict between man and nature in the Yukon. 14 minutes; film or videocassette.

Julie of the Wolves. McGraw-Hill Media, 1985. While running away from her pre-arranged marriage, a thirteen-year-old Eskimo girl becomes lost on the Alaskan tundra and must make friends with a wolf pack to survive. 38 minutes; videocassette.

My Side of the Mountain. Films Incorporated, 1976. This learning kit features an adaptation of the novel by Jean George about a thirteen-year-old boy who vows he will live off the land for a year after being inspired by the writings of Thoreau. 43 minutes; 3 filmstrips and 3 audiocassettes, teacher's guide, 15 activity cards, and a copy of the book.

Never Give Up—Imogen Cunningham by Ann Hershey. Phoenix Films, Inc., 1975. A visit with a noted elderly portrait photographer is recorded on film. 28 minutes; film or videocassette.

To Climb a Mountain. BFA Educational Media, 1974. A group from the Braille Institute sets out with determination to scale a rugged part of the Sierras. 15 minutes; film or videocassette.

A Winner Never Quits by Ralph Taragan and Richard Oretsky. Phoenix Films, Inc., 1977. This documentary about a high school football team raises questions about values and the wide range of attitudes toward them. 18 minutes; film or videocassette.

Community/School

• School guidance counselors
• Placement and employment agencies
• Scout leaders
• Scouts who have reached the highest level of achievement

- Organizations for people with disabilities
- The National Inventors Hall of Fame
  Patent and Trademark Office
  2021 Jefferson Davis Highway
  Arlington, Virginia 22202
  (moving to Akron, Ohio)

Concept Board

Remind students that as in previous units, the class will keep a **Concept Board to record new information learned about the explorable concepts in this unit.** Designate an area of the classroom for the Concept Board. You may wish to begin the Concept Board after the students have had an opportunity to raise important questions about perseverance and have some idea of where they are going with the unit. Throughout the reading of the unit, encourage the students to review the information on the Concept Board and explain how it changed or altered their original ideas about perseverance.

Question Board

Designate an area for the **Question Board. Remind the students to post any questions they have as they proceed through the unit,** beginning with questions related to their original ideas and theories about perseverance. Remember to periodically review the questions on the board and to add new questions or remove old questions when they no longer warrant consideration. This review will provide an opportunity for students to rethink their original ideas about perseverance and clear up any misconceptions they may have had prior to reading the unit. Students should also be encouraged to use the Question Board to generate ideas to pursue in their independent exploration.

Both boards will allow the students to display and share their ideas and to see who has common questions and interests, a step toward building a community of scholars. For a review of information about the **Question Board** and the **Concept Board**, see **Teacher Tool Card 123.**

UNIT PREVIEW BY THE STUDENTS

Activating Prior Knowledge

- Have the students discuss what they already know about perseverance. Encourage them to share their differences of opinion. This is an opportunity to determine any misconceptions they may have about perseverance. For example, they may believe that people who have accomplished extraordinary goals are the only ones who persevere. They may be unaware that most people persevere to accomplish ordinary, everyday goals.
- If the Concept Board has been started, add important information to it about the contributions of groups or individuals who have persevered to attain a goal. Throughout the reading of the unit, refer to these statements on the Concept Board to help students add to their prior knowledge or to clear up any misconceptions that they may have. It is

important that the students feel free to voice their opinions and discuss them. Misconceptions can be addressed as the students proceed through the unit.

Setting Reading Goals and Expectations

- Have the students examine and discuss the unit opener on pages 12–13 of the student anthology—the illustration and unit title.
- Have the students spend a few minutes browsing the selections in the unit. Encourage them to list on the chalkboard the people they think they will be reading about in the unit.
- Let the students report on and discuss things they believe are important that they have noticed in their browsing and raise any questions they may have. Have them post these questions on the Question Board.
- Explain to the students that throughout this unit they will be participating in activities that will extend their experiences and deepen and expand their knowledge of perseverance. These **exploratory activities** may include **narrative writing, drama, art, interviews, debates, and panel discussions.** The students will be allowed ample opportunity to reflect on and discuss the activities they complete. Perseverance is a subject for which there is abundant material and one that naturally leads into many interesting problems on the nature of human ideals and motivation. The activities will provide a framework for inquiry that is driven by the students' own wonderings and conjectures.

❯ Have the students complete page 64 in their Explorer's Notebook and share their responses. Also have them suggest and record on the Question Board questions they would like to pursue in their reading of the unit.

Knowledge About Perseverance

This is what I know about perseverance before reading the unit.

_____
_____
_____
_____
_____
_____
_____
_____
_____
_____
_____

These are some things I would like to know about perseverance.

_____
_____
_____
_____
_____
_____
_____
_____
_____
_____
_____
_____

Reminder: I should read this page again when I get to
the end of the unit to see how much I've learned about
perseverance.

64 EN   Perseverance/Unit 4

Copyright © 1995 Open Court Publishing Company

Explorer's Notebook, page 64

Learning Unit: Perseverance

SELECTION	LINK TO THE UNIT CONCEPTS
● ▲ ■ **Saint George and the Dragon,** pages 16–39 legend retold by Margaret Hodges, illustrated by Trina Schart Hyman Caldecott Medal, 1985; ALA Notable Book, 1984; New York Times Best Illustrated Children's Book of the Year, 1984	Worthwhile goals are accomplished through perseverance.
● **Miracle at the Pump House,** pages 40–59 biography from *The Helen Keller Story* by Catherine Owens Peare, illustrated by Ron Himler Sequoyah Award, 1962; William Allen White Children's Book Award, 1962	Positive changes can occur when even the most severe problems are viewed as challenges to be overcome through sensitivity, intelligence, and perseverance.
ON YOUR OWN ● **The Fire Builder,** pages 60–73 realistic fiction from *Hatchet* by Gary Paulsen, illustrated by Leah Palmer Preiss Newbery Honor Book, 1987; ALA Notable Book, 1987; Notable Children's Trade Book in the Field of Social Studies, 1987	Persistence and imagination are important factors related to perseverance.
● **Amaroq, the Wolf,** pages 74–95 realistic fiction from *Julie of the Wolves* by Jean Craighead George, illustrated by Gail Piazza Newbery Medal, 1973; National Book Award Finalist, 1973; ALA Notable Book, 1972	Persevering to survive can be difficult and grueling. Is it different from persevering to do a job well?
FINE ART pages 96–99 *Four Jockeys Riding Hard,* Théodore Géricault; *The Village School,* Giuseppe Constantini; **Man chasing after his hat in the wind,** Japanese	Perseverance can be expressed through the visual arts.
POETRY pages 100–107 ● **Mother to Son** poem by Langston Hughes, illustrated by Susan Keeter	There is value in setting high goals and persevering to attain those goals.
● **It Can't Beat Us,** pages 108–129 historical fiction from *The Long Winter* by Laura Ingalls Wilder, illustrated by Garth Williams Newbery Honor Book, 1941	Persevering in times of hardship often brings people together in a cooperative effort.
ASSESSMENT **The Sticky Secret,** pages 130–145 informational article from *Micromysteries: Stories of Scientific Detection* by Gail Kay Haines, illustrated by Robert Byrd	Perseverance is important even when the situation seems hopeless. Nothing important gets done without someone sticking to the task.
● **Back to the Drawing Board,** pages 146–167 biography from *The Wright Brothers: How They Invented the Airplane* by Russell Freedman Newbery Honor Book, 1991; Boston Globe-Horn Book Award Honor Book, 1991; SLJ Best Books of the Year, 1991	Seemingly impossible goals can often be accomplished by persistence in pursuing a dream. Perseverance and determination go hand in hand.

Unit Wrap-up, pages 168–169

● **Award-winning authors and/or illustrators**   ▲ **Full-length trade books**   ■ **Dramatized on audiocassette**

Exploration Through Reflective Activities

SELECTION-BASED MINILESSONS		REFLECTIVE ACTIVITIES
TEACHER'S GUIDE	TEACHER TOOLBOX	
Plot Setting	Precise Verb Use, Providing Comparisons	Group discussions Writing a story/Speaking to class Interviewing someone who has persevered
Sensory Description	Characterization, Providing Multiple Effects for a Cause	Information search
Students choose a writer's craft to focus on.	Genre—Adventure, Adverbs	News article search Role playing Inviting a speaker to class
Developing Problems and Solutions Establishing Setting/Realistic Fiction	Elaboration by Providing Noncausal Reasons, Sensory Description	Group discussions Debate Role-playing a news-conference situation
Discussing Poetry		Writing poetry
Providing Multiple Effects for a Cause	Description, Providing Problems and Solutions	Investigating and comparing ideas
Choice of a writer's craft to study is part of assessment.		Biography search
Indicators of Location Using Quotations to Support Ideas	Strong Topic Sentences, Writing Captions for Photographs	Preparing a pictorial history Biography/quotation search
		Sharing of group knowledge, insights, and ideas

Assessment available for this unit includes Teacher's Observation Log, Self-Assessment Questionnaire, Concept Connections, Portfolios, and separate Comprehension assessment and Essay and Writing assessment.

Saint George and the Dragon

1 READING THE SELECTION

About the Selection

This classic English legend of *Saint George and the Dragon* gets a lift with Margaret Hodges' refreshing retelling. When the monstrous dragon unleashes his reign of terror across the kingdom, only Una, the king's daughter, is brave enough to leave the safety of the castle to seek help. Upon hearing Una's plea, a courageous but inexperienced knight follows her back to the castle. There, the young Red Cross Knight confronts his vicious foe, only to be struck down. Will the good knight conquer the evil demon who has turned far more experienced opponents into dust? Will the knight earn his given name?

The tightly woven plot develops rapidly in this tale of good and evil. Readers will delight in Hodges' fast-paced, powerful descriptions of the battles between the courageous knight and the giant dragon. An added dimension to this version of the story includes soothing lyric passages which provide a particularly effective contrast to the harrowing descriptions of conflict. This merger of the two styles expands readers' enjoyment.

Link to the Unit Concepts

The story of Saint George and the Dragon, pages 14–25, helps students think about the conditions of a time that called for brave and honorable men and women, and connects the past to the present by stressing overcoming problems. This selection may lead students to compare legendary heroic deeds with the actions of ordinary people conquering present-day problems. It may cause them to examine their own ideas about what makes something a worthy goal, and to wonder whether the greatest accomplishments are achieved by trying to do worthwhile things. Students may also question whether perseverance is necessarily a force for good.

LESSON OVERVIEW

Saint George and the Dragon, retold by Margaret Hodges, pages 14–25

READING THE SELECTION

Materials
Student anthology, pp. 14–25
Explorer's Notebook, p. 65
Assessment Master 1

FYI
Learning Framework Cards
- Setting Reading Goals and Expectations, 1A
- Responding to Text, 1B
- Checking Understanding, 1C
- Exploring Through Discussion, 2

Teacher Tool Cards
- Classroom Supports: Modeling and Generating Think-Alouds, 118
- Classroom Supports: Writer's Notebook, 122

READING WITH A WRITER'S EYE

Minilessons
Writer's Craft: Plot
Writer's Craft: Setting

Materials
Reading/Writing Connection, pp. 27–28
Reproducible Masters 15, 40

FYI
Teacher Tool Card
- Spelling and Vocabulary: Building Vocabulary, 77

Options for Instruction
Writer's Craft: Precise Verb Use
Writer's Craft: Providing Comparisons
(Use Teacher Tool Cards listed below.)

GUIDED AND INDEPENDENT EXPLORATION

Materials
Home/School Connection 27–28
Reproducible Masters 41–44
Explorer's Notebook, pp. 68–69
Assessment Master 1

FYI
Learning Framework Cards
- Exploring Through Reflective Activities, 3
- Independent Workshop, 5

Optional Materials from Student Toolbox

Audiocassette

Tradebook Connection Cards
- *Call It Courage* by Armstrong Sperry

Cross-curricular Activity Cards
- 14 Social Studies—Heraldry
- 11 Art—Castle Architecture

Independent Workshop

Student Tool Cards
- Writer's Craft/Reading: Plot, 15
- Writer's Craft/Reading: Setting, 14
- Writer's Craft/Reading: Choosing Precise and Vivid Verbs, 22
- Writer's Craft/Reading: Comparing and Contrasting, 37

FYI
Teacher Tool Cards
- Writer's Craft/Reading: Plot, 15
- Writer's Craft/Reading: Setting, 14
- Writer's Craft/Reading: Choosing Precise and Vivid Verbs, 22
- Writer's Craft/Reading: Elaboration Through Providing Comparison and Contrast, 37

N O T E S

Asterisks (*) throughout the lesson indicate learning frameworks. Learning Framework Cards and Teacher Tool Cards can be found in the Teacher Toolbox.

About the
Author

Saint George and the Dragon is an English legend from *The Faerie Queene* by Edmund Spenser, retold by award-winning author Margaret Hodges. In 1984, *Saint George and the Dragon* was named an American Library Association Notable Book. Margaret Hodges was born in 1911 in Indianapolis, Indiana. Hodges has written many books for children, including retellings of folk tales, biographies, and real-life stories, which she says "are based on the adventures and misadventures of my three sons." *Lady Queene Anne: A Biography of Queen Anne of England, The Making of Joshua Cobb,* and *The Wave* are but a few award-winning books written by this outstanding children's author.

About the
Illustrator

Trina Schart Hyman knew from the time she was four years old that she wanted to illustrate children's books. After graduating from the Boston Museum School of Art, she and her husband moved to Stockholm, Sweden, where she got her first job illustrating a book called *Toffe and the Little Car.* After moving back to the United States, she was assigned more illustration jobs, which led to her position as art director for *Cricket* magazine, a position she held for five years. She has received many awards for her work, including the Caldecott Medal in 1985 for *Saint George and the Dragon.*

"I've always longed to be the sort of artist who simply paints pictures—big, mysterious, grown-up paintings on canvas—with oil paint. But I can't. I can't because there are too many stories in the world, too many books waiting to be illustrated, and not enough time to illustrate them all or to learn how to do it well enough."

INFORMATION FOR THE STUDENT

Tell the students that the selection they are about to read was written by Margaret Hodges and illustrated by Trina Schart Hyman. As appropriate, you may want to share other information about the author or illustrator with the students. The author profile on page 25 of the student anthology explains how Hodges became interested in this story, and the illustrator profile tells of the research Hyman did before illustrating *Saint George and the Dragon.*

Have students tell what they know about legends. Like many tales and legends, the story of *Saint George and the Dragon* has been told and retold. Some students may be familiar with the story. Remind the students that there are many versions of this legend and that this version may be somewhat different from others they know. Explain that as legends like this one are told over and over, details often change, but the main point of the story remains the same. This version contains italicized passages interspersed throughout the story that create a different feeling from that of the fast-paced narrative selections.

Legends

*

COGNITIVE AND RESPONSIVE READING

Activating Prior
Knowledge

Ask students to share anything they know about knights in general or knights as they are portrayed in legends.

Setting Reading Goals and Expectations

Explain to the students that before they read they will **set reading goals and expectations.** To do this, they will **browse the first page** of the selection and **use the clues/problems/wondering procedure.** On the chalkboard under the headings clues, problems, and wonderings, write in brief note form the observations the students generate during browsing. For example, students might list the genre of the selection under clues; they might list unfamiliar words under problems; and they might note any questions that arise during browsing under wonderings. Students will return to these observations after reading. For a review of browsing, see **Learning Framework Card 1A, Setting Reading Goals and Expectations.**

Recommendations for Reading the Selection

Allow the students time to discuss how they would like to read the story. Although the selection is simple in nature and students would have little difficulty reading it silently, the text is also good for expressive reading. Because of the archaic speech patterns, oral reading may increase students' enjoyment and understanding of the selection. Reading the story aloud can also help them appreciate the magnitude of the oral tradition of the legend as they listen to it. Since lyrical italicized passages alternate with fast-paced prose, you might want to have a group of volunteers read the italicized parts as a chorus, and individual volunteers read the faster-moving narrative passages.

If the students elect to read orally, you should refer to the think-aloud prompts provided with the page miniatures. Instead of or in addition to using these prompts, encourage the students to provide their own think-alouds while reading.

This would also be a good selection for **responding to text by telling feelings while reading aloud.** Model this response, and then invite the students to do the same.

If the students elect to read silently, have them discuss problems, reactions, and strategies after reading. Let them know, however, that they can raise their hands anytime during reading to ask questions or to identify problems for discussion with the group.

About the Reading Strategies

Due to the nature of the legend, students will naturally suspend their sense of reality to picture the world created in the text. **Visualizing** is one strategy that might help the students to understand the story. Additionally, some passages go beyond the literal meaning and will naturally evoke a variety of interpretations from students. **Interpreting** is another strategy the students may find useful. For a review of **visualizing** and **interpreting,** see **Learning Framework Cards 1B and 1C.**

Think-Aloud Prompts for Use in Oral Reading

The think-aloud prompts are placed with the page miniatures. These are merely suggestions for helping students use the strategies. Remind the students to use whatever strategies they need to help them understand the selection. Refer them to the **reading strategy posters,** if necessary. Encourage them to share which strategies they use as they read. For a review of information about **modeling and generating think-alouds,** see **Teacher Tool Card 118.**

THINK ALOUD PROMPTS

These prompts may be used as guides to promote cognitive and responsive reading.

1 This italicized passage is distinguished from the other text in typeface and in writing style. Some students may be confused by this and may suggest a **clarification strategy**. Encourage volunteers to explain in their own words what they think this passage means and how the language or writing style in the passage differs from the other text in the story. If necessary, model a clarification strategy for dealing with figurative language. In your model, you might respond to the poetic quality of lines.

SAINT GEORGE AND THE DRAGON

 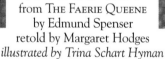

from THE FAERIE QUEENE
by Edmund Spenser
retold by Margaret Hodges
illustrated by Trina Schart Hyman

In the days when monsters and giants and fairy folk lived in England, a noble knight was riding across a plain. He wore heavy armor and carried an ancient silver shield marked with a red cross. It was dented with the blows of many battles fought long ago by other brave knights.

The Red Cross Knight had never yet faced a foe, and did not even know his name or where he had been born. But now he was bound on a great adventure, sent by the Queen of the Fairies to try his young strength against a deadly enemy, a dragon grim and horrible.

Beside him, on a little white donkey, rode a princess leading a white lamb, and behind her came a dwarf carrying a small bundle of food. The lady's lovely face was veiled and her shoulders were covered with a black cloak, as if she had a hidden sorrow in her heart. Her name was Una.

The dreadful dragon was the cause of her sorrow. He was laying waste to her land so that many frightened people had left their homes and run away. Others had shut themselves

14

inside the walls of a castle with Una's father and mother, the king and queen of the country. But Una had set out alone from the safety of the castle walls to look for a champion who would face the terrible dragon. She had traveled a long, long way before she found the Red Cross Knight.

Like a sailor long at sea, under stormy winds and fierce sun, who begins to whistle merrily when he sees land, so Una was thankful.

Now the travelers rode together, through wild woods and wilderness, perils and dangers, toward Una's kingdom. The path they had to follow was straight and narrow, but not easy to see. Sometimes the Red Cross Knight rode too far ahead of Una and lost his way. Then she had to find him and guide him back to the path. So they journeyed on. With Una by his side, fair and faithful, no monster or giant could stand before the knight's bright sword.

After many days the path became thorny and led up a steep hillside, where a good old hermit lived in a little house by himself. While Una rested, the Red Cross Knight climbed with the hermit to the top of the hill and looked out across the valley. There against the evening sky they saw a mountaintop that touched the highest heavens. It was crowned with a glorious palace, sparkling like stars and circled with walls and towers of pearls and precious stones. Joyful angels were coming and going between heaven and the High City.

Then the Red Cross Knight saw that a little path led up the distant mountain to that city, and he said, "I thought that the fairest palace in the world was the crystal tower in the city of the Fairy Queen. Now I see a palace far more lovely. Una and I should go there at once."

But the old hermit said, "The Fairy Queen has sent you to do brave deeds in this world. That High City that you see is in another world. Before you climb the path to it and hang your shield on its wall, go down into the valley and fight the dragon that you were sent to fight.

"It is time for me to tell you that you were not born of fairy folk, but of English earth. The fairies stole you away as a baby while you slept in your cradle. They hid you in a farmer's field, where a plowman found you. He called you George, which means 'Plow the Earth' and 'Fight the Good Fight.' For you were born to be England's friend and patron saint, Saint George of Merry England."

Then George, the Red Cross Knight, returned to Una, and when morning came, they went together down into the valley. They rode through farmlands, where men and women working

🐍 16 🐍

in their fields looked up and cheered because a champion had come to fight the dragon, and children clapped their hands to see the brave knight and the lovely lady ride by.

"Now we have come to my own country," said Una. "Be on your guard. See, there is the city and the great brass tower that my parents built strong enough to stand against the brassy-scaled dragon. There are my father and mother looking out from the walls, and the watchman stands at the top, waiting to call out the good news if help is coming."

Then they heard a hideous roaring that filled the air with terror and seemed to shake the ground. The dreadful dragon lay stretched on the sunny side of a great hill, like a great hill himself, and when he saw the knight's armor glistening in the sunlight, he came eagerly to do battle. The knight bade his lady stand apart, out of danger, to watch the fight, while the beast drew near, half flying, half running. His great size made a wide shadow under his huge body as a mountain casts a shadow on a valley. He reared high, monstrous, horrible, and vast, armed all over with scales of brass fitted so closely that no sword or spear could pierce them. They clashed with every movement. The dragon's wings stretched out like two sails when the wind fills them. The clouds fled before him. His huge, long tail, speckled red and black, wound in a hundred folds over his scaly back and swept the land behind him for almost half a mile. In his tail's end, two sharp stings were fixed. But sharper still were his cruel claws. Whatever he touched or drew within those claws was in deadly danger. His head was more hideous than tongue can tell, for his deep jaws gaped wide, showing three rows of iron teeth ready to devour his

🐍 17 🐍

2 The ideas presented in this passage are important for the students' understanding of the story. Students may be trying to understand the importance of the hermit's words to the Red Cross Knight. **Interpreting** is one strategy they may find useful to determine the meaning. If necessary, model this strategy. In your model, you might compare the hermit's message to a sports coach's pep talk to a star player—an appeal to the player's higher sense of duty. Encourage the students to share their interpretations.

prey. A cloud of smothering smoke and burning sulfur poured from his throat, filling the air with its <u>stench</u>. His blazing eyes, flaming with rage, glared out from deep in his head. So he came toward the knight, raising his speckled breast, clashing his scales, as he leaped to greet his newest victim.

The knight on horseback fiercely rode at the dragon with all his might and <u>couched</u> his spear, but as they passed, the pointed steel glanced off the dragon's hard hide. The wrathful beast, surprised at the strength of the blow, turned quickly, and, passing the knight again, brushed him with his long tail so that horse and man fell to the ground.

Once more the Red Cross Knight mounted and attacked the dragon. Once more in vain. Yet the beast had never

🦢 *18* 🦢

before felt such a mighty stroke from the hand of any man, and he was furious for <u>revenge</u>. With his waving wings spread wide, he lifted himself high from the ground, then, stooping low, snatched up both horse and man to carry them away. High above the plain he bore them as far as a bow can shoot an arrow, but even then the knight still struggled until the monster was forced to lower his paws so that both horse and rider fought free. With the strength of three men, again the knight struck. The spear <u>glanced</u> off the scaly neck, but it pierced the dragon's left wing, spread broad above him, and the beast roared like a raging sea in a winter storm. Furious, he snatched the spear in his claws and broke it off, throwing forth flames of fire from his nostrils. Then he hurled his hideous tail about and wrapped it around the legs of the horse, until, striving to loose the knot, the horse threw its rider to the ground.

Quickly, the knight rose. He drew his sharp sword and struck the dragon's head so fiercely that it seemed nothing could withstand the blow. The dragon's crest was too hard to take a cut, but he wanted no more such blows. He tried to fly away and could not because of his wounded wing.

Loudly he bellowed—the like was never heard before—and from his body, like a wide devouring oven, sent a flame of fire that scorched the knight's face and heated his armor red-hot. Faint, weary, sore, burning with heat and wounds, the knight fell to the ground, ready to die, and the dragon clapped his iron wings in victory, while the lady, watching from afar, fell to her knees. She thought that her champion had lost the battle.

But it happened that where the knight fell, an ancient spring of silvery water bubbled from the ground. In that cool water the knight lay resting until the sun rose. Then he, too, rose to do battle again. And when the dragon saw him, he could hardly believe his eyes. Could this be the same knight, he wondered, or another who had come to take his place?

The knight <u>brandished</u> his bright blade, and it seemed sharper than ever, his hands even stronger. He <u>smote</u> the crested head with a blow so mighty that the dragon reared up like a hundred raging lions. His long, stinging tail threw down high trees and tore rocks to pieces. Lashing forward, it pierced the knight's shield and its point stuck fast in his shoulder. He tried to free himself from that barbed sting, but when he saw that his struggles were in vain, he raised his fighting sword and struck a blow that cut off the end of the dragon's tail.

Heart cannot think what outrage and what cries, with black smoke and flashing fire, the beast threw

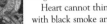

forth, turning the whole world to darkness. Gathering himself up, wild for revenge, he fiercely fell upon the sunbright shield and gripped it fast with his paws. Three times the knight tried and failed to pull the shield free. Then, laying about him with his trusty sword, he struck so many blows that fire flew from the dragon's coat like sparks from an <u>anvil</u>, and the beast raised one paw to defend himself. Striking with might and main, the knight <u>severed</u> the other paw, which still clung to the shield.

Now from the furnace inside himself, the dragon threw huge flames that covered all the heavens with smoke and <u>brimstone</u> so that the knight was forced to retreat to save his body from the scorching fire. Again, weary and wounded with his long fight, he fell. When gentle Una saw him lying motionless, she trembled with fear and prayed for his safety.

But he had fallen beneath a fair apple tree, its spreading branches covered with red fruit, and from that tree dropped a

20

3 This paragraph signals a turning point in the story. The students should sense that something exciting is about to happen. It would be natural for them to **predict** what might happen next. Encourage volunteers to share their predictions and to explain how previous information in the story helped them make their predictions. Remind them to follow up on their predictions later.

Throughout the story, the students may suggest **visualizing** the many descriptive action scenes to help them understand the characters and their emotions. Have them comment on the physical and emotional changes in the knight.

healing dew that the deadly dragon did not dare to come near. Once more the daylight faded and night spread over the earth. Under the apple tree the knight slept.

Then dawn chased away the dark, a lark mounted up to heaven, and up rose the brave knight with all his hurts and wounds healed, ready to fight again. When the dragon saw him, he began to be afraid. Still he rushed upon the knight, mouth gaping wide to swallow him whole. And the knight's bright weapon, taking advantage of that open jaw, ran it through with such strength that the dragon fell dead, breathing his last in smoke and cloud. Like a mountain he fell, and lay still. The knight himself trembled to see that fall, and his dear lady did not dare to come near to thank her faithful knight until she saw that the dragon would stir no more.

4 *Now our ship comes into port. Furl the sails and drop anchor. Safe from storm, Una is at her journey's end.*

The watchman on the castle wall called out to the king and queen that the dragon was dead, and when the old king saw that it was true, he ordered the castle's great brass gates to be opened so that the tidings of peace and joy might spread through all the land. Trumpets sounded the news that the great beast had fallen. Then the king and queen came out of the city with all their nobles to meet the Red Cross Knight. Tall young men led the way, carrying laurel branches to lay at the hero's feet. Pretty girls wore wreaths of flowers and made music on tambourines. The children came dancing, laughing and singing, with a crown of flowers for Una. They gazed in wonder at the victorious knight.

 22

But when the people saw where the dead dragon lay, they dared not come near to touch him. Some ran away, some pretended not to be afraid. One said the dragon might still be alive; one said he saw fire in the eyes. Another said the eyes were moving. When a foolish child ran forward to touch the dragon's claws, his mother scolded him. "How can I tell!" she said. "Those claws might scratch my son, or tear his tender hand." At last someone of the bolder men began to measure the dragon to prove how many acres his body covered.

The old king embraced and kissed his daughter. He gave gifts of gold and ivory and a thousand thanks to the dragon-slayer. But the knight told the king never to forget the poor people, and gave the rich gifts to them. Then back to the palace all the people went, still singing, to feast and to hear the story of the knight's adventures with Una.

23

4 Students may connect this italicized passage to the previous italicized passage and try to figure out the meanings in relation to the story. **Interpreting** is one strategy they might find useful. Have the students collaborate and discuss their ideas to determine the meaning of the passages. Naturally there will be multiple viewpoints. Encourage students to look for clues as they read further in the text to determine the meaning of these passages relative to the story.

When the tale ended the king said, "Never did living man sail through such a sea of deadly dangers. Since you are now safely come to shore, stay here and live happily ever after. You have earned your rest."

But the brave knight answered, "No, my lord, I have sworn to give knight's service to the Fairy Queen for six years. Until then, I cannot rest."

The king said, "I have promised that the dragonslayer should have Una for his wife, and be king after me. If you love each other, my daughter is yours now. My kingdom shall be yours when you have done your service for the Fairy Queen and returned to us."

Then he called Una, who came no longer wearing her black cloak and her veil, but dressed in a lily-white gown that shimmered like silver. Never had the knight seen her so beautiful.

Whenever he looked at the brightness of her sunshiny face, his heart melted with pleasure.

So Una and the Red Cross Knight were married and lived together joyfully. But the knight did not forget his promise to serve the Fairy Queen, and when she called him into service, off he rode on brave adventures until at last he earned his name, Saint George of Merry England.

That is how it is when jolly sailors come into a quiet harbor. They unload their cargo, mend ship, and take on fresh supplies. Then away they sail on another long voyage, while we are left on shore, waving good-bye and wishing them Godspeed. **5**

MEET MARGARET HODGES, AUTHOR
Margaret Hodges became interested in the story of Saint George and the Dragon when one of her colleagues told of reading the tale to his four-year-old granddaughter. After Hodges saw the story acted out in a puppet show, she began noticing the figure of Saint George depicted in various art forms—in sculpture, stained glass, and paintings. Saint George's bravery and virtue have made him an admired figure in folk literature. Margaret Hodges decided to do her own telling of his tale, based on Edmund Spenser's Faerie Queene.

MEET TRINA SCHART HYMAN, ILLUSTRATOR
Before undertaking the illustrations for Saint George and the Dragon, Trina Schart Hyman did extensive research on the historical setting of the pre-Arthurian period, and even on the correct portrayal of the dragon.

"I studied lizard scales very carefully, as they have a notched shape quite different from snake scales, and used them in my illustrations. My dragon's entire physiognomy is correct for a reptile, except for the wings, which were inspired by images of a pterodactyl."

25

5 The figurative language in this passage may cause confusion for some students. **Visualizing** is one strategy they may find useful. Encourage the students to discuss the feeling or mood created in the passage. They may wish to go back and read all of the italicized passages together. Encourage the students to collaborate and share their ideas about what the passage means and the feeling the author was trying to convey. Ask a volunteer to explain the results of their collaboration.

Discussing Strategy Use
Encourage students to discuss any problems they had as they read this story and to tell what strategies they used to solve those problems.

* EXPLORING THROUGH DISCUSSION

Reflecting on the Selection
Whole-Group Discussion

The whole group discusses the selection and any **personal thoughts, reactions, problems, or questions** that it raises. During this time, students may also be invited to **return** to the **clues, problems, and wonderings** they noted on the board during browsing to determine whether the clues were borne out by the selection, whether and how their problems were solved, and whether their wonderings were answered or deserve further discussion and exploration. Avoid treating their ideas like a list to be discussed and eliminated in a linear fashion. Instead, let the **students decide which items deserve further discussion.** To stimulate discussion, the **students** can **ask** one another the kinds of **questions that good readers ask themselves** about a text: **What did I find interesting? What is important here? What was difficult to understand? Why would someone want to read this?** Your own participation in the discussion might take the form of expressing and modeling your reactions to characters or to other aspects of the story. It is important for the students to see you as a contributing member of the group.

To emphasize that you are part of the group, actively **participate in the handing-off process:** Raise your hand to be called on by the last speaker when you have a contribution to make. Point out unusual and interesting insights verbalized by the students so that these insights are recognized and discussed. As the year progresses, the **students will take more and more responsibility for the discussions** of the selections. The handing-off process is a good way to get them to take on this responsibility. To review the **discussion process,** see **Learning Framework Card 2, Exploring Through Discussion.**

Assessment

In a successful discussion, it should not be necessary for you to ask questions to assess the students' understanding of the text. If necessary, however, engage in a discussion to determine whether students have grasped the following ideas:
- how the knight came to fight the dragon
- how the knight dealt with each challenge
- how the knight was changed by the end of the story

Response Journal

If the students would like to remember any additional thoughts about the story, have them record these in their personal response journal. For a review of information about the **response journal,** see **Teacher Tool Card 122.**

Exploring Concepts Within the Selection
Small-Group Discussion

Small groups should discuss the relationship of this selection to the unit concepts. Circulate among the groups and observe discussions. Remind the students to refer to the Question Board and the Concept Board to keep their discussions focused.

ASSESSMENT TIP This may be a good opportunity to observe students working in groups and to mark observations in your Teacher's Observation Log.

Sharing Ideas
About Explorable
Concepts

Have the groups **report their ideas** and **discuss them** with the rest of the class. It is crucial that the students' ideas determine this discussion.

- Students may point out that the knight exhibited the characteristics of perseverance because he was *willing* to face a problem, had the *courage* to try to overcome obvious dangers, and *kept trying* when problems arose. They may compare the idea of *persevering* with that of *being brave* and clarify the difference by identifying the factor of persistence that distinguishes perseverance.
- Some students may suggest that the dragon also persevered. They may discuss whether perseverance always serves a good cause.
- Some students may suggest that the knight persevered because others expected him to.
- They may point out that the king rewarded the knight, and may discuss whether perseverance is necessarily rewarded.
- Although this selection is based on fantasy, students may compare the main idea of fighting for the "good cause" with the ideas in the stories in unit 3, Taking A Stand. Specifically, they may connect St. George to Gandhi. Both were committed to making life better for the people of their land.

As these ideas and others are stated, have the students **add them to** the **Question Board** or the **Concept Board**.

Recording Ideas

As students complete the above discussions, ask them to **sum up what they have learned from their conversations and to tell how they might use this information** in further explorations. Any special information or insights may be recorded on the **Concept Board**. Any further questions that they would like to think about, pursue, or investigate may be recorded on the **Question Board**. They may want to discuss the progress that has been made on their questions. They may also want to cross out any questions that no longer warrant consideration.

❯ The students should also record their ideas and impressions about the selection and the concepts on page 65 of their Explorer's Notebook.

TEACHING TIP Students should be generating their own questions and ideas. Each class will construct its own unique discussion. Ideas offered here are merely suggestions.

Connections
Across Units

Recording Concept Information

As I read each selection, this is what I added to my understanding of perseverance.

Saint George and the Dragon, retold by Margaret Hodges

_____
_____
_____
_____
_____
_____
_____
_____
_____
_____
_____

"Miracle at the Pump House" by Catherine Owens Peare

_____
_____
_____
_____
_____
_____
_____
_____
_____
_____
_____

Unit 4/Perseverance   EN 65

Explorer's Notebook, page 65

2 READING WITH A WRITER'S EYE

MINILESSONS

Writer's Craft:
Plot

Ask students what they have learned about **developing the plot** in a story. Have them describe any examples they can remember about the elements of plot from previous reading or writing.

❯ Then distribute copies of Reproducible Master 40 and discuss the elements of plot. The discussion should include the following ideas:

• In the beginning of a story, the author usually **introduces the main character, describes the setting**, and **establishes a problem.**

• Additional **conflicts** develop as the main character struggles to overcome the problem.

• Often the story has a **climax**, or major **turning point,** an event that leads to a **solution** to the problem.

• The story usually concludes with the **resolution** of all conflicts.

Then discuss the plot line diagram at the bottom of Reproducible Master 40. Remind students to draw a plot line similar to this whenever they want to keep track of the plot elements of a story they are reading or writing. Have them place this page in the Story Elements section of their Writer's Notebook.

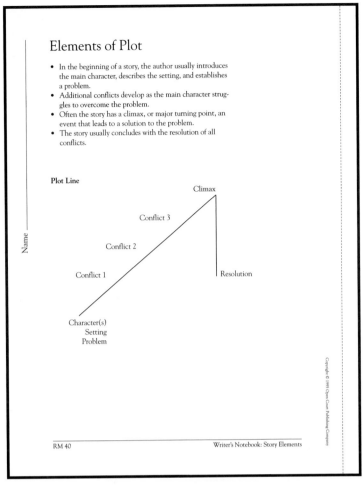

Elements of Plot

- In the beginning of a story, the author usually introduces the main character, describes the setting, and establishes a problem.
- Additional conflicts develop as the main character struggles to overcome the problem.
- Often the story has a climax, or major turning point, an event that leads to a solution to the problem.
- The story usually concludes with the resolution of all conflicts.

Plot Line

Climax

Conflict 3

Conflict 2

Conflict 1

Resolution

Character(s)
Setting
Problem

Name

Copyright © 1995 Open Court Publishing Company

RM 40   Writer's Notebook: Story Elements

Reproducible Master 40

Tell students that Margaret Hodges defines the setting, the characters, and the problem at the beginning of *Saint George and the Dragon.* Explain that writers often organize their stories with a plot line to help them develop their ideas. To illustrate how the author structured the plot, have a volunteer read the first two paragraphs of the selection on page 14. Ask students to identify the characters, the setting, and to explain what clues in the text indicate a problem. If necessary, help the students to recall that the main character tries to reach a goal.

*Selective Reading:
Focus on Plot*

Have students identify and read aloud passages from the text on pages 17 and 18 that show the first conflict between the dragon and the knight. Some examples students may point out include the following:

- page 17, paragraph 2: "Then they heard a hideous roaring"
- page 18, line 3: "he came toward the knight"
- page 18, paragraph 1: "The knight . . . rode at the dragon"
- page 18, paragraph 1: "horse and man fell to the ground"

Selection-Based Practice

You might want to draw a plot line on the chalkboard similar to the one on Reproducible Master 40 and fill it in to indicate the story's conflict(s), moving from the bottom upward. Have students identify passages in which Hodges keeps the plot moving at a rapid pace. Encourage them to point out examples of details that created suspense. For example:

Saint George and the Dragon

Plot

Fill in the plot elements for Saint George and the Dragon.

Setting: _____

_____

Characters: _____

_____

Problem/conflict: _____

_____

_____

Two events: _____

_____

_____

_____

_____

_____

_____

_____

Turning point: _____

_____

Climax, or high point: _____

_____

End of conflict: _____

_____

Conclusion: _____

_____

_____

Refer to this page when writing to make sure your stories
contain these important story elements.

Name

Copyright © 1995 Open Court Publishing Company

Story Elements

Unit 4/Perseverance   R/WC 27

Reading/Writing Connection, page 27

- page 19, line 13: "Then he hurled . . . the horse threw its rider to the ground."
- page 20, paragraph 1: "Quickly, the knight rose."

Independent Practice: Plot

➤ To extend their discussion of what Hodges did in her writing to develop the plot, have the students work independently or in small groups to complete the plot elements for *Saint George and the Dragon* on Reading/Writing Connection, page 27. Provide time for students to share and compare their ideas. Encourage them to discuss each plot element as it corresponds to the selection and to express their idea about how Hodges resolves the story.

Writer's Craft: Setting

Ask students what they have learned about **setting** and **have them** describe any examples they can remember from their reading or writing about setting, especially in fiction. Explain that a writer's purpose in establishing the setting is to **bring the story to life** for readers, to **help them understand** the story, and to **make it interesting.**

Refer students to Reproducible Master 5 in the Story Elements section of their Writer's Notebook, Elements of Setting. Discuss the following points about the setting of a story:

- The setting of a story tells **where** and **when** the events of a story occur.

- The setting must help the reader **visualize** where the action is occurring. An author does this by including **vivid sensory details** about the setting to aid the reader as she or he pictures the action.
- The setting of any story, realistic or imaginary, must be **believable** so that the reader can visualize the time and place.
- The setting should help **create a mood** for the story—warm, happy, lonely, sad, frightening, or humorous. Authors do this by using just the **right words**. And artists help create a mood with their **illustrations** of a setting.

Tell students that Margaret Hodges established the setting in *Saint George and the Dragon* by using carefully detailed, vivid descriptions **to help the reader visualize an imaginary place**. To illustrate how the author reveals setting, have a volunteer read aloud the first paragraph from the story on page 14. Ask students to identify words and phrases in the passages that the author used to establish when and where the story takes place ("In the days when . . . lived in England").

Selective Reading:
Focus on Setting

Have volunteers identify and read aloud two or three additional passages from the story that illustrate the setting. (Almost any page from the story contains a description of the setting.) Ask students to identify words and phrases in the passages that are used to describe what the characters see, feel, hear, taste, or smell, and that describe the place. You may wish to write on the chalkboard words and phrases that help establish the setting.

Independent Practice:
Setting

➤ Have students work independently or in small collaborative groups, using Reading/Writing Connection, page 28, to extend their discussion of how authors of fictional stories establish settings in interesting ways to bring imaginary places to life.

WRITING

Linking Reading to Writing

To provide opportunities for the students to develop interesting plots and create vivid settings in their writing, encourage them to do any or all of the following:
- Look in their own writing for examples of ways in which they used story elements to develop plot and add these to their Writer's Notebook.
- Look in their own writing for pieces that they can improve by revising the plot. Encourage them to add events that lead up to the climax, or high point, and to change, add to, or refine the settings.
- Write a new story and list possible plots and settings.

✱ Writing Process

Some students may want to write a new story that takes place in an imaginary setting. Encourage them to develop a plot that includes a character or characters that could not really exist, and events that could

Saint George and the Dragon

Setting

In *Saint George and the Dragon* or in any other stories you have read, look for examples of how authors establish settings. Write down the story titles and list some of the details the authors use to describe the settings. Note anything that distinguishes the imaginary settings in the stories from realistic settings.

Title: _____ Page: _____
Setting details: _____
_____
_____
_____
_____
_____
_____

Title: _____ Page: _____
Setting details: _____
_____
_____
_____
_____
_____
_____
_____

Name

Story Elements
28 R/WC   Perseverance/Unit 4

Copyright © 1995 Open Court Publishing Company

Reading/Writing Connection, page 28

Vocabulary Exploration

Word: _____
Why you chose this word: _____
_____

Definition as used in the selection: _____
_____

Other meanings: _____
_____

Any antonyms you can think of: _____

Any synonyms you can think of: _____

Where else have you found this word? _____
_____

How might you use this word in your writing? _____
_____

Your sentence using the word: _____
_____
_____

Remember to use this word in speaking as well as in writing.

Name

Copyright © 1995 Open Court Publishing Company

Writer's Notebook: Personal Dictionary   RM 15

Reproducible Master 15

not really happen as described. Have students share their plot ideas with their classmates and seek feedback to clarify their ideas during this prewriting step.

VOCABULARY

➤ Words from the story that are related to perseverance and that may have come up in discussion include *perils, wrathful,* and *striving.* Allow time for the students to complete copies of Vocabulary Exploration form, Reproducible Master 15, for those words they wish to remember and use or for those that are important to the unit concepts. Remind them to add these or any other words and phrases from the story to the Personal Dictionary section of their Writer's Notebook. Then provide an opportunity for volunteers to share words and phrases they've added and to tell why they chose them. For additional opportunities to build vocabulary, see **Teacher Tool Card 77.**

Adding to Personal Dictionary

3 GUIDED AND INDEPENDENT EXPLORATION

Guided
Exploration

* Exploring
Through
Reflective
Activities

Students will engage in activities of their own choosing that allow them to explore the subject of perseverance more deeply, using the questions they have raised. These explorations may relate to the current selection or to a number of selections, but they must revolve around the unit concepts. The following is a menu of possible activities from which the students may choose:

- **A literature search** to pursue a question or a problem. Discussion or writing may follow.
- **An original playlet or puppet show** based on perseverance-related situations.
- **A role-playing game** to work out a problem about perseverance.
- **A panel discussion** with audience participation on a question or a problem. (This discussion would have a leader and could be video-taped.)
- **A debate** on an issue related to perseverance. (Debaters would form teams. They would be required to follow some basic rules of debate, providing reasoned support for their side of the issue.)
- **An advice column** dealing with concept-related problems.
- **A personal experience story** related to perseverance.
- **An interview** with someone on a subject related to perseverance.
- **A picture or photo essay** about concepts related to perseverance.

Display the **Exploration Activities poster** listing the activities above so that the students may readily select from them.

Students may work on these activities alone, in pairs, or in small groups, with an option to write about them or to present them to the group. To review information about exploration, see **Learning Framework Card 3, Exploring Through Reflective Activities.**

If the students need help in deciding on an activity, here are some suggestions to get them started.

- Some students may want to examine and discuss their own ideas about what makes some people keep trying to accomplish a goal after others have given up. Suggest they share specific experiences they have had with overcoming obstacles or rising to meet challenges, such as learning to swim, learning a new game, learning to play a musical instrument, or speaking in front of a group. Encourage them to discuss motivational factors that helped them to keep trying. Some students may wish to write a story about their problems, attempts, and solutions, or to prepare a brief talk to present to the class about why some people persevere while others do not.
- The students may choose to interview a person they admire and who they think has persevered in an endeavor. During the interview, they should ask open-ended questions to find out what perseverance means to that person and whether perseverance is always a good thing.

> Students may complete Explorer's Notebook, page 68, to help them with the interview. After the interview, suggest that the students decide on the type of report they might write to share their findings with the class.

> Distribute Home/School Connection 27–28, which explains some of the unit concepts and contains a brief bibliography for students and families to share together.

Generating Questions to Explore

Encourage the students to raise questions about perseverance that they may wish to explore. Remind them that as they read further into the unit they may discover new ideas or ways to explore the concepts and that they may want to present some of the things they discover about perseverance to their classmates. Since this is the first selection of this unit, the students will simply be generating ideas at this time. They will revisit this set of questions and choose concepts for exploration after they have read and thought more about perseverance.

At this point, explain to the students that throughout the unit they may want to discuss their explorations with each other or to write about them.

Explorer's Notebook, page 68

Conducting an Interview

Choose a person whom you admire. Conduct an interview with that person to find out what perseverance means to him or her. Be sure to get the person's ideas on whether perseverance is always good or is sometimes harmful and elicit examples. Share your findings with your classmates.

• Make the necessary arrangements.

Name: _____ Date/time: _____

• Make notes about where you will conduct the interview. The setting can give you some insight into your subject and can also be of interest to your audience.

Notes: _____
_____

• Decide how you will record the answers (notebook, tape recorder).

_____

• Write out a list of the questions you would like to ask. Ask open-ended questions, not questions that can be answered with *yes* or *no*.

_____
_____
_____
_____

• Inform your subject of how you intend to report the information.

68 EN   Perseverance/Unit 4

Home/School Connection 27

Saint George and the Dragon

A message from _____

The subject of unit 4 in our reading anthology is perseverance. The students will learn about many aspects of perseverance that can lead to interesting reflections on the nature of human ideals and motivation. Some ideas that we will discuss and explore include the following: the meaning of perseverance and why it is often difficult; the importance of perseverance in our everyday lives; and the importance of perseverance in history. Here are some books about perseverance that you might like to read with your child:

The Adventures of the Negro Cowboys by Philip Durham and Everett L. Jones. Of the estimated 35,000 cowboys who rode the herds north, about one-third were African-American. Through cloudbursts and burning sun, through mud and choking dust, these cowboys did their jobs, and did them well.

Frozen Fire: A Tale of Courage by James Houston. Matthew and his Eskimo friend Kayak take off in a snowmobile in a secret search to find Matthew's father, a prospecting geologist. Struggling against bone-chilling wind, storms, starvation, wild beasts, and lawless men, the two boys battle for life.

Homecoming by Cynthia Voigt. Dicey leads her sister and two brothers, abandoned by their mother at a shopping center in Connecticut, to the home of their reclusive grandmother in Maryland. When they are not warmly welcomed, they persevere, working to make a home with her by helping revive her neglected farm.

The Incredible Journey by Sheila Burnford. A Siamese cat, an English bull terrier, and a golden retriever head for their old home across several hundred miles of Canadian wilderness.

Island of the Blue Dolphins by Scott O'Dell. A Native-American girl, Karana, lives alone on an island for years, keeping herself alive by building a shelter, making weapons, finding food, and fighting off wild dogs.

continued

Unit 4/Perseverance   H/SC 27

Copyright © 1995 Open Court Publishing Company

Saint George and the Dragon

continued

Ride the Red Cycle by Harriet G. Robinet. Jerome Johnson, disabled by a disease when he was a baby, dreams of riding a bicycle—and his stubbornness, pride, and courage take him beyond his dreams.

They Triumphed Over Their Handicaps by Joan Harries. Six people—including musician Ray Charles, stunt woman Kitty O'Neil, and private detective Jay J. Armes—attain their goals by overcoming obstacles with hard work and determination.

Here are some video titles you might like to obtain from your local video store and view with your child:

Mask. Universal, 1985. A young man with an incurable, fatal disease that causes his head to grow to twice its normal size struggles, with the help of his determined mother, to live a normal life. 120 minutes; videocassette.

National Velvet. MGM/UA Home Video, 1944. A young girl strives to train an unruly horse so that she can ride him in the Grand National steeplechase. 124 minutes; videocassette.

Stand and Deliver. Warner Home Video, 1988. With the help of an inspiring teacher, Jaime Escalante, a school class unexpectedly achieves record high scores in the state's advanced placement calculus exam. 103 minutes; videocassette.

Copyright © 1995 Open Court Publishing Company

Unit 4/Perseverance H/SC 28

Home/School Connection 28

Recording Questions

Record any questions about perseverance that your reading and exploration bring to mind. As you continue through the unit, keep adding questions that arise from your exploration of the unit concepts. Compare your ideas with those of your classmates.

1. _____
2. _____
3. _____
4. _____
5. _____
6. _____
7. _____
8. _____
9. _____
10. _____
11. _____

Copyright © 1995 Open Court Publishing Company

Unit 4/Perseverance EN 69

Explorer's Notebook, page 69

▶ Be sure students record on the **Question Board** any questions they have about perseverance. Have them use Explorer's Notebook, page 69, to help them start recording their questions about perseverance.

▶ Distribute copies of the unit bibliography, Reproducible Masters 41–44, so that students will have bibliographies available when they start their exploration. Remind them also to use the bibliography on pages 132–133 of their student anthology.

Bibliography

Books related to perseverance are listed below. You may use these as references along with other books and magazine articles you find that are related to the explorable concepts.

Notes

Alexander Graham Bell by Richard Tames. Bell, who was a teacher of the deaf, worked long and hard on various machines to aid the deaf and accidentally discovered a principle that led to the invention of the modern-day telephone.

ANPAO: An American Indian Odyssey by Jamake Highwater. To earn the right to marry the beautiful Ko-ko-mik-e-is, Anpao undertakes a long and dangerous quest over mountains, deserts, and prairies to find the home of the Sun.

Avalanche! by Ron Roy. Scott and his brother Tony find themselves caught in an avalanche in Aspen and must finally learn to get along if they are going to survive.

The Contest, an Armenian folktale adapted by Nonny Hogrogian. Two thieves discover that they are engaged to the same girl and begin a contest for her hand in marriage. The one who proves himself the cleverer at his trade will be the winner.

Dear Dr. Bell . . . Your friend, Helen Keller by Judith St. George. Dr. Bell, the famous inventor of the telephone, was also a teacher of the deaf and a lifelong friend of Helen Keller.

Reproducible Master 41

Bibliography *continued*

Notes

Dreamers & Doers: Inventors Who Changed Our World by Norman Richards. Each of these men had a dream—Goddard, Goodyear, Edison, Eastman—and though they faced failure at times, they learned from their failures and went on trying until they succeeded.

Dreams into Deeds: Nine Women Who Dared by Linda Peavy and Ursula Smith. The nine women profiled in this book all had the courage to envision fulfilling lives for themselves, lives others thought were unrealistic if not downright dangerous, but through their perseverance they achieved remarkable personal and social goals.

Eight Black American Inventors by Robert C. Hayden. These are the stories of eight men of determination who fought the odds and became inventors of devices that saved lives and revolutionized industries.

Franklin Delano Roosevelt by Russell Freedman. Freedman has written a fascinating biography of the man who led the nation through the Great Depression and most of World War II while fighting his own battle with the aftereffects of polio.

The Incredible Journey of Lewis and Clark by Rhoda Blumberg. Nothing could stop a team of daring explorers who set out to chart the vast wilderness—said to be a place where monsters roamed. The pluck and the perseverance that made Lewis and Clark's expedition an enduring success is described here in a lively narrative style.

Reproducible Master 42

Bibliography *continued*

Notes

Matthew Henson: Black Explorer by Edward F. Dolan, Jr. Orphaned at thirteen, Matt Henson leads a life of adventure and peril, from China to Nicaragua to the North Pole. Henson fights off charging walruses, learns to drive a pack of dogs, and despite his lack of formal education becomes one of Admiral Peary's most valuable team members in his explorations of the arctic.

Move Over, Wheelchairs Coming Through! by Ron Roy. Seven young people discuss how they cope with their physical disabilities.

Pioneer Plowmaker: A Story about John Deere by David R. Collins. The young blacksmith John Deere had not let impossibility and disaster stop him before, and he wasn't about to now. Deere built a self-scouring plow; and with this small start, he founded the famous farm-implement manufacturing business—John Deere and Company.

Sadako and the Thousand Paper Cranes by Eleanor Coerr. Sadako Sasaki was only two when an atom bomb was dropped on her city, Hiroshima, Japan. At twelve she developed leukemia as a result of radiation and faced her illness with courage, persevering to make one thousand paper cranes for good luck. Today she is a heroine to the children of Japan.

Sarah Bishop by Scott O'Dell. Sarah, left alone after the deaths of her brother and father during the American Revolutionary War, follows a path that takes her from the kitchen of a country inn to the crowded city, to a British prison, and at last to a wilderness refuge. There, drawing on strengths and skills she did not know she possessed, she begins a new life.

Reproducible Master 43

Bibliography *continued*

Notes

Sir Gawain and the Green Knight, retold by Constance Hieatt. Only Sir Gawain dared to confront the huge warrior with the green beard and the great green-bladed battle-ax. The challenge was absurd and simple: each warrior was to take one swing at the other's neck to try to behead him; but the challenge took more than a year to complete.

The Swiss Family Robinson by Johann Wyss. This is the classic story of a family who is stranded on a deserted island and whose clever use of island materials keeps it alive.

Trial by Wilderness by David Mathieson. A small plane crashes off the rugged coast of British Columbia, and one lone passenger fights her way to shore and into a world as harsh as that of the Stone Age. Her survival and eventual escape will depend entirely on her own courage and ingenuity.

Add books or articles you find.

- _____
- _____
- _____
- _____
- _____

Reproducible Master 44

BIBLIOGRAPHY

A Boat To Nowhere by Maureen Crane Wartski. Fleeing from agents of the new communist government in Vietnam, an old man and three children begin an endless and seemingly hopeless struggle for survival as boat people.

The Call of the Wild by Jack London. The year is 1897 and a dog named Buck is stolen from his master by would-be prospectors during the Alaskan Gold Rush. On the trek across Alaska's savage terrain, Buck battles with the other dogs on the sled team to gain the coveted position of lead dog.

The Cay by Theodore Taylor. This is the story of young Phillip's struggle to survive after being shipwrecked on a desert island with an old sailor named Timothy.

The Endless Steppe by Esther Hautzig. Ten-year-old Esther Rudimon and her family fight to survive five years of exile in the harsh Siberian steppes during World War II.

🐚 132 🐚

Lyddie by Katherine Paterson. In 1843, teenager Lyddie Worthen takes a job in a textile mill. There she endures long hours of exhausting work in murky, lint-filled air in order to earn the money to regain her family's farm.

The River by Gary Paulsen. In this sequel to *Hatchet*, Brian Robeson is back in the wilderness documenting his survival techniques for the government. All goes well until someone gets hit by lightning!

Where the Lilies Bloom by Vera and Bill Cleaver. A strong-willed Appalachian teenager attempts to conceal her father's death from nosy neighbors who would send her and her siblings to the county charity home.

Words by Heart by Ouida Sebestyen. In a story set during Reconstruction, an African-American family struggles for acceptance in a predominantly white southern community.

🐚 133 🐚

Professional Checkpoint: Guided and Independent Exploration

The discussions and explorations are designed to expand and deepen the students' understanding of the concepts related to perseverance. Encourage students to share with each other how their ideas have changed. They should readily discuss and accept each other's points of view.

Notes:

*INDEPENDENT WORKSHOP
Building a Community of Scholars

Student-Directed Reading, Writing, and Discussion

Remind the class that the Independent Workshop is a block of time during which they will work on a variety of activities. During the first part of Independent Workshop, they will work cooperatively with their classmates in a self-directed manner on unit explorations. The second part may be devoted to options of their choice.

Remind students that the most important thing to remember about Independent Workshop is that it is a time for them to work together and to help each other learn more about the unit concepts.

At this time, the students might choose to return to their Explorer's Notebook to complete any unfinished pages or to discuss ideas with their classmates. To review information about **Independent Workshop**, see **Learning Framework Card 5**.

WORKSHOP TIPS

Remind students to share information freely. Encourage them to use the Question Board and the Concept Board often as they formulate questions, develop ideas, and acquire new knowledge.

Collaborative Groups Since students will not be quite ready at this point to decide on one aspect of perseverance that they want to explore, encourage them to check the Question Board or to discuss ideas they may have with their classmates.

After small-group work, some students may wish to **locate some of the books about perseverance** listed on their bibliographies. This may help them think further about the concept and how to explore it.

Assessment This may be a good opportunity to observe students working in groups and to mark observations in your Teacher's Observation Log.

Additional Opportunities for Independent Reading, Writing, and Cross-curricular Activities

✳ Reading Roundtable

Encourage the students to read other books by Margaret Hodges, such as *The Wave,* about a wise old man who saves his people from a tidal wave; and *The Fire Bringer: A Paiute Indian Legend,* about a Paiute boy and his friend, Coyote, who leads the boy on a quest for fire. *Call It Courage* by Armstrong Sperry is a Tradebook Connection selection that relates well to the unit concepts. Remind the students that if they read the book, they can do the activities on the Tradebook Connection Card in the Student Toolbox.

✳ Writing Seminar

Before students begin writing a new piece, remind them to write down their goal in writing the piece and make brief notes on ideas they want to include in their writing. Encourage them to ask for peer input as they brainstorm ideas. Remind the students to use the writing process as they work on any new writing pieces or revise those in their writing folders.

Cross-curricular Activity Cards

The following Cross-curricular Activity Cards in the Student Toolbox are appropriate for this selection:
- 14 Social Studies—Heraldry
- 11 Art—Castle Architecture

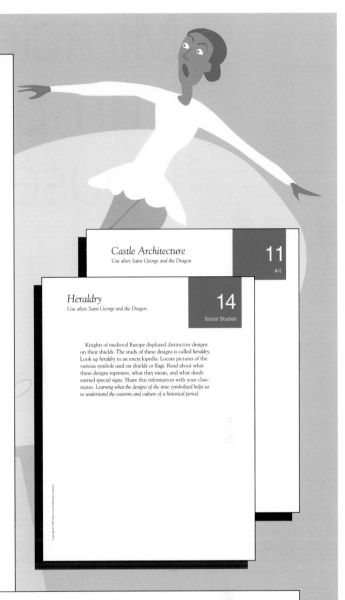

> **Castle Architecture**
> Use after Saint George and the Dragon
> **11**
> Art

> **Heraldry**
> Use after Saint George and the Dragon
> **14**
> Social Studies
>
> Knights of medieval Europe displayed distinctive designs on their shields. The study of these designs is called *heraldry.* Look up *heraldry* in an encyclopedia. Locate pictures of the various symbols used on shields or flags. Read about what these designs represent, what they mean, and what deeds earned special signs. Share this information with your classmates. *Learning what the designs of the time symbolized helps us to understand the customs and culture of a historical period.*

Additional Opportunities for Solving Learning Problems

Tutorial

Use this time to work with those students who need help in any area. Remember to use peer tutoring with those for whom it would be appropriate. Encourage the students to ask for help when they feel the need. The following Teacher Tool Cards are available in the Teacher Toolbox for your convenience:
- Writer's Craft/Reading: Plot, Teacher Tool Card 15
- Writer's Craft/Reading: Setting, Teacher Tool Card 14
- Writer's Craft/Reading: Choosing Precise and Vivid Verbs, Teacher Tool Card 22
- Writer's Craft/Reading: Elaboration Through Providing Comparison and Contrast, Teacher Tool Card 37

Miracle at the Pump House

1 READING THE SELECTION

INFORMATION FOR THE TEACHER

About the Selection

From Catherine Owens Peare's masterful biography *The Helen Keller Story*, "Miracle at the Pump House" sensitively captures the complexity of Anne Sullivan's heroic role in Helen Keller's life. Blind and deaf since early childhood, six-year-old Helen Keller displays uncontrollable rage at her own helplessness. She feels like "a bird trapped in a cage." Keller's behavior becomes even more disruptive and violent when her teacher, Anne Sullivan, arrives on the scene.

The virtue of this story lies in sensory images so vivid and yet so ordinary they touch the child in us all. Readers can experience both sadness and great joy through descriptions that reproduce the impact of fear, the weight of despair, and the glow of hope.

Link to the Unit Concepts

"Miracle at the Pump House," pages 26–37, illustrates the positive changes that can occur when even the most severe problems are viewed as challenges to be overcome through sensitivity, intelligence, and perseverance.

Today diverse new technology is available to assist the teaching process. The efforts of parent groups and professional organizations have resulted in some improvement in the functioning of our institutions to provide for people with special needs. But the willingness of a parent, teacher, or friend to understand the kinds of feelings that accompany an individual's problem can make all the difference.

This selection may lead students to ask what they can do to become a source of encouragement to the people around them. They may also begin to explore how people with limitations have gone on to persevere and overcome their problems and, consequently, have developed methods to make things easier for others with similar problems.

LESSON OVERVIEW

"Miracle at the Pump House" by Catherine Owens Peare, pages 26–37

READING THE SELECTION

Materials
Student anthology, pp. 26–37
Explorer's Notebook, p. 65
Assessment Master 1

FYI
Learning Framework Cards
• Setting Reading Goals and Expectations, 1A
• Exploring Through Discussion, 2

READING WITH A WRITER'S EYE

Minilesson
Writer's Craft: Sensory Description

Materials
Reading/Writing Connection, p. 29
Reproducible Master 15

FYI
Learning Framework Card
• Writing Process, 7

Teacher Tool Cards
• Spelling and Vocabulary: Building Vocabulary, 77

• Classroom Supports: Peer Conferencing, 120
• Classroom Supports: Writer's Notebook, 122

Options for Instruction
Writer's Craft: Characterization
Writer's Craft: Providing Multiple Effects for a Cause
(Use Teacher Tool Cards listed below.)

GUIDED AND INDEPENDENT EXPLORATION

Materials
Home/School Connection 29
Explorer's Notebook, pp. 70–71

Independent Workshop

Optional Materials from Student Toolbox
Tradebook Connection Cards

Cross-curricular Activity Cards
• 15 Social Studies—Sign Language
• 16 Social Studies—Today's Miracles

Student Tool Cards
• Writer's Craft/Reading: Giving Descriptions, 40
• Writer's Craft/Reading: Characterization, 13
• Writer's Craft/Reading: Showing Cause and Effect, 31

FYI
Learning Framework Card
• Reading Roundtable, 6

Teacher Tool Cards
• Writer's Craft/Reading: Elaboration Through Providing Descriptions, 40
• Writer's Craft/Reading: Characterization, 13
• Writer's Craft/Reading: Causal Indicators, 31

NOTES

Asterisks (*) throughout the lesson indicate learning frameworks. Learning Framework Cards and Teacher Tool Cards can be found in the Teacher Toolbox.

About the
Author

"Miracle at the Pump House" is from *The Helen Keller Story*, a biography by Catherine Owens Peare. In 1962, Peare's biography, *The Helen Keller Story*, won a Sequoyah Award and the William Allen White Children's Book Award. Peare was born in Perth Amboy, New Jersey, in 1911 and is an award-winning author of many biographies written for children. Some of her works include biographies of writers, such as Mark Twain and Louisa May Alcott, and biographies of political figures, such as Herbert Hoover and Franklin Delano Roosevelt.

About the
Illustrator

Ron Himler is the award-winning illustrator of "Miracle at the Pump House." He was born in Cleveland, Ohio, and attended the Cleveland Institute of Art and the Cranbook Academy of Art in Michigan. In addition to illustrating children's books, he has worked as a technical sculptor and a toy designer. His books, *Baby* and *Rocket in My Pocket* both received the American Institute of Graphic Arts award. Himler's illustrations show how important details create time and place. One of the best known books Himler has illustrated is Byrd Baylor's *The Best Town in the World*.

INFORMATION FOR THE STUDENT

Tell the students that the selection they are about to read was written by Catherine Owens Peare and illustrated by Ron Himler. As appropriate, you may want to share other information about the author or the illustrator.

As a child Anne Sullivan suffered from trachoma, a virus that causes blindness. Partial sight was returned to her after several operations. Sullivan's own experience with blindness prepared her to teach Keller. During the course of Anne Sullivan's life, she continued her work with Helen Keller. Sullivan married John Macy in 1905 and died in 1936.

About the Characters

In 1904, Keller graduated from Radcliffe College and went on to become an international author and lecturer. Some of Helen Keller's works include *The Story of My Life*, *The World I Live In*, *A Chant of Darkness*, and *Teacher: Anne Sullivan Macy*. Helen Keller led an active life until the age of 87. She died in June 1968. Reading about these extraordinary women helps us to see not only the qualities that we admire in them, but also the problems that made them human.

✳ COGNITIVE AND RESPONSIVE READING

Activating Prior
Knowledge

Students may be familiar with Helen Keller or Anne Sullivan. You might want to ask volunteers to talk about anything they know about these two women.

Setting Reading
Goals and
Expectations

Have the children **browse the selection, using the clues/problems/ wondering procedure.** Children will return to these observations after reading. For a review of **browsing**, see **Learning Framework Card 1A, Setting Reading Goals and Expectations.**

Recommendations for Reading the Selection

Allow the students time to discuss how they would like to read the story. The simplicity of the language in this story makes it a good one for silent reading. Whether the selection is read silently or orally, it should not pose many problems for most students. During **oral reading, use and encourage think-alouds.** During **silent reading,** allow discussion as needed. Discuss problems, strategies, and reactions after reading.

This would also be a good selection **for responding to text by expressing feelings** while reading aloud. Model this response, and then invite the students to respond similarly.

TEACHING TIP Before assigning a reading selection, skim the text for difficulties that you will want to discuss before, during, and after reading.

About the Reading Strategies

Because of the nature of biographical literature, students will naturally wonder about the lives of people different from themselves. They may try to understand ideas that can be answered by making inferences from the text. **Wondering** is a strategy that the students might find themselves using to make sense of their reading. In addition, students will decide what impact the text has on the way they look at things. **Interpreting** is another strategy that they may find helpful.

STEPS TOWARD INDEPENDENCE By this time in the year, students should be taking responsibility for using these strategies on their own.

Think-Aloud Prompts for Use in Oral Reading

Notice the think-aloud prompts placed with the page miniatures. These are merely suggestions for helping students use the strategies. Remind the students to use whatever strategies they need to help them understand the selection. Refer them to the **reading strategy posters,** if necessary. Encourage them to share with each other the strategies they use to solve problems as they read. If you have sight-, speech-, or hearing-impaired students in your classroom, use them as a resource in helping other students clarify unfamiliar ideas discussed in the selection.

THINK ALOUD PROMPTS

These prompts may be used as guides to promote cognitive and responsive reading.

1 Some students may **wonder** about the term *finger alphabet*. If necessary, model your own wondering. For example,

I wonder what a finger alphabet is. I've seen people talk with their hands. Maybe they are spelling words with their fingers. Does anyone else wonder about this?

If some students are familiar with the manual alphabet, ask them to explain or demonstrate how letters are represented by different finger positions pressed into another's hand. If students are not familiar with this method of communication, encourage them to look for clues as they read further in the text to help them understand the term *finger alphabet.*

MIRACLE AT THE PUMP HOUSE

from THE HELEN KELLER STORY
by Catherine Owens Peare
illustrated by Ron Himler

On 27 June 1880, a baby girl was born to Arthur and Kate Keller on their farm in Tuscumbia, Alabama. They christened her Helen Adams Keller. Helen was a happy, healthy child until February 1882, when she was stricken with a high fever that left her blind and deaf.

Young Helen was baffled by the dark and silent world into which she had been propelled, and she became bad-tempered and unruly. She threw tantrums and got into mischief. No one in the family seemed able to control her behavior.

When Helen was six years old, Mrs. Keller read a book by Charles Dickens called American Notes. In the book, Dickens discussed Perkins Institution for the Blind, located in Boston. He told about Laura Bridgman, a blind and deaf girl who learned to communicate by means of a finger alphabet—a method that was revolutionary at the time. Captain and Mrs. Keller traveled to Perkins and discussed their daughter's condition with Mr. Anagnos who worked with the handicapped children at the institution. After hearing their story, Mr. Anagnos chose one of his former students, twenty-year-old Anne Sullivan, to be Helen Keller's governess and teacher.

26

Anne Sullivan had come to Perkins Institution as a blind child, and later her vision had been partially restored by surgery. She wanted to spend the winter weeks studying the records on Laura Bridgman, before going to Alabama, and so could be expected at the Keller's home on the first of March.

"Just a few more months," thought Kate Keller. "Just a few more months, and there will be someone to take care of my little girl."

And while the robust and undisciplined Helen tyrannized the household with her pranks—locking doors and hiding keys, yanking tablecloths filled with dishes to the floor—Kate Keller fastened her hopes on Anne Sullivan and the first of March.

"James will drive you to the station to meet her," said the Captain when the day came.

Anxious and tense, Mrs. Keller sat on the front seat of the carriage beside her stepson. He allowed the reins to lie slack on the back of the motionless horse, and they both stared along the railway tracks watching for that first puff of soft-coal smoke in the distance.

"How will we know her?" Mrs. Keller wondered aloud.

"She will probably be the only passenger, Mother. It will be all right. Don't worry."

"She is coming such a long way to help us!"

James noticed the train first.

"There it is," he said and climbed out of the carriage.

The train pulled in and ground to a stop before the little wooden station house. A man in the baggage compartment

27

tossed a sack of mail to the local agent, and the train pulled out. No passenger disembarked.

Without a word James Keller climbed back into his seat, jerked the reins, and turned the horse's head toward home. Kate Keller fumbled for a handkerchief and began to cry.

"There's another train this afternoon, and we are going to meet it!" declared Mrs. Keller firmly.

Anne Sullivan didn't appear on the first of March, nor on the second.

"We are going to meet every train until she comes!" insisted Helen's mother.

On the third of March, 1887, Kate and James sat in the carriage at the railway station once more, waiting for a late afternoon train. This time a passenger did get off, a young girl dressed in burdensome woolen clothing, looking frightened and tired, her eyes red from weeping and the irritation of the soft-coal dust.

"Miss Sullivan?"

"Yes."

James helped her into the carriage, and placed her bag and trunk in the back.

"We were afraid you weren't coming," said Mrs. Keller.

"I am sorry," said Anne Sullivan. "I had the wrong kind of ticket somehow, and I had to change trains at Philadelphia and Baltimore. Then I had to wait over a whole day at Washington for a train coming to Tuscumbia."

"Oh, that is too bad."

"It's all right, now," said Miss Sullivan. "I'm only thinking of your little girl. I want to see my pupil as soon as possible."

28

The carriage drew into the yard at last and Captain Keller came forward to help them down. Miss Sullivan didn't seem to be listening to the introduction. She was looking at the open doorway of the house where a young mortal stood—blank-faced and hostile—nearly seven years old.

Miss Sullivan left the Kellers and hurried forward to gather the little "phantom" into her arms.

"Phantom"—Helen Keller's own name for herself as a child—stood in the doorway sensing the excitement of a new arrival. She felt the vibration of a strange footstep on the porch, then another footstep, coming closer. Strangers were often enemies. She bent her head down and charged into the newcomer, and the newcomer fell back. Again the footsteps came toward her, and the stranger tried to put arms around her. Helen drove off Miss Sullivan's embrace with kicks and punches.

She discovered that the stranger had a bag, and she grabbed the bag and darted into the house. When her mother caught up with her and tried to take the bag away she fought, because she knew her mother would give in. Mother always gave in.

But Anne Sullivan encouraged her to keep the bag and carry it up the stairs. Soon a trunk was brought into the room, and Helen flung herself against it, exploring the lid with her fingers until she found the lock. Miss Sullivan gave her the key and allowed her to unlock it and lift the lid. Helen plunged her hands down into the contents, feeling everything.

The newcomer lifted a doll out of the trunk and laid it in Helen's arms, and after that she did something very strange indeed. She held one of Helen's hands and in its palm formed

29

2 Students may ask for clarification of the word *phantom.* Some may try to determine the meaning of the word as it is used in this **context.** You might encourage them to make connections to what they already know about the word "phantom" and to think about the nature of something that only appears to exist, such as a hologram. Have volunteers share their **clarification strategies** and explain why Helen regarded herself as a phantom.

curious figures with her own fingers. First she held her own thumb and middle finger together while her index finger stood upright. Then she formed a circle by joining her thumb and first finger, and finally she spread her thumb and index finger as far apart at they would go.

With a sudden wild leap Helen darted for the door, but the stranger caught hold of her and brought her back, forcing her into a chair. Helen fought and raged, but the stranger was strong. She did not give in like family and servants. Helen was startled to feel a piece of cake being placed in her hand, and she gobbled it down quickly before it could be taken away. The stranger did another trick with her fingers. On Helen's palm she formed an open circle with thumb and first finger, next closed her fist for a moment, following that by placing her thumb between her second and third fingers and curling her last two fingers under, and finally held all her fingertips together against her thumb.

That was enough! Helen tore loose and bolted out of the room and down the stairs, to Mother, to Father, to her stepbrother, to the cook, to anybody whom she could manage.

But at dinner the stranger sat next to her. Helen had her own way of eating, and no one had ever tried to stop her. She stumbled and groped her way from place to place, snatching and grabbing from other people's plates, sticking her fingers into anything at all. When she came to the visitor, her hand was slapped away. Helen reached out for the visitor's plate again. Another slap! She flung herself forward and was lifted bodily back. Now she was being forced into her own chair again, being made to sit there, and once more she was raging, fighting, kicking. She broke away and found all the other

30

3 There is a great deal of action occurring at this point in the story. **Visualizing** is one strategy the students may find helpful as they try to picture the interaction between the two characters. You might want to encourage volunteers to act out the sequence of events to help students picture what is happening in the text and to gain a better understanding of the significance of the exchange between Anne Sullivan and Helen Keller.

Some students might point out the additional information given about the term *finger alphabet.*

chairs empty. Her family had deserted her, left her alone with this enemy!

Again the enemy took hold of her, made her sit down, forced a spoon into her hand, made her eat from her own plate.

When the ordeal finally ended, she broke away and ran out of the dining room—to Mother, to Mother's arms. Mother's eyes were wet. Mother was crying. Mother was sorry.

Every day there were battles with the newcomer. There were battles when she had to take her bath, comb her hair, button her shoes. And always those finger tricks; even Mother and Father were doing them. Since the trick for cake usually brought her a piece of cake, Helen shrewdly began to learn others.

If battles with her new governess grew too unbearable, Helen could seek out Martha Washington, a child her own age, daughter of their Negro cook, and bully and boss her. Martha's pigtails were short because Helen had once clipped them off with a pair of scissors.

Or she could simply romp with her father's hunting dogs and forget there was such a thing in the house as a governess. She could help feed the turkey gobblers, or go hunting for the nests of the guinea hens in the tall grass. She loved to burrow her way in amongst the big flowering shrubs; completely surrounded by the prickly leaves of the mimosa she felt safe and protected.

There was real comfort in revenge. She knew about keys and locks, and she found a day when she could lock the awful intruder in her room and run away with the key. The

32

big day of revenge came when, in one of the enemy's unguarded moments, Helen raised her fists in the air and brought them down on Miss Sullivan's face. Two teeth snapped off.

An abrupt change occurred in her life right after that.

Miss Sullivan took her by the hand and they went for a carriage drive. When the carriage stopped, they alighted and entered a different house. Helen groped her way about the room, recognizing nothing, until her companion placed one of her own dolls in her arms. She clung to the familiar thing. But as soon as Helen realized that she was alone with the stranger in a strange place, she flung the doll away in a rage. She refused to eat, refused to wash, and gave the governess a long, violent tussle when it came time to go to bed.

The governess did not seem very tall, but she was strong and stubborn, and for the first time in her life Helen began to experience defeat. She grew tired, wanted to lie down and sleep, but still she struggled against the stranger's will. She would sleep on the floor, or in the chair! But each time she was dragged back to the bed. At last Helen felt herself giving in, and, exhausted by her own efforts, and huddled close to the farthest edge of the big double bed, she fell asleep.

When Helen awoke in the morning, she flung herself out of bed prepared to give further resistance, but somehow her face was washed with less effort than the night before, and after she had dressed and eaten her breakfast she felt her companion's determined but gentle hands guiding her fingers over some soft, coarse yarn, guiding them again along a thin bone shaft with a hooked end. In a very little while Helen had grasped the idea of crocheting, and as she became interested in making a chain she forgot to hate Anne Sullivan.

33

4 This passage signals a turning point in the story. The students should sense from the action that something exciting is going to happen. Some students may naturally want to **predict** what will happen next. Encourage volunteers to share their predictions and explain how previous information in the story helped them make their predictions.

5 The notion of a virtual stranger taking a little deaf and blind girl away from her loving family may appear to be cruel and frightening. Students may **wonder** why Miss Sullivan took Helen away from her home. If necessary, model your own wondering. In your model, you might wonder aloud about doing something one way and, when that doesn't seem to work, trying another way.

Each day in the new house after that brought new skills to be learned—cards to sew, beads to string.

After about two weeks, Helen had begun to accept her routine, her table manners, her tasks, her companion. The whole world seemed to grow gentler as her own raging disposition subsided.

She cocked her head suddenly one afternoon and sniffed the air, detecting a new odor in the room, something familiar—one of her father's dogs! Helen groped about until she found the silken, long-haired setter, Belle. Of all the dogs on the farm, Belle was Helen's favorite, and she quickly lifted one of Belle's paws and began to move the dog's toes in one of the finger tricks. Miss Sullivan patted Helen's head, and the approval made her feel almost happy.

Miss Sullivan soon took her by the hand and led her out the door, across a yard, to some front steps, and instantly Helen realized where she was. She was home! She had been in the little annex near her home all this time. Mother and Father had not been far away. She raced up the steps and into the house and flung herself at one adult after another. She was home! Scrambling up the stairs to the second floor, she found her own room just the same, and when she felt Miss Sullivan standing behind her she turned impulsively and pointed a finger at her and then at her own palm. Who was she?

"T-e-a-c-h-e-r," Anne Sullivan spelled into her hand.

But the finger trick was too long to be learned at once.

Every day after that Teacher and Helen were constant companions indoors and out, and gradually Helen learned to see with her fingers. Teacher showed her how to explore plants and animals without damaging them—chickens, grasshoppers,

35

6 The miraculous change in Helen's behavior after two weeks may cause some students to be surprised or skeptical. **Interpreting** is a strategy that might help them better understand Helen's behavior. If necessary, model your own interpretation. In your model, you might want to compare Helen's behavior with the behavior of young children who haven't yet learned how to talk. They cry and carry on to make their needs known, but once they learn to communicate, their behavior changes. Encourage the students to share their ideas and feelings about the dramatic changes in Helen's behavior.

rabbits, squirrels, frogs, wildflowers, butterflies, trees. Grass-hoppers had smooth, clear wings; the wings of a butterfly were powdery. The bark of a tree had a curious odor, and through its huge trunk ran a gentle humming vibration.

Hand-in-hand they wandered for miles over the country-side, sometimes as far as the Tennessee River where the water rushed and churned over the mussel shoals.

For everything she felt or did there was a finger trick: wings, petals, river boats—walking, running, standing, drinking.

One morning when she was washing her face and hands, Helen pointed to the water in the basin, and Teacher spelled into her hand: "w-a-t-e-r." At the breakfast table later Helen pointed to her mug of milk, and Teacher spelled: "m-i-l-k." But Helen became confused. "D-r-i-n-k" was milk, she insisted. Helen pointed to her milk again and Teacher spelled, "m-u-g." Was m-u-g d-r-i-n-k? In another second Helen's mind was a jumble of wiggling fingers. She was frustrated, bewildered, angry, a bird trapped in a cage and beating her wings against the bars.

Quickly Teacher placed an empty mug in her hand and led her out-of-doors to a pump that stood under a shed in the yard. Helen stood before the pump, mug in hand, as Teacher indi-cated, and felt the rush of cold water over her hands. Teacher took one of her hands and spelled, "w-a-t-e-r." While water rushed over one hand Helen felt the letters, w-a-t-e-r, in the other.

Suddenly Helen was transfixed, and she let her mug crash to the ground forgotten. A new, wonderful idea . . . back into her memory rushed that infant's word she had once spoken: "wah-wah." She grew excited, her pulse raced, as understanding

🌿 36 🌿

lighted her mind. Wah-wah was w-a-t-e-r. It was a word! These finger tricks were words! There were words for everything. That was what Teacher was trying to tell her.

She felt Teacher rush to her and hug her, and Teacher was as excited as she, crying and laughing, because at last Helen understood the concept of words.

Joyfully they ran back into the house, and Helen was sur-rounded by an excited household. All the rest of the day she demanded words, words, words. What was this? What was that? Even the Keller's new infant Mildred? What was that? "B-a-b-y." And once more Helen pointed a persistent finger at Miss Sullivan and demanded the word that would identify her.

"T-e-a-c-h-e-r," Anne Sullivan spelled. "T-e-a-c-h-e-r."

The last shred of hostility and hate vanished from Helen's soul as she glowed with her sudden happiness. She felt her fin-gers being lifted to Teacher's face to explore its expression. The corners of the mouth were drawn up and the cheeks were crin-kled. Helen imitated the expression, and when she did her face was no longer blank, because Helen Keller was smiling.

When bedtime finally arrived, she put her hand will-ingly into Teacher's and mounted the stairs, and before climbing into bed she slipped her arms around Teacher's neck and kissed her—for the first time.

---

7 The contradictory feelings of joy and frustration presented in this passage may be confusing to students. **Interpreting** is a strategy that may help them express the feelings conveyed by the figura-tive language, ". . . bird trapped in a cage. . . ." Encourage them to tell what they think the author is trying to say about Helen's feelings.

Discussing Strategy Use
Encourage the students to share any problems or confusion they encountered while reading "Miracle at the Pump House" and to discuss the strategies they used to solve these difficulties.

*
EXPLORING THROUGH DISCUSSION

Reflecting on the Selection
Whole-Group Discussion

The whole group discusses the selection and any thoughts or questions that it raises. During this time, children also **return to the clues, problems, and wonderings** they noted on the board during browsing.

To review information about the discussion process, see **Learning Framework Card 2, Exploring Through Discussion.**

Assessment

To assess the children's understanding of the text, **engage in a discussion to determine whether the children have grasped the following ideas:**
- how Anne Sullivan faced the challenges in her relationship with Helen Keller
- what the rewards of perseverance were for both Anne Sullivan and Helen Keller

Response Journal

Students may wish to record their personal responses to the selection.

Exploring Concepts Within the Selection
Small-Group Discussion

Small groups discuss the relationship of the selection to perseverance. Circulate among the groups and **observe discussions.** Remind the students to refer to the Question Board and Concept Board to keep the discussions focused. Encourage students to consider whether their original ideas about perseverance have changed as a result of reading this selection.

ASSESSMENT TIP This may be a good opportunity to observe students working in groups and to mark observations in your Teacher's Observation Log.

Sharing Ideas About Explorable Concepts

Have the groups **report their ideas** and **discuss them** with the rest of the class. It is crucial that the students' ideas determine this discussion.
- Students who identify with Helen or Miss Sullivan may discuss what they might have done or how they might have felt in the same situation.
- Students may notice that Anne Sullivan did not give up when Helen did not initially respond to her. They may introduce the adage, "Where there's a will, there's a way."
- Students may notice that Miss Sullivan's approach to Helen was firm, yet sensitive to her feelings. They may discuss the advantages and disadvantages of using force or using sensitivity to accomplish a goal.

As these ideas and others are stated, have the students **add them** to the **Question Board** or the **Concept Board.**

Have students look at the fine art pieces on pages 70–71 of the student anthology and examine the painting *The Village School* by Giuseppe Constantini. Encourage students to discuss their impressions and ideas about the painting. They may wish to compare the classroom representation in the painting with the special challenges faced by Keller in learning and by Sullivan in teaching.

Fine Art

Exploring
Concepts Across
Selections

Ask students whether this story reminds them of anything else they have read. They might make connections with other selections.

- Some students might point out a similarity between Anne Sullivan and the Red Cross Knight in *Saint George and the Dragon*. Both made a commitment and had a job to do. Both persevered until their goal was achieved.

- Some students may be reminded of the story "Ray and Mr. Pit" in the unit on music and musicians. They may point out that both Helen Keller and Ray Charles were blind and were enormously influenced by their teachers. They may want to list the qualities that characterize the perseverance of student and teacher in each selection. Encourage the students to share their lists.

> Connections
> Across Units

Recording Ideas

As the students complete the above discussions, ask them to **sum up what they have learned from their conversations and to tell how they might use this information** in further explorations. Any special information or insights may be recorded on the **Concept Board.** Any further questions that they would like to think about, pursue, or investigate may be recorded on the **Question Board.** They may want to discuss the progress that has been made on their questions. They may also want to cross out any questions that no longer warrant consideration.

❯ After discussion, students should record their ideas on page 65 of their Explorer's Notebook.

Explorer's Notebook, page 65

Recording Concept Information

As I read each selection, this is what I added to my understanding of perseverance.

Saint George and the Dragon, retold by Margaret Hodges

_____
_____
_____
_____
_____
_____
_____
_____
_____
_____
_____

"Miracle at the Pump House" by Catherine Owens Peare

_____
_____
_____
_____
_____
_____
_____
_____
_____
_____
_____
_____

Unit 4/Perseverance   EN 65

2 READING WITH A WRITER'S EYE

MINILESSON

Writer's Craft: Sensory Description

Have the students talk about anything they have learned about providing **sensory descriptions** in stories. Encourage them to describe any examples they can remember from their reading or writing. If necessary, explain that writers often use words or phrases to describe what characters in the story hear, smell, taste, touch, and see. This creates sense impressions to help readers picture or feel what is happening in the story. To provide students with a better understanding of sense impressions, you might encourage them to look out a window and tell what they see, using the best words they can think of to let someone else know what sense impressions they are receiving. Or you might want to have them close their eyes, think about what they hear and smell, and then write it down so they can share their sensory descriptions with the class.

Tell the students that Catherine Owens Peare used sensory descriptions effectively in "Miracle at the Pump House." Instead of simply describing a character, an emotion, an experience, or an object, Peare was able to re-create for readers the sense impressions the characters received. To illustrate, have a volunteer read aloud paragraph 5 on page 27. "Anxious and tense . . . watching for that first puff of soft-coal smoke in the distance." Encourage students to identify the descriptive words or phrases in the passage and to identify the senses to which they appeal.

Selective Reading: Focus on Sensory Description

To help the students focus on Catherine Owens Peare's use of sensory description, ask volunteers to identify and read aloud parts of the story that were especially helpful to their understanding of the appearance, sounds, tastes, or feelings of the characters in the Keller household. Pause to discuss each example. Have the students identify the person or object being described and then point out specific words or phrases the author used to create sense impressions. Have students write the words they identify on the chalkboard. Encourage them to discuss what makes the words or phrases effective. If students do not offer suggestions, point out the strong verbs, precise nouns, and carefully selected adjectives the author uses.

The following are a few examples the students may point out:

- page 28, paragraph 5: ". . . young girl dressed in burdensome woolen clothing . . . eyes red from weeping and the irritation of the soft-coal dust."
- page 29, paragraph 3: "She felt the vibration of a strange footstep . . . then another . . . coming closer."
- page 29, paragraph 5: "Helen flung herself . . . exploring the lid . . . lock . . . plunged . . . "

Selection-Based Practice

"Miracle at the Pump House"

Sensory Description

Look again at "Miracle at the Pump House," or at any other stories you have read, for a good example of sensory description. Identify the person or object being described and the overall feeling of the passage. Classify the sensory words according to the appropriate sense.

Selection: _____ Page: _____

Person or Object Described:		
Overall Feeling:		
Sight	Smell	Sound
Taste	Touch	

Name

Copyright © 1995 Open Court Publishing Company

Unit 4/Perseverance

Description
R/WC 29

Reading/Writing Connection, page 29

Independent Practice: Sensory Description

❯ Have the students work individually or in small collaborative groups, using Reading/Writing Connection, page 29, to extend their discussion of how writers use sensory description. Provide time for them to share their ideas.

WRITING

Linking Reading to Writing

To provide opportunities for the students to apply the writer's craft of providing sensory descriptions, encourage them to do the following:

- Look in their own writing for examples in which they provided description and add the examples to their Writer's Notebook.
- Look for places they can improve their own writing by providing descriptions that include precise nouns, strong verbs, and carefully selected adjectives that create vivid sensory impressions.
- Revise a piece from their writing folders, using descriptions to develop clear and effective word pictures by emphasizing at least one or more of the senses.

To review information about the **Writer's Notebook,** see **Teacher Tool Card 122.**

* Writing Process

If the students have elected to revise a piece from their writing folders, encourage them to meet with their classmates to discuss ideas and to ask for feedback on ways to improve their writing. For information about **peer conferencing**, see **Teacher Tool Card 120.** To review the **writing process**, see **Learning Framework Card 7.**

VOCABULARY

Words related to perseverance you might discuss include *burdensome, frustrated, bewildered,* and *persistent.* Remind the students to use copies of Vocabulary Exploration form, Reproducible Master 15, and add words and phrases to the Personal Dictionary section of their Writer's Notebook. Then provide an opportunity for volunteers to share words and phrases they've added and to tell why they chose them. For additional opportunities to build vocabulary, see **Teacher Tool Card 77.**

VOCABULARY TIP Wide reading is an effective way to build vocabulary. Encourage students to read other books related to perseverance.

Professional Checkpoint: Reading with a Writer's Eye

An environment in which writing is central provides a multifaceted context for the development of higher-order thinking. Students learn to plan, which allows them to work out ideas in their heads; to set goals, which promotes interest and the ability to monitor progress; to edit, which enables the creation of text that conforms to conventional standards and heightens its acceptability; and to revise content, which engages students in the reworking and rethinking activities that elevate writing from a craft to a tool for discovery.

Notes:

3 GUIDED AND INDEPENDENT EXPLORATION

Guided
Exploration

The following activities do not all have to be completed within the time allotted for this lesson.

Students will select activities in which they explore the unit concepts. Refer them to the **Exploration Activities poster** and give them time to choose an activity. Allow them to discuss what they wish to explore and how they wish to go about it. If the students need further help, here are some suggestions:

Conduct a search to find out about people who have had to overcome difficulties in order to accomplish something personally important to them. Some of the aids and devices we use today—such as eyeglasses, telephones, or the Braille system—were developed by people with special needs to help themselves overcome difficulties and to help others with similar problems. Have students find out who some of these people were, what they did, where they came from, and what caused them to pursue their goals. Students may choose to share their findings with their classmates.

❯ Have students use page 70 in their Explorer's Notebook to record their findings.

> ✱ *Exploring Through Reflective Activities*

Explorer's Notebook, page 70

Perseverance Triumphs

Many of the aids and devices that we use today—such as the telephone, eyeglasses, or the Braille system—were developed by people with special needs to help themselves overcome difficulties.

Find out who some of these people were, what work they did, where they came from, and what caused them to pursue their goals. Find out about their inventions and learn about the improvements that have been made on those inventions over the years.

Name of inventor: _____

Problem or Cause That Sparked Invention	
Invention or New Method	
Improvements Made on Invention	

70 EN   Perseverance/Unit 4

Copyright © 1995 Open Court Publishing Company

❯ Distribute Home/School Connection 29. Encourage students, if possible, to watch and discuss the movie *Mask* with their families. Students may identify the evidence of perseverance exhibited by the characters in the film and point out the problem, the cause of the problem, the ways the characters overcame the problem, and whether or how the problem was resolved.

Generating Questions to Explore

Have the students review the questions currently on the Question Board. Encourage them to continue raising questions about perseverance that they may wish to explore. This is a good time to post those questions on the Question Board with names or initials of the students who asked them. Students can then form collaborative groups based on shared interests.

❯ Have students use page 71 in their Explorer's Notebook to help them plan their exploration and to begin forming collaborative groups with which they can work.

Remind students to add to Explorer's Notebook page 69 if they have additional questions they want to think about and explore.

Home/School Connection 29

"Miracle at the Pump House"

A message from _____

In our unit on perseverance, we have just read "Miracle at the Pump House," an excerpt from the biography *The Life of Helen Keller*. The story focuses on Anne Sullivan, Helen Keller's teacher, and her efforts to teach the blind and deaf Keller to communicate. We have discussed the importance of determination in accomplishing something worthwhile.

The motion picture *Mask* is another story about a sensitive and determined woman helping a youngster to overcome pain and loneliness. *Mask* is based on the story of Rocky Dennis. Rocky is a disfigured teenager whose face resembles a mask. With the help of his mother's uncompromising determination, Rocky overcomes prejudice. He becomes an inspiration to his classmates and teachers. If possible, locate this film or the book. Watch the movie or read the book with your child. Discuss why it was important for Rocky and his mother to change his status from that of outcast to that of outstanding young man. Then have your child list the problem, the cause of the problem, the ways Rocky's mother helped him, and the results they achieved. Have your child take notes below and then return this page to school to compare ideas with the rest of the class.

Problem: _____

_____

_____

Cause of the problem: _____

_____

_____

Attempts to overcome the problem: _____

_____

_____

Results: _____

_____

_____

Copyright © 1995 Open Court Publishing Company

Unit 4/Perseverance   H/SC 29

Exploration Plans

The question about perseverance that I'd most like to explore:

_____
_____
_____
_____
_____

The team that I may work with:

_____   _____
_____   _____
_____   _____
_____   _____

The resources that we may use:

_____
_____
_____
_____

The people that we may talk to:

_____   _____
_____   _____
_____   _____
_____   _____

Copyright © 1995 Open Court Publishing Company

Unit 4/Perseverance   EN 71

Explorer's Notebook, page 71

Professional Checkpoint: Guided and Independent Exploration

Learning to work collaboratively in groups is essential for success. You should encourage the students to take responsibility within their group. Allow them to choose projects based on their group's interest. Give the students time to work out group problems before you offer them advice.

Notes:

✳ INDEPENDENT WORKSHOP
Building a Community of Scholars

Student-Directed Reading, Writing, and Discussion

Remind the students that during the first part of Independent Workshop they will work in their collaborative groups to explore concepts related to perseverance. Provide time for individuals or small groups to use the library as needed to locate reference materials and information. The second part of Independent Workshop can be used by students for options of their choice. At this time, the students might also choose to return to their Explorer's Notebook to complete pages and discuss ideas with their classmates.

WORKSHOP TIP

Remind students to ask for feedback on their ideas or their writing from you and their peers.

Additional Opportunities for Independent Reading, Writing, and Cross-curricular Activities

✱ Reading Roundtable

Encourage the students to read other books by Catherine Owens Peare, such as *The FDR Story*, a biography of our thirty-second president, Franklin Delano Roosevelt; and *The Woodrow Wilson Story,* about the twenty-eighth President of the United States. Also remind them to use the Tradebook Connection cards in the Student Toolbox. For additional ideas for **Reading Roundtable,** see **Learning Framework Card 6.**

✱ Writing Seminar

Remind students to focus on both ideas and content when revising their writing. Encourage them to get suggestions from their peers and their teacher for improving their writing. As they collect more information, they should be moving sentences around, elaborating, and deleting. Remind them that writing is an ongoing process and that they may revise any given piece of writing more than once.

Teacher-Conferencing Tip If your students are using the optional Writer's Handbook, remind them to refer to it when they have questions about their writing.

Portfolio

Remind the students to think about which pieces of writing they might choose to put into their portfolios.

Cross-curricular Activity Cards

The following Cross-curricular Activity Cards in the Student Toolbox are appropriate for this selection:
- 15 Social Studies—Sign Language
- 16 Social Studies—Today's Miracles

Additional Opportunities for Solving Learning Problems

Tutorial

Use this time to work with those students who need help in any area. Remember to use peer tutoring with those for whom it would be appropriate. Encourage the students to ask for help when they feel the need. The following Teacher Tool Cards are available in the Teacher Toolbox for your convenience:
- Writer's Craft/Reading: Elaboration Through Providing Descriptions, Teacher Tool Card 40
- Writer's Craft/Reading: Characterization, Teacher Tool Card 13
- Writer's Craft/Reading: Causal Indicators, Teacher Tool Card 31

On Your Own

The Fire Builder

1 READING THE SELECTION

About the
Selection

In this compelling realistic adventure, thirteen-year-old Brian Robeson is the sole survivor of a plane crash in the northern Canadian woods. Alone, famished, and in pain, Brian arduously battles brutal wilderness conditions. If only he could start a fire. Then he might be able to stave off the bears and other hungry wild creatures—and prevent them from feasting on his flesh. Readers who relish the sheer technique of story-telling and the gripping details of natural setting cannot afford to miss "The Fire Builder" by Gary Paulsen.

Link to the
Unit Concepts

"The Fire Builder," pages 38–51, portrays the physical survival, increased emotional maturity, and perseverance of a young boy. This story shows students how someone much like themselves wrestles with fear and persists in attempting to overcome difficulties in spite of obstacles. This selection may lead students to investigate how others have triumphed over the forces of nature. The students will naturally identify the factors that motivate someone to strive for survival and compare them with the factors that motivate someone to accomplish something that is not a matter of life or death. This selection may also cause students to think about the importance of combining what they already know with their imaginative skills to discover new ways to accomplish something.

About the
Author

"The Fire Builder" is from the book *Hatchet*, written by award-winning children's author, Gary Paulsen. In 1987, *Hatchet* was named an American Library Association Notable Book. That same year, the Child Study Children's Book Committee also honored it as one of their Children's Books of the Year, and it was acclaimed as a Notable

LESSON OVERVIEW

"The Fire Builder" by Gary Paulsen, pages 38–51

READING THE SELECTION

Materials
Student anthology, pp. 38–51
Explorer's Notebook, p. 66
Assessment Master 2

FYI
Learning Framework Card
• Setting Reading Goals and
  Expectations, 1A

READING WITH A WRITER'S EYE

Minilesson
On Your Own

Materials
Reproducible Master 15

FYI
Teacher Tool Card
• Spelling and Vocabulary: Building
  Vocabulary, 77

Options for Instruction
Writer's Craft: Genre—Adventure
Grammar, Mechanics, and Usage:
  Adverbs
(Use Teacher Tool Cards listed below.)

GUIDED AND INDEPENDENT EXPLORATION

Materials
Home/School Connection 30
Explorer's Notebook, pp. 69, 71–72
Assessment Master 1

Independent Workshop

**Optional Materials from
Student Toolbox**
Tradebook Connection Cards
• *The Sign of the Beaver* by Elizabeth
  George Speare

Cross-curricular Activity Cards
• 17 Social Studies—Taming Fire
• 18 Social Studies—Tools of the Past

Student Tool Cards
• Writer's Craft/Reading: Reading and
  Writing Adventure Tales, 7
• Grammar, Mechanics, and Usage:
  Using Adjectives and Adverbs, 68

FYI
Learning Framework Card
• Writing Seminar, 8

Teacher Tool Cards
• Writer's Craft/Reading: Genre—
  Adventure, 7
• Grammar, Mechanics, and Usage:
  Using Adjectives and Adverbs, 68
• Classroom Supports: Question Board
  and Concept Board, 123

N O T E S

Asterisks (*) throughout the lesson indicate learning frameworks. Learning Framework Cards and Teacher Tool Cards can be found in the Teacher Toolbox.

Children's Trade Book in the Field of Social Studies. In 1988, *Hatchet* was also named a Newbery Honor Book.

Gary Paulsen was born in Minneapolis, Minnesota, in 1939. With his myriad experiences working as a trapper, rancher, truck driver, and farmer, it is little wonder that most of his novels feature an outdoor theme. He even drove in the grueling Iditarod dogsled race in Alaska and used that experience to write one of his best known novels, *Dogsong*. Two of Paulsen's other books written for upper elementary grade students are *The Island* and *Dancing Carl*.

INFORMATION FOR THE STUDENT

Tell the students that the selection they are about to read was written by Gary Paulsen and illustrated by Leah Palmer Preiss. As appropriate, you may wish to share other information about the author with the students. Have them read the author and illustrator profiles on page 51 of their student anthology.

Note: When students have finished reading the selection, they may express curiosity about the method used to start the fire. If this occurs, you might want to suggest that they not experiment with the fire-building method described in this story unless they are accompanied by an adult.

COGNITIVE AND RESPONSIVE READING

Activating Prior Knowledge

Ask the students to tell what they know about fire and the many uses people have for fire. Those who have been involved in scouting may want to share what they know about building a fire.

Setting Reading Goals and Expectations

Before students read the selection, have them **browse the first page** of the selection **using the clues/problems/wondering procedure**. For a review of **browsing**, see **Learning Framework Card 1A**.

Recommendations for Reading the Selection

This selection has been designated as an On Your Own selection. Tell the students that they will read the selection independently. Remind them to use strategies they have learned when confronted with difficulties in the text. Encourage them to use the **reading strategy posters** if they encounter a reading problem or are unsure about how to use a strategy. Remind them to feel free to raise their hands at any time during silent reading to discuss particular problems or to wonder about things. Following the reading of the selection, the students will complete a Self-Assessment Questionnaire.

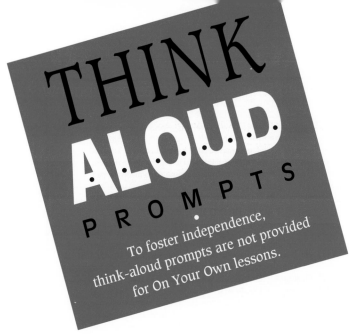

THINK ALOUD PROMPTS

To foster independence, think-aloud prompts are not provided for On Your Own lessons.

THE FIRE BUILDER
from HATCHET by Gary Paulsen
illustrated by Leah Palmer Preiss

Three days ago, Brian Robeson, age thirteen, boarded a Cessna 406 airplane to visit his father who lives in the Canadian wilderness. During the flight, the pilot suffered a heart attack and died. Despite Brian's desperate attempts to make radio contact and to land the plane safely, the plane crashed into a lake in the northern Canadian woods. Brian, the only passenger, survived.

Now that he has survived the crash, he must survive the Canadian wilderness. In the past three days, he has been attacked by hordes of vicious mosquitos and flies, has been racked with hunger, and has seen a bear. The only tool he has is the hatchet his mother gave him before he boarded the airplane in New York. So far he has found a rock shelter and has managed to satisfy some of his hunger with berries.

It is the third night of Brian's ordeal and he is sleeping in his shelter.

38

At first he thought it was a growl. In the still darkness of the shelter in the middle of the night his eyes came open and he was awake and he thought there was a growl. But it was the wind, a medium wind in the pines had made some sound that brought him up, brought him awake. He sat up and was hit with the smell.

It terrified him. The smell was one of rot, some musty rot that made him think only of graves with cobwebs and dust and old death. His nostrils widened and he opened his eyes wider but he could see nothing. It was too dark, too hard dark with clouds covering even the small light from the stars, and he could not see. But the smell was alive, alive and full and in the shelter. He thought of the bear, thought of Bigfoot and every monster he had ever seen in every fright movie he had ever watched, and his heart hammered in his throat.

Then he heard the slithering. A brushing sound, a slithering brushing sound near his feet—and he kicked out as hard as he could, kicked out and threw the hatchet at the sound, a noise coming from his throat. But the hatchet missed, sailed into the wall where it hit the rocks with a shower of sparks, and his leg was instantly torn with pain, as if a hundred needles had been driven into it. "Unnnngh!"

Now he screamed, with the pain and fear, and skittered on his backside up into the corner of the shelter, breathing through his mouth, straining to see, to hear.

The slithering moved again, he thought toward him at first, and terror took him, stopping his breath. He felt he could see a low dark form, a bulk in the darkness, a shadow that lived, but now it moved away, slithering and scraping

39

it moved away and he saw or thought he saw it go out of the door opening.

He lay on his side for a moment, then pulled a rasping breath in and held it, listening for the attacker to return. When it was apparent that the shadow wasn't coming back he felt the calf of his leg, where the pain was centered and spreading to fill the whole leg.

His fingers gingerly touched a group of needles that had been driven through his pants and into the fleshy part of his calf. They were stiff and very sharp on the ends that stuck out, and he knew then what the attacker had been. A porcupine had stumbled into his shelter and when he had kicked it the thing had slapped him with its tail of quills.

40

He touched each quill carefully. The pain made it seem as if dozens of them had been slammed into his leg, but there were only eight, pinning the cloth against his skin. He leaned back against the wall for a minute. He couldn't leave them in, they had to come out, but just touching them made the pain more intense.

So fast, he thought. So fast things change. When he'd gone to sleep he had satisfaction and in just a moment it was all different. He grasped one of the quills, held his breath, and jerked. It sent pain signals to his brain in tight waves, but he grabbed another, pulled it, then another quill. When he had pulled four of them he stopped for a moment. The pain had gone from being a pointed injury pain to spreading in a hot smear up his leg and it made him catch his breath.

Some of the quills were driven in deeper than others and they tore when they came out. He breathed deeply twice, let half of the breath out, and went back to work. Jerk, pause, jerk—and three more times before he lay back in the darkness, done. The pain filled his leg now, and with it came new waves of self-pity. Sitting alone in the dark, his leg aching, some mosquitos finding him again, he started crying. It was all too much, just too much, and he couldn't take it. Not the way it was.

I can't take it this way, alone with no fire and in the dark, and next time it might be something worse, maybe a bear, and it wouldn't be just quills in the leg, it would be worse. I can't do this, he thought, again and again. I can't. Brian pulled himself up until he was sitting upright back in the corner of the cave. He put his head down on his arms across

41

his knees, with stiffness taking his left leg, and cried until he was cried out.

He did not know how long it took, but later he looked back on this time of crying in the corner of the dark cave and thought of it as when he learned the most important rule of survival, which was that feeling sorry for yourself didn't work. It wasn't just that it was wrong to do, or that it was considered incorrect. It was more than that—it didn't work. When he sat alone in the darkness and cried and was done, was all done with it, nothing had changed. His leg still hurt, it was still dark, he was still alone and the self-pity had accomplished nothing.

At last he slept again, but already his patterns were changing and the sleep was light, a resting doze more than a deep sleep, with small sounds awakening him twice in the rest of the night. In the last doze period before daylight, before he awakened finally with the morning light and the clouds of new mosquitos, he dreamed, of his father at first and then of his friend Terry.

In the initial segment of the dream his father was standing at the side of a living room looking at him and it was clear from his expression that he was trying to tell Brian something. His lips moved but there was no sound, not a whisper. He waved his hands at Brian, made gestures in front of his face as if he were scratching something, and he worked to make a word with his mouth but at first Brian could not see it. Then the lips made an *mmmmm* shape but no sound came. *Mmmmm—maaaa.* Brian could not hear it, could not understand it and he wanted to so badly; it was so important to understand his father, to know what he was saying. He was

42

trying to help, trying so hard, and when Brian couldn't understand he looked cross, the way he did when Brian asked questions more than once, and he faded. Brian's father faded into a fog place Brian could not see and the dream was almost over, or seemed to be, when Terry came.

He was not gesturing to Brian but was sitting in the park at a bench looking at a barbecue pit and for a time nothing happened. Then he got up and poured some charcoal from a bag into the cooker, then some starter fluid, and he took a flick type of lighter and lit the fluid. When it was burning and the charcoal was at last getting hot he turned, noticing Brian for the first time in the dream. He turned and smiled and pointed to the fire as if to say, see, a fire.

But it meant nothing to Brian, except that he wished he had a fire. He saw a grocery sack on the table next to Terry. Brian thought it must contain hot dogs and chips and mustard and he could think only of the food. But Terry shook his head and pointed again to the fire, and twice more he pointed to the fire, made Brian see the flames, and Brian felt his frustration and anger rise and he thought all right, all right, I see the fire but so what? I don't have a fire. I know about fire; I know I need a fire.

I know that.

His eyes opened and there was light in the cave, a gray dim light of morning. He wiped his mouth and tried to move his leg, which had stiffened like wood. There was thirst, and hunger, and he ate some raspberries from the jacket. They had spoiled a bit, seemed softer and mushier, but still had a rich sweetness. He crushed the berries against the roof of his mouth with his tongue and drank the sweet juice as it ran

43

down his throat. A flash of metal caught his eye and he saw his hatchet in the sand where he had thrown it at the porcupine in the dark.

He scootched up, wincing a bit when he bent his stiff leg, and crawled to where the hatchet lay. He picked it up and examined it and saw a chip in the top of the head.

The nick wasn't large, but the hatchet was important to him, was his only tool, and he should not have thrown it. He should keep it in his hand, and make a tool of some kind to help push an animal away. Make a staff, he thought, or a lance, and save the hatchet. Something came then, a thought as he held the hatchet, something about the dream and his father and Terry, but he couldn't pin it down.

"Ahhh . . ." He scrambled out and stood in the morning sun and stretched his back muscles and his sore leg. The hatchet was still in his hand, and as he stretched and raised it over his head it caught the first rays of the morning sun. The first faint light hit the silver of the hatchet and it flashed a brilliant gold in the light. Like fire. That is it, he thought. What they were trying to tell me.

Fire. The hatchet was the key to it all. When he threw the hatchet at the porcupine in the cave and missed and hit the stone wall it had showered sparks, a golden shower of sparks in the dark, as golden with fire as the sun was now.

The hatchet was the answer. That's what his father and Terry had been trying to tell him. Somehow he could get fire from the hatchet. The sparks would make fire.

Brian went back into the shelter and studied the wall. It was some form of chalky granite, or a sandstone, but imbedded

🐾 44 🐾

in it were large pieces of a darker stone, a harder and darker stone. It only took him a moment to find where the hatchet had struck. The steel had nicked into the edge of one of the darker stone pieces. Brian turned the head backward so he would strike with the flat rear of the hatchet and hit the black rock gently. Too gently, and nothing happened. He struck harder, a glancing blow, and two or three weak sparks skipped off the rock and died immediately.

He swung harder, held the hatchet so it would hit a longer, sliding blow, and the black rock exploded in fire. Sparks flew so heavily that several of them skittered and jumped on the sand beneath the rock and he smiled and struck again and again.

There could be fire here, he thought. I will have a fire here, he thought, and struck again—I will have fire from the hatchet.

Brian found it was a long way from sparks to fire.

Clearly there had to be something for the sparks to ignite, some kind of tinder or kindling—but what? He brought some dried grass in, tapped sparks into it and watched them die. He tried small twigs, breaking them into little pieces, but that was worse than the grass. Then he tried a combination of the two, grass and twigs.

Nothing. He had no trouble getting sparks, but the tiny bits of hot stone or metal—he couldn't tell which they were—just sputtered and died.

He settled back on his haunches in exasperation, looking at the pitiful clump of grass and twigs.

He needed something finer, something soft and fine and fluffy to catch the bits of fire.

Shredded paper would be nice, but he had no paper.

"So close," he said aloud, "so close . . ."

He put the hatchet back in his belt and went out of the shelter, limping on his sore leg. There had to be something, had to be. Man had made fire. There had been fire for thousands, millions of years. There had to be a way. He dug in his pockets and found a twenty-dollar bill in his wallet. Paper. Worthless paper out here. But if he could get a fire going . . .

He ripped the twenty into tiny pieces, made a pile of pieces, and hit sparks into them. Nothing happened. They just wouldn't take the sparks. But there had to be a way—some way to do it.

Not twenty feet to his right, leaning out over the water were birches and he stood looking at them for a full half-minute before they registered on his mind. They were a beautiful white with bark like clean, slightly speckled paper.

Paper.

🐾 46 🐾

He moved to the trees. Where the bark was peeling from the trunks it lifted in tiny tendrils, almost fluffs. Brian plucked some of them loose, rolled them in his fingers. They seemed flammable, dry and nearly powdery. He pulled and twisted bits off the trees, packing them in one hand while he picked them with the other, picking and gathering until he had a wad close to the size of a baseball.

Then he went back into the shelter and arranged the ball of birchbark peelings at the base of the black rock. As an afterthought he threw in the remains of the twenty-dollar bill. He struck and a stream of sparks fell into the bark and quickly died. But this time one spark fell on one small hair of dry bark—almost a thread of bark—and seemed to glow a bit brighter before it died.

The material had to be finer. There had to be a soft and incredibly fine nest for the sparks.

I must make a home for the sparks, he thought. A perfect home or they won't stay, they won't make fire.

He started ripping the bark, using his fingernails at first, and when that didn't work he used the sharp edge of the hatchet, cutting the bark in thin slivers, hairs so fine they were almost not there. It was painstaking work, slow work, and he stayed with it for over two hours. Twice he stopped for a handful of berries and once to go to the lake for a drink. Then back to work, the sun on his back, until at last he had a ball of fluff as big as a grapefruit—dry birchbark fluff.

He positioned his spark nest—as he thought of it—at the base of the rock, used his thumb to make a small depression in the middle, and slammed the back of the hatchet down across the black rock. A cloud of sparks rained down, most of them

🐾 47 🐾

missing the nest, but some, perhaps thirty or so, hit in the depression and of those six or seven found fuel and grew, smoldered and caused the bark to take on the red glow.

Then they went out.

Close—he was close. He repositioned the nest, made a new and smaller dent with his thumb, and struck again.

More sparks, a slight glow, then nothing.

It's me, he thought. I'm doing something wrong. I do not know this—a cave dweller would have had a fire by now, a Cro-Magnon man would have a fire by now—but I don't know this. I don't know how to make a fire.

Maybe not enough sparks. He settled the nest in place once more and hit the rock with a series of blows, as fast as he could. The sparks poured like a golden waterfall. At first they

🐾 48 🐾

seemed to take, there were several, many sparks that found life and took briefly, but they all died.

Starved.

He leaned back. They are like me. They are starving. It wasn't quantity, there were plenty of sparks, but they needed more.

I would kill, he thought suddenly, for a book of matches. Just one book. Just one match. I would kill.

What makes fire? He thought back to school. To all those science classes. Had he ever learned what made a fire? Did a teacher ever stand up there and say, "This is what makes a fire . . ."

He shook his head, tried to focus his thoughts. What did it take? You have to have fuel, he thought—and he had that. The bark was fuel. Oxygen—there had to be air.

He needed to add air. He had to fan on it, blow on it.

He made the nest ready again, held the hatchet backward, tensed, and struck four quick blows. Sparks came down and he leaned forward as fast as he could and blew.

Too hard. There was a bright, almost intense glow, then it was gone. He had blown it out.

Another set of strikes, more sparks. He leaned and blew, but gently this time, holding back and aiming the stream of air from his mouth to hit the brightest spot. Five or six sparks had fallen in a tight mass of bark hair and Brian centered his efforts there.

The sparks grew with his gentle breath. The red glow moved from the sparks themselves into the bark, moved and grew and became worms, glowing red worms that crawled up the bark hairs and caught other threads of bark and grew

🐾 49 🐾

until there was a pocket of red as big as a quarter, a glowing red coal of heat.

And when he ran out of breath and paused to inhale, the red ball suddenly burst into flame.

"Fire!" He yelled. "I've got fire! I've got it, I've got it, I've got it . . ."

But the flames were thick and oily and burning fast, consuming the ball of bark as fast as if it were gasoline. He had to feed the flames, keep them going. Working as fast as he could he carefully placed the dried grass and wood pieces he had tried at first on top of the bark and was gratified to see them take.

But they would go fast. He needed more, and more. He could not let the flames go out.

He ran from the shelter to the pines and started breaking off the low, dead small limbs. These he threw in the shelter, went back for more, threw those in, and squatted to break and feed the hungry flames. When the small wood was going well he went out and found larger wood and did not relax until

that was going. Then he leaned back against the wood brace of his door opening and smiled.

I have a friend, he thought—I have a friend now. A hungry friend, but a good one. I have a friend named fire.

"Hello, fire . . ."

The curve of the rock back made an almost perfect drawing <u>flue</u> that carried the smoke up through the cracks of the roof but held the heat. If he kept the fire small it would be perfect and would keep anything like the porcupine from coming through the door again.

A friend and a guard, he thought.

So much from a little spark. A friend and a guard from a tiny spark.

MEET GARY PAULSEN, AUTHOR

Gary Paulsen has worked as a teacher, electronics field engineer, soldier, actor, director, farmer, rancher, truck driver, trapper, professional archer, migrant farm worker, singer, and sailor. He says that he writes "because it's all I can do. Every time I've tried to do something else I cannot, and have to come back to writing. . . ."

He has written more than forty books and enjoys writing for young people.

MEET LEAH PALMER PREISS, ILLUSTRATOR

In creating her illustrations for "The Fire Builder," Leah Palmer Preiss tried to imagine how it would feel to be in Brian Robeson's situation, lost and alone in the wilderness. She tried to capture for the reader the mixture of fear and determination that Brian experienced throughout his ordeal. Preiss used colored pencil on black silk-screened paper to contrast the dark cave against the glowing fire. It was an artistic challenge to portray Brian in the cave and "to make his expression clear without losing the dark and . . . threatening quality of the scene."

🐾 51 🐾

* **EXPLORING THROUGH DISCUSSION**

Reflecting on the Selection
Whole-Group Discussion

The whole group discusses the selection and any thoughts or questions that it raises. During this time, children also **return to the clues, problems,** and **wonderings** they noted on the chalkboard during browsing.

Assessment

To assess the students' understanding of the text, engage in a discussion to determine whether students have grasped the following ideas:
- why the fire was so important and so necessary to Brian
- how Brian dealt with the physical and emotional problems he faced

Response Journal

Students may wish to record any personal thoughts or responses to the selection in their response journals.

Exploring Concepts Within the Selection
Small-Group Discussion

While small groups discuss the relationship of the selection to perseverance, **circulate and observe the discussions.** Remind the students to refer to the Question Board and the Concept Board to keep their discussions focused.

Sharing Ideas About Explorable Concepts

Have the groups **report their ideas and discuss them** with the rest of the class. It is crucial that the students' ideas determine this discussion.
- Students may notice that Brian's persistence was motivated by self-preservation.
- Students who identify with Brian Robeson may discuss what they might have done in his situation.
- Some students may suggest that Brian used what he already knew and combined that with persistence and imagination to accomplish his goal.

As these ideas and others are stated, have the students **add them to the Question Board** or the **Concept Board**.

TEACHING TIP Questions stimulated by the reading of selections provide good springboards for exploring ideas. Always ask the students what each selection makes them wonder about. Encourage students to verbalize their inquiries.

Exploring Concepts Across Selections

Ask students whether this story reminds them of anything else they have read. They may make connections with selections in this unit or other units.
- Some students may compare Brian Robeson's conflict to the knight's conflict in *Saint George and the Dragon.* They may identify such similarities as physical pain and the struggle for survival.

Recording Ideas

As students complete the above discussions, ask them to **sum up what they have learned from their conversations and to tell how they might use this information** in further explorations. Any special information or insights may be recorded on the **Concept Board.** Any further questions that they would like to think about, pursue, or investigate may be recorded on the **Question Board.** They may want to discuss the progress that has been made on their questions. They may also want to cross out any questions that no longer warrant consideration.

Evaluating Discussions

Recording Concept Information continued

"The Fire Builder" by Gary Paulsen

_____
_____
_____
_____
_____

"Amaroq, the Wolf" by Jean Craighead George

_____
_____
_____
_____
_____

"Mother to Son" by Langston Hughes

_____
_____
_____
_____
_____
_____

Copyright © 1995 Open Court Publishing Company

Explorer's Notebook, page 66

Self-Assessment Questionnaire

Date

1. How would you rate this selection?
   ○ easy   ○ medium   ○ hard

2. If you checked **medium** or **hard**, answer these questions.
   • Which part of the selection did you find especially difficult?
   • What strategy did you use to understand it?

   _____
   _____

   • Were some of the words hard?
   • What did you do to figure out their meaning?

   _____
   _____

INDIVIDUAL

3. What do you feel you need to work on to make yourself a better reader?

   _____
   _____
   _____

Name

4. Give an example of something you said in the group.
   Tell why you said it.

   _____
   _____
   _____

5. Give an example of something that people in the group helped you
   understand about the selection.

   _____
   _____
   _____

GROUP

Self-Assessment Questionnaire   Assessment Master 2

Copyright © 1995 Open Court Publishing Company

Assessment Master 2

❯ Students should also record their thoughts about the selection and the unit concepts on page 66 of their Explorer's Notebook.

Self-Assessment Questionnaire

Distribute Assessment Master 2, Self-Assessment Questionnaire, which can be found in the booklet, Masters for Continuous Assessment, in the Teacher Toolbox. Tell the students to answer the questionnaires after they have completed this lesson. Collect the completed questionnaires so that you can compare students' current self-assessments with later self-assessments when they again answer the same questionnaires. You might also examine their responses to see if the students' assessments of themselves are compatible with your assessments of them in your Teacher's Observation Log.

Professional Checkpoint: Cognitive and Responsive Reading

Look for increases in students' abilities to come up with their own ideas about perseverance in relation to the story and to make their own connections. This should further reinforce the notion that students' ideas are more important than any we might impose on them.

Notes:

2 READING WITH A WRITER'S EYE

On Your Own

MINILESSON

Remind the students that in each selection they've read, they have discussed something that the writer did particularly well. For example, in *Saint George and the Dragon,* they discussed Margaret Hodges' skillful **weaving of plot** in her retelling of the story as well as her ability to **establish setting. Review** also the discussion about **sensory description** in "Miracle at the Pump House."

Tell students that since they read "The Fire Builder" on their own, you would like them to try to identify something they think Gary Paulsen did especially well in the story. Does something about the writing stand out? They might think back to a portion of the story that they particularly enjoyed. Their positive reaction might be a clue to especially good writing.

Allow time for students to skim the story, if necessary, to refresh their memories. If they seem to be having difficulty expressing how they felt about the writing in this selection, you might wish to share your feelings about things you felt were noteworthy. For example, you might want to point out how the author established the **setting** of the story and how the setting helped you to visualize the conflict between the main character and nature. Again, encourage students to identify anything they really like about the writing and explain what the author did to achieve the effect.

WRITING

Linking Reading to Writing

Encourage the students to use in their own writing any of Paulsen's writing techniques they especially liked. Encourage them to review their writing folders for a piece they might revise to include a writing device that they felt was used well in this story.

✱ Writing Process

Although no specific writing assignment is recommended here, students may concentrate on an appropriate phase of the writing process for any writing on which they are currently working. Remind them that peer-conferencing and the input they receive is an important part of the writing process.

VOCABULARY

Words and phrases from the selection that are related to the unit concepts and that students might discuss include *survived, desperate attempts, ordeal, exasperation,* and *painstaking work.* Allow time for the students to complete copies of Vocabulary Exploration form, Reproducible Master 15, for these or any other words they wish to remember and use. Remind the students to add these to the Personal Dictionary section of their Writer's Notebook. Then provide an opportunity for volunteers to share words and phrases they've selected and to

Adding to Personal Dictionary

tell why they chose them. For additional opportunities to build vocabulary, see **Teacher Tool Card 77.**

3 GUIDED AND INDEPENDENT EXPLORATION

Guided
Exploration

EXPLORING CONCEPTS BEYOND THE TEXT

The following activities do not have to be completed within the days devoted to this lesson.

Students will select activities in which they explore the unit concepts. Refer them to the **Exploration Activities poster** and give them time to choose an activity. Allow them to discuss what they wish to explore and how they wish to go about it. If the students need further help, here are some suggestions:

- Some students may choose to find out about people who have survived conflicts with nature or other disasters (hurricanes, tornadoes, earthquakes, plane crashes). Locate magazine, newspaper, or book articles that tell about how people persevered and survived. Students may present a brief summary of their article and discuss it with the class. Encourage the students to identify the factors that led people to keep trying and the factors that led to discouragement. If it is significant to the story, students might identify the qualities of the people who emerged as leaders.

- As an extension of the previous activity, students might choose a particularly exciting example from among the articles presented and role-play the situation.

- Some students may want to invite a scout master, outdoor education teacher, or another appropriate community member to speak to the class about perseverance related to survival in the wilderness.

❭ From their reading, discussions, and research, students have found out about some of the ways in which people have persevered to reach a goal. Encourage them to set their own priorities for goals they would like to accomplish. Have them use the chart on page 72 of their Explorer's Notebook to rank their goals according to seriousness, list problems they may encounter, and note how they plan to accomplish the goals that are important to them. They can check back to note any progress they have made in pursuing their goals or to revise their priorities, as they continue through the unit.

❭ Distribute Home/School Connection 30 and encourage students to collaborate with their families to locate and discuss newspaper or magazine articles about people who have survived harsh conditions of nature. Have the students share the article with their classmates and describe what they found interesting or surprising about the effects of the disaster on human behavior.

✱ *Exploring Through Reflective Activities*

Setting Goals

People persevere to accomplish something that is important to them. What do you want to accomplish? Fill out this chart to rank your goals in order of their importance to you. Check your progress and continue to add to the list or to revise your priorities as you learn more about perseverance throughout this unit.

Goal	Problem	Ideas for Solving Problem or Accomplishing Goal	Comments
1.			
2.			
3.			

Perseverance/Unit 4

Copyright © 1995 Open Court Publishing Company

Explorer's Notebook, page 72

"The Fire Builder"

A message from _____

In our unit on perseverance, we have just read the story "The Fire Builder," which is about a young boy's struggle for survival in the wilderness. If possible, locate a news article about someone who has survived harsh conditions of nature. Read it with your child and discuss the main factors that threatened the individual's physical survival. Discuss what your child found most interesting or surprising about the effects of disaster on human behavior. Have your child take notes below on what the individual did to overcome hardship and keep hope alive. Encourage your child to return this page and the article to school to share with the rest of the class.

Individual: _____

Geographic location: _____

Reason for being there: _____

Weather conditions: _____

Shelter: _____

Food: _____

Clothing: _____

Medical care: _____

Other: _____

Copyright © 1995 Open Court Publishing Company

Unit 4/Perseverance   H/SC 30

Home/School Connection 30

Continuing Exploration

Encourage students to share what they have learned about perseverance from their discussions and their reading. If important concepts about perseverance have emerged, be sure to have students add these to the **Concept Board.** Tell the students that this is also a good time to post questions on the **Question Board.** Remind them to feel free to go to the Question Board or the Concept Board at any time during their exploration to add questions or ideas.

Based on the contents of the Concept Board and the Question Board, students may wish to return to and revise or add to ideas they previously recorded on page 69 of their Explorer's Notebook. Work with groups that need further direction. Then allow time for collaborative groups to work on their exploration. Remind them to return to page 71 in their Explorer's Notebook to review their plans and ideas for collaborative group work. To review information about the **Concept Board** and the **Question Board,** see **Teacher Tool Card 123.**

*INDEPENDENT WORKSHOP
Building a Community of Scholars

Student-Directed Reading, Writing, and Discussion

Remind the students that the first part of Independent Workshop will be spent in their collaborative groups, working together on ideas for exploring perseverance.

Encourage the students to brainstorm as a group about the various aspects of perseverance and possible questions related to perseverance they might explore. Remind them to check the bibliography in their student anthology as well as the one on Reproducible Masters 41–44 for books they might want to use.

At this time, the students might choose to return to their Explorer's Notebook to discuss ideas with their classmates.

WORKSHOP TIP

Assessment This might be a good opportunity to observe students working in groups and to mark observations in your Teacher's Observation Log.

Additional Opportunities for Independent Reading, Writing, and Cross-curricular Activities

✱ Reading Roundtable

Encourage the students to read the other books by Gary Paulsen. *Hatchet* is the book from which "The Fire Builder" was excerpted. Another book by Paulsen that students might enjoy is *Dancing Carl,* about two boys who learn to respect a war veteran who had a traumatic experience. *The Sign of the Beaver* by Elizabeth George Speare is a selection from the Tradebook Connection that relates particularly well to the unit concepts. It tells about a young boy, left alone in the Maine wilderness, who is befriended by an Indian chief and his grandson. If the students read the book, remind them to complete the activities related to it on the Tradebook Connection Card in the Student Toolbox.

✱ Writing Seminar

Encourage the students to continue revising their writing. While revising, remind them to pinpoint parts that can be made clearer or more interesting. Have them ask for feedback from classmates and have them identify confusing or incorrect information. For additional ideas for **Writing Seminar,** see **Learning Framework Card 8.**

Cross-curricular Activity Cards

The following Cross-curricular Activity Cards in the Student Toolbox are appropriate for this selection:
- 17 Social Studies—Taming Fire
- 18 Social Studies—Tools of the Past

Additional Opportunities for Solving Learning Problems

Tutorial

Use this time to work with those students who need help in any area. Remember to use peer tutoring with those for whom it would be appropriate. Encourage the students to ask for help when they feel the need. The following Teacher Tool Cards are available in the Teacher Toolbox for your convenience:
- Writer's Craft/Reading: Genre—Adventure, Teacher Tool Card 7
- Grammar, Mechanics, and Usage: Using Adjectives and Adverbs, Teacher Tool Card 68

Amaroq, the Wolf

1 READING THE SELECTION

INFORMATION FOR THE TEACHER

About the
Selection

"Amaroq, the Wolf" transports readers to a world ruled by nature's harsh law of survival. Lost on the North Slope of the frozen Alaskan wilderness, Miyax, a thirteen-year-old Eskimo girl, faces life-or-death peril. "The barren slope stretches for three hundred miles. . . . Winds scream across it, and the view in every direction is exactly the same." Miyax's only hope for survival is to make friends with the wolves—animals that she both fears and admires. Amaroq, the proud leader of the wolf pack, will not even glance her way. Will Miyax make friends with the wolves? Will she survive?

"Amaroq, the Wolf" is excerpted from the riveting adventure *Julie of the Wolves* by Jean Craighead George. George combines rich descriptions with distinctive characters, both human and animal, to produce a tale that is both touching and enlightening. Readers will feel the desperation of Miyax, admire her determination, and gain a close-up, true-to-life view of wolf behavior in the Arctic.

Link to the
Unit Concepts

"Amaroq, the Wolf," pages 52–69, illustrates the courage and the resourcefulness that it takes to cope in a hostile environment. After reading this selection, students may begin to understand why the very act of persevering often seems difficult and grueling. This selection may lead them to compare the perseverance that is involved in the struggle to survive with the perseverance that it takes to do a job well. It may also lead them to investigate the culture, the customs, and the history of the people who live in certain geographic locations and the ways in which they have persevered to survive the forces of nature or the destruction caused by humans.

LESSON OVERVIEW

"Amaroq, the Wolf" by Jean Craighead George, pages 52–69

READING THE SELECTION

Materials

Student anthology, pp. 52–69
Explorer's Notebook, p. 66
Assessment Master 1
Map or globe

FYI

Teacher Tool Card
• Classroom Supports: Modeling and Generating Think-Alouds, 118

READING WITH A WRITER'S EYE

Minilessons

Writer's Craft: Developing Problems and Solutions
Writer's Craft: Establishing Setting/Realistic Fiction

Materials

Reading/Writing Connection, pp. 30–31
Reproducible Masters 15, 45

FYI

Teacher Tool Card
• Spelling and Vocabulary: Building Vocabulary, 77

Options for Instruction

Writer's Craft: Elaboration by Providing Noncausal Reasons
Writer's Craft: Sensory Description (Use Teacher Tool Cards listed below.)

GUIDED AND INDEPENDENT EXPLORATION

Materials

Home/School Connection 31
Explorer's Notebook, pp. 69, 73

FYI

Learning Framework Cards
• Exploring Through Reflective Activities, 3
• Independent Workshop, 5

Independent Workshop

Optional Materials from Student Toolbox

Tradebook Connection Cards
• *The Shark Beneath the Reef* by Jean Craighead George

Cross-curricular Activity Cards
• 10 Science—Wild Food
• 11 Science—Wolf Behavior

Student Tool Cards
• Writer's Craft/Reading: Giving Problem and Solution, 45
• Writer's Craft/Reading: Setting, 14
• Writer's Craft/Reading: Giving Reasons or Causes, 38
• Writer's Craft/Reading: Giving Descriptions, 40

FYI

Teacher Tool Cards
• Writer's Craft/Reading: Elaboration Through Providing Problem and Solution, 45
• Writer's Craft/Reading: Setting, 14
• Writer's Craft/Reading: Elaboration Through Giving Reasons or Causes, 38
• Writer's Craft/Reading: Elaboration Through Providing Descriptions, 40

N O T E S

Asterisks (*) throughout the lesson indicate learning frameworks. Learning Framework Cards and Teacher Tool Cards can be found in the Teacher Toolbox.

About the
Author

"Amaroq, the Wolf" is a story excerpted from *Julie of the Wolves* by award-winning author Jean Craighead George. In 1972 *Julie of the Wolves* was named an American Library Association Notable Book, and in 1973 it was awarded a Newbery Medal and became a finalist for the National Book Award.

George was born in Washington, D.C., in 1919. Since 1948 George has written nearly fifty fascinating books about nature for young people. Her books are distinguished by authentic detail blended with vivid description. For writing *Julie of the Wolves*, George traveled to Alaska to research wolves. There she met an Inuit woman and her husband, from whom she learned about the native culture. George based the character of Julie on this Inuit woman whom she had met by chance. Other books written by George include *The Wounded Wolf* and *My Side of the Mountain*.

About the
Illustrator

Gail Piazza is the illustrator of "Amaroq, the Wolf." Some children may remember that Piazza also illustrated the cover of Volume 6, Book 1 of *Collections for Young Scholars*. She likes to add something special to her illustrations. To show the sky and the tundra more effectively in "Amaroq, the Wolf," Piazza added a watered wash to her colored-pencil drawings. Piazza notes that usually her pictures are put together like a puzzle. For example, in her final illustration for this story, she used a model—a girl at her daughter's school—and had her wear a parka, get down on all fours in front of a ladder, and pat the chin of a teddy-bear prop. Then Piazza took a photograph of the scene and painted it, piecing in for the face of the teddy bear a separate drawing of an angry wolf's face, based on a photograph that she had found in a library book.

Currently, Piazza is concentrating on illustrations for children. She lives in Maryland with her husband and two children.

INFORMATION FOR THE STUDENT

Tell the students that the selection they are about to read is taken from the book *Julie of the Wolves* by Jean Craighead George. It is illustrated by Gail Piazza. As appropriate, you may want to share other information about the author or illustrator with the students.

Explain to the students that this story takes place in the northernmost part of the state of Alaska—as stated on page 53 of the selection—from the Brooks Range to the Arctic Ocean and from the Chukchi to the Beaufort Sea. If possible, display a map or a globe and have students locate the area in which the story takes place. Discuss with them the proximity of this area to the North Pole and to their own region.

*Geographical
Setting*

* ### COGNITIVE AND RESPONSIVE READING

Activating Prior
Knowledge

Students may be familiar with the physical appearance, the habitats, the diet, or the sounds of wolves. Ask volunteers to tell what they know about wolves.

Setting Reading Goals and Expectations

Have the students **browse** the **first page** of the selection, using the **clues/problems/wonderings procedure.** Students will return to these observations after reading.

Recommendations for Reading the Selection

Ask the students how they would like to read the selection. Because of the variety of information presented in this selection, the students may need assistance. Most students would probably benefit from reading the selection aloud.

During oral reading, use and encourage think-alouds. During silent reading, allow discussion as needed. Discuss problems, strategies, and reactions after reading.

This would also be a good selection for **responding to text by visualizing** while reading aloud. Model this response, and then invite the students to respond similarly.

Note: Notice that "Amaroq, the Wolf" has been divided into two parts. If the students do not finish reading the selection in one class period, the suggested breaking point is on page 61. The second part is indicated by a large initial capital letter.

About the Reading Strategies

Students will naturally be picturing the vividly described characters and setting in the text. **Visualizing** is one strategy that may help the students understand the story. Additionally, because of the real-life setting and the nature of the factual information, **question asking** is another strategy that students may want to use.

STEPS TOWARD INDEPENDENCE By this time in the year, on the basis of their browsing, students should be able to suggest strategies to use while reading.

Think-Aloud Prompts for Use in Oral Reading

Think-aloud prompts are placed with the page miniatures. These are merely suggestions for helping students use the strategies. Remind them to use whatever strategies they need to help them understand the selection. Refer them to the **reading strategy posters** if necessary. Encourage them to share the strategies they use as they read. For a review of information about **modeling think-alouds,** see **Teacher Tool Card 118.**

THINK ALOUD PROMPTS

These prompts may be used as guides to promote cognitive and responsive reading.

1 This selection contains many important concept words that may be new or confusing to students. As they encounter unfamiliar words, the students may need to clarify them. Encourage them to stop and clarify any unfamiliar words by using the **clarification strategies** they have learned. Encourage them to collaborate with classmates when necessary.

AMAROQ, THE WOLF
from JULIE OF THE WOLVES
by Jean Craighead George
illustrated by Gail Piazza

1 Miyax pushed back the hood of her sealskin parka and looked at the Arctic sun. It was a yellow disc in a lime-green sky, the colors of six o'clock in the evening and the time when the wolves awoke. Quietly she put down her cooking pot and crept to the top of a dome-shaped frost heave, one of the many earth buckles that rise and fall in the crackling cold of the Arctic winter. Lying on her stomach, she looked across a vast lawn of grass and moss and focused her attention on the wolves she had come upon two sleeps ago. They were wagging their tails as they awoke and saw each other.

Her hands trembled and her heartbeat quickened, for she was frightened, not so much of the wolves, who were shy and many harpoon-shots away, but because of her desperate predicament. Miyax was lost. She had been lost without food for many sleeps on the North Slope of Alaska. The barren slope stretches for three hundred miles from the Brooks Range to the Arctic Ocean, and for more than eight hundred miles from the Chukchi to the Beaufort Sea. No roads cross it; ponds and lakes freckle its immensity. Winds scream across it, and the view in every direction is exactly the same. Somewhere in this cosmos was Miyax; and the very life in her body, its spark and warmth, depended upon these wolves for survival. And she was not so sure they would help.

Miyax stared hard at the regal black wolf, hoping to catch his eye. She must somehow tell him that she was starving and ask him for food. This could be done she knew, for her father, an Eskimo hunter, had done so. One year he had camped near

🐾 52 🐾

🐾 53 🐾

a wolf den while on a hunt. When a month had passed and her father had seen no game, he told the leader of the wolves that he was hungry and needed food. The next night the wolf called him from far away and her father went to him and found a freshly killed caribou. Unfortunately, Miyax's father never explained to her how he had told the wolf of his needs. And not long afterward he paddled his kayak into the Bering Sea to hunt for seal, and he never returned.

She had been watching the wolves for two days, trying to discern which of their sounds and movements expressed goodwill and friendship. Most animals had such signals. The little Arctic ground squirrels flicked their tails sideways to notify others of their kind that they were friendly. By imitating this signal with her forefinger, Miyax had lured many a squirrel to her hand. If she could discover such a gesture for the wolves she would be able to make friends with them and share their food, like a bird or a fox.

Propped on her elbows with her chin in her fists, she stared at the black wolf, trying to catch his eye. She had chosen him because he was much larger than the others, and because he walked like her father, Kapugen, with his head high and his chest out. The black wolf also possessed wisdom, she had observed. The pack looked to him when the wind carried strange scents or the birds cried nervously. If he was alarmed, they were alarmed. If he was calm, they were calm.

Long minutes passed, and the black wolf did not look at her. He had ignored her since she first came upon them, two sleeps ago. True, she moved slowly and quietly, so as not to alarm him; yet she did wish he would see the kindness in her eyes. Many animals could tell the difference between hostile

❦ 54 ❦

hunters and friendly people by merely looking at them. But the big black wolf would not even glance her way.

A bird stretched in the grass. The wolf looked at it. A flower twisted in the wind. He glanced at that. Then the breeze rippled the wolverine ruff on Miyax's parka and it glistened in the light. He did not look at that. She waited. Patience with the ways of nature had been instilled in her by her father. And so she knew better than to move or shout. Yet she must get food or die. Her hands shook slightly and she swallowed hard to keep calm.

Miyax was a classic Eskimo beauty, small of bone and delicately wired with strong muscles. Her face was pearl-round and her nose was flat. Her black eyes, which slanted gracefully, were moist and sparkling. Like the beautifully formed polar bears and foxes of the north, she was slightly short-limbed. The frigid environment of the Arctic has sculptured life into compact shapes. Unlike the long-limbed, long-bodied animals of the south that are cooled by dispensing heat on extended surfaces, all live things in the Arctic tend toward compactness, to conserve heat.

The length of her limbs and the beauty of her face were of no use to Miyax as she lay on the lichen-speckled frost heave in the midst of the bleak tundra. Her stomach ached and the royal black wolf was carefully ignoring her.

"Amaroq, ilaya, wolf, my friend," she finally called. "Look at me. Look at me."

She spoke half in Eskimo and half in English, as if the instincts of her father and the science of the gussaks, the white-faced, might evoke some magical combination that would help her get her message through to the wolf.

❦ 55 ❦

---

2 A great deal of information has been presented about the geography of the Arctic and the behavior of animals that inhabit the tundra. Students may want to **sum up** at this point.

Throughout the story, the author uses vivid language to describe the land, the animals, and Miyax. The students may suggest **visualizing** the scenes to help them understand the story. Encourage them to share their visualizations with the class.

Amaroq glanced at his paw and slowly turned his head her way without lifting his eyes. He licked his shoulder. A few matted hairs sprang apart and twinkled individually. Then his eyes sped to each of the three adult wolves that made up his pack and finally to the five pups who were sleeping in a fuzzy mass near the den entrance. The great wolf's eyes softened at the sight of the little wolves, then quickly hardened into brittle yellow jewels as he scanned the flat tundra.

Not a tree grew anywhere to break the monotony of the gold-green plain, for the soils of the tundra are permanently frozen. Only moss, grass, <u>lichens</u>, and a few hardy flowers take root in the thin upper layer that thaws briefly in summer. Nor do many species of animals live in this rigorous land, but those creatures that do dwell here exist in bountiful numbers. Amaroq watched a large cloud of Lapland longspurs wheel up into the sky, then alight in the grasses. Swarms of crane flies, one of the few insects that can survive the cold, darkened the tips of the mosses. Birds wheeled, turned, and called. Thousands sprang up from the ground like leaves in a wind.

The wolf's ears cupped forward and tuned in on some distant message from the tundra. Miyax tensed and listened, too. Did he hear some brewing storm, some approaching enemy? Apparently not. His ears relaxed and he rolled to his side. She sighed, glanced at the vaulting sky, and was painfully aware of her predicament.

Here she was, watching wolves—she, Miyax, daughter of Kapugen, adopted child of Martha, citizen of the United States, pupil at the Bureau of Indian Affairs School in Barrow, Alaska, and thirteen-year-old wife of the boy Daniel. She shivered at the thought of Daniel, for it was he who had

56

driven her to this fate. She had run away from him exactly seven sleeps ago, and because of this she had one more title by gussak standards—the child divorcée.

The wolf rolled to his belly.

"Amaroq," she whispered. "I am lost and the sun will not set for a month. There is no North Star to guide me."

Amaroq did not stir.

"And there are no berry bushes here to bend under the polar wind and point to the south. Nor are there any birds I can follow." She looked up. "Here the birds are buntings and longspurs. They do not fly to the sea twice a day like the puffins and sandpipers that my father followed."

The wolf groomed his chest with his tongue.

"I never dreamed I could get lost, Amaroq," she went on, talking out loud to ease her fear. "At home on Nunivak Island where I was born, the plants and birds pointed the way for wanderers. I thought they did so everywhere . . . and so, great black Amaroq, I'm without a compass."

It had been a frightening moment when two days ago she realized that the tundra was an ocean of grass on which she was circling around and around. Now as that fear overcame her again she closed her eyes. When she opened them her heart skipped excitedly. Amaroq was looking at her!

"*Ee-lie*," she called and scrambled to her feet. The wolf arched his neck and narrowed his eyes. He pressed his ears forward. She waved. He drew back his lips and showed his teeth. Frightened by what seemed a snarl, she lay down again. When she was flat on her stomach, Amaroq flattened his ears and wagged his tail once. Then he tossed his head and looked away.

57

3 Some interesting scientific information is presented in this passage. Students may want to be sure that they understand what they have read and suggest using the strategy of **question asking** here. If no one does, however, you might model the strategy out loud:

Why do so few plants and animals live in the Arctic?

Then model finding the answer in the text.

Discouraged, she wriggled backward down the frost heave and arrived at her camp feet first. The heave was between herself and the wolf pack and so she relaxed, stood up, and took stock of her home. It was a simple affair, for she had not been able to carry much when she ran away; she took just those things she would need for the journey—a backpack, food for a week or so, needles to mend clothes, matches, her sleeping skin, and ground cloth to go under it, two knives, and a pot.

She had intended to walk to Point Hope. There she would meet the *North Star*, the ship that brings supplies from the States to the towns on the Arctic Ocean in August when the ice pack breaks up. The ship could always use dishwashers or laundresses, she had heard, and so she would work her way to San Francisco where Amy, her pen pal, lived. At the end of every letter Amy always wrote: "When are you coming to San Francisco?" Seven days ago she had been on her way— on her way to the glittering, white, postcard city that sat on a hill among trees, those enormous plants she had never seen. She had been on her way to see the television and carpeting in Amy's school, the glass buildings, traffic lights, and stores full of fruits; on her way to the harbor that never froze and the Golden Gate Bridge. But primarily she was on her way to be rid of Daniel, her terrifying husband.

She kicked the sod at the thought of her marriage; then shaking her head to forget, she surveyed her camp. It was nice. Upon discovering the

❧ 58 ❧

wolves, she had settled down to live near them in the hope of sharing their food, until the sun set and the stars came out to guide her. She had built a house of sod, like the summer homes of the old Eskimos. Each brick had been cut with her *ulo*, the half-moon shaped woman's knife, so versatile it can trim a baby's hair, slice a tough bear, or chip an iceberg.

Her house was not well built for she had never made one before, but it was cozy inside. She had windproofed it by sealing the sod bricks with mud from the pond at her door, and she had made it beautiful by spreading her caribou ground cloth on the floor. On this she had placed her sleeping skin, a moosehide bag lined with soft white rabbit skins. Next to her

bed she had built a low table of sod on which to put her clothes when she slept. To decorate the house she had made three flowers of bird feathers and stuck them in the top of the table. Then she had built a fireplace outdoors and placed her pot beside it. The pot was empty, for she had not found even a lemming to eat.

Last winter, when she had walked to school in Barrow, these mice-like rodents were so numerous they ran out from under her feet wherever she stepped. There were thousands and thousands of them until December, when they suddenly vanished. Her teacher said that the lemmings had a chemical similar to antifreeze in their blood, that kept them active all winter when other little mammals were hibernating. "They eat grass and multiply all winter," Mrs. Franklin had said in her singsong voice. "When there are too many, they grow nervous at the sight of each other. Somehow this shoots too much antifreeze into their bloodstreams and it begins to poison them. They become restless, then crazy. They run in a frenzy until they die."

Of this phenomenon Miyax's father had simply said, "The hour of the lemming is over for four years."

Unfortunately for Miyax, the hour of the animals that prey on the lemmings was also over. The white fox, the snowy owl, the weasel, the jaeger, and the siskin had virtually disappeared. They had no food to eat and bore few or no young. Those that lived preyed on each other. With the passing of the lemmings, however, the grasses had grown high again and the hour of the caribou was upon the land. Healthy fat caribou cows gave birth to many calves. The caribou population increased, and this in turn increased the number of wolves

꒛ 60 ꒐

who prey on the caribou. The abundance of the big deer of the north did Miyax no good, for she had not brought a gun on her trip. It had never occurred to her that she would not reach Point Hope before her food ran out. **④**

A dull pain seized her stomach. She pulled blades of grass from their sheaths and ate the sweet ends. They were not very satisfying, so she picked a handful of caribou moss, a lichen. If the deer could survive in winter on this food, why not she? She munched, decided the plant might taste better if cooked, and went to the pond for water. **⑤**

As she dipped her pot in, she thought about Amaroq. Why had he bared his teeth at her? Because she was young and he knew she couldn't hurt him? No, she said to herself, it was because he was speaking to her! He had told her to lie down. She had even understood and obeyed him. He had talked to her not with his voice, but with his ears, eyes, and lips; and he had even commended her with a wag of his tail.

She dropped her pot, scrambled up the frost heave and stretched out on her stomach.

"Amaroq," she called softly, "I understand what you said. Can you understand me? I'm hungry—very, very hungry. Please bring me some meat."

The great wolf did not look her way and she began to doubt her reasoning. After all, flattened ears and a tail-wag were

꒛ 61 ꒐

④ If you and your class cannot finish the selection during this period, this is a good place to stop reading.

⑤ Before beginning to read the second part of the selection, students may want to **sum up** what they remember from the first part. Their summaries should include only the important points.

scarcely a conversation. She dropped her forehead against the lichens and rethought what had gone between them.

"Then why did I lie down?" she asked, lifting her head and looking at Amaroq. "Why did I?" she called to the yawning wolves. Not one turned her way.

Amaroq got to his feet, and as he slowly arose he seemed to fill the sky and blot out the sun. He was enormous. He could swallow her without even chewing.

"But he won't," she reminded herself. "Wolves do not eat people. That's gussak talk. Kapugen said wolves are gentle brothers."

The black puppy was looking at her and wagging his tail. Hopefully, Miyax held out a pleading hand to him. His tail wagged harder. The mother rushed to him and stood above him sternly. When he licked her cheek apologetically, she pulled back her lips from her fine white teeth. They flashed as she smiled and forgave her cub.

"But don't let it happen again," said Miyax sarcastically, mimicking her own elders. The mother walked toward Amaroq.

"I should call you Martha after my stepmother," Miyax whispered. "But you're much too beautiful. I shall call you Silver instead."

Silver moved in a halo of light, for the sun sparkled on the guard hairs that grew out over the dense underfur and she seemed to glow.

The reprimanded pup snapped at a crane fly and shook himself. Bits of lichen and grass spun off his fur. He reeled unsteadily, took a wider stance, and looked down at his sleeping sister. With a yap he jumped on her and rolled her to her feet. She whined. He barked and picked up a bone. When he was sure she was watching, he ran down the slope with it. The sister tagged after him. He stopped and she grabbed the bone, too. She pulled; he pulled; then he pulled and she yanked.

Miyax could not help laughing. The puppies played with bones like Eskimo children played with leather ropes.

"I understand *that*," she said to the pups. "That's tug-o-war. Now how do you say, 'I'm hungry'?"

Amaroq was pacing restlessly along the crest of the frost heave as if something were about to happen. His eyes shot to Silver, then to the gray wolf Miyax had named Nails. These glances seemed to be a <u>summons</u>, for Silver and Nails glided to him, spanked the ground with their forepaws and bit him gently under the chin. He wagged his tail furiously and took Silver's slender nose in his mouth. She crouched before him, licked his cheek and lovingly bit his lower jaw. Amaroq's tail flashed high as her mouthing charged him with vitality. He nosed her affectionately. Unlike the fox who met his mate only in the breeding season, Amaroq lived with his mate all year.

Next, Nails took Amaroq's jaw in his mouth and the leader bit the top of his nose. A third adult, a small male, came slinking up. He got down on his belly before Amaroq, rolled trembling to his back, and wriggled.

"Hello, Jello," Miyax whispered, for he reminded her of the quivering gussak dessert her mother-in-law made.

She had seen the wolves mouth Amaroq's chin twice before and so she concluded that it was a ceremony, a sort of "Hail to the Chief." He must indeed be their leader for he was clearly the wealthy wolf; that is, wealthy as she had known the meaning of the word on Nunivak Island. There the old Eskimo hunters she had known in her childhood thought the riches of life were intelligence, fearlessness, and love. A man with these gifts was rich and was a great spirit who was admired in the same way that the gussaks admired a man with money and goods.

The three adults paid tribute to Amaroq until he was almost smothered with love; then he bayed a wild note that sounded like the wind on the frozen sea. With that the others sat around him, the puppies scattered between them. Jello hunched forward and Silver shot a fierce glance at him. Intimidated, Jello pulled his ears together and back. He drew himself down until he looked smaller than ever.

❦ 64 ❦

Amaroq wailed again, stretching his neck until his head was high above the others. They gazed at him affectionately and it was plain to see that he was their great spirit, a royal leader who held his group together with love and wisdom.

Any fear Miyax had of the wolves was dispelled by their affection for each other. They were friendly animals and so devoted to Amaroq that she needed only to be accepted by him to be accepted by all. She even knew how to achieve this—bite him under the chin. But how was she going to do that?

She studied the pups hoping they had a simpler way of expressing their love for him. The black puppy approached the leader, sat, then lay down and wagged his tail vigorously. He gazed up at Amaroq in pure adoration, and the royal eyes softened.

Well, that's what I'm doing! Miyax thought. She called to Amaroq. "I'm lying down gazing at you, too, but you don't look at *me* that way!"

When all the puppies were wagging his praises, Amaroq yipped, hit a high note, and crooned. As his voice rose and fell, the other adults sang out and the puppies yipped and bounced.

The song ended abruptly. Amaroq arose and trotted swiftly down the slope. Nails followed, and behind him ran Silver, then Jello. But Jello did not run far. Silver turned and looked him straight in the eye. She pressed her ears forward aggressively and lifted her tail. With that, Jello went back to the puppies and the three sped away like dark birds.

Miyax hunched forward on her elbows, the better to see and learn. She now knew how to be a good puppy, pay

❦ 65 ❦

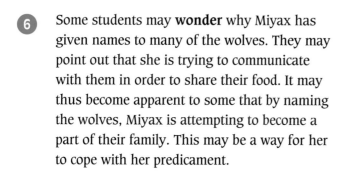

6 Some students may **wonder** why Miyax has given names to many of the wolves. They may point out that she is trying to communicate with them in order to share their food. It may thus become apparent to some that by naming the wolves, Miyax is attempting to become a part of their family. This may be a way for her to cope with her predicament.

tribute to the leader, and even to be a leader by biting others on the top of the nose. She also knew how to tell Jello to baby-sit. If only she had big ears and a tail, she could lecture and talk to them all.

Flapping her hands on her head for ears, she flattened her fingers to make friends, pulled them together and back to express fear, and shot them forward to display her aggression and dominance. Then she folded her arms and studied the puppies again.

The black one greeted Jello by tackling his feet. Another jumped on his tail, and before he could discipline either, all five were upon him. He rolled and tumbled with them for almost an hour; then he ran down the slope, turned, and stopped. The pursuing pups plowed into him, tumbled, fell, and lay still. During a minute of surprised recovery there was no action. Then the black pup flashed his tail like a semaphore signal and they all jumped on Jello again.

Miyax rolled over and laughed aloud. "That's funny. They're really like kids."

When she looked back, Jello's tongue was hanging from his mouth and his sides were heaving. Four of the puppies had collapsed at his feet and were asleep. Jello flopped down, too, but the black pup still looked around. He was not the least bit tired. Miyax watched him, for there was something special about him.

He ran to the top of the den and barked. The smallest pup, whom Miyax called Sister, lifted her head, saw her favorite brother in action and, struggling to her feet, followed him devotedly. While they romped, Jello took the opportunity to

🐾 66 🐾

rest behind a clump of sedge, a moisture-loving plant of the tundra. But hardly was he settled before a pup tracked him to his hideout and pounced on him. Jello narrowed his eyes, pressed his ears forward, and showed his teeth.

"I know what you're saying," she called to him. "You're saying, 'lie down.'" The puppy lay down, and Miyax got on all fours and looked for the nearest pup to speak to. It was Sister.

"Ummmm," she whined, and when Sister turned around she narrowed her eyes and showed her white teeth. Obediently, Sister lay down.

"I'm talking wolf! I'm talking wolf!" Miyax clapped, and tossing her head like a pup, crawled in a happy circle. As she was coming back she saw all five puppies sitting in a row watching her, their heads cocked in curiosity. Boldly the black pup came toward her, his fat backside swinging as he trotted to the bottom of her frost heave, and barked.

"You are *very* fearless and *very* smart," she said. "Now I know why you are special. You are wealthy and the leader of the puppies. There is no doubt what you'll grow up to be. So I shall name you after my father Kapugen, and I shall call you Kapu for short."

Kapu wrinkled his brow and turned an ear to tune in more acutely on her voice.

"You don't understand, do you?"

Hardly had she spoken than his tail went up, his mouth opened slightly, and he fairly grinned.

"Ee-lie!" she gasped. "You do understand. And that scares me." She perched on her heels. Jello whined an undulating note and Kapu turned back to the den.

🐾 67 🐾

7 Miyax has observed a great deal of interaction among the wolves. Some students may suggest **summing up** all that she has seen. They may then want to **predict** what Miyax will do with all of this information. Remind them to follow up on their predictions later.

Miyax imitated the call to come home. Kapu looked back over his shoulder in surprise. She giggled. He wagged his tail and jumped on Jello.

She clapped her hands and settled down to watch this language of jumps and tumbles, elated that she was at last breaking the wolf code. After a long time she decided they were not talking but roughhousing, and so she started home. Later she changed her mind. Roughhousing was very important to wolves. It occupied almost the entire night for the pups.

"Ee-lie, okay," she said. "I'll learn to roughhouse. Maybe then you'll accept me and feed me." She pranced, jumped, and whimpered; she growled, snarled, and rolled. But nobody came to roughhouse.

Sliding back to her camp, she heard the grass swish and looked up to see Amaroq and his hunters sweep around her frost heave and stop about five feet away. She could smell the sweet scent of their fur.

The hairs on her neck rose and her eyes widened. Amaroq's ears went forward aggressively and she remembered that wide eyes meant fear to him. It was not good to show him she was afraid. Animals attacked the fearful. She tried to narrow them, but remembered that was not right either. Narrowed eyes were mean. In desperation she recalled that Kapu had moved forward when challenged. She pranced right up to Amaroq. Her heart beat furiously as she grunt-whined the sound of the puppy begging adoringly for

🐾 68 🐾

attention. Then she got down on her belly and gazed at him with fondness.

The great wolf backed up and avoided her eyes. She had said something wrong! Perhaps even offended him. Some slight gesture that meant nothing to her had apparently meant something to the wolf. His ears shot forward angrily and it seemed all was lost. She wanted to get up and run, but she gathered her courage and pranced closer to him. Swiftly she patted him under the chin.

The signal went off. It sped through his body and triggered emotions of love. Amaroq's ears flattened and his tail wagged in friendship. He could not react in any other way to the chin pat, for the roots of this signal lay deep in wolf history. It was inherited from generations and generations of leaders before him. As his eyes softened, the sweet odor of <u>ambrosia</u> arose from the gland on the top of his tail and she was drenched lightly in wolf scent. Miyax was one of the pack.

*

EXPLORING THROUGH DISCUSSION

Reflecting on the Selection
Whole-Group Discussion

The **whole group discusses** the selection and any thoughts or questions that it raises. During this time, students also **return to the clues, problems, and wonderings** that they noted on the chalkboard during browsing.

Assessment

To assess their understanding of the text, engage the students in a discussion to determine whether they have grasped the following ideas:
- why and how Miyax made friends with the wolves
- how Miyax dealt with isolation

Response Journal

Students may wish to record in their response journals any personal thoughts or reactions they had to the selection.

Exploring Concepts Within the Selection
Small-Group Discussion

Circulate among the groups and observe discussions. Remind the students to refer to the Question Board and the Concept Board to keep the discussions focused. Encourage students to consider whether their original ideas about perseverance have changed as a result of reading this story.

ASSESSMENT TIP This might be a good time to observe students working in groups and to mark observations in your Teacher's Observation Log.

Sharing Ideas About Explorable Concepts

Have the groups **report their ideas** and **discuss them** with the rest of the class. It is crucial that the students' ideas determine this discussion.
- The students may realize that the wolves were not Miyax's enemies. Instead, her adversary was the cold, harsh tundra.
- Some students may point out the spirit of sharing within the wolf family and comment on how animals cooperate with one another to survive.
- Some students may wonder what role perseverance plays in non-life-or-death situations.

As these ideas and others are stated, have the students add them to the Question Board or the Concept Board.

Exploring Concepts Across Selections

Ask students whether this story reminds them of anything else they have read. They may make connections with other selections in this unit or in other units.
- Students may notice that like Brian in "The Fire Builder," Miyax was motivated to struggle to survive because of her natural instinct for self-preservation, which caused her to run away in the first place. However, some students may comment that unlike Brian, who tried to keep animals away, Miyax made the decision to make friends with the wolves because of what she knew about them.

Recording Ideas

As they complete the above discussions, ask the students to **sum up what they have learned from their conversations and to tell how they might use this information** in further explorations. Any special information or insights may be recorded on the **Concept Board.** Any

Evaluating Discussions

Recording Concept Information continued

"The Fire Builder" by Gary Paulsen

_____

_____

_____

_____

_____

_____

_____

"Amaroq, the Wolf" by Jean Craighead George

_____

_____

_____

_____

_____

_____

"Mother to Son" by Langston Hughes

_____

_____

_____

_____

_____

_____

66 EN   Perseverance/Unit 4

Explorer's Notebook, page 66

further questions that they would like to think about, pursue, or investigate may be recorded on the **Question Board.** They may want to discuss the progress that has been made on their questions. They may also want to cross out any questions that no longer warrant consideration.

❯ Students should record their ideas about the selection and the unit concepts on page 66 of their Explorer's Notebook.

2 READING WITH A WRITER'S EYE

MINILESSONS

Writer's Craft:
Developing
Problems and
Solutions

Ask the students to talk about anything they have learned about **developing problems and solutions** in stories and to describe any examples they can remember about problems and solutions from their reading or writing. Explain to the students that writers create problems in stories to develop excitement so that their readers will keep reading—often to discover whether and how the problem is solved.

❯ Distribute Reproducible Master 45 and discuss with students some of the common elements of stories about problems and solutions. Then have the students place the page in the Story Elements section of their Writer's Notebook. The following points should be among those discussed:

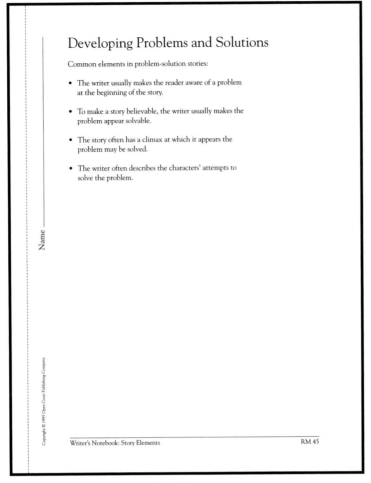

Developing Problems and Solutions

Common elements in problem-solution stories:

- The writer usually makes the reader aware of a problem at the beginning of the story.

- To make a story believable, the writer usually makes the problem appear solvable.

- The story often has a climax at which it appears the problem may be solved.

- The writer often describes the characters' attempts to solve the problem.

Name

Copyright © 1995 Open Court Publishing Company

Writer's Notebook: Story Elements   RM 45

Reproducible Master 45

- The writer usually makes the reader aware of a problem at the beginning of the story.
- To make a story believable, the writer usually makes the problem appear solvable.
- The story often has a climax at which it appears the problem may be solved.
- The writer often describes the characters' attempts to solve the problem.

Tell students that in "Amaroq, the Wolf," Jean Craighead George developed a problem and solution to create interest for the reader. For example, on pages 52 and 53 the problem is identified (Miyax is lost, cold, and hungry). George then tells how Miyax thought about solving her hunger problem (asking the wolves for food).

Write the problem and the possible solution on the chalkboard. Point out that one problem and its solution often leads to a new problem.

- **Problem:** Miyax is lost and hungry in the wilderness. She is alone except for the wolves.
- **Possible solution:** The wolves may share their food with Miyax.
- **New problem:** Miyax must convince the wolves to share their food with her.
- **Possible solution:** Miyax will try to talk to the wolves. She knows that her father had done so.

Developing Problems and Solutions

Look again at "Amaroq, the Wolf" or at any other stories you have read in which the author develops problems for a character. Identify the story, the character, and one or more problems that he or she encounters. Complete the rest of the page, using information from the story.

Story: _____ Page: _____

Character: _____

Problem: _____

_____

Possible solution: _____

New problem: _____

Possible solution: _____

Is the character's search for a solution consistent with his or her personality? Explain.

_____

_____

_____

How is the problem solved? _____

_____

_____

_____

_____

Problem/Solution Text

30 R/WC   Perseverance/Unit 4

Copyright © 1995 Open Court Publishing Company

Name

Reading/Writing Connection, page 30

Setting/Realistic Fiction

In "Amaroq, the Wolf" or in any other stories you have read, look for ways in which authors establish the settings of their stories. For each example, write down the story title, a general description of the setting, and some of the details the author uses to describe the setting. Explain what the author does to make the setting seem real.

Title: _____

Setting: _____ Details: _____

_____ _____

_____ _____

What makes the setting seem real? _____

_____

Title: _____

Setting: _____ Details: _____

_____ _____

_____ _____

What makes the setting seem real? _____

_____

Use this page when you need help in establishing a setting in your own writing.

Story Elements

Unit 4/Perseverance   R/WC 31

Copyright © 1995 Open Court Publishing Company

Name

Reading/Writing Connection, page 31

Selection-Based Practice

Selective Reading: Focus on Developing Problems and Solutions

Have a volunteer identify and read aloud one or two passages from the selection that show (1) how Miyax thinks through the various actions that she could take to solve her problem and (2) how she contemplates the reasons. Encourage students to focus on the approach Miyax uses to solve her problem and the possible consequences of the solutions.

One problem the students may identify is introduced on page 54.

- **Problem:** Miyax needs food. In order to get it she must make friends with the wolves. How can she do this?
- **Possible solutions:** (1) She must observe them. Page 54, paragraph 1: "She had been watching the wolves for two days. . . ." (2) She must discover the sounds and movements that express friendship. Page 54, paragraph 1: "If she could discover such a gesture. . . ."

Independent Practice: Developing Problems and Solutions

▶ For additional practice in recognizing how an author creates problems and solutions in a story, have students work in small groups to discuss and complete Reading/Writing Connection, page 30.

Writer's Craft: Establishing Setting/Realistic Fiction

Ask students to talk about anything they have learned about establishing **setting** in realistic stories and to describe any examples they can remember from their reading or writing. If necessary, remind students that writers establish the setting to help the reader understand **where and when the story takes place.** Remind them of their discussion of setting in an imaginary story after they read the selection *Saint George and the Dragon.* Refer them to Reproducible Master 5 in the Story Elements section of their Writer's Notebook, and review with them the points to remember about a story setting.

Then discuss the importance of the setting in "Amaroq, the Wolf." Point out that without a clearly established setting, readers would have trouble understanding the life-or-death situation that Miyax faces.

Explain that since this story is a piece of realistic fiction—that is, it is not true but it could happen—the author provides a very real setting. For example, she begins to establish her setting in the very first paragraph:

- "Miyax . . . looked at the Arctic sun" (place).
- "It was a yellow disc . . . six o'clock . . ." (time of day).
- "Quietly she put down . . . the Arctic winter (time of year).

Selective Reading: Focus on Setting/Realistic Fiction

Have volunteers identify and read aloud other passages from the story in which the setting is described. Almost every page of the story contains some description of setting. Ask students to identify passages in which the author describes what the characters see, feel, hear, and smell as well as the geographic location. Encourage students to consider and discuss what George did in her writing to establish a realistic setting—one that encourages readers to believe such a place could exist.

Selection-Based Practice

Independent Practice: Setting/Realistic Fiction

❯ Have students work individually or in small collaborative groups, using Reading/Writing Connection, page 31, to extend their discussion of how authors establish settings in interesting ways so as to make their stories more believable.

WRITING

Linking Reading to Writing

Remind students that it is important for writers to keep readers interested in their stories by establishing settings and by creating problems for the characters to solve. Remind them that they may want to revise pieces of their own writing to include interesting settings or problems for a character to solve. When dealing with a problem-solution story, they should focus on events that build to a climax at which the problem can be solved. They should also remember to keep a character's search for a solution consistent with the personality of the character.

✱ Writing Process

Some students may want to begin a new writing piece in which they create for a character a difficult problem that will keep the reader interested. Encourage students to share and discuss their own experiences with classmates to generate strong problem-solution ideas during their prewriting activities. Other students may wish to begin a piece of writing with a realistic setting that will appeal to readers. You might allow time for students to research the locations of their stories in order to provide realistic details for their settings. Suggest that students conference with peers and ask for feedback about their ideas.

You might discuss the following words from the selection related to perseverance: *rigorous, barren, phenomenon,* and *dominance.* Remind students to fill out Vocabulary Exploration forms, Reproducible Master 15, for these or any other words or phrases from the story that they want to remember and use. Have them add these to the Personal Dictionary section of their Writer's Notebook. Allow time for them to share with classmates the words they chose and their reasons for choosing them. For additional opportunities to build vocabulary, see **Teacher Tool Card 77.**

VOCABULARY TIP Have students choose from the selections words that they may find useful in their speaking and writing about the explorable concepts. Add these words to the Concept Board.

3 GUIDED AND INDEPENDENT EXPLORATION

EXPLORING CONCEPTS BEYOND THE TEXT

Guided Exploration

Students will select activities in which they explore the unit concepts. Refer them to the **Exploration Activities poster** and give them time to choose an activity. Allow them to discuss what they wish to explore and how they wish to go about it. If the students need further help, here are some suggestions:

- Some students may wish to take part in a small discussion group to compare perseverance in a life-or-death situation with perseverance in the pursuit of a goal that is important but that is not a matter of life or death. Encourage students to discuss the differences and the similarities in the situations—motivation, risk factors, and priorities. The students should take notes and refer to them later in the unit to see whether their ideas change.

- Students may wish to debate the following statement: *Reaching a goal depends more on luck than on perseverance.* Have volunteers choose sides on the basis of whether they agree or disagree with the statement. The rest of the class can act as the audience and ask questions afterward.

- Some students may want to role-play a news-conference situation. They should decide who will take the roles of news reporters and who will take the role of Miyax from the story. News reporters should prepare questions to ask Miyax about her experiences. The student playing Miyax should respond as Miyax would respond, on the basis of what she has learned about Miyax's character and experiences. Students can prepare for this activity by reading the entire book from which "Amaroq, the Wolf" was taken, *Julie of the Wolves* by Jean Craighead George. Students should consider the problems that Julie faced, the difficulties that she encountered in trying to overcome those problems, the new information that she acquired, and her reasons for persevering. Students are encouraged to switch roles to offer their

✱ Exploring Through Reflective Activities

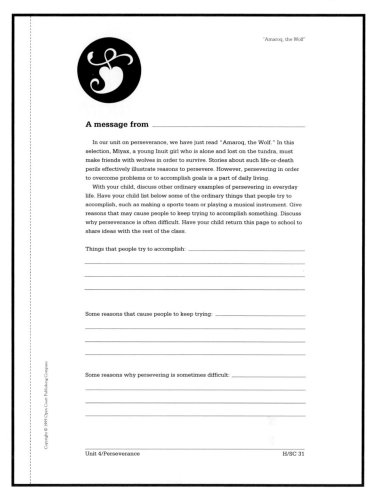

Exploring Perseverance Through Role-Playing

If you have chosen to role-play a news-conference situation in which reporters interview Miyax about her experience on the tundra, use this page to record questions and answers. Remember that as a reporter, you want to uncover the factors that caused a person to persevere and not to give up. The person who plays Miyax should base her or his responses on what you have learned about Miyax's character and her experiences. Switch roles from time to time so that everyone who wants to play Miyax will have the opportunity to do so.

Questions that a news reporter might ask Miyax:

_____

_____

_____

_____

_____

_____

_____

Responses that Miyax might give:

_____

_____

_____

_____

_____

_____

_____

_____

Copyright © 1995 Open Court Publishing Company

Unit 4/Perseverance   EN 73

Explorer's Notebook, page 73

"Amaroq, the Wolf"

A message from _____

In our unit on perseverance, we have just read "Amaroq, the Wolf." In this selection, Miyax, a young Inuit girl who is alone and lost on the tundra, must make friends with wolves in order to survive. Stories about such life-or-death perils effectively illustrate reasons to persevere. However, persevering in order to overcome problems or to accomplish goals is a part of daily living.

With your child, discuss other ordinary examples of persevering in everyday life. Have your child list below some of the ordinary things that people try to accomplish, such as making a sports team or playing a musical instrument. Give reasons that may cause people to keep trying to accomplish something. Discuss why perseverance is often difficult. Have your child return this page to school to share ideas with the rest of the class.

Things that people try to accomplish: _____

_____

_____

_____

Some reasons that cause people to keep trying: _____

_____

_____

_____

Some reasons why persevering is sometimes difficult: _____

_____

_____

_____

Copyright © 1995 Open Court Publishing Company

Unit 4/Perseverance   H/SC 31

Home/School Connection 31

---

unique insights into Miyax's behavior and to compare their ideas with those of their classmates.

❯ Students can use page 73 in their Explorer's Notebook to help them if they choose a role-playing activity.

❯ Distribute Home/School Connection 31. Stories about life-or-death perils effectively illustrate "good" reasons to persevere. However, perseverance in order to overcome problems or to accomplish a goal is a part of everyday life. Students and their families can discuss other examples of persevering in everyday life and list some of the ordinary things that people try to accomplish, such as making a sports team or playing a musical instrument.

Continuing Exploration

By this time, students should have narrowed their focus and decided on specific aspects of perseverance that they would like to explore further. Have them revisit the questions that they previously raised and choose concepts for exploration that they are interested in.

Have the students return to their Explorer's Notebook, page 69, to record any additional questions they have about the unit concepts.

To review information about **Exploring Through Reflective Activities,** see **Learning Framework Card 3.**

*INDEPENDENT WORKSHOP
Building a Community of Scholars

Student-Directed Reading, Writing, and Discussion

Remind the students that they will work with their collaborative groups during the first part of Independent Workshop. Afterward they are free to make independent choices about their explorations. Discuss questions with students. Assist them in narrowing the focus of their explorations and in locating resources. To review information about **Independent Workshop,** see **Learning Framework Card 5.**

WORKSHOP TIP

Remind students to return to their Explorer's Notebook to complete unfinished pages or to discuss ideas with their classmates.

Additional Opportunities for Independent Reading, Writing, and Cross-curricular Activities

✱ Reading Roundtable

Encourage the students to read other books by Jean Craighead George, such as *The Cry of the Crow* about problems that result when wild creatures are tamed; *River Rats,* about two boys struggling for survival with the help of a wild boy; or *The Shark Beneath the Reef,* a Tradebook Connection selection that relates well to the unit concepts. If they read the latter book, remind them to do the activities on the Tradebook Connection Card in the Student Toolbox.

✱ Writing Seminar

When students are revising their writing, remind them to reorganize ideas or information to achieve their purposes. Have them share their writing with their classmates and ask for feedback.

Portfolio

Remind students to think about pieces of writing to put in their portfolios.

Cross-curricular Activity Cards

The following Cross-curricular Activity Cards in the Student Toolbox are appropriate for this selection:
- 10 Science—Wild Food
- 11 Science—Wolf Behavior

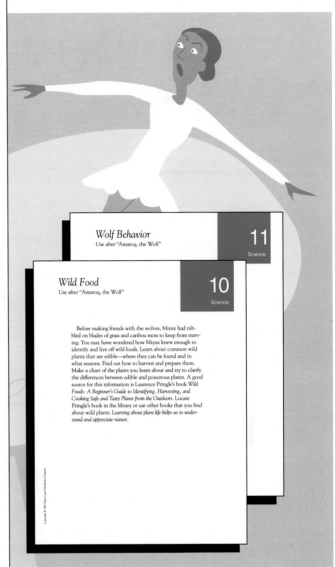

Wolf Behavior
Use after "Amaroq, the Wolf"

11
Science

Wild Food
Use after "Amaroq, the Wolf"

10
Science

Before making friends with the wolves, Miyax had nibbled on blades of grass and caribou moss to keep from starving. You may have wondered how Miyax knew enough to identify and live off wild foods. Learn about common wild plants that are edible—where they can be found and in what seasons. Find out how to harvest and prepare them. Make a chart of the plants you learn about and try to clarify the differences between edible and poisonous plants. A good source for this information is Laurence Pringle's book *Wild Foods: A Beginner's Guide to Identifying, Harvesting, and Cooking Safe and Tasty Plants from the Outdoors.* Locate Pringle's book in the library or use other books that you find about wild plants. *Learning about plant life helps us to understand and appreciate nature.*

Additional Opportunities for Solving Learning Problems

Tutorial

Use this time to work with students who need help in any area. Remember to arrange peer tutoring for those for whom it would be appropriate. Encourage the students to ask for help when they feel the need. The following Teacher Tool Cards are available in the Teacher Toolbox for your convenience:
- Writer's Craft/Reading: Elaboration Through Providing Problem and Solution, Teacher Tool Card 45
- Writer's Craft/Reading: Setting, Teacher Tool Card 14
- Writer's Craft/Reading: Elaboration Through Giving Reasons or Causes, Teacher Tool Card 38
- Writer's Craft/Reading: Elaboration Through Providing Descriptions, Teacher Tool Card 40

Fine Art

DISCUSSING FINE ART

Included here is some background information about the pieces of fine art shown on pages 70–71. Share with the students whatever you feel is appropriate. Some works may be familiar to them. Encourage them to express their reactions to each piece—for example, what the piece has to do with perseverance, whether they think it is related to this unit, and why. Encourage them to find out more about artists or artistic styles that interest them. For additional information on discussing fine art, refer to **Teacher Tool Card 125.**

Four Jockeys Riding Hard. c. 1815.
Théodore Géricault. Oil on canvas.

The French artist Théodore Géricault (1791–1824) was one of the most original figures of the Romantic movement in European art, music, literature, and philosophy. Eighteenth- and nineteenth-century Romanticists, reacting against rationalism and growing industrialization, stressed a belief in individual experience and a break with the restrictive classical traditions of Western art and thought.

Géricault painted contemporary events as scenes of heroic drama and action. His most famous work, *The Raft of the Medusa,* portrays the survivors of the shipwreck of a government ship, the *Medusa,* which went down off the coast of West Africa with hundreds of men on board. In an effort to achieve authenticity, Géricault interviewed survivors, had a model of the raft made, and studied corpses and severed limbs at the morgue. He later painted a series of portraits of individual patients in the clinic of his friend, Dr. Georget, a pioneer in modern psychiatry.

Four Jockeys Riding Hard. c. 1815. Théodore Géricault.
Oil on canvas. Musée Bonnat, Bayonne. Photo: Giraudon/Art Resource

The Village School. 1846. Giuseppe Constantini.
Oil on canvas. Centro Didattico Nazionale di Studi e Documentazione, Florence. Photo: SCALA/Art Resource

FINE ART
PERSEVERANCE

Man chasing after his hat in the wind. c. 18th–19th century. Japanese.
Woodblock print. Photo: Art Resource

71

Géricault was an enthusiastic horseman. He painted jockeys and horse races in France and in England, greatly influenced by eighteenth-century British animal painters. In *Four Jockeys Riding Hard*, Géricault captures the riders' emotional intensity and persistence. Their postures depict their refusal to give up and their determination to reach their goal, the finish line.

Théodore Géricault died at the age of thirty-three as the result of a riding accident.

The Village School. 1846.
Guiseppe Constantini. Oil on canvas.

Guiseppe Constantini was a nineteenth-century genre painter, born in Nola, in the Italian province of Napoli (Naples) in the region of Campania. (Genre painting depicts scenes of everyday life and activities, usually in a realistic style.) Constantini was from southern Italy, called the Mezzogiorno (meaning midday or noon), which historically has been and continues to be the poorest area of Italy. When *The Village School* was painted, Italy was not yet a unified nation; Austria controlled much of the country, either through direct rule or through local rulers who were loyal to the Austrian king.

The French Revolution (which began in 1789) influenced Italy more than it did any other European country. The idea of an Italian republic began to spread, and throughout the peninsula secret clubs favoring the creation of such a republic were formed. During the 1820s and 1830s, several unsuccessful revolts took place against certain local rulers. Talk of reform continued, especially among the educated and the professional classes and some liberal members of the nobility. In 1848 revolution broke out in every major Italian city. Constitutions were granted by their rulers to the people of the kingdoms of Sardinia and Naples. The Austrian army was driven out of Milan. Venice, Rome, and the Tuscan region all declared their own republics. However, because of the inexperience of, and divisions among, the new republican leaders, Austria was able to put down the revolutions. Austria's hold on Italy was nonetheless weakened, and by 1859, with the aid of French soldiers, the Austrians had been pushed eastward, and those rulers who had cooperated with Austria were expelled. In 1860 the great Italian hero Giuseppe Garibaldi sailed to Sicily with one thousand volunteers to help the Sicilians in their fight for freedom against the Kingdom of Naples. After defeating the larger professional army of the king of Naples, Garibaldi and his troops, called the red shirts, captured southern Italy and the city of Naples. In 1871 Rome became the capital of a united Italy.

When Constantini painted *The Village School,* one of the reforms most discussed was increasing education. Almost 80 percent of the Italian people were illiterate, and the figures were even worse for the poorer, agricultural south. *The Village School* depicts an ideal, one that was probably largely unrealized when Constantini created his work. Barefoot peasant boys (the education of girls in such a setting would generally have been unconsidered) are gathered with their schoolmaster in a one-room rural schoolhouse to learn about Italy and the world, ancient and modern. Under the watchful eye of the schoolmaster, one boy works at math problems on the blackboard. Other boys read, write, and discuss amongst themselves. A map of the world hangs on the wall, along with a painting of Mary and the Infant Jesus, reminding the children of their Roman Catholic faith (Italy has been predominately Roman Catholic for many centuries). In the wall niche to the right, an ancient vase is displayed, reminding the boys of their history, dating back to the Etruscans, the Greeks, and the Romans. On a lighter note, one boy sitting on the floor in the left foreground of the painting wears a dunce cap (once worn by slow or lazy students as a punishment; also called a fool's cap). The letters *ASIN* can be made out; the letter that cannot be seen by the viewer would be *O.* The Italian word *asino* means "donkey," "stupid fellow," or "dunce." However, the dunce-capped student takes his mischievous revenge by sketching an unflattering likeness of his teacher. A hazy glow softens the poverty of the surroundings.

This was the reformist's dream in mid-nineteenth-century Italy during the great national revival called the *Risorgimento* ("rebirth"): an education for all citizens, who, regardless of their origins, might become, if they persevered, the new leaders of a strong and unified Italy, a vital part of a modern Europe.

Man chasing after his hat in the wind. c. 18th–19th century. Japanese. Artist unknown. Woodblock print.

The piece shown here is representative of Japanese prints from the seventeenth through the nineteenth centuries, prints that depicted ordinary scenes from daily life as well as scenes from the theater and other popular entertainments and amusements. Such transitory moments were referred to as the "floating world," and the prints that portrayed them were "pictures of the floating world," or *ukiyoe.*

Unlike modern print production, the production of old Japanese woodblock prints did not involve the use of a printing press or of colors made from inks. The process required the work of three different craftspeople: the artist who created and drew the design, the engraver who transferred the design to wood, and the printer.

The artist drew the original design on thin paper with a brush dipped in Chinese ink. This was passed on to the engraver, who pasted it onto a block of wood (usually cherry wood) and, using a special knife, cut through the paper, transferring the outlines of the design to the block. The excess wood between the lines was removed with various chisels and gouges. A printer then applied the color by hand in the form of paints mixed with rice paste. Black and white prints were made from one block of wood, color prints from one block for each color used. Fresh color was reapplied for each impression made, thus allowing multiple copies of a print to be produced. The final design was printed on sheets of mulberry-bark paper.

Prints were favored by middle-class buyers for whom paintings were too expensive. *Ukiyoe* dealt with subjects and themes beyond the formal conventions of traditional Japanese art, conveying a sense of the passing scene that was shared by the print artist and by everyday Japanese people alike.

The man in the print shown fights the forces of nature, standing up to the wind even though the wind will battle hard for its prize. The man perseveres, unwilling to give in to the powerful and stubborn strength of the wind.

Poetry
Mother to Son

1 READING THE POEM

INFORMATION FOR THE TEACHER

About the Poem

Unparalleled in its honesty, deceptively simple, but extremely effective, "Mother to Son" by Langston Hughes presents an image of a mother speaking to her son about the importance of not letting life's inevitable problems get him down. "Mother" is the voice of experience when she says, "Life for me ain't been no crystal stair." The diction and rhythm Hughes wrapped into the language of this poem conjures the musical quality of a "blues" or "jazz" tune describing everyday life with its hardships, hopes, and desires.

Link to the
Unit Concepts

"Mother to Son," pages 72–73, expresses the nature of the human condition—that in life, problems are bound to occur, and when they do, we have to face them and not take the easy way out. It also illustrates the value of setting high goals and working to attain them. The selection will naturally cause students to recall advice their mothers or other adults have given to them about setting goals and not giving up. In addition, students may be inclined to explore the ways ordinary people persevere in spite of everyday problems, and discuss whether it is better to persevere toward a goal with little hope of accomplishing it or to redirect efforts toward a more readily attainable goal.

About the Poet

Langston Hughes was born in Joplin, Missouri, in 1902. He was the son of a successful businessman who wanted Langston to become an engineer. In high school, however, Hughes was especially impressed by the poetry of Carl Sandburg and decided to become a writer. Hughes's father may have been disappointed, but society as a whole has benefited greatly from the writings of the enormously gifted author. Hughes spent his life composing fiction, drama, children's books, histories, opera

LESSON OVERVIEW

"Mother to Son" by Langston Hughes, pages 72–73

READING THE SELECTION

Materials

Student anthology, pp. 72–73

Explorer's Notebook, p. 66

READING WITH A WRITER'S EYE

Minilesson

Discussing Poetry

Materials

Reproducible Master 15

FYI

Teacher Tool Cards

- Writer's Craft/Reading: Genre— Poetry, 10
- Spelling and Vocabulary: Building Vocabulary, 77

GUIDED AND INDEPENDENT EXPLORATION

Independent Workshop

Optional Materials from Student Toolbox

Tradebook Connection Cards

- *Roll of Thunder, Hear My Cry* by Mildred D. Taylor

Cross-curricular Activity Cards

- 12 Art—Feelings
- 9 Music—The Sounds of Music

FYI

Learning Framework Card

- Reading Roundtable, 6

N O T E S

Asterisks (*) throughout the lesson indicate learning frameworks. Learning Framework Cards and Teacher Tool Cards can be found in the Teacher Toolbox.

librettos, radio scripts, and essays in addition to poetry. In his best-known poetry, Hughes wrote proudly and optimistically about African Americans. He experimented with poetic meter, using in his poetry the rhythms of African-American music of the time. A number of his poems were designed for musical accompaniment. Among his many books, *The Dream Keeper* is one of his finest poetry collections.

INFORMATION FOR THE STUDENT

Share with the students any information about the poet that you think may be of interest to them.

* COGNITIVE AND RESPONSIVE READING

Activating Prior Knowledge

Tell students that this poem is a mother's advice to her son. Ask them to talk about any advice they have received from an adult.

Setting Reading Goals and Expectations

Have the students **browse the poem** and comment on its title, form, and illustration. Then, you may wish to have them talk briefly about poetry and discuss what makes reading a poem different from reading a story or an article.

Recommendations for Reading the Poem

Have the students read the poem themselves in whatever way is most comfortable for them. Then ask a volunteer to read the poem aloud. Since the poem is brief, you may wish to have several readings. Each volunteer can lend her or his unique style to the reading.

This would be a good opportunity for the students to **respond to the text by telling feelings and by connecting to their own experiences.** Model these responses and invite the students to do the same.

* EXPLORING THROUGH DISCUSSION

Reflecting on the Poem
Whole-Group Discussion

Have the **students discuss the poem** and any personal thoughts, reactions, or questions it raises. Encourage them to think about how this poem adds to their knowledge of perseverance.

- Some students may identify the use of figurative language, such as "tacks" and "splinters," to represent minor problems encountered in everyday life. They may suggest that "boards torn up" represents major difficulties to be overcome.
- The students may discuss how their own mothers or other adults have given similar advice to them.
- Some students may not agree with the advice in the poem and may want to tell their reasons for disagreeing.

Have students look at the fine-art pieces on pages 70–71 and examine the painting *Four Jockeys Riding Hard* by Théodore Géricault. Have volunteers give their impressions and ideas about the painting and explain what they think the painting might have to do with perseverance. Ask them to draw comparisons between the ideas presented in the painting

Fine Art

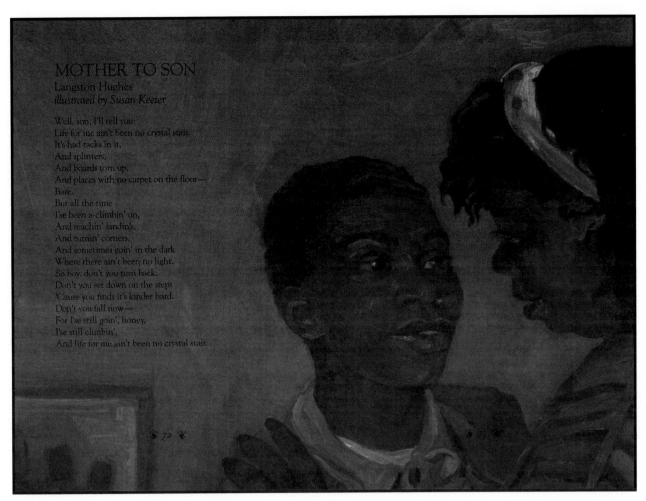

MOTHER TO SON
Langston Hughes
illustrated by Susan Keeter

Well, son, I'll tell you:
Life for me ain't been no crystal stair.
It's had tacks in it,
And splinters,
And boards torn up,
And places with no carpet on the floor—
Bare.
But all the time
I'se been a-climbin' on,
And reachin' landin's,
And turnin' corners,
And sometimes goin' in the dark
Where there ain't been no light.
So boy, don't you turn back.
Don't you set down on the steps
'Cause you finds it's kinder hard.
Don't you fall now—
For I'se still goin', honey,
I'se still climbin',
And life for me ain't been no crystal stair.

72

and the ideas presented in the poem "Mother to Son." Some students may notice that the jockeys are looking straight ahead to the finish line. Students may connect this to "Mother's" advice. Both works suggest setting a goal and striving toward it, whatever it takes.

Response Journal   Poetry evokes very personal reactions. Students who are keeping personal response journals should be given time to record their thoughts and feelings about the poem.

Recording Ideas   As students complete the above discussions, ask them to **sum up what they have learned from their conversations and to tell how they might use this information** in further explorations. Any special information or insights may be recorded on the Concept Board. Any further questions that they would like to think about, pursue, or investigate may be recorded on the Question Board. They may want to discuss the progress that has been made on their questions. They may also want to cross out any questions that no longer warrant consideration.

❯ After discussion, students should record their thoughts and impressions about the selection and the unit concepts on page 66 of their Explorer's Notebook.

Recording Concept Information continued

"The Fire Builder" by Gary Paulsen

_____
_____
_____
_____
_____
_____
_____
_____

"Amaroq, the Wolf" by Jean Craighead George

_____
_____
_____
_____
_____
_____
_____

"Mother to Son" by Langston Hughes

_____
_____
_____
_____
_____
_____
_____
_____

Copyright © 1995 Open Court Publishing Company

66 EN   Perseverance/Unit 4

Explorer's Notebook, page 66

2 READING WITH A WRITER'S EYE

MINILESSON

Discussing Poetry

Ask the students if there was anything about the poem that they especially enjoyed. Remind them that the sounds and rhythms of a poem are important. Poetry is often read aloud so that the listener can hear and enjoy the sounds and patterns of the words, phrases, and stanzas. Encourage the students to share the emotions the poem may have elicited and to tell how the **author's choice of words or rhythm** affect the mood of the poem. Some students may wish to share with the class their interpretations of the figurative language used in the poem. To review ideas for **discussing poetry**, see **Teacher Tool Card 10**.

WRITING

Linking Reading to Writing

Encourage the students to use in their own poetry writing any of the writing techniques they discussed.

✱ Writing Process

Encourage students who have decided to write poetry to use the writing process, as needed, to help them develop their poems. If your class is using the optional Writer's Handbook, remind students to use it for tips and ideas to make their writing better.

VOCABULARY

Allow time for the students to complete copies of Vocabulary Exploration form, Reproducible Master 15, for words they wish to use and remember or for those that are important to the unit concepts. For additional opportunities to build vocabulary, see **Teacher Tool Card 77.**

VOCABULARY TIP Encourage students to use new vocabulary in their speaking and writing and praise them when they do so.

3
GUIDED AND INDEPENDENT EXPLORATION

EXPLORING CONCEPTS BEYOND THE TEXT

Guided
Exploration

After reading this poem, students may want to consider advice they remember getting from their mother, father, grandparents, or other adults. Perhaps they remember a particularly important piece of wisdom or advice that they use often and would like to share with their classmates. They may choose to share this advice in the form of a poem, as Langston Hughes did.

Other students may have their own tidbits of advice that they would like to pass on to younger, less experienced students. They may wish to write an advice poem to share with a class of first-, second-, or third-graders.

* *Exploring Through Reflective Activities*

TEACHING TIP By this point you should be directing your attention to the students' misconceptions about the subject of perseverance and encouraging students with different points of view to discuss their differences.

*INDEPENDENT WORKSHOP
Building a Community of Scholars

Student-Directed Reading, Writing, and Discussion

The students will work in their collaborative groups for the first part of Independent Workshop. They can discuss additional ideas about perseverance that have come up and work together to explore these ideas further. Some students may choose to complete unfinished pages in their Explorer's Notebook and continue with their independent exploration.

Additional Opportunities for Independent Reading, Writing, and Cross-curricular Activities

✶ Reading Roundtable

Students may be interested in reading other poems by Langston Hughes, such as "Dreams," in which Hughes provides vivid descriptions of what life would be like without dreams. This poem and others can be found in *The Dream Keeper*, a poetry collection. *Roll of Thunder, Hear My Cry* by Mildred D. Taylor is a Tradebook Connection book that relates well to perseverance. If the students read the book, remind them to do the activities on the Tradebook Connection Card in the Student Toolbox. For additional ideas for **Reading Roundtable,** see **Learning Framework Card 6.**

✶ Writing Seminar

The students may continue following the writing process for any writing on which they are working. If students have elected to publish any previously written, revised, and proofread pieces, encourage them to place the pieces in the classroom library to share with the rest of the class.

Portfolio

Remind students to think about which pieces of writing they might place in their portfolio.

Cross-curricular Activity Cards

The following Cross-curricular Activity Cards in the Student Toolbox are appropriate for this poem:

* 12 Art—Feelings
* 9 Music—The Sounds of Music

The Sounds of Music
Use after "Mother to Son"

9
Music

Feelings
Use after "Mother to Son"

12
Art

Langston Hughes was an enormously gifted African-American writer. He wrote poems, children's books, essays, plays, and histories. His poems often express the hopes and desires of people in earlier eras of American history. Locate the poem "Dreams" by Langston Hughes. You can find it in *The Dream Keeper* or other collections of his poetry. Read the poem and draw a sketch to illustrate the feelings you think the author is trying to convey in the poem. *Art is a good way to express your feelings creatively.*

Additional Opportunities for Solving Learning Problems

Tutorial

Use this time to give extra help to individuals or small groups who need it. Encourage students to discuss with you any areas in which they are having difficulties.

It Can't Beat Us

1 READING THE SELECTION

INFORMATION FOR THE TEACHER

About the Selection

Once again Laura Ingalls Wilder skillfully pulls readers to the heart of her pioneer family. The Ingalls family draws strength from the interdependence of pioneer life and the rhythms of the seasons. In "It Can't Beat Us," Wilder balances the frightening effects of a cruel, relentless winter on a close-knit family with heartwarming events that provide a realistic glimpse of early pioneer life. With the very first lines of the introduction—"Strange signs in nature, as well as an old Indian's warning, convinced Pa Ingalls that the winter of 1880–1881 would be a hard one in Dakota Territory. So Pa moved his family . . . from their homestead in the country into town"—readers are invited to experience a feeling of closeness with America's favorite pioneer family. Wilder's homespun, spare prose and Garth Williams' wonderfully atmospheric illustrations prove to be a winning combination that readers cannot resist.

Link to the Unit Concepts

"It Can't Beat Us," pages 74–95, depicts the tremendous challenges self-sufficient pioneer families dealt with daily, and shows how they struggled to meet those challenges. This selection may lead students to understand and develop closer ties with the past by examining the relationships between pioneer family values and present-day family values. It may also cause students to wonder if hardship usually brings people together in a cooperative effort, or if it may cause people to go their separate ways.

About the Author

"It Can't Beat Us" is an excerpt from *The Long Winter,* one of the Little House books by Laura Ingalls Wilder. In 1941, *The Long Winter* was named a Newbery Honor Book. Wilder's stories sound as if they were written down immediately after an incident occurred, but she actually wrote the stories describing the period of her life between 1870 and

LESSON OVERVIEW

"It Can't Beat Us" by Laura Ingalls Wilder, pages 74–95

READING THE SELECTION

Materials
Student anthology, pp. 74–95
Explorer's Notebook, p. 67

FYI
Learning Framework Cards
- Setting Reading Goals and Expectations, 1A
- Checking Understanding, 1C

Teacher Tool Card
- Classroom Supports: Question Board and Concept Board, 123

READING WITH A WRITER'S EYE

Minilesson
Writer's Craft: Providing Multiple Effects for a Cause

Materials
Reading/Writing Connection, p. 32
Reproducible Master 15

FYI
Teacher Tool Card
- Spelling and Vocabulary: Building Vocabulary, 77

Options for Instruction
Writer's Craft: Description
Writer's Craft: Providing Problems and Solutions
(Use Teacher Tool Cards listed below.)

GUIDED AND INDEPENDENT EXPLORATION

Materials
Home/School Connection 32
Explorer's Notebook, pp. 70, 74

Independent Workshop

Optional Materials from Student Toolbox

Tradebook Connection Cards
- *A Gathering of Days* by Joan Blos

Cross-curricular Activity Cards
- 19 Social Studies—To Be a Pioneer
- 12 Science—Pioneer Foods

Student Tool Cards
- Writer's Craft/Reading: Showing Cause and Effect, 31
- Writer's Craft/Reading: Giving Descriptions, 40
- Writer's Craft/Reading: Giving Problem and Solution, 45

FYI
Learning Framework Card
- Writing Seminar, 8

Teacher Tool Cards
- Writer's Craft/Reading: Causal Indicators, 31
- Writer's Craft/Reading: Elaboration Through Providing Descriptions, 40
- Writer's Craft/Reading: Elaboration Through Providing Problem and Solution, 45

NOTES

Asterisks (*) throughout the lesson indicate learning frameworks. Learning Framework Cards and Teacher Tool Cards can be found in the Teacher Toolbox.

1889 much later—from 1926 to 1943. The Ingalls family moved many times throughout Laura's childhood. In her books Laura recounts the difficult life on the prairie—the financial difficulties, women's labor, everyday hardships—and how the family worked together to build a life. Other Little House books by Wilder include *Little House in the Big Woods, Little House on the Prairie, On the Banks of Plum Creek,* and *By the Shores of Silver Lake.*

About the Illustrator

Garth Williams is the award-winning illustrator of *The Long Winter.* Williams is best known for his full-color illustrations of personified animals in Golden Books; for his illustrations of E. B. White's two classics, *Stuart Little* and *Charlotte's Web*; and for the pictures in the 1953 reissue of Laura Ingalls Wilder's semiautobiographical Little House books. Recalling the time the publisher invited Williams to illustrate the reissue, Williams admits, "My knowledge of the West at that time was almost zero. . . . And so I decided to visit Mrs. Wilder in Mansfield, Missouri and then follow the route which the Ingalls family took in their covered wagon."

INFORMATION FOR THE STUDENT

Tell the students that the selection they are about to read was written by Laura Ingalls Wilder and illustrated by Garth Williams. As appropriate, you may want to share other information about the author, illustrator, or historical setting with the students.

* COGNITIVE AND RESPONSIVE READING

Activating Prior Knowledge

Most students will recognize the name of the author, Laura Ingalls Wilder, and be familiar with some of her stories. Invite the students to discuss what they know about pioneer life as described in Wilder's stories or about any of the difficulties early pioneers may have faced.

Setting Reading Goals and Expectations

Have the students **browse the first page** of the selection, using the **clues/problems/wondering procedure.** Students will return to these observations after reading. For a review of **browsing,** see **Learning Framework Card 1A.**

Recommendations for Reading the Selection

Have students decide how they want to read the selection. The simplicity of the language in this story makes it a good one for silent reading. Whether the selection is read silently or orally, it should not pose any problems for most students.

During oral reading, use and encourage think-alouds. During silent reading, allow discussion as needed. Discuss problems, strategies, and reactions after reading.

This would be a good selection for **responding to text by connecting** while reading aloud. Model this response, and then invite the students to respond similarly.

Note: In case the students do not finish reading the selection in one class period, the selection has been divided into two parts. The second part begins on page 86 and is indicated by a large initial capital letter.

About the Reading Strategies

Because of the time period and the sequence of events covered in the story, students may naturally want to sum up what is happening in the text. **Summing up** is one strategy that might help the students to better understand the story. To review the strategy of **summing up,** see **Learning Framework Card 1C, Checking Understanding.**

Think-Aloud Prompts for Use in Oral Reading

The think-aloud prompts are placed with the page miniatures. These are merely suggestions for helping students use the strategies. Remind the students to use whatever strategies they need to help them understand the selection. Refer them to the **reading strategy posters**, if necessary. Encourage them to share with their classmates strategies they use as they read.

TEACHING TIP Keep thinking out in the open. Reveal your thinking to students and ask them to reveal theirs.

THINK ALOUD PROMPTS

These prompts may be used as guides to promote cognitive and responsive reading.

IT CAN'T BEAT US

from THE LONG WINTER
by Laura Ingalls Wilder
illustrated by Garth Williams

Strange signs in nature, as well as an old Indian's warning, convinced Pa Ingalls that the winter of 1880–1881 would be a hard one in the Dakota Territory. So Pa moved his family—his wife, Caroline, and four daughters, Mary (who was blind), Laura, Carrie, and Grace—from their homestead in the country into town. Blizzards soon snowed the little town under, cutting off all supplies from the outside. By the end of March, many families in town had only a sack of wheat for food. The blizzards were still striking regularly.

74

Winter had lasted so long that it seemed it would never end. It seemed that they would never really wake up.

In the morning Laura got out of bed into the cold. She dressed downstairs by the fire that Pa had kindled before he went to the stable. They ate their coarse brown bread. Then all day long she and Ma and Mary ground wheat and twisted hay as fast as they could. The fire must not go out; it was very cold. They ate some coarse brown bread. Then Laura crawled into the cold bed and shivered until she grew warm enough to sleep.

Next morning she got out of bed into the cold. She dressed in the chilly kitchen by the fire. She ate her coarse brown bread. She took her turns at grinding wheat and twisting hay. But she did not ever feel awake. She felt beaten by the cold and the storms. She knew she was dull and stupid but she could not wake up.

There were no more school lessons. There was nothing in the world but cold and dark and work and coarse brown bread and winds blowing. The storm was always there, outside the walls, waiting sometimes, then pouncing, shaking the house, roaring, snarling, and screaming in rage.

Out of bed in the morning to hurry down and dress by the fire. Then work all day to crawl into a cold bed at night and fall asleep as soon as she grew warm. The winter had lasted so long. It would never end.

Pa did not sing his trouble song in the mornings any more.

On clear days he hauled hay. Sometimes a blizzard lasted only two days. There might be three days of clear cold, or

75

even four days, before the blizzard struck again. "We're out-wearing it," Pa said. "It hasn't got much more time. March is nearly gone. We can last longer than it can."

"The wheat is holding out," Ma said. "I'm thankful for that."

The end of March came. April began. Still the storm was there, waiting a little longer now perhaps but striking even more furiously. There was the bitter cold still, and the dark storm days, the wheat to be ground, the hay to be twisted. Laura seemed to have forgotten summer; she could not believe it would ever come again. April was going by.

"Is the hay holding out, Charles?" Ma asked.

"Yes, thanks to Laura," Pa said. "If you hadn't helped me in the haying, Little Half-Pint, I'd not have put up enough hay. We would have run short before this."

Those hot days of haying were very far away and long ago. Laura's gladness because Pa said that seemed far away too. Only the blizzard and the coffee mill's grinding, the cold and the dusk darkening to night again, were real. Laura and Pa were holding their stiff, swollen red hands over the stove, Ma was cutting the coarse brown bread for supper. The blizzard was loud and furious.

"It can't beat us!" Pa said.

"Can't it, Pa?" Laura asked stupidly.

"No," said Pa. "It's got to quit sometime and we don't. It can't lick us. We won't give up."

Then Laura felt a warmth inside her. It was very small but it was strong. It was steady, like a tiny light in the dark, and it burned very low but no winds could make it flicker because it would not give up.

76

They ate the coarse brown bread and went through the dark and cold upstairs to bed. Shivering in the cold bed Laura and Mary silently said their prayers and slowly grew warm enough to sleep.

Sometime in the night Laura heard the wind. It was still blowing furiously but there were no voices, no howls or shrieks in it. And with it there was another sound, a tiny, uncertain, liquid sound that she could not understand.

She listened as hard as she could. She uncovered her ear to listen and the cold did not bite her cheek. The dark was warmer. She put out her hand and felt only a coolness. The little sound that she heard was a trickling of waterdrops. The eaves were dripping. Then she knew.

She sprang up in bed and called aloud, "Pa! Pa! The Chinook is blowing!"

"I hear it, Laura," Pa answered from the other room. "Spring has come. Go back to sleep."

The Chinook was blowing. Spring had come. The blizzard had given up; it was driven back to the north. Blissfully Laura stretched out in bed; she put both arms on top of the quilts and they were not very cold. She listened to the blowing wind and dripping eaves and she knew that in the other room Pa was lying awake, too, listening and glad. The Chinook, the wind of spring, was blowing. Winter was ended. **1**

In the morning the snow was nearly gone. The frost was melted from the windows, and outdoors the air was soft and warm.

Pa was whistling as he came from doing the chores.

"Well, girls," he said gaily. "We beat old Winter at last! Here it is spring, and none of us lost or starved or frozen!"

77

1 The students have read a lot of information about the effects of the winter on the Ingalls family. They may wish to **sum up** what they have read so far. Have a volunteer explain what has happened up to this point in the story.

Anyway, not *much* frozen," and he felt tenderly of his nose. "I do believe it is longer," he said anxiously to Grace, and his eyes twinkled. He looked in the glass. "It is longer, and red, too."

"Stop worrying about your looks, Charles," Ma told him. " 'Beauty is only skin deep.' Come eat your breakfast."

She was smiling and Pa chucked her under the chin as he went to the table. Grace scampered to her chair and climbed into it laughing.

Mary pushed her chair back from the stove. "It is really too warm, so close to the fire," she said.

How marvelous it was that anyone could be too warm.

Carrie would hardly leave the window. "I like to see the water run," she explained.

Laura said nothing; she was too happy. She could hardly believe that the winter was gone, that spring had come. When Pa asked her why she was so silent, she answered <u>soberly</u>, "I said it all in the night."

"I should say you did! Waking us all from a sound sleep to tell us the wind was blowing!" Pa teased her. "As if the wind hadn't blown for months!"

"I said the Chinook," Laura reminded him. "That makes all the difference."

"We've got to wait for the train," Pa said. "We can't move to the claim till it comes."

Tightly as he had nailed and battened the tar-paper to the shanty, blizzard winds had torn it loose and whipped it to shreds, letting in the snow at

❧ 78 ❧

sides and roof. And now the spring rains were beating in through the cracks. The shanty must be repaired before anyone could live in it and Pa could not repair it until the train came, for there was no tar-paper at the lumberyard.

 The snow had all disappeared from the prairie. In its place was the soft green of new grass. All the <u>sloughs</u> brimmed with water that had run into them when the deep snow melted. Big Slough had spread until it was a part of Silver Lake and Pa must drive miles around it to reach the homestead from the south.

One day Mr. Boast came walking into town. He explained that he could not drive in, because much of the road was under water. He had walked the railroad track on the long fill that crossed the slough.

Mrs. Boast was well, he told them. She had not come with him because of the slough-lakes spreading everywhere. He had not known whether he could reach town by the railroad track. He promised that Mrs. Boast would walk in with him some day soon.

One afternoon Mary Power came, and she and Laura took Mary walking on the high prairie west of town. It was so long since Laura had seen Mary Power that they felt like strangers again, beginning to get acquainted.

All over the softly green prairie the sloughs were a broken network of water, reflecting the warm, blue sky. Wild geese and ducks were flying high overhead, their clamoring calls coming faintly down. None of them stopped at Silver Lake. They were hurrying, late, to their nesting grounds in the North.

❧ 79 ❧

Soft spring rains fell all day long from harmless gray skies and swelled still wider the brimming sloughs. Days of sunshine came and then again rain. The feed store was locked and vacant. The Wilder brothers had hauled the seed wheat around the slough north of town to their claims. Pa said that they were sowing the wheat on their big fields.

And still the train did not come. Still, day after day, Laura and Mary and Carrie took turns at the endless grind of the coffee mill, and morning and evening they ate the coarse brown bread. The wheat was low in the sack. And the train did not come.

The blizzard winds had blown earth from the fields where the sod was broken, and had mixed it with snow packed so tightly in the railroad cuts that snowplows could not move it. The icy snow could not melt because of the earth mixed with it, and men with picks were digging it out inch by inch. It was slow work because in many big cuts they must dig down twenty feet to the steel rails.

April went slowly by. There was no food in the town except the little wheat left from the sixty bushels that young Mr. Wilder and Cap had brought in the last week of February. Every day Ma made a smaller loaf and still the train did not come.

"Could something be hauled in, Charles?" Ma asked.

"We've talked that over, Caroline. None of us see how," Pa answered. He was tired from working all day with a pick. The men from town were digging away at the cut to the west, for the stranded work train must go on to Huron before a freight train could come on the single track.

🐚 80 🐚

"There's no way to get a team and wagon out to the east," Pa said. "All the roads are under water, the sloughs are lakes in every direction, and even on the uplands a wagon would mire down in the mud. If worst comes to worst, a man can walk out on the railroad ties, but it's more than a hundred miles to Brookings and back. He couldn't carry much and he'd have to eat some of that while he was getting here."

"I've thought of greens," Ma said. "But I can't find any weeds in the yard that are big enough to pick yet."

"Could we eat grass?" Carrie asked.

"No, Nebuchadnezzar," Pa laughed. "You don't have to eat grass! The work crews at Tracy are more than half way through the big cut already. They ought to get the train here inside of a week."

"We can make the wheat last that long," said Ma. "But I wish you wouldn't work so hard, Charles."

Pa's hands were shaking. He was very tired from working all day with pick and shovel. But he said that a good night's sleep was all he needed. "The main thing is to get the cut clear," he said.

On the last day of April the work train went through to Huron. It seemed to wake the whole town up to hear the train whistle again and see the smoke on the sky. Puffing and steaming and clanging its bell, it stopped at the depot, then pulled out, whistling loud and clear again. It was only a passing train that brought nothing, but a freight train was coming tomorrow.

In the morning Laura woke thinking, "The train is coming!" The sun was shining brightly; she had overslept, and

🐚 81 🐚

2 Some students may be confused when Pa calls Carrie "Nebuchadnezzar." They may ask for clarification. Allow volunteers to suggest a **clarifying strategy** that would be helpful. If necessary, explain that Nebuchadnezzar was an ancient king of Babylonia. It is written that during spells of madness he imagined himself an ox and would go out into the fields and eat grass. This should clarify Pa's reference.

Remind students to use a clarification strategy whenever they are confused.

Ma had not called her. She jumped out of bed and hurried to dress.

"Wait for me, Laura!" Mary begged. "Don't be in such a hurry, I can't find my stockings."

Laura looked for them. "Here they are. I'm sorry, I pushed them out of the way when I jumped out of bed. Now hurry! Come on, Grace!"

"When will it get here?" Carrie asked breathless.

"Any minute. Nobody knows when," Laura answered, and she ran downstairs singing:

> "If you're waking call me early,
> Call me early, mother dear."

Pa was at the table. He looked up and laughed at her. "Well, Flutterbudget! you're to be Queen of the May, are you? And late to breakfast!"

"Ma didn't call me," Laura made excuse.

"I didn't need help to cook this little bit of breakfast," Ma said. "Only one biscuit apiece, and small ones at that. It took the last bit of the wheat to make them."

"I don't want even one," Laura said. "The rest of you can divide mine. I won't be hungry till the train comes in."

"You will eat your share," Pa told her. "Then we'll all wait till the train brings more."

They were all merry over the biscuits. Ma said that Pa must have the biggest one. When Pa agreed to that, he insisted that Ma take the next size. Mary's of course came next. Then there was some doubt about Laura and Carrie; they had to have the two most nearly alike. And the smallest one was for Grace.

❧ 82 ☙

"I thought I made them all the same size," Ma protested.

"Trust a Scotchwoman to manage," Pa teased her. "You not only make the wheat come out even with the very last meal before the train comes, but you make the biscuits in sizes to fit the six of us."

"It is a wonder, how evenly it comes out," Ma admitted.

"You are the wonder, Caroline," Pa smiled at her. He got up and put on his hat. "I feel good!" he declared. "We really got winter licked now! with the last of the blizzards thrown out of the cuts and the train coming in!"

Ma left the doors open that morning to let in the spring air, moist from the sloughs. The house was fresh and fragrant, the sun was shining, and the town astir with men going toward the depot. Clear and long across the prairie, the train whistle sounded and Laura and Carrie ran to the kitchen window. Ma and Grace came, too.

They saw the smoke from the smokestack rolling up black against the sky. Then puffing and chuffing the engine came hauling the line of freight cars toward the depot. A little crowd of men on the depot platform stood watching the engine go by. White steam puffed up through its smoke and its clear whistle came after every puff. Brakemen along the top of the train were jumping from car to car and setting the brakes.

The train stopped. It was really there, a train at last.

"Oh, I do hope that Harthorn and Wilmarth both get all the groceries they ordered last fall," said Ma.

After a few moments the engine whistled, the brakemen ran along the tops of the cars loosening the brakes. Clanging its bell, the engine went ahead, then backed, then went ahead again and rushed on away to the west, trailing its smoke

❧ 83 ☙

and its last long whistle. It left behind it three freight cars standing on the sidetrack.

Ma drew a deep breath. "It will be so good to have enough of everything to cook with again."

"I hope I never see another bite of brown bread," Laura declared.

"When is Pa coming? I want Pa to come!" Grace insisted. "I want Pa to come now!"

"Grace," Ma reproved her, gently but firmly, and Mary took Grace into her lap while Ma added, "Come, girls, we must finish airing the bedding."

84

It was almost an hour before Pa came. At last even Ma wondered aloud what could be keeping him. They were all impatiently waiting before he came. His arms were filled with a large package and two smaller ones. He laid them on the table before he spoke.

"We forgot the train that was snowed in all winter," he said. "It came through, and what do you suppose it left for De Smet?" He answered his own question, "One carload of telegraph poles, one carload of farm machinery, and one emigrant car."

"No groceries?" Ma almost wailed.

"No. Nothing," Pa said.

"Then what is this?" Ma touched the large package.

"That is potatoes. The small one is flour and the smallest is fat salt pork. Woodworth broke into the emigrant car and shared out what eatables he could find," said Pa.

"Charles! He ought not to do that," Ma said in dismay.

"I'm past caring what he ought to do!" Pa said savagely. "Let the railroad stand some damages! This isn't the only family in town that's got nothing to eat. We told Woodworth to open up that car or we'd do it. He tried to argue that there'll be another train tomorrow, but we didn't feel like waiting. Now if you'll boil some potatoes and fry some meat, we'll have us a dinner."

Ma began to untie the packages. "Put some hay in the stove, Carrie, to make the oven hot. I'll mix up some white-flour biscuits, too," she said.

85

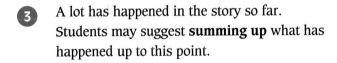 **A lot has happened in the story so far. Students may suggest summing up what has happened up to this point.**

This is a good place to stop reading if you and your class cannot finish the selection during this period. Before beginning to read the second part of the selection, have the students sum up the information in the first part of the selection once again to refresh their memory. Their summaries should include only the important points.

Next day the second train came. After its departing whistle had died away, Pa and Mr. Boast came down the street carrying a barrel between them. They upended it through the doorway and stood it in the middle of the front room.

"Here's that Christmas barrel!" Pa called to Ma.

He brought his hammer and began pulling nails out of the barrel-head, while they all stood around it waiting to see what was in it. Pa took off the barrel-head. Then he lifted away some thick brown paper that covered everything beneath.

Clothes were on top. First Pa drew out a dress of beautifully fine, dark-blue flannel. The skirt was full pleated and the neat, whaleboned <u>basque</u> was buttoned down the front with cut-steel buttons.

"This is about your size, Caroline," Pa beamed. "Here, take it!" and he reached again into the barrel.

He took out a fluffy, light-blue <u>fascinator</u> for Mary, and some warm flannel underthings. He took out a pair of black leather shoes that exactly fitted Laura. He took out five pairs of white woolen stockings, machine-knit. They were much finer and thinner than home-knit ones.

Then he took out a warm, brown coat, a little large for Carrie, but it would fit her next winter. And he took out a red hood and mittens to go with it.

Next came a silk shawl!

"Oh, Mary!" Laura said. "The most beautiful thing—a shawl made of silk! It is dove-colored, with fine stripes of green and rose and black and the richest, deep fringe with all those colors shimmering in it. Feel how soft and rich and heavy the silk is," and she put a corner of the shawl in Mary's hand.

🌱 86 🌿

"Oh, lovely!" Mary breathed.

"Who gets this shawl?" Pa asked, and they all said, "Ma!" Such a beautiful shawl was for Ma, of course. Pa laid it on her arm, and it was like her, so soft and yet firm and well-wearing, with the fine, bright colors in it.

"We will all take turns wearing it," Ma said. "And Mary shall take it with her when she goes to college."

"What is there for you, Pa?" Laura asked jealously. For Pa there were two fine, white shirts, and a dark brown plush cap.

"That isn't all," said Pa, and he lifted out of the barrel one, two little dresses. One was blue flannel, one was green-and-rose plaid. They were too small for Carrie and too big for Grace, but Grace would grow to fit them. Then there was an A-B-C book printed on cloth, and a small, shiny Mother Goose book of the smoothest paper, with a colored picture on the cover.

There was a pasteboard box full of bright-colored yarns and another box filled with embroidery silks and sheets of perforated thin cardboard, silver-colored and gold-colored. Ma gave both boxes to Laura, saying, "You gave away the pretty things you had made. Now here are some lovely things for you to work with."

Laura was so happy that she couldn't say a word. The delicate silks caught on the roughness of her fingers, scarred from twisting hay, but the beautiful colors sang together like music, and her fingers would grow smooth again so that she could embroider on the fine, thin silver and gold.

"Now I wonder what this can be?" Pa said, as he lifted from the very bottom of the barrel something bulky and lumpy that was wrapped around and around with thick brown paper.

🌱 87 🌿

4 This paragraph signals a turning point in the story. The students should sense that something important has changed in the story. Some students may want to **predict** what will happen next. Encourage volunteers to share their predictions and explain how previous information in the story helped them make their predictions.

"Je-ru-salem crickets!" he exclaimed. "If it isn't our Christmas turkey, still frozen solid!"

He held the great turkey up where all could see. "And fat! Fifteen pounds or I miss my guess." And as he let the mass of brown paper fall, it thumped on the floor and out of it rolled several cranberries.

"And if there isn't a package of cranberries to go with it!" said Pa.

Carrie shrieked with delight. Mary clasped her hands and said, "Oh my!" But Ma asked, "Did the groceries come for the stores, Charles?"

"Yes, sugar and flour and dried fruit and meat—Oh, everything anybody needs," Pa answered.

"Well, then, Mr. Boast, you bring Mrs. Boast day after tomorrow," Ma said. "Come as early as you can and we will celebrate the springtime with a Christmas dinner."

"That's the ticket!" Pa shouted, while Mr. Boast threw back his head and the room filled with his ringing laugh. They all joined in, for no one could help laughing when Mr. Boast did.

"We'll come! You bet we'll come!" Mr. Boast chortled. "Christmas dinner in May! That will be great, to feast after a winter of darn near fasting! I'll hurry home and tell Ellie."

Pa brought groceries that afternoon. It was wonderful to see him coming in with armfuls of packages, wonderful to see a whole sack of white flour, sugar, dried apples, soda crackers, and cheese. The kerosene can was full. How happy Laura was to fill the lamp, polish the chimney, and trim the wick. At suppertime the light shone through the clear glass

88

onto the red-checked tablecloth and the white biscuits, the warmed-up potatoes, and the platter of fried salt pork.

With yeast cakes, Ma set the sponge for light bread that night, and she put the dried apples to soak for pies.

Laura did not need to be called next morning. She was up at dawn, and all day she helped Ma bake and stew and boil the good things for next day's Christmas dinner.

Early that morning Ma added water and flour to the bread sponge and set it to rise again. Laura and Carrie picked over the cranberries and washed them. Ma stewed them with sugar until they were a mass of crimson jelly.

Laura and Carrie carefully picked dried raisins from their long stems and carefully took the seeds out of each one. Ma stewed the dried apples, mixed the raisins with them, and made pies.

"It seems strange to have everything one could want to work with," said Ma. "Now I have cream of tartar and plenty of saleratus, I shall make a cake."

All day long the kitchen smelled of good things, and when night came the cupboard held large brown-crusted loaves of white bread, a sugar-frosted loaf of cake, three crisp-crusted pies, and the jellied cranberries.

"I wish we could eat them now," Mary said. "Seems like I can't wait till tomorrow."

"I'm waiting for the turkey first," said Laura, "and you may have sage in the stuffing, Mary."

She sounded generous but Mary laughed at her. "That's only because there aren't any onions for you to use!"

89

"Now, girls, don't get impatient," Ma begged them. "We will have a loaf of light bread and some of the cranberry sauce for supper."

So the Christmas feasting was begun the night before.

It seemed too bad to lose any of that happy time in sleep. Still, sleeping was the quickest way to tomorrow morning. It was no time at all, after Laura's eyes closed, till Ma was calling her and tomorrow was today.

What a hurrying there was! Breakfast was soon over, then while Laura and Carrie cleared the table and washed the dishes, Ma prepared the big turkey for roasting and mixed the bread-stuffing for it.

The May morning was warm and the wind from the prairie smelled of springtime. Doors were open and both rooms could be used once more. Going in and out of the large front room whenever she wanted to, gave Laura a spacious and rested feeling, as if she could never be cross again.

Ma had already put the rocking chairs by the front windows to get them out of her way in the kitchen. Now the turkey was in the oven, and Mary helped Laura draw the table into the middle of the front room. Mary raised its drop-leaves and spread smoothly over it the white tablecloth that Laura brought her. Then Laura brought the dishes from the cupboard and Mary placed them around the table.

Carrie was peeling potatoes and Grace was running races with herself the length of both rooms.

Ma brought the glass bowl filled with glowing cranberry jelly. She set it in the middle of the white tablecloth and they all admired the effect.

❦ 90 ❦

"We do need some butter to go with the light bread, though," Ma said.

"Never mind, Caroline," said Pa. "There's tar-paper at the lumberyard now. I'll soon fix up the shanty and we'll move out to the homestead in a few days."

The roasting turkey was filling the house with scents that made their mouths water. The potatoes were boiling and Ma was putting the coffee on when Mr. and Mrs. Boast came walking in.

"For the last mile, I've been following my nose to that turkey!" Mr. Boast declared.

"I was thinking more of seeing the folks, Robert, than of anything to eat," Mrs. Boast chided him. She was thin and the lovely rosy color was gone from her cheeks, but she was the same darling Mrs. Boast, with the same laughing black-fringed blue eyes and the same dark hair curling under the same brown hood. She shook hands warmly with Ma and Mary and Laura and stooped down to draw Carrie and Grace close in her arms while she spoke to them.

"Come into the front room and take off your things, Mrs. Boast," Ma urged her. "It is good to see you again after so long. Now you rest in the rocking chair and visit with Mary while I finish up dinner."

"Let me help you," Mrs. Boast asked, but Ma said she must be tired after her long walk and everything was nearly ready.

"Laura and I will soon have dinner on the table," said Ma, turning quickly back to the kitchen. She ran against Pa in her haste.

"We better make ourselves scarce, Boast," said Pa. "Come along, and I'll show you the *Pioneer Press* I got this morning."

❦ 91 ❦

"It will be good to see a newspaper again," Mr. Boast agreed eagerly. So the kitchen was left to the cooks.

"Get the big platter to put the turkey on," Ma said, as she lifted the heavy dripping-pan out of the oven.

Laura turned to the cupboard and saw on the shelf a package that had not been there before.

"What's that, Ma?" she asked.

"I don't know. Look and see," Ma told her, and Laura undid the paper. There on a small plate was a ball of butter.

"Butter! It's butter!" she almost shouted.

They heard Mrs. Boast laugh. "Just a little Christmas present!" she called.

Pa and Mary and Carrie exclaimed aloud in delight and Grace squealed long and shrill while Laura carried the butter to the table. Then she hurried back to slide the big platter carefully beneath the turkey as Ma raised it from the dripping-pan.

While Ma made the gravy Laura mashed the potatoes. There was no milk, but Ma said, "Leave a very little of the boiling water in, and after you mash them beat them extra hard with the big spoon."

The potatoes turned out white and fluffy, though not with the flavor that plenty of hot milk and butter would have given them.

When all the chairs were drawn up to the well-filled table, Ma looked at Pa and every head bowed.

"Lord, we thank Thee for all Thy bounty." That was all Pa said, but it seemed to say everything.

"The table looks some different from what it did a few days ago," Pa said as he heaped Mrs. Boast's plate with turkey and

❦ 92 ❦

stuffing and potatoes and a large spoonful of cranberries. And as he went on filling the plates he added, "It has been a long winter."

"And a hard one," said Mr. Boast.

"It is a wonder how we all kept well and came through it," Mrs. Boast said.

While Mr. and Mrs. Boast told how they had worked and contrived through that long winter, all alone in the blizzard-bound shanty on their claim, Ma poured the coffee and Pa's tea. She passed the bread and the butter and the gravy and reminded Pa to refill the plates.

When every plate had been emptied a second time Ma refilled the cups and Laura brought on the pies and the cake.

They sat a long time at the table, talking of the winter that was past and the summer to come. Ma said she could hardly wait to get back to the homestead. The wet, muddy roads were the difficulty now, but Pa and Mr. Boast agreed that they would dry out before long. The Boasts were glad that they had wintered on their claim and didn't have to move back to it now.

At last they all left the table. Laura brought the red-bordered table cover and Carrie helped her to spread it to cover neatly out of sight the food and the empty dishes. Then they joined the others by the sunny window.

Pa stretched his arms above his head. He opened and closed his hands and stretched his fingers wide, then ran them through his hair till it all stood on end.

"I believe this warm weather has taken the stiffness out of my fingers," he said. "If you will bring me the fiddle, Laura, I'll see what I can do."

❦ 93 ❦

Laura brought the fiddle-box and stood close by while Pa lifted the fiddle out of its nest. He thumbed the strings and tightened the keys as he listened. Then he <u>rosined</u> the bow and drew it across the strings.

 A few clear, true notes softly sounded. The lump in Laura's throat almost choked her.

Pa played a few bars and said, "This is a new song I learned last fall, the time we went to Volga to clear the tracks. You hum the <u>tenor</u> along with the fiddle, Boast, while I sing it through the first time. A few times over, and you'll all pick up the words."

They all gathered around him to listen while he played again the opening bars. Then Mr. Boast's tenor joined the fiddle's voice and Pa's voice singing:

"This life is a difficult riddle,
For how many people we see
With faces as long as a fiddle
That ought to be shining with glee.
I am sure in this world there are plenty
Of good things enough for us all,
And yet there's not one out of twenty
But thinks that his share is too small.

Then what is the use of <u>repining</u>,
For where there's a will, <u>there's</u> a way,
And tomorrow the sun may be shining,
Although it is cloudy today.

🎵 94 🎵

Do you think that by sitting and sighing
You'll ever obtain all you want?
It's cowards alone that are crying
And foolishly saying, 'I can't!'
It is only by plodding and striving
And laboring up the steep hill
Of life, that you'll ever be thriving,
Which you'll do if you've only the will."

They were all humming the melody now and when the chorus came again, Mrs. Boast's <u>alto</u>, Ma's <u>contralto</u>, and Mary's sweet <u>soprano</u> joined Mr. Boast's tenor and Pa's rich <u>bass</u>, singing the words, and Laura sang, too, soprano:

"Then what is the use of repining,
For where there's a will, there's a way,
And tomorrow the sun may be shining,
Although it is cloudy today."

5

And as they sang, the fear and the suffering of the long winter seemed to rise like a dark cloud and float away on the music. Spring had come. The sun was shining warm, the winds were soft, and the green grass growing.

🎵 95 🎵

5 Students may point out that this song is almost a summary of what life was like for the Ingalls family that winter. If students do not do so on their own, ask a volunteer to **interpret** the words of the song.

Discussing Strategy Use

Have students share whatever strategies they used while reading to help make sense of the text. Encourage those students who have developed their own strategies to explain them to their classmates.

* **EXPLORING THROUGH DISCUSSION**

**Reflecting on
the Selection**
Whole-Group
Discussion

The whole group discusses the selection and any personal thoughts or questions that it raises. During this time, students also **return to the clues, problems, and wonderings** they noted on the board during browsing.

Assessment

To assess the students' understanding of the text, engage in a discussion to determine whether the students have grasped the following ideas:

- the challenges that the Ingalls family faced and how they met those challenges
- the extent to which this family was self-sufficient and yet dependent on others for certain things

Response Journal

If students have additional thoughts about or reactions to the selection, suggest that they record these in their personal response journals.

**Exploring
Concepts Within
the Selection**
Small-Group Discussion

While small groups discuss the relationship of the selection to perseverance, circulate and observe discussions. Remind the students to refer to the Question Board and the Concept Board to keep the discussions focused. To review information about the **Question Board** and the **Concept Board**, see **Teacher Tool Card 123.**

**Sharing Ideas
About Explorable
Concepts**

Have the groups **report their ideas** and **discuss them** with the rest of the class. It is crucial that the students' ideas determine this discussion.

- Students may point out that the pioneers lacked many of the modern conveniences we have today to make living easier. They may discuss how everyday life to the pioneers would be very rugged conditions to us.
- Other students may point out that they have, on occasion, felt the way Laura did—that they didn't want to get out of bed on a cold morning—and then compare their own reasons for getting up to Laura's reasons.
- Because each season brought a particular set of difficulties to the pioneers, students may discuss whether perseverance can develop into habit. They may discuss whether trying to overcome a problem that occurs on a regular basis is an example of perseverance, or whether it may not be considered perseverance at all.

As these ideas and others are stated, have the students add them to the **Question Board** or the **Concept Board.**

**Exploring
Concepts Across
Selections**

Ask the students whether this reminds them of anything else they have read. They may make connections with other selections in this unit or in other units.

- Students may compare the elements of sharing and cooperation demonstrated by the Ingalls family to the cooperation of the wolf pack in the story "Amaroq, the Wolf." They may point out that Pa Ingalls

STEPS TOWARD INDEPENDENCE By now the students should be taking charge of the commentary during and after reading the selection, with little or no teacher intervention. If this is not happening, invite students to talk more often, and reinforce their efforts.

battled harsh conditions to bring food to his family in much the same way that Amaroq led the hunt to secure food for the wolves.

- Some students may point out a connection between this story and "The Pretty Pennies Picket" from unit 3, Taking a Stand. They may suggest that the Pretty Pennies persevered in their fight against Mr. Putterham. They didn't give up, just as the Ingalls family didn't let the harsh weather beat them.

Connections Across Units

Recording Ideas

As students complete the above discussions, ask them to sum up what they have learned from their conversations and to tell how they might use this information in further explorations. Any special information or insights may be recorded on the Concept Board. Any further questions that they would like to think about, pursue, or investigate may be recorded on the Question Board. They may want to discuss the progress that has been made on their questions. They may also want to cross out any questions that no longer warrant consideration.

❯ Students should also record their thoughts and ideas about the selection on page 67 of their Explorer's Notebook.

Explorer's Notebook, page 67

"It Can't Beat Us" by Laura Ingalls Wilder

_____
_____
_____
_____
_____
_____
_____

"The Sticky Secret" by Gail Kay Haines

_____
_____
_____
_____
_____
_____
_____

"Back to the Drawing Board" by Russell Freedman

_____
_____
_____
_____
_____
_____
_____

Copyright © 1995 Open Court Publishing Company

Unit 4/Perseverance   EN 67

Professional Checkpoint: Cognitive and Responsive Reading

Summing up serves to refocus the students' attention on the selection after a break for clarifying or predicting, or after a change of readers. It is not an end in itself, but a springboard back into the selection. At the lowest grades, it involves a simple retelling of what has just happened. By sixth grade, the students briefly sum up only the main gist of the selection in their own words.

It is important that summing up not become intrusive. Therefore, it should be done quickly, and only a few times in the course of active reading. The summing up at the end of a selection can be a more complete recounting of the main thread of the whole selection.

Notes:

2 READING WITH A WRITER'S EYE

MINILESSON

Writer's Craft: Providing Multiple Effects for a Cause

Ask the students to talk about anything they have learned about **causes and effects in writing**, and to describe any examples they can remember from their reading or writing. A discussion should include the following points:

- One event (a cause) can result in another event (an effect).
- A cause precedes an effect.
- An effect can become the cause of later events (effects).
- Certain clue words, such as *since, now,* or *because,* sometimes point to the cause. And certain clue words, such as *thus, so, as a result,* and *therefore,* can sometimes indicate effects.

Tell students that Laura Ingalls Wilder made use of multiple effects for a cause to let the reader know what events occurred in the story and why they happened. For example, Wilder uses multiple effects for a cause on page 79. Write the headings Cause and Effects on the chalkboard and then list the cause-and-effect relationships from the page. For example:

Cause	Effects
Spring rains	caused melting snow
	caused road to be underwater
	could not drive
	had to walk

Selection-Based
Practice

Selective Reading:
Focus on Multiple
Effects

Now have students identify and read aloud parts of pages 80–82 that indicate a cause and its multiple effects. The students' ideas may vary. One example is listed below.

Cause	Effect/Cause	Effects
blizzard winds	blew sod mixed with snow on railroad tracks	Snowplows couldn't move it. Men had to dig it out. The train couldn't get through. A work train had to go through before the freight train with food.

Encourage the students to focus on how an effect can become the cause of subsequent events (effects).

Independent Practice:
Multiple Effects

➤ Have the students complete Reading/Writing Connection, page 32, to extend their discussion of the use of multiple effects for a cause. Encourage students to discuss their ideas with their classmates after completing the page.

Reading/Writing Connection, page 32

"It Can't Beat Us"

Multiple Effects for a Cause

Look again at "It Can't Beat Us" or at any other stories you have read. Find one event (cause) that results in additional events (effects). Write these on the proper lines below. Do the effects you have written down lead to further events, or effects? If so, follow the arrows and write down the additional effects.

Cause   Effects

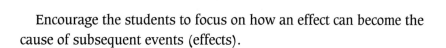

Further Effects

Name

Cause and Effect
32 R/WC   Perseverance/Unit 4

Copyright © 1995 Open Court Publishing Company

Linking Reading to Writing

To provide opportunities for the students to apply the writer's craft of creating multiple effects for a cause in their own writing, encourage them to look for pieces that they can revise and improve by adding or changing causes and effects. They could add effects that become causes for subsequent effects, or use clue words to signal causes and effects.

* Writing Process

If students have elected to revise a piece from their writing folders, encourage them to meet with their classmates to discuss idea and content changes that may improve their writing and make it clearer for the reader.

VOCABULARY

Words from the selection that students may wish to discuss include *stranded, dismay, chided, repining,* and *plodding.* Allow time for the students to complete Vocabulary Exploration forms, Reproducible Master 15, for those words they wish to remember and use or that are important to the unit concepts. Remind the students to add these or any other words and phrases to the Personal Dictionary section of their Writer's Notebook. Then provide an opportunity for volunteers to share words they've chosen and to tell why they chose them. For additional opportunities to build vocabulary, see **Teacher Tool Card 77.**

> *Adding to Personal Dictionary*

3 GUIDED AND INDEPENDENT EXPLORATION

EXPLORING CONCEPTS BEYOND THE TEXT

Guided Exploration

Students will select activities in which they explore the unit concepts. Refer them to the **Exploration Activities poster** and give them time to choose an activity. Allow them to discuss what they wish to explore and how they wish to go about it. If the students need further help, a suggestion follows.

Some students may wish to investigate the problems and perseverance of the pioneers, comparing them with those of today's families. Encourage them to locate information about the difficulties early pioneers faced and what they did to overcome their problems. Students may wish to categorize problem areas, such as food, transportation, economics, child rearing, and so on, as they focus on the ways in which both groups persevere and solve their problems. Remind students to identify the qualities that are characteristic of perseverance in their comparisons. Have them share their writing and ideas with their classmates.

> ** Exploring Through Reflective Activities*

❯ Students can use Explorer's Notebook, page 74, to help them complete this activity.

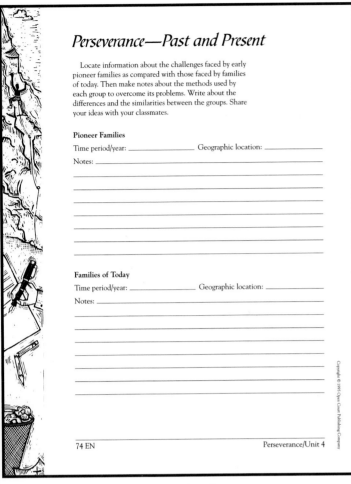

Perseverance—Past and Present

Locate information about the challenges faced by early pioneer families as compared with those faced by families of today. Then make notes about the methods used by each group to overcome its problems. Write about the differences and the similarities between the groups. Share your ideas with your classmates.

Pioneer Families

Time period/year: _____ Geographic location: _____

Notes: _____

_____

_____

_____

_____

_____

_____

Families of Today

Time period/year: _____ Geographic location: _____

Notes: _____

_____

_____

_____

_____

_____

_____

_____

74 EN   Perseverance/Unit 4

Copyright © 1995 Open Court Publishing Company

Explorer's Notebook, page 74

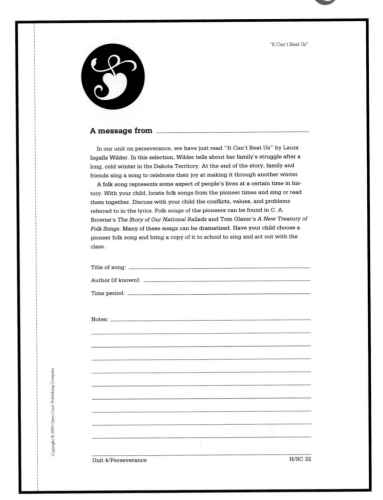

"It Can't Beat Us"

A message from _____

In our unit on perseverance, we have just read "It Can't Beat Us" by Laura Ingalls Wilder. In this selection, Wilder tells about her family's struggle after a long, cold winter in the Dakota Territory. At the end of the story, family and friends sing a song to celebrate their joy at making it through another winter.

A folk song represents some aspect of people's lives at a certain time in history. With your child, locate folk songs from the pioneer times and sing or read them together. Discuss with your child the conflicts, values, and problems referred to in the lyrics. Folk songs of the pioneers can be found in C. A. Browne's *The Story of Our National Ballads* and Tom Glazer's *A New Treasury of Folk Songs*. Many of these songs can be dramatized. Have your child choose a pioneer folk song and bring a copy of it to school to sing and act out with the class.

Title of song: _____

Author (if known): _____

Time period: _____

Notes: _____

_____

_____

_____

_____

_____

_____

_____

_____

_____

Unit 4/Perseverance   H/SC 32

Copyright © 1995 Open Court Publishing Company

Home/School Connection 32

> Distribute Home/School Connection 32. Have students and their families locate folk songs of the pioneers that present information about the struggles of the period.

Continuing Exploration

Collaborative groups should meet to check progress, ask questions, and give help to members who are uncertain how to proceed. Remind students to return to the pages in their Explorer's Notebook to which they can add information based on new knowledge they have acquired. For example, perhaps after researching problems of pioneer life, they may have found out about inventions they could add to Explorer's Notebook, page 70.

*INDEPENDENT WORKSHOP
Building a Community of Scholars

Student-Directed Reading, Writing, and Discussion

Students will continue to work in their collaborative groups during the first part of Independent Workshop. They can discuss their ideas in small groups and make individual assignments as needed. Provide time to discuss questions to explore with the students. Assist them in narrowing the focus of their exploration and in locating resources.

Additional Opportunities for Independent Reading, Writing, and Cross-curricular Activities

✳ Reading Roundtable

Encourage students to read and share other books by Laura Ingalls Wilder, such as *On the Banks of Plum Creek,* about the Ingalls' move to Minnesota, or *These Happy Golden Years*, which describes Laura's becoming a teacher. *A Gathering of Days* by Joan Blos is a Tradebook Connection selection that relates well to the unit concepts. The story is about the hardships and joys of pioneer life as seen through the eyes of a young girl. If students read the book, they can do the accompanying activities on the Tradebook Connection Card in the Student Toolbox.

✳ Writing Seminar

Have the students continue using the writing process as they work on any new writing pieces or revise and proofread those in their writing folders. Encourage the students to collaborate with their classmates and ask for feedback on their writing. Remind them to use Reproducible Master 20 from the Checking My Work section of their Writer's Notebook if they are proofreading a piece of their writing. To review information about **Writing Seminar**, see **Learning Framework Card 8.**

Portfolio

Remind the students to think about which pieces of work created during this lesson they might choose to put into their portfolios.

Cross-curricular Activity Cards

The following Cross-curricular Activity Cards in the Student Toolbox are appropriate for this selection:
- 19 Social Studies—To Be a Pioneer
- 12 Science—Pioneer Foods

Pioneer Foods
Use after "It Can't Beat Us"

12
Science

To Be a Pioneer
Use after "It Can't Beat Us"

19
Social Studies

If you could travel back in time to the days of the pioneers, in which frontier area of the United States would you choose to live? Do some research to find out where the pioneers settled. Find out about the land and the climate of the frontier region that you choose. What kind of homes did the settlers build there? What foods did they eat? Write a brief report about your area, and tell why you chose it. Share your report with your classmates. *Learning about the conditions of the past helps us to understand the ways in which people lived and worked.*

Additional Opportunities for Solving Learning Problems

Tutorial

Use this time to work with those students who need help in any area. Encourage the students to ask for help when they feel the need. The following Teacher Tool Cards are available in the Teacher Toolbox for your convenience:
- Writer's Craft/Reading: Causal Indicators, Teacher Tool Card 31
- Writer's Craft/Reading: Elaboration Through Providing Descriptions, Teacher Tool Card 40
- Writer's Craft/Reading: Elaboration Through Providing Problem and Solution, Teacher Tool Card 45

Assessment

The Sticky Secret

1 READING THE SELECTION

INFORMATION FOR THE TEACHER

About the Selection

"The Sticky Secret" is a chronicle of Charles Goodyear's bumbling, unconventional search for the missing ingredient that would change rubber into an all-purpose material. In his search, Goodyear makes himself a spiffy rubber suit of clothes, only to have the hot smelly rubber melt while he is wearing it. Then, living on borrowed money with barely enough food for his family, Goodyear lands in debtor's prison. His persistence knows no bounds. Even in prison Goodyear continues work on the mystery of the missing ingredient. Will Goodyear's relentless pursuit pay off? Maybe not in the way we expect. Gail Kay Haines blends the real-life tragedies that beset Goodyear with just a dash of humor to create this bittersweet account of Goodyear's quest.

Link to the Unit Concepts

"The Sticky Secret," pages 96–111, is about one person's determination to fulfill his dream, even though he is almost completely dependent on the kindness and generosity of others. This selection may lead students to explore the question of what causes particular people to persist in trying to attain their goals. Students may also wonder whether anything worthwhile can be accomplished without perseverance and may try to determine the difference between persevering and being stubborn.

About the Author

"The Sticky Secret" is taken from the book entitled *Micromysteries* by Gail Kay Haines. Haines, the daughter of a foreman at an atomic plant, grew up excited about chemistry, worked after college as a chemist, and became a member of the American Chemical Society. Haines says, however, that she always wanted to be a writer and found that "the most interesting thing" she could do was to be a science writer. In speaking about *Micromysteries*, she reveals that she likes "learning about what

LESSON OVERVIEW

"The Sticky Secret" by Gail Kay Haines, pages 96–111

READING THE SELECTION

Materials
Student anthology, pp. 96–111
Explorer's Notebook, p. 67
Assessment Masters 1–2, 6

FYI
Learning Framework Card
• Setting Reading Goals and Expectations, 1A

READING WITH A WRITER'S EYE

Minilesson
Assessment

Materials
Reproducible Master 15

FYI
Teacher Tool Card
• Spelling and Vocabulary: Building Vocabulary, 77

GUIDED AND INDEPENDENT EXPLORATION

Materials
Home/School Connection 33
Explorer's Notebook, p. 75

FYI
Learning Framework Card
• Exploring Through Reflective Activities, 3

Independent Workshop

Optional Materials from Student Toolbox
Tradebook Connection Cards

Cross-curricular Activity Cards
• 13 Art—It Was a "Goodyear"
• 20 Social Studies—Discovery

N O T E S

Asterisks (*) throughout the lesson indicate learning frameworks. Learning Framework Cards and Teacher Tool Cards can be found in the Teacher Toolbox.

happens and why, and I like digging out information. Books like this one lured me into becoming a chemist and then a writer."

About the Illustrator

Having drawn since childhood, but never aware that this talent could lead to a profession until he entered art school thirty years ago, Robert Byrd is today an accomplished illustrator of science books and story books for children. "Children's book illustration gave me the greatest satisfaction of all my work," he has said. "It is my 'fine art.' It keeps me going aesthetically." As a teacher of illustration at the University of the Arts in Philadelphia, Byrd passes this enthusiasm on to his students.

INFORMATION FOR THE STUDENT

Tell the students that the selection they are about to read was written by Gail Kay Haines and illustrated by Robert Byrd. Share any other information that you think is appropriate.

COGNITIVE AND RESPONSIVE READING

Activating Prior Knowledge

Students may be familiar with the name Goodyear, as in Goodyear tire or Goodyear Blimp. You may want to have students talk about what they know about the name Goodyear or about products bearing that name.

Setting Reading Goals and Expectations

Even though this selection has been designated as an assessment selection, the class will proceed as usual with the setting of reading goals and expectations. Have the students **browse the selection**, using the **clues/problems/wondering procedure**. Students will return to these observations after reading. For a review of **browsing**, see **Learning Framework Card 1A**.

Recommendations for Reading the Selection

Explain to the students that they will read this selection to assess what they have learned about the unit concepts. Place the students in small groups. Tell them that they will decide in their small groups how they would like to read this selection. For example, the groups may choose to

- read silently but stay in groups, stopping to ask each other questions when they need help understanding
- alternate reading and summarizing a section at a time
- read silently on their own

Encourage the students to use the strategies that they think will best help them understand and appreciate the story. They should feel free to refer to the **reading strategy posters** as needed. Encourage them to collaborate with others in their groups by asking questions when they encounter reading difficulties and by offering suggestions to others who need help.

Concept Connections

1. Explain what this selection is about. Write a short summary.

   _____
   _____
   _____
   _____
   _____
   _____

2. Tell what this selection has to do with perseverance.

   _____
   _____
   _____
   _____
   _____

Tell how this selection is like other selections you have read in this unit.

   _____
   _____
   _____
   _____
   _____

4. You have read many selections about people who persevered. How did *this* selection change your ideas about perseverance?

   _____
   _____
   _____
   _____
   _____

Date

Name

Copyright © 1995 Open Court Publishing Company

Unit 4/Perseverance   Assessment Master 6

Assessment Master 6

❯ Distribute copies of Assessment Master 6, Concept Connections for unit 4, Perseverance. Tell the students that after reading the selection in their small groups, they will write responses on the page independently. They will then regroup and share their findings, changing any ideas that they wish.

THINK ALOUD PROMPTS

To foster independence, think-aloud prompts are not provided for Assessment lessons.

THE STICKY SECRET

Gail Kay Haines

illustrated by Robert Byrd

The original bumbling detective may have been Christopher Columbus. As the old story goes, when he set off he didn't know where he was going. When he landed, he didn't know where he was. When he got back, he didn't know where he had been, and he did it all on borrowed money.

In spite of that, Columbus discovered the Americas and helped solve a major mystery about the size and shape of the earth. Another bumbling detective, Charles Goodyear, faced even worse problems when he investigated a mysterious substance called rubber.

According to reports, when Columbus landed in Haiti he saw natives bouncing balls made from a strange elastic gum. Columbus (who thought he was in India) had never seen a material so odd. How could a ball hit the ground and then fly back into the air? He packed one of the mysterious toys to show his backer, Queen Isabella. He probably was the first to bring the substance to Europe.

The bouncing balls intrigued Columbus's crew, but riches —gold and jewels—interested them more. No one suspected that the strange gum might someday be valuable.

96

When Charles Goodyear entered the scene, more than three hundred years later, "India rubber"—the strange elastic gum from the New World—had become the latest craze. It stretched. It shed water. It could be made into waterproof shoes and wagon covers and whatever the customer needed. It looked like a quick path to riches.

But instead of quick riches, rubber plunged Goodyear into a nightmare of poverty, prison, and even near death. It led him straight into a major mystery.

Goodyear needed money. His family hardware business had failed, and frail, sickly Charles, thirty-four years old, owed almost everyone. A trip to New York, to borrow more money, failed too. Then Charles happened to glance into a New York shop window.

When Charles Goodyear stepped inside the Roxbury India Rubber Company store in spring, 1834, business was booming. Customers grabbed at the disappearing stacks of black rubber shoes and hats, wagon covers, and rubber-coated raincoats.

Too short to see over the crowd, Goodyear picked up a rubber life preserver from the window display. When he tried to blow it up, the valve stuck.

Instantly, Charles had a fabulous money-making idea. He would invent a better valve. He spent the last two dollars and fifty cents in his pocket to buy the rubber "doughnut," and he took it home to Philadelphia.

Weeks later, Goodyear walked back into the same store with a new valve he had designed (much like the valve used in inflatable toys today). First, he sniffed. A terrible smell hung in the air.

Then he looked around, astonished. No eager shoppers, no merchandise! The store stood empty, except for the manager, handing out refunds to a couple of angry customers.

Stunned, Goodyear listened to the manager's list of miseries. Thirty thousand dollars worth of once-perfect shoes had been returned, melted by a summer heat wave into sticky black blobs. Everything else had melted, too. And everything stunk.

In fact, the warehouse reeked with the nauseating odor of disintegrating rubber. Many of the items smelled so bad that the company finally buried them in a deep pit near the factory.

In England, where the rubber industry started, summers are cool. Rubber products had lasted fairly well. But in the United States, rubber was turning into a disaster. In hot weather, it softened into a sticky mess. And in cold weather, rubber turned hard and brittle.

No one knew what to do. No one understood rubber's chemistry. Thousands of manufacturing dollars now hinged on a scientific mystery—how could rubber be controlled? The industry seemed sure to collapse unless someone found a solution.

Charles Goodyear couldn't sell his valve to a bankrupt company, but he loved hearing about the mystery. Rubber "is such a wonderful substance," he said. There had to be a way to handle it. Goodyear decided to turn his inventing talents to rubber.

Charles Goodyear came from a family of inventors. His father's steel pitchfork had revolutionized a farmhand's job, and patents on it and other inventions had been keeping his family fed since the store failed. Charles's own valve worked, even if the life preserver didn't.

Unfortunately, as soon as Goodyear stepped off the train, back home in Philadelphia, police arrested him. In those days, prison was the usual punishment for debt. Goodyear, with far more debts than money, had served time in debtor's prison before.

In fact, Goodyear had done some of his best inventing there. He already held patents for some farm machinery, a safe-eye metal button which would not fray thread, and a new type of faucet. Hours of the work had been done from a jail cell.

Now, from a new cell, he tackled the new project. In a little cottage on the prison grounds, Goodyear began chopping chunks of sticky, gummy rubber, mixing them with chemicals and rolling them out with his wife's rolling pin. Charles's wife, Clarissa, and one of the jailors kept him supplied with materials. Buying supplies wasn't easy, because Clarissa and their three children barely had enough money to eat.

Most American chemists favored turpentine for mixing with rubber. Fortunately, turpentine, used for thinning paint, was cheap. So was raw rubber. Charles mixed the pungent-smelling oil with tiny chunks of rubber and kneaded them into black "dough" with his hands. Then he worked in other chemicals to see what would happen. Finally, he rolled the mixtures out on a marble slab.

At first it looked easy. Goodyear, with no scientific training, discovered several different chemicals that could make rubber appear dry and smooth.

Then everything he had made started to sag out of shape. All his work melted into a sticky, decaying lump. Goodyear found himself back where he had started.

Selling a couple of old patents bought his way out of jail, and Goodyear began to work full time on the rubber mystery. For food and materials money, he pawned the furniture.

Next he tried kneading magnesia powder with sticky lumps of rubber. Mixing rubber with half its own weight of magnesia produced a smooth, white, dry surface. (Possibly Charles had the chemical on hand because he suffered from severe indigestion, then called "dyspepsia." Magnesia is a medication used to treat indigestion.)

Goodyear rolled out sheets of the mixture and made some into a waterproof book cover. It soon became soft and sticky.

Undaunted, he began coating cloth with the same mixture. Using $100 borrowed from an old friend, and with help from Clarissa and the children, he sewed rubber-coated fabric into hundreds of pairs of shoes. The Goodyears decorated them with bright patterns and colors, until they looked as elegant as any shoes in the shops. Goodyear stored them in a shed, as a test.

On the next really hot day, the shoes began to melt. The sticky mess soon smelled so foul that Charles had to bury it all.

The friend who had lent him that money refused to lend more, so Goodyear sold the rest of the furniture. Other friends advised him to give up and get a job.

Goodyear moved his family to a cheaper house and found a room in New York where he could experiment, rent-free. A druggist friend gave him the chemicals he needed. Without wasting time, Goodyear got back on the track of the mystery.

His next effort involved boiling a powdered chemical called quicklime with rubber and turpentine. Smooth, unsticky sheets of rubber soon rolled off his marble slab. Goodyear saw success ahead. He quickly made up some articles to sell and even took out a patent "for a new discovery in India rubber."

102

Unfortunately, the results only "cured" the surface. Inside, rubber stayed as sticky as ever. And spilling an acid as mild as apple juice on the rubber could destroy the "curing" completely.

Since lime on the surface didn't work, Goodyear tried mixing quicklime throughout the rubber "dough." Lime is caustic to the touch. Kneading the sticky black mass as it cooled burned skin off his hands.

Then Goodyear found a small factory, three miles away, which would let him use some mixing equipment. He carried a large ball of rubber under his arm and a huge jar of lime on his shoulder, back and forth every day. Broke, as usual, he couldn't afford a horse and wagon.

Lime-treated rubber cloth looked gorgeous, and Goodyear thought of a special way to advertise his new product. He made himself an entire suit of rubber-coated clothes. "If you see a man who has on an India rubber cap, <u>stock</u>, coat, vest, and shoes, with an India rubber purse without a cent of money in it, that is I," Goodyear said about himself.

This time he thought for sure he had the mystery solved. Then his fancy rubber clothes began to fall apart. The burning effects of lime eventually destroyed the rubber. Another failure.

103

India rubber came from the milky juice of South American trees called cachuchu (spelling varies). The "India" part came from Columbus, and a British chemist named it "rubber" because he found it could rub out pencil marks better than the moist bread crumbs most people used. Rubber erasers once sold for as much as twenty dollars in today's money. But in Goodyear's time, "rubber" was fast becoming a synonym for "financial disaster."

Meanwhile, Charles already knew what to try next. Goodyear had used nitric acid to wash metallic paint off one of his decorated samples of rubber. The surface seemed to shrivel, and Goodyear threw it into the trash.

A few days later he dug it out, just in case it could be reused for something. Most of the sample stuck to his hands and to itself. But to Goodyear's amazement, the acid-washed spot felt smooth and dry. This looked like the best clue yet to the mystery.

Enthusiasm high, Goodyear plunged into experiments with acid and rubber. He took out another patent, for his new "acid-gas" process. The rubber sheets it produced looked fantastic—smooth and sleek and totally unsticky.

Goodyear began to sell some of the articles he made. He even earned enough money to bring his family to New York, into a better house, and to buy some new furniture.

The new process won Goodyear medals from a trade fair. It drew in new investors and earned Goodyear the use of an abandoned rubber factory. President Andrew Jackson praised it.

Then disaster struck. Goodyear, who never had any training in chemistry, mixed some unnamed acids and metallic

104

salts together in a small, windowless room. Poisonous gas began to seep into the air. Before he knew what was happening, he had generated enough poison to knock himself unconscious.

Workmen found Charles, some time later, sprawled on the laboratory floor. Goodyear hovered near death for days.

Strength of will and Clarissa's nursing helped Goodyear survive the deadly gas. He spent seven weeks in bed, recovering. As soon as he could sit up, Goodyear covered the bedspread with papers, plans, and sheets of rubber.

Charles didn't want to waste a minute, because he was certain this time he had to be right. And he did seem to be right. Thinner articles of acid-gas-treated rubber held their shape well, although thicker items still deteriorated in the first heat wave. He found a new backer and borrowed more money.

This time, a new disaster struck. The whole U.S. <u>economy</u> sagged. A general <u>recession</u> dried up sources of money, and Goodyear's backer went bankrupt. The factory had to close. Charles couldn't find anyone else willing to risk a cent on rubber.

Rubber had become a joke. People said it ought to be left where it came from, in the Amazon jungle, with the snakes and the headhunting natives. And people said Goodyear ought to give up and find a way to support his family. He lost the new house and had to move his wife and children into the factory. Soon he began pawning the new furniture.

More ups and downs over the next year landed Goodyear at a shut-down rubber plant in Woburn, Massachusetts. There, he uncovered a major clue to the rubber mystery.

Working almost alone at the abandoned factory, a British rubber worker, Nathaniel Hayward, tried a fresh idea. He mixed small amounts of a foul-smelling yellow chemical called sulfur, with his rubber. Then he dried it in the sun. According to his own first report, he used fumes of sulfur as a bleach. Instead of black, his rubber was almost white.

Hayward's rubber seemed to stay dry a little longer than Goodyear's efforts. Always scrupulously honest, Goodyear suggested that Hayward patent his "solarization" process. He did, and Goodyear bought the patent for three thousand dollars—of borrowed money.

Hayward could not even write his own name. He made "his mark" on a contract to work for Goodyear and to share "all his knowledge," for $800 a year. Goodyear took over the plant.

Goodyear decided if a little sulfur helped, a lot of sulfur should work even better. It did.

Combining sulfur with the acid-gas process, Goodyear and Hayward began making everything from life preservers to tents to ladies' cloaks out of rubber. Prosperity began to boom. At last the Goodyears could afford to redeem their furniture from the pawnshop.

For the first time in years, rubber began to get good publicity. Best of all, Goodyear was awarded a contract to produce 150 waterproof mailbags for the U.S. Post Office out of sulfur and acid-treated rubber. The *Boston Post* predicted rubber would begin to replace other materials everywhere "should they succeed, as there can be but little doubt they will." The *Boston Courier* called rubber "very durable," and free of "obnoxious smells." The publishers printed a few copies of the June 19, 1838, paper on rubber sheets Charles sent them.

But the whole future of rubber seemed to hinge on the mailbags. Could Goodyear finally deliver a perfect product? Was the mystery of rubber finally solved?

Charles and Clarissa worked for weeks to sew and decorate all the bags. Then they hung them in the shed.

The weather turned unusually hot. A few days later, an awful odor seeped out from under the shed door.

Inside, the heavy bags had begun to ferment. Their painted surfaces still looked beautiful and smooth, but layers of uncured rubber underneath had begun to spoil.

A few weeks later most bags, hung by their handles, had sagged all the way to the floor. Everyone in town knew Goodyear had a contract with the Post Office and everyone in town knew he had failed to deliver. Again.

Customers started returning the ruined, foul-smelling life preservers and other rubber objects they had bought. The acid-gas-sulfur process still couldn't solve the mystery.

Unfortunately for Goodyear, the real problem took place deep inside the rubber. The real mystery of rubber involved its structure—molecules far too tiny to see.

Charles Goodyear did not even understand what he was trying to do. Rubber still baffled chemists all across the world. In 1838, they had no idea how complex a tiny molecule could be.

Natural rubber comes in long, skinny molecules made of thousands of chemical "units," linked together end-to-end, like a chain. Each unit is identical to the rest, combining five carbon and eight hydrogen atoms.

Modern chemists label rubber $(C_5H_8)n$. The "n" stands for the number of units, or "links," usually from 4,000 to 5,000.

Goodyear's efforts to tame rubber didn't work because the chemicals he added always worked their way to the surface of the rubber. Inside, long (but far too small to see) chainlike molecules slithered around on top of each other, something like a pile of slippery snakes. Heat always made them slide apart and sag to the floor in a heap.

Meanwhile, Goodyear and Hayward had been ignoring a vital clue. Sulfur worked best on rubber dried in the sun. Neither man thought to try using heat. No one had ever used heat to cure rubber. As far as they knew, heat always destroyed rubber.

Stories differ on how Goodyear actually solved the mystery. His own account doesn't say exactly where it happened, but in January 1839, somehow Goodyear accidentally dropped a chunk of sulfur-cured rubber on a hot stove.

Expecting a melted, smelly mess, he tried snatching the hot rubber off. To Goodyear's absolute amazement, the rubber had not melted the slightest bit. Rubber *always* melted under extreme heat! What could be happening?

Goodyear examined the sample. Some parts had charred, almost like leather, but most of the piece felt smooth and elastic. In fact, it seemed stronger and more stable than any rubber he had ever touched. Heating the sulfur-cured rubber had made an amazing difference.

Goodyear shouted with excitement and showed everyone in the room his discovery. No one even paid attention. They had all heard it too many times before.

That night, Goodyear tacked the piece of sulfur and heat-cured rubber outside on the wall. Winter nights in Massachusetts are bitterly cold. But the next morning, his sample felt as smooth and elastic as before.

To test the change, he tried boiling pieces of rubber in hot sulphur-water, as hot as he could make it. The rubber should have melted, but it didn't. Strong, foul-smelling fumes of sulfur rolled off the kettle, but nothing affected the rubber. In fact, Goodyear could not get any sample of sulfur-treated rubber to melt, no matter how hard he tried.

Goodyear didn't know it, but inside the rubber, vital changes had taken place. He had finally hit on a chemical process that worked!

Atoms of sulfur, aided by heat, attached themselves to the individual links in rubber's long, chainlike molecules and then cross-linked the chains together. Instead of slithery snakes, the rubber now acted like a chainlink fence. It still had rubber's elastic "give," but now it always returned to its original shape. The cross-linking gave the tiny molecules no choice.

The inside of the rubber could no longer slither away. Without knowing how or why it had happened (chemists didn't figure it out for another hundred years), Goodyear had solved the mystery of rubber.

Naturally, life didn't get simple for the Goodyear family. Charles' amazing rubber cure, which came to be called *vulcanization*, turned out to be so simple that other inventors and manufacturers started using it without recognizing Goodyear's patent. Even Nathaniel Hayward changed his story and said the sulfur-and-heat idea had originally been his. He had seen it "in a dream," he told the court.

Money poured in, but lawsuits put Goodyear further in debt than ever. When the French general Napoleon awarded him a medal, Goodyear accepted it from jail. Money and medals never mattered as much to Charles Goodyear as solving the mystery he set out to solve. Today, vulcanization is still the process which cures natural and synthetic rubber for use in all kinds of tires and other rubber objects.

Charles Goodyear spent years chasing a mystery. He blundered upon the key. Once he solved the puzzle, he didn't understand what he had done, and, like Columbus, he did it all on borrowed money. And like Columbus, his discovery changed the world.

EXPLORING THROUGH DISCUSSION

Reflecting on the Selection

As the students read the selection, circulate among the groups to **observe the students' understanding of the concepts** as well as their **collaboration** in solving difficulties in understanding the selection.

As you note the **collaborative group discussions**, mark your Teacher's Observation Log for individuals in one or two groups. Take a moment to reflect on how each student is changing in his or her **ability to use strategies** to solve problems in reading from unit to unit.

Have the groups break while the students respond to Concept Connections, Assessment Master 6.

ASSESSMENT TIP This is an ideal time to mark observations in your Teacher's Observation Log.

Exploring Concepts Within the Selection

Allow the students to regroup to compare and discuss their responses to the Concept Connections. During these discussions you will have more opportunities to observe students and mark your Teacher's Observation Log. Then gather the Concept Connections pages and continue with the lesson as usual.

ASSESSMENT TIP This is another ideal time to mark observations in your log.

Sharing Ideas About Explorable Concepts

Have the groups **report their ideas** and **discuss them** with the rest of the class. It is crucial that the students' ideas determine this discussion.

- Some students may notice that Mr. Goodyear's family and friends were greatly supportive of his efforts and discuss the ways in which their support and cooperation helped him to persevere and to achieve his goal.
- The students may point out that Goodyear himself may not have noticed how much his family helped him and discuss the differences between persevering in the pursuit of a goal and being stubborn about it.
- Goodyear's relentless pursuit may cause some students to suggest reasons that in some cases selfishness might be linked to perseverance.
- Again, some students may wonder whether it is possible for anybody to succeed at anything without perseverance.

As these ideas and others are stated, have the students add them to the **Question Board** or the **Concept Board.**

Exploring Concepts Across Selections

Students may make connections with previous selections in this unit or in other units.

- The students may compare the ways in which Goodyear responded to his family's support with the way in which Pa Ingalls responded to his family's support in "It Can't Beat Us." They may point out the different problems, motivational factors, and aspects of perseverance between the men in the two selections.
- Some students may see a connection between this selection and "The Man Who Wrote *Messiah*" in the unit on music and musicians. Both selections deal with a person who refused to give up—even when his life was at a very low point—but continued to strive for the success that was eluding him.

Connections Across Units

Recording Ideas

As they complete the above discussions, ask the students to **sum up what they have learned from their conversations and to tell how they might use this information** in further explorations. Any special information or insights may be recorded on the Concept Board. Any further questions that they would like to think about, pursue, or investigate may be recorded on the Question Board. They may want to discuss the progress that has been made on their questions. They may also want to cross out any questions that no longer warrant consideration.

▶ Students should also record their ideas about the selection and the unit concepts on page 67 of their Explorer's Notebook.

Self-Assessment Questionnaire

▶ After these aspects of the lesson have been completed, you may wish to distribute the Self-Assessment Questionnaire, Assessment Master 2. Allow plenty of time for the students to complete this important assessment piece.

Explorer's Notebook, page 67

"It Can't Beat Us" by Laura Ingalls Wilder

"The Sticky Secret" by Gail Kay Haines

"Back to the Drawing Board" by Russell Freedman

Assessment Master 2

Self-Assessment Questionnaire

1. How would you rate this selection?
   ○ easy   ○ medium   ○ hard

2. If you checked **medium** or **hard**, answer these questions.
   • Which part of the selection did you find especially difficult?
   • What strategy did you use to understand it?

   • Were some of the words hard?
   • What did you do to figure out their meaning?

3. What do you feel you need to work on to make yourself a better reader?

4. Give an example of something you said in the group. Tell why you said it.

5. Give an example of something that people in the group helped you understand about the selection.

2 READING WITH A WRITER'S EYE

MINILESSON

Assessment

Remind the students that in each selection they have read so far, you have discussed something the writer did particularly well. For example, in "Amaroq, the Wolf," Jean Craighead George established a realistic setting to make the fictional story seem more believable, and in "It Can't Beat Us," Laura Ingalls Wilder showed the multiple effects of a single cause to help her readers understand the story better.

Ask the students to work in small groups and identify something in this selection the author did especially well. Have them point to anything about the writing style that stands out. Remind them to think back to a part of the story that they reacted to or particularly enjoyed as they read. These responses may be clues to good writing.

Allow time for the students to skim the story, if necessary, to refresh their memory. If they seem to be having difficulty expressing how they felt about the writing in this selection, model a response for them by pointing out things that you found noteworthy.

WRITING

Linking Reading to Writing

Encourage the students to use in their own writing any techniques used by Haines that they especially liked. Invite them to search their writing folders for a piece of writing that they could revise to include some writing device that was used effectively in this story.

✱ Writing Process

Although no specific writing assignment is recommended, students may concentrate on an appropriate phase of the writing process for any writing on which they are currently working.

VOCABULARY

You might discuss the following words from the selection that are related to the unit concepts: *blundered, intrigued*, and *undaunted*. Provide an opportunity for the students to fill out Vocabulary Exploration forms, Reproducible Master 15, for these or any other words they wish to remember and use. Have them add these to the Personal Dictionary section of their Writer's Notebook. For additional opportunities to build vocabulary, see **Teacher Tool Card 77**.

VOCABULARY TIP Students need multiple exposures to new vocabulary words. Encourage them to read other books about perseverance.

3 GUIDED AND INDEPENDENT EXPLORATION

EXPLORING CONCEPTS BEYOND THE TEXT

Guided Exploration

Students will select activities in which they explore the unit concepts. Refer them to the **Exploration Activities poster** and give them time to choose an activity. Allow them to discuss what they wish to explore and how they wish to go about it. To review information about **exploring the concepts,** see **Learning Framework Card 3, Exploring Through Reflective Activities.** If the students need further help, here is a suggestion:

Some students may wish to discuss an individual with whom they are personally familiar who has persevered to accomplish a task or reach a goal that was important to him or her. They may wish to do a biography search to find passages illustrating perseverance in biographies of famous persons and share these with the rest of the class. You might remind students who are familiar with Michael Jordan, the former professional basketball player who some consider the finest athlete ever to play the game, that he was once cut from his high-school basketball team. Jordan obviously did not give up, but went on to become the best at what he did.

* Exploring Though Reflective Activities

Explorer's Notebook, page 75

Famous People Who Persevered

Read about famous people who became successful through perseverance. Use this chart to record what you find out.

Name			
Cause of Fame			
Incident That Illustrates Perseverance			
Name			
Cause of Fame			
Incident That Illustrates Perseverance			

Copyright © 1995 Open Court Publishing Company

Unit 4/Perseverance   EN 75

"The Sticky Secret"

A message from _____

In our unit on perseverance, we have just read "The Sticky Secret," a story about Charles Goodyear's unconventional approach to discovering how to stop rubber from becoming sticky when it got hot. Ask your child to tell you about it.

The students have also done some exploring to find examples of how famous people persevered to achieve their success. Perhaps you know of relatives, neighbors, or friends who have worked hard and refused to give up in order to become successful at something—a sport, a profession, or a musical skill, for example. Discuss with your child individuals fitting this description whom you both know. Your child may wish to talk to some of these individuals. Have your child jot down notes below about these individuals to share with the rest of the class.

Notes: _____

_____

_____

_____

_____

_____

_____

_____

_____

_____

_____

_____

_____

_____

_____

_____

Unit 4/Perseverance　　　　　　　　　　　　　　　H/SC 33

Copyright © 1995 Open Court Publishing Company

Home/School Connection 33

❯ Have students use page 75 in their Explorer's Notebook to record what they find out in their biography search. Have them add to this page as they find out more about people who have persevered.

❯ Distribute Home/School Connection 33, and have students discuss with their families examples of perseverance among family members, neighbors, and friends.

Professional Checkpoint: Guided and Independent Exploration

A student's comprehension of a selection is affected by what occurs before, during, and after reading. As the students discuss the selection and its relation to the concepts, notice students who are having difficulty using concept-related terms or making connections between selections. These students may need additional, explicit strategy instruction or modeling in the use of prior knowledge to make sense of new information. Modeling and corrective feedback are powerful tools for improving and refining comprehension skills.

Notes:

✳ INDEPENDENT WORKSHOP
Building a Community of Scholars

Student-Directed Reading, Writing, and Discussion

Meet with the entire class as needed to assess the progress of the students' exploration activities. Groups that want to share information from their explorations should be preparing that information for presentation.

Additional Opportunities for Independent Reading, Writing, and Cross-curricular Activities

✳ Reading Roundtable

Encourage students to read other stories by Gail Kay Haines. They may want to locate and read *Micromysteries*, from which "The Sticky Secret" was taken. Remind them that the Tradebook Connection Cards in the Student Toolbox contain activities connected to many well-known children's books.

✳ Writing Seminar

When the class is revising and proofreading, provide time for students to meet and read each other's written work. Encourage the students to use a thesaurus when they are revising so that they can vary their word choices.

Cross-curricular Activity Cards

The following Cross-curricular Activity Cards from the Student Toolbox are appropriate for this selection:

- 13 Art—It was a "Goodyear"
- 20 Social Studies—Discovery

Discovery
Use after "The Sticky Secret"

20
Social Studies

It Was a "Goodyear"
Use after "The Sticky Secret"

13
Art

Some of the illustrations in "The Sticky Secret" add a little humor to the story. Try your hand at being a cartoonist. In a three-frame cartoon strip, draw three events from "The Sticky Secret" that led up to Charles Goodyear's discovery. *Art is a good way to visualize events and understand them better. Art also helps you to use your creative skills.*

Additional Opportunities for Solving Learning Problems

Tutorial

Use this time to work with individuals or small groups of students who need help in any area. Encourage students to ask for help when they need it and to discuss with you any questions that they have.

Back to the Drawing Board

1 READING THE SELECTION

INFORMATION FOR THE TEACHER

About the Selection

Aspiring aviators can prepare for takeoff when they read this engaging story about two men with a dream that changed the world. "Back to the Drawing Board" is about the experiences leading up to Orville and Wilbur Wright's first flight. Russell Freedman's text, with details of the brothers' experiments, original photographs, and quotations, contains enough eye-opening material to interest all readers.

Link to the Unit Concepts

Until the turn of the century, the notion of a person's being able to fly was thought impossible. "Back to the Drawing Board," pages 112–131, is an illustration of the wonders that can be accomplished by pursuing a dream or goal and a testament to the power of determination and persistence. After reading this selection, students may be inclined to identify other things that are thought to be impossible by most people and to investigate the possibilities. Students may wonder, however, about the economic realities of chasing a dream when the dreamer has other obligations.

About the Author

"Back to the Drawing Board" is an excerpt from *The Wright Brothers: How They Invented the Airplane*, a biography by Russell Freedman. Freedman, born in San Francisco, California, in 1929, is the award-winning author of many biographies written for children. Among his best-known works are *Immigrant Kids*, named a Notable Children's Book of 1980 by the American Library Association; *Children of the Wild West*, named a Notable Children's Book of 1983 by the American Library Association and also a winner of the Western Heritage Award by the National Cowboy Hall of Fame in 1984; and *Cowboys of the Wild West*, named a Notable Children's Book of 1985 by the American Library Association.

LESSON OVERVIEW

"Back to the Drawing Board" by Russell Freedman, pages 112–131

READING THE SELECTION

Materials

Student anthology, pp. 112–131
Explorer's Notebook, p. 67
Assessment Master 1

FYI

Learning Framework Cards
- Checking Understanding, 1C
- Clarifying Unfamiliar Words and Passsages, 1D

READING WITH A WRITER'S EYE

Minilessons

Writer's Craft: Indicators of Location
Writer's Craft: Using Quotations to Support Ideas

Materials

Reading/Writing Connection, pp. 33–34
Reproducible Master 15

FYI

Teacher Tool Card
- Spelling and Vocabulary: Building Vocabulary, 77

Options for Instruction

Writer's Craft: Strong Topic Sentences
Writer's Craft: Writing Captions for Photographs
(Use Teacher Tool Cards listed below.)

GUIDED AND INDEPENDENT EXPLORATION

Materials

Home/School Connection 34
Explorer's Notebook, pp. 76–77

Independent Workshop

Optional Materials from Student Toolbox

Tradebook Connection Cards

Cross-curricular Activity Cards
- 21 Social Studies—Report from Kitty Hawk
- 13 Science—Airplanes

Student Tool Cards
- Writer's Craft/Reading: Signal Words Showing Place and Location, 30
- Writer's Craft/Reading: Using Quotations in Writing, 32
- Writer's Craft/Reading: Strong Topic Sentences, 25
- Writer's Craft/Reading: Using and Understanding Captions, 36

FYI

Teacher Tool Cards
- Writer's Craft/Reading: Indicators of Place and Location, 30
- Writer's Craft/Reading: Using Quotations in Writing, 32
- Writer's Craft/Reading: Strong Topic Sentences, 25
- Writer's Craft/Reading: Using and Understanding Captions, 36

NOTES

Asterisks (*) throughout the lesson indicate learning frameworks. Learning Framework Cards and Teacher Tool Cards can be found in the Teacher Toolbox.

About the
Original
Photographs

Wilbur and Orville Wright left a detailed pictorial record of their work. The story "Back to the Drawing Board" includes photographs of their early gliders, a replica of a pioneering wind tunnel, and their living quarters—where they ate, slept, and worked. As in everything else, Wilbur and Orville were partners in photography; they took turns behind the camera.

INFORMATION FOR THE STUDENT

Tell the students that the selection they are about to read was written by Russell Freedman. As appropriate, you may want to share other information about the author.

Wilbur Wright was born in Millville, Indiana, in 1867. Orville was born in Dayton, Ohio, where the family settled, in 1871. Neither brother had special training in engineering. They were good students, with an amazing mechanical aptitude that they believed had been inherited from their mother, Susan. Although it was said that their father "couldn't hammer a nail straight," Milton Wright is credited with teaching his sons that working hard would bring results.

Aviation has come a long way since the Wright brothers' first flight at the turn of the century. The Boeing 747 can fly nearly ten miles in fifty-nine seconds, and it is only a medium-speed aircraft. The Lockheed SR-71 flies at six hundred miles per hour, and that is just cruising speed; and the Concorde cruises at Mach 2, twice the speed of sound, at over thirteen hundred miles per hour. There can be no doubt that through their determination to pursue their dream, Orville and Wilbur Wright greatly influenced aviation as we know it today.

*About the
Characters*

* COGNITIVE AND RESPONSIVE READING

Activating Prior
Knowledge

Some students may be familiar with the Wright brothers and their work. Invite them to discuss what they know about airplanes.

Setting Reading
Goals and
Expectations

Have the students **browse the selection**, using the **clues/problems/ wondering procedure**. Students will return to these observations after reading.

Note: Notice that "Back to the Drawing Board" has been divided into two parts. If the students do not finish reading the selection in one class period, the second part begins on page 123 and is indicated by a large initial capital letter.

Recommen-
dations for
Reading the
Selection

Ask the students how they would like to read the selection. Because of the scientific nature of the detailed information presented in this selection, the students may need assistance. Oral reading is recommended.

During oral reading, use and encourage think-alouds. During silent reading, allow discussion as needed. Discuss problems, strategies, and reactions after reading.

This would be a good selection for **responding to text by making connections** while reading aloud. Model this response, and then invite the children to respond similarly.

About the Reading Strategies

Students will naturally be trying to figure out the meanings of words, phrases, and ideas to help them to understand the story. They may need to use **clarification strategies** to help make sense of their reading. Additionally, because of the amount of factual information in the text, **question asking** may also be helpful. To review the **clarification strategies** and the strategy of **question asking**, see **Learning Framework Cards 1C and 1D**.

Think-Aloud Prompts for Use in Oral Reading

The think-aloud prompts placed with the page miniatures are merely suggestions for helping students use the strategies. Remind the students to use whatever strategies they need to help them understand the selection. Refer them to the **reading strategy posters**, if necessary. Encourage them to share which strategies they use as they read.

These prompts may be used as guides to promote cognitive and responsive reading.

1 In reading expository literature, students must immediately understand the facts presented in order to avoid confusion as they read further. Consequently, before reading on, students may try to clarify the ideas in this passage to make sure that their understanding is accurate. If no one asks for clarification, you might prompt students with a discussion starter such as the following:

This is somewhat puzzling. I thought that scientific data were supposed to be reliable. I wonder why these data were so unreliable. Does anyone have any ideas?

Allow volunteers to share their thoughts.

BACK TO THE DRAWING BOARD

from THE WRIGHT BROTHERS:
HOW THEY INVENTED THE AIRPLANE
by Russell Freedman
*with original photographs
by Wilbur and Orville Wright*

Flying a glider as a kite.

The year was 1899. In the workroom of their bicycle shop in Dayton, Ohio, two brothers designed and built their first experimental aircraft—a biplane glider flown as a kite. With its successful flight, Wilbur and Orville Wright's next step was to build a man-carrying glider. The performance of this glider, which they tested at Kitty Hawk, North Carolina, in the fall of 1900, left the brothers hopeful. They returned to Kitty Hawk in July 1901, to test a bigger, newly designed glider, but experienced one problem after another. By the end of August, Wilbur and Orville, puzzled and discouraged, went back to Dayton. Wilbur later wrote, "We doubted that we would ever resume our experiments. When we looked at the time and money which we had expended, and considered the progress made and the distance yet to go, we considered our experiments a failure. At this time I made the prediction that man would sometime fly, but that it would not be in our lifetime."

The experiments that Wilbur and Orville had carried out with their latest glider in 1901 were far from encouraging. Reflecting on their problems, Wilbur observed: "We saw that the <u>calculations</u> upon which all flying machines had been based were unreliable, and that all were simply groping in the dark. Having set out with absolute faith in the existing scientific data, we were driven to doubt one thing after another, till finally, after two years of experiment, we cast it all aside, and decided to rely entirely on our own investigations."

In the gaslit workroom behind their bicycle shop, Wilbur and Orville began to compile their own data. They wanted to test different types of wing surfaces and obtain accurate

1

113

air-pressure tables. To do this, they built a wind tunnel—a wooden box 6 feet long with a glass viewing window on top and a fan at one end. It wasn't the world's first wind tunnel, but it would be the first to yield valuable results for the construction of a practical airplane.

The materials needed to make model wings, or *airfoils*, and the tools to shape them were right at hand. Using tin shears, hammers, files, and a soldering iron, the brothers fashioned as many as two hundred miniature wings out of tin, galvanized iron, steel, solder, and wax. They made wings that were thick or thin, curved or flat, wings with rounded tips and pointed tips, slender wings and stubby wings. They attached these experimental airfoils to balances made of bicycle spokes and old hacksaw blades. Then they tested the wings in their wind tunnel to see how they behaved in a moving airstream.

For several weeks they were absorbed in painstaking and systematic lab work—testing, measuring, and calculating as they tried to unlock the secrets of an aircraft wing. The work

A replica of the Wrights' pioneering wind tunnel.

§ 114 ₢

was tedious. It was repetitious. Yet they would look back on that winter as a time of great excitement, when each new day promised discoveries waiting to be made. "Wilbur and I could hardly wait for morning to come," Orville declared, "to get at something that interested us. *That's* happiness."

The Wrights knew that they were exploring uncharted territory with their wind-tunnel tests. Each new bit of data jotted down in their notebooks added to their understanding of how an airfoil works. Gradually they replaced the calculations of others with facts and figures of their own. Their doubts vanished, and their faith in themselves grew. When their lab tests were finally completed, they felt confident that they could calculate in advance the performance of an aircraft's wings with far greater accuracy than had ever before been possible.

Armed with this new knowledge, they designed their biggest glider yet. Its wings, longer and narrower than before, measured 32 feet from tip to tip and 5 feet from front to rear. For the first time, the new glider had a tail—two 6-foot-high vertical fins, designed to help stabilize the machine during turns. The hip cradle developed the year before to control wing warping was retained. The craft weighed just under 120 pounds.

With growing anticipation, Wilbur and Orville prepared for their 1902 trip to the Outer Banks of North Carolina. "They really ought to get away for a while," their sister Katharine wrote to her father. "Will is thin and nervous and so is Orv. They will be all right when they get down in the sand where the salt breezes blow. . . . They think that life at Kitty Hawk cures all ills, you know.

§ 115 ₢

"The flying machine is in process of making now. Will spins the sewing machine around by the hour while Orv squats around marking the places to sew [the cotton wing covering]. There is no place in the house to live but I'll be lonesome enough by this time next week and wish I could have some of their racket around."

The brothers reached the Outer Banks at the end of August with their trunks, baggage, and crates carrying the glider parts. At Kill Devil Hills, their launching site, they found that their wooden shed from the year before had been battered by winter storms. They set to work making repairs and remodeling the building, so they could use it instead of a tent as their new living quarters.

"We fitted up our living arrangements much more comfortably than last year," Wilbur reported. "Our kitchen is immensely improved, and then we have made beds on the second floor and now sleep aloft. It is an improvement over cots. We also have a bicycle which runs much better over the sand than we hoped, so that it takes only about an hour to make the round trip to Kitty Hawk instead of three hours as before. There are other improvements . . . so we are having a splendid time."

By the middle of September they had assembled their new glider and were ready to try it out. This year they took turns in the pilot's position, giving Orville a chance to fly for the first time. To begin with, they were very cautious. They would launch the machine from the slope on Big Hill and glide only a short distance as they practiced working the controls. Steering to the right or left was accomplished by warping the wings, with the glider always turning toward the lower wing.

🐦 *116* 🐦

"Our kitchen is immensely improved . . .

. . . we have made beds on the second floor and now sleep aloft."

2 Quite a bit of information has been presented so far. Students may find it helpful to **sum up** at this point. If they do not suggest it, point out that this is an appropriate place to sum up.

Wilbur and Dan Tate launch the 1902 glider with Orville at the controls.

Up-and-down movements were controlled by the forward elevator.

In a few days they made dozens of short but successful test glides. At this point, things looked more promising than ever. The only mishap occurred one afternoon when Orville was at the controls. That evening he recorded the incident in his diary:

"I was sailing along smoothly without any trouble . . . when I noticed that one wing was getting a little too high and that the machine was slowly sliding off in the opposite direction. . . . The next thing I knew was that the wing was very high in the air, a great deal higher than before, and I thought I must have worked the twisting apparatus the wrong way. Thinking of nothing else . . . I threw the wingtips

118

to their greatest angle. By this time I found suddenly that I was making a descent backwards toward the low wing, from a height of 25 or 30 feet. . . . The result was a heap of flying machine, cloth and sticks in a heap, with me in the center without a bruise or scratch. The experiments thereupon suddenly came to a close till repairs can be made. In spite of this sad catastrophe we are tonight in a hilarious mood as a result of the encouraging performance of the machine."

A few days' labor made the glider as good as new. It wasn't seriously damaged again during hundreds of test glides, and it repeatedly withstood rough landings at full speed. Wilbur and Orville became more and more confident. "Our new machine is a very great improvement over anything we had built before and over anything anyone has built," Wilbur told his father. "Everything is so much more satisfactory that we now believe that the flying problem is really nearing its solution."

And yet the solution was not yet quite at hand. As they continued their test flights, a baffling new problem arose. On most flights, the glider performed almost perfectly. But every so often—in about one flight out of fifty—it would spin out of control as the pilot tried to level off after a turn.

"We were at a loss to know what the cause might be," wrote Wilbur. "The new machine . . . had a vertical tail while the earlier ones were tailless; and the wing tips were on a line with the center while the old machines had the tips drawn down like a gull's wings. The trouble might be due to either of these differences."

First they altered the wingtips and went back to Big Hill for more test flights. Again, the glider spun out of control during a turn. Then they focused their attention to the machine's

119

3 In order to make sure that they understand what is happening, some students may suggest **summing up** at this point.

6-foot-high double-vaned tail, which was fixed rigidly in place. They had installed this tail to help stabilize the glider during turns, but now, it seemed, something was wrong.

Lying in bed one sleepless night, Orville figured out what the problem was. The fixed tail worked perfectly well most of the time. During some turns, however—when the airspeed was low and the pilot failed to level off soon enough—pressure was built up on the tail, throwing the glider off balance and into a spin. That's just what happened to Orville the day of his accident. The cure was to make the tail movable—like a ship's rudder or a bird's tail.

The next morning at breakfast, Orville told Wilbur about his idea. After thinking it over for a few minutes, Wilbur agreed. Then he offered an idea of his own. Why not connect the new movable tail to the wing-warping wires? This would allow the pilot to twist the wings and turn the tail at the same time, simply by shifting his hips. With the wings and tail coordinated, the glider would always make a smooth banked turn.

They removed the original tail and installed a movable single-vaned tail 5 feet high. From then on, there were no more problems. The movable tail rudder finally gave the Wright brothers complete control of their glider. "With this improvement our serious troubles ended," wrote Wilbur, "and thereafter we devoted ourselves to the work of gaining skill by continued practice."

As the brothers worked on their glider, their camp was filling up with visitors again. Their older brother Lorin arrived at the end of September to see what Wilbur and Orville were up to. Then Octave Chanute, a civil engineer who had also conducted gliding experiments, showed up, along with two other

120

Lorin Wright took this photo of his brothers and their visitors at Kill Devil Hills in October 1902. From left: Octave Chanute, Orville, Wilbur, Augustus M. Herring, George A. Spratt, Dan Tate.

gliding enthusiasts. Now six bunks were jammed into the narrow sleeping quarters up in the rafters. At night, the sounds of Wilbur's harmonica, Orville's mandolin, and a chorus of male voices drifted across the lonely dunes.

With their movable tail rudder, the Wrights felt confident that their glider could master the winds. They practiced flying at every opportunity, staying on at their camp until late in October, long after all their visitors had left. "Glides were made whenever weather conditions were favorable," Wilbur recalled. "Many days were lost on account of rain. Still more were lost on account of light winds. Whenever the breeze fell below six miles an hour, very hard running was required to get the machine started, and the task of carrying it back up the hill was real labor . . . but when the wind rose to 20 miles an hour, gliding was a real sport, for starting was easy and the labor of carrying the machine back uphill was performed by the wind."

One day they had a wind of about 30 miles an hour and were able to glide in it without any trouble. "That was the

121

4 Quite a bit of scientific theory has been discussed so far. In order to check their understanding, students may suggest using the strategy of **question asking.** Allow volunteers to formulate questions based on what they have read. The following is one question that they may ask:

What does Orville think might help solve the problem of the glider's instability?

Some students may **make connections** with what they already know about some logical principles of physics.

"When the wind rose to 20 miles an hour, gliding was a real sport . . ."

highest wind a gliding machine was ever in, so that we now hold all the records!" Orville wrote home. "The largest machine ever handled . . . the longest distance glide (American), the longest time in the air, the smallest angle of descent, and the highest wind!!! Well, I'll leave the rest of the 'blow' till we get home." That season the Wrights had designed, built, and flown the world's first fully controllable aircraft. The three-dimensional system of aircraft control worked out by the brothers is the basic system used even today in all winged vehicles that depend on the atmosphere for support.

Except for an engine, their 1902 glider flew just as a Boeing 747 airliner or a jet fighter flies. A modern plane "warps" its wings in order to turn or level off by moving the ailerons on the rear edges of the wings. It makes smooth banking turns with the aid of a movable vertical rudder. And it noses up or down by means of an elevator (usually located at the rear of the plane).

Wilbur and Orville made hundreds of perfectly controlled glides in 1902. They proved that their laboratory tests were accurate. The next step was to build a powered airplane.

122

"Before leaving camp," Orville wrote, "we were already at work on the general design of a new machine which we proposed to propel with a motor."

The Wright brothers could not just take a motor and put it into one of their gliders. First they needed a motor that was light yet powerful. Then they had to design propellers that would produce enough <u>thrust</u> to drive a flying machine through the air. Finally they had to build an aircraft body sturdy enough to carry the weight and withstand the vibrations of the motor and propellers.

Wilbur wrote to several manufacturers of gasoline engines, asking if they could supply an engine that would produce at least 8 horsepower, yet weigh less than 200 pounds. No company was willing to take on the assignment. Wilbur and Orville decided to build the motor themselves with the help of Charlie Taylor, a mechanic they had hired to help out in the bicycle shop.

"We didn't make any drawings," Taylor later recalled. "One of us would sketch out the part we were talking about on a piece of scratch paper and I'd spike the sketch over my bench." In just six weeks, they had the motor on the block testing its power. A marvel of lightness and efficiency, it weighed 179 pounds and generated more than 12 horsepower.

The propellers were much more difficult, since no reliable data on aerial propellers existed. "What at first seemed a simple problem became more complex the longer we studied it," wrote Orville. "With the machine moving forward, the air flying backward, the propellers turning sideways, and nothing standing still, it seemed impossible to find a starting point

123

⑤ If your class reads the selection in two class periods, remind the students to **sum up** the information given in the first part of the selection before beginning the second part. Their summaries should include only the important points.

from which to trace the various simultaneous reactions. . . . Our minds became so obsessed with it that we could do little other work."

During several months of study, experiments, and discussion, Wilbur and Orville filled no less than five notebooks with formulas, diagrams, tables of data, and computations. They were the first to understand that an aerial propeller works like a rotary wing. The same physical laws that produce upward lift when a curved wing slices through the air will also produce forward thrust when a curved propeller blade rotates. Once they had grasped this idea, the Wrights were able to design propeller blades with the right diameter, pitch, and area for their needs.

"Isn't it astonishing that all these secrets have been preserved for so many years just so that we could discover them!!!" Orville told a friend. "Well, our propellers are so different from any that have been used before that they will have to either be a good deal better, or a good deal worse."

They decided to use two propellers turning in opposite directions, so that any twisting effect on the aircraft would be neutralized. The propellers were connected to the motor through a sprocket-and-chain transmission, like the kind used to drive a bicycle. The motor rested on the lower wing, to the right of the pilot, so it would not fall on him in case of a headlong crash. To balance the motor's extra weight, the right wing was 4 inches longer than the left.

In the Wright brothers' gliders, the wing-warping wires had twisted the entire wing up or down. In their new powered machine, the front edge of each wing was fixed rigidly in place. Only the rear outer edges of the wingtips could now be

❦ 124 ❦

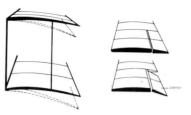

Wing warping in the 1903 Wright Flyer served the same function as ailerons on a modern aircraft.

flexed, much like the movements of ailerons on a modern aircraft. The controls were similar to those in the 1902 glider—a padded hip cradle to operate the wing warping and the tail rudder, and a wooden hand lever to control the forward elevator. With a wingspan of just over 40 feet, the new machine was their biggest yet. They called it their first "Flyer."

There wasn't enough space in the bicycle shop workroom to assemble the entire machine. The center section alone was so big that it blocked the passage leading to the front of the shop. When a customer walked in, one of the brothers had to go out a side door and walk around to the front to wait on the customer. They didn't see their Flyer in one piece until the parts were shipped to the Outer Banks and assembled there.

Wilbur and Orville returned to their camp at Kill Devil Hills on September 25, 1903, and again found a storm-ravaged camp building. They made repairs and put up a second building to use as a workshop for assembling and housing their Flyer. On days with good winds, they took out their old 1902 glider for practice flights. On calm or rainy days, they worked on the new machine indoors.

Their progress was slowed by frustrating problems with the propeller shafts and the transmission sprocket wheels,

❦ 125 ❦

6 In this paragraph significant laws of physics are stated. Students may wish to use a **clarification strategy** to help them understand how an aerial propeller works. Have students restate the paragraph in their own words and point to clues in the text that helped them understand the idea.

which kept coming loose as the motor was being tested. Meanwhile, winter arrived early. Rain, snow, and freezing winds buffeted their camp. The water in their washbasin was frozen solid in the morning. They converted an old <u>carbide</u> can into a woodburning stove and piled on the blankets when they went to bed.

"We have no trouble keeping warm at nights," Wilbur wrote home. "In addition to the classifications of last year, to wit, 1, 2, 3 and 4 blanket nights, we now have 5 blanket nights, & 5 blankets & 2 quilts. Next come 5 blankets, 2 quilts & fire; then 5, 2, fire, & hot-water jug. This is as far as we have got so far. Next come the addition of sleeping without undressing, then shoes & hats, and finally overcoats. We intend to be comfortable while we are here."

The propeller shafts gave them so much trouble that Orville had to go all the way back to Dayton to have new ones made. He was returning to North Carolina on the train when he read a newspaper story about Samuel Pierpont Langley's second and last attempt to launch a man-carrying airplane on December 8, 1903. Once again, the *Great Aerodrome* and its pilot had crashed into the Potomac—and so had the $73,000 Langley had spent on it. So far, the Wrights had spent less than $1,000 on their still untested Flyer.

Orville reached Kill Devil Hills with the new propeller shafts on December 11. The brothers were anxious to test their Flyer before the weather got any worse. To launch the machine, they had built a movable starting track—a 60-foot-long wooden rail made of four 15-foot sections. The top of the rail was covered with a thin metal strip. For takeoff, the Flyer would be placed over this track with its landing skids

❧ *126* ❦

resting on a small two-wheeled dolly, or "truck" as the Wrights called it, which ran freely along the rail. When the propellers started to turn, the Flyer would ride down the monorail on its truck, heading into the wind until it gained enough airspeed to lift off and fly. The Wrights called this starting track their "Grand Junction Railroad."

They were ready for their first trial on Monday, December 14, but the wind that day wasn't strong enough to permit a launching from level ground. Instead of waiting any longer, they decided to try a downhill launching from the side of Big Kill Devil Hill.

7 They hoisted a red signal flag to the top of a pole, alerting the lifesaving station a mile away. Before long, five men, two small boys, and a dog came trudging up the beach. The

The Flyer sits atop its movable 60-foot starting track.

7 This paragraph signals a turning point in the selection. The students should sense from the mounting action that something exciting is going to happen. Some students may **predict** upcoming events on the basis of their previous knowledge about the Wright brothers' success. Encourage volunteers to share their predictions and explain how facts they knew before reading this selection helped them make their predictions.

lifesavers had agreed to act as witnesses and help move more than 700 pounds of flying machine over the sand.

Everyone pitched in. Balancing the Flyer by hand, they rolled it along the starting rail, moving each 15-foot section of track from the rear to the front as they went along. When they reached the bottom of Big Hill, the entire 60-foot track was laid on the hillside. Then the Flyer was pulled up the rail and placed in position. "With the slope of the track, the thrust of the propellers, and the machine starting directly into the wind, we did not anticipate any trouble in getting up flying speed on the 60-foot monorail track," Orville recalled.

They started the motor. The propellers turned over, paddling loudly. The transmission chains clattered. The motor popped and coughed, and the whole machine seemed to shudder and shake. The two small boys took one look, backed away, and went racing across the sand dunes with the dog at their heels.

Wilbur and Orville tossed a coin to decide who should try first. Wilbur won. He lay down on the lower wing, sliding his hips into the padded wing-warping cradle. Orville took a position at one of the wings to help balance the machine as it roared down the starting track. Then Wilbur loosened the restraining rope that held the Flyer in place. The machine shot down the track with such speed that Orville was left behind, gasping for breath.

After a 35- to 40-foot run, the Flyer lifted up from the rail. Once in the air, Wilbur tried to point the machine up at too steep an angle. It climbed a few feet, stalled, settled backward, and smashed into the sand on its left wing. Orville's stopwatch showed that the Flyer had flown for just 3½ seconds.

 128

Wilbur in the damaged Flyer after his unsuccessful trial on December 14. His hand still grips the wooden control lever.

Wilbur wasn't hurt, but it took two days to repair the damage to the Flyer. They were ready to try again on Thursday, December 17, 1903.

They woke up that morning to freezing temperatures and a blustery 27-mile-an-hour wind. Puddles of rainwater in the sand hollows around their camp were crusted with ice. They spent the early part of the morning indoors, hoping the wind would die down a little. At 10 o'clock, with the wind as brisk as ever, they decided to attempt a flight. "The conditions were very unfavorable," wrote Wilbur. "Nevertheless, as we had set our minds on being home by Christmas, we determined to go ahead."

They hoisted the signal flag to summon the lifesavers. Then, in the biting wind, they laid down all four sections of

129

---

the starting track on a level stretch of sand just below their camp. They had to go inside frequently to warm their hands by the carbide-can stove.

By the time the starting track was in place, five witnesses had shown up—four men from the lifesaving station and a teenage boy from the nearby village of Nags Head. They helped haul the Flyer over to the launching site.

Now it was Orville's turn at the controls. First he set up his big box camera, focused on a point near the end of the track, and inserted a glass-plate negative. Then he placed the rubber bulb that tripped the shutter in the big hand of John Daniels, one of the lifesaving men, and asked him to squeeze the bulb just as the Flyer took off.

The brothers shook hands. "We couldn't help but notice how they held onto each other's hand," one of the lifesavers recalled, "sort of like two folks parting who weren't sure they'd ever see one another again."

Orville took the pilot's position, his hips in the wing-warping cradle, the toes of his shoes hooked over a small supporting rack behind him. Like his brother, he was wearing a dark suit, a stiff collar, a necktie, and a cap. Wilbur turned to the lifesaving men and told them "not to look so sad, but to . . . laugh and holler and clap . . . and try to cheer Orville up when he started."

"After running the motor a few minutes to heat it up," Orville recalled, "I released the wire that held the machine to the track, and the machine started forward into the wind. Wilbur ran at the side of the machine, holding the wing to balance it on the track. Unlike the start on the 14th, made in a calm, the machine, facing a 27-mile-per-hour wind, started

130

---

very slowly. Wilbur was able to stay with it till it lifted from the track after a forty-foot run. [John] snapped the camera for us, taking a picture just as the machine had reached the end of the track and had risen to a height of about two feet."

Wilbur had just let go of the wing when John Daniels tripped the shutter. The lifesavers broke into a ragged cheer. The Flyer was flying!

Orville couldn't hear them. He hung on to the control lever and stared straight ahead as the icy wind whistled past his ears and the motor clattered beside him. Buffeted by gusts, the Flyer lurched forward like a drunken bird. "The course of the flight up and down was exceedingly _erratic_," wrote Orville, "partly due to the irregularity of the air, and partly to lack of experience in handling this machine. . . . As a result the machine would rise suddenly to about ten feet, and then as suddenly dart for the ground. A sudden dart when a little over a hundred feet from the end of the track, or a little over 120 feet from the point at which it rose into the air, ended the flight. . . .

"This flight lasted only 12 seconds, but it was nevertheless the first in the history of the world in which a machine carrying a man had raised itself by its own power into the air in full flight, had sailed forward without reduction of speed, and had finally landed at a point as high as that from which it had started."

It had happened so quickly. A boy could have thrown a ball as far as the Flyer had flown. But the Wright brothers were _elated_. They had launched a flying machine that could actually fly.

131

* **EXPLORING THROUGH DISCUSSION**

Reflecting on the Selection
Whole-Group Discussion

The whole group discusses the selection and any **thoughts or questions** that it raises. During this time, students also **return to the clues, problems, and wonderings** that they noted on the board during browsing.

Assessment

To assess their understanding of the text, engage the students in a discussion to determine whether they have grasped the following ideas:
- the difficulties the Wright brothers encountered and how they reacted to defeat and disappointment
- how the Wright brothers met each new challenge and the factors that contributed to their success

Response Journal

If students have additional thoughts or reactions to the selection, suggest that they record these in their response journals.

Exploring Concepts Within the Selection
Small-Group Discussion

Circulate among the groups and observe discussions. Remind the students to refer to the Question Board and the Concept Board to keep the discussions focused on their original ideas about perseverance and to see whether those ideas have changed as a result of reading this selection.

ASSESSMENT TIP This might be a good time to observe students working in groups and to mark observations in your Teacher's Observation Log.

Sharing Ideas About Explorable Concepts

Have the groups report their ideas and discuss them with the rest of the class. It is crucial that the students' ideas determine this discussion.
- Students may identify the ways in which Orville and Wilbur Wright shared responsibilities and cooperated with one another in their attempts to attain their goal.
- Students may point out that with each scientific discovery, the Wright brothers were encouraged to investigate further, and that even when it failed, each new experiment led them closer to attaining their goal.
- Students may point out that Orville and Wilbur Wright did not have to support themselves. They may discuss the economic realities of trying to accomplish a goal when other obligations exist.

TEACHING TIP As the students share ideas, be sure that they give reasons for their conclusions or tell why they feel the way they do.

As these ideas and others are stated, have the students add them to the **Question Board** or the **Concept Board.**

Have the students turn to the fine-art pieces on pages 70–71 of their student anthology and examine the painting on page 71. Have them discuss their ideas about the painting as it relates to the ideas presented in the selection that they just read. They may suggest that the hat symbolizes a dream and compare the man's chasing his hat to the Wright brothers' chasing their dream. Invite them to discuss any thoughts they have about the painting.

Fine Art

Exploring Concepts Across Selections

Ask the students whether this selection reminds them of anything else they have read. They may make connections with other selections in this unit or other units.

- Some students will naturally compare this selection with "The Sticky Secret": they may point out the similarities and differences between the characters in the two selections and between the ways in which they met challenges and dealt with their frustrations and difficulties. They may also compare Goodyear's determination in pursuing his quest with that of the Wright brothers. In their comparisons, students may point out that both inventions led to enormously successful industries whose products affect the way we live today.

Recording Ideas

As they complete the above discussions, ask the students to **sum up what they have learned from their conversations and to tell how they might use this information** in further explorations. Any special information or insights may be recorded on the Concept Board. Any further questions that they would like to think about, pursue, or investigate may be recorded on the Question Board. The students may want to discuss the progress that has been made on their questions. They may also want to cross out any questions that no longer warrant consideration.

❯ Students should also record their ideas about the selection and the unit concepts on page 67 of their Explorer's Notebook.

STEPS TOWARD INDEPENDENCE The students should be becoming more adept at making comparisons between selections. If some students need help with this, model comparing selections on the basis of ideas they have discussed about perseverance.

Evaluating Discussions

Explorer's Notebook, page 67

"It Can't Beat Us" by Laura Ingalls Wilder

_____
_____
_____
_____
_____
_____

"The Sticky Secret" by Gail Kay Haines

_____
_____
_____
_____
_____
_____

"Back to the Drawing Board" by Russell Freedman

_____
_____
_____
_____
_____
_____

Unit 4/Perseverance   EN 67

Copyright © 1995 Open Court Publishing Company

2 READING WITH A WRITER'S EYE

MINILESSONS

Writer's Craft: Indicators of Location

Ask students to talk about anything that they have learned about indicators of location. Have them describe any examples that they can remember from their reading or writing. Tell them that when writing about the process of building or making something, writers often use **words to show the location of where things appear.**

Tell students that Russell Freedman made use of words that indicate location when describing a building process to help readers picture where things are located. As an example, read the first complete sentence at the top of page 114. Ask students to identify words and phrases that indicate where the parts of the wind tunnel are located. For example:

- "a glass viewing window *on top*"
- "a fan *at one end*"

Have the students explain in what ways Freedman's details in the sentence helped them to understand what the wind tunnel looked like.

Selective Reading: Focus on Indicators of Location

Encourage the students to skim the selection and find other examples of words that indicate location. Have volunteers read and discuss each of their examples. Encourage the students to identify the words and phrases that indicate location and then discuss how each makes the passage clearer. The following examples are some that might be suggested:

- page 118, paragraph 2: "The next thing . . . the wing was *very high in the air*. . . ."
- page 119, paragraph 3: ". . . the wing tips were *on a line with the center*. . . ."
- page 121, line 2: ". . . sleeping quarters *up in the rafters*."

Selection-Based Practice

Independent Practice: Indicators of Location

❯ Have the students work independently or in small groups, using Reading/Writing Connection, page 33, to extend their discussion of words used to indicate location to make the story clearer.

Writer's Craft: Using Quotations to Support Ideas

Remind students that writers often use quotations to support or to elaborate on their ideas. Ask students to talk about anything they have learned about **using quotations to support their ideas** and to give any examples that they can remember from their reading or writing. Tell them that in biographical stories, authors often use quotations to make their writing more interesting and credible. Not all quotations, however, are used to support the main idea. Some are used merely to add interest. Remind students that the main idea of a selection or a paragraph is the most important idea; supporting details are pieces of information used to tell more about the main idea.

Tell students that Russell Freedman made extensive use of quotations to support the important ideas presented in this story. As an example, read pages 118–119 (from "In a few days" to "of the machine"). Ask

"Back to the Drawing Board"

Indicators of Location

Look again at "Back to the Drawing Board" or at other stories that you have read and find words that indicate location. List the location words or phrases the author uses and explain how each helps you better understand the passage.

Story: _____ Page: _____

Words or phrases that indicate location: _____

_____

_____

How this makes the passage clearer: _____

_____

_____

_____

Story: _____ Page: _____

Words or phrases that indicate location: _____

_____

_____

How this makes the passage clearer: _____

_____

_____

_____

Story: _____ Page: _____

Words or phrases that indicate location: _____

_____

_____

How this makes the passage clearer: _____

_____

_____

_____

Indicators of Location

Copyright © 1995 Open Court Publishing Company

Reading/Writing Connection, page 33

"Back to the Drawing Board"

Using Quotations to Support Ideas

In "Back to the Drawing Board" or in other stories that you have read, find passages that contain quotations supporting or elaborating on a main idea. Write down the main idea and list the supporting details given in the quotation.

Story: _____

Page number for quotation: _____

Main idea: _____

_____

Details: _____

_____

_____

_____

Story: _____

Page number for quotation: _____

Main idea: _____

_____

Details: _____

_____

_____

_____

Story: _____

Page number for quotation: _____

Main idea: _____

_____

Details: _____

_____

_____

_____

Quotations to Support Ideas

Copyright © 1995 Open Court Publishing Company

Reading/Writing Connection, page 34

---

students to identify the main idea of the passage. They should note that the passage is about the one mishap that occurred. Discuss the details. Invite students to give their impressions of Orville's account and to discuss why the direct quotation is more effective than the author's third-person account would have been.

Selective Reading: Focus on Using Quotations to Support Ideas

Throughout this selection the author used many quotations to support his ideas. Encourage the students to skim the selection to find other examples of quotations used to support important ideas. Have volunteers read and discuss each of their examples. They should name the person speaking, identify the important idea, and give the details that support the idea.

Selection-Based Practice

Independent Practice: Using Quotations to Support Ideas

▶ Have the students work independently or in small groups, using Reading/Writing Connection, page 34, to extend their discussion of using direct quotations to support ideas.

WRITING

Linking Reading to Writing

To provide opportunities for the students to apply the writer's craft of using indicators of location in descriptions or using quotations to support ideas, encourage them to revise a piece from their writing folders by adding words that indicate location to make ideas clearer or by adding quotations to support their ideas. If they are revising to add quotations, remind them to check materials in the library to see what others have had to say about their subject.

∗ Writing Process

Some students may wish to start a new piece of writing in which they describe the process of making or building something. Encourage them to use indicators of location to make their description clear. Remind students about the differences between writing about a process and providing a set of instructions. A process description is informational and not something the writer expects someone to carry out. A set of instructions is written for people to carry out.

VOCABULARY

Words from the selection that are related to the unit concepts and that you might discuss with the students include *painstaking, tedious, repetitious,* and *uncharted territory.* Allow time for the students to complete Vocabulary Exploration forms, Reproducible Master 15, for those words they wish to remember and use or that are important to the unit concepts. Have them add these to the Personal Dictionary section in their Writer's Notebook. Then provide an opportunity for volunteers to share the words and phrases that they have added and to tell why they chose them. For additional opportunities to build vocabulary, see **Teacher Tool Card 77.**

VOCABULARY TIP The Vocabulary Exploration form allows students to use new words in a variety of ways and to make associations between words and words or concepts they already know to improve their vocabulary.

Professional Checkpoint: Reading with a Writer's Eye

Proofreading sessions allow the students time to apply grammar, mechanics, and usage skills to their own writing. Because you have a large sample of every student's writing, you know where the written language problems of each lie. Sometimes these problems are persistent. In proofreading sessions you can deal with these problems in a constructive way.

Notes:

3 GUIDED AND INDEPENDENT EXPLORATION

EXPLORING CONCEPTS BEYOND THE TEXT

Guided
Exploration

Students will select activities in which they explore the concepts related to perseverance. Refer them to the **Exploration Activities poster** and give them time to choose an activity. Allow them to discuss what they wish to explore and how they wish to go about it. If the students need further help, here are some suggestions:

* Some students may wish to prepare a photographic or a pictorial history depicting a person who is striving toward a goal. They could take their own photographs, or use those from old magazines or newspapers, or draw illustrations or sketches and then write a caption under each illustration. The captions should include the place, the time, or the date and a description of the main character and action. Explain to the students that the rigor and dedication needed for success in any goal can be captured in photographs or sketches and can illustrate the day-to-day struggles as well as the joys of aspiring individuals.

* Some students may wish to find out what successful people have said about perseverance. Have the students read biographies and books about people who have been successful in pursuing their dreams— former presidents, industrial leaders, their favorite authors, or anyone they find interesting. Students might choose an appropriate quotation from one of the persons whom they have read about and discuss with classmates why they agree or disagree with the ideas expressed in the quotation.

❯ Students may use pages 76–77 in their Explorer's Notebook if they choose to search for quotes.

❯ Distribute Home/School Connection 34 and have students and their families read a biography about a person who persevered in a discipline that students are interested in learning more about. Have them share anything that they have learned about the person or the field of interest with their classmates.

* Exploring
Through
Reflective
Activities

Presenting
Exploration
Results

If any groups have information or ideas on perseverance that they wish to present to the class, allow time for presentations. Encourage the students to make their presentations as interesting to the audience as possible. Provide any necessary audiovisual equipment.

After each presentation, encourage classmates to respond to the presentation. What did they enjoy most about the presentation? What new facts did they learn? Can they link information from the presentation with something they learned during the course of the unit?

Perseverance and Success

Find out what successful people have said about perseverance. Read biographies, autobiographies, and other books about people who have been successful in pursuing their dreams. Look in books about U.S. presidents, industrial leaders, your favorite authors, or any other individuals you find interesting. Write down quotations from your reading that deal with perseverance. Identify the speaker and the source in which you found the quotation. Note any similarities among the ideas presented in the various quotations.

Quotation: _____
_____
Speaker or writer: _____
Book/source: _____
_____

Quotation: _____
_____
Speaker or writer: _____
Book/source: _____
_____

Quotation: _____
_____
Speaker or writer: _____
Book/source: _____
_____

 Copyright © 1995 Open Court Publishing Company

Explorer's Notebook, page 76

Quotation: _____
_____
Speaker or writer: _____
Book/source: _____
_____

Quotation: _____
_____
Speaker or writer: _____
Book/source: _____

Now choose one quotation and discuss it with your classmates. Do you agree or disagree with the speaker or writer? Why? Write down notes and ideas from your discussion.

_____
_____
_____
_____
_____
_____
_____
_____
_____

Copyright © 1995 Open Court Publishing Company

Explorer's Notebook, page 77

"Back to the Drawing Board"

A message from _____

In our unit on perseverance, we have just read "Back to the Drawing Board," a story about the Wright brothers' efforts to build a machine with which people could fly. With your child locate and read a biography or an autobiography about a person who persevered in a discipline that your child is interested in learning more about. Discuss why the individual was motivated to pursue the goal and how she or he acquired knowledge and expertise, coped with disappointment, and kept her or his dream alive. Also discuss with your child what steps might be taken to build knowledge and expertise in the discipline. Have your child write a summary of the book and bring it to school to share ideas with the class.

Title of book: _____
Subject of biography or autobiography: _____
Author: _____
Summary: _____
_____
_____
_____
_____
_____
_____
_____
_____
_____
_____
_____

Copyright © 1995 Open Court Publishing Company

*INDEPENDENT WORKSHOP
Building a Community of Scholars

Student-Directed Reading, Writing, and Discussion

Collaborative groups should be completing their explorations on perseverance. Suggest that they share any special ideas they have with the rest of the class and discuss the manner in which they would like to do so.

Additional Opportunities for Independent Reading, Writing, and Cross-curricular Activities

✱ Reading Roundtable

If students enjoyed reading "Back to the Drawing Board," encourage them to read *The Wright Brothers: How They Invented the Airplane*, the book from which the selection was excerpted. Other books by Russell Freedman that they might enjoy include *Lincoln: A Photobiography* about Abraham Lincoln, or *Indian Chiefs,* about six Native-American chiefs who led their people in historic moments of crisis. Remind them that if they read a Tradebook Connection selection, they can do the accompanying activities on the Tradebook Connection Card in the Student Toolbox.

✱ Writing Seminar

Remind the students to look through their writing folders for pieces that they might like to prepare for publishing. Remind them to proofread before they publish. If your class is using the optional Writer's Handbook, refer students to the handbook when they hit a stumbling block in trying to revise their writing.

Portfolio

Remind the students to think about pieces of writing to put into their portfolios.

Cross-curricular Activity Cards

The following Cross-curricular Activity Cards in the Student Toolbox are appropriate for this selection:
- 21 Social Studies—Report from Kitty Hawk
- 13 Science—Airplanes

Airplanes
Use after "Back to the Drawing Board"

13
Science

Report from Kitty Hawk
Use after "Back to the Drawing Board"

21
Social Studies

It is December 17, 1903. You are a news reporter covering the Wright brothers' first flight. Write an imaginary interview with Wilbur and Orville Wright and spectators. To prepare for your report, locate a book about the Wright brothers, such as *The Wright Brothers: How They Invented the Airplane*. Draw up a list of questions to ask the brothers about their experience. Also prepare a few questions to ask spectators about their reactions to the flight. Have some of your classmates play the roles of the interviewees. Start your report by stating the location and describing the conditions. Present your report to the class. *Preparing a news report helps you practice research and organizational skills.*

Additional Opportunities for Solving Learning Problems

Tutorial

Use this time to work with those students who need help in any area. Remember to use peer tutoring with those for whom it would be appropriate. Encourage the students to ask for help when they feel the need. The following Teacher Tool Cards are available in the Teacher Toolbox for your convenience:
- Writer's Craft/Reading: Indicators of Place and Location, Teacher Tool Card 30
- Writer's Craft/Reading: Using Quotations in Writing, Teacher Tool Card 32
- Writer's Craft/Reading: Strong Topic Sentences, Teacher Tool Card 25
- Writer's Craft/Reading: Using and Understanding Captions, Teacher Tool Card 36

Unit Wrap-up

Initiate a general class discussion on the unit. The Concept Board can help the students recall the knowledge that they have gained from this unit. In addition, have students turn to Explorer's Notebook, page 64, to remind themselves of what they knew about perseverance as they began the unit and what they expected to learn by completing the unit. The discussion may be extended to include

- an evaluation of the unit selections. Which selections did students find the most interesting? Which were the least interesting?
- an evaluation of the unit activities. Which activities did students find enjoyable or informative? Which did not seem valuable?
- an evaluation of the overall unit. How well did the unit cover the explorable concepts? Was perseverance a worthwhile subject to examine? Why?
- suggestions of ideas related to perseverance worth further exploration, beginning with questions left on the Question Board.

Small-Group Discussion

As an alternative, you might have the students **work in small groups to discuss the unit.** To refresh their memory on important ideas raised in the unit, encourage the group participants to refer to the Concept Board, browse the anthology selections, and **review their Explorer's Notebook pages** for unit 4. Then have the groups share the important points and conclusions from their discussions.

ASSESSMENT

Informal Assessment

▶ Give the students the opportunity to make individual evaluations of their experiences during this unit by completing pages 78–79 in their Explorer's Notebook. Meet with students to discuss their evaluations.

End-of-Unit Assessment

At this point, you might wish to carry out end-of-unit assessment for unit 4, Perseverance. You will find the following end-of-unit assessment booklets in the Teacher Toolbox:

Comprehension Assessment
- Understanding the Selection
- Making Connections Across Selections
- Checking Skills

- Multiple-Choice Option
Essay and Writing Assessment

You may pick and choose among the various assessment components to find the right mix for assessing areas you want to stress. See *Formative Assessment: A Teacher's Guide* for specific suggestions on how to use these assessment materials.

UNIT CELEBRATION

Have the students suggest ways to celebrate their completion of this unit. Their suggestions may include the following:
- Creating a perseverance mural or collage showing ordinary, everyday activities in which people persevere—learning, sports, working, building or making something—and extraordinary quests in which people persevere—working to overcome prejudice or persevering to overcome the effects of natural disasters. In small groups, students could plan and draw illustrations or use photographs depicting scenes from their own experiences.
- Inviting family members or another class to the classroom to see the displays on persevering.
- Having students write questions about people and perseverance on note cards. Use these questions in a quiz-game format.

Explorer's Notebook, page 78

Explorer's Notebook, page 79

Unit Wrap-up

How did you feel about this unit?
- ☐ I enjoyed it very much.　☐ I liked it.
- ☐ I liked some of it.　☐ I didn't like it.

How would you rate the difficulty of the unit?
- ☐ easy　☐ medium　☐ hard

How would you rate your performance during this unit?
- ☐ I learned a lot about perseverance.
- ☐ I learned some new things about perseverance.
- ☐ I didn't learn much about perseverance.

Why did you choose this rating?
_____
_____
_____
_____

What was the most interesting thing that you learned about perseverance?
_____
_____
_____
_____

Is there anything else about perseverance that you would like to learn? What?
_____
_____
_____
_____

78 EN　　　　Perseverance/Unit 4

Copyright © 1995 Open Court Publishing Company

What did you learn about perseverance that you didn't know before?
_____
_____
_____
_____

What did you learn about yourself as a learner?
_____
_____
_____
_____

As a learner, what do you need to work on?
_____
_____
_____
_____

What resources (books, films, magazines, interviews, tool cards, other) did you use on your own during this unit? Which of these were the most helpful? Why?
_____
_____
_____
_____
_____
_____

Copyright © 1995 Open Court Publishing Company

Unit 4/Perseverance　　　　EN 79

Ecology

UNIT INTRODUCTION

BACKGROUND INFORMATION FOR THE TEACHER

Explorable
Concepts

Nearly all human activities have by-products of some kind—garbage, water and air pollution, sewage. This is true even of a process as peaceable as publishing a book; the printing of this book released volatile organic compounds into the atmosphere, quite apart from the energy used in making paper, turning the presses, binding the book, and shipping it to your school. At each of these stages, exhaust fumes and a small amount of heat got into the atmosphere.

Until recently, the human population of the earth was so small, and these by-products were generated in such small quantities, that the impact of those by-products on our natural surroundings (our environment) could be ignored. We didn't worry too much about what happened to the exhaust from our car once it left the tailpipe or about what became of our garbage once it was collected. But now, both the number of human beings on earth and the scale of our activities have grown so enormously that it is impossible to overlook the impact of our by-products on the world. We have become more aware that all the living things in any given area are connected in a single system, adapted to that particular geographic area, its climate, its altitude, its water supplies, and so on. Each living thing in that system depends on many others, and they live in a sort of balance with one another. Today we have become aware that human activities, and their by-products, can disrupt

ECOLOGY

that system, causing damage not just to one part of it but to the system as a whole. For example, by eliminating certain insect pests we may also endanger birds that needed those insects for food—and then the absence of birds means too many insects again.

The study of such systems of living things is called ecology, and the systems themselves are called ecosystems. The study of ecology, as a part of biology, goes back to the early years of this century, but it was not a popular or widely discussed area of study until the 1960s and 1970s, when the impact of human activities on the environment first became strikingly evident. Since then, ecology has become part of our everyday vocabulary; and it is almost impossible to understand a large part of present-day political debate, or anything else in the news, without knowing a little about ecology. This unit is designed to introduce students to these ideas.

Most students will already have heard of some basic concepts of ecology. Words like *environment, recycling,* and *endangered species* have become part of the everyday vocabulary of television and other media. Very often, however, popular media use these concepts in a very superficial or misleading manner. So it is unlikely that students have developed a deep understanding of these concepts or had the opportunity to think them through. This unit can give students that opportunity. The goal in this unit, as in other units, is not to ensure that students emerge with

some particular body of knowledge about ecology but to promote a
broader understanding and interest in the subject than the one they
started with.

Ecology raises a wide variety of questions. To stimulate your own
thinking, you might ask yourself questions such as the following:

• If everyone in the world were as well-off as the average American
(i.e., able to afford a car, a cooking stove, a television, a telephone,
and other pieces of technology), what would be the impact on the
earth's atmosphere?

• Poor countries often do not have the same controls on pollution that
exist in more affluent countries. It is often said that with such extreme
poverty, these countries can't afford the expense of pollution control.
What is more important, a decent standard of living or a clean environment?

• Some environmentalists say that people will not willingly give up
habits that destroy the natural world. Other environmentalists suggest
that society should set up ways to make people want to give up these
habits voluntarily, because pollution control can make or save money
for them. Which approach is better?

• Much of the pollution we create comes from the technology we need to
sustain our everyday lives in an industrialized society—cars, refrigerators, and so forth. But technology has also been the most important
way to reduce pollution. Will it be possible to maintain our current
level of industrialization if we reduce pollution to a level that does not
endanger the environment? Or will we eventually destroy ourselves?

Resources   Among the following resources are **professional reference books,
audiovisual materials, and community/school resources.** The reference books are intended to help you develop the concepts and organize
information to share with the students in whatever way you choose.
Among the audiovisual materials are some that your students will not be
able to obtain and others that will be available to both you and your students. For a complete list of audiovisual sources, see page 519. The
community/school resources include people, agencies, and institutions
that may be helpful in your exploration.

In addition to the resources listed here, **bibliographies for the students** appear in the student anthology, on **Reproducible Masters 46–51,**
and on **Home/School Connection 35–36.** Encourage the students to use
these bibliographies as they explore the concepts in this unit.

You should also read books from the students' bibliographies.
Reading stories about ecology written for children will help you understand the nature of the information the students are learning.

Professional
Reference Books

Bonnet, Robert L., and Keen, G. Daniel. *Environmental Science: 49 Science Fair Projects.* TAB Books, 1990. Procedures are given for projects concerning soil, habitat and life cycles, weeds and insects, decomposition, and resources and conservation.

Brooks, Paul. *Speaking for Nature: How Literary Naturalists from Henry Thoreau to Rachel Carson Have Shaped America.* Houghton Mifflin, 1980. America would be a much different place today had it not been for the contribution of these men and women, who felt an immense concern for nature and who also possessed the superb gift of being able to write about it. John Muir, John Wesley Powell, Theodore Roosevelt, and Aldo Leopold are among the writers discussed.

Cox, Barry; Moor, Peter D.; and Whitfield, Philip. *The Atlas of the Living World.* Houghton Mifflin, 1989. Patterns affecting living things—including Global Patterns, Habitat Patterns, and Niche Patterns,—are explored and developed with specific examples that come to life with lavish illustrations and photographs.

Dekkers, Midas. *The Nature Book: Discovering, Exploring, Observing, Experimenting with Plants and Animals at Home and Outdoors.* Macmillan Publishing Company, 1988. Help your students learn more about nature by using some of the simple or much more ambitious projects in this book.

DiSilvestro, Roger L. *The Endangered Kingdom: The Struggle to Save America's Wildlife.* Wiley Science Editions, 1989. The author provides a moving account of the plight of North American wildlife today, including the successes and failures of wildlife management policies. The relationship between wildlife management and hunters is explored. The introduction is filled with imagery of the former abundance of American wildlife before turning to the situation today, the result of the unthinking slaughter of such creatures as the great auk, the sea mink, and the passenger pigeon.

Fanning, Odom. *Opportunities in Environmental Careers.* VGM Career Horizons, 1991. A well-organized guide that lists the centers for environmental education opportunities, goes on to cover the four main setors of environmental careers: The Sciences of Living Things, Environmental Protection and Public Health, Natural Resources, and Land Use and Human Settlements. Job descriptions, education requirements, work locations, earnings, and job outlooks are all discussed.

Franck, Irene, and Brownstone, David. *The Green Encyclopedia.* Prentice Hall General Reference, 1992. The body of this reference contains entries describing animals, environmental concerns and catastrophes, activists, concepts, and organizations, along with a twenty-three-page listing of Endangered and Threatened Wildlife and Plants and a twenty-nine-page list of Superfund Sites.

Garber, Steven D. *The Urban Naturalist.* John Wiley & Sons, Inc., 1987. Garber introduces plants and animals to be found even in urban and suburban ecosystems, along with hundreds of interesting but little-known facts.

The Grolier World Encyclopedia of Endangered Species. The Grolier Educational Corporation, 1993. Ten volumes are organized alphabetically by geographic region. The index volume also contains both a listing of national parks throughout the world and an indispensible glossary.

Mitchell, John Hanson. *A Field Guide to Your Own Back Yard.* W. W. Norton & Company, 1985. Mitchell's very readable book shares information on the "wilderness" that exists in your own backyard. It also presents the ecological patterns and dynamics that occur in the smallest of natural settings. The author intersperses his own experiences with nature throughout the book, which is arranged according to season.

Reid, George K. *Pond Life.* Golden Press, 1967. A perfect guide to pond ecology, *Pond Life* discusses broad concepts as well as specific plants and animals. It is well illustrated.

Richardson, D'Arcy. *The Rainforests.* Smithmark Publishers, Inc., 1991. This gorgeous photographic tour emphasizes the interdependence of all the creatures and plant life found in rain forests. Also pictured are some of the results of rain forest destruction.

Rittner, Don. *Ecolinking: Everyone's Guide to Online Environmental Information.* Peachpit Press, Inc., 1992. Have instant access to environmental information. Find out how to link up your personal computer with major environmental information networks.

Tesar, Jenny. *Global Warming.* Facts on File, 1991. For a thorough, up-to-date overview of the many aspects of global warming, check this out. You may choose to read aloud some sections to the students.

A Zoo for All Seasons: The Smithsonian Animal World. W. W. Norton & Company, 1979. This is a beautifully photographed look at the National Zoo in Washington, D.C., its animal occupants, and its human caretakers. Related zoo and research issues are also covered.

10

Read-Alouds

Adams, Richard. *Watership Down.* Macmillan Publishing Co., Inc., 1972. One of the rabbits has prophesied imminent destruction to its warren, little knowing that humans are planning a housing development for that spot. When the rabbits ignore the warning, Fiver and his brother Hazel leave with a small group of believers to find a new home.

Earthworks Group. *50 Simple Things You Can Do to Save the Earth.* Earthworks Press, 1989. Threats to the environment are briefly described. The book then details fifty ways of helping the environment along with reasons for the importance of this help. Ideas are given for both the casual and the committed conservationist.

Facklam, Margery. *Wild Animals, Gentle Women.* Harcourt Brace Jovanovich, 1978. The professional work of eleven women who have made great contributions in the field of ethology, the study of an animal in its own habitat, are chronicled. Best known are Jane Goodall and Dian Fossey, but also included are Belle Benchley, former director of the San Diego Zoo, and Ruth Harkness, who brought the giant panda to worldwide attention.

Fleischman, Paul. *Joyful Noise: Poems for Two Voices.* Trumpet Club, 1988. With a partner—a student or another teacher—read aloud these duet poems about insects from this Newbery-Award winner.

George, Jean Craighead. *The Moon of the Mountain Lions.* HarperCollins Publishers, Inc., 1991. Though part of Craighead's The Thirteen Moons series, which features a different night-prowling animal for each of the lunar months, this volume is complete in itself. The descriptive prose is realistic and detailed, giving the listener a feel for the natural surroundings and daily routine of the mountain lion.

Hanson, Jeanne K., and Morrison, Deane. *Of Kinkajous, Capybaras, Horned Beetles, Seladangs, and the Oddest and Most Wonderful Mammals, Insects, Birds, and Plants of Our World.* HarperCollins Publishers, Inc., 1991. Help students to love and appreciate the diversity of the animal and plant world by reading aloud from this perfect browsing compendium, which contains descriptions of the most unique and unusual life forms on our planet.

Mowat, Farley. *Never Cry Wolf.* Atlantic Monthly Press, 1963. In this true, first-person account, a young, inexperienced biologist alone in the Arctic learns about himself and the habits of the wolves he has been sent to study.

Conserving America: A Four-Part Series. WQED-TV in association with The National Wildlife Federation, 1988/1990. Featuring inspiring portraits of concerned people working together for the environment and magnificent scenes of the landscapes and animals they are campaigning to protect, each PBS program includes a detailed workbook, with class exercises, field activities, and a bibliography. Titles include *Champions of Wildlife, The Challenge on the Coast, The Rivers,* and *The Wetlands.* 58 minutes each; videocassette.

Giants of the Sky. Robert Hartkopf, 1975. Chronicling the reestablishment of a population of the world's largest wild goose (previously thought to have been extinct since the 1930s), the film serves as a model of how to reverse the trend toward wildlife extinction. 16 minutes; film or videocassette.

Greenhouse Crisis: The American Response. Union of Concerned Scientists, 1988. This fast-paced video shows the direct relationship between energy consumption, the greenhouse effect, and global warming. There is a discussion guide included. 11 minutes; videocassette.

Never Cry Wolf. Walt Disney Productions, 1983. This feature film is based on Farley Mowat's book. 105 minutes; videocassette.

Our Forest. Sefra Films and SHB Media Center, 1992. The importance of forests as a biological system to mankind and nature is shown. 24 minutes; film or videocassette.

Our Fragile Earth. Beth Pike and Stephen Hudnell, 1991. Both programs in this two-part series are information packed and emphasize the connection between students' lives and the environment. Titles include "Recycling" (16 minutes) and "Energy Efficiency and Renewables" (22 minutes); videocassette.

Our Threatened Heritage. The National Wildlife Federation, 1988. Fifty acres of tropical rain forest are destroyed each minute, with serious ecological implications. This film presents an overview of the destruction of the rain forests and the action needed to stop this threat. 19 minutes; videocassette.

Spaceship Earth: Our Global Environment. Worldlink, 1990. Hosted by young people, this program emphasizes the interdependence of human, natural, and technological systems and examines three critical issues: deforestation, global warming, and ozone depletion. A teacher's guide is included. 25 minutes; videocassette.

Time for Survival. A National Audubon Production, 1980. Emphasizing that environmental stability depends on natural diversity, this documentary film is a visually exquisite lesson in the workings of ecological interdependence. 25 minutes; film or videocassette.

Treehouse. Earth Science Curriculum Project and Environmental Studies Project, 1969. Land use is explored in this unfinished story of the destruction of a boy's treehouse to make room for a housing development. Students can discuss the boy's possible course of action. 9 minutes; film or videocassette.

When the Spill Hit Homer. Edith Becker, 1991. See and hear a firsthand account of the devastating effect of the *Exxon Valdez* oil spill and the inadequate cleanup efforts in its aftermath. 27 minutes; videocassette.

Community/School

- State offices of the Environmental Protection Agency
- Local branches of environmental groups, such as the Audubon Society, Greenpeace, the Nature Conservancy, the Sierra Club, or the Wilderness Society
- Instructors in biology or environmental science from local universities
- Museums of natural science
- Public-information offices of local zoos and park systems
- Directors or naturalists of local forest preserves or animal reserves
- The Cousteau Society, 930 West Twenty-first Street, Norfolk, VA 23517
- Kids for Saving the Earth Club, P.O. Box 47247, Plymouth, MN 55447
- The Kids' Earthworks Group, Box 25,1400 Shattuck Avenue, Berkeley, CA 94709
- National Wildlife Federation, 1400 Sixteenth Street NW, Washington, DC 20036
- Student Conservation Association, Inc., P.O. Box 550, Charlestown, NH 03603

Concept Board

Remind the students that, as in previous units, **the class will keep a Concept Board to record new information learned about explorable concepts in this unit.** Designate an area of the classroom for the Concept Board. You may wish to begin the Concept Board after the students have had an opportunity to raise important questions about ecology and have some idea of where they are going with the unit. Throughout the reading of the unit, encourage the students to review the information on the Concept Board and explain how it changed or altered their original ideas about ecology.

Question Board

Designate an area for the Question Board. **Remind the students to post any questions they have as they proceed through the unit,** beginning with questions related to their original ideas and theories about ecology. Remember to periodically review the questions on the board, and add new questions or remove old questions when they have been answered or are no longer of interest. This review will provide an opportunity for students to rethink their original ideas about ecology and to clear up any misconceptions they had prior to reading the unit. Students should also be encouraged to use the Question Board to generate ideas to pursue in their independent research.

Both boards will allow the students to display and share their ideas and to see who has common questions and interests, a step toward building a community of scholars.

UNIT PREVIEW BY THE STUDENTS

Activating Prior Knowledge

- Have the students discuss what they already know about ecology and natural resources. Encourage the students to share their differences of opinion. This is an opportunity to determine whether they have any misconceptions about ecology. For example, some students may be unaware that ecology covers the relationship between plants, animals, and humans both in the wild and in populated areas. Students may also be unaware that specialists from many diverse subject areas—including botany, zoology, microbiology, chemistry, and even communications—contribute to the study of ecology. Students may not realize that ecology involves the protection, conservation, and restoration of wildlife.

- If the Concept Board has been started, add important information about the links between various environmental problems. For example, oil spills in the oceans harm sea animals. They also kill off algae, which provide oxygen for the atmosphere. Throughout the reading of the unit, refer to these statements on the Concept Board to help students add to their prior knowledge or clear up any misconceptions they might have had. It is important that students feel free to voice their opinions and discuss them. Misconceptions can be addressed as the students proceed through the unit.

- Using a topographical map, invite students to point out areas and locations they think are interesting and to tell why. Over the course of the unit, students will learn more about different habitats around the world. It will be helpful to keep a physical map or topographical map of the world easily accessible.

Setting Reading Goals and Expectations

- Have the students examine and discuss the unit title and the illustration that appears on pages 134–135.
- Have the students spend a few minutes browsing the selections in the unit. Encourage them to list on the chalkboard ecological issues they think they will be reading about in the unit.
- Let the students report on and discuss things they feel are important that they might not have noticed in their browsing and raise any questions they might have. Have the students post these questions on the Question Board.

Note: This initial browsing will provide the students with many research ideas. It is best for the students to generate problems or questions for research before they have had an opportunity to consult encyclopedias or other reference books. In this way, their ideas are more likely to be driven by their natural interests than by what they think will be easy to research.

- Tell the students that this unit has been designated as a **research unit.** Ecology is a **subject** for which there is **abundant factual material** and one that might naturally **pose intellectual problems or arouse curiosity.** The **Research Cycle** will provide a **systematic scientific framework** for inquiry that is driven by the students' wonderings and conjectures. Display the Research Cycle poster so that the students may refer to it during their explorations of ecology. It might be helpful for you to post notes on the poster showing where each research group is in the cycle as it proceeds in its exploration.

➤ Have the students complete page 80 in their Explorer's Notebook and share their responses.

- Have them suggest and record on the Question Board the questions they would like to pursue in their reading of the unit.

Explorer's Notebook, page 80

Knowledge About Ecology

These are some of my ideas about ecology before reading the unit.

_____
_____
_____
_____
_____
_____
_____
_____
_____
_____
_____

These are some things I would like to know about ecology.

_____
_____
_____
_____
_____
_____
_____
_____
_____
_____
_____
_____
_____

Reminder: I should read this page again when I get to the end of the unit to see how much I've learned about ecology.

Ecology/Unit 5

Copyright © 1995 Open Court Publishing Company

Learning Unit: Ecology

SELECTION	LINK TO THE UNIT CONCEPTS
▲ *Protecting Wildlife*, pages 182–213 nonfiction by Malcolm Penny	As active participants who destroy or rebuild habitats and kill or protect wildlife, humans play a vital role in any ecosystem.
POETRY pages 214–223 ● ■ The Passenger Pigeon, poem by Paul Fleischman, illustrated by Diane Blasius	Passenger pigeons became extinct within a period of seventy-five years because they were killed for game.
ON YOUR OWN ● Windows on Wildlife, pages 224–243 nonfiction by Ginny Johnston and Judy Cutchins IRA Teachers' Choice, 1990; Outstanding Science Trade Book for Children, 1990	Today's zoo and park officials support wildlife protection, breed endangered animals, and construct realistic habitats for the animals in their care.
FINE ART pages 244–247 *Dust Bowl*, Alexandre Hogue; *Meltdown Morning*, Neil Jenney; *Impalas grazing*, **Kenya**, Ernst Haas	Ecology can be expressed through visual arts.

● A Natural Force, pages 248–267
nonfiction from *Natural Fire: Its Ecology in Forests* by
   Laurence Pringle
New York Academy of Science, Children's Science Book Award
   Honorable Mention, 1985; ALA Best Science Book for
   Children, 1985; AAAS Best Science Book for Children, 1983
	In an ecosystem, wildlife depend upon natural occurences, such as fire, for survival.

ASSESSMENT
● ▲ *Saving the Peregrine Falcon*, pages 268–283
nonfiction by Caroline Arnold, photographs by
   Richard R. Hewett
SLJ Best Book of the Year, 1985; ALA Notable Book, 1985;
   Outstanding Science Trade Book for Children, 1985
	Introducing toxins into the environment can affect all of the animal species linked together in a food chain.

● ▲ *The Day They Parachuted Cats on Borneo*, pages 284–303 play by Charlotte Pomerantz, illustrated by Jose Aruego New York Times Outstanding Book of the Year, 1972	An action that affects the lives of one species in an ecosystem may, in turn, affect the lives of other species in that ecosystem.

Unit Wrap-Up, pages 304–305

● Award-winning authors and/or illustrators   ▲ Full-length trade books   ■ Dramatized on audiocassette

Exploration Through Research

SELECTION-BASED MINILESSONS		RESEARCH
TEACHER'S GUIDE	TEACHER TOOLBOX	
Writing Paragraphs Stating Opinions Note Taking	Casual Indicators, Using Captions	Problem Phase 1 Problem Phase 2 Protecting Wildlife and Their Habitats Ecological Problems and Solutions
Providing Comparisons	Elaboration Through Providing Comparison and Contrast, Genre—Poetry	Conjecture Phase Catalog of Endangered or Extinct Species
Students choose a writer's craft to focus on.	Elaboration Through Providing Examples, Phrases, Using Commas in a Series	Needs and Plans Phase 1 Needs and Plans Phase 2 The Dietary Needs of Wildlife Habitats Around the World Specialists in the Field of Ecology
Defining Unfamiliar Terms Using the *Reader's Guide to Periodical Literature*	Elaboration Through Giving Reasons or Causes, Elaboration Through Providing Specific Facts	Research Cycle Trees, Plants, and Flowers That Grow in a Forest
Choice of a writer's craft to study is part of assessment.		Research Cycle Urban Wildlife
Providing Multiple Effects for a Single Cause	Genre—Play/Drama; Providing Problems and Solutions; Using Parentheses, Dashes, and Ellipses	Research Cycle Creating a Food Web
		Sharing of group knowledge, insights, and ideas

Assessment available for this unit includes Teacher's Observation Log, Self-Assessment Questionaire, Concept Connections, Portfolios, and separate Comprehension, Essay and Writing, and Research assessments.

Protecting Wildlife

1 READING THE SELECTION

About the Selection

In *Protecting Wildlife,* Malcolm Penny examines the plight of wild animals in a world where humans, out of ignorance or greed, are invading, polluting, and destroying nature, pushing wildlife into smaller and remoter habitats. Not only are the habitats threatened, but the animals themselves are threatened by those who hunt and kill for sport or profit and by those who introduce pesticides and other toxins into the environment. Yet, according to Penny, humans can educate themselves about ways to reverse the destruction that has occurred and in so doing preserve and protect our precious lands and the even more precious wildlife that inhabits them.

Link to the Unit Concepts

In *Protecting Wildlife,* pages 136–157, Penny explains the ways in which human beings are a part of the ecology of a place. As invaders and destroyers, we pose a threat to all wildlife. Yet, as environmentalists, we are also wildlife's best hope for surviving.

After reading the selection, students may ask themselves how their lives and attitudes would change if they lived within a wildlife habitat. They may also ask whether humans have greater rights to the land, air, and water than do plants and animals.

About the Author

Malcolm Penny is a graduate in zoology from Bristol University, England. Penny has been a producer of television wildlife documentaries, and his many expeditions have given him an acute awareness of the problems that animals face in the modern world. A prolific author on natural history, Penny has written an eleven-volume series entitled the Animal Kingdom. In volumes such as *Animal Camouflage* and

LESSON OVERVIEW

Protecting Wildlife by Malcolm Penny, pages 136–157

READING THE SELECTION

Materials

Student anthology, pp. 136–157
Explorer's Notebook, p. 81
Assessment Master 1

FYI

Learning Framework Cards
- Setting Reading Goals and Expectations, 1A
- Exploring Through Discussion, 2

Teacher Tool Card
- Classroom Supports: Writer's Notebook, 122

READING WITH A WRITER'S EYE

Minilessons

Writer's Craft: Writing Paragraphs
Writer's Craft: Stating Opinions

Materials

Reading/Writing Connection, pp. 35–36
Reproducible Master 15

FYI

Teacher Tool Card
- Spelling and Vocabulary:Building Vocabulary, 77

Options for Instruction

Writer's Craft: Causal Indicators
Writer's Craft: Using Captions
(Use Teacher Tool Cards listed below.)

GUIDED AND INDEPENDENT EXPLORATION

Minilesson

Research Aid: Note Taking

Materials

Explorer's Notebook, pp. 84–90
Home/School Connection 35–36
Reproducible Masters 46–51

FYI

Learning Framework Cards
- Exploring Through Research, 4
- Problem Phase 1 and 2, 4A
- Reading Roundtable, 6
- Writing Seminar, 8

Optional Materials from Student Toolbox

Tradebook Connection Cards

Cross-curricular Activity Cards
- 14 Art—Sketching Habitats
- 14 Science—Tracking Wildlife
- 15 Science—Alligators of the Everglades
- 22 Social Studies—Making a Map of the World's Rain Forests

Independent Workshop

Student Tool Cards
- Writer's Craft/Reading: Writing Paragraphs, 24
- Writer's Craft/Reading: Writing to Persuade, 33
- Writer's Craft/Reading: Showing Cause and Effect, 31
- Writer's Craft/Reading: Using and Understanding Captions, 36
- Study and Research: Note Taking, 111

FYI

Teacher Tool Cards
- Writer's Craft/Reading: Writing Paragraphs, 24
- Writer's Craft/Reading: Persuasive Writing, 33
- Writer's Craft/Reading: Causal Indicators, 31
- Writer's Craft/Reading: Using and Understanding Captions, 36
- Study and Research: Note Taking, 111
- Classroom Supports: Collaborative Groups, 119

NOTES

Asterisks (*) throughout the lesson indicate learning frameworks. Learning Framework Cards and Teacher Tool Cards can be found in the Teacher Toolbox

Endangered Animals, he looks at animal behavior around the world. Penny directly explores ecological issues in several of his books, including *Pollution and Conservation* and *Protecting Wildlife.*

Share information about the author with the students. You might also display a topographical map or globe so that they can become familiar with the locations of the habitats mentioned in the selection.

*

Activating Prior Knowledge

Ask the students what they know about wildlife and wildlife habitats. Invite them to share any information they wish. Students who are familiar with certain wildlife habitats might point out their locations on a map.

Setting Reading Goals and Expectations

Explain to the students that before they read, they will **set reading goals and expectations.** To do this, they will **browse the selection** and **use the clues/problems/wondering procedure.** On the chalkboard under the headings clues, problems, and wonderings, write in brief note form the observations the students generate during browsing. For example, students might list the genre of the selection under clues; they might list unfamiliar words under problems; and they might note any questions that arise during browsing under wonderings. Students will return to these observations after reading. For a review of the **browsing** procedure, see **Learning Framework Card 1A, Setting Reading Goals and Expectations.**

> **TEACHING TIP** Before reading an expository text, students should scan the title and the subheads to familiarize themselves with the topics discussed in the selection and the order of presentation.

Recommendations for Reading the Selection

Ask the students how they would like to read the selection. The selection is long and is divided into two parts. It also contains much new information and many new words. You might suggest that students begin reading aloud and then continue reading silently once they feel they can handle the content and the vocabulary. As they read silently, the students may find it helpful to paraphrase passages containing new ideas or information.

If the students elect to **read orally,** you should **refer to the think-aloud prompts that are provided with the page miniatures.** Instead of or in addition to using these prompts, encourage the students to provide their own think-alouds while reading.

This would also be a good selection for **responding** to text **by visualizing** and **telling feelings** while reading aloud. Model these responses and invite the students to do the same.

If the students elect to **read silently,** have them **discuss problems, reactions,** and **strategies** after reading. Let them know, however, that they can raise their hands at any time during reading to ask questions or to identify problems for discussion with the group.

Note: *Protecting Wildlife* has been divided into two parts in case the students are not able to finish reading the selection in one class period. The second part begins on page 150 and is indicated by a large initial capital letter. Notice that the Research Cycle in part 3 of this lesson, Guided and Independent Exploration, is also divided into two parts.

About the
Reading
Strategies

Protecting Wildlife contains a lot of factual information and words that may be new to many students. **Summing up** is one strategy that may help the students better understand what they are reading. Remind the students that summing up will help them focus on the most important information in the selection, and that it is an especially effective strategy to use when reading long articles. Remind the students to use the **clarifying strategies** whenever they encounter unfamiliar words or names. If **decoding, applying context clues,** and **rereading the passage** do not help, students should **check the Glossary or a dictionary** for the meaning of a word.

Think-Aloud Prompts
for Use in Oral Reading

The think-aloud prompts are placed where the students may want to use strategies to help them understand the text better. These are merely suggestions. Remind the students to refer to the strategy posters and to use any strategy that will help them make sense of what they are reading. Encourage the students to collaborate with classmates when confronted with reading difficulties.

THINK ALOUD PROMPTS

These prompts may be used as guides to promote cognitive and responsive reading.

PROTECTING WILDLIFE
Malcolm Penny

Indris survive only in a few remaining patches of Madagascar's rain forest.
© O. Langrand/Bruce Coleman Limited

INTRODUCTION

It is dawn in the rain forest of Madagascar. An unearthly howl arises from among the trees. It is joined by another, then several more. Soon a chorus is ringing through the forest, making a weird harmony in the morning mist.

≥ 136 ≤

The singers are lemurs, a primitive group of animals related to monkeys. This particular species, called the indri, regularly greets the dawn by calling from the borders of its territory. Soon the indris will begin to feed, pulling branches to their mouths, biting off leaves and fruit.

They are tall, slender animals, covered in dense fur—brown, with silver-gray arms and legs. They move between the trees in long, athletic leaps in an upright position. When they drop to the ground to cross a clearing, they hop on both feet together, with their arms outstretched.

Some of the females have babies riding on their backs. Indri females bear their single babies only every three years: indris are very slow breeders. They are also very rare.

Some time after dawn, other voices are heard in the forest. Soon, there is the sound of chopping, and smoke drifts through the clearings. The local human inhabitants are preparing a new field to grow crops. They have already removed the larger trees for timber and fuel; now they are felling and burning the undergrowth to clear the land. This technique is called slash and burn.

The new vegetable plot will last only for two or three years, before the soil becomes sandy and loses all its fertility. Then the people will move on to clear a new area of forest. There are similar situations all over the world, where protecting wildlife has become an urgent problem.

The Malagasy people brought this style of agriculture with them when they came to Madagascar from Malaysia about 1,500 years ago. It worked well in the ancient forests they left behind: fields they abandoned soon recovered, going back to forest within a few years. The forests of Madagascar

≥ 137 ≤

Where once hills were forest covered, only
dry grasslands are left.
© David Curl/Oxford Scientific Films from Earth Scenes

cannot recover in the same way, and after centuries of this method of agriculture there is little left of them—just bare hills where nothing but cattle can flourish.

The result is that the people are hungry, as the dusty soil is swept from the hills by heavy rain; and the indri, along with the other species of lemurs, are practically homeless. A few small groups of them survive in carefully protected patches of forest.

HABITAT DESTRUCTION

The destruction of the forests of Madagascar is typical of the loss of wildlife habitat that is going on all over the world. The areas most at risk are rain forests.

The richness of rain forests. Rain forests are moist, warm forests that thrive in tropical parts of South and Central America, Africa, and Southeast Asia. They have existed for

≥ 138 ≤

tens of millions of years and contain the richest diversity of plants and animals to be found on earth. Many of the world's best-known animals live in rain forests: chimpanzees, gorillas, gibbons, and most monkey species; tigers and jaguars; nocturnal bush babies and lorises; and the world's most beautiful birds, from hummingbirds and parrots to birds of paradise. In addition, there are endless kinds of snakes and tree frogs, plus millions of insects—far too many to be identified.

When rain forests are destroyed, their unique wildlife is also doomed. For the past thirty years, rain forests have been cut down to supply the timber and farmland that are badly

Clouds and mist are trapped by trees in the rain forest of Sabah in Malaysia.
In this way, the rain forest creates its own climate.
© Doug Wechsler/Earth Scenes

1 In the introduction Penny gives his first example of an animal whose home and well-being has been adversely affected by the behavior of a people. Students might **think about** how the farming practices of the Malagasy people affect the indri and **how this information makes the students feel** and why.

needed by the local people. However, the rate of destruction has greatly <u>accelerated</u> with modern technology. Already about half of the world's rain forests have been cleared. Unless effective action is taken, all our rain forests will have disappeared by early next century. With them will go their marvelous plant and animal life.

The dangers of erosion. A rain forest is sometimes called "a desert covered with trees." While the trees are standing, their roots hold the soil in place, where it is fed by the leaves and other debris falling from above. When the trees are gone, the soil has nothing to feed it. It becomes loose and sandy, and will soon be eroded, washed away by the heavy tropical rainstorms.

Erosion is one of the most serious threats to all farmland, especially in the tropics. As the rainwater carries the soil away, it forms channels that get deeper and deeper until they reach the underlying rock. The soil is carried down rivers until they reach the sea. As they flow more slowly, the rivers drop the soil in the form of silt. This chokes the riverbed and increases the danger of floods.

The loss of grasslands. Most <u>habitat</u> destruction arises from the need for farmland to feed the world's

Floods caused by deforestation in the foothills of the Himalayas make people homeless in Bangladesh, far downstream.
AP/Wide World

≥ 140 ≤

Bison once roamed the prairies of North America in vast numbers. Today only a few are left: these grazing bison are protected in Yellowstone National Park, Wyoming.
© Jeff Foott/Bruce Coleman Limited

rapidly increasing human population. Grasslands may be destroyed as a wildlife habitat when they are fenced off and sprayed with weedkillers, in order to raise cattle and grow corn. On the American prairies, for example, large grazing animals, such as deer and buffalo, are no longer able to move freely in search of food. Smaller animals, such as insects, and reptiles and birds that feed on them, are made homeless when the "weeds" are killed.

Other habitats are being destroyed as well. In many parts of the world, wetlands, such as ponds and marshes, are drained to make farmland or commercial forestry plantations. Rivers are <u>dredged</u>, improving the drainage of the

≥ 141 ≤

Wetland plants like marsh rose-mallow have become
much rarer, as most of the damp meadows in which they grow have
been drained to make farmland.

© Jeff Lepore/Photo Researchers

surrounding land, but at the same time destroying the habitat of creatures that live among reedbeds and in shallow streams. Land reclamation, especially beside estuaries, has made farmland out of what were once the feeding and roosting places of millions of birds.

It is vital that sufficient crops are grown to feed people. In developing countries it is hard to grow enough food crops, while in Europe there is a glut of food, leading to surplus grain and milk. Excess food in the U.S. is stored, sold to other countries, or fed to livestock. Many environmentalists agree that, in areas of overproduction, it would be better to reduce farmland and leave areas to become natural grassland and woodland, for wild animals.

②

⤵ *142* ⤶

HUNTING AND KILLING

Humans have always killed other animals to eat. In a few places this is still part of everyday life: Indians in the Amazon jungles, Bushmen in Botswana, and some tribes of Inuit in North America and the Commonwealth of Independent States still hunt in the traditional way for food and raw materials.

Most people no longer have to hunt for food. Nevertheless, hunting still causes the death of many millions of wild animals every year. Many animals are killed by farmers, to protect their crops and their livestock. These "enemies" of the farmer range in size from elephants and tigers to beetles and greenflies.

Most of the wild animals killed every year are fish. Because the demand for fish rises as the human population increases, some fisheries are in danger of running out. The fishery around South Georgia, one of the Falkland islands in the South Atlantic Ocean, is the latest area to be affected by overfishing.

Puffins, shags, and kitiwakes nest safely on remote cliffs, but their numbers in
the Shetland Islands have been severely reduced by a loss of the sand eels.

© John Markham/Bruce Coleman Limited

② The students have read about the destruction of several kinds of habitats. They may find it helpful to **sum up** the ways in which these habitats have been destroyed and the effects of the destruction on the wildlife that lived in them. They could list the information on the chalkboard for later reference.

Sand eels—small fish that are collected by trawling in shallow northern waters—have suffered badly from overfishing. This has affected the large bird populations that depend on them for food during their breeding season. Arctic terns, skuas, and puffins in the Shetland Islands, to the north of Scotland, have all fallen sharply in numbers. In 1981, there were 54,000 kittiwakes in the Shetlands; by 1988, there were only a few hundred left.

Hunting for sport. There is another kind of unnecessary hunting. Many people, all over the world, enjoy hunting and killing wild animals as a sport. Not very long ago, it was considered very brave and sporting to go out into the bush of Africa, or the jungles of India, to shoot lions, elephants, or tigers. Today, most people consider this type of hunting barbaric and destructive, and it has almost completely stopped. All the same, especially in North America, the shooting of wild animals is big business, with a whole industry devoted to making and selling guns and special clothing for hunters. The number of animals that may be killed is carefully controlled by the authorities.

Victims of our vanity. The very worst kind of killing is poaching: hunting protected animals because they are worth a lot of money. Spotted cats are protected all over the world, but because there are still some people who like to wear their beautiful skins as coats, there are others who will hunt and kill the rarest leopard or cheetah to supply the market.

In the Far East, rhinoceros horn is regarded as a powerful medicine. In one Arab country, North Yemen, it is used to make the handles of the ceremonial daggers worn by adult

≥ *144* ≤

Surprisingly, there are still people who think it is chic to wear the skins of spotted cats, mainly because they are very expensive. Until such people change their minds, animals like the Asian snow leopard will continue to be very rare because they are hunted for their coats.
© Michael Dick/Animals Animals

men. These people are prepared to pay enormous sums of money for rhino horns. A North Yemeni ceremonial dagger with a rhino horn handle can cost over $50,000. Chinese pharmacists can sell powdered or flaked horn for as much as $5,500 per pound. Knowing this, it is easy to understand why the black rhino is hunted so extensively in Africa north of the Zambezi River.

3

≥ *145* ≤

3 In this section the author discusses some hunting and fishing practices that are detrimental to animal and fish populations. Students may **sum up** what these practices are and how they are destructive. They may also wonder what can be done to persuade people to change their behavior.

POLLUTION

The oldest and most common form of air pollution is smoke. Coal fires and factory chimneys fill the air with soot, blackening buildings and causing thick fog in damp weather. Now burning forests add to the pollution.

All burning fuel releases carbon dioxide. The layer of carbon dioxide in the earth's atmosphere is becoming thicker, so that it traps heat that would otherwise escape into space. This is known as the "greenhouse effect," and scientists suspect it is causing the earth to become warmer. There is a danger that the polar icecaps might start to melt, causing the sea level to rise. If this happens, it will <u>alter</u> the climate,

The steam produced by this power station in the U.S. is harmless, but the fumes from the fossil fuels burned at the station cause acid rain.

© Robert Carr/Bruce Coleman Limited

especially the distribution of rainfall. Wildlife as well as people will be in great danger. If the climate changes abruptly, they will be unable to adapt quickly enough to survive.

The fumes from burning fossil fuels contain oxides of sulfur and nitrogen, which react with damp air to make sulfuric and nitric acids. Often, the fumes drift downwind until they come to a place where the air is damp; then they form acids, and fall as rain. Acid rain can kill fish in lakes and rivers, and has been blamed for causing the death of trees over large areas of the northern U.S., Canada, Europe, and Scandinavia.

The atmosphere at risk. A very dangerous form of air pollution is caused by CFCs, or chlorofluorocarbons, which are used in some <u>aerosols</u>, refrigerators, and <u>polystyrene</u> fast-food cartons. They drift up into the ozone layer, far above the earth's surface, and break down the <u>ozone</u> molecules. The ozone layer protects the earth from the harmful effects of sunlight. As it becomes thinner, more ultraviolet light will come through. This will help to raise the earth's temperature, already elevated because of the greenhouse effect. It will also increase the risk of skin cancer among people. Its effect on animals and plants is hard to predict.

The radioactive fuel used in nuclear power stations gives off radiation that is extremely dangerous, if it escapes into the air. Even small amounts can damage human cells, causing cancer, and interfering with the development of unborn babies. The effects of radiation on wildlife are not known, but it seems most likely that they will be very similar to those on human beings. Certainly, large numbers of sheep in Britain, and reindeer in Lapland, are still radioactive following the 1986 accident at the Chernobyl nuclear power station in the

4 The term *greenhouse effect* is nicely explained. However, students may not understand why the word *greenhouse* is used to describe this phenomenon of global warming. If students wonder about this term, explain that—as in a greenhouse—plants take in oxygen and release carbon dioxide; the carbon dioxide collects inside the greenhouse and has a warming effect on the inside temperature. Students should then be able to make the connection between what happens when carbon dioxide collects in a greenhouse and what happens when carbon dioxide is trapped in the earth's atmosphere.

Commonwealth of Independent States. This released a dangerous level of radioactivity into the atmosphere, which drifted over much of Europe.

An ocean of chemicals. Water pollution, like air pollution, is made more serious now by the numbers of people involved, and the types of harmful substances that they produce.

Oil pollution has very serious effects on wildlife. It poisons fish and coastal animals like crabs and shellfish, and also clogs the feathers of seabirds. When the birds preen the oil from their feathers, it poisons them. Most oil spills are accidental, but some are deliberate, for example when a tanker captain washes out his tanks at sea. Such actions are illegal, but they save time and money, and they can be carried out far at sea, out of sight of land.

Oil spilled into the sea kills thousands of birds every year. Only a few are cleaned, like these penguins in South Africa.
© Gerald Cubitt/Bruce Coleman Limited

The greatest threat to the marine environment is no longer oil pollution. Industrial chemicals have been invented that are far more poisonous and long-lasting. Among them is a group known as PCBs (polychlorinated biphenyls), which are used for various industrial processes. These very strong chemicals can be destroyed by burning, but because this is expensive,

≥ 148 ≤

they are most often buried in dumps on land, or allowed to pass down rivers into the sea.

PCBs are directly poisonous, but they also weaken the immune system of many animals, so that they become <u>vulnerable</u> to diseases which they would normally resist. The seal plague in the North Sea and the Baltic, first noticed in 1988, was probably made much worse because many of the seals were affected by PCBs.

Poisonous <u>pesticides</u>. Wild animals and plants are also harmed by pesticides and weedkillers, because these substances do not only kill the pests they are intended to, but other creatures, too. The strong chemicals contained in pesticides have harmed many insects, like butterflies, while weedkillers have killed off plants on which caterpillars feed.

Pesticides can harm many animals because they are passed along the food chain. For example, a field mouse may eat grains of wheat treated with pesticide. The pesticide chemicals are not used up, but stored in the mouse's body.

Harvest mice flourish in fields of wheat. They suffered in the past from the use of pesticides, and from modern harvesting machinery, which cuts the crop very close to the ground and destroys their nests. Now it appears their population is recovering.
© Sean Morris/Oxford Scientific Films from Earth Scenes

≥ 149 ≤

5 If the mouse is caught by a barn owl, the harmful chemicals will be passed on to the owl. Since barn owls catch many mice, they will in time receive a poisonous dose of pesticides. The <u>accumulated</u> chemicals harm their eggs and the owlets that hatch from them.

6

RESERVES AND NATIONAL PARKS

The idea of protecting large areas of wild land was first put into practice in the U.S. in 1872, when Yellowstone National Park was opened. Since then, national parks have been founded in almost every country in the world.

When Yellowstone was founded, wildlife in the Rocky Mountains was not in any danger. The park was set up to protect the extraordinary landscape of geysers and sulfur springs, so that visitors could marvel at it forever. The fact that it was full of wildlife, including buffalo, grizzly bears, and herds of elk, was a secondary consideration.

Later, national parks were established to protect particular species of animal, usually from overhunting. The first of these was in Italy, when in 1922 the king gave his hunting preserve at Gran Paradiso to the nation, to protect the <u>alpine ibex</u>. Since then, most parks have been established to protect the whole environment, including all its animals and plants.

The future of national parks. For a national park to be a success, there must be a balance between the needs of the local people and those of the animals. A good example is Royal Chitwan National Park, in Nepal. It is partly forest,

≋ 150 ≋

Ibex were one of the first animals to be given protection in a national park. The national park of Switzerland not only protects ibex but also provides a safe home for many other alpine animals and plants.
© Stephen Meyers/Animals Animals

and partly elephant grass over 6 feet tall. Tigers and one-horned rhinoceroses live there, together with two different species of crocodile. However, the park is surrounded by villages, whose people need firewood from the forest and grass from the plain, to build houses and feed cattle.

To save arguments, the local people are allowed into the park at certain times of year to collect grass. The park staff collect dead wood from the forest, and driftwood from the rivers, for the villagers to use as fuel. The villagers are encouraged to plant "firewood forests," around the edge of the park, to provide a renewable fuel supply. The park is safe, and the people no longer feel it is taking land that they need.

One of the oldest and largest national parks in the U.S., the Florida Everglades, is suffering from a similar conflict.

≋ 151 ≋

5 The students have read about several kinds of pollution. Some students may find it helpful to **sum up** at this time. Students might also **think about how the information in the first part of the selection makes them feel** and why.

Note: The first part of the selection ends on page 150. This is a good place to stop reading if the selection cannot be finished during this class period.

6 If they read the first part of *Protecting Wildlife* during another class period, have the students **sum up** the important information before they begin the second part of the article.

The millions of water birds that live in the Everglades National Park
include spoonbills, egrets, and herons.
© Erwin & Peggy Bauer/Bruce Coleman Limited

The park relies on a steady flow of clean water from the
north. Unfortunately, the water is also needed for agriculture. More and more people are moving to Florida and it is
necessary to drain land to build houses, and to provide people with water. This drainage removes some of the water
from the edges of the park. The water that comes from the
farmland is often polluted with fertilizer. This polluted water
enters the tidal swamp, causing an excessive growth of some
green algae. Eventually the algae will cover the water,
removing all oxygen from it. If the problem is not solved
soon, the Everglades will be lost, with all its wonderful
scenery, and the millions of superb birds, snakes, and alligators that live there.

The Everglades is considered so important that it has
been declared a World Heritage Site, a matter of concern to
the whole world. Some other World Heritage Sites are
Mount Everest, the Grand Canyon, the Serengeti in Africa,

152

and Lake Ichkeul in Tunisia, an important wetland used by
migrant birds.

National parks are vital to the whole world, because they
will be the only way for future generations to know what the
world looked like before farmland and cities took over.
Many of them are also the last home of animals that used to
be common.

In Africa, the only hope for the black rhinoceros is to be
protected in national parks, with armed guards to keep the
poachers away. Biologists have discovered ways of making
rhinoceroses breed more quickly, by adjusting the numbers
in each park.

7

A black rhinoceros mother and her calf have been rescued from
farmland, transported by truck, and released into Etosha National Park,
Namibia. Such efforts are often necessary to protect endangered
rhinoceroses from poachers.
© Jen & Des Bartlett/Survival Anglia

7 Students may find it helpful to **sum up** the information about national parks and forest preserves.
They may also **make connections** between what
they have learned in the first part of the article
and what they are reading in the second part.

CHANGING OUR BEHAVIOR.

The best hope for the black rhino is for people to change their beliefs about the value of its horn, so that the trade in daggers and medicines collapses. Many other changes in beliefs and behavior will be necessary if the natural world is to survive for much longer.

The program to persuade villagers in Nepal to plant trees for firewood is being carried out, not only on the plains near Royal Chitwan National Park, but also in the foothills of the Himalayas. As more trees are planted there, the land will become more stable, instead of being washed away down the rivers, and there will be less danger of flooding in faraway Bangladesh.

Pollution can be reduced as well, for example, by discouraging people from using pesticides and artificial fertilizers on farmland. Today a growing number of people are realizing that soil can be enriched, and pests controlled, by organic methods. Such methods are less suited to large-scale farming, but farmers can use less-harmful chemicals.

The use of CFCs has already been greatly reduced, and there are moves to ban the manufacture and use of most of the PCBs, which have caused so much damage to the environment in the short time since they were invented.

Scientists are working hard to find other ways of providing energy. "Alternative energy sources," as they are called, include wind and water power, and solar energy. Finding alternative energy sources is important for two reasons: they will reduce the pollution from burning fossil fuels, and they will postpone the time when the fossil fuels are used up.

◁ 154 ▷

Saving the rain forests. The destruction of rain forests can also be reduced, by changing the way in which people clear the land, and by using the land better when it has been cleared. The main problem with rain forest soil is that it is very soft, made up of leaves that have fallen over thousands of years. If the trees are cleared with heavy machinery, this fragile soil is squashed flat. It quickly becomes waterlogged, and bad for growing plants. If the trees are cleared by people on foot, the soil survives much better.

To help the forests and their animals to survive, it would be better if the clearings were much smaller, leaving "corridors" of forest between them. The animals would still have somewhere to live, and the trees would still be there to produce seeds. Thus the clearings would recover more quickly when the soil was no longer suitable for growing crops.

There are plans to slow down the destruction of rain forests in countries as far apart as Mexico and Madagascar,

This patch of Brazilian rain forest was the home of the rare golden lion tamarin.
© Dr. Nigel Smith/Animals Animals

but at present they are on a small scale. It is important that more areas of rain forest be protected, while there are still some worthwhile areas of forest left.

WHAT YOU CAN DO

There are many organizations that exist to safeguard the environment. By joining, and supporting a local group, you can let the authorities know that you, too, are concerned with what is happening to the natural world.

Conservation does not have to be a public matter: it can be personal, too. On a walk in the country, for example, a good motto is "Look, don't touch." In some nature reserves there may be a sign that says "Take only photographs, leave only footprints." If everyone followed this advice, there would be much less damage to the plants and animals that make the countryside such a marvelous place.

Making room for wildlife. If you have a garden or yard, you can make your own nature reserve. To encourage butterflies, for example, you could plant a shrub called Buddleia or "butterfly bush." Butterflies love the nectar from it sweet-scented flower spikes.

You can encourage many butterflies to breed, too, by growing various plants and flowers. Among cultivated annuals, plants that grow for only one season, are alyssum, marigolds, and verbena. Some choices of cultivated perennials, plants that grow for several years, include butterfly weed, daisies, phlox, and primroses. Wild, prickly thistle or nettles, are also good choices. Avoid using chemical weedkillers.

≥ 156 ≤

In the suburbs of Australian towns, where they are not under pressure from farmers, gray kangaroos can become very tame.
© Mickey Gibson/Animals Animals

In the countryside, ditches and ponds are often drained, or become polluted by fertilizers and weedkillers. By creating a pond in your garden, you can provide an alternative home for frogs and many freshwater insects, including beautiful dragonflies.

You can also help wild birds in winter. Birdfeeders and bird baths are especially valuable to birds in winter, when food is scarce and water may be frozen. Once birds know that food and water are available in your garden, or on the terrace of your apartment, many different species may come to feed there. When small birds visit a garden in winter, they help to control pests by eating the eggs of aphids that lie under the bark of trees.

If we successfully conserve the rich wild life we still have now, the world will be a much nicer place in the future. **8**

≥ 157 ≤

8 The selection ends with several concrete suggestions for protecting wildlife, wildlife habitats, and the environment. Students may **sum up** this information and think about how the article *Protecting Wildlife* has made them feel.

Discussing Strategy Use
Encourage the students to share the strategies they used while reading *Protecting Wildlife* and discuss how these strategies helped them understand the selection. Ask the students to share their thoughts about the subheads in the article. Ask those who found the subheads helpful to explain how.

EXPLORING THROUGH DISCUSSION

Reflecting on the Selection
Whole-Group Discussion

The whole group discusses the selection and any **personal thoughts, reactions, problems,** or **questions** that it raises. During this time, students may also be invited to **return** to the **clues, problems, and wonderings** they noted on the board during browsing to determine whether the clues were borne out by the selection, whether and how their problems were solved, and whether their wonderings were answered or deserve further discussion and exploration. Avoid treating the students' ideas like a list to be discussed and eliminated in a linear fashion. Instead, let the **students decide which items deserve further discussion.** To stimulate discussion, the **students** can **ask** one another the kinds of **questions that good readers ask themselves** about a text: **What did I find interesting? What is important here? What was difficult to understand? Why would someone want to read this?** Your own participation in the discussion might take the form of expressing and modeling your reactions to the article. It is important for the students to see you as a contributing member of the group.

To emphasize that you are part of the group, actively **participate in the handing-off process:** Raise your hand to be called on by the last speaker when you have a contribution to make. Point out unusual or interesting insights verbalized by the students so that these insights can be recognized and discussed. As the year progresses, the **students will take more and more responsibility for the discussions** of the selections. The handing-off process is a good way to get them to take on this responsibility. For a review of **Exploring through Discussion**, see **Learning Framework Card 2.**

Assessment

In a successful discussion, it should not be necessary for you to ask questions to assess the students' understanding of the text. If necessary, however, engage the students in a discussion **to determine whether they have grasped the following ideas:**

- how the needs of an increasing human population threaten the survival of wildlife and its habitats
- how the behaviors of humans are destroying wildlife and the environment
- the ways in which the needs of wildlife and the needs of humans are being balanced through reserves and national parks

Response Journal

Students may wish to record their personal responses to the selection. For a review of the response journal, see **Teacher Tool Card 122, Writer's Notebook.**

Exploring Concepts Within the Selection
Small-Group Discussion

Remind the students to check the Concept Board and the Question Board to determine whether their original perceptions about ecology have changed as a result of their reading this selection. Circulate among the groups to see whether any of the groups have difficulty connecting the information in this selection with the unit concepts.

ASSESSMENT TIP This may be a good opportunity to observe students working in groups and to mark observations in your Teacher's Observation Log.

Sharing Ideas
About Explorable
Concepts

Have the groups **report their ideas** and **discuss them** with the rest of the class. It is crucial that the students' ideas determine this discussion.

- The students may mention that the problems of habitat destruction and environmental pollution can be solved when humans begin caring about wildlife and changing their farming, hunting, fishing, and industrial practices.
- The students may notice that protecting wildlife is something that everyone can do by educating herself or himself to the needs of wildlife and living in a way that would help satisfy those needs.

As these ideas and others are stated, have the students **add them to** the **Question Board** or the **Concept Board.**

Have the students examine the fine-art pieces on pages 182–183 of the student anthology and briefly discuss Ernst Haas's photograph of impalas, Alexandre Hogue's painting *Dust Bowl,* and Neil Jenney's painting *Meltdown Morning.* The students may wish to express their thoughts and feelings about these works and to suggest connections between the fine-art pieces and the article they have just read.

Recording Ideas

As they complete the above discussions, ask the students to **sum up what they have learned from their conversations and to tell how they might use this information** in further explorations. Any special information or insights may be recorded on the **Concept Board.** Any further questions that they would like to think about, pursue, or investigate may be recorded on the **Question Board.** They may want to discuss the progress that has been made on their questions. They may also want to cross out any questions that no longer warrant consideration.

➤ After discussion, students should individually record their ideas on page 81 of their Explorer's Notebook.

STEPS TOWARD INDEPEND-ENCE By now the students should be taking charge of the commentary during and after reading the selection, with little or no teacher intervention. If this is not happening, invite the students to talk more often, and reinforce their efforts.

Fine Art

Evaluating Discussions

Recording Concept Information

As I read each selection, this is what I added to my understanding of ecology.

Protecting Wildlife by Malcolm Penny

_____
_____
_____
_____
_____
_____
_____
_____
_____
_____
_____

"The Passenger Pigeon" by Paul Fleischman

_____
_____
_____
_____
_____
_____
_____
_____
_____
_____
_____
_____

Copyright © 1995 Open Court Publishing Company

Unit 5/Ecology   EN 81

Explorer's Notebook, page 81

2 READING WITH A WRITER'S EYE

MINILESSONS

**Writer's Craft:
Writing
Paragraphs**

Ask students to talk about anything they have learned about writing paragraphs and to give examples they can remember from their reading or writing. Remind the students that a paragraph **contains one or more sentences and deals with a single thought or topic.** Point out that usually one sentence within the paragraph states the main thought. This sentence, often placed at the beginning, is called the **topic sentence,** or stated main idea. Sometimes the main idea is not stated but implied. In this case, the reader has to infer the main idea by reading the whole paragraph. Remind the students that a paragraph begins on a new, usually indented line. A paragraph may include a description, an idea and examples, a series of steps, or a set of related actions or facts.

**Selective Reading:
Focus on Writing
Paragraphs**

Most of the paragraphs in Malcolm Penny's *Protecting Wildlife* contain topic sentences. In the paragraph on page 136, a topic sentence is followed by details about dawn in the rain forest of Madagascar. Other examples of paragraphs with topic sentences can be found on the following pages:

*Selection-Based
Practice*

- page 139, paragraph 1: "When rain forests are destroyed, their unique wildlife is also doomed."
- page 140, paragraph 2: "Erosion is one of the most serious threats to all farmland, especially in the tropics."

Two examples of paragraphs with implied main ideas can be found on the following pages:

- page 137, paragraph 2: how the indri look and behave
- page 137, paragraph 4: how humans (the Malagasy) destroy the rain forest

Have the students find examples of paragraphs with topic sentences and paragraphs in which the main idea is implied. In their examples of paragraphs with topic sentences, encourage the students to describe how the sentences in the paragraph are related. For example, the paragraphs may contain a topic sentence followed by a **description, reasons or examples,** or a **series of steps.** Here are two examples from the selection:

- page 141, paragraph 1: topic sentence followed by description
- page 143, paragraph 1: topic sentence followed by examples

Independent Practice: Writing Paragraphs

▶ For additional practice in recognizing the elements of a paragraph, have the students work in small groups to discuss and complete Reading/Writing Connection, page 35.

Reading/Writing Connection, page 35

Protecting Wildlife

Writing Paragraphs

Find examples of paragraphs in *Protecting Wildlife* or in any other selections you have read in which the author elaborates on a main idea by giving a description, reasons, examples, or a series of steps.

Title: _____ Page: _____ Paragraph: _____

What is the main idea of the paragraph? _____

_____

_____

Is the main idea stated in a topic sentence or implied? _____

How are the sentences related? _____

_____

_____

_____

Title: _____ Page: _____ Paragraph: _____

What is the main idea of the paragraph? _____

_____

_____

Is the main idea stated in a topic sentence or implied? _____

How are the sentences related? _____

_____

_____

Use this page as a guide when you want to write good, clear paragraphs.

Name

Copyright © 1995 Open Court Publishing Company

Unit 5/Ecology

Writing Paragraphs

R/WC 35

Writer's Craft:
Stating Opinions

Ask the students to talk about anything they have learned about stating opinions and to give any examples they can remember from their reading or writing. Point out that, in this selection, Malcolm Penny **states his opinions in order to clarify the purpose of his writing. He supports his opinions with reasons and examples.** Remind the students that opinions are often stated in the same way that facts are stated, but unlike facts, opinions cannot be proven. Nevertheless, opinions can be supported with reasons and examples.

Point out that statements of opinion often include **judgment words,** such as *good, bad, unfortunate,* or *best.* Judgment words place a value on ideas, situations, people, or things. For example, on page 137, paragraph 6, the author claims that the Malagasy style of agriculture worked *well* in the ancient forests of Malaysia. Then he backs up his opinion with facts.

Selective Reading:
Focus on Stating
Opinions

Have the students find passages that contain statements of opinion. Ask volunteers to read a statement of opinion, identify the word or words that indicate that it is an opinion, and tell how the opinion is supported—whether by giving reasons or by giving examples. Some examples can be found on the following pages:

- page 142, paragraph 1: "It is *vital* that sufficient crops are grown to feed people," by giving examples
- page 144, paragraph 3: "The very *worst* kind of killing is poaching . . . ," by giving reasons

Selection-Based Practice

Independent Practice:
Stating Opinions

❯ For additional practice in recognizing statements of opinion in writing, have the students work in small groups to discuss and complete Reading/Writing Connection, page 36.

WRITING

Linking Reading
to Writing

Remind the students that **in expository pieces** it is very **important to write clearly defined paragraphs and to support opinions.** Encourage the students to look through their **writing folders** for pieces of their own writing that they could improve by adding facts, examples, and other supporting details to opinion statements. Remind the students to make sure that in each paragraph the sentences relate to one idea. Also remind them that sometimes the topic of a paragraph can be implied rather than specifically stated. When the students have had sufficient time to choose and revise a piece of writing, invite volunteers to read their original and rewritten versions and to explain how the changes they made improved the quality of their writing.

✳ Writing Process

Be sure that the students concentrate on an appropriate phase of the writing process in any writing on which they are currently working. If they are revising a piece of writing to include opinion statements, suggest that they conference with their peers to get additional input. If your class is using the optional Writer's Handbook, refer the students to it for help with their writing.

WRITER'S NOTEBOOK TIP
Have the students review all sections of their Writer's Notebook from time to time. Encourage them to keep their notebook updated and to refresh their memories about its contents.

Stating Opinions

Protecting Wildlife

Find examples in *Protecting Wildlife* or in any other selections you have read in which the author states opinions.

Title: _____ Page: _____

Opinion: _____

_____

Word or words that indicate it is an opinion: _____

_____

How the opinion is supported: _____

_____

Title: _____ Page: _____

Opinion: _____

_____

Word or words that indicate it is an opinion: _____

_____

How the opinion is supported: _____

_____

Title: _____ Page: _____

Opinion: _____

_____

Word or words that indicate it is an opinion: _____

_____

How the opinion is supported: _____

_____

Stating Opinions

36 R/WC   Ecology/Unit 5

Name

Copyright © 1995 Open Court Publishing Company

Reading/Writing Connection, page 36

Vocabulary Exploration

Word: _____

Why you chose this word: _____

_____

Definition as used in the selection: _____

_____

Other meanings: _____

_____

Any antonyms you can think of: _____

Any synonyms you can think of: _____

_____

Where else have you found this word? _____

_____

How might you use this word in your writing? _____

_____

Your sentence using the word: _____

_____

_____

Remember to use this word in speaking as well as in writing.

Writer's Notebook: Personal Dictionary   RM 15

Name

Copyright © 1995 Open Court Publishing Company

Reproducible Master 15

VOCABULARY

❯ Words and phrases related to ecology that you might discuss include *habitat, erosion, grasslands, wetlands, trawling, poaching, greenhouse effect, atmosphere, ozone layer, radioactive fuel, CFCs, PCBs, pesticides, World Heritage Site, alternative energy sources,* and *fossil fuels.* Have copies of Vocabulary Exploration form, Reproducible Master 15, available so that students can add these or any other words and phrases from the selection to the Personal Dictionary section of their Writer's Notebook. Some students may wish to share the words they have selected. For additional opportunities to build vocabulary, see **Teacher Tool Card 77.**

3 GUIDED AND INDEPENDENT EXPLORATION

EXPLORING CONCEPTS BEYOND THE TEXT

Guided Exploration

The following activities do not have to be completed within the days devoted to this lesson:

• With the students, locate books and articles about recycling, organic farming, selective logging, and alternative energy sources. Share these resources and encourage the students to discuss how each measure helps protect wildlife. Allow the students to organize an ecology display in one corner of the classroom. Ideas for what to include should be their own. If, however, they need help getting started, you might suggest some of the following items: recycling bins, samples of organic foods, seedlings of redwood trees or of other commonly logged trees, and solar-powered objects such as calculators.

- Engage the students in a discussion of how we can minimize our negative impact on the environment by being ecology minded. The students may suggest ways of behaving responsibly toward the environment, such as buying organic foods, which are grown without pesticides; buying wood products from tree farms instead of old-growth forests; avoiding products with a lot of packaging; recycling whenever possible; and using solar collectors or windmills to help power our homes.

- Some students might be interested in adding a piece of persuasive writing to their writing folders. This piece could be a letter to a newspaper suggesting steps that the community could take to minimize its adverse impact on the environment.

- Modern life is full of dilemmas that result from the conflicting needs of wildlife and humans. In the Northwest, for example, citizens are trying to resolve a conflict between the spotted owl's need for its habitat and the loggers need to fell the trees in that habitat. Students may find and collect newspaper and magazine articles about dilemmas concerning the opposing needs of wildlife and humans. These articles could be posted on a current-events bulletin board or pasted on a poster board or in a scrapbook and shared with classmates.

❯ Tell the students that although wildlife continues to be threatened, ecologists are making great progress in protecting animals and wildlife habitats. As they read this selection and others in the unit, the students will record in their Explorer's Notebook, page 88, some of the ways in which ecologists protect wildlife. Provide time for students to share their findings with their classmates.

❯ Point out to the students that many of the problems that threaten wildlife have understandable causes and workable remedies. Tell them that as they read the selections in the unit and begin their research, they will record these problems, their causes, and possible solutions in their Explorer's Notebook, on pages 84–85. Provide time for the students to share their findings with their classmates.

❯ Distribute Home/School Connection 35–36, a bibliography of books and videos about various ecological subjects that the students and their families can explore together.

Explain to the students that since this unit has been designated a research unit, they will produce and publish in some way the results of

Ecological Problems and Solutions

Most ecological problems that threaten wildlife, its habitats, and the environment in general have specific causes and workable solutions. As you read and do research for this unit, record ecological problems, their causes, and some of the remedies that have been proposed.

Problem: _____

Cause(s): _____

Solution(s): _____

Problem: _____

Cause(s): _____

Solution(s): _____

Problem: _____

Cause(s): _____

Solution(s): _____

84 EN   Ecology/Unit 5

Explorer's Notebook, page 84

Problem: _____

Cause(s): _____

Solution(s): _____

Problem: _____

Cause(s): _____

Solution(s): _____

Problem: _____

Cause(s): _____

Solution(s): _____

Problem: _____

Cause(s): _____

Solution(s): _____

Unit 5/Ecology   EN 85

Explorer's Notebook, page 85

Protecting Wildlife and Its Habitats

Ecologists have helped protect many forms of wildlife and its habitats. As you read and do research for this unit, record examples of wildlife or of habitats that have been protected and the methods that have been used to protect each one.

Animal	Habitat	Methods Used to Protect
Black rhinoceros		moved to national parks; learn ways to increase their breeding cycles

88 EN   Ecology/Unit 5

Explorer's Notebook, page 88

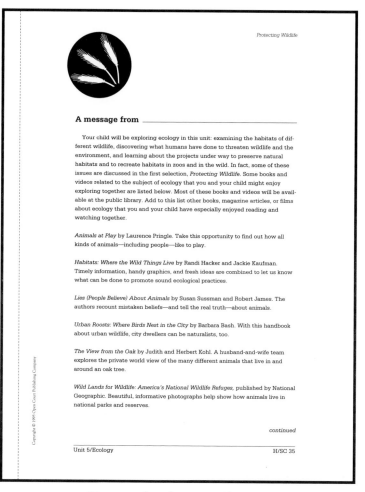

A message from _____

Your child will be exploring ecology in this unit: examining the habitats of different wildlife, discovering what humans have done to threaten wildlife and the environment, and learning about the projects under way to preserve natural habitats and to recreate habitats in zoos and in the wild. In fact, some of these issues are discussed in the first selection, *Protecting Wildlife*. Some books and videos related to the subject of ecology that you and your child might enjoy exploring together are listed below. Most of these books and videos will be available at the public library. Add to this list other books, magazine articles, or films about ecology that you and your child have especially enjoyed reading and watching together.

Animals at Play by Laurence Pringle. Take this opportunity to find out how all kinds of animals—including people—like to play.

Habitats: Where the Wild Things Live by Randi Hacker and Jackie Kaufman. Timely information, handy graphics, and fresh ideas are combined to let us know what can be done to promote sound ecological practices.

Lies (People Believe) About Animals by Susan Sussman and Robert James. The authors recount mistaken beliefs—and tell the real truth—about animals.

Urban Roosts: Where Birds Nest in the City by Barbara Bash. With this handbook about urban wildlife, city dwellers can be naturalists, too.

The View from the Oak by Judith and Herbert Kohl. A husband-and-wife team explores the private world view of the many different animals that live in and around an oak tree.

Wild Lands for Wildlife: America's National Wildlife Refuges, published by National Geographic. Beautiful, informative photographs help show how animals live in national parks and reserves.

continued

Unit 5/Ecology　　　　　　　　　　　　　　　　　　　　H/SC 35

Home/School Connection 35

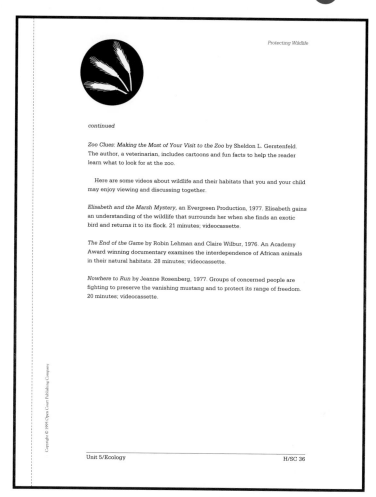

continued

Zoo Clues: Making the Most of Your Visit to the Zoo by Sheldon L. Gerstenfeld. The author, a veterinarian, includes cartoons and fun facts to help the reader learn what to look for at the zoo.

Here are some videos about wildlife and their habitats that you and your child may enjoy viewing and discussing together.

Elisabeth and the Marsh Mystery, an Evergreen Production, 1977. Elisabeth gains an understanding of the wildlife that surrounds her when she finds an exotic bird and returns it to its flock. 21 minutes; videocassette.

The End of the Game by Robin Lehman and Claire Wilbur, 1976. An Academy Award winning documentary examines the interdependence of African animals in their natural habitats. 28 minutes; videocassette.

Nowhere to Run by Jeanne Rosenberg, 1977. Groups of concerned people are fighting to preserve the vanishing mustang and to protect its range of freedom. 20 minutes; videocassette.

Unit 5/Ecology　　　　　　　　　　　　　　　　　　　　H/SC 36

Home/School Connection 36

their exploration of and research on ecology. They are free to decide what problems or questions to explore, whom to work with, and how to present their finished products. They may publish a piece of writing, produce a poster, write and perform a play, make a video, or in some other manner present the written results of their exploration and research. They may work with partners or in small groups, as they wish. For additional information on the Research Cycle, see **Learning Framework Card 4, Exploring Through Research.**

> Distribute copies of Reproducible Masters 46–51 so that the students will have this **bibliography** available when they begin their research. Remind them also to consult the bibliography on pages 234–235 of the student anthology. The students should **examine the bibliographies for possible research topics.**

Research Cycle: Problem Phase 1

Note: If your class read the selection in two parts, complete Problem Phase 1 after the first part and Problem Phase 2 after the second part.

Outline the research-project schedule for the students: how long the project in the Ecology unit is expected to take, how much time will be available for research, when the first presentation will be due. This schedule will partly determine the size of problems that students should be encouraged to work on. It is suggested that the projects be completed

＊Exploring Through Research

Bibliography

Books related to ecology are listed below. You may use these sources and others as you explore the concepts of ecology.

Notes

Acid Rain by Eileen Lucas. This book explains what makes acid rain; why it is so harmful to lakes, farms, and forests; and how sulfur dioxide harms the very air we breathe.

Animals and the New Zoos by Patricia Curtis. A comparison of outdated zoos and refurbished zoos shows the great progress being made to accommodate the natural needs of even the most endangered animals.

Careers in Conservation by Ada and Frank Graham. Profiles of thirteen people in a variety of conservation careers illustrate how much is being done to improve and protect the environment.

Cars: An Environmental Challenge by Terri Willis and Wallace B. Black. The machine that has revolutionized the world may also revolutionize our future because of the pollution it brings. Read about the harmful substances produced by cars, their ill effects, and a variety of possible solutions to the problems.

Cartons, Cans, and Orange Peels: Where Does Your Garbage Go? by Joanna Foster. Landfilling, burning, recycling, and composting are some of the different ways of disposing of the 1,300 pounds of garbage that each American produces every year.

Name

Copyright © 1995 Open Court Publishing Company

RM 46 Unit 5/Ecology

Reproducible Master 46

Bibliography *continued*

Notes

Chains, Webs and Pyramids: The Flow of Energy in Nature by Laurence Pringle and Jan Adkins. Nutrients are passed from one animal to another in a complex chain of energy use, explained here in a manner suitable for a beginner in environmental science.

Coastal Rescue: Preserving Our Seashores by Christina G. Miller and Louise A. Berry. The natural and man-made problems that face our seashores are concisely explained.

Disappearing Wetlands by Helen J. Challand. In this book you'll find out about marshes, swamps, and bogs that, contrary to what most people think, are not wastelands but areas with a rich ecology.

Eight Words for Thirsty: A Story of Environmental Action by Ann E. Sigford. Learn about deserts, the life forms that have adapted to their dry, harsh surroundings, and the endangered pupfish and squawfish.

Endangered Habitats (Our Fragile Planet series) by Jenny Tesar. Threatened areas of the world are highlighted to show what they need to survive and what is currently being done to save them.

Endangered Species by Sunni Bloyd. Read about species that have become extinct, about others saved from extinction, and about the overall causes of extinction.

Name

Copyright © 1995 Open Court Publishing Company

Unit 5/Ecology RM 47

Reproducible Master 47

Bibliography *continued*

Notes

The Endangered World: Using and Understanding Maps, edited by Scott E. Morris. Each region of the earth is highlighted with text, maps, graphs, and illustrations showing the major ecological threats to that locale.

Environmental America (series) by D. J. Herda. The books in this series examine the state of the environment in six major regions of the United States—Northeastern, North Central, Northwestern, Southeastern, South Central, and Southwestern.

The Greenhouse Effect: Life on a Warmer Planet by Rebecca L. Johnson. Scientists predict that, due to the greenhouse effect, life on earth is faced with the possibility of great changes in climate.

Jungle Rescue: Saving the New World Tropical Rain Forests by Christina G. Miller annd Louise A. Berry. The encroachment of development that is causing the destruction of the tropical rain forest ecosystem with its wealth of natural resources has worldwide consequences and merits worldwide action.

Land Use and Abuse by Terri Willis. Read how centuries of abuse and of destructive use of land through mining, pollution, logging, and poor farming practices are contributing to worldwide environmental problems and to starvation for the residents of some areas.

Oil Spills by Jean F. Blashfield and Wallace B. Black. The devastating ecological effects of an oil spill and suggestions for coping with them are outlined.

Name

Copyright © 1995 Open Court Publishing Company

RM 48 Unit 5/Ecology

Reproducible Master 48

Bibliography *continued*

Notes

The Ozone Layer (Earth at Risk series) by Marshall Fisher. We've all heard about the ozone layer, but here is an explanation of precisely what it is, why it is so important, and how it is threatened.

Plants in Danger by Edward R. Ricciuti. Find out about earth's vanishing species of plants—the giant, the strange, and the beautiful—and why they are threatened.

Pollution: The Land We Live On by Claire Jones, Steve J. Gadler, and Paul H. Engstrom. These authors offer a thorough discussion both of the causes of pollution and of the problems created by it.

Predator! by Bruce Brooks. The balance of nature in the food chain is maintained by the ongoing battle between the prey with its defenses and the predator with its specialized tools for hunting.

Rachel Carson (American Women of Achievement series) by Marty Jezer. Scientist-writer Rachel Carson is the author of one of the most influential books on the environment, *Silent Spring*, which unveiled the dangers of the irresponsible use of pesticides.

Rads, Ergs, and Cheeseburgers: The Kids' Guide to Energy and the Environment by Bill Yanda. Katy and Mark, guided by Ergon, the personification of energy, go on an adventure that helps them understand energy wastefulness, energy sources, and the dangers of radiation.

Name

Copyright © 1995 Open Court Publishing Company

Unit 5/Ecology RM 49

Reproducible Master 49

Bibliography *continued*

Notes

Restoring Our Earth by Laurence Pringle. Scientists and volunteers are working to restore land that has been destroyed by misuse and mismanagement.

A Sand County Almanac by Aldo Leopold. Timeless essays of a nature lover are enhanced with superb photographs of a famous area along the Wisconsin River, which includes the Sand County farm rebuilt by the author and his family.

Tall Grass and Trouble by Ann E. Sigford. The author describes the once-vast prairies of North America, shows they've been destroyed, and outlines what steps must be taken to restore them.

Then There Were None by Charles E. Roth. It is natural for species to change or become extinct over time, but the "life expectancy" of a bird species used to be two million years and of a mammal species 600,000 years. Human activities have greatly shortened those spans, forcing many bird and mammal species into extinction.

Toxic Cops by D. J. Arneson. After exploring earth's various pollution threats, find out about America's Environmental Enforcement police, the men and women who bring to justice those responsible for our "planetary pollution."

Vanishing Habitats by Noel Simon. A compact overview is devoted to each of the earth's many different wildlife habitats, describing them and discussing the main ecological problems each faces.

Name

Copyright © 1995 Open Court Publishing Company

RM 50   Unit 5/Ecology

Reproducible Master 50

Bibliography *continued*

Notes

Waste War (Operation Earth series) by Jeremy Leggett. Specific types of garbage are treated in specific ways.

Wilderness Preservation (Earth at Risk series) by Richard Amdur. Wilderness—what is it, where is it, what laws govern it, and what are the challenges facing it?

Wildlife, Making a Comeback: How Humans Are Helping by Judith E. Rinard. People are helping some species on the brink of extinction to reestablish themselves.

Add the titles of books and articles that you find.

- _____
- _____
- _____
- _____
- _____
- _____
- _____
- _____

Name

Copyright © 1995 Open Court Publishing Company

Unit 5/Ecology   RM 51

Reproducible Master 51

BIBLIOGRAPHY

And Then There Was One: The Mysteries of Extinction by Margery Facklam. This book examines why some animals—like the dinosaur, passenger pigeon, and saddleback tortoise—have disappeared from the face of the earth.

Blackface Stallion by Helen Griffiths. Griffiths tells the story of a wild mustang foal named Blackface—how he grew up and how he faced the challenges from an often harsh environment and from the other horses in his herd.

Fight Against Albatross Two by Colin Thiele. Read this book to discover how an oil drilling accident affects the wildlife and citizens of Ripple Bay on the southern coast of Australia.

The Glass Ark: The Story of Biosphere 2 by Linnea Gentry and Karen Liptak. Four men and women and 4,000 species of plants and animals live together in a self-contained structure in the Arizona desert.

234

Home: How Animals Find Comfort and Safety by Laurence Pringle. Why do animals choose the homes they do? Pringle describes animals' relationships with other things, both living and nonliving.

The Living Planet by David Attenborough. This is the story of the earth's surface and how it became colonized by plants and animals.

Moon Dark by Patricia Wrightson. In Wrightson's fantasy about a community of animals living in the Australian wilds, something has happened to upset the balance of nature. Can anything be done?

Who Really Killed Cock Robin? An Ecological Mystery by Jean Craighead George. The citizens of Saddleboro have a mystery to solve: what imbalance in the environment killed Cock Robin? Can you solve the mystery?

235

Project Planning

Use the calendar to help you schedule your Ecology unit project. Fill in the dates. Make sure that you mark any days you know you will not be able to work on the project. Then choose your starting date and the date on which

Sunday	Monday	Tuesday	Wednesday

Copyright © 1995 Open Court Publishing Company

you hope to finish the project. You may also find it helpful to mark the dates on which you hope to finish different parts of the project. Record what you accomplish each day.

Thursday	Friday	Saturday

Copyright © 1995 Open Court Publishing Company

Explorer's Notebook, page 86

Explorer's Notebook, page 87

by the time you finish the unit itself. Remind the students, however, that some projects may take longer. Additional information on pacing is provided on **Learning Framework Card 4, Exploring Through Research.**

❯ Have the students enter key dates, such as the starting and ending dates you have selected, on the calendar in their Explorer's Notebook, pages 86–87. Encourage them to record on the calendar what they accomplish each day. This will help the students monitor their progress and enable you to assist them in managing their time. Explain to the students that the type of research they will conduct will take many weeks and that it will require them to make important decisions about managing their time. Suggest that they record dates on the calendar in pencil, since schedules often need to be revised.

Have the students **examine their original questions and ideas about ecology** on the Question Board and the Concept Board. Encourage them to **use these initial questions and theories about the explorable concepts to suggest research ideas.** Have them **post on the Question Board any additional questions** raised by *Protecting Wildlife.* Remind them that they can post questions at any time throughout the unit. Encourage the students to consult the board periodically to **answer posted questions, to look for ideas for exploration, or to find out who has similar interests so that they can exchange ideas and**

Research Cycle: Problem Phase 1

A good problem to research:

_____
_____
_____
_____
_____
_____
_____

Why this is an interesting research problem:

_____
_____
_____
_____
_____
_____
_____

Some other questions about this problem:

_____
_____
_____
_____
_____
_____
_____
_____

Copyright © 1995 Open Court Publishing Company

Unit 5/Ecology   EN 89

Explorer's Notebook, page 89

information. Remember that you should also post your own questions from time to time.

To start the Problem Phase of the Research Cycle, conduct a free-floating discussion of problems and questions of interest to the students. Explain to the students that a good research problem or question not only will require them to consult multiple sources but will add to the group's knowledge of ecology, be engaging, and generate further questions.

❯ Help the students think about problems related to ecology that they might like to research. Generate a list of these on the chalkboard. Model for the students how to turn their research ideas into good research problems, especially if their initial responses are topics rather than problems. For additional information on modeling the formation of good research problems or questions, see **Learning Framework Card 4A, Problem Phase 1 and 2.** When the discussion is completed, assign page 89 of their Explorer's Notebook to be completed during Independent Workshop.

TEACHING TIP By this point in the year, the students should be initiating most of the research questions. If their questions are leaning toward ones that might be answered in a single encyclopedia entry, help the students upgrade their questions to more interesting and difficult ones that would be worthy of more extensive investigation.

Research Cycle: Problem Phase 2

By this point each student should have completed the Problem Phase 1 page in their Explorer's Notebook. The next step is for students to discuss one another's proposed problems, which will lead to the creation of research groups to work on selected problems.

* Exploring Through Research

Research Cycle: Problem Phase 2

My research group's problem:

_____
_____
_____
_____
_____
_____

What our research will contribute to the rest of the class:

_____
_____
_____
_____
_____
_____

Some other questions about this problem:

_____
_____
_____
_____
_____
_____
_____

90 EN   Ecology/Unit 5

Explorer's Notebook, page 90

Have students present their proposed problems, along with reasons for their choices, allowing open discussion of how promising and interesting various proposed problems are. Remind the students that a good problem cannot be answered by examining one encyclopedia entry but must add to the group's understanding of the explorable concepts. This constant emphasis on group knowledge building will help set a clear purpose for the students' research. The students are not to reproduce information aimlessly, but are to find information that will help them and their classmates increase their understanding of ecology.

To aid the formation of groups, students may record their problems on the chalkboard. During the discussion, arrows may be drawn to link related problems. For example, students interested in how humans have polluted the environment and those interested in how hunting for sport or profit has affected certain animal species might form a group to research the behaviors that endanger the lives of birds and animals. For additional information on helping the students tackle more challenging and puzzling problems, see **Learning Framework Card 4A, Problem Phase 1 and 2.**

Final groups should be constituted in the way you find best for your class—by self-selection, by assignment on the basis of common interests, or by some combination of methods. For information on forming **collaborative groups,** see **Teacher Tool Card 119.**

TEACHING TIP If the students progress through the Research Cycle faster than expected, proceed to the next phase of the cycle. This will provide additional time for gathering materials, collecting information, and sharing findings.

❯ Assign the next steps for students to carry out during Independent Workshop: Each group will meet to agree on and state the problem that it will work on and what that work will contribute to the rest of the class's knowledge. Have them record their statements in the Explorer's Notebook, page 90.

MINILESSON

Research Aid: Note Taking

Remind the students that good note-taking skills will help improve their performance as readers, researchers, and writers. Ask them if they remember what good note taking involves: **deciding what ideas and facts are the most important to remember and evaluating those ideas and relating them to their own experience or knowledge.**

Guided Practice: Note Taking

Review the following guidelines for good note taking with the students. Answer any questions they have about taking notes. Together with the class, use the guidelines to take notes on the material under the subhead Habitat Destruction on pages 138–142 of the selection.

Guidelines for Taking Notes

- Note the main ideas or points that an author is making. Paraphrasing this information in your own words will ensure that you understand the text.
- Organize your notes so that main ideas are easy to find. This may mean leaving a line space between a main idea and the important facts you list below it, or it may mean highlighting the main ideas with a colored marker.
- Note the most important facts about a main idea. Remember that not all facts are equally important.
- Use spacing well. Some people like to indent the facts under a main idea so that both are easily distinguished. Some people like to leave plenty of space in the left or right margin of their papers so that they can ask questions about the text or add references to related material in other parts of an article.
- Review your notes and add information from other sources you have seen and from your own experience.
- Include in your notes your opinions about noted information and how it fits in with other information you have gathered on the subject.

Independent Practice: Note Taking

Review with the students Explorer's Notebook, page 36, about note-taking tips. Have the students choose another passage in the selection and take notes. After they have taken notes, they might share with their classmates the ideas and facts they wrote down, the format they chose for taking notes, whether they added personal comments and other information to their notes, and whether they are satisfied with the results. **Remind the students that they will be continuing to do research on some aspect of ecology and that effective note taking is an essential part of doing research.**

✳ INDEPENDENT WORKSHOP
Building a Community of Scholars

Student-Directed Reading, Writing, and Discussion

Remind the students that they will devote the first part of each day's Independent Workshop to **collaborative work with peers on their unit projects.** The remainder of Independent Workshop time can be spent on options of their choice.

Resources The students will need as many resources as possible to help them choose a topic and research it. Provide as many of the suggested resources as you can. If necessary, provide students with additional library time to look for resources and to share their findings with their groups.

Research Cycle: Problem Phase 1 Students should complete the Problem Phase 1 page in their Explorer's Notebook. Try to get them to elaborate on their reasons for wanting to research their stated problems. They should go beyond simple expressions of interest or liking and indicate what is puzzling, important, potentially informative, and so forth, about their chosen problems. If they are having difficulties generating problems or questions for research, have them browse the Cross-curricular Activity Cards in the Student Toolbox for ideas. If they are having difficulty turning their ideas into questions or problems for research, see **Learning Framework Card 4A** for helpful hints on focusing their ideas. The following questions might be helpful: *What is it about the topic that really interests you? Can you turn that into a question?*

Research Cycle: Problem Phase 2 Each newly formed research group should meet to agree on a precise statement of its research problem, the nature of the expected research contribution, and a list of related questions (which may help later in assigning individual roles). These should be entered in their Explorer's Notebook on page 90. Remind the students to add any new information to their planning calendars on pages 86–87 of their Explorer's Notebook.

Additional Opportunities for Independent Reading, Writing, and Cross-curricular Activities

✻ Reading Roundtable

Encourage the students to look for books about protecting wildlife, such as *Saving Our Wildlife* by Laurence Pringle or *The Green Lifestyle Handbook,* edited by Jeremy Rifkin. In both books the interdependence between plants and animals is examined. Also encourage the students to read other books by Malcolm Penny, many of which deal with endangered species.

Model good reading habits for the students by doing your own free reading at this time whenever possible. Also, share with the students information from any interesting and informative books that you have read on the subject of ecology. For additional ideas for **Reading Roundtable**, see **Learning Framework Card 6.**

✻ Writing Seminar

It is important for the students to keep in mind that writing is a recursive process. They should always be looking for ways to revise and improve their writing. For additional ideas about **Writing Seminar**, see **Learning Framework Card 8.**

Portfolio

Remind the students to think about choosing pieces of writing to put into their portfolios.

Cross-curricular Activity Cards

The following Cross-curricular Activity Cards in the Student Toolbox are appropriate for this selection:

- 14 Art—Sketching Habitats
- 14 Science—Tracking Wildlife
- 15 Science—Alligators of the Everglades
- 22 Social Studies—Making a Map of the World's Rain Forests

Making a Map of the World's Rain Forests
Use after *Protecting Wildlife*
22 Social Studies

Alligators of the Everglades
Use after *Protecting Wildlife*
15 Science

Tracking Wildlife
Use after *Protecting Wildlife* or *Saving the Peregrine Falcon*
14 Science

Sketching Habitats
Use after *Protecting Wildlife* or "Windows on Wildlife"
14 Art

One way of taking part of the wilderness home with you without disturbing the wildlife or its environment is to sketch the nests or habitats of animals and the animals themselves if you catch sight of them. Find a quiet area in a park, a forest preserve, or even a zoo. Sit quietly until the animals forget that you are present. Then sketch the animals, their activities, and their surroundings. Share your drawings with the class. *Drawings are an important source of information.*

Additional Opportunities for Solving Learning Problems

Tutorial

Invite students to discuss with you any subject or area in which they need extra help. Work with individuals or small groups who need help in a particular area. Some students may benefit from giving or receiving peer tutoring. Have tutoring pairs refer to the appropriate Student Tool Cards to guide their work. The following aids are available in the Teacher Toolbox for your convenience:

- Writer's Craft/Reading: Writing Paragraphs, Teacher Tool Card 24
- Writer's Craft/Reading: Persuasive Writing, Teacher Tool Card 33
- Writer's Craft/Reading: Causal Indicators, Teacher Tool Card 31
- Writer's Craft/Reading: Using Captions, Teacher Tool Card 36
- Study and Research: Note Taking, Teacher Tool Card 111

Poetry
The Passenger Pigeon

1 READING THE POEM
INFORMATION FOR THE TEACHER

About the Poem

This poem for two voices is the imagined narrative of a passenger pigeon, the last remaining member of his species. He speaks from his cage in the Cincinnati Zoo and with great pathos reminisces about the magnificent flocks of pigeons that once covered the continent but that have now completely vanished from the earth, their numbers extinguished forever. Fleischman's use of the first person underscores the desolation of this lonely passenger pigeon, who died in his cage in 1914.

Link to the Unit Concepts

"The Passenger Pigeon," pages 158–159, illustrates the bond between wildlife and its environment and the extent to which human behavior can affect the survival of a species. Though passenger pigeons seemed too numerous ever to be endangered, they became extinct largely because hunters killed so many of them.

About the Poet

The son of noted children's author Sid Fleischman, Paul Fleischman traces his interest in the sound of words back to his childhood when his father "tried out" chapters from his stories by reading them aloud to his family. Paul also credits his "ear" for language to the fact that all the Fleischmans played musical instruments. Fleischman says he would be a composer "in an instant" and give up writing books—if he had the talent.

I Am Phoenix, the book from which "The Passenger Pigeon" has been excerpted, has been declared a "groundbreaking collection"—two-voiced, read-aloud poems that intertwine their alternating lefthand and right-hand readers "as in a musical duet." The entire book celebrates various birds.

Whether in stories or in poetry, Fleischman's manner of writing is constant. "If I can please my readers' ears while telling my tale, such that a listener who knew no English would enjoy it read aloud purely for its music," he told *Horn Book,* "so much the better."

LESSON OVERVIEW

"The Passenger Pigeon" by Paul Fleischman, pages 158–159

READING THE SELECTION

Materials
Student anthology, pp. 158–159
Explorer's Notebook, p. 81

READING WITH A WRITER'S EYE

Minilesson
Writer's Craft: Providing Comparisons

Materials
Reading/Writing Connection, p. 37
Reproducible Master 15

FYI
Teacher Tool Cards
- Writer's Craft/Reading: Genre—
  Poetry, 10
- Spelling and Vocabulary: Building
  Vocabulary, 77

GUIDED AND INDEPENDENT EXPLORATION

Materials
Explorer's Notebook, pp. 91–92

FYI
Learning Framework Card
- Conjecture Phase, 4B

Independent Workshop

**Optional Materials from
Student Toolbox**

Tradebook Connection Cards

Cross-curricular Activity Cards
- 23 Social Studies—Creating a Time
  Line
- 3 Math—Counting Pigeons

Student Tool Cards
- Writer's Craft/Reading: Comparing
  and Contrasting, 37
- Writer's Craft/Reading: Reading and
  Writing Poetry, 10

FYI
Teacher Tool Cards
- Writer's Craft/Reading: Elaboration
  Through Providing Comparison and
  Contrast, 37
- Writer's Craft/Reading: Genre—
  Poetry, 10

Asterisks (*) throughout the lesson indicate learning frameworks. Learning Framework Cards and Teacher Tool Cards can be found in the Teacher Toolbox

INFORMATION FOR THE STUDENT

Share with the students the information about Paul Fleischman that you think will interest them. You might point out that Fleischman meant this poem to be read by two people or by two choruses of voices, as is apparent by the layout of the poem on the page. This type of reading, he hoped, would produce the effect of a vocal duet.

✳ COGNITIVE AND RESPONSIVE READING

Setting Reading Goals and Expectations

Have the students quickly **browse the poem,** noticing the title, form, and illustration. Encourage comments concerning what the poem may be about and how it might relate to ecology.

Recommendations for Reading the Selection

Students can acquaint themselves with the rhythm and mood of the poem by **reading** it **silently** before they read it aloud. This poem is meant to be read by "two voices," so it is recommended that the students read the poem in pairs or in two groups.

"The Passenger Pigeon" contains some hyperbole and figurative language: numeric comparisons of passenger pigeons to stars, grains of sand, and buffaloes; and the phrase "Humblers of the sun" will probably require interpretation by some students. During their discussion of the poem, you might tell the students that passenger pigeons did, at one time, number in the billions.

This would be a good opportunity for the students to **respond** to the text **by visualizing** and **showing surprise.** Model these responses, and then invite the students to do the same.

✳ EXPLORING THROUGH DISCUSSION

Reflecting on the Poem
Whole-Group Discussion

Have the students **discuss** the poem and any **personal thoughts, reactions, or questions** that it raises. Encourage them to think about how this poem adds to their knowledge of ecology. The reasons for the passenger pigeon's demise are not directly stated in the poem, but students might make connections between this poem and what they learned in *Protecting Wildlife* about the ways in which humans pose a threat to wildlife.

Response Journal

Poetry often evokes very personal responses. The students may wish to record their special thoughts and feelings about the poem at this time.

Recording Ideas

➤ Have the students **sum up their discussion and record their ideas and impressions** about the poem and the unit concepts on the **Concept Board** and on page 81 of their Explorer's Notebook.

Evaluating Discussions

THE PASSENGER PIGEON

Paul Fleischman
illustrated by Diane Blasius

We were counted not in

    thousands

nor

    millions

but in

billions.

    billions.
    We were numerous as the

stars

    stars
    in the heavens

As grains of
sand
at the sea

    sand

buffalo

    As the
    buffalo
    on the plains.

When we burst into flight

    we so filled the sky

that the
sun
was darkened

    sun

day

    and
    day
    became dusk.

158

Humblers of the sun
we were!
The world
<u>inconceivable</u>

Yet it's 1914,
and here I am
alone

the last

    Humblers of the sun
    we were!

    inconceivable
    without us.

    alone
    caged in the Cincinnati Zoo,

    of the passenger pigeons.

MEET PAUL FLEISCHMAN, POET

Paul Fleischman has had an interest in music ever since he was a child. When he was in college, he once wrote a song for three voices called "Fruit Melange." Years later when Paul was writing a poetry book about birds, he remembered "Fruit Melange." He decided to write poems that involved two readers and to combine them with his song. The result was the book I Am Phoenix: Poems for Two Voices.

Fleischman said the poems came to him quickly and easily. "I was in Paradise, as close to writing music as I'll ever get." For Fleischman, writing books is very similar to writing music. He believes that "every word has a meaning and a music to it."

159

Recording Concept Information

As I read each selection, this is what I added to my understanding of ecology.

Protecting Wildlife by Malcolm Penny

_____
_____
_____
_____
_____
_____
_____
_____
_____

"The Passenger Pigeon" by Paul Fleischman

_____
_____
_____
_____
_____
_____
_____
_____
_____
_____
_____

Copyright © 1995 Open Court Publishing Company

Explorer's Notebook, page 81

2 READING WITH A WRITER'S EYE

MINILESSON

Writer's Craft: Providing Comparisons

Ask the students to discuss anything they have learned about providing comparisons and to describe any examples they can remember from their reading or writing. Point out that **comparisons** can clarify ideas by helping a reader **make connections between unfamiliar things or ideas and those that are familiar. Literal comparisons** provide facts about a subject, and **figurative comparisons** help create an impression.

In "The Passenger Pigeon," Paul Fleischman provides literal and figurative comparisons to help the reader understand both the glory and the downfall of the passenger pigeon. As an example, read to the students the comparison on page 158, lines 7–9, between passenger pigeons and stars in the heavens. Have a volunteer state the comparison and tell whether it is literal or figurative. Students may realize that the impression of great flocks of passenger pigeons filling the sky is connected to certain facts about the stars.

- They are too numerous to be counted.
- They seem eternal.
- Humans cannot affect them.

Selective Reading: Focus on Providing Comparisons

Now have the students find other comparisons in the poem that clarify a fact or create an impression. Encourage volunteers to state a comparison, tell whether it is literal or figurative, and tell how it affects their understanding of the fate of passenger pigeons. What idea is clarified or what image is created? Some possible examples follow:

- page 158, lines 10–12: "As grains of sand at the sea" (figurative—passenger pigeons too numerous to count)
- page 158, lines 16–23: "When we burst into flight we so filled the sky that the sun was darkened and day became dusk." (literal—passenger pigeons so numerous that they blocked out the sunlight)

Independent Practice: Providing Comparisons

❯ Students may use Reading/Writing Connection, page 37, to record comparisons found in "The Passenger Pigeon" or in other selections they have read. The students will then note the type and purpose of each comparison. For additional ideas for **discussing poetry**, see **Teacher Tool Card 10.**

WRITING

Linking Reading to Writing

Remind the students that it is very important for writers to make concepts and images clear to the reader. Encourage the students to look through their writing folders for samples of writing that could be improved by providing comparisons. When the students have had sufficient time to choose and revise a piece of writing, invite volunteers to read their original passage and their rewritten version and to explain how the changes made the writing better.

Copyright © 1995 Open Court Publishing Company

"The Passenger Pigeon"

Providing Comparisons

Find examples in "The Passenger Pigeon" or in selections you have read in other units in which the author uses comparisons to clarify an idea or to create an image or an impression.

Title: _____ Page: _____
Comparison _____
If figurative, what impression or image is created? _____
_____
If literal, what idea is being clarified? _____
_____

Title: _____ Page: _____
Comparison _____
If figurative, what impression or image is created? _____
_____
If literal, what idea is being clarified? _____
_____

Title: _____ Page: _____
Comparison _____
If figurative, what impression or image is created? _____
_____
If literal, what idea is being clarified? _____
_____

Providing Comparisons

Unit 5/Ecology   R/WC 37

Name

Reading/Writing Connection, page 37

✷Writing Process

Encourage the students who have decided to write poetry to use the writing process, as needed, to help them develop their poems.

VOCABULARY

Words from the poem that students may want to discuss and record for future reference are *billions, numerous, humblers,* and *inconceivable.* Provide copies of Vocabulary Exploration form, Reproducible Master 15, so that the students can add these or any other words and phrases from the poem to the Personal Dictionary section of their Writer's Notebook. For additional opportunities to build vocabulary, see **Teacher Tool Card 77.**

Adding to Personal Word Lists

3 GUIDED AND INDEPENDENT EXPLORATION

Guided Exploration

The following activities do not have to be completed within the days devoted to this lesson:

Have the students check the card catalog in their school or community library for the names of birds and land or sea animals that have become extinct or are in danger of extinction. Have them bring this information to class and list the names on the chalkboard. Then ask each of them to choose an animal from the board, read about it, and share with their classmates such information as where the animal lives or lived, why it is in danger of extinction, or how and when it became extinct.

❯ During their research into ecology, students may record information about endangered or extinct animals on page 91 of their Explorer's Notebook.

Research Cycle: Conjecture Phase

❯ Explain to the students that a conjecture is a kind of educated guess, a conclusion that is based on incomplete evidence. Conjectures may be proved right, proved wrong, or modified in some way by the evidence. Have the students work on the Conjecture Phase of the Research

* *Exploring Through Research*

Explorer's Notebook, page 91

Catalog of Endangered or Extinct Species

As you read and do research for this unit, list the names of endangered and extinct species. If possible, record when the species became endangered or extinct. If the species is endangered, list how many animals are known to exist in the wild. Information about endangered species is constantly changing; if you find different sources of information, use the most recent one.

Species	Status	Date of Status	Approximate Number in the Wild
passenger pigeon	extinct	1914	0

Unit 5/Ecology — EN 91

Copyright © 1995 Open Court Publishing Company

Cycle on page 92 in their Explorer's Notebook. Prior to this, it would be helpful to have a group discussion and an opportunity to model conjectures. You might choose a problem that has already been suggested for research but that has not been chosen by any group. Using this problem, the whole class can engage in conjecturing without taking anything away from any individual's project. (The problems and conjectures will be useful in a later lesson, so you may want to record them on the chalkboard.) Explain to the students that it is not necessary to come to a consensus at this point. As they begin their research, they will revisit their conjectures and make revisions on the basis of new information. If necessary, explain that the phases of the Research Cycle are recursive; therefore, they will continually return to the previous phases of the cycle to assess how the problem and the conjectures have changed and to determine what new information is necessary.

If they are comfortable with the conjecture phase of the Research Cycle, the students can go directly to work on their research problem in Independent Workshop. However, if the students are having difficulties with forming conjectures, refer to **Learning Framework Card 4B, Conjecture Phase,** for ideas. Encourage them to record their own ideas even if these are vague or limited. The important thing is that they progress toward more sophisticated conjectures in subsequent cycles.

RESEARCH TIP Some students may have difficulty finding an adequate amount of material if their focus is too narrow. If this happens, encourage the students to think of other research questions and conjectures that will broaden the scope of their research.

Explorer's Notebook, page 92

Research Cycle: Conjecture Phase

Our problem:

_____
_____
_____
_____
_____
_____
_____

Conjecture (my first theory or explanation):

_____
_____
_____
_____
_____
_____
_____
_____
_____
_____
_____
_____
_____
_____
_____

As you collect information, your conjectures will change. Return to this page to record your new theories or explanations about your research problem.

92 EN   Ecology/Unit 5

Copyright © 1995 Open Court Publishing Company

✳ INDEPENDENT WORKSHOP
Building a Community of Scholars

Student-Directed Reading, Writing, and Discussion

Research Cycle: Conjecture Phase Each student should develop his or her own conjectures regarding the group's research question or problem and enter them on page 92 of their Explorer's Notebook. Then groups should meet to discuss their conjectures.

As you observe the groups discussing their conjectures, encourage students to record the ideas of everyone in the group. Tell them that they can refine their conjectures as they collect information. Remind them that the purpose of their research is to improve their conjectures. Rephrasing the students' conjectures will help you elicit additional information from them and will help them clarify and refine their ideas. Remind the students that they will return to this page later in their research.

WORKSHOP TIP

Remember that students should be sharing information freely. They should be encouraged to use the Concept Board and the Question Board often. They should write in their Explorer's Notebook questions, notes, or information from either board that they think will be useful. It is important that they share ideas and information from their Explorer's Notebook with their classmates.

Additional Opportunities for Independent Reading, Writing, and Cross-curricular Activities

✴ Reading Roundtable

Remind the students that nature has been a popular topic for poets throughout the ages. Encourage the students to find and read other poems about nature by poets such as Robert Frost, Christina Rosetti, E. B. White, Walt Whitman, and Jack Prelutsky.

✴ Writing Seminar

If students have elected to begin a new piece of writing at this time, encourage them to make brief notes on ideas they want to include in their writing. Have them follow the writing process as they develop their writing.

Portfolio

Remind the students to think about putting the best examples of their writing into their portfolios.

Cross-curricular Activity Cards

The following Cross-curricular Activity Cards in the Student Toolbox are appropriate for this selection:
- 23 Social Studies—Creating a Time Line
- 3 Math—Counting Pigeons

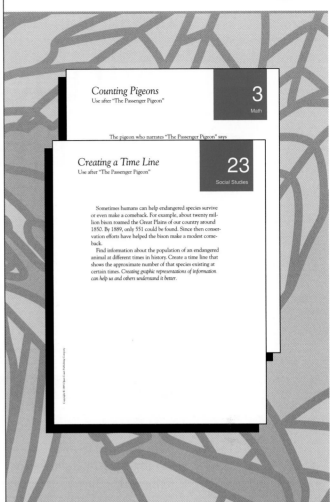

Counting Pigeons
Use after "The Passenger Pigeon"

3 Math

The pigeon who narrates "The Passenger Pigeon" says

Creating a Time Line
Use after "The Passenger Pigeon"

23 Social Studies

Sometimes humans can help endangered species survive or even make a comeback. For example, about twenty million bison roamed the Great Plains of our country around 1850. By 1889, only 551 could be found. Since then conservation efforts have helped the bison make a modest comeback.

Find information about the population of an endangered animal at different times in history. Create a time line that shows the approximate number of that species existing at certain times. *Creating graphic representations of information can help us and others understand it better.*

Additional Opportunities for Solving Learning Problems

Tutorial

You may want to use this time to work with those students who need some extra help. The following aids are available in the Teacher Toolbox for your convenience:
- Writer's Craft/Reading: Elaboration Through Providing Comparison and Contrast, Teacher Tool Card 37
- Writer's Craft/Reading: Genre—Poetry, Teacher Tool Card 10

On Your Own

Windows on Wildlife

1 READING THE SELECTION

About the Selection

In this selection, authors Ginny Johnston and Judy Cutchins describe how some zoos, aquariums, and zoological parks are creating and maintaining realistic habitats for the animals in their care. Building realistic habitats can be a technological challenge. How, for example, does one build a rain forest in the middle of an American city or replicate the weather and the seasons of the Antarctic in an indoor aquarium? Constructing habitats may be challenging work, but it is worthwhile, since many of the animals who will live in them would be endangered in their native lands.

Link to the Unit Concepts

In "Windows on Wildlife," pages 160–181, the authors emphasize the positive ways in which human beings influence the fate of wildlife. Without specialized habitats in which to live and breed safely, many more species would now be extinct. Today's zoological gardens and reserves bear little resemblance to the rows of cages that once characterized zoos. Now, instead of simply warehousing and displaying animals, zoo and park officials support wildlife protection, breed endangered animals, and provide visitors with a more realistic view of animals in the wild.

After reading this selection, students may ask themselves why zoos were first created. They may raise questions about the ethical issues surrounding animal captivity or about the difference between surviving and thriving in captivity.

About the Authors

Ginny Johnston and Judy Cutchins write about many different topics related to biology, including animals in the wild, wildlife habitats, and museum exhibits showing how animals live in the wild. They see themselves as teachers first and writers second. Thus, a conservation message underlies all their natural-science books. They hope to encourage in their readers a respect and an appreciation for animals.

LESSON OVERVIEW

"Windows on Wildlife" by Ginny Johnston and Judy Cutchins, pages 160–181

READING THE SELECTION

Materials
Student Anthology, pp. 160–181
Explorer's Notebook, p. 82
Assessment Masters 1–2

FYI
Learning Framework Card
• Setting Reading Goals and
  Expectations, 1A

READING WITH A WRITER'S EYE

Minilesson
On Your Own

Materials
Reproducible Master 15

FYI
Teacher Tool Card
• Spelling and Vocabulary: Building
  Vocabulary, 77

Options for Instruction
Writer's Craft: Elaboration Through
  Providing Examples
Grammar, Mechanics, and Usage:
  Phrases
Grammar, Mechanics, and Usage: Using
  Commas in a Series
(Use Teacher Tool Cards listed below.)

GUIDED AND INDEPENDENT EXPLORATION

Materials
Explorer's Notebook, pp. 93–97
Home/School Connection 37

FYI
Learning Framework Card
• Needs and Plans Phase 1 and 2, 4C

Independent Workshop

**Optional Materials from
Student Toolbox**
Tradebook Connection Cards

Cross-curricular Activity Cards
• 15 Art—Paint a Mural of a Natural
  Habitat
• 16 Art—Designing an Aviary

Student Tool Cards
• Writer's Craft/Reading: Giving
  Examples, 39
• Grammar, Mechanics, and Usage:
  Phrases, 50
• Grammar, Mechanics, and Usage:
  Using Commas in a Series, 52

FYI
Teacher Tool Cards
• Writer's Craft/Reading: Elaboration
  Through Providing Examples, 39
• Grammar, Mechanics, and Usage:
  Phrases, 50
• Grammar, Mechanics, and Usage:
  Using Commas in a Series, 52

N O T E S

Asterisks (*) throughout the lesson indicate learning frameworks. Learning Framework Cards and Teacher Tool Cards can be found in the Teacher Toolbox

Share with the students any information about the authors that you feel is appropriate.

* COGNITIVE AND RESPONSIVE READING

Activating Prior Knowledge

Have the students read the title of the selection. Ask them what they know about habitat exhibits.

Setting Reading Goals and Expectations

Before they **read the selection independently,** have the students **browse the selection using the clues/problems/wondering procedure.** For a review of the browsing procedure, see **Learning Framework Card 1A, Setting Goals and Expectations.**

Recommendations for Reading the Selection

This selection has been designated as an On Your Own selection. Tell the students that they will read "Windows on Wildlife" **silently on their own.** Remind them to use any of the reading strategies that they have learned to help them understand the selection. Encourage them to check the **reading strategy posters** if they encounter a reading problem or if they are unsure about how to use a strategy. You may wish to review briefly the reading strategies that have already been introduced in this unit. Explain to the students that relating their own experiences to what they read will help them understand the selection better. They should feel free to raise their hands at any time during silent reading to discuss particular problems or to wonder about things. Following the reading of the selection, they will complete a Self-Assessment Questionnaire.

ASSESSMENT TIP This may be a good opportunity to observe students working in groups and to mark observations in your Teacher's Observation Log.

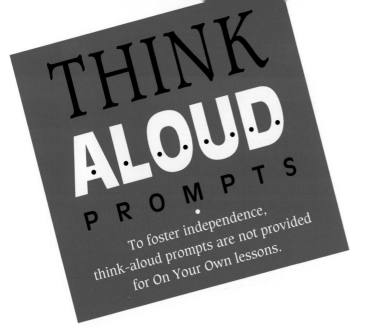

THINK ALOUD PROMPTS

To foster independence, think-aloud prompts are not provided for On Your Own lessons.

WINDOWS ON WILDLIFE

Ginny Johnston and Judy Cutchins

WHAT ARE HABITAT EXHIBITS?

The excitement of watching an animal in the wild is unforgettable. What a thrill it is to hear gorillas growl and hoot or watch them care for their young. But few people get a chance to venture into African forests where the great apes live. Many of the world's most fascinating creatures live in habitats too far away or too difficult to visit. However, most people can watch them by visiting a zoo or aquarium.

Until recently, animals in such places were usually caged behind bars, and people walked by to stare at them. The visit held none of the excitement of seeing animals in the wild.

Today, modern zoos, aquariums, and wildlife parks are showing plants and animals in natural-habitat exhibits. These exhibits duplicate a part of an animal's true environment as closely as possible. Since many animals are endangered in their native lands, habitat exhibits may be the only places they can survive.

Building these realistic habitats is not a simple job. It is challenging to build a "river" for hippos or grow a forest indoors. Making rain or snow fall under a roof requires special equipment. Also, before a habitat exhibit can be developed, scientists must spend a great deal of time studying plants,

⇟ 160 ⇟

animals, and their natural environment. They watch each species to learn about its way of life and special needs. The scientists then work with exhibit specialists to design a habitat that will be as authentic as they can make it.

Visitors may see more in natural-habitat exhibits than they would see in nature. Windows, for example, allow people to remain warm and dry while watching penguins "fly" under icy water or waddle across snow-covered rocks. Naturalistic exhibits are not only more fun for visitors, but healthier and more comfortable for captive wildlife.

These modern exhibits are much more expensive than cages with bars, but it is worth the money to provide the best possible environment for captive species. The well-being of the plants and animals is the number one goal. Scientists believe that zoo animals live longer and have more babies in naturalistic settings. Raising more young, especially if a species is rare or endangered, will prevent the species from becoming extinct. American zoos no longer take rare animals from the wild for exhibits, so raising these babies is extremely important.

FOREST FOR GORILLAS

Slowly the square, white door of the gorilla building slid open. A huge head appeared, and two dark eyes scanned quickly in every direction. It was the gorilla's first look outside in his twenty-seven years at the zoo in Atlanta, Georgia. Captured as a three-year-old in Africa, the male lowland gorilla had lived alone since then in an indoor cage with bars. Now he was about to enter the outdoor area of his new habitat

⇟ 161 ⇟

exhibit, the Ford African Rain Forest at Zoo Atlanta. Just outside the gorilla's habitat, the zoo director, exhibit designers, keepers, and news reporters watched anxiously. They wondered what the gorilla's first reaction to the outdoors would be.

The 458-pound gorilla cautiously left the building and moved a few feet away. Hearts beat faster as people watched the powerful ape investigate his new home. He picked up leaves and sniffed them. He felt the grass and looked up at the cloudy sky. The gorilla's old indoor cage of concrete and tile had none of the wonderful smells and sights of the outdoors. A gentle rain began to fall. Confused and startled by the falling drops, the gorilla dashed back inside to safety. Later

After twenty-seven years indoors, this western lowland gorilla explores the
Ford African Rain Forest exhibit at Zoo Atlanta.
Judy Cutchins

The sloping, grass-covered hillside was designed to look like a clearing
in an African rain forest.
Judy Cutchins

that day, he ventured out again. Bravely, he ambled farther and investigated every tree and rock on the hillside of the simulated African rain forest. Fallen trees, high grass, and bamboo gave the sloping hillside the appearance of a forest clearing. The curious gorilla seemed to be quite content in his naturalistic home.

Of all the people watching the gorilla that first day, no one was more pleased than his keeper for the past fourteen years. The zookeeper knew the magnificent gorilla would, at last, have a large, interesting place to live. Although the great ape would still go indoors at night, he would spend each day exploring outside.

In just a few weeks, the lone gorilla had next-door neighbors. The Ford African Rain Forest exhibit was designed for several families of lowland gorillas. The four-and-one-half-acre exhibit is divided so that each family has a separate area. A gorilla family is led by an adult male called a silverback. Since silverbacks in captivity are very protective of their families and their territories, they must be kept apart or they will

≥ 163 ≤

The gorilla habitats
are separated by steep-
sided double moats.
Judy Cutchins

fight. Moats with steep dirt banks separate the families from each other and from zoo visitors. Each moat is twelve feet deep and fifteen feet across. These moats do not have water in them; instead, thick, soft grass grows at the bottom in case a gorilla tumbles in. The silverbacks can see, smell, and hear each other across the moats, but they cannot get too close.

This realistic habitat design, with families near each other, allows the gorillas to behave much as they would in the wild. In an African forest, gorilla families sometimes meet other families as they search for food. As they approach each other, one male will beat his chest, slap the ground or trees, and run toward the other silverback. This show of strength usually results in one family's moving away, with no actual fighting between the males. In the zoo exhibit, the gorillas cannot reach each other, but they can still display their feelings across the moats. The gorillas, especially the silverbacks, are alert and aware of the activities of the apes living nearby.

At night and in bad weather, the gorillas are kept inside. The holding building for them is hidden behind a wall of giant artificial rocks at the top of the hillside. Each family has

≥ 164 ≤

A young female
gorilla, searching for
food in the forest
clearing, fascinates
visitors.
Judy Cutchins

its own sliding door into the building. Inside, the families have large, separate, barred cages. During the day, the gorillas eat fruits and vegetables scattered outside by the keepers. Each evening, they receive their main meal of dried food and milk indoors before they sleep.

The gorilla-habitat exhibit looked nothing like a rain forest before builders got started. Twenty-six thousand tons of soil were moved to build a hillside. More than 3,500 trees, shrubs, and flowers were planted to fill in around several hundred trees already growing in the area. Stands of bamboo were planted to make the area look like a sun-filled opening in an African rain forest. The key to success was finding plants that would simulate the look and feel of a rain forest but would survive in Atlanta's cooler, drier climate. For example, southern magnolias that grow in Atlanta were planted because their wide shiny leaves look very much like the leaves of tropical plants. Some of the exhibit plants must be taken inside a greenhouse for the winter, but most can remain in the exhibit all year round. Rocks and cliffs were made of Gunite, a concrete mixture sprayed over steel wires. The Gunite forms were painted

≥ 165 ≤

Watching how gorilla families behave is an important part of the research being done at Zoo Atlanta.
Judy Cutchins

to resemble rocks photographed in Africa. Before the gorillas were released into the exhibit, rock climbers from a nearby university were invited to climb the walls and find any places over which a gorilla might escape.

At Zoo Atlanta, future zookeepers, veterinarians, and scientists will observe gorilla families as part of their training. The Ford African Rain Forest offers close encounters with great apes. Trails wind along outside all four gorilla habitats. At each turn, through the leaves and branches, visitors may spot a gorilla munching bamboo or resting in the sunshine. It is intriguing to watch the delicate and deliberate way apes eat and the gentle way they groom each other. At one place the trail leads through an information building where visitors can learn about gorillas while they watch real ones through a huge

≥ 166 ≤

window. Gorillas, especially the younger ones, often come close to or even touch the glass. It seems they are curious about people, too.

In western Africa, rain forests have been cut and cleared for farms and lumber. As their habitats disappear, gorillas are becoming very rare. Until recently, zoos have not been very successful in raising young gorillas. Fortunately, as more is learned about the needs of the great apes, American zoos are raising larger numbers of healthy youngsters. Since wild gorillas are never captured for American zoos, in a few years, only those born and raised in captivity will be in exhibits.

ICY HOME FOR PENGUINS

It is 9:00 A.M. at Sea World's Penguin Encounter in Orlando, Florida. A perky rockhopper penguin, just eighteen inches tall, bounces from one ice-covered rock to another. Around him dozens of gentoo, chinstrap, and crested macaroni penguins waddle by. Tall king penguins strut about with their flipperlike wings outstretched and orange bills pointed up. An exhibit keeper, dressed in warm, waterproof clothes, carries a

Each of the exhibit's two hundred penguins is hand-fed three times a day.
Sea World, Inc.

bucket filled with fresh fish for the penguins' morning feeding. Each fish was stuffed with vitamins before being placed in the bucket. The keeper holds a small herring in front of an Adélie penguin. The hungry bird gulps the fish headfirst.

Visitors to Penguin Encounter travel on a moving sidewalk in front of windows that are ninety-five feet long. Every day thousands of people look into a simulated Antarctic habitat without disturbing the penguins. Each glass window is three inches thick to hold the tremendous amount of water in the sea pool and to maintain the near-freezing temperatures inside the exhibit. The window panels extend below the water so people can watch the penguins swimming in the deep pool. Since the glass is cleaned five times a day, visitors always have a clear view of the penguins.

To duplicate the seasonal changes of sunlight in the Antarctic and to make the penguins feel at home, special lighting is used at Penguin Encounter. When it is summer in North America, it is winter at the South Pole. The sun cannot be seen for several weeks during the Antarctic winter. Imitating this season means keeping the exhibit lights dim

Through thick glass windows, visitors watch penguins "fly" underwater like black-and-white torpedoes.
Sea World, Inc.

from late May until the end of July. The lights are not turned out completely because visitors would not be able to see the penguins. In August, the keepers turn the lights up a little more each morning. By early October, the lights are bright for twenty-four hours a day. This would be like summer at the South Pole, when the sun shines all day and all night.

Simulating the below-zero temperatures of the penguins' natural habitat is not possible at Penguin Encounter, but the birds are kept comfortable by giant air-cooling machines. These machines keep the temperature in the exhibit near freezing all the time. Other machines in the ceiling produce 6,000 pounds of "snow" every twenty-four hours. This finely ground ice falls softly and steadily. Twice a day, keepers shovel it into a smooth layer that melts very slowly. A clear saltwater pool runs the length of the exhibit, and the water is always a chilly 50 degrees. That's about 30 degrees colder than most swimming pools!

A penguin's body is protected by a marvelous feather coat. About seventy shiny, bristly feathers grow from each square inch of skin. These stiff feathers overlap like shingles on a roof. They trap body heat to keep the penguin warm even during Antarctic blizzards, when the temperature can be 100 degrees below zero. Each day, a penguin uses its curved bill to straighten its feathers. The bird also spreads oil over them from a gland near its tail. The oil and tight, overlapping fit of the feathers keep the skin dry even while the penguin is swimming.

Like those of all birds, a penguin's outer feathers wear out in about a year. These old feathers are shed during the molting season. For one month, while a new set of feathers is

≥ 169 ≤

growing in, a penguin cannot enter the ocean to find food. Without its warm, waterproof layer, a penguin would quickly die in the icy water. In Antarctica, a penguin may lose nearly half of its body weight while waiting for new feathers. At Penguin Encounter, keepers continue to feed the birds during the molting season.

The Penguin Encounter at Sea World in Orlando, Florida, is not the only Penguin Encounter in the United States. Other exhibits are in California, Ohio, and Texas. Before any were built, teams of scientists studied in Antarctica for six years. They hoped to learn enough about penguins to create suitable habitats for them in America. The scientists watched penguins swim, tumble off rocks into the icy sea, sled across the snow on their bellies, build nests, and raise young. Researchers observed several different species of penguins living close together. They learned that penguins were curious about humans, but not frightened by them.

When the researchers returned to the United States, they worked with a design team to create the first naturalistic exhibit for penguins. It was built at Sea World of San Diego, California, in 1983. Adult penguins were brought to San Diego from Antarctica. They seemed to feel comfortable and behaved very naturally in their indoor home. Some mated and produced eggs.

All the penguins in Penguin Encounters in Ohio, Texas, and Florida were hatched from eggs laid in San Diego. No other adults have been taken from the wild. Although penguins are not an <u>endangered</u> species, it is best not to remove animals from their natural habitat or disturb their environment if another way to study them can be found.

≥ 170 ≤

Since the penguins look so much alike, color-coded bands help researchers and keepers identify each bird.
Sea World, Inc.

Thanks to years of research and careful planning at Penguin Encounters, scientists at last are able to study and raise penguins without traveling thousands of miles to Antarctica. Visitors to the exhibits gain a better understanding of penguins and their unusual, icy habitat.

INDOOR JUNGLE

Stepping inside the huge JungleWorld building at the Bronx Zoo, a visitor enters another world. Not far from the busy streets and bustling crowds of New York City, this simulated Asian rain forest is a jungle adventure. Sounds of birds and insects are everywhere. Splashing waterfalls pour into streams that flow into quiet pools. Tremendous trees, more than fifty feet tall, reach almost out of sight toward sky-

≥ 171 ≤

lights in the exhibit ceiling. For the visitor, every sense is awakened because JungleWorld looks, sounds, and even smells like a real rain forest.

This rain forest is completely indoors, so the temperature and amount of moisture in the air can be carefully controlled. Above one of the exhibit's four waterfalls, fog machines spray mist into the air. The moisture forms clouds that drift over the jungle. It is always warm and steamy here, just as it is in a tropical forest. Heating coils hidden beneath the realistic riverbanks at JungleWorld simulate sun-warmed basking areas for monitor lizards and crocodilelike <u>gharials</u>.

To add to the rain forest adventure, sounds of insects, birds, and frogs ring out from speakers hidden around the exhibit. These voices were recorded in faraway forests. Live Jungle-

Gharials live in JungleWorld's river. Three separate pools allow the males to set up individual territories.
© Everett H. Scott

World animals answer with calls of their own. JungleWorld actually includes several rain forest habitats. In a <u>mangrove</u> swamp, playful small-clawed otters grab the tails of proboscis monkeys that perch on low branches; gharials cool themselves in a simulated river; the forest canopy high overhead provides a realistic habitat for troops of monkeys. More than eighty-seven different animal species live under one huge roof at JungleWorld.

In the exhibit, some animals need to be separated from the visitors and from each other. Instead of traditional cages with bars, exhibit builders cleverly used naturalistic barriers. Visitor trails were placed just a little too far from the trees for the proboscis monkeys to leap onto them. Simulated mudbanks are so steep the gharials cannot climb them. Rocky cliffs extend to the ceiling behind spectacular waterfalls. These cliffs provide barriers to separate the three species of monkeys that would not live so close together in the wild. Sleek clouded

There are no bars between visitors and this group of rare proboscis monkeys at JungleWorld.
© Everett H. Scott

leopards stretch lazily and watch monkeys play just a few feet away. A clean, almost invisible glass separates the leopards from the monkeys. Predators are not allowed to hunt living prey as they would in the wild, so the leopards must be separated from other animals.

At night most of the animals enter individual holding shelters hidden behind the plants and rockwork of the exhibit. They move readily into their overnight enclosures because this is where they are fed their big meals of the day. Each animal's diet is carefully planned to contain the necessary vitamins and minerals. Once the animals are secured inside their holding pens, keepers observe each individual closely and act quickly if one needs special attention. Every morning while the animals are still in their holding areas, keepers vacuum the floors of the pools and streams. They rake or wash down the jungle floor. Cleanliness is most important in keeping animals healthy.

In the wild, rain forest animals spend much of their time searching for food. To duplicate their natural activities, keepers put some food in the exhibit for the animals to "discover." Fresh leaves, sunflower seeds, and raisins are hidden for the monkeys. This extra food helps keep the leaf eaters from nibbling on the real plants. Crickets are tossed onto the mudbank for the otters. A special "feeding tree" was built for the gibbons. This artificial tree has a secret, bark-covered door in the trunk. Inside, a container is filled with nuts or seeds. Every so often, a device in the tree turns and a few treats fall through pipes and land in openings around the trunk. The quick-learning gibbons search the tree often because they

≈ 174 ≈

sometimes find a tasty reward. Scientists believe searching for food helps keep the captive animals alert.

Hundreds of exotic ferns, shrubs, and small trees grow throughout the exhibit. But giant rain forest trees could not be brought to JungleWorld. Artificial trees were made with a framework of steel and fiberglass. The "bark" is a layer of hard plastic that was hand carved and painted. Miles of vines wind through the trees of a real rain forest. Gibbons and silvered leaf monkeys use vines to travel quickly through the treetops. Neither of these species spends much time on the ground. But the miles of vines used by the monkeys could not be grown easily in the exhibit. The young, slow-growing vines would constantly be broken by the acrobatic monkeys. So sturdy artificial vines were especially designed for such active climbers.

The vines were made by threading thin steel wires through long nylon ropes. Then the ropes were "slimed." Workers spread gooey rubber all over the ropes. Brown and green colors were mixed into the rubber. When the rubber hardened, the vines were shaped and painted to look as though they were covered with mosses and lichens. Then the vines were twisted and hung all through the tree branches. Some were hung near, but not too near, the trails so visitors can enjoy a close view of long-tailed acrobats in action.

Artists at JungleWorld re-created giant rain forest trees.
New York Zoological Society

Painted murals realistically show cloud-covered mountains as they look in an Asian rain forest.
New York Zoological Society

JungleWorld is truly a zoo work of art. It is the first exhibit to combine so many different kinds of animals in one complex indoor habitat. Visitors leave knowing and caring more about the beautiful and valuable rain forest environment where tropical plants and wildlife thrive.

HABITAT FOR TROPICAL BIRDS

One hundred fifty colorful birds with unusual names such as crested barbet, white-fronted bee-eater, and red-faced mousebird sing and call throughout the R. J. Reynolds Forest Aviary. Part of the North Carolina Zoological Park, the aviary is as big as an auditorium. Glass walls and a transparent roof allow sunlight to warm the aviary, creating a giant greenhouse. This indoor woodland simulates the tropical forests of Africa, Asia, and South America. Exotic birds from around the world share this lush enclosure.

Visitors do not watch the birds from behind a window. Instead, they can enter the exhibit and walk among the

≈ 176 ≈

White African spoonbills and South American scarlet ibises share an artificial stream in the North Carolina Zoo's forest aviary.
Judy Cutchins

fascinating birds. A booklet with color pictures helps people identify and name them. With thousands of people visiting the aviary, it might seem that some of the quick-flying birds would accidentally escape through the doorways. Yet this almost never happens. The aviary, which is only open during daylight hours, is always brightly lit by the sun. The entrance and exit hallways are dark. Birds will not fly into the dark area. There are two sets of doors in the hallway just in case, but birds rarely leave the lighted aviary.

Inside, a winding pathway takes visitors past trickling streams and rock outcrops that were realistically planned by the zoo's design team. Fig trees from Asia and Africa reach the ceiling to form the forest canopy, or highest level. These tall trees were carefully planted so the soaring birds would have plenty of flying space. Palm, banana, and rubber trees do not grow as tall as the fig trees and so form an understory

≈ 177 ≈

The green woodhoopoe darts around the understory in search of insects.
Judy Cutchins

layer. Canopy and understory trees provide shade and protect the lower levels from the sun's strong rays. Shrubs, vines, and ferns from tropical countries cover the ground. More than 2,000 plants create the multilayered bird habitat. The dense greenery provides hiding places, perches, and nesting materials for fifty-five species of birds.

The one hundred fifty birds must be observed regularly by the keepers. To make identification of the birds possible, every bird is banded with colored leg bands. No two are alike. Keepers must use binoculars to see the colored bands on tiny lavender finches or scarlet-chested sunbirds. If any bird is not spotted once a month, a serious effort is made to find it. Finding each bird regularly helps the keepers know if one is sick or injured.

The most exciting time of the year in the aviary is nesting season. Each spring, keepers watch for signs of mating and nest building. Bird lovers walking along the curving pathways also search for hidden nests.

When the exhibit was first built, one of the birds gave keepers a special challenge at nesting time. The gray-headed

178

The bright red of the scarlet ibis from South America makes this bird one of the first to be spotted by a keeper or an aviary visitor.
Judy Cutchins

kingfisher from Africa usually digs into mudbanks along creeks and rivers to make its nest. Since the aviary's "mudbanks" are made of wire coated by a layer of rock-hard Gunite, keepers had to give the tunnel nesters a helping hand. They cut a kingfisher-sized hole in the bank and pushed a long plastic tube into it. This duplicated the smooth tunnel made by a kingfisher. It took only a few days for the kingfishers to discover the tunnel and move in to nest. Like most of the aviary birds, they successfully raised young.

Any bird not hatched in the aviary must be introduced to the indoor habitat very carefully. A new arrival is not allowed near the other birds for thirty days in case it has some illness that could spread. During this time, the bird has a complete medical checkup. Before its release, the newcomer is placed in a cage on the floor of the aviary for a few nights. This gives the stranger time to get used to the sights and sounds of its future home. Three or four flight feathers on each wing are clipped to slow its flying speed. If the bird flies fast at first, it might crash into the clear walls or roof and be seriously hurt. Clipped feathers are shed and replaced by new ones when the

179

bird molts. By that time, the bird is familiar with the aviary and rarely flies into the glass.

Soon after its release, a bird learns where food bowls are placed. Because of the variety of birds, seven different diets are prepared each morning. In addition, some of the nectar feeders drink the sweet juices from orchids and other flowers. Fruit-eating birds gobble up berries as they ripen. Insect eaters catch pests on leaves and flowers. A few birds at the aviary require special diets. For example, the white-fronted bee-eater from Africa eats only insects it catches in the air, so the keepers toss out live insects for the bee-eater to grab.

Since its opening in 1982, the R. J. Reynolds Forest Aviary has become a very successful habitat exhibit. Between forty and fifty baby birds are raised each year. Some of the youngsters are sold to other tropical aviaries. This makes it unnecessary to capture birds in their natural habitats for exhibit purposes.

In the aviary, just as in nature, there is much for visitors to discover. If they look quickly and carefully, they will see

The six-sided aviary building has a clear, domed ceiling four stories high.
Judy Cutchins

brilliantly colored birds fly overhead and disappear into the dense forest. The aviary is what a realistic wildlife exhibit should be—a lifelike home for animals and an educational treat for people.

LIFE IN THE WILD VERSUS LIFE IN CAPTIVITY

Natural-habitat exhibits are exciting places and fun to visit. They are realistic homes away from home for plants and animals, and they let people peek into those fascinating worlds.

But artificial habitats are not perfect. Designers know that nature is far too complex to be duplicated. Some parts of a naturalistic exhibit are very different from the wild. In captivity, for example, plants and animals are tended by keepers specializing in their care. Many exhibit animals are taken indoors at night and during bad weather. Protected from their enemies, zoo animals receive expert medical attention and perfectly balanced meals. Even with such care, zookeepers may not meet every need of a captive species because all of its needs are not yet understood.

Living freely in its own natural environment is, of course, ideal for any living thing. But many wildlife habitats are disappearing. In much of the world people have moved in, cleared the land, and even killed the animals for their own needs. Thousands of plant and animal species are nearing extinction. As conservationists fight to save natural areas, zoos and aquariums have taken on the challenge of protecting some of the rare and endangered species. Natural-habitat exhibits provide safe and healthy places for plants and animals while helping visitors understand their world a little better.

181

* **EXPLORING THROUGH DISCUSSION**

Reflecting on the Selection
Whole-Group Discussion

The whole group discusses the selection and any thoughts or questions that it raises. During this time, students also **return to the clues, problems, and wonderings** that they noted on the chalkboard during browsing.

Assessment

To assess their understanding of the text, engage the students in a discussion to determine whether they have grasped the following ideas:
- the contributions made by modern zoos, aquariums, and wildlife parks to the conservation of plants and animals
- the scientific and technological knowledge required to build and maintain a naturalistic habitat

Response Journal

Students may wish to record their thoughts and impressions about "Windows on Wildlife" in their response journals.

Exploring Concepts Within the Selection
Small-Group Discussion

Small groups discuss the selection's relationship to ecology. Circulate among the groups and observe the discussions. Refer the students to the **Question Board** and the **Concept Board** to keep them focused on their original ideas about ecology and to see whether those original perceptions have changed as a result of their reading this selection.

Sharing Ideas About Explorable Concepts

Have the groups **report their ideas** and **discuss them** with the rest of the class. It is crucial that the students' ideas determine this discussion.
- Students may notice that, although both traditional and modern zoos are interested in protecting rare and endangered species, modern zoos create an environment in which animals will thrive, not just survive.
- Students may suggest that naturalistic habitats may change and improve as scientists learn more about the special needs of captive animals.
- Students may comment that naturalistic wildlife habitats benefit humans as well as animals; through them we can experience environments and their wildlife that we could not otherwise experience.

As these ideas and others are stated, have the students **add them to** the **Question Board** or the **Concept Board.**

Have the students turn to page 183 of the student anthology and examine Ernst Haas's photograph of impalas grazing in Kenya. They may wish to express their thoughts and feelings about this particular work and comment on any connections they think it has to the article they have just read.

Fine Art

Exploring Concepts Across Selections

Ask the students how this selection reminds them of other selections that they have read. Students may make connections with selections in this or other units.
- Some students may compare the efforts to reconstruct wildlife habitats outside of the wild in "Windows on Wildlife" and the efforts to preserve and protect natural wildlife habitats in *Protecting Wildlife.*

TEACHING TIP Questions that arise from the reading of selections provide good springboards for research ideas. Always ask the students what each selection makes them wonder about. Encourage them to verbalize their questions.

- Some students may wonder whether the fate of the passenger pigeons in "The Passenger Pigeon" would have been different if the Cincinnati Zoo had contained a forest aviary like the one in the North Carolina Zoological Park.
- Some students may remember that in *The Nightingale* (from the unit on music), the mechanical nightingale was an unsatisfactory substitute for the real thing. The author of *The Nightingale,* like the authors of this selection, emphasized the preciousness and irreplaceability of wildlife.

Recording Ideas

As they complete the above discussions, ask the students to **sum up what they have learned from their conversations and to tell how they might use this information** in further explorations. Any special information or insights may be recorded on the **Concept Board.** Any further questions that they would like to think about, pursue, or investigate may be recorded on the **Question Board.** They may want to discuss the progress that has been made on their questions. They may also want to cross out any questions that no longer warrant consideration.

➤ After discussion, students should individually record their thoughts and ideas about the selection on page 82 of their Explorer's Notebook. As they work in their Explorer's Notebook, identify students who are having trouble relating the selection to ecology. Work with those who are confused or form peer groups to help clear up confusion.

Self-Assessment Questionnaire

➤ Distribute copies of Assessment Master 2, Self-Assessment Questionnaire, which you will find in the Masters for Continuous Assessment booklet in the Teacher Toolbox. Tell the students to answer the questionnaires after they have completed this lesson. Collect the completed questionnaires so that you can compare students' current self-assessments with previous self-assessments. You might also compare the students' assessments with your assessments of them in your Teacher's Observation Log.

Connections Across Units

Evaluating Discussions

Recording Concept Information continued

"Windows on Wildlife" by Ginny Johnston and Judy Cutchins

_____
_____
_____
_____
_____
_____
_____
_____
_____
_____
_____

"A Natural Force" by Laurence Pringle

_____
_____
_____
_____
_____
_____
_____
_____
_____
_____
_____

82 EN   Ecology/Unit 5

Copyright © 1995 Open Court Publishing Company

Explorer's Notebook, page 82

Self-Assessment Questionnaire

Date

1. How would you rate this selection?
   ○ easy   ○ medium   ○ hard

2. If you checked **medium** or **hard**, answer these questions.
   • Which part of the selection did you find especially difficult?
   • What strategy did you use to understand it?

   _____
   _____

   • Were some of the words hard?
   • What did you do to figure out their meaning?

   _____
   _____

INDIVIDUAL

3. What do you feel you need to work on to make yourself a better reader?

   _____
   _____
   _____

4. Give an example of something you said in the group. Tell why you said it.

   _____
   _____
   _____

Name

5. Give an example of something that people in the group helped you understand about the selection.

GROUP

   _____
   _____
   _____

Self-Assessment Questionnaire   Assessment Master 2

Copyright © 1995 Open Court Publishing Company

Assessment Master 2

Professional Checkpoint: Cognitive and Responsive Reading

Students who do not seem to be using the reading strategies "on their own" should be prompted to think about, choose, and use strategies as they read. They should listen to strategy-using class-mates read aloud and discuss strategies during the lesson. Students will probably notice that once they have been learned, reading strategies, come naturally and enhance their understanding and enjoyment of a selection.

Notes:

2 READING WITH A WRITER'S EYE

MINILESSON

On Your Own

Remind the students that in most of the selections they have read this year, they have discussed something the writer did especially well. For example, in *Protecting Wildlife,* they discussed how Malcolm Penny clarified his purpose for writing by stating his opinions; and in "The Passenger Pigeon," they discussed how Paul Fleischman used comparisons to emphasize the plight of an almost-extinct species.

Tell the students that since they have read "Windows on Wildlife" on their own, you would like them to try to identify something they think Ginny Johnston and Judy Cutchins did especially well. Is there something about the writing that stands out? They might think back to a portion of the article that they particularly enjoyed. Their positive reaction may be a clue to especially good writing.

Allow time, if necessary, for the students to skim the selection to refresh their memories. If they have difficulty expressing their feelings about the writing, model a response for them by pointing out things that you found noteworthy. For example, you might wish to point out that Johnston and Cutchins are especially good at **using descriptive language.** On pages 162–163, they describe a gorilla's first foray into his newly constructed naturalistic habitat. The authors' interesting choice of adverbs and adjectives make this scene especially believable and easy to visualize.

STEPS TOWARD INDEPENDENCE By this time in the year, students should be able to notice and point out aspects of good writing.

WRITING

Linking Reading to Writing

Encourage the students to use in their own writing any of the techniques used by Johnston and Cutchins that they especially liked. Invite them to search their writing folders for a piece of writing that they could revise by using a writing device that they liked in this story.

* Writing Process

Although no specific writing assignment is recommended here, students should use the writing process with any writing on which they are currently working. Remind those who are currently revising a piece of their writing to ask their peers for feedback on the effectiveness and clarity of the piece. If your class is using the optional Writer's Handbook, refer the students to it for help with their writing.

VOCABULARY

Words and phrases related to ecology that you might discuss include *naturalistic, captive species, silverback, simulation, habitat exhibit, aviary,* and *exotic.* Provide Vocabulary Exploration forms, Reproducible Master 15, so that the students can add these or any other words and phrases from the story to the Personal Dictionary section of their

VOCABULARY TIP During discussions with the students, use words that are related to the explorable concepts so as to model the utility of these words.

Writer's Notebook. Then provide an opportunity for volunteers to share the words and phrases that they have selected and to tell why they have chosen them. For additional opportunities to build vocabulary, see **Teacher Tool Card 77.**

3

Guided
Exploration

GUIDED AND INDEPENDENT EXPLORATION

EXPLORING CONCEPTS BEYOND THE TEXT

The following activities do not have to be completed within the days devoted to this lesson:

- The students might want to construct a naturalistic habitat for an animal. If possible, borrow a small animal, such as a bird or a reptile, from a science center or a neighborhood zoo or a pet store and bring it to class. Help the students create a suitable miniature habitat for the animal in the classroom. Ask some students to study the dietary needs of the animal and then, on a rotating schedule, assign students the task of providing meals to the animal. Students might take notes on the information they learn about the animal, its habitat, and its dietary needs and list this information on a chart that hangs above the "habitat." At the end of this experiment, the animal can be taken back to the organization that lent it to the students.

- Zoologists carefully study the diets of wild animals that are to be kept in captivity. Sometimes their normal diets can be supplied; sometimes suitable substitutes must be found. Students might interview a zookeeper or a zoo dietitian about the diets of some of the animals in the zoo. Students might choose the diet of one or two of these animals; collect (or find replicas of) the various plants, animals, or insects that make up the diets; and display these in the classroom.

❯ As a result of their reading or their interviews with zoo officials, students can record on page 93 of their Explorer's Notebook the diets of some fish, fowl, and animals that live in the wild. Invite the students to share their findings with their classmates.

❯ Point out to students that many different specialists collaborate in order to create suitable habitats for the animals in their care. As they read the selections in the unit and do independent research, have the students turn to their Explorer's Notebook and record information about wildlife habitats on page 94 and about conservation professionals on page 95.

❯ Distribute Home/School Connection 37, which encourages the students and a family member to visit a zoo or zoological park or aviary that features naturalistic habitats, to take pictures of the animals, and to record information about the animals and their habitats.

The Dietary Needs of Wildlife

Zoologists carefully study the diets of wild animals so that they can provide them with suitable diets in captivity. As you read, do research, and conduct interviews with wildlife specialists, record below information about the diets of fish, fowl, and other animals that live in the wild. Share your findings with your classmates.

Animal: _____ Where it lives: _____

Diet: _____

Animal: _____ Where it lives: _____

Diet: _____

Animal: _____ Where it lives: _____

Diet: _____

Animal: _____ Where it lives: _____

Diet: _____

Unit 5/Ecology — EN 93

Explorer's Notebook, page 93

Habitats Around the World

Throughout your reading and research for this unit, record what you have learned about some of the types of wildlife habitats around the world. Below, record their climates and geographical characteristics, their locations, and species of wildlife that live in them. Physical maps and atlases are helpful resources to use in your research.

Type of Habitat	Climate and Geographical Characteristics	Locations	Wildlife Species
grassland	dry, hot, flat	Central U.S., Africa	bison, deer, giraffe

94 EN — Ecology/Unit 5

Explorer's Notebook, page 94

Specialists in the Field of Ecology

The field of ecology requires the skills of many kinds of specialists, including biologists, geologists, chemists, engineers, and writers. Throughout your reading and research for the unit, list the types of specialists who are working to help the environment, the education and credentials they need to work in their fields, and their primary responsibilities.

Specialist: _____
Education needed: _____
Responsibilities: _____

Specialist: _____
Education needed: _____
Responsibilities: _____

Specialist: _____
Education needed: _____
Responsibilities: _____

Specialist: _____
Education needed: _____
Responsibilities: _____

Unit 5/Ecology — EN 95

Explorer's Notebook, page 95

"Windows on Wildlife"

A message from _____

In our unit on ecology, we have just read "Windows on Wildlife" by Ginny Johnston and Judy Cutchins. This selection is about some zoos, zoological parks, and aviaries that are constructing naturalistic habitats for the animals that are kept in captivity. Johnston and Cutchins describe the great care that is taken in reconstructing native habitats and in studying the dietary needs of the animals. If you live near a zoological park or an aviary that features naturalistic habitats, visit it with your child and do the following things. Notice and discuss the ways in which the zoo has attempted to reconstruct the animals' native habitats. If possible, take photographs of the wildlife in their habitats. As you take each picture, jot down (at the bottom of this page or in a small notebook) a number for each photograph and a description of the habitat. Tell what the animals are doing, what they are eating, and anything else of significance. Allow your child to bring the photographs and photographic summaries to school to share with his or her classmates.

Photographic summaries: _____

Unit 5/Ecology — H/SC 37

Home/School Connection 37

**Research Cycle:
Needs and Plans
Phase 1**

The students should already have produced individual conjectures regarding their chosen research problems and discussed them in their research groups. A whole-class discussion of these may now be conducted, in which problems and conjectures are briefly presented and all students have a chance to contribute suggestions, criticisms, and questions. These ideas should help the research groups as they enter the next phase, Needs and Plans.

Remind the students that the term *needs* refers to information they need to find out or to understand. To help groups get started in identifying knowledge needs related to their problems, you might focus on one of the conjectures that came out of Guided Exploration during the previous lesson. Relevant questions are, *What facts will we need to help us decide whether this conjecture is right? What do we need to understand to make our conjecture better? What would an expert on this problem know that we do not know?*

> Have the students examine the resources listed on page 96 of their Explorer's Notebook. If they are unfamiliar with any of these resources, briefly explain the purpose of each and where some can be found. The students may be unaware of other sources of information, such as interviews, films, and primary source materials. Highlight these sources of information and have the students discuss how each might be useful in their research. Remind the students to review the annotations in the bibliographies previously distributed and in those in the student anthology. Explain to them that these annotations will help them narrow their search for information by letting them know whether the book deals with their research problem. Tell the students that the way in which they decide to present their research may also affect their choice of resources. For example, if they want to make a poster, they might want to collect photographs and illustrations from magazines to place on the poster. Encourage them to begin thinking of interesting ways to present the information they will collect. These might include reports, posters, dioramas, video presentations, plays, or a combination of methods. If necessary, remind the students that the Cross-curricular Activity Cards in the Student Toolbox can provide them with ideas. Following this discussion, assign Explorer's Notebook, page 96, where the students will list knowledge needs and possible sources of information. Have the students begin collecting and examining resources. When students have finished Needs and Plans Phase 1, have them go to Needs and Plans Phase 2 before they read the next selection. This will provide them with enough time to conduct their research. For additional information on the Research Cycle, see **Learning Framework Card 4C, Needs and Plans Phase 1 and 2.**

**Research Cycle:
Needs and Plans
Phase 2**

Before the research groups meet to settle on definite research plans, whole-class discussion will be important to accomplish the following goals:
- Help students who are having trouble identifying knowledge needs related to their conjectures. It is important for students to recognize

* Exploring Through Research

* Exploring Through Research

Research Cycle: Needs and Plans Phase 1

My group's problem:

_____
_____
_____
_____
_____
_____

Knowledge Needs—Information I need to find or figure out in order to help explore the problem:

A. _____
B. _____
C. _____
D. _____
E. _____

Source	Useful?	How?
Encyclopedias		
Books		
Magazines		
Newspapers		
Videotapes, filmstrips, etc.		
Television		
Interviews, observations		
Museums		
Other		

Copyright © 1995 Open Court Publishing Company

96 EN   Ecology/Unit 5

Explorer's Notebook, page 96

what they need to know before they embark on gathering information; otherwise their research is liable to proceed aimlessly.

- Remind the research groups that they can still change their research problems. Some groups may have discovered by this time that their problem is not very promising. A group may choose to keep the same general problem but reformulate more precisely. (It is also possible that some students will want to change groups because they have become more interested in the problem of another group.)
- Provide any other needed discussion or guidance before students embark on formulating and carrying out their research plans.

▶ Assign page 97 of their Explorer's Notebook, to be completed after each planning group has agreed on a final statement of its problem, its knowledge needs, and its individual job assignments. As you observe the groups making their job assignments, encourage the students to take on tasks that are related to their strengths and likings. For example, a student who loves to draw might particularly enjoy planning and making the visual portion of the research project or examining photographs, illustrations, and diagrams for useful information. A student with good verbal skills might benefit from conducting interviews, while a less verbal child might primarily contribute information located in books,

Research Cycle: Needs and Plans Phase 2

Our problem:

_____

_____

_____

_____

_____

_____

_____

Knowledge Needs—Information we need to find or figure out in order to help explore the problem:

A. _____

B. _____

C. _____

D. _____

E. _____

F. _____

Group Members	Main Jobs

Hint: To save rewriting Knowledge Needs in the Main Jobs section, put in the capital letter marking the Knowledge Needs line.

Unit 5/Ecology   EN 97

Copyright © 1995 Open Court Publishing Company

Explorer's Notebook, page 97

magazines, and other reference materials. Whatever the job assignment, it is important that each child have a significant role in the group and be able to provide valuable information to help the group in its investigation and to add to its increasing understanding of ecology.

✳ INDEPENDENT WORKSHOP
Building a Community of Scholars

Student-Directed Reading, Writing, and Discussion

Research Cycle: Needs and Plans Phase 1 Working individually, students can list knowledge needs and resources on page 96 of their Explorer's Notebook. Then they can discuss their lists in their research groups, adding to their individual notebooks any items that may arise from the discussion. Remind the students to add scheduled activities, such as days on which they will go to the library, to their planning calendars. The students should also be collecting resources that relate to their research problem.

Research Cycle: Needs and Plans Phase 2 Students should work together in their research groups to complete the group plan in their Explorer's Notebook, page 97. Group members should agree on each item so that their group plans are the same. It is important that each member have a copy for future reference. Have the students examine their planning calendars. Assist them in allotting enough time to conduct their research and complete their research projects before the ending date. It may be helpful to record on the research cycle poster, using stick-on notes, where each group is in the cycle. Provide additional library time, if possible. Meet with the whole class as needed to assess the progress of each research group.

Additional Opportunities for Independent Reading, Writing, and Cross-curricular Activities

✱ Writing Seminar

If they have elected to begin a new piece of writing, encourage the students to think about their own observations and, with their classmates, to generate ideas during the prewriting and writing stages.

Explain to the students that most science writing and other informative articles are examples of expository writing. In expository pieces, the authors explain facts and concepts about a subject and may give their personal opinions, or they may explain a process or describe a problem and its causes. Encourage interested students to add expository pieces to their portfolios.

Cross-curricular Activity Cards

The following Cross-curricular Activity Cards in the Student Toolbox are appropriate for this selection:

- 15 Art—Paint a Mural of a Natural Habitat
- 16 Art—Designing an Aviary

Designing an Aviary
Use after "Windows on Wildlife"
16 Art

Paint a Mural of a Natural Habitat
Use after "Windows on Wildlife"
15 Art

The selection "Windows on Wildlife" contains photographs of various naturalistic habitat exhibits. Included are African and Asian rain forests; a tropical rain forest such as those found in Africa, Asia, and Central and South America; and a bit of the Antarctic. Use a large sheet of paper to paint a mural of one of the habitats illustrated in the selection. Use paint or magic marker. Look at the picture on page 176 of the student anthology to get an idea of the kind of painting you might try to create on a smaller scale. *You can learn a lot about a habitat by capturing it in a drawing or painting.*

Additional Opportunities for Solving Learning Problems

Tutorial

Use this time to work with individuals or small groups who need help in any area. This is also a good time for peer tutoring. If you have students who would benefit from giving or receiving peer tutoring, match them accordingly and have them refer to the proper Student Tool Card to guide their work together. Encourage the students to discuss with you any subject or area in which they need extra help. The following aids are available in the Teacher Toolbox for your convenience:

- Writer's Craft/Reading: Elaboration Through Providing Examples, Teacher Tool Card 39
- Grammar, Mechanics, and Usage: Phrases, Teacher Tool Card 50
- Grammar, Mechanics, and Usage: Using Commas in a Series, Teacher Tool Card 52

Fine Art

DISCUSSING FINE ART

Included here is some background information about the pieces of fine art shown on pages 182–183. Share with the students whatever you feel is appropriate. Some works may be familiar to them. Encourage them to express their reactions to each piece—for example, what the piece has to do with ecology, whether it is related to this unit, and why. Encourage them to find out more about artists or artistic styles that interest them. For additional information on **discussing fine art,** refer to **Teacher Tool Card 125.**

Dust Bowl. 1933.
Alexandre Hogue. Oil on canvas.

Alexandre Hogue, the son of a Presbyterian minister, was born in Memphis, Missouri, in 1898. He was six when his family moved to Texas. Hogue worked for a time on a cattle ranch in the Texas Panhandle. He saw firsthand the influx of "suitcase farmers" who were seeking short-term profits in the booming wheat market. A suitcase farmer lived outside the farming community and came to the farm only during the plowing, seeding, and harvesting seasons. Thus, he had no real connections with the land and no stake in the long-term survival of the farm. To plant wheat, these farmers plowed up grazing land, turning up roots that had never before been broken. Hogue often heard long-time ranchers say, "If you plow up this land, it will blow away." He would later see this prediction come true. For a time Hogue attended the Minneapolis Art Institute. In 1921, he moved to New York, where he spent four years "hanging around New York art galleries." He decided, however, that his best chance of enjoying life and painting life as he knew it was back in Texas.

Hogue would get his chance to paint the life he knew during the Great Depression. One of the government programs started at the time was the

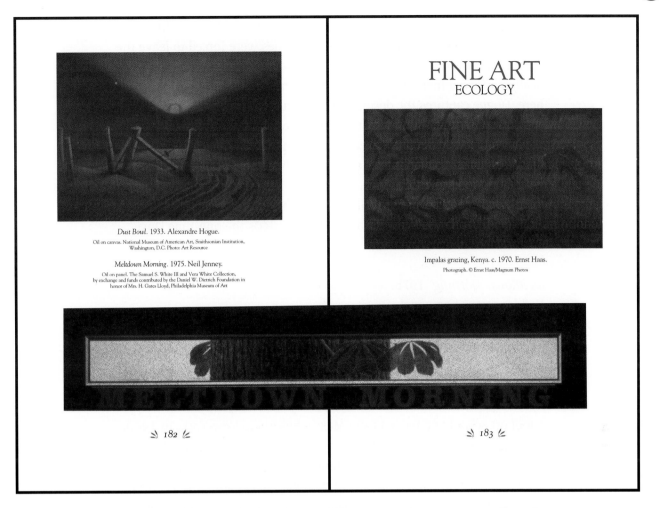

FINE ART
ECOLOGY

Dust Bowl. 1933. Alexandre Hogue.
Oil on canvas. National Museum of American Art, Smithsonian Institution,
Washington, D.C. Photo: Art Resource

Meltdown Morning. 1975. Neil Jenney.
Oil on panel. The Samuel S. White III and Vera White Collection,
by exchange and funds contributed by the Daniel W. Dietrich Foundation in
honor of Mrs. H. Gates Lloyd, Philadelphia Museum of Art

Impalas grazing, Kenya. c. 1970. Ernst Haas.
Photograph. © Ernst Haas/Magnum Photos

182

183

Section of Fine Arts (SFA), which employed artists to create murals and
sculptures for federal buildings, mostly post offices. It was the belief of
the government that everyone, including the poor, needed cultural
enrichment as well as material assistance. The goal of the SFA was to
produce accessible works of art that would be neither academic nor
avante-garde but statements about contemporary American life based on
common experience. The SFA commissioned artists from all over the
country, many of whom were unknown, to create works of art in every
type of community, not just urban or wealthy areas. These artists seized
the opportunity to create art for the "real people" rather than the academic art world. Many people, especially those in small rural towns, had
never seen original works of art.

Hogue certainly understood the experience of the displaced and finan-
cially ruined Dust Bowl farmers. The region consisting of the panhandles
of Oklahoma and Texas, southeastern Colorado, southwestern Kansas,
and northeastern New Mexico came to be known as the Dust Bowl
because of the conditions that struck it in the 1930s. Those suitcase
farmers that Hogue had witnessed as a young man were a large part of
the problem. Prior to World War I the grasslands had largely supported
cattle grazing. The grass that was plowed up to make way for cash crops
was essential to the maintenance of the topsoil: the roots held the soil
down and retained moisture in a region that received very little rainfall
per year. When high winds and drought struck the land in the 1930s,
the topsoil simply "blew away," as the old ranchers had said it would.

"Black blizzards" of airborne dirt would block out the sun and form drifts. As a result, tens of thousands of families were forced to leave the region. In his 1939 book *The Grapes of Wrath,* John Steinbeck realistically portrayed their dismal plight. In his painting *Dust Bowl,* shown here, Hogue captures the desolation of the area as the unyielding sun burns steadily on the barren, dust-smothered landscape.

Sympathetic to the devastated farmers, the newly elected New Deal government enacted a bill that suspended the foreclosure of farms in the area for a period of three years. Eventually, the wind erosion was stemmed by the planting of millions of young trees as windbreaks and by the restoration of the grasslands. By the 1940s the one-time Dust Bowl had returned to normal.

Meltdown Morning. 1975.
Neil Jenney. Oil on panel.

Neil Jenney, born in 1945, grew up in the Berkshire hills of Massachusetts, a fact that cannot be forgotten while viewing his paintings and their strong environmentalist messages. As Jenney puts it, "Being a little biological organism on the third stone from the sun, you can't help but be in awe of what's around you." In 1966, Jenney dropped out of art school and moved from Massachusetts to New York. In 1969, after trying his hand at sculpture for three years and living the life of a starving artist, he switched to painting. Jenney developed a slightly abstract realism as his style. His early paintings are stark and ironic comparisons: between birds and planes, a girl and a doll, an American jet and a Soviet jet. The viewer is left to draw his or her own conclusions from these comparisons; in the works themselves, Jenney offers none. One of these paintings, *Forest and Lumber,* depicts a row of standing trees and a row of fallen trees; the two rows are divided by a row of tree stumps. Jenney himself thinks of this painting as "tragic."

The titles of Jenney's paintings are very important to the understanding of his work—so important, in fact, that they are often emblazoned in huge letters on the picture frames. The title becomes, in effect, a part of the work itself. "I put a title on the picture frame to reinforce what you're seeing or to expand it," explains Jenney.

Meltdown Morning depicts the narrowest slice of a tree and a spare brace of leaves with a faint candy-colored mushroom cloud in the background. Because of its shape, the cloud emitted at the detonation of a nuclear device is called a mushroom cloud. One can see in that bare slice of tree not just one tree but all of the world's ecosystems. One can see in that mushroom cloud not just the threat of one nuclear blast, or even nuclear power generally but the dark and disenchanting side of technology, the potentially destructive side of human scientific advancement. The exaggerated shape of the painting (it is twelve times longer than it is tall) suggests the view a gunner might have looking through a gun turret, illustrating the continuing battle between humanity and the natural world.

"Art is a social science," Jenney maintains, and most of his work has a clear social agenda. It celebrates the North American wilderness but warns of and exposes the forces that threaten it. Realism, his chosen painting style, allows Jenney to "address the issues of today," he claims. "There is no confusion."

Impalas grazing, Kenya. c. 1970.
Ernst Haas. Photograph.

Ernst Haas (1921–1986) was born in Vienna, Austria. After studying medicine briefly, he turned to photography. In 1947 the American Red Cross headquarters in Vienna showed his photographs of returning POWs (prisoners of war), captured during World War II (1939–1945). The pictures and accompanying story eventually appeared in *Life* magazine. Haas's first one-person exhibition opened at the Museum of Modern Art in New York in 1962. Haas began teaching photography workshops in the early 1970s. During his lifetime, Haas won numerous awards, and his work was published in many books.

One hundred years ago, the woodlands and plains of Africa were abundant with a great variety of wild animals. The impala, a graceful antelope that at times has been recorded to leap as far as thirty feet and run as fast as eighty miles per hour, grazed a range of land that extended almost all the way across the continent. Impalas are still seen in many of the eastern game reserves, but their numbers are now greatly reduced.

The male impala, with its red-brown upper body and pure white chest and stomach, has horns that can grow up to twenty-nine inches long. Although they are long and beautifully curved, its horns have never been prized as having any extraordinary value, unlike those of the elephant or the rhinoceros. In spite of efforts by the government and ecologists, the elephant and the rhinoceros have nearly become extinct because of illegal hunting, or poaching. Poachers risk severe punishment, sometimes even death, to obtain rhinoceros horns, still considered in some cultures to have medicinal properties, and elephant tusks, often referred to as "white gold," for its use as ivory.

Poachers are not the only problem confronting Africa's wildlife. Increasing human populations, encroaching cities, pollution, and growing demands upon the land through farming and domestic breeding have forced many animals from their natural habitats. Encroachment upon natural migration routes has also affected their survival. In some cases, animals may die of starvation or thirst because they are unable to reach food and water supplies that are only seasonally available.

Fortunately, many African countries, like Kenya, have created game reserves for the preservation of endangered species. Under the protection of the law, many animals have been able to rebuild their numbers and repopulate their herds. Some animals that are extinct in the wild have been able to breed well in captivity. Programs have been developed to reintroduce the captive animals back into their natural habitats. With continued interest and concern, we may be able to save animals like the impala from extinction.

A Natural Force

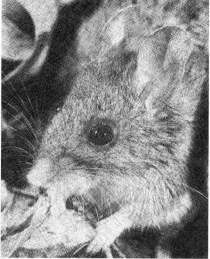

1 READING THE SELECTION

About the Selection

Until recently, most people thought that fire was destructive to forests and the wildlife that lives in them. Now scientists are discovering that certain types of fires are actually beneficial to a forest ecosystem. In "A Natural Force," Laurence Pringle explains how forest fires help many species of plants and animals to thrive and survive. From its provocative introduction to its surprising conclusion, this selection captures the reader's attention and destroys some common misconceptions about forest fires.

Link to the Unit Concepts

In "A Natural Force," pages 184–197, the author explains that forest fires are natural occurrences and that plant life in a forest ecosystem depends on fires for survival. In fact, since fires have been occurring naturally for many thousands of years, many plants have adapted to survive them. Fires clear out the undergrowth of a forest and allow some plants and trees to release seeds. Fires also open up to sunlight areas of the forest that may previously have been choked from the sunlight. When leaves and twigs burn on the forest floor, nutrients are released into the soil and are recycled into the roots of living plants. All of these occurrences are beneficial to the flora and fauna of a forest ecosystem.

After reading this selection, students may wonder to what extent humans should intervene during natural events like forest fires.

About the Author

Laurence Pringle was once the editor of the children's magazine *Nature and Science,* and his articles and photographs have appeared in many journals. He has also written numerous children's books about nature and science, with one of his main goals being to stimulate children's interest in these subjects.

LESSON OVERVIEW

"A Natural Force" by Laurence Pringle, pages 184–197

READING THE SELECTION

Materials
Student anthology, pp. 184–197
Explorer's Notebook, p. 82

FYI
Learning Framework Card
• Setting Reading Goals and Expectations, 1A

READING WITH A WRITER'S EYE

Minilesson
Writer's Craft: Defining Unfamiliar Terms

Materials
Reading/Writing Connection, p. 38
Reproducible Masters 15, 52
Assessment Master 1

FYI
Teacher Tool Card
• Spelling and Vocabulary: Building Vocabulary, 77

Options for Instruction
Writer's Craft: Elaboration Through Giving Reasons or Causes
Writer's Craft: Elaboration Through Providing Specific Facts
(Use Teacher Tool Cards listed below.)

GUIDED AND INDEPENDENT EXPLORATION

Minilesson
Research Aid: Using the *Reader's Guide to Periodical Literature*

Materials
Explorer's Notebook, pp. 98–99
Home/School Connection 38

Independent Workshop

Optional Materials from Student Toolbox

Tradebook Connection Cards

Cross-curricular Activity Card
• 16 Science—Plant Rubbings

Student Tool Cards
• Writer's Craft/Reading: Giving Definitions, 44
• Writer's Craft/Reading: Giving Reasons or Causes, 38
• Writer's Craft/Reading: Telling Important Facts, 41
• Study and Research: Using the *Reader's Guide to Periodical Literature* and the *Children's Magazine Guide*, 105

FYI
Teacher Tool Cards
• Writer's Craft/Reading: Elaboration Through Providing Definitions in Text, 44
• Writer's Craft/Reading: Elaboration Through Giving Reasons or Causes, 38
• Writer's Craft/Reading: Elaboration Through Providing Specific Facts, 41
• Study and Research: Using the *Reader's Guide to Periodical Literature* and the *Children's Magazine Guide*, 105

NOTES

Asterisks (*) throughout the lesson indicate learning frameworks. Learning Framework Cards and Teacher Tool Cards can be found in the Teacher Toolbox

Pringle is committed to preserving nature, and many of his books explain the damage to the earth brought about by humans. He writes that his books "tend to encourage readers to feel a kinship with other living things and a sense of membership in the earth's ecosystem." The titles of some of his books bear out his concern for saving our earth: *Living Treasure: Saving Earth's Threatened Biodiversity; Water: The Next Resource Battle; Restoring Our Earth; Rain of Troubles: The Science and Politics of Acid Rain;* and *Oil Spills.*

INFORMATION FOR THE STUDENT

Share with students any information about Laurence Pringle that may be of interest to them. You might also refer them to page 197 of the student anthology so that they can read about Pringle's background and his ideas about nature and science before they begin "A Natural Force."

COGNITIVE AND RESPONSIVE READING

Activating Prior Knowledge

Ask the students what they know about forest fires. You might want to write their responses on the chalkboard so that after reading the selection, they can pinpoint any misconceptions they had about forest fires.

Setting Reading Goals and Expectations

Have the students **browse the selection, using the clues/problems/wondering procedure.** Students will return to these observations after reading. For a review of **browsing**, see **Learning Framework Card 1A, Setting Reading Goals and Expectations.**

Recommendations for Reading the Selection

Ask students how they would like to read the selection. Since they may have questions about the content of this nonfiction piece, oral reading is recommended. During oral reading, use and encourage think-alouds. During silent reading, allow discussion as needed. Discuss problems, strategies, and reactions after reading. This would also be a good selection for **responding** to text by **visualizing** and by **showing surprise** while reading aloud. Model these responses, and then invite the students to do the same.

About the Reading Strategies

"A Natural Force" may contain terms and ideas that are unfamiliar to the students. Remind them that **asking questions** is a strategy that good readers use frequently to check their understanding of what they have read.

Think-aloud Prompts for Use in Oral Reading

The think-aloud prompts are placed where the students may want to use strategies to help them better understand the text. These are merely suggestions. Remind the students to refer to the **reading strategy posters** and to use any strategy they find helpful as they read.

TEACHING TIP Offer an example of how good readers might work out a reading problem to make certain that they understand what they are reading.

THINK ALOUD PROMPTS

These prompts may be used as guides to promote cognitive and responsive reading.

A NATURAL FORCE

Laurence Pringle

A lightning bolt flashes in the summer night. It sizzles and spirals down a tree trunk. Wisps of smoke rise from dead pine needles on the forest floor. Flames glow in the night, and a forest fire begins.

The fire spreads quickly. Flames leap up to the <u>crowns</u> of trees, which explode into fireballs. Overhead the fire leaps from tree to tree. A wall of flames moves through the woods, gaining speed. The forest fire seems like a terrible beast with a mind of its own. It roars; it changes direction. It hungrily sucks oxygen from the air and kills almost everything in its path.

Some of the fastest wild animals are able to escape. The unlucky and the less swift perish—burned to death or robbed of oxygen by the fire. Sometimes a dying rabbit becomes an agent of the fire; its fur ablaze, it dashes crazily through the woods, setting fires as it goes.

At last the fire comes to an end. It dies because of rain, or the efforts of fire fighters, or a combination of factors. But the land is blackened, studded with tree skeletons, littered with dead animals. The soil is vulnerable to terrible erosion, and many years pass before the land heals itself with new plant growth and wildlife.

৯১ 184 ৶

© Bob McKeever/Tom Stack & Associates

Northwestern foresters deliberately set surface fires in order to help the growth of new trees.

© Scott Blackman/Tom Stack & Associates

This scene of death and destruction exists in the imaginations of millions of people—*and seldom anywhere else*. Each year there are more than 100,000 forest fires in the United States. Most are started by people, either accidentally or on purpose. Some are started by lightning. Most lightning-caused fires go out, by themselves, after burning less than a quarter acre of land. And most forest fires of any size are beneficial to plants and animals.

Their good effects have been recognized for many years in the Southeastern United States. Each year forest managers there routinely set ablaze two million acres where pine trees grow. In the West, some wildfires are now allowed to burn for months in national parks and forests. This practice upsets people who feel that all forest fires are "bad."

Whether a forest fire is "bad" or "good" depends on many factors. No one advocates that fires be allowed to burn homes or valuable timber. But fire has been a natural force on land for millions of years, not just in forests but on prairies and savannahs (grasslands mixed with trees and shrubs). Fire became part of our planet's environment as soon as there was vegetation dry enough to be lit by lightning. From then on, periodic fires have been as natural as rain over much of the Earth's land surface. Rain can sometimes be destructive. So

⇒ *186* ⇐

can fire. But a great deal of the Earth's plant and animal life has been "born and bred" with fire and thrives under its influence.

After many years of suppressing forest fires at all costs, ideas about them are changing. In the past few decades scientists have learned a lot about ecology—the study of relationships between living things and their environment. Now they are learning about ecopyrology—the ecology of fire.

The study of fire ecology is complex and fascinating because there are many kinds of forests and many kinds of fires. To understand the natural role of fire, scientists observe current fires and also investigate fires that occurred centuries ago.

They learn about past fires by examining fire scars. When a fire injures a tree's zone of growing cells (the cambium) and the wound heals, a mark that is eventually covered by bark is left. This scar can be seen later, when the tree is cut down. A cross-section near the tree's base reveals many of the fire scars that formed during the tree's life.

Studies of these scars show that fire was a normal occurrence in most of the original forests of North America. In California, scientists discovered that fires have happened about every eight years since the year 1685—as far back as they could date the cedar trees studied. They also found that few fire scars had formed after 1900, when people began preventing forest fires.

Ecologists have concluded that low-intensity fires, burning along the ground, were common in Western forests of ponderosa pine and sequoia. They also occurred frequently in Southeastern pine forests. With the exception of swamps

⇒ *187* ⇐

1 To understand the text that follows, the students will need to grasp the meaning of the italicized phrase, that is, that the scene described previously represents a popular misconception about forest fires. **Asking questions** is one strategy that may help students to determine the meaning of Pringle's statement.

Crown fires are inevitable in some Western forests where fuel has
accumulated over many years.
© Bob McKeever/Tom Stack & Associates

≥ 188 ≤

and other year-round wet environments, fire used to be a regular happening in many parts of North America.

In many forests of the Pacific Northwest and Northern
Rockies, fires were less frequent and usually more intense.
Flames reached the crowns of trees, which were often killed or
damaged. Forest managers have accepted the idea that crown
fires are <u>inevitable</u> in parts of the West. The cool, dry climate
prevents much decay of dead leaves and other natural litter
on the forest floor. Plenty of fuel is available when ideal fire
weather occurs, as it does in these northern forests every fifty
to one hundred years or so.

Since fires have been a part of forest environments for
many thousands of years, many plants have <u>adapted</u> to survive them. These plants might be called "fire species."
Among them are the major forest trees of the Northern Rockies: ponderosa pine, white pine, lodgepole pine, larch, and
Douglas fir.

These trees have especially thick bark, which can withstand fire damage better than the bark of other species. Fire
species also include such plants as aspen, willow, and pine
grass, which send up many sprouts after suffering fire damage.

One group of Western shrubs, known as *Ceanothus*, is especially dependent on fire. It includes redstem, wedgeleaf, snow
brush, and deer brush. *Ceanothus* shrubs are three to nine feet
tall and thrive where plenty of sunlight reaches the forest
floor. Once damaged by fire, the shrubs produce abundant
new sprouts. Furthermore, *Ceanothus* seeds must be exposed
to high temperatures in order to sprout.

Ordinarily, vital moisture cannot get through the hard seed
coat to the embryo plant inside. Heat from the fires causes

≥ 189 ≤

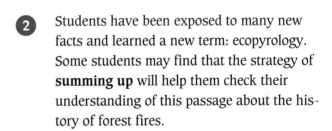

2 Students have been exposed to many new
facts and learned a new term: ecopyrology.
Some students may find that the strategy of
summing up will help them check their
understanding of this passage about the history of forest fires.

Ceanothus shrubs thrive where fires occur. Western deer and elk feed
on the shrubs, especially in wintertime.
© Jack Wilburn/Earth Scenes

the seed coat to open permanently. The seedling can then
develop when conditions are right. After a forest fire, ecologists
have counted as many as 242,000 *Ceanothus* seedlings on an
acre of land.

The reproduction of jack pine, lodgepole pine, and some
other evergreens depends partly on forest fire. These species
have sticky resins that hold together the scales of their seed-
bearing cones. The cones remain on the trees for many years,
storing thousands of pine seeds. In time, a fire releases them. A
temperature of about 122 degrees Fahrenheit is needed for the
resins to melt so that the seeds can pop out onto the ground.

Fire also burns away all or most of the leaves and other natural litter. Many more seedlings grow from such an exposed
seedbed than from a surface covered with a deep layer of leaves.

In a plant community that depends on periodic fire, not all
species are well-adapted to it. Some take over if fire is kept out
of the forest. Without fire, pines in the Southeast are gradually

≥ *190* ≤

Seed pods opening after a fire. A ponderosa
pine seedling flourishes on a forest floor where,
once, the leaves were burned and seeds fell
directly onto the soil.
Top: © David C. Fritts/Earth Scenes. *Right:* National Park Service

replaced by such deciduous trees as oaks. If no fire occurs for
many years in a lodgepole-pine forest in the Rocky Mountains, the old pines are eventually replaced by Engelmann
spruce and fir trees. The entire plant community changes
unless a forest fire halts the process. A fire would kill many
spruce and fir trees, which are less able to withstand the damage than lodgepole pine. And the fire would help release the
seeds that represent a new generation of lodgepole pines.

Ponderosa pine is another fire species. It covers thirty-six
million acres of Western land, from Nebraska to the Pacific
Ocean and from Mexico to Canada. The large needles of ponderosa pine seem designed to encourage fire. Many needles
are dropped each year. Because of their size they do not pack
down much, and so they dry quickly. They also contain resins.
Thus, the needles decay slowly and burn easily.

As long as ponderosa-pine forests have occasional surface
fires, the trees thrive and grow in grassy, parklike stands. A

≥ *191* ≤

ponderosa-pine forest without fire is doomed. When young pines are not thinned out by fire, they grow so close together they are called "dog hair thickets." These thickets are a tremendous crown-fire hazard. Biologists sometimes call these dense stands of trees "biological deserts," because there is so little variety of life in them.

A lack of occasional fires in pine woods may produce a dog hair thicket of young trees.
© Micky Gibson/Earth Scenes

Without fire, white fir and Douglas fir gradually replace the ponderosa pines. The entire forest environment changes. Fir trees have dense crowns, which allow little light to reach the forest floor. Grasses and other surface plants dwindle in numbers and variety—and so do the animals that depend on them. Ecologists have concluded that fire is vital for the survival of beauty and variety in ponderosa-pine forests.

3 Fire obviously plays a key role in allowing some major plant communities to thrive. Just as there are plant fire species, there are also animal fire species. Elk and deer rely heavily on *Ceanothus* shrubs for winter food in the West. Their health and numbers depend in part on forest fires, which cause *Ceanothus* to thrive. Periodic fires also affect the availability of aspen, a favorite food of moose.

The very survival of the endangered Kirtland's warbler seems to depend on fire. About four hundred of these tiny,

≥ 192 ≤

colorful birds nest in part of Michigan and nowhere else in the world. They are also known as jack-pine birds, because they build nests under or near young jack pines. This species may never have had a very big range. However, its numbers have declined because of fire control in Michigan jack-pine forests. In an attempt to prevent the Kirtland warblers from dying out, foresters now deliberately plan and set some fires to maintain the kind of nesting habitat needed by them.

Forest fires seldom kill wildlife. Most of them do not occur during the season when birds and other animals have young in nests or dens. Many kinds of animals seem able to sense a fire and its direction, and they move out of its way. Even slow-moving creatures like snakes usually escape. **4**

Every forest fire is different and may have different effects. During most of the fire's life it moves slowly. Rain, lack of wind, or lack of fuel may bring the fire almost to a halt for several days. (Some have been known to smolder all winter long, then resume burning in the spring.) Fires have a daily rhythm too, slowing at night when winds usually die down.

A fire's biography may include a wind-pushed rapid spread when some slow-moving animals are overtaken. It may also burn with great heat in certain areas and suffocate some animals hidden in burrows. Overall, however, wildlife populations are not usually harmed.

Deer, elk, and other large mammals often feed calmly near a surface fire. Usually fire fighters, not flames, are what frighten them away. Foresters working in Southern pine woods report that hawks are attracted by smoke. It may be a signal to them that rodents and other prey are on the move. Eagles and other predatory birds in Africa have also been observed

≥ 193 ≤

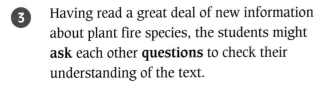

3 Having read a great deal of new information about plant fire species, the students might **ask** each other **questions** to check their understanding of the text.

4 Students may **wonder** why forest fires seldom kill animal wildlife or how certain animals are able to sense a fire and its direction. Students may discover some satisfactory answers to their wonderings if they **make connections** between the text and what they already know about wildlife.

Elk in Wyoming feed on willow and cottonwood, plants that produce
new sprouts after a fire.
© Gregory K. Scott/Photo Researchers

catching insects, lizards, and rodents that are flushed from
hiding places by an advancing fire.

Wildlife is attracted to freshly burned land too. Mice and
other seed-eating rodents appear in great numbers after a forest fire, sometimes to the dismay of foresters who are concerned about getting a new crop of seedling trees.

For elk, deer, and other plant-eating animals, the end of a
forest fire marks the beginning of a period of plentiful and
nutritious food. Plants that grow after a fire are usually richer
than normal in protein, calcium, phosphate, potash, and
other nutrients.

In some ways the burning process is like the process of
decay speeded up. As leaves and twigs decay, nutrients are
released slowly, over a period of months or years. When leaves
and twigs burn, the nutrients are released quickly. From the
soil they are gradually recycled into the roots of plants. This
sudden dose of nutrients shows up in plant tissues for about
two years after a forest fire.

≥ 194 ≤

Whether the new growth is shrub sprouts, new grasses, or
other plants, it is nutritious, tender, and perhaps better-tasting
than normal. Elk have been observed eating new sprouts of
plants that they usually avoid when the plants are older.

A forest fire also produces a more varied "menu" of plants.
The burning away of dead leaves, release of nutrients, and

Deer mice and red squirrels find abundant seeds after a forest fire. These
plentiful seed-eating mammals are hunted by hawks and other predators.

Top left: © Gary Milburn/Tom Stack & Associates. *Top right:* © Robert C. Simpson/Tom Stack
& Associates. *Bottom:* © Kerry T. Givens/Tom Stack & Associates

This photograph was taken immediately after the Elk Creek Fire
in Yellowstone National Park in 1988.
© J.H. Robinson/Earth Scenes

The same place, photographed a year later, is covered by plant growth
that was nourished by nutrients from ashes.
© J.H. Robinson/Earth Scenes

increased sunlight on the forest floor help create an environment in which a great variety of plants can grow. After a forest fire swept through an Idaho Douglas-fir forest, ninety- nine different kinds of plants appeared where only fifty-one species had been found before.

Ecologists suspect that periodic forest fires have other good effects. Woodsmoke seems to inhibit the growth of fungi, which sometimes harm living trees. Fire also affects populations of insects, including some pests, which spend part of their lives in the leafy litter of forest floors.

Forests and forest fires vary a lot. Scientists still have much to learn in order to understand and manage the fires that affect the forested one-third of the United States. There is no doubt, however, that the return of periodic fires will be good **5** for most forests and their wildlife.

≥ 196 ≤

MEET LAURENCE PRINGLE, AUTHOR

Laurence Pringle became interested in wildlife and the environment as a child growing up in rural New York. After earning degrees in wildlife conservation, Pringle decided to become a writer rather than a wildlife biologist. He says that he writes his books like a teacher would plan a lesson. He discusses the key ideas and tries to spark some enthusiasm about them.

Pringle wants readers to understand that humans are part of a large ecosystem that includes all living creatures. Although he makes his living as a writer, Pringle still uses his science training to help his writing. He says that challenging authority and accepted truths is a basic part of the scientific process. Therefore, many of his books clarify popular misconceptions about subjects like forest fires, vampire bats, wolves, coyotes, and killer bees. Through his books, Pringle tries to show that scientific explorations give us a better understanding of the world.

≥ 197 ≤

---

5 **Summing up** now may help the students to keep in mind all that they have learned about how forest fires benefit the wildlife of the forest.

Discussing Strategy Use

Encourage the students to share with each other any problems they had while reading the article and the strategies they used to solve them. Have any students who developed their own strategies for solving problems share these with their classmates.

*   **EXPLORING THROUGH DISCUSSION**

Reflecting on the Selection
Whole-Group Discussion

The whole group discusses the selection and any thoughts or questions that it raises. During this time, students also **return to the clues, problems, and wonderings** that they noted on the chalkboard during browsing.

Assessment

To assess their understanding of the text, engage the students in a discussion to determine whether they have grasped the following ideas:
- some common misconceptions about forest fires
- the ways in which fires are helpful to plant and animal species

Response Journal

"A Natural Force" introduced the students to some interesting and surprising facts about forest fires. Students who are keeping a response journal may wish to record their personal thoughts and impressions about the selection.

Exploring Concepts Within the Selection
Small-Group Discussion

While small groups discuss the **selection's relationship to ecology,** circulate and observe the discussions. Remind the students to **refer to the Question Board and the Concept Board** to keep their discussions focused.

Sharing Ideas About Explorable Concepts

Have the groups **report their ideas** and **discuss them** with the rest of the class. It is crucial that the students' ideas determine this discussion.
- Students may notice that during most of the twentieth century, people suppressed forest fires because of a mistaken belief that these fires irrevocably destroyed the plant and animal life of the forest; when facts replaced assumptions, ideas about forest fires began to change.
- Students may comment that, although a fire may cause some casualties in an ecosystem, the ecosystem as a whole benefits from the effects of a fire.

As these ideas and others are stated, have the students **add them to the Question Board** or the **Concept Board.**

Have students examine and briefly discuss the painting *Dust Bowl* by Alexandre Hogue on page 182 of the student anthology. They may wish to express their thoughts and feelings about this particular work and comment on any connections they see between the painting and the article they have just read.

Fine Art

Exploring Concepts Across Selections

Ask the students whether this selection reminds them of other selections that they have read. Students may make connections with other selections in this unit or in previous units.
- Students may compare the positive and negative ways in which humans have affected plant and animal life mentioned in this selection with those behaviors mentioned in *Protecting Wildlife* and "Windows on Wildlife."

STEPS TOWARD INDEPEN-DENCE The students should be becoming more adept at making comparisons between selections. If some students need help, model comparing selections on the basis of ideas that they have discussed about ecology.

- Students may compare the attitudes and concerns of ecologists and conservationists with those of abolitionists, suffragists, and human rights activists such as Sarah and Angelina Grimké, Martin Luther King, Jr., and Gandhi in the unit Taking a Stand.

Connections Across Units

Evaluating Discussions

Recording Ideas

As they complete the above discussions, ask the students to **sum up what they have learned from their conversations and to tell how they might use this information** in further explorations. Any special information or insights may be recorded on the **Concept Board.** Any further questions that they would like to think about, pursue, or investigate may be recorded on the **Question Board.** They may want to discuss the progress that has been made on their questions. They may also want to cross out any questions that no longer warrant consideration.

❱ The students should record their ideas and impressions about the selection on page 82 of their Explorer's Notebook.

Explorer's Notebook, page 82

Recording Concept Information continued

"Windows on Wildlife" by Ginny Johnston and Judy Cutchins

"A Natural Force" by Laurence Pringle

---

82 EN   Ecology/Unit 5

Copyright © 1995 Open Court Publishing Company

2 READING WITH A WRITER'S EYE
MINILESSON

**Writer's Craft:
Defining
Unfamiliar Terms**

Ask the students to discuss anything that they have learned about defining unfamiliar terms and to give any examples that they can remember from their reading or writing. Point out that in "A Natural Force," author Laurence Pringle **defines new terms and concepts** for his readers. Good writers provide definitions of unfamiliar terms so that readers can understand what they read without having to stop and use a dictionary.

As an example, read to the students paragraphs 1 and 2 on page 187. Invite a volunteer to identify the terms being defined and the definitions given. Are Pringle's definitions clear and understandable? Note that **some terms are defined in appositive—phrases that are set off by commas, dashes, or parentheses. Other terms are made clear by the context in which they are used.** You may want to point out that a complete definition of *ecopyrology* includes the definition of *ecology,* which came before it in the text, and that although *ecopyrology* is defined in paragraph 1, the concept is explained in paragraph 2.

**Selective Reading:
Focus on Defining
Unfamiliar Terms**

Now have the students find other passages in the selection in which the author defines new terms or concepts. Encourage volunteers to read a passage, identify the term defined, and tell how it is defined: with an appositive, by it's use in a context that makes its meaning clear, or by an explanation in the text. One example can be found on page 187, paragraph 3. In this paragraph the term *cambium* is in apposition with its meaning, "growing cells." Other examples can be found on the following page:

- page 189, paragraph 1: "crown fires" (used in context)
- page 189, paragraph 2: "fire species" (explained in the text)

*Selection-Based
Practice*

**Independent Practice:
Defining Unfamiliar
Terms**

❯ For additional practice in recognizing how an author provides definitions, have the students work in small groups to discuss and complete Reading/Writing Connection, page 38.

❯ Distibute Reproducible Master 52, Examples of Defintions, and suggest that the students record good examples of definitions as they read throughout the year. Have them insert this page in the Author's Style section of their Writer's Notebook. Encourage students to refer to these examples and use them as models when they write. Make available additional copies of this master as needed.

ASSESSMENT TIP This may be a good opportunity to observe students working in groups and to write observations in your Teacher's Observation Log.

Defining Unfamiliar Terms

"A Natural Force"

In "A Natural Force" or other selections that you have read, find examples in which the author provides definitions to explain or to clarify new terms and concepts. Write the selection title, the term or the concept being defined, and the number of the page where the definition appears. Notice the various styles that authors use to define terms and concepts.

Title: _____

Term or concept defined: _____ Page: _____

Method used to define term or concept: _____

_____

Title: _____

Term or concept defined: _____ Page: _____

Method used to define term or concept: _____

_____

Title: _____

Term or concept defined: _____ Page: _____

Method used to define term or concept: _____

_____

Title: _____

Term or concept defined: _____ Page: _____

Method used to define term or concept: _____

_____

Look back at this page for help when you want to define unfamiliar terms in your writing.

Defining Terms
_____
38 R/WC   Ecology/Unit 5

Name

Copyright © 1995 Open Court Publishing Company

Reading/Writing Connection, page 38

Examples of Definitions

An example of a good definition is _____

_____

From the article _____

by _____

The author used this method to define the term or concept: _____

An example of a good definition is _____

_____

From the article _____

by _____

The author used this method to define the term or concept: _____

An example of a good definition is _____

_____

From the article _____

by _____

The author used this method to define the term or concept: _____

An example of a good definition is _____

_____

From the article _____

by _____

The author used this method to define the term or concept: _____

RM 52   Writer's Notebook: Author's Style

Name

Copyright © 1995 Open Court Publishing Company

Reproducible Master 52

WRITING

Linking Reading to Writing

Remind the students that **they can define terms and concepts in their own writing** to make it easier for their readers to understand a piece. To provide opportunities for the students to apply the techniques of defining terms, encourage them to look through their **writing folders** for stories or articles that could be improved by adding definitions of unfamiliar terms and concepts. When the students have had sufficient time to choose and revise a piece of writing, invite volunteers to read their original passages and their rewritten versions and to explain how the changes have made their writing better.

∗ Writing Process

Remind students who are proofreading and revising their work to refer to Reproducible Master 21, Proofreader's Marks, in the Checking My Work section of their Writer's Notebook. Encourage any students who have elected to publish previously written, revised, and proofread pieces to place these in the classroom library so that they may be shared with the rest of the class.

WRITER'S NOTEBOOK TIP Have the students review all the sections in their Writer's Notebook to make sure the contents are updated and complete.

VOCABULARY

Concept-related words or phrases from the selection that the students may want to remember and use in their speaking and writing include *vegetation, ecopyrology, cambium, cross-section, low-intensity, crown, abundant, embryo, resins, periodic, deciduous, fire species, vital, smolder,* and *nutrients.* Have copies of Vocabulary Exploration form, Reproducible Master 15, available so that the students can add these or any other words or phrases to the Personal Dictionary section of their Writer's Notebook. Then encourage volunteers to share their words and tell why they chose them. For additional opportunities to build vocabulary, see Teacher Tool Card 77.

Professional Checkpoint: Reading with a Writer's Eye

The students should be continually adding to the Writing Ideas section in their Writer's Notebook. Reinforce often that they should put ideas in their Writer's Notebook at any time they occur, not just during writing time. Remind students that they need not use every idea that they record in their notebook, or even most of them. They should not be afraid to jot down ideas that they are not sure about. These ideas may prove helpful later.

Notes:

3 GUIDED AND INDEPENDENT EXPLORATION

Guided Exploration

The following activities do not have to be completed within the days devoted to this lesson.

❯ In "A Natural Force," the students read about some varieties of trees and plants, such as the lodgepole pine tree and the *Ceanothus* shrub. Working in small groups, the students could choose and gather information about a variety of tree, plant, or flower (one type per group) that often grows in a forest. What environmental conditions does it need in order to thrive? How does it reproduce? What does it look like? What animals like to eat it? Would it survive a forest fire? Students could draw pictures of their subjects and display them in the classroom. They should record their findings on page 98 of their Explorer's Notebook.

❯ Distribute Home/School Connection 38. Family members are encouraged to visit a natural history museum where they can view exhibits of the plants and animals that make up a forest ecosystem.

Research Cycle

Invite each research group to present its research plan for discussion and possible refinement. From this point onward, there will be no specific suggestions for Guided Exploration in the Research Cycle. Meet with the whole class, as needed, for the following purposes:

* to arrange schedules and update calendars
* to discuss problems that children are having with their research
* to hear preliminary presentations and discussions of findings
* to arrange more formal presentations of children's research
* to provide guidance to ensure that groups progress through the phases of the Research Cycle—obtaining information; revising problems, conjectures, needs, and plans (perhaps with input resulting from a presentation to the class); and proceeding to a further cycle of a problem, conjecture, and so forth.

❋ Exploring Through Research

Research Aid: Using the *Reader's Guide to Periodical Literature*

Introduce the students to the *Reader's Guide to Periodical Literature.* This guide is an author and subject index to selected general interest periodicals. Entries are listed alphabetically by author's last name or by subject. An entry contains the title of the article; the author's name; the name of the magazine in which the article appears; the volume number, page number, and date of publication of the magazine.

Sometimes an entry will contain cross references to other headings in the *Guide* that are related to the subject. For example, if one looks up ecology, one may find other subject headings having to do with ecology, such as adaptation, environment, food chains, or forest ecology.

Once the researcher has found an article in the *Reader's Guide* that he or she wants to read, the next step is to find the magazine in the periodicals section of the library. In most libraries back issues of magazines are

Trees, Plants, and Flowers That Grow in a Forest

In "A Natural Force," you read about some of the trees and plants that grow in a forest. As you research these or other trees, plants, and flowers that grow in forests, note important facts about them below.

Name of tree, plant, or flower: _____

Notes: _____

Name of tree, plant, or flower: _____

Notes: _____

Name of tree, plant, or flower: _____

Notes: _____

Name of tree, plant, or flower: _____

Notes: _____

Name of tree, plant, or flower: _____

Notes: _____

98 EN   Ecology/Unit 5

Explorer's Notebook, page 98

"A Natural Force"

A message from _____

Many people assume that fire is an enemy of the forest, but in "A Natural Force," Laurence Pringle points out that fires are a natural part of forest life. The burning of ground cover speeds up the decaying process and helps release nutrients into the soil. From the enriched soil, these nutrients are recycled into the roots of other plants, which become a healthier food supply for animals. Fire also causes some cone-bearing trees and plants to release their seeds, allowing a new and healthier crop of plants to grow. Fire also opens up areas of the forest to sunlight. More sunlight and more nutrients in the soil allow a greater variety of plants to grow and thrive in the forest. Rarely are the animals that live in a forest hurt or destroyed by fire.

You and your child might visit a natural history museum to learn more about forest life. The museum may have exhibits of trees, plants, and animals that live in forests. It may even have information on forest fires. Some of the most interesting facts that you and your child learn about forest life may be written below. Your child can bring this page back to the classroom to share with his or her classmates.

Interesting facts about forest life:

_____

Unit 5/Ecology   H/SC 38

Home/School Connection 38

---

bound together and labeled by year and months. Students who are unfamiliar with the periodicals section of their library should ask the reference librarian to show them around the periodicals area and to point out signs that will guide them to the periodicals they want.

Guided Practice: Using the *Reader's Guide to Periodical Literature*

With the students, look up *ecology* in the *Reader's Guide to Periodical Literature.* Ask students to name some of the magazine articles and the cross-referenced headings that appear underneath this heading. Copy these entries on the chalkboard. With the students, choose an article to look up in the school library. Make certain that the students copy from the entry the information they will need in order to find the magazine in the library. In the library, familiarize the students with the periodicals section. Guide them through the process of finding the magazine article they are searching for.

Independent Practice: Using the *Reader's Guide to Periodical Literature*

▶ Encourage students to use the *Reader's Guide to Periodical Literature* as they continue to do research in ecology. Students who need practice using the *Reader's Guide* should list entries they are interested in finding on page 99 of the Explorer's Notebook. After finding and reading the articles, students should evaluate whether or not the articles are relevant to their research topic.

Using the Reader's Guide to Periodical Literature

List below four articles that are listed in the *Reader's Guide to Periodical Literature* that you would like to find in the periodicals section of your library. After you have found and read the articles, evaluate whether the information they contain is suitable for your research project. As you begin gathering suitable resource materials, use this page as a quick reference.

Subject heading: _____

Title of article: _____

Author: _____ Magazine: _____

Volume: _____ Pages: _____ Date: _____ Suitable? _____

Subject heading: _____

Title of article: _____

Author: _____ Magazine: _____

Volume: _____ Pages: _____ Date: _____ Suitable? _____

Subject heading: _____

Title of article: _____

Author: _____ Magazine: _____

Volume: _____ Pages: _____ Date: _____ Suitable? _____

Subject heading: _____

Title of article: _____

Author: _____ Magazine: _____

Volume: _____ Pages: _____ Date: _____ Suitable? _____

Unit 5/Ecology   EN 99

Copyright © 1995 Open Court Publishing Company

Explorer's Notebook, page 99

Professional Checkpoint: Guided and Independent Exploration

Provide ample opportunity for individuals, research groups, and the whole class to consider possible revisions to their work. During discussions regarding revisions, most of the real thinking and knowledge building occurs. Knowledge does not come simply from the acquisition of new information but from reconsidering current beliefs and conjectures in the light of new information and trying to make sense of them in combination. The principles for successful revision discussions are the same as those for successful discussions in general: constructive commenting, handing-off, refocusing, and participant modeling.

Notes:

✳ INDEPENDENT WORKSHOP
Building a Community of Scholars

Student-Directed Reading, Writing, and Discussion

Provide additional library time and assistance for students who are locating resources for their research. Encourage them to use sources other than books and encyclopedias. Remind the students that many of the Student Tool Cards, such as Note Taking or Using the Card Catalog, in the Student Toolbox can assist them in using resources and collecting information. Provide a space in the classroom in which sources can be stored and shared. In order to keep the research focused, it might be helpful to ask the students during individual conferences questions such as, *What did you look up? What are you finding out? What else might you need to find out? Can you give me more details about that fact or idea? How does this information help you? What does this information tell you that you didn't already know?*

WORKSHOP TIP

Remind the students that they may choose at this time to return to their Explorer's Notebook to complete any unfinished pages or to share ideas and information with their classmates.

Additional Opportunities for Independent Reading, Writing, and Cross-curricular Activities

✳ Reading Roundtable

Encourage the students to look for books about woodlands, such as *Because of a Tree* by Louis J. Milne and Margery Milne or *America's Wild Woodlands* published by the National Geographic Society. In both books the authors discuss the connections between the health of trees and the health of the other wildlife in a forest. Also encourage the students to read other books by Laurence Pringle, many of which deal with ecological issues. Whenever possible, model good reading habits for the students by doing your own free reading at this time. Also, share with the students the names of any interesting and informative books you have found on ecology that may be useful in their independent explorations.

✳ Writing Seminar

Students may use this time to continue revising any of their writing work in progress. Remind them to ask for peer input. Encourage them to refer to the writing strategy posters whenever they need help with their writing.

Cross-curricular Activity Cards

The following Cross-curricular Activity Card in the Student Toolbox is appropriate for this selection:

- 16 Science—Plant Rubbings

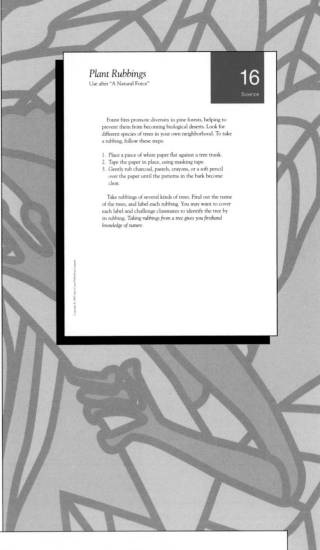

Additional Opportunities for Solving Learning Problems

Tutorial

Remember that the group of students who need tutoring may change from one period to another as well as from one day to another. You may want to use this time to work with students who need extra help. The following teaching aids are available in the Teacher Toolbox for your convenience:

- Writer's Craft/Reading: Elaboration Through Providing Definitions in Text, Teacher Tool Card 44
- Writer's Craft/Reading: Elaboration Through Giving Reasons or Causes, Teacher Tool Card 38
- Writer's Craft/Reading: Elaboration Through Providing Specific Facts, Teacher Tool Card 41
- Study and Research: Using the *Reader's Guide to Periodical Literature* and the *Children's Magazine Guide,* Teacher Tool Card 105

Assessment

Saving the Peregrine Falcon

1 READING THE SELECTION

About the Selection

Peregrine falcons have been prized and admired for centuries. They are now becoming an endangered species, however, because of the insecticide DDT. Peregrines that ingest DDT produce eggs too delicate to survive the rigors of incubation. When parent birds sit on the eggs to keep them warm, the thin shells often break and the chick growing inside dies. To combat the harmful effects of DDT, scientists have begun kidnapping and hatching peregrine eggs and then reintroducing baby peregrines into the wild. This selection describes the procedures followed and the dedication and skill of the scientists who are saving this glorious bird from extinction.

Link to the Unit Concepts

Saving the Peregrine Falcon, pages 198–215, shows how introducing toxins into the environment can affect all of the animal species that are linked together in a food chain. When peregrine falcons prey upon smaller birds that have eaten grains and insects sprayed with DDT, the toxin accumulates in the falcons' bodies, eventually causing them to lay eggs with very thin shells. Peregrine embryos are less likely to develop normally and hatch from thin-shelled eggs. Fewer chicks mean fewer peregrine falcons, and suddenly a species' chances of surviving are endangered.

After reading this selection, students may wonder how people can change their behavior to reverse the harm they are doing to the environment. Students also may reflect upon the amount of effort that is required to save a single endangered species from extinction.

About the Author

Caroline Arnold writes mostly about subjects that fascinate her and her children. She enjoys "the challenge of writing about complicated

LESSON OVERVIEW

Saving the Peregrine Falcon by Caroline Arnold, pages 198–215

READING THE SELECTION

Materials
Student anthology, pp. 198-215
Explorer's Notebook, p. 83
Assessment Masters 1–2, 7

FYI
Learning Framework Card
• Setting Reading Goals and
  Expectations, 1A

READING WITH A WRITER'S EYE

Minilesson
Assessment

Materials
Reproducible Master 15

FYI
Teacher Tool Card
• Spelling and Vocabulary: Building
  Vocabulary, 77

GUIDED AND INDEPENDENT EXPLORATION

Materials
Explorer's Notebook, p. 100

FYI
Learning Framework Card
• Needs and Plans Phase 1 and 2, 4C

Independent Workshop

**Optional Materials from
Student Toolbox**

Tradebook Connection Cards

Cross-curricular Activity Cards
• 14 Science—Tracking Wildlife
• 17 Science—Capturing Prey
• 24 Social Studies—The Sport of
  Falconry

N O T E S

Asterisks (*) throughout the lesson indicate learning frameworks. Learning Framework Cards and Teacher Tool Cards can be found in the Teacher Toolbox

subjects" using language that children can comprehend, and she is spurred on "by my own and other children's eagerness to know more about the world around them." Arnold, a teacher of writing and art, has written more than eighty children's books, often about endangered species of animals. Her recent book *The Ancient Cliff Dwellers of Mesa Verde* (with photographs by Richard Hewett) explores the mystery of the sudden disappearance, in about 1300, of the Anasazi—Native-American inhabitants of intricate adobe buildings in a high tableland in south-western Colorado. Your students may have read this book, which appears in the student bibliography for the Ancient Civilizations unit.

About the Illustrator

By the time he was twelve years old, noted freelance photojournalist Richard Hewett already had his own darkroom. His photographs have appeared in such magazines as *Life* and *TV Guide.* In collaboration with his wife, Joan, he has produced several books for children about political science and cultural awareness.

However, Hewett is best known for his collaboration with Caroline Arnold on a series of children's science books. *Saving the Peregrine Falcon* was a *School Library Journal* Best Book in 1985. Eight other books by this author-photographer team were named Outstanding Science Trade Books for Children by the National Science Teachers Association.

Hewett's photograph of a bloodhound named Stretch hangs in the Metropolitan Museum in New York City.

INFORMATION FOR THE STUDENT

Tell the students that *Saving the Peregrine Falcon* was written by Caroline Arnold and photographed by Richard Hewett. The students may be interested in reading on student anthology page 215 about how this author-photographer team works together to create a book. Share other information about Arnold and Hewett that you think will interest the students.

* COGNITIVE AND RESPONSIVE READING

Activating Prior Knowledge

Invite the students to discuss what they know about falcons or about other wild birds, like the falcon, that have now become city dwellers.

Setting Reading Goals and Expectations

Even though this selection has been designated as an Assessment selection, the class will proceed as usual with the setting of reading goals and expectations. To do this, they will **browse the selection** and **use the clues/problems/wondering procedure.** On the chalkboard under the headings clues, problems, and wonderings, write in brief note form the observations the students generate during browsing. The students will return to these observations after reading. For a review of **browsing,** see **Learning Framework Card 1A, Setting Reading Goals and Expectations.**

Recommendations for Reading the Selection

Explain to the students that they will read this selection to assess what they have learned about ecology. Place the students in small groups. Tell them that they will decide in their small groups how they would like to read this selection. For example, the groups may choose to do the following:

- read silently but stay in groups, stopping to ask each other questions when they need help understanding
- alternate reading and summarizing one section at a time
- read silently on their own

Encourage the students to use the strategies that they think will best help them to understand and appreciate the selection. They should feel free to refer to the reading strategy posters as needed. Encourage them to collaborate with others in their group by asking questions when they encounter reading difficulties and by offering suggestions to others who need help. Remind them also to **respond** to text **by connecting and giving opinions** as they read.

➤ Distribute copies of Assessment Master 7, Concept Connections for unit 5, Ecology, which you will find in the booklet Masters for Continuous Assessment. Tell the students that after reading the selection in their small groups, they will write responses on the page independently. They will then regroup and share their findings, changing any ideas they wish.

Assessment Master 7

Concept Connections

1. Explain what this selection is about. Write a short summary.

2. Tell what this selection has to do with ecology.

3. Tell how this selection is like other selections you have read in this unit.

4. You have read many selections about ecology. How did *this* selection change your ideas about ecology?

Date

Name

Copyright © 1995 Open Court Publishing Company

Unit 5/Ecology   Assessment Master 7

THINK ALOUD PROMPTS

To foster independence, think-aloud prompts are not provided for Assessment lessons.

SAVING THE PEREGRINE FALCON

Caroline Arnold

photographs by
Richard R. Hewett

High above a tall bank building in downtown Los Angeles, a peregrine falcon soars in the air looking for food below. The peregrine falcon is a wild bird that we do not normally think of as a city dweller. Yet the peregrine is at home among the high-rise buildings, which in many ways are like the cliffs and mountains where peregrines usually live. Window and roof ledges make good places to perch and to lay eggs, and the streets below are filled with pigeons, starlings, sparrows, and other small birds that peregrines like to eat. Today more and more peregrines are becoming part of city life as part of a special program to try to save this beautiful and powerful bird from extinction.

198

For centuries the peregrine was prized by kings and fal-coners who used it to hunt. Bird lovers too have always admired the peregrine. Yet a few years ago it was feared that soon there would be no more peregrines. Man's pollution of the environment with the poison DDT had interfered with the birds' ability to produce babies. The total number of peregrines was growing smaller each year. In 1970 there were only two known pairs of nesting peregrines in California. Until the 1940s, when DDT began to be used, there had been nearly two hundred. In the eastern United States the peregrine had already become extinct by 1970. Only with man's help could the peregrine be saved.

Peregrine falcons are found all over the world. The scientific name for those found in the United States is *Falco peregrinus anatum*. Other falcons living in the United States are the gyrfalcon, the prairie falcon, the merlin, and the kestrel. Although the numbers of these other falcons have been reduced by man, none of them is endangered like the peregrine.

199

Falcons are similar in many ways to birds in the hawk family. When flying, however, a falcon has pointed wings, which are better suited to speed, whereas a hawk has widespread wing feathers, which are better suited to soaring.

You can recognize an adult peregrine because it appears to wear a large black moustache. Both males and females have the same color markings but, as with all hawks and falcons, the female is larger and stronger than the male. A female peregrine is usually about twenty inches long and weighs about thirty ounces. A male is about fifteen inches long and weighs about eighteen ounces. The male is sometimes called a tiercel from the French word meaning "third" because he is about a third smaller than the female peregrine.

Falcons, like hawks, eagles, and owls, catch and eat other animals. They are predators. The peregrine specializes in a diet of birds. In the United States, peregrines used to be called duck hawks because they were seen around marshes and occasionally hunted ducks.

The peregrine's body, like those of other predatory birds, is well adapted for hunting. Its strong feet and sharp talons are ideal for catching and carrying, and its beak is designed for tearing. The peregrine's eyesight is so keen that it has been compared to a person being able to read a newspaper a

mile away! A soaring peregrine can see a bird hundreds of feet below.

After spotting a bird, the peregrine points its head down, tucks in its wings and feet, and transforms its body into the shape of a speeding bullet. As it begins to dive, it pumps its wings to increase its speed up to 200 miles per hour! No bird alive is faster than a diving peregrine. When the peregrine reaches its prey, it grabs it with its feet, then quickly kills it by breaking its neck. The peregrine then either carries the dead bird to a protected place and eats it, or brings it back to the nest to feed hungry babies.

Baby peregrines are usually called chicks, although a chick in a wild nest is also called an eyas. Unfortunately for most peregrines in the United States, there have been fewer and fewer hungry chicks in wild nests to feed.

Most of the smaller birds that peregrines in the United States eat spend the winter in Central and South America. There they eat grains and insects that have been sprayed with DDT. DDT is a poison used by farmers to kill insects that are harmful to crops. When the birds eat food with DDT on it, the poison is stored in their bodies. Later, when the peregrines eat these birds, they eat the poison too. The more birds the peregrines eat, the more DDT they store.

Scientists have found that DDT causes birds to lay eggs with shells that are too thin. When they measure the shells

201

of hatched or broken eggs, they find that the thinnest shells are those with the most DDT in them. When parent birds sit on these eggs to keep them warm, the thin shells often break. Thin-shelled eggs also lose moisture faster than thick-shelled eggs. Often the chick growing inside the egg dies because the egg dries out too much. By helping the eggs with thin shells to hatch, scientists can combat some of the effects of DDT.

Most wild peregrines nest on high ledges on rocky cliffs. These nest sites are called eyries. A pair of peregrines makes a nest in an eyrie by scraping clean a small area in the stones or sand. In the scrape the female usually lays three eggs. Scientists carefully watch each peregrine nest. Then if they feel that the eggs are unlikely to hatch without help, they borrow them for a while, but first they let the birds sit on the eggs for five days. This seems to improve the eggs' chances of hatching in the laboratory.

202

Because the cliffs where peregrines nest are so steep, only a mountain climber can reach a nest. When he approaches the nest, the angry parents screech and swoop at him. The mountain climber quickly and carefully puts each speckled egg into a padded box. He then replaces the eggs he has taken with plaster eggs which look just like real peregrine eggs. These fake eggs will fool the parent birds. After the mountain climber leaves, the parents will return to the nest and sit on the plaster eggs as if they were their own.

It is important to keep the parent birds interested in the nest. After the eggs have hatched, the mountain climber will bring the babies back so that the parents can take care of them.

When the mountain climber gets back to the top of the cliff, he puts the eggs into a portable incubator. The incubator will keep them safe and warm on their ride back to the laboratory.

Three places in the United States where peregrine eggs are hatched are in Ithaca (New York), Boise (Idaho), and Santa Cruz (California). Brian Walton and the staff of the Santa Cruz Predatory Bird Research Group (SCPBRG) collect eggs and release birds throughout the western United States. The laboratory at the SCPBRG center is used for hatching eggs and caring for the newly hatched peregrine chicks.

In the laboratory each egg is carefully weighed. Then it is held in front of a bright light in a dark room. This is called candling. When an egg is candled, the shadow of the chick growing inside and a lighter area at the large end of the egg can be seen. The lighter area is called the air pocket.

Then the egg is placed on a rack inside an incubator. The incubator keeps the egg warm and moist. Each day the egg will be weighed and candled again. As the chick grows, water slowly evaporates from the egg, making room for the air pocket to get bigger. The egg's weight shows how much water it is losing. If it is losing water too quickly, the incubator can be made more moist.

Wild birds turn their eggs constantly as they move around in the nest. But in the laboratory, people must carefully turn each egg four or five times each day. This prevents the

≥ 204 ≤

growing chick from sticking to the inside of the eggshell. If the eggs are not turned, they will not hatch.

Sometimes eggs are found with shells so thin that they have already begun to crack. Then people in the laboratory try to repair them with glue. Sometimes eggs are also waxed to prevent them from losing moisture. Everything possible is done to make sure that each egg hatches into a healthy peregrine chick.

The eggs are kept in the incubator until they are $31^1/2$ days old. Then they are carefully watched for the first signs of hatching.

Each chick has a hard pointed knob on the top of its beak. This is called an egg tooth. The chick pushes against the inside of the shell with its egg tooth and breaks the shell.

The first crack in the egg is called the pip. When the pip appears, the egg is moved to a special hatching chamber. There the egg will take 24

≥ 205 ≤

to 48 hours to hatch. During this time somebody watches it all the time. Some chicks are too weak to break out of their shells. Then the scientists are there to help them.

Often two eggs begin to hatch at about the same time. Then they are put next to each other in the hatcher. When a chick is ready to hatch, it begins to peep inside its shell. The two chicks can hear each other peep. This seems to encourage them to move around and break their shells. Sometimes where there is only one egg, the scientists make peeping sounds for the chick to hear.

Starting at the pip, the chick slowly turns, pressing its egg tooth against the shell. Soon the crack becomes a ring around the shell. Then the chick pushes its head against the top of the shell, and the shell pops open. After hatching, the egg tooth is no longer needed, and in a week or so it falls off.

The newly hatched chick is wet and its down feathers are matted together. A cotton swab is used to clean the feathers. If necessary, ointment is put on the chick's navel to prevent infection. In the shell the chick gets nutrients from the yolk through its navel. Normally, by the time a chick hatches, the yolk has been totally absorbed and the navel has closed.

In the wild, a mother bird broods her chicks by sitting on top of them to keep them warm and dry. In the laboratory, the dry chick is placed with one or more other chicks in a small container called a brooder. A heater keeps the chicks warm. The chick will rest in the brooder for eight to twelve hours. Then it will be ready for its first meal.

In the wild, the father peregrine hunts birds and brings them back to the nest. Then he and the mother peregrine tear off small bits of meat to feed each chick. The hungry chicks beg for food by peeping and opening their mouths wide.

Bird meat is also used to feed chicks in the laboratory. Usually the chicks are fed quail, although adult birds are also fed pigeon and chicken meat. First the meat is put through a meat grinder to break it into small pieces. The newly hatched

≥ 207 ≤

chicks are then fed tiny pieces with tweezers. For somewhat older chicks the ground meat can be squeezed through a bag with a nozzle.

Like many birds, falcons have pouches in their necks to store food. These are called crops. Food first goes to the crop and then to the stomach. A bird feeder knows that a chick has had enough when the crop begins to bulge.

During the day, young peregrine chicks need to be fed every three to five hours. At night they sleep eight hours between feedings.

Even though the peregrine chicks are cared for by people, it is important that they remain wild. During the first week or so, the chicks cannot see very well. Then it does not matter if people feed them directly. But as they get older, their contact with people must be limited.

Young animals identify with the other animals they see during the first weeks of life. This is called imprinting. Most young animals see only their parents in early life, and they imprint on them.

≥ 208 ∕

Peregrines raised in the laboratory that will be returned to the wild must be imprinted on adult peregrines. One way to help them do this is to feed them with a peregrine-shaped puppet. The puppet fools the peregrine chicks and they behave as if it were a real bird.

When a peregrine chick is three days to a week old, it is put into the nest of an adult bird that has been imprinted on people. At the SCPBRG center, adult birds are kept in barnlike buildings. Each large, open-air room in these buildings has bars across the top to let in air and light. Each room also has perches and nesting ledges for the birds.

Unfortunately there are not enough adult peregrines at the center to care for all the hatched chicks. Another more common bird, the prairie falcon, is very much like the peregrine, and it is often used as a substitute parent for very young peregrine chicks. During the breeding season, a

≥ 209 ∕

female prairie falcon will care for adopted peregrine chicks. She will keep them warm and feed them as if they were her own. When the chicks are one to two weeks old, they are put into nests of peregrines which are not imprinted on people. Then, at the age of three weeks, the young peregrines are ready to go back to wild nests.

Before a bird goes back to the wild, a metal band is put on its leg. The band identifies the bird and helps people keep track of it as it grows up.

Then the chicks are put into a special wooden pack and taken to the nest site. There the mountain climber puts the pack on his back and climbs to the nest. He removes the plaster eggs and puts in the young chicks. Then he leaves as quickly as possible. He does not want to disturb the parent birds any more than necessary.

The parent birds soon return to the nest. Although they are surprised at first to find healthy chicks instead of eggs in their nest, the parents quickly accept their new babies. The hungry chicks beg for food, and the parents' natural response is to feed them. The chicks are on their way to growing up as wild peregrines.

Most wild birds do not breed well in captivity. They are easily disturbed by people and by loud noises. The cages at the SCPBRG center are made so that the birds rarely see people, although people can see the birds through tiny peepholes.

In the bird buildings a radio is constantly played. The sound blocks out most noises from outside. The radio also helps the birds become used to people's voices. Then they are less likely to be startled when people make noises outside their chambers.

Pairs of peregrine falcons at the SCPBRG center build nests and breed just as birds do in the wild. Their chicks can be released to help increase the number of wild peregrines.

Both in the wild and in captivity, peregrines normally raise only one nest of chicks each year. If the eggs are destroyed, however, the birds will lay a second set. In the wild, peregrine eggs might be eaten by other birds or animals. At the center, scientists purposely take away the first eggs from each pair of breeding falcons and hatch them in an incubator. The birds then lay another set of eggs. In this way each pair of birds can produce twice as many chicks as usual.

During its six weeks in the nest, a peregrine grows from a fluffy chick covered with soft down to a fully feathered bird

≥ 211 ∕

the size of its parents. These first juvenile feathers are a mottled brown color. The peregrine will get its adult feathers at the beginning of its second year.

Three-week-old peregrine chicks are put into known wild nests that have parent birds on them when possible, but because there are so few peregrines left in the wild, soon all the wild peregrine nests are filled. Some peregrine chicks are put into wild prairie falcon nests. Others are released on their own when they are old enough to fly.

In the wild, a young peregrine is ready to fly at the age of six weeks. Then it leaves the nest and tries to hunt for food. At first it is not a very good hunter. Its parents will help it and continue to feed it. When juvenile peregrines from the laboratory are put into the wild, they have no parents to help them. Then people must help them instead.

Usually the birds are released near cliff tops or mountain ledges far away from where people live. They are placed in a box at the release site when they are about five weeks old. Sometimes the box must be carried to the release site by a helicopter.

The box has bars across one side, but the people involved try to stay out of the birds' sight. From behind, they drop meat into the box for the birds. Then after a week, the box is opened and the birds are allowed to fly free.

⫍ 212 ⫎

Predatory Bird Research Group

People stay at the site and put food out each day until the birds learn to take care of themselves. This may take four to five weeks. When the birds no longer need to return to the release site for food, the people's job is finished.

In addition to its identification band, each bird also wears a small radio transmitter. The radio makes beeping sounds which can be heard with a radio receiver. During the first few weeks on its own, a bird sometimes gets lost or in trouble. Then people can find it by tracking the beeps over the radio receiver. After a few weeks the transmitter will no longer be needed, and it will fall off the bird.

Most birds are set free in wild places where peregrines once lived but are now gone. It is hoped that the new peregrines will stay there, build nests, and bring up chicks of their own.

Some peregrines are released in cities, and they seem to adapt well to city life. Los Angeles, New York, Washington, Baltimore, Edmonton, London, and Nairobi are just some of the cities around the world where peregrines live. Some live on the ledges of office buildings. Others have built nests on tall bridges. In England peregrines lived for many years in the spire of Salisbury Cathedral.

In cities peregrines are usually released from the tops of tall buildings. As in the wild, people stay and feed the birds until they can take care of themselves. After a pair of peregrines has claimed a building ledge as a nest site, scientists

Predatory Bird Research Group

⫍ 213 ⫎

sometimes build a nest there for the birds. They may even put a fake egg into the nest. They hope that this will encourage the birds to begin laying their own eggs.

Peregrines usually do not mate and have young until their third year. In their first breeding years in the wild, peregrines can raise their own chicks. But as the birds get older and store more and more DDT in their bodies, their egg shells will become dangerously thin. As long as people use DDT as an insecticide, peregrines will be endangered and will continue to need man's help to survive.

Peregrines must survive many dangers before they are old enough to produce their own chicks. Many hurt themselves when they collide with man-made objects such as fences or telephone and electric wires. Others are shot by unthinking people. Centers like the SCPBRG help sick and wounded peregrines. Endangered birds like peregrines need all the help they can get.

The peregrine falcon is a beautiful bird, and it would be sad to let it become extinct simply through ignorance or carelessness. Many animals that once roamed the earth are now gone because man destroyed or polluted their environments. For the present, the peregrine falcon has been saved from extinction. Through the work of many people around the world its numbers are increasing each year. If you are lucky, maybe where you live, you can see one of these magnificent birds soaring high in the sky.

⫍ 214 ⫎

MEET CAROLINE ARNOLD, AUTHOR,
AND RICHARD HEWETT, PHOTOGRAPHER

When author Caroline Arnold and photographer Richard Hewett work together to create a book, they believe that the text and the photographs are equally important. Arnold thinks that the best ideas for writing come from first-hand observation. When she writes about animals, she likes to see what they look like, smell like, and feel like. To do this, she works with Hewett when he takes photographs for their books. Hewett and Arnold often work in wildlife parks or zoos so they can get close-up pictures of animals. Arnold enjoys doing research and talking to wildlife researchers the most. When all the pictures are taken, Arnold can finish writing the text to match the photos. Then she and Hewett put together the pictures and text to make a complete story.

⫍ 215 ⫎

*

EXPLORING THROUGH DISCUSSION

Reflecting on the Selection

As the students read the selection, circulate among the groups to **observe their understanding of the concepts** as well as their **collaboration** in solving difficulties in understanding the selection.

As you note their **collaborative group discussions,** mark your Teacher's Observation Log for the individuals in one or two of the groups. Take a moment to reflect on how each student is changing in his or her **ability to use strategies** to solve problems in reading from unit to unit.

Have the groups break while the students respond independently to the Concept Connections on Assessment Master 7.

ASSESSMENT TIP This is an ideal time to mark observations in your Teacher's Observation Log.

Exploring Concepts Within the Selection

Allow the students to regroup to compare and discuss their responses to the Concept Connections. During these discussions you will have more opportunities to observe students and mark your Teacher's Observation Log. Then gather the Concept Connections pages and continue with the lesson as usual.

ASSESSMENT TIP This is another ideal time to mark observations in the log.

Sharing Ideas About Explorable Concepts

Have the groups **report their ideas** and **discuss them** with the rest of the class. It is crucial that the students' ideas determine this discussion.

- Students may observe that, until toxic substances such as DDT are no longer introduced into the environment, the survival of animals such as the peregrine falcon will continue to be endangered.
- Students may suggest that placing wild animals in urban settings may help humans learn to understand their needs and to live in greater harmony with them.

As these ideas and others are stated, have the students **add them to** the **Question Board** or the **Concept Board.**

Exploring Concepts Across Selections

Ask the students whether this selection reminds them of any others they have read in this unit. If so, in what ways? Students might make connections with other selections in this unit or in previous units.

- The students may compare the plight of the peregrine falcon with that of the passenger pigeon, noting the similarities and differences of the two situations.
- Some students may remember the scientists' efforts in *Protecting Wildlife* to save birds that were the victims of an oil spill in South Africa.
- Some students may make a connection between this selection and "Amaroq, the Wolf" in the unit on perseverance. They may recall that Miyax took great pains to learn the wolves' language and behavior in order to be accepted by them.

Connections Across Units

Recording Ideas

As students complete the above discussions, ask them to **sum up what they learned from their conversations and to tell how they might use this information** in further explorations. Any special information or insights may be recorded on the **Concept Board.** Any further questions that they would like to think about, pursue, or investigate may be recorded on the **Question Board.** They may want to discuss the progress that has been made on their questions. They may also want to cross out any questions that no longer warrant consideration.

Evaluating Discussions

➤ Students should record their ideas about the selection on page 83 of their Explorer's Notebook.

Self-Assessment Questionnaire

➤ After all aspects of this lesson have been completed, you may wish to distribute the Self-Assessment Questionnaire, Assessment Master 2. Allow plenty of time for the students to complete this important assessment piece.

Explorer's Notebook, page 83

Saving the Peregrine Falcon by Caroline Arnold

_____

_____

_____

_____

_____

_____

_____

_____

_____

_____

The Day They Parachuted Cats on Borneo by Charlotte Pomerantz

_____

_____

_____

_____

_____

_____

_____

_____

_____

_____

_____

Unit 5/Ecology   EN 83

Assessment Master 2

Self-Assessment Questionnaire

Date

Name

INDIVIDUAL

GROUP

1. How would you rate this selection?
   ○ easy   ○ medium   ○ hard

2. If you checked **medium** or **hard**, answer these questions.
   • Which part of the selection did you find especially difficult?
   • What strategy did you use to understand it?

   _____

   • Were some of the words hard?
   • What did you do to figure out their meaning?

   _____

3. What do you feel you need to work on to make yourself a better reader?

   _____

   _____

4. Give an example of something you said in the group.
   Tell why you said it.

   _____

   _____

5. Give an example of something that people in the group helped you understand about the selection.

   _____

   _____

Self-Assessment Questionnaire   Assessment Master 2

2 READING WITH A WRITER'S EYE

Assessment

MINILESSON

Remind the students that in each selection they have read thus far, you have discussed something that the writer did particularly well. For example, in "The Passenger Pigeon," Paul Fleischman's use of comparisons, both literal and figurative, created powerful imagery for the reader while getting across a difficult concept. Laurence Pringle, in "A Natural Force," provided the reader with well-written and clearly understood definitions for the terms he used in his article. He varied the style of his definitions, which made his article interesting to read. Tell the students that because they read *Saving the Peregrine Falcon* on their own, you would like them to **try to identify something they think that Caroline Arnold did especially well.** Does something about the writing stand out? They might think back to a portion of the article that they reacted to or particularly enjoyed. Their reaction could be a clue to especially good writing.

Allow time, if necessary, for the students to **skim the article** to refresh their memories. If they have difficulty expressing their feelings about the writing in this selection, model a response for them by pointing out things that you felt were noteworthy.

For example, you might wish to point out that Arnold does an especially effective job of **explaining the procedures** involved in caring for peregrine eggs and chicks and releasing falcons into the wild or into urban areas.

WRITING

Linking Reading to Writing

Encourage the students to use in their own writing any techniques that they particularly enjoyed in Caroline Arnold's writing. Invite them to go into their writing folders and see what piece of writing they might revise to include writing techniques they noticed and liked in this article.

★ Writing Process

Although no specific writing assignment is recommended here, the students may concentrate on the writing process for any writing on which they are currently working. If your class is using the optional Writer's Handbook, refer the students to it for help with their writing.

VOCABULARY

Encourage the students to discuss words or phrases from the selection that they might want to use in their speaking and writing or in their research for this unit. Words related to ecology you might discuss include *DDT, eyries, incubator, pip, crop,* and *imprinting.* Provide Vocabulary Exploration forms, Reproducible Master 15, so that the students can add these or any other words and phrases from the selection to the Personal Dictionary section of their Writer's Notebook. For additional opportunities to build vocabulary, see **Teacher Tool Card 77.**

VOCABULARY TIP Encourage the students to choose words they think are important or interesting and to record them on vocabulary exploration forms. Student choice leads to student ownership of words.

3 GUIDED AND INDEPENDENT EXPLORATION

Guided Exploration

The following activities do not have to be completed within the days devoted to this lesson:

- In *Saving the Peregrine Falcon,* students learned that scientists are releasing some peregrine falcons into cities to live. The students might be interested in reading about other types of wildlife that live in urban areas and discussing what they learn with classmates. If possible, students might try to find out whether and how an urban setting changes the lives of wild birds and animals. After their research has ended, students could get together and compare information.

  ❯ Students should record their findings in Explorer's Notebook, page 100.

- Remind students of the poem they read earlier by Paul Fleischman, "The Passenger Pigeon." The students might enjoy writing a poem about the peregrine falcon. Fleischman wrote his poem from the pigeon's point of view. Perhaps some students would enjoy attempting to tell the falcon's story from its point of view. Perhaps they would also like to illustrate their poem and display it somewhere in the classroom.

Research Cycle

Meet with the whole class, as needed, for the following purposes:
- to arrange schedules and update calendars
- to discuss problems that students are encountering with their research
- to hear preliminary presentations and discussions of interesting findings
- to arrange more formal presentations of students' research
- to provide guidance to ensure that groups progress through phases of the Research Cycle—obtaining information; revising problems, conjectures, needs, and plans (perhaps with input resulting from a presentation to the class); and proceeding to a further cycle of problem, conjecture, and so forth

> ✱ *Exploring Through Research*

Students will begin presenting their final research projects during the days devoted to reading and discussing the next selection, *The Day They Parachuted Cats on Borneo.* Students should be given as much time as they need to give an effective presentation, even though this may mean devoting more than one class period to this activity. For additional ideas for informal presentations, see **Learning Framework Card 4C, Needs and Plans Phase 1 and 2.** A few presentation ideas include the following:
- Minidebate: Group members who have opposing conjectures present them, along with evidence and arguments, for the rest of the class's reaction.

TEACHING TIP These informal presentations should take some of the emphasis off the final research product and give the students a better sense of research as a continuous process.

Urban Wildlife

You learned in *Saving the Peregrine Falcon* that scientists are releasing some peregrine falcons into cities to live. Do some research and find out about other types of animal wildlife that live in urban areas. Record your findings below and discuss what you've learned with your classmates.

Animal: _____ Where it lives: _____

What it eats: _____

How it has adapted to city life: _____

_____

_____

_____

Other facts about its life in the city: _____

_____

_____

_____

_____

Animal: _____ Where it lives: _____

What it eats: _____

How it has adapted to city life: _____

_____

_____

_____

Other facts about its life in the city: _____

_____

_____

_____

_____

100 EN   Ecology/Unit 5

Copyright © 1995 Open Court Publishing Company

Explorer's Notebook, page 100

- Problem presentations: Groups that are stuck, unable to find relevant material, or are finding something puzzling or inconsistent, present their problem for suggestions from their peers.
- Poster session: When not enough time is available, groups put up small displays (including posters, graphs, and summaries) of any kind showing their preliminary findings. The students examine these displays during Independent Workshop and give feedback to their peers.

*INDEPENDENT WORKSHOP
Building a Community of Scholars

Student-Directed Reading, Writing, and Discussion

If students have not already done so, have them select an organized way to store their research information. Have them continue recording information on their planning calendars. If necessary, remind them that the next selection ends the unit. Many students should be ready to begin making plans for their final research projects.

WORKSHOP TIP

Remind the students that they may choose at this time to return to their Explorer's Notebook to complete any unfinished pages or to share ideas and information with their classmates.

Additional Opportunities for Independent Reading, Writing, and Cross-curricular Activities

✻ Reading Roundtable

Encourage students to read more books by Caroline Arnold and other writers who examine the subject of endangered wildlife. For example, they might read Gene Stuart's *Wildlife Alert: The Struggle to Survive,* which outlines the steps being taken to help endangered animals around the world; or Paula Hendrich's *Saving America's Birds,* which explores why some species are endangered and describes the methods that are being used to save them.

✻ Writing Seminar

Remind the students that they may want to look through their writing folders as a last chance to prepare any pieces of writing for publishing. Remind them to proofread carefully before publishing.

Cross-curricular Activity Cards

The following Cross-curricular Activity Cards in the Student Toolbox are appropriate for this selection:
- 14 Science—Tracking Wildlife
- 17 Science—Capturing Prey
- 24 Social Studies—The Sport of Falconry

The Sport of Falconry
Use after *Saving the Peregrine Falcon*
24 Social Studies

Capturing Prey
Use after *Saving the Peregrine Falcon*
17 Science

Tracking Wildlife
Use after *Protecting Wildlife* or *Saving the Peregrine Falcon*
14 Science

Once, hunting was a necessary activity for most people. Now, very few people in the United States need to hunt for food. Yet many people enjoy walking in nature and searching for wildlife. One way to hunt without harming wildlife is to track wild birds and animals in their natural settings. Look for evidence of wild birds and animals in parks, forests, or even your backyard. (A pair of binoculars or a magnifying glass may be especially helpful in spotting the tracks and clues that animals leave behind.) Stop to draw the tracks, food leavings, droppings, nests, and other evidence of animal life that you discover. Use the information you sketch to guess what animal or animals you have tracked down. You may have to do some research in an encyclopedia to determine whether your guess was valid. Share your information with your classmates. *Tracking animals can provide information about their life styles.*

Additional Opportunities for Solving Learning Problems

Tutorial

Steps Toward Independence By this time in the year, students should be taking the initiative in identifying problem areas.

Use this time to give extra help to individuals or small groups who need it. This is also a good time for peer tutoring. Have the students refer to the appropriate Student Tool Cards to guide their work together. Encourage them to discuss with you any questions they may have.

The Day They Parachuted Cats on Borneo

1 READING THE SELECTION

About the Selection

This selection, a drama, is based on the chain of events that occurred on the island of Borneo in 1969 after the island was sprayed with the pesticide DDT to kill mosquitos that carried the dreaded disease malaria. What the islanders soon discovered was that DDT killed mosquitoes but not cockroaches. It slowed down geckoes but not the caterpillars that they fed on. It destroyed cats but not the rats that were their prey. In short, DDT upset the balance of an ecosystem, and this imbalance caused some distressing and surprising results. The government concocted what it thought was a solution to a problem—but was it really?

Link to the Unit Concepts

The Day They Parachuted Cats on Borneo, pages 216–233, demonstrates the intricacy of the relationships that exist among the creatures within an ecosystem. The author stresses the need for ecologists to anticipate how an action that affects one member of an ecosystem will, in turn, affect other members of that ecosystem. An action that was taken to solve the problem of malaria actually produced conditions that would increase the incidence of plague. This play is also a cautionary tale about introducing toxic substances into the environment.

After reading this selection, students may wonder how humans could solve ecological problems without destroying the balance of nature.

About the Author

Charlotte Pomerantz has been writing since she was a child. She had had a career in writing for adults before turning, in her mid-thirties, to writing children's books. In 1972 *The Day They Parachuted Cats on Borneo* was chosen as an Outstanding Book of the Year by the *New York Times.* It was one of the ten U.S. books selected for the International Year of the Child, 1977–1978, by the International Board on Books for Young People. Pomerantz notes that her own children provide her with ideas about which to write.

LESSON OVERVIEW

The Day They Parachuted Cats on Borneo by Charlotte Pomerantz, pages 216–233

READING THE SELECTION

Materials

Student anthology, pp. 216–233
Explorer's Notebook, p. 83
Assessment Master 1
World map or globe

FYI

Learning Framework Card
• Setting Reading Goals and
  Expectations, 1A

READING WITH A WRITER'S EYE

Minilesson

Writer's Craft: Describing the Multiple
  Effects of a Single Cause

Materials

Reading/Writing Connection, p. 39
Reproducible Master 15
Assessment Master 1

FYI

Teacher Tool Card
• Spelling and Vocabulary: Building
  Vocabulary, 77

Options for Instruction

Writer's Craft: Genre—Play
Writer's Craft: Providing Problems and
  Solutions
Grammar, Mechanics, and Usage: Using
  Parentheses, Dashes, and Ellipses
(Use Teacher Tool Cards listed below.)

GUIDED AND INDEPENDENT EXPLORATION

Materials

Explorer's Notebook, p. 101
Home/School Connection 39

Independent Workshop

**Optional Materials from
Student Toolbox**

Tradebook Connection Cards

Cross-curricular Activity Cards
• 8 Drama—Role Play
• 4 Math—Just How Big Is Borneo,
  Anyway?
• 5 Math—Malaria Mortality

Student Tool Cards
• Writer's Craft/Reading: Showing
  Cause and Effect, 31
• Writer's Craft/Reading: Reading and
  Writing Plays/Drama, 11
• Writer's Craft/Reading: Giving
  Problem and Solution, 45

• Grammar, Mechanics, and Usage:
  Using Parentheses, Dashes, and
  Ellipses, 54

FYI

Teacher Tool Cards
• Writer's Craft/Reading: Causal
  Indicators, 31
• Writer's Craft/Reading: Genre—
  Play/Drama, 11
• Writer's Craft/Reading: Elaboration
  Through Providing Problem and
  Solution, 45
• Grammar, Mechanics, and Usage:
  Using Parentheses, Dashes, and
  Ellipses, 54

NOTES

Asterisks (*) throughout the lesson indicate learning frameworks. Learning Framework Cards and Teacher Tool Cards can be found in the Teacher Toolbox

About the
Illustrator

Jose Aruego, born in Manila, the Phillipines, earned a law degree before coming to the United States in the mid-1950s to realize his ambition of becoming a commercial artist. He eventually became a cartoonist and in 1968 began a full-time career as a book illustrator, adapting his cartoon style to children's stories in a mannner popularized by Dr. Seuss and, later, by Steven Kellogg. He has written and illustrated eight books and has illustrated—often in partnership with his former wife, Ariane Dewey—more than fifty others.

In 1972 Aruego shared honors with author Charlotte Pomerantz for *The Day They Parachuted Cats on Borneo* when it was chosen as a *New York Times* Best Illustrated Children's Book of the Year. Among his other honors are four ALA Notable Book selections, three appearances in the American Institute of Graphic Arts list of Children's Books of the Year, and a *Boston Globe-Horn Book* honor award.

His storybook *We Hide, You Seek* (1979), in which more than seventy East African animals play hide and seek with a rhino, is considered a classic of its type. Aruego often depicts unpopular animal species, such as piranhas and boars, and delights in showing "funny animals doing funny things."

INFORMATION FOR THE STUDENT

Tell the students that *The Day They Parachuted Cats on Borneo* is a play written by Charlotte Pomerantz and illustrated by Jose Aruego. As appropriate, you may share any information about the author and illustrator that you consider important. Additional information about Pomerantz and Aruego can be found on page 233 of the student anthology.

The play takes place on the island of Borneo. Ask the students if they know where Borneo is located. If any students know, ask one of them to point out the island on a map of the world for the benefit of the other students.

*

COGNITIVE AND RESPONSIVE READING

Activating Prior
Knowledge

Ask the students to discuss what they know about the balance of nature within an ecosystem.

Setting Reading
Goals and
Expectations

Have the students **browse the selection, using the clues/problems/wondering procedure.** Students will return to these observations after reading the selection. For a review of **browsing,** see **Learning Framework Card 1A, Setting Reading Goals and Expectations.**

Recommen-
dations for
Reading the
Selection

Ask students how they would like to read the selection. Because it is written as a drama, to be spoken and acted, the students may wish to **read the selection aloud,** perhaps even several times. Reading the selection aloud will help the students appreciate the rhythm and the poetic language. Students could be assigned to read the parts of the many "characters" in the play. In that way the play would be read in the same fashion in which it would be acted.

During oral reading, use and encourage think-alouds. During silent reading, allow discussion as needed. Discuss problems, strategies, and reactions after reading.

This would also be a good selection for **responding to text by connecting** and **showing surprise** while reading aloud. Model these responses and then invite the students to do the same.

Note: *The Day They Parachuted Cats on Borneo* has been divided into two parts, in case the students are not able to finish reading the selection in one class period. The second part begins on page 255 with section XII.

About the Reading Strategies

Because of the complex nature of the events described in the play, students may find it helpful to **ask questions** as they read. Encourage them to stop at any time to do so.

Think-Aloud Prompts for Use in Oral Reading

The think-aloud prompts are placed where the students may want to use strategies to help them better understand the text. These are merely suggestions. Remind the students to refer to the **reading strategy posters** and to use any strategy they find helpful as they read. Encourage them to call upon classmates when confronted with problems while reading.

TEACHING TIP Remind students to be aware of the different speakers that are relating the events in the drama.

These prompts may be used as guides to promote cognitive and responsive reading.

THE DAY THEY PARACHUTED CATS ON BORNEO
A DRAMA OF ECOLOGY
Charlotte Pomerantz
illustrated by Jose Aruego

This play is based on an actual event reported in the New York Times, *November 13, 1969.*

CAST IN ORDER OF APPEARANCE AND DISAPPEARANCE

≥ 216 ≤

I
I am the island of Borneo,
Where the farmer—poor farmer—bends low, bends low.
I have honey bears, rhinos, and tiger cats,
Great falcons, flamingoes, and foxy-faced bats.
I have gold and quicksilver, rubber and rice,
Cane sugar and spice—but not everything nice:
   A land of harsh ridges and savage monsoon,
   Of jungles as dark as the dark of the moon.
   Land of thundering rains and earthquakes and heat,
   Where the farmer's life is more bitter than sweet.
   Land of mosquitoes, which carry with ease
   The dreaded malaria, scourge and disease.

≥ 217 ≤

II

I am malaria, dreaded disease.
I cause men to ache and to shake and to freeze.
Three hundred million a year do I seize.
One million I kill with remarkable ease.
But I'm not the big killer I used to be
In the good old days before—ugh!—DDT;
'Cause that stuff kills mosquitoes—one, two, three . . .

And the death of them
is the death of me.

III

My name is dichloro-diphenyl-trichloroethane,
Which you've got to admit is a heck of a name.
But, perhaps, some of you have heard tell of me
By my well-known initials, which are DDT.
An organo-chlorine insecticide,
I come in a powder or liquified.
I'm death to mosquitoes outside or inside.
I was brought here by copter to Borneo,
Where the farmer—now hopeful—bends low, bends low.

1 My job is to kill that cruel killer of man:
A worthy and wise ecological plan.

If you don't know
what ecology means,
you'll soon find out.

IV

We are the mosquitoes who roam day and night,
Bringing death to the farmer with one small bite.
We like the farmer's hut—it buzzes with life.
There's the farmer, of course, his kids and his wife.
The caterpillars chew on the roof beams there,
While the geckoes, or lizards, roam everywhere.
There are lots of cockroaches, and always some cats
Who pounce on the lizards and scare away rats.
All of us are busy—busy looking for food.
Sometimes we eat each other, which may seem rather crude.
But imagine yourself in that hut, and I bet
You would rather eat someone than find yourself et.

Now suddenly—zap!—there is no place to hide,
For they sprayed all the huts with insecticide.
That's the end of our tale.

≥ *219* ≤

Postscriptum: we died.

---

1 Since the story line is introduced in sections I–III, the students may want to **sum up** the information before they continue reading. These passages may also contain unfamiliar words. The students may find it helpful to **apply decoding skills** and to **use context clues** when trying to pronounce and clarify unfamiliar words.

People are so anti-roach.

V

We are the cockroaches, homeloving pests.
In most people's huts we are unwelcome guests.
When we all got sprayed with that DDT stuff,
The mosquitoes got killed—not us. We're too tough.
We just swallowed hard and kept right on a-crawling,
Despite the rude comments and vicious name-calling.

VI

We're the hungry caterpillars of Borneo,
Where the farmer—also hungry—bends low, bends low.
We live on the roof beams, eating and hatching.
We make all our meals out of roof beams and thatching.
Nosh-nosh, nibble-nibble, munch-munch-munch,
For breakfast, supper, high tea and lunch.
Our life is as pleasant as green tea and roses,
Except when the lizards (gulp) poke in their noses.
Then nosh-nosh, nibble-nibble, munch-munch-munch,
The lizards ate half our cousins for lunch.
Those four-legged reptiles ruin our meals . . .

You'd have to be eaten
to know how it feels.

≥ 220 ≤

VII

We are the lizards, or geckoes, by name.
To the farmer we're useful, we're charming, we're tame.
Over the floors, walls and roof beams we roam,
Of every tropical home sweet home.
For us, cockroaches are scrumptious to eat.
Almost as tasty as caterpillar meat.

VIII

Then the copters sprayed, and we lost our appetite.
Now we laze away the days, we snooze the balmy night.
For every roach we eat, though they *do* taste yummy,
Adds DDT to our little lizard tummy.
And makes our tiny nervous system sluggish and slow.
We geckoes—leaping lizards!—got no get-up-and-go.

≥ 221 ≤

It's true we're not dying of DDT,
But a slooow gecko ain't nooo gecko,
As the caterpillars can plainly see.
We watch them eating roof beams like there's no tomorrow,
While we lizards hold our tummies in pain and sorrow.

At night the caterpillars and the roaches
Walk right up to us and say, *Buenas Noches*.

IX

We're the cats on the island of Borneo
Where the farmer—who loves us—bends low, bends low.
Eating all those lizards, or geckoes, by name,
Is turning out to be (sigh) a dying shame,
'Cause those lizards are poisoned from tail to head,
And killing those lizards is killing us dead.
We poor cats got a massive overdose.
What's left to say
(Sob)
Except *adios*.

Be careful of the lizard you eat.
The life you take may be your own.

222

X

We're the rivers, the rivers of Borneo.
We watch little man come and go, come and go.
We watched him kill mosquitoes with pesticide.
Saw the roaches poisoned, though not one cockroach died
Till . . .
The hungry lizards ate them, one by one by one.
Oh what a feast they had—it seemed like good clean fun.
But every roach they ate, though they *did* taste yummy,
Added DDT to their little lizard tummy.
Then the lizards were filled with deadly pesticide.
They felt pretty punchy, though not one lizard died
Till . . .
The hungry cats devoured them, one by one by one.
Oh what a feast they had—it seemed like good clean fun.
But every liz they ate, though they *did* taste yummy,
Killed the cats by poisoning their DD Toxic tummy.
Now this poor old island is steeped in poison air.
Our waters, too, are poisoned. Little man, take care!

Whoever thought that little man could affect
us mighty rivers? But the rain has washed the
DDT into our waters, and our tenants, the
friendly fish, are feeling pretty rocky.

2 The students have now read how some of the animals in the food chain on Borneo were affected by the pesticide DDT. They can check their understanding of these events by **asking** each other **questions** and by **summing up** information.

XI

We're the rats on the island of Borneo,
We never had it so good—heigh—dee—ho.
When the cats who had swallowed the geckoes lay dying,
We crawled in by thousands from forests outlying.
    When the farmers saw us, they raised an anguished cry:
    "Rats bring plague! Fly in help, or we shall surely die.
    Help us, men of science, help us kill the rats;
    For the DDT you sprayed has killed off all our cats!"
"Borneo for rent," we sang. "Inquire, please, within.
When the cats die off from DDT, we rats—move—in."

And then the helicopters came . . .

≥ 224 ≤

XII

We're the copters who've just flown in thousands of cats
And chuted them down on the armies of rats,
On the plague-threatened island of Borneo,
A bright green jewel in the blue sea below.

Once we came with DDT; now we come with cats.
Once we sprayed mosquitoes; now we'll fix the rats.
Looks like no one really thought the whole thing through . . .
Soon all the cats and rats will have a deadly rendezvous.

It was, all told,
a rather unusual assignment.

XIII

We're the parapussycats they parachuted down
On every cat-killed, rat-filled little village and town
On the dead-cat, dread-rat island of Borneo,
Where the farmer—strictly catless—bends low, low, low.

It's better than hanging
around fish markets.

3 If none of the students can define the word *plague,* explain that plague is a highly infectious, usually fatal, epidemic disease that is transmitted to humans from infected rats by means of the bites of fleas.

Note: The first part of the selection ends at the bottom of page 224. This is a good place to stop reading if the selection cannot be finished during this class period. Students may want to **sum up** before beginning to read the second part.

XIV

When we parapussycats were dropped to the ground,
What a feast we had—there were rats all around.
Everywhere you looked there were rats and rats and rats
Pursued by our élite corps of parapussycats.
We chased the rats for days, till most of them had fled,
And those who didn't run fast enough were—biff bam!—dead.

XV

The good farmers gave us a ticker-tape parade.
They heaped us with ivory, gold and silk brocade.
They said they would grant us our most fantastic wish—
So we asked them for five hundred kettles of fish.
We were wined, we were dined, we slept in king-size beds,
Till we heard a strange creaking just over our heads . . .
KA-RASH!

But let the roof beams
tell their own story.

XVI

We're the roof beams of thatched huts in Borneo,
Where the farmer—enduring—bends low, bends low.
If a man, now and then, did some roof patching,
Replaced chewed-up beams and half-eaten thatching,
We could keep out the wind, the rain, and the sun,
And shelter a man when his labors were done.
Despite caterpillars, we roof beams stayed strong,
And the lizards, by eating them, helped us along.
For the lizard, you see, was the number-one killer
Of the beam-eating (nosh-nosh) cater- (nosh-nosh) pillar.

Now we mourn the little lizards—may they rest in peace—
While the greedy caterpillars (burp) get more and more obese.

XVII

Good day, I'm a farmer in Borneo,
Where the coconut palm and the mango grow.
Here are honey bears, rhinos, and tiger cats.
Great falcons, flamingoes, and foxy-faced bats.
Here are gold and quicksilver, rubber and rice,
Cane sugar and spice—but not everything nice:
    When they sprayed my hut with insecticide,
    My rat-catching cat soon sickened and died.
    When the rats crawled in, I was filled with fear:
    The plague can kill more than malaria here.
    When my roof beams caved in, I moved next door,
    Until *their* roof beams collapsed to the floor.
But please do not think I wish to offend,
For DDT is the farmer's good friend.

227

---

4 Pomerantz introduces a note of irony in this passage when she has the farmer, despite all that has happened, call DDT his "good friend." You may need to explain to the students that irony is the use of words to convey the opposite of their literal meaning. For example, DDT is not the farmer's friend, since it has upset the balance of nature in his community, and this imbalance has caused the farmer some serious problems.

Still, perhaps you'll allow a poor man to say,
He hopes men of science will soon find a way
To kill the mosquitoes till all, all are dead—
But save the roof beams which are over my head,
As well as my most useful rat-catching cat.
How grateful I'd be if you'd only do that!
    Then, men of science, I would not complain.
    But now I must look to my roof—I smell rain!

XVIII

I am an ecologist. Ecology is the study of living things in relation to the world around them—everything around them—air, water, rocks, soil, plants, and animals, including man.

If a tree is cut down, I try to find out what will happen to the birds in the nests, the squirrels in the branches, the insects at the roots. I know that the roots of the tree hold the earth, that the earth holds the rainwater, and that the rainwater keeps the soil moist, so that plants can grow. I am concerned if too many trees are cut down, for then the rain will run off the surface of the soil, making the rivers rise, overflow their banks and flood the land. This is the kind of thing an ecologist thinks about.

Borneo is a huge island in Southeast Asia—the third largest in the world and bigger than all of Texas. It straddles the equator, which is why the climate is hot and steamy. Someone has said that there are two seasons in Borneo—a wet season and a less wet season.

The people are mainly Malays and Dyaks. The Malays, who live near the coast, are rice farmers and fishermen. Some

≥ 228 ≤

work on rubber plantations or in the oil fields, for Borneo is rich in oil. Inland are high mountain ranges, where most of the Dyaks live. Until recently, they were headhunters—the wild men of Borneo—and they still hunt with blowguns and poisoned darts. The women grow rice, yams, and sugarcane in tiny forest clearings.

Most of Borneo is part of the Republic of Indonesia. Some of it belongs to Malaysia, and a tiny part is an independent state called Brunei. It is an island of dense tropical forests, where vines grow as high as a thousand feet, where orangutans swing through the trees, and where the giant long-nosed proboscis monkey can grow as tall as a man. There is also a great variety of insects, including the anopheles mosquito. This mosquito carries malaria and is the reason I was sent to Borneo.

Mosquitoes breed in wet places, and there are many swamps and rain holes in Borneo. In the old days, we used to fight mosquitoes by draining swamps, when possible, and by spraying a thin film of oil on stagnant waters during the breeding season. Those who could afford to, put screens on doors, windows, and openings to keep the mosquitoes out. All this helped to keep malaria down, but millions of people still got sick.

Then, during World War II, a scientist discovered that a certain chemical compound, called dichloro-diphenyl-trichloroethane—DDT for short—was a marvelous insect killer. The discoverer, Dr. Paul Mueller of Switzerland, received the Nobel Prize for his discovery.

In Borneo, we sprayed the walls and insides of the huts with DDT. You know what happened: we killed the mosquitoes—and ended up with no cats. We had not realized how much DDT can accumulate in the fatty tissues of animals. Even a

≥ 229 ≤

tiny amount of DDT in food or drinking water, with repeated meals, builds up and up until the quantity is large enough to poison a large animal, such as a cat.

As you know, with the cats dead, the rats took over and brought the threat of plague. So cats were flown in to stop the rats. Then, just when matters seemed under control—the roofs fell down. This is but a small example of the complex and subtle connections and balances which exist among all living things.

Because of the poisonous effects of DDT, it has been banned or restricted in the United States, the Commonwealth of Independent States, and other industrial countries. In December, 1969, at a world conference of the Food and Agricultural Organization (a body of the United Nations), an attempt was made to ban the use of DDT all over the world. But the majority of scientists, representing the nonindustrial countries, refused to go along with the ban. They knew DDT was dangerous to health, but they needed it to control malaria and other diseases, and to protect food crops from insect destruction. The alternatives to DDT are expensive, and the nonindustrial countries, which contain about eighty percent of the world's population, cannot afford them, for they are very poor.

The wealthy nations pointed out that the danger of pesticides is everyone's responsibility, for when you pollute the atmosphere, and the waters which flow to the oceans, everyone suffers. Ecologically, the nations of the earth are one.

The poor nations replied that the wealthy nations are not faced with malaria epidemics, wholesale destruction of the food supply, and mass starvation. They can afford to worry

≥ 230 ≤

about the future of the environment. The poor nations can only think of day-to-day survival. Seventy-five per cent of the people in the world go to bed hungry, and the great majority of them are in the poor, nonindustrial countries.

Ecologists from underdeveloped countries, faced with starvation and disease, can only choose the lesser evil—DDT. But the real answer to their problem is to find new solutions. Work is going forward on drugs for the prevention of malaria. Unfortunately, some of these drugs have bad side effects. Others are not effective for all kinds of malaria. And all drugs are very expensive.

A more fruitful road is for scientists to seek an insecticide that kills mosquitoes and nothing else. Scientists have discovered that under crowded conditions, some mosquitoes release a toxic chemical that kills young mosquitoes. If they can isolate and synthesize that chemical, it would be a great step forward in malaria control.

Another possibility, which shows considerable promise, is to breed a variety of mosquito which leaves seventy-five per cent of the female eggs unfertilized. Released among other mosquitoes, this new strain transmits its infertility to all the offspring. Thus each generation would breed fewer and fewer mosquitoes.

We've been talking about DDT and the farmers of Borneo, but ecological problems are extremely varied and serious, and they cover the whole world. For example, the fumes of automobile exhausts have greatly increased the number of people who get lung diseases. Atomic radiation has increased the incidence of certain types of cancer. The hot water

≥ 231 ≤

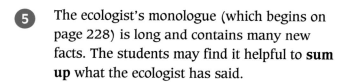

from power plants, when poured into lakes and rivers, kills the fishes.

There is pollution by lumber mills in Lake Baikal in the Commonwealth of Independent States. There is too much sewage in the canals of Amsterdam and Venice. The Danube is no longer blue. One can no longer swim in the Rhine in Germany, or in the Seine in Paris, or in our own Hudson River. Whole stretches of beaches in Italy, South America, England, and the United States have been polluted with oil slicks from the sea.

This is bad enough, but if the oil spills continue, worse will follow: a thin film of oil will spread over all the oceans. This will cut down the sunlight which very tiny plants, called diatoms, need both to reproduce and to live. These tiny plants, billions and billions of them, are the source of food for all the fishes of the sea. Further, these tiny plants use sunlight to combine with water to form carbon dioxide (used as food by them) and oxygen which is released into the air. Eighty per cent of all the oxygen in the world comes from these tiny plants. If sunlight is cut down and the amount of oxygen is reduced, the whole animal kingdom, including man, will suffer.

We need to know these things, so that we can do something to keep the air and water clean for all the people, as well as for all the animals and plants in the world. The ecologist should not protect the farmer against malaria with one hand and bring the roof down on his head with the other. But the answer is not for the ecologist to do nothing, but to be wiser about what he does. This is the <u>moral</u> of Borneo.

⑤

≥ 232 ≤

MEET CHARLOTTE POMERANTZ, AUTHOR

Charlotte Pomerantz was inspired to write The Day They Parachuted Cats on Borneo *by a newspaper article in the* New York Times. *Just the idea of cats parachuting was enough to spark her imagination. She was also fascinated by the chain of events that led to the parachuting of the cats. The children's book* The House That Jack Built *came to mind when she read the article because of the way the events built upon each other.*

Pomerantz believes that the message of the play is as important today as it was in 1971 when she wrote it. She has recently thought about doing an animated version which might reach a new audience. She hopes that by reading (or performing) her play, children will become more aware of and cautious about environmental problems. Pomerantz says that her children have made her more aware of today's ecological problems. "My children are very good about collecting glass bottles and plastic containers for recycling. Thinking about their futures also has an effect on me. So I try to help them with that as much as I can," she says.

MEET JOSE ARUEGO, ILLUSTRATOR

Jose Aruego was very happy to illustrate The Day They Parachuted Cats on Borneo. *Aruego thought the plot was interesting and worth telling. He was also excited because the story takes place on the island of Borneo, which is near his homeland of the Philippines. The drawings in* The Day They Parachuted Cats on Borneo *were easy for Aruego because he was already familiar with the animals and the scenery. Aruego says that he loves to work on books that are about Asia or that have Asian characters.*

Aruego has seen the play performed on his many visits to classrooms and says that students love performing it. He is very proud of the book because it has an important message to tell. Aruego believes that everyone should be concerned about the environment. "We should make every day count," he says. "We all should start now to do what we can to make the future better for everyone."

≥ 233 ≤

⑤ The ecologist's monologue (which begins on page 228) is long and contains many new facts. The students may find it helpful to **sum up** what the ecologist has said.

Discussing Strategy Use

Encourage the students to share any problems they had while reading *The Day They Parachuted Cats on Borneo.* If they used the **clarifying strategies** while reading, ask them to share how clarifying ideas helped them predict events and understand causes and effects.

* **EXPLORING THROUGH DISCUSSION**

Reflecting on the Selection
Whole-Group Discussion

The whole group discusses the selection and any thoughts or questions that it raises. During this time, students also **return to the clues, problems, and wonderings** that they noted on the chalkboard during browsing.

Assessment

To assess their understanding of the text, engage the students in a discussion to determine whether they have grasped the following ideas:
- how DDT affected each of the species living on Borneo in 1969
- why DDT is still being used in poor countries
- what scientists are doing to make the use of DDT unnecessary

Response Journal

Charlotte Pomerantz's play is both entertaining and thought provoking. Students who are keeping a response journal may want to record their thoughts and impressions of the selection now.

Exploring Concepts Within the Selection
Small-Group Discussion

Remind the students to refer to the **Concept Board** and the **Question Board** to keep their discussions focused. Circulate among the groups and encourage the students to consider their original ideas about ecology as they discuss this selection's relationship to the unit concepts.

ASSESSMENT TIP This may be a good opportunity to observe students working in groups and to write observations in your Teacher's Observation Log.

Sharing Ideas About Explorable Concepts

Have the groups **report their ideas** and **discuss them** with the rest of the class. It is crucial that the students' ideas determine this discussion.
- Students may notice that ecologists are learning to anticipate how one change within an ecosystem may affect all of the plants and animals in that ecosystem; this knowledge helps them find solutions to ecological problems without upsetting the balance of nature.
- Some students may comment that in order to stop the use of toxic substances like DDT to solve pest problems, scientists are beginning to look at nature, and thus, for natural ways of solving these problems.

As these ideas and others are stated, have the students **add them to the Question Board** or the **Concept Board.**

Exploring Concepts Across Selections

Ask the students whether this selection reminds them of other works they have read. Students may make connections with other selections in this or previously read units.
- Students may notice that DDT has also endangered the peregrine falcon, about which they read in *Saving the Peregrine Falcon.* The birds' health, like the health of the cats in this selection, was affected by eating animals that had ingested DDT.
- The ecologist in Pomerantz's play comments that scientists are trying to find acceptable alternatives to DDT that nonindustrialized countries can afford to use. Students may remember from *Protecting Wildlife* that conservationists who are establishing wildlife preserves are also taking into consideration the needs of the native population.

Recording Ideas

As they complete the above discussions, ask the students to **sum up what they have learned from their conversations and to tell how they might use this information** in further explorations. Any special information or insights may be recorded on the **Concept Board.** Any further questions that they would like to think about, pursue, or investigate may be recorded on the **Question Board.** The students may want to discuss the progress that has been made on their questions. They may also want to cross out any questions that no longer warrant consideration.

Evaluating Discussions

❯ After discussion, have the students individually record their ideas on page 83 of their Explorer's Notebook.

Explorer's Notebook, page 83

Saving the Peregrine Falcon by Caroline Arnold

_____
_____
_____
_____
_____
_____
_____
_____
_____
_____

The Day They Parachuted Cats on Borneo by Charlotte Pomerantz

_____
_____
_____
_____
_____
_____
_____
_____
_____

Copyright © 1995 Open Court Publishing Company

Unit 5/Ecology   EN 83

2 READING WITH A WRITER'S EYE

MINILESSON

Writer's Craft: Describing the Multiple Effects of a Single Cause

Ask students to discuss anything they have learned about using multiple effects of a single cause in writing and to cite any examples they can remember from their reading and writing. Remind the students that **writers enumerate the multiple effects of a single cause when they want to emphasize the far-reaching results of one action.** In *The Day They Parachuted Cats on Borneo,* Charlotte Pomerantz describes the **many effects** that resulted **from the spraying of the island with DDT.** For example, in part VIII on page 221, she tells the reader that after eating roaches that were sprayed with DDT, the geckoes both lost their appetite and became sluggish. Affected in these ways, the geckoes were not able to eat the caterpillars that noshed on the roof beams. This, in turn, caused something else to happen.

Selective Reading: Focus on Multiple Effects of a Single Cause

Have the students find other examples of how DDT affected the people and animals on Borneo. Encourage volunteers to read aloud the examples that they find. Other examples can be found on the following pages:

- page 222, part VIII: Since the geckoes are not eating the caterpillars, the caterpillars are destroying the farmers' roof beams.
- page 222, part IX: The cats are eating the DDT-infected geckoes and are becoming ill and dying.
- page 223, part X: DDT has gotten into the rivers and is poisoning the fish.
- page 224, part XI: Now, with the cats lying dead or dying, the rats are moving into the villages from the outlying forests.

Selection-Based Practice

Independent Practice: Multiple Effects of a Single Cause

▶ Have the students work in small groups, using Reading/Writing Connection, page 39, to extend their discussion of recounting multiple effects of a single cause.

WRITING

Linking Reading to Writing

Remind the students that in their writing it is very important to give the effects of actions and events. Giving more than one effect helps the reader understand a topic or an issue from more than one perspective. Encourage the students to look through their writing folders for pieces of their own writing that they could improve by showing the multiple effects of a single cause. When the students have had sufficient time to choose and revise a piece of writing, invite volunteers to read their original passages and their rewritten versions and to explain how the changes improved their writing.

∗ Writing Process

Suggest to the students that they complete any writing that they have been revising. They may want to prepare some pieces for publishing.

The Day They Parachuted Cats on Borneo

Describing Multiple Effects of a Single Cause

Find examples from *The Day They Parachuted Cats on Borneo* or from any other selections you have read in which the author describes the multiple effects of a single cause. Note how one event can sometimes have far-reaching results.

Title: _____ Page: _____

Cause: _____

_____

Effect no. 1: _____

_____

Effect no. 2: _____

_____

Effect no. 3: _____

_____

Effect no. 4: _____

_____

Title: _____ Page: _____

Cause: _____

_____

Effect no. 1: _____

_____

Effect no. 2: _____

_____

Effect no. 3: _____

_____

Effect no. 4: _____

_____

Name

Copyright © 1995 Open Court Publishing Company

Unit 5/Ecology

Cause and Effect

R/WC 39

Reading/Writing Connection, page 39

VOCABULARY

Encourage the students to discuss words or phrases from the selection that they might want to use in their speaking and writing or in their research for this unit. Words that you might discuss include *malaria, scourge, liquified, postscriptum, steeped, rendezvous, parapussycats, plague,* and *straddles.* Have Vocabulary Exploration forms, Reproducible Master 15, available so that the students can add to the Personal Dictionary section of their Writer's Notebook these or any other words or phrases from the selection that they want to remember and use. For additional opportunities to build vocabulary, see **Teacher Tool Card 77.**

VOCABULARY TIP Examine the students' writings for their use of new words learned during this unit. Record your observations in your Teacher's Observation Log.

Professional Checkpoint: Reading with a Writer's Eye

Revising and proofreading activities offer perfect opportunities to help the students better understand grammar and mechanics. Use the students' own writings to show both examples of errors that need to be corrected and examples of good work.

Notes:

3 GUIDED AND INDEPENDENT EXPLORATION

EXPLORING CONCEPTS BEYOND THE TEXT

Guided
Exploration

The following activity does not have to be completed within the days devoted to this lesson.

The students have just discussed how DDT set off a chain of reactions on Borneo that affected species from the mosquito to the cat. This link between animals that eat one another is called a food chain. Complex food chains, in which animals have more than one predator or prey, are called food webs. Point out that DDT affected the entire food web on the island. Encourage the students to research the food web of the animals native to their communities. Remind those who live in urban areas that wildlife exists in cities as well.

❯ Students may record their food webs in their Explorer's Notebook, page 101.

❯ This would be an appropriate time to distribute Home/School Connection 39 and have students and their families think of something that happened to them or to someone they know that set off a whole chain of events.

Explorer's Notebook, page 101

Creating a Food Web

A food web shows the complex, interrelated food chains of the animals that live in a habitat. It shows the animals that prey on more than one insect or animal and that, in turn, may be preyed upon by one or more other animals. Learn about the food web of the animals that are native to your community; then create a food web in the space provided below. Show your web to classmates and explain to them how it works.

Copyright © 1995 Open Court Publishing Company

Unit 5/Ecology   EN 101

Home/School Connection 39

The Day They Parachuted Cats on Borneo

A message from _____

The students have just read Charlotte Pomerantz's ecology play, *The Day They Parachuted Cats on Borneo,* which describes how one event (spraying the island of Borneo with DDT) caused a chain reaction of problems for both the animals and the people on the island. Have your child explain this chain of events to you. Then, together with your child, think of a similar occurrence in your life or in the life of someone you know, in which one event caused several other things to happen. Have your child summarize the story below and return it to school so that it may be shared with her or his classmates.

Event: _____

First result: _____

Second result: _____

Third result: _____

Fourth result: _____

Copyright © 1995 Open Court Publishing Company

Unit 5/Ecology   H/SC 39

Research Cycle

Meet with the whole class, as needed, for the following purposes:

- to arrange schedules and update calendars
- to discuss problems that students are having with their research
- to hear preliminary presentations and discussions of interesting findings
- to arrange more formal presentations of students' research
- to provide guidance to ensure that groups progress through the phases of the Research Cycle—obtaining information; revising problems, conjectures, needs, and plans (perhaps with input resulting from a presentation to the class); and proceeding to a further cycle of problem, conjecture, and so forth

* Exploring Through Research

Professional Checkpoint: Guided and Independent Exploration

You should spend some time in individual conferences with the students during Independent Workshop to help them with their writing and research projects. Here are a few specific pointers for these conferences:

- Focus first on the student's stated problem. Determine whether the student is having real difficulty or just needs reassurance from you.
- If there is a difficulty, analyze the student's approach. If that approach is not working, discuss alternative approaches.
- Review peer feedback.
- Determine with the student the next step or goal.
- Refer the student to helpful resources, such as the Writer's Handbook and the Student Tool Cards in the Student Toolbox.

Notes:

✳ INDEPENDENT WORKSHOP
Building a Community of Scholars

Student-Directed Reading, Writing, and Discussion

Meet with the whole class, as needed, to assess the progress of each research group. By this point, the students should be revising any written work that is to be presented.

If any groups are ready to present their research projects, set aside time for the presentations. Have the students add to the Concept Board any information learned from the presentations.

Additional Opportunities for Independent Reading, Writing, and Cross-curricular Activities

✱ Reading Roundtable
Encourage the students to look for books about food webs or about the interdependence of the animals within an ecosystem.

✱ Writing Seminar
Remind the students to proofread carefully before they publish a piece of writing.

Portfolio
Remind the students to think about choosing pieces of work created during this unit to put in their portfolios.

Cross-curricular Activity Cards
The following Cross-curricular Activity Cards in the Student Toolbox are appropriate for this selection:
- 8 Drama—Role Play
- 4 Math—Just How Big Is Borneo, Anyway?
- 5 Math—Malaria Mortality

Additional Opportunities for Solving Learning Problems

Tutorial
You may want to use this time to work with students who need extra help. For your convenience, the following aids are available in the Teacher Toolbox:
- Writer's Craft/Reading: Causal Indicators, Teacher Tool Card 31
- Writer's Craft/Reading: Genre—Play/Drama, Teacher Tool Card 11
- Writer's Craft/Reading: Elaboration Through Providing Problem and Solution, Teacher Tool Card 45
- Grammar, Mechanics, and Usage: Using Parentheses, Dashes, and Ellipses, Teacher Tool Card 54

Unit Wrap-up

After all the projects have been shared, initiate a general class discussion on the unit. The Concept Board and research project displays can help the students recall the knowledge they have gained from this unit. In addition, the students might open their Explorer's Notebook to page 80 to remind themselves of what they knew about ecology as they began the unit and what they expected to learn by completing the unit. The discussion may be extended to include

- an evaluation of the unit selections. Which selections did students find most interesting? Which were the least interesting?
- an evaluation of the unit activities. Which activities did students find the most enjoyable or informative? Which did not seem valuable?
- an evaluation of the overall unit. How well did the unit cover the explorable concepts? Was ecology a worthwhile subject to examine? Why or why not?
- suggestions of ideas related to ecology worth further exploration, beginning with questions left on the Question Board.

Small Group Discussion

As an alternative, you might have the students work in small groups to discuss the unit. Encourage the group participants to refer to the Concept Board, browse the anthology selections, and review their Explorer's Notebook pages for unit 5 to refresh their memories on important ideas raised in the unit. Then have the groups share their important points and conclusions from their discussions.

ASSESSMENT

Informal Assessment

▶ Have students evaluate their experiences with this unit by completing Explorer's Notebook, pages 102–103. Meet with students to discuss their evaluations.

End-of-Unit Assessment

At this point, you might wish to carry out end-of-unit assessment for unit 5, Ecology. You will find the following end-of-unit assessment booklets in the Teacher's Toolbox:
Comprehension Assessment
- Understanding the Selection
- Making Connections Across Selections

Unit Wrap-up

How did you feel about this unit?
☐ I enjoyed it very much.   ☐ I liked it.
☐ I liked some of it.   ☐ I didn't like it.

How would you rate the difficulty of the unit?
☐ easy   ☐ medium   ☐ hard

How would you rate your performance during this unit?
☐ I learned a lot about ecology.
☐ I learned some new things about ecology.
☐ I didn't learn much about ecology.

Why did you choose this rating?
_____
_____
_____
_____

What was the most interesting thing you learned about ecology?
_____
_____
_____

Is there anything else about ecology that you would like to learn? What?
_____
_____
_____
_____

102 EN   Ecology/Unit 5

Copyright © 1995 Open Court Publishing Company

Explorer's Notebook, page 102

What did you learn about ecology that you didn't know before?
_____
_____
_____
_____

What did you learn about yourself as a learner?
_____
_____
_____

As a learner, what do you need to work on?
_____
_____
_____

What resources (books, films, magazines, interviews, tool cards, other) did you use on your own during this unit? Which of these were the most helpful? Why?
_____
_____
_____
_____
_____
_____

Unit 5/Ecology   EN 103

Copyright © 1995 Open Court Publishing Company

Explorer's Notebook, page 103

- Checking Skills
- Multiple-Choice Option

Essay and Writing Assessment

Research Assessment

You may pick and choose among the various assessment components to find the right mix for assessing areas you want to stress. See *Formative Assessment: A Teacher's Guide* for specific suggestions on how to use these assessment materials.

UNIT CELEBRATION

Have the students suggest how they might celebrate the completion of this unit. Their suggestions may include the following:
- Create a poster that includes pictures and information about a habitat and its wildlife. Include arrows to show how the plants and animals are related in a food web.
- Invite family members and/or another class in for a "tour" of the classroom. Students could act as tour guides.
- Encourage the students to make up a game in which they write important ecology questions on notecards and quiz one another.

Value

UNIT INTRODUCTION

BACKGROUND INFORMATION FOR THE TEACHER

Explorable
Concepts

The idea of trade-offs is fundamental to economics; it is also fundamental to basic life choices. It cannot be avoided. The only way that you can decide how much you want something—how much you value something—is to decide what you are willing to give up for it. Choices are necessary because all resources are finite. Therefore, we cannot just decide, in isolation from all of our other choices, how much we want something; we have to balance the desirability of having it against the undesirability of not having something else. This unit—which could also have been called Trade-offs or Choices—is about that inescapable fact.

The necessity of making choices and the consequences of trying to avoid them are common themes in literature. If you have the time or the energy or the money for only one thing out of three or four but are unwilling to forgo any of them, you end up making compromises, being careless, doing justice to none of them. Economists refer to the cost of a thing in terms of what is given up to get it as the "opportunity cost." It is not enough to want something very badly; you also have to decide what to give up for it, or you will get less of everything.

The word *value* appears to have different meanings in its different contexts. On the one hand, we talk about "getting good value" when we go shopping, which means that we would have been willing to pay more than we did for what we got (or that we got something better than what we would ordinarily have gotten for the price we paid). On the other

hand, we talk about "our deepest and most cherished values" as the beliefs or customs that are of greatest importance to us, those that define us as individuals, families, and cultures. What these usages have in common is the idea of trade-offs and choices. Our deepest values determine the choices we will make. "Getting good value" means getting what we wanted and giving up less than we expected for it. In both cases— whether or not money is involved—we are making trade-offs, deciding what to do with our basic resources of time, energy, attention, and love.

Many basic choices do not appear to involve money directly—choices about where to live, what job to take, who to marry or live with, how many children to have, how hard to work. Very often, however, these choices involve a trade-off between money and other things—some jobs pay more than others, some places cost more to live in, and so on. Still, money is not the most important element in reaching a decision; it may influence what we choose when we do not care very much, but rarely will it be the determining factor in a really important choice. In making these major choices, we go through the same thought process—the same kind of evaluation—as in making smaller choices, like those we make when we go shopping.

In this unit, the inquiry will probably not take the form of research, though it may. Students may want to follow up on the idea of trade-offs in economics and find out how economists analyze choices, or they may wish to probe the ways in which marketers attempt to influence choices. Advertising is widely available for all to see, discuss, and analyze; and market research is widely discussed and reported in the business and marketing press. Students may want to ask whether advertising works and how it influences people's values. Many other approaches to research are possible. The most important thing is that students come to understand the idea of trade-offs and opportunity costs in a wide variety of human situations, not just in those involving money.

Value raises a wide variety of questions. To stimulate your own thinking, you might ask yourself questions like the following:

- In the marketplace, value is determined by supply and demand. Does supply and demand also affect value when money is not involved?
- Is it more important to work at what one enjoys doing or to earn an adequate living?
- How do an individual's values correspond to and interrelate with the values of the society in which he or she lives?
- Why is it so difficult to explain or articulate basic values?

Resources

Among the following resources are **professional reference books, read-alouds, audiovisual materials,** and **community/school resources.** The reference books are intended to help you develop the concepts and organize information to share with the students in whatever way you choose. The read-alouds are books and short stories that fit the concepts well and that offer the listener pleasure because of their rich language and vivid imagery. Among the audiovisual materials are some that your students may not be able to obtain and others that will be available to both you and your students. For a complete list of audiovisual sources, see page 519. The community/school resources include people, agencies, and institutions that may be helpful in your exploration.

In addition to the resources listed here, bibliographies for the students appear in the student anthology, on Reproducible Masters 53–58, and on Home/School Connection 40–41. Encourage the students to use these bibliographies as they explore the concepts in this unit.

You should also choose and read books from the students' bibliographies. Reading stories about value written for younger audiences will help you understand the nature of the information the students are learning.

Professional Reference Books

Davis, Ken, and Taylor, Tom. *Kids and Cash.* Oak Tree Publications, Inc., 1979. *Kids and Cash* explains methods that adults can use to help young people learn to deal with money, using many true-to-life examples. It also explains monetary concepts and the importance of jobs for young people and offers ideas of ways young people can go into business for themselves.

Dolan, Edward F., Jr. *Money Talk.* Julian Messner, 1986. This dictionary of financial terms is clearly written and would be a good classroom resource.

Drew, Bonnie. *Money Skills: 101 Activities to Teach Your Child About Money.* The Career Press, 1992. These worthwhile activities are divided into age-appropriate sections, with forty activities targeted for nine-to-twelve-year-olds. Many of these activities could be done at school or in cooperation with adults at home.

Miller, Gordon Porter. *Teaching Your Child to Make Decisions: How to Raise a Responsible Child.* Harper & Row, 1984. Teachers and parents alike will find this a useful guide to helping children learn to be good decisionmakers. It includes "A Brief Course in Decisionmaking"—seven steps to becoming an effective decisionmaker, based on the values that each individual chooses as important.

Roberts, Wess. *Straight A's Never Made Anybody Rich: Lessons in Personal Achievement.* HarperCollins Publishers, 1991. Numerous sections in this book—especially chapter 11, "The Phony Lure of Fame and Fortune"—refer to real values.

Schulman, Michael, and Mekler, Eva. *Bringing Up a Moral Child.* Addison-Wesley Publishing Company, Inc., 1985. Parents and other adults who wish to implant a strong set of moral values in children will find this a most helpful book. No specific set of morals is espoused. The emphasis is, rather, on the three processes used to develop moral values: internalizing, empathizing, and developing personal standards. Of special interest for this unit is a section in chapter 10 entitled "Money and Morals in a Competitive Society."

Simon, Sidney B.; How, Leland W.; Kirschenbaum, Howard. *Values Clarification: A Handbook of Practical Strategies for Teachers and Students*. Hart Publishing Co., 1972, 1978. The teacher can choose from among the seventy-nine different values-clarification strategies contained in this book. There are exercises applicable to all age levels.

Read-Alouds   Coatsworth, Elizabeth. *The Cat Who Went to Heaven.* Scholastic, Inc., printed 1987 (paperback). Copyright Macmillan, 1958. This Newbery Award–winning book begins as a poor artist's housekeeper brings home a three-colored cat. As such cats are supposed to be lucky, the artist calls the humble creature "Good Fortune." When the artist is asked to paint a picture of Buddha for the temple, he must choose between his future success and his love for his cat.

Trelease, Jim. *Hey! Listen to This: Stories to Read Aloud.* Viking, 1992. Included in this anthology in a section devoted to "Classic Tales" is a wonderful updated, read-aloud version of the Greek myth of King Midas, who learns that there are things more valuable than gold when he is granted his wish and briefly possesses "The Golden Touch."

Wilde, Oscar. *The Happy Prince.* Creative Education, Inc., 1983. With the help of a small swallow, a richly decorated statue sacrifices the gold and gems that adorn him to help the poor and needy in his town.

Banks: The Money Movers. A Greenhouse Film Production, 1977. A miser named Arthur Scrooge is visited late one night by the Spirit of Banking. In a humorous adventure, Scrooge learns about bank services, the economy, and government safeguards. 15 minutes; film or videocassette.

Magic Orchard. Kratky Film Prague, 1986. This animated fairy tale is about a group of poor desert people who want only to live a simple, peaceful life, but instead are terrorized by marauders. After finding a pot of gold, they unselfishly give it away. They are rewarded with a magic feather that enables them to live their peaceful life protected from the marauders. 16 minutes; film or videocassette.

The No-Guitar Blues. Gary Templeton, 1991. Based on the unit selection by Gary Soto, this film follows young Fausto Sanchez on his quest to earn money to buy a guitar. 27 minutes; film or videocassette.

Thank You, Ma'am. Andrew Sugarman, 1976. Based on Langston Hughes's short story, this video concerns a youth who tries to steal an older woman's purse. The woman catches him, takes him home, and gives him some valuable life-changing advice. 12 minutes; film or videocassette.

The Wave: A Japanese Folktale. Stephen Busustow Production, 1968. Grandfather sacrifices the village rice fields by setting fire to them, drawing the townspeople to the hill and saving them from the tidal wave that destroys the village. 9 minutes; film or videocassette.

What Are Values? Wayne Mitchell Film, 1977. The film delineates what values are, what people's actions reveal about their values, and what methods can be used to make difficult value decisions. 9 minutes; film or videocassette.

What Is the Good Life?: The Human Image. Eli Hollander, 1974. A series of interviews explores the answer to the title's question. 16 minutes; film or videocassette.

Additional resources that may be helpful in the exploration of value include the following:
- School counselor
- Leaders of volunteer services and charitable organizations
- Local bankers or financial planners

The following sources can provide information about economics and money by mail:

Federal Reserve Bank of Philadelphia
Public Information Department
P.O. Box 66
Philadelphia, PA 19105-0066
Free booklets: *Coins of the Ancient Mediterranean World; Money in Colonial Times*

Federal Reserve Bank of New York
Public Information Department
33 Liberty Street
New York, NY 10045
Free booklets: *Once Upon a Dime* (the history of bartering and money); *The Arithmetic of Interest Rates; Story of Consumer Credit* (English or Spanish)
Free comic book: *The Story of Checks and Electronic Payment*

Office of Public Affairs
U.S. Savings Bond Division
Department of the Treasury
Washington, DC 20226
Free booklets: *U.S. Savings Bonds Buyers' Guide; The Savings Bond Question and Answer Book; U.S. Savings Bonds: Now Tax-Free for Education*

Commonwealth of Massachusetts
Executive Office of Consumer Affairs
One Ashburton Place
Boston, MA 02108
Free pamphlet: *Kids Are Consumers Too!*

Concept Board

Designate an area of the classroom for the **Concept Board.** Remind the students that, as in the previous unit, the class will keep a Concept Board to **record information learned about the unit concepts.** You may wish to begin the Concept Board after the students have had an opportunity to raise important questions about value and have some idea of where they are going with the unit. Throughout the reading of the unit, encourage the students to review the information on the Concept Board and explain how their growing understanding has changed or altered their original ideas about value.

Question Board

Designate another area for the **Question Board.** Remind the students to **post any questions that they have about value** as they proceed through the unit. Take time to review these questions periodically so that students can add new questions or remove old questions when they no longer warrant consideration.

For a review of information about the **Question Board** and the **Concept Board**, see **Teacher Tool Card 123**.

Activating Prior Knowledge

Have the students talk about the things that they think are important in their lives. If no one wants to begin, reveal some things that are important to you; for example, you might mention that you enjoy teaching and learning from your students.

Add to the Concept Board important ideas arising from this discussion. Throughout the reading of the unit, refer to the statements on the Concept Board to help students focus. It is important that the students feel free to voice their opinions and discuss them.

Setting Reading Goals and Expectations

- Have students **examine the unit title and the illustration** that appear on pages 236–237.
- Have the students spend a few minutes **browsing the selections.** Have them list on the chalkboard different issues related to value that they think they will read about in the unit.
- Encourage them to **share and discuss** anything in the text or the illustrations that catches their attention.
- Explain to the students that throughout this unit they will be participating in activities that will extend their experiences and deepen and expand their knowledge of value. These **exploratory activities** may include narrative writing, drama, art, interviews, debates, and panel discussions. The students will be allowed ample opportunity to reflect on and discuss the activities they complete.

For a review of **browsing,** see **Learning Framework Card 1A, Setting Reading Goals and Expectations.**

❯ Have students complete page 104 in their Explorer's Notebook and share their responses with the rest of the class.

Knowledge About Value

These are some of my ideas about value before reading the unit.

_____
_____
_____
_____
_____
_____
_____
_____
_____
_____
_____

These are some things about value that I would like to discuss and understand
better.

_____
_____
_____
_____
_____
_____
_____
_____
_____
_____
_____
_____

Reminder: I should read this page again when I get to
the end of the unit to see how much my ideas about value
have changed.

Copyright © 1995 Open Court Publishing Company

Explorer's Notebook, page 104

Learning Unit: Value

SELECTION	LINK TO THE UNIT CONCEPTS
The Miser, pages 318–333 fable by Aesop, illustrated by Jean and Mou-sien Tseng	The true value of money lies not in having money, but in using money.

● **Money Matters**, pages 334–353
realistic fiction from *Tough Tiffany* by Belinda Hurmence,
    illustrated by Marcy Ramsey
ALA Notable Book, 1980; Notable Children's Trade Book in the
    Field of Social Studies, 1980
	Money should be neither hoarded nor carelessly spent; money is most valuable when it is put to meaningful use.

A Gift for a Gift, pages 354–367 folk tale adapted by Eric Protter, illustrated by Krystyna Stasiak	A humble gift that is given sincerely may be more valuable than an expensive one that is given for dishonest reasons.
ON YOUR OWN **What Money Is**, pages 368–381 nonfiction from *Nickels, Dimes, and Dollars: How Currency Works* by R. V. Fodor	Money is valuable only because we agree that it is.

● **The Shoeshine Stand**, pages 382–407
realistic fiction from *Shoeshine Girl* by Clyde Robert Bulla,
    illustrated by Susan David
Sequoyah Children's Book Award, 1978; South Carolina Children's
    Book Award, 1980; Southern California Council Notable Book,
    1976
	Money means more when one must earn it oneself.

▲ ■ **The Gold Coin**, pages 408–425 folk tale by Alma Flor Ada, illustrated by Neil Waldman	Friendship and a place in the community are far more rewarding than mere money.
FINE ART pages 426–429 *The Thankful Poor*, Henry Ossawa Tanner; *One Dollar Silver Certificate*, Victor Dubreuil; *Peasant Wedding*, Pieter Bruegel the Elder	Value can be expressed through the visual arts.
● **President Cleveland, Where Are You?**, pages 430–451 realistic fiction by Robert Cormier, illustrated by Mary Beth Schwark and Bob Kuester Notable Children's Trade Book in the Field of Social Studies, 1980	Sometimes loyalty to family is more important than personal gain.
ASSESSMENT ● **The No-Guitar Blues**, pages 452–465 realistic fiction by Gary Soto, illustrated by Andy San Diego ALA Best Books for Young Adults, 1991	Personal integrity is not worth trading for material gain.

● Award-winning authors and/or illustrators   ▲ Full-length trade books   ■ Dramatized on audiocassette

Exploration Through Reflective Activities

SELECTION-BASED MINILESSONS		REFLECTIVE ACTIVITIES
TEACHER'S GUIDE	**TEACHER TOOLBOX**	
Using Interesting Verbs	Genre—Fable, Indicators of Time and Order, Introductory Phrases	Small-group discussions Writing an essay
Dialogue—Speaker Tags Describing Characters' Thoughts and Feelings	Genre—Realistic Fiction, Compound Words	Taking a survey
Theme in Folk Tales	Dependent and Independent Clauses, Punctuating Dialogue	Group discussions Writing personal experience stories Comparing and contrasting values
Students choose a writer's craft to focus on.	Genre—Expository Text, Elaboration Through Providing Specific Facts	Group discussions Organizing a "barter day"
Characterization Dialogue	Point of View, Contractions	Group discussions Illustrating or writing about prized possessions
Story Structure Using Sensory Descriptions	Indicators of Place and Location	Small-group discussions Exploring volunteer organizations Inviting an expert to class/Interview
Using Adverbs Story Elements—Plot, Setting, Characterization	Using Parentheses, Dashes, and Ellipses	Exploring the value of trading cards Exploring collectibles
Choice of a writer's craft to study is part of assessment.		Debating an issue Small-group discussions

Assessment available for this unit includes Teacher's Observation Log,
Self-Assessment Questionnaire, Concept Connections, Portfolios, and
separate Comprehension assessment and Essay and Writing assessment.

Learning Unit: Value

SELECTION	LINK TO THE UNIT CONCEPTS
POETRY pages 466–473 ● **The Courage That My Mother Had** poem by Edna St. Vincent Millay, illustrated by Luis Vasquez **The Coin** poem by Sara Teasdale, illustrated by Luis Vasquez	Intangible things are often more valuable than material objects.

● ▲ ■ **The Hundred Penny Box**, pages 474–497
realistic fiction by Sharon Bell Mathis, illustrated by Leo and
  Diane Dillon
Newbery Honor Book, 1976; Boston Globe-Horn Book Award,
  1975; Notable Children's Trade Book in the Field of Social
  Studies, 1975
	The sentimental value of prized possessions may be far greater than their monetary value.

Unit Wrap-up, pages 498–499	

● Award-winning authors and/or illustrators   ▲ Full-length trade books   ■ Dramatized on audiocassette

Exploration Through Reflective Activities

SELECTION-BASED MINILESSONS		REFLECTIVE ACTIVITIES
TEACHER'S GUIDE	**TEACHER TOOLBOX**	
Discussing Poetry		Group discussions
Point of View Describing Characters' Thoughts and Feelings	Dialogue	Role-playing
		Sharing of group knowledge, insights, and ideas

Assessment available for this unit includes Teacher's Observation Log,
Self-Assessment Questionnaire, Concept Connections, Portfolios, and
separate Comprehension assessment and Essay and Writing assessment.

The Miser

1 READING THE SELECTION

INFORMATION FOR THE TEACHER

About the Selection

This thought-provoking fable teaches, in only three paragraphs, a lesson that many people don't learn in a lifetime. Lush illustrations, rich with detail, illuminate the text.

Link to the Unit Concepts

In "The Miser," pages 238–239, students will encounter a man who valued having his gold more than he valued using it. Even when he loses all of his gold, the man's way of living probably remains unchanged. The fable may cause students to ponder the question of what money is really good for.

About the Author

Aesop was a Greek slave who was given his freedom by his master. He lived sometime during the sixth century B.C. This is pretty much all that is known about the man who has been credited with creating some of the best-known stories in the world. Whether he actually created the stories is disputed by some historians. Fables were written in Sumeria and in India, long before Aesop's time, and indeed, these earlier fables are often similar in form and content to some of those credited to Aesop. However, the fact that Aesop was revered as a fabulist by such scholars as Plato, Aristotle, Xenophon, and Aristophanes suggests that he had earned at least some of his reputation. One possible reason is that Aesop was purported to be especially adept at using fables to make his point in discussions.

LESSON OVERVIEW

"The Miser" by Aesop, pages 238–239

READING THE SELECTION

Materials
Student anthology, pp. 238–239
Explorer's Notebook, p. 105

FYI
Learning Framework Card
- Setting Reading Goals and Expectations, 1A

READING WITH A WRITER'S EYE

Minilesson
Writer's Craft: Using Interesting Verbs

Materials
Reading/Writing Connection, p. 40
Reproducible Master 15

FYI
Teacher Tool Card
- Spelling and Vocabulary: Building Vocabulary, 77

Options for Instruction
Writer's Craft: Genre—Fable
Writer's Craft: Indicators of Time and Order
Grammar, Mechanics, and Usage: Introductory Phrases
(Use Teacher Tool Cards listed below.)

GUIDED AND INDEPENDENT EXPLORATION

Materials
Home/School Connection 40–41
Reproducible Masters 53–58
Explorer's Notebook, p. 109

FYI
Learning Framework Card
- Exploring Through Reflective Activities, 3

Independent Workshop

Optional Materials from Student Toolbox
Tradebook Connection Cards

Cross-curricular Activity Card
- 6 Math—Gold!

Student Tool Cards
- Writer's Craft/Reading: Choosing Precise and Vivid Verbs, 22
- Writer's Craft/Reading: Reading and Writing Folk Tales and Fables, 1
- Writer's Craft/Reading: Signal Words Showing Time and Order, 29
- Grammar, Mechanics, and Usage: Phrases, 50

FYI
Teacher Tool Cards
- Writer's Craft/Reading: Choosing Precise and Vivid Verbs, 22
- Writer's Craft/Reading: Genre—Folk Tale and Fable, 1
- Writer's Craft/Reading: Indicators of Time and Order, 29
- Grammar, Mechanics, and Usage: Phrases, 50
- Classroom Supports: Question Board and Concept Board, 123

NOTES

Asterisks (*) throughout the lesson indicate learning frameworks. Learning Framework Cards and Teacher Tool Cards can be found in the Teacher Toolbox.

INFORMATION FOR THE STUDENT

Inform the students that "The Miser" is a fable. Fables are short stories that are meant to teach a moral truth. Often their purpose was to instruct children by presenting an instance of particular human behavior and then offering a moral or maxim to point out how the instance represents human behavior in general. In many fables, animals were used in place of humans to entertain the children as well as to teach them a lesson. However, there was another reason that fables used animals to represent people. During a time when speaking freely was dangerous in Greece, storytellers sometimes dared to criticize or make fun of public officials. By using animals instead of people as the characters in their stories, they could protect themselves in case a listener thought he or she recognized someone important in the story. Thus, both to entertain children and to protect the author from punishment, fables often used talking animals to represent humans. However, this is not the case in "The Miser."

Explain that this short piece was written by Aesop. The children are probably familiar with some of Aesop's fables such as "The Tortoise and the Hare," "The Fox and the Grapes," and "The Crow and the Pitcher." However, they may not know much about the purpose or form of fables or about Aesop himself, so provide them with some of the background information included above and in About the Author.

Fables

*

COGNITIVE AND RESPONSIVE READING

Setting Reading Goals and Expectations

Tell students to open their books to page 238. Have them **browse** the first few lines of the fable. If the students have observations about the selection, list them on the chalkboard **using the clues/problems/ wondering procedure.** For example, students might list the genre of the selection under clues; they might list unfamiliar words under problems; and they might note any questions that arise during browsing under wonderings. Students will return to these observations after reading. For a review of **browsing,** see **Learning Framework Card 1A, Setting Reading Goals and Expectations.**

Recommendations for Reading the Selection

Ask the students how they would like to read the selection. Because the selection is brief and fairly simple, the students should have little difficulty **reading** it **silently** to themselves.

If the students choose to read orally, use and encourage think-alouds. If they elect to read silently, allow discussion as needed. Discuss problems, strategies, and reactions after reading.

This would also be a good selection for **responding** to text **by giving opinions.** Model this response, and then invite the students to do the same.

TEACHING TIP Observe students' nonverbal reactions as they read. Watch for puzzled frowns, long pauses, looks of surprise, smiles, and so on. When you see such reactions, ask students to share their questions and their comments.

About the
Reading
Strategies

Think-Aloud Prompts
for Use in Oral Reading

"The Miser" is so short and straightforward that it should not present many problems for the students. If some students do have difficulties, clarifying through the use of **context clues** may be helpful.

Notice the suggested think-aloud prompts with the page miniatures. These are merely suggestions for using the strategies where they might be most helpful for the students. Remind students that what they are reading should make sense. If a passage doesn't make sense, they should apply whatever strategy is necessary to clear it up. By now they should have a good working knowledge of the reading strategies; however, remind them to refer to the **reading strategy posters** if they need help deciding which strategy to use. Encourage students to stop and ask for help if they are confused about something or to share any reactions they may have as they read.

THINK ALOUD PROMPTS

These prompts may be used as guides to promote cognitive and responsive reading.

1 Some students may **wonder** how the miser could have a garden wall if he had "sold all his property." Allow students to speculate on the meaning of the paragraph, but help them understand that the miser obviously sold everything but his house and his land.

Some students may be unfamiliar with the word *gloat*. Encourage them to **use context clues** to figure out the meaning of the word. Remind them that illustrations as well as text can help them make sense of new words.

THE MISER
Aesop
illustrated by Jean and Mou-sien Tseng

1 A miser, who never stopped worrying about the safety of his many possessions, sold all his property and <u>converted</u> it into a huge lump of gold. This he buried in a hole in the ground near his garden wall, and every morning he went to visit it and gloat over the size of it.

The miser's strange behavior aroused the curiosity of the town thief. Spying upon the rich man, the thief saw him place the lump of gold back in the hole and cover it up. As soon as the miser's back was turned, the thief went to the spot, dug up the gold and took it away.

The next morning when the miser came to gloat over his treasure he found nothing but an empty hole. He wept and tore his hair, and so loud were his <u>lamentations</u> that a neighbor came running to see what was the trouble. As soon as he had learned the cause of it, he said comfortingly: "You are foolish to distress yourself so over something that was buried in the earth. Take a stone and put it in the hole, and think that it is your lump of gold. You never meant to use it anyway. Therefore it will do you just as much good to fondle a lump of granite as a lump of gold."

The true value of money is not in its possession but in its use.

238

*

Reflecting on the Selection
Whole-Group Discussion

The whole group discusses the selection and any personal thoughts, reactions, or questions that it raises. At this time, students also **return to the clues, problems, and wonderings** noted on the chalkboard during browsing.

Assessment

In a successful discussion, it should not be necessary for you to ask questions to assess the students' understanding of the story. If necessary, however, engage them in a discussion **to determine whether the students have grasped the following ideas:**
- why the miser converted his possessions to gold
- how the neighbor's advice suited the miser's situation

Response Journal

Remind students to enter, if they wish, their personal reactions to the fable in their response journals.

Exploring Concepts Within the Selection
Small-Group Discussion

Small groups discuss the selection's relationship to value. **Circulate among the groups** and observe the discussions. Remind the students to refer to the Concept Board and the Question Board to help keep their discussions focused.

Sharing Ideas About Explorable Concepts

Have the groups **report their ideas** and **discuss them** with the rest of the class.
- Students may speculate whether or not the miser's life will truly be any different without his gold.

As these and other ideas and concepts are stated, have the students add them to the **Question Board** or the **Concept Board**.

Recording Ideas

As the students complete the above discussions, ask them to **sum up what they have learned from their conversations and to tell how they might use this information** in their further explorations. Any special information or insights may be recorded on the **Concept Board**. Any further questions that they would like to think about, pursue, or investigate may be recorded on the **Question Board**. Students may want to discuss the progress that has been made on their questions, and they may also want to cross out any questions that no longer warrant consideration.

➤ After the discussion, remind the students to record their ideas and impressions about the selection on page 105 of their Explorer's Notebook.

Evaluating Discussions

Recording Concept Information

As I read each selection, this is what I added to my understanding of value.

"The Miser" by Aesop

_____
_____
_____
_____
_____
_____
_____
_____
_____

"Money Matters" by Belinda Hurmence

_____
_____
_____
_____
_____
_____
_____
_____

Unit 6/Value   EN 105

Copyright © 1995 Open Court Publishing Company

Explorer's Notebook, page 105

Professional Checkpoint: Cognitive and Responsive Reading

Asking the students to get just the facts from text can stifle the development of interpretational habits. Interpretations are natural. Do everything possible throughout the day to encourage students to form their own conclusions about what they read and hear.

Notes:

2 READING WITH A WRITER'S EYE

MINILESSON

Writer's Craft: Using Interesting Verbs

Explain to the students that in a short piece of writing, such as a fable, it is especially important for writers to choose words that create a vivid and clear picture of what is happening. One way to do this is to use interesting verbs—verbs that are descriptive or precise. Ask the students to share what they have learned about using interesting verbs. If necessary, remind them that **verbs are the action words in a sentence** and that using descriptive and precise verbs will make their writing more interesting and help to create a picture in their reader's mind.

Selective Reading: Focus on Interesting Verbs

Point out that precise verbs are used in this story rather than general words that are not very descriptive. Then have the students find examples of interesting verbs in the fable. Verbs the students may mention include *converted, gloat, wept, tore,* and *fondle.* Take time to discuss the examples identified by the students.

You might then ask the students to suggest tools they could use to help them come up with the most interesting and appropriate verbs to use in their own writing. Point out, if the students do not, the following sources:

- a thesaurus
- the Personal Dictionary or the Author's Style section of their Writer's Notebook
- peer input

Independent Practice: Interesting Verbs

❯ To extend their discussion of interesting verbs, have the students complete Reading/Writing Connection, page 40. Provide time for the sharing of ideas.

WRITING

Linking Reading to Writing

Have the students look through their writing folders to see whether any pieces might be improved by replacing general, nondescript verbs with more precise, interesting verbs. Encourage the students to use peer input, a thesaurus, or appropriate sections of their Writer's Notebook to get ideas for ways to describe the action of their stories more accurately and vividly.

✳ Writing Process

Students who are ready to begin a new piece of writing may be interested in writing a fable of their own. Remind them that fables should contain a lesson about human behavior, should usually be short, and may use animal characters instead of humans. Interested students might begin prewriting by brainstorming with other classmates who wish to try writing a fable.

Using Interesting Verbs

The verbs used in this fable make the story vivid and interesting. Write down examples of interesting verbs from "The Miser" and from other stories you have read that enable you to picture clearly the action that is occurring.

Title: _____ Page: _____
Interesting verbs: _____
_____
_____

Title: _____ Page: _____
Interesting verbs: _____
_____
_____

Title: _____ Page: _____
Interesting verbs: _____
_____
_____

Title: _____ Page: _____
Interesting verbs: _____
_____
_____

Refer to this page to get ideas for interesting verbs that you can use as you write and revise your own work.

Verbs _____

40 R/WC   Value/Unit 6

Name

Copyright © 1995 Open Court Publishing Company

Reading/Writing Connection, page 40

Vocabulary Exploration

Word: _____
Why you chose this word: _____
_____
_____

Definition as used in the selection: _____
_____

Other meanings: _____
_____

Any antonyms you can think of: _____

Any synonyms you can think of: _____

Where else have you found this word? _____

How might you use this word in your writing? _____
_____
_____

Your sentence using the word: _____
_____
_____

Remember to use this word in speaking as well as in writing.

Writer's Notebook: Personal Dictionary   RM 15

Name

Copyright © 1995 Open Court Publishing Company

Reproducible Master 15

VOCABULARY

❯ Concept-related words from "The Miser" which students may want to remember and use include *miser* and *possessions.* In addition, students may wish to discuss the words *gloat, lamentation,* and *distress,* which appear in the selection. Finally, the word *hoard* might be introduced during discussion. Have copies of Vocabulary Exploration form, Reproducible Master 15, available for students who wish to add these or any other words or phrases from the story to the Personal Dictionary section of their Writer's Notebook. For additional opportunities to build vocabulary, see **Teacher Tool Card 77.**

Adding to Personal Word Lists

3 GUIDED AND INDEPENDENT EXPLORATION

EXPLORING CONCEPTS BEYOND THE TEXT

Guided Exploration

Students will engage in **activities of their own choosing** that allow them to explore the concepts related to value more deeply and to use the questions they have raised to do so. These explorations may relate to the current selection or to a number of selections, but they must revolve around the explorable concepts. The following is a **menu of possible activities** from which the students may choose:

* A **literature search** to pursue a question or a problem. Discussion or writing may follow.
* **An original playlet or puppet show** based on value-related situations.
* A **role-playing game** to work out a problem related to value.
* A **panel discussion** with audience participation on a question or a problem. (This discussion would have a leader and could be video-taped.)
* A **debate** on an issue related to value. (Debaters would form teams. They would be required to follow some basic rules of debate, providing reasoned support for their side of the issue.)
* **An advice column** dealing with problems related to value.
* A **personal experience story** related to value.
* **An interview** with someone on a subject related to value.
* A **picture or photo essay** about concepts related to value.

Display the **Exploration Activities poster** listing the activities above so that the students may readily select from them.

Students may work on these activities alone, in pairs, or in small groups, with an option to write about them or to present them to the group. To review information about exploration, see **Learning Framework Card 3, Exploring Through Reflective Activities.**

If the students need help deciding on an activity, here is a suggestion:

* Some students may wish to form small groups to discuss things other than gold that people have been known to hoard. Often in times of impending disaster, people hoard canned foods and gasoline. Students might offer examples of things that they themselves have hoarded. Some students may wish to explore further and then write an essay about this topic.

❯ Distribute Home/School Connection 40–41, a bibliography of books and videos about value that the students and their families can explore together.

Generating Questions to Explore

Have the students discuss value, noting any ideas or questions that they may wish to explore. Tell students that as they read further in the unit they may discover other ideas for ways to explore the concept of value. For example, they might talk to friends about things that they

* Exploring Through Reflective Activities

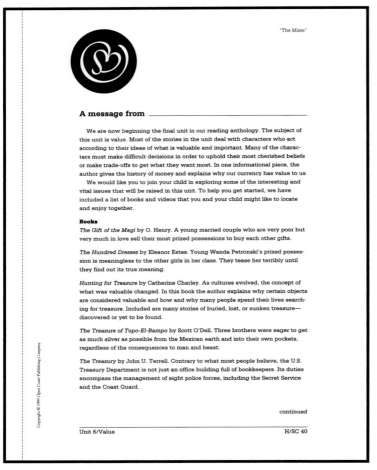

"The Miser"

A message from _____

We are now beginning the final unit in our reading anthology. The subject of this unit is value. Most of the stories in the unit deal with characters who act according to their ideas of what is valuable and important. Many of the characters must make difficult decisions in order to uphold their most cherished beliefs or make trade-offs to get what they want most. In one informational piece, the author gives the history of money and explains why our currency has value to us.

We would like you to join your child in exploring some of the interesting and vital issues that will be raised in this unit. To help you get started, we have included a list of books and videos that you and your child might like to locate and enjoy together.

Books

The Gift of the Magi by O. Henry. A young married couple who are very poor but very much in love sell their most prized possessions to buy each other gifts.

The Hundred Dresses by Eleanor Estes. Young Wanda Petronski's prized possession is meaningless to the other girls in her class. They tease her terribly until they find out its true meaning.

Hunting for Treasure by Catherine Charley. As cultures evolved, the concept of what was valuable changed. In this book the author explains why certain objects are considered valuable and how and why many people spend their lives searching for treasure. Included are many stories of buried, lost, or sunken treasure—discovered or yet to be found.

The Treasure of Topo-El-Bampo by Scott O'Dell. Three brothers were eager to get as much silver as possible from the Mexican earth and into their own pockets, regardless of the consequences to man and beast.

The Treasury by John U. Terrell. Contrary to what most people believe, the U.S. Treasury Department is not just an office building full of bookkeepers. Its duties encompass the management of eight police forces, including the Secret Service and the Coast Guard.

continued

Copyright © 1995 Open Court Publishing Company

Unit 6/Value   H/SC 40

Home/School Connection 40

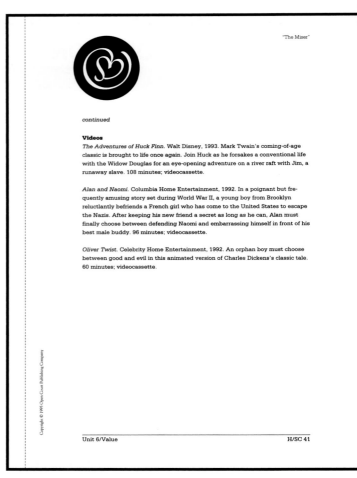

"The Miser"

continued

Videos

The Adventures of Huck Finn. Walt Disney, 1993. Mark Twain's coming-of-age classic is brought to life once again. Join Huck as he forsakes a conventional life with the Widow Douglas for an eye-opening adventure on a river raft with Jim, a runaway slave. 108 minutes; videocassette.

Alan and Naomi. Columbia Home Entertainment, 1992. In a poignant but frequently amusing story set during World War II, a young boy from Brooklyn reluctantly befriends a French girl who has come to the United States to escape the Nazis. After keeping his new friend a secret as long as he can, Alan must finally choose between defending Naomi and embarrassing himself in front of his best male buddy. 96 minutes; videocassette.

Oliver Twist. Celebrity Home Entertainment, 1992. An orphan boy must choose between good and evil in this animated version of Charles Dickens's classic tale. 60 minutes; videocassette.

Copyright © 1995 Open Court Publishing Company

Unit 6/Value   H/SC 41

Home/School Connection 41

value, or they might analyze books or movies in terms of what the main characters consider most valuable.

Remind the students to add to the Question Board any new questions that they have about value. Be sure to tell them to include their name or initials with each question so that students with similar questions can get together to exchange ideas. Remember that you are a part of the group. Feel free to post your own questions from time to time. For a review of the **Question Board,** see **Teacher Tool Card 123.**

➤ Distribute copies of the unit bibliography, Reproducible Masters 53–58, so that students will have it available as they explore. Remind them also to refer to the bibliography on pages 368–369 in the student anthology.

➤ Have the students use Explorer's Notebook, page 109, to help them formulate questions about value.

Bibliography

Books related to value are listed below. You may use these sources and others as you explore concepts related to value.

Notes

Aladdin and the Enchanted Lamp, retold by Marianna Mayer. Aladdin and his poor mother fall into the hands of an evil sorcerer, who uses them to obtain a magic lamp. Follow their fortunes and misfortunes in this ancient tale of wealth and greed.

All About Your Money by Dan Fitzgibbon. This is a good introduction to money management: how to create a budget, how to spend money, and how to avoid misspending it.

The Beatinest Boy by Jesse Stuart. David didn't want to live with his grandmother, but a genuine family feeling develops between them. When Christmas comes, David struggles to buy his grandmother a special gift and learns the value of things that are right at hand.

Black Diamonds by James Houston. Searching in the rocks for some gold nuggets they once saw, Matthew and Kayak discover a pool covered with iridescent oil. When they try to make a strike, they cause a disaster that nearly costs the lives of everyone involved.

The Black Pearl by Scott O'Dell. When the young pearl diver Ramon finds the Great Pearl of Heaven, its value to his family and to his small village has nothing to do with its monetary worth.

Copyright © 1995 Open Court Publishing Company

Name

Unit 6/Value RM 53

Reproducible Master 53

Bibliography *continued*

Notes

Buried Treasures of the South by W. C. Jameson. Read about thirty-eight lost treasures that are said to be somewhere in the southern United States—among them the treasure of Red Bone Cave and the lost Clapham silver mine.

Coins Have Tales to Tell by Frances W. Brown. This lively history of American coinage includes descriptions of rare mintings, coin values today, barter, and foreign coins used in the United States.

Coins of the Ancient World by Ya'akov Meshorer. Learn about silver shekels, bronze Roman coins marked with zodiac signs, and tetradrachmas bearing the image of the goddess Athena. Learn also how the ancients minted their coins.

The Department of the Treasury by Mark Walston. As part of the Know Your Government series, this book will introduce you to the U.S. Treasury Department and explain its history and function.

Eddie, Incorporated by Phyllis Reynolds Naylor. Everyone else in Eddie's family is in business, so Eddie decides he wants to be in business, too. The problem is that he is not as smart as his brother, as creative as his mother, or as happy around vegetables as his father. In searching for something to sell, Eddie discovers the true value of work.

Extra Cash for Kids by Larry Belliston and Kurt Hanks. This book provides dozens of ideas on how kids under sixteen years of age can earn money. Creative ideas include raising worms, addressing envelopes, making and selling sandwiches, and hauling away junk.

Copyright © 1995 Open Court Publishing Company

Name

RM 54 Unit 6/Value

Reproducible Master 54

Bibliography *continued*

Notes

A Gift for Mama by Esther Hautzig. For birthdays and other holidays, Sara always has to make a gift, but this time she wants to buy her mother some fancy black slippers to go with the fancy black robe that she never wears. After weeks of part-time work mending clothes to earn the money, Sara is unpleasantly surprised by her mother's reaction.

Good Luck, Arizona Man by Rex Benedict. A half-white Apache boy sets out to solve the mystery of his own origins and the hiding place of a treasure in gold. Legend says that whoever finds the gold of the Guadalupes must die, but the curse is only part of the boy's problem.

The Hand-Me-Down Kid by Francine Pascal. Ari suspects that she has been adopted just so there will be someone to use her sister's old clothes. When the school bully strongly suggests that Ari "borrow" her sister's new Peugeot bike for the race in the park, real trouble begins.

It Will Never Be the Same Again by Mike Neigoff. This is a summer that fifteen-year-old Sid will never forget. After his father loses his job, Sid must work to earn money for a trip. The lessons he learns while working bring changes to his father's life and cause Sid to reassess the value of the trip.

Jingo Django by Sid Fleischman. An orphan boy resolves to follow a treasure map he finds inscribed on a whale tooth.

Kid Power by Susan Beth Pfeffer. When she innocently uses the slogan *No job too big or too small* to start her own business, Janie learns that some jobs *are* too big and that not every job is worth doing.

Copyright © 1995 Open Court Publishing Company

Name

Unit 6/Value RM 55

Reproducible Master 55

Bibliography *continued*

Notes

The King, the Princess, and the Tinker by Ellen K. McKenzie. King John spends all his days and most of his nights in his treasure room playing with his gold and jewels and ignoring his children. It takes a disobedient young princess and a humble tinker to teach him about the wonders of the world.

The Lost Umbrella of Kim Chu by Eleanor Estes. In the Year of the Dragon, a special umbrella with a secret in its bamboo handle was presented to Kim's father. One day Kim borrows the umbrella—without permission—and it is subsequently stolen. Join Kim on a frantic chase through the streets of New York City as she tries to retrieve the umbrella.

My Mom, the Money Nut by Betty Bates. Fritzi's mom seems to care only about money. Fritzi cannot get her attention at all until she is chosen to sing a solo at the school choral recital. Then Fritzi learns a secret about her mother's past, and suddenly she doesn't feel so alone.

Nelda by Pat Edwards. When a wealthy woman offers Nelda a much-needed job, Nelda's migrant-worker parents are shocked to learn that it will mean the breakup of their family.

The Nitty Gritty by Frank Bonham. An A student in English, Dogtown resident Charlie Matthew has earned his teacher's encouragement. Charlie's father, however, still thinks that there is no future in education for an African American and that Charlie is better off skipping school to work in the shoeshine parlor. As he schemes to earn money and leave Dogtown, Charlie discovers what is really valuable to him.

Copyright © 1995 Open Court Publishing Company

Name

RM 56 Unit 6/Value

Reproducible Master 56

Bibliography *continued*

Notes

Rusty Timmons' First Million by Joan Carris. Rusty learns the value of a true friendship when it must withstand the trials of running a summer business.

Salt, retold by Jane Langton. In this Russian folk tale, three brothers are sent off in grand ships to find their fortunes. Only the "foolish" brother succeeds. You will laugh as you find out how he does it.

Song of the Trees by Mildred D. Taylor. Cassie's trees are her friends, and they have been there for centuries. When her family decides to sell them to a road-construction crew, a fierce battle erupts.

Sonia Begonia by Joanne Rocklin. Sonia desperately wants her own business and eagerly starts a house-watching service for neighborhood vacationers. She soon learns, though, that single-minded devotion to a business is not all that is needed for success.

Standing Up for America: A Biography of Lee Iacocca by Patricia Haddock. Iacocca believes in honesty and wants people to stand up for what they believe. Tranforming his values into a company that is both successful and responsive to people's needs is his recipe for success and happiness.

The Treasure of Tolmec by Louis A. Stinetorf. After a volcano erupted and buried the old church in Jorge's Mexican village, thieves arrive to try to dig treasure out of the rubble. When they force Jorge to help, Jorge turns the tables on them, causing them to wish that they had left him alone in his mother's poor home.

Copyright © 1995 Open Court Publishing Company

Name

Reproducible Master 57

Bibliography *continued*

Notes

The Trumpeter of Krakow by Eric P. Kelly. "It was late July of the year 1461" when a man, his wife, and their son journeyed to the large and beautiful city of Krakow to escape a band of thieves who burned every building of their farm and dug holes in the land looking for treasure. To earn money, the father becomes a church trumpeter. Eventually the boy's memory of an earlier trumpeter of Krakow helps him to save his father's life and restore the treasure his family has guarded.

Walking Through the Dark by Phyllis Reynolds Naylor. In 1931—when Ruth Wheeler and her mother visit Hooverville, a makeshift village inhabited by the unemployed—Ruth decides to help her own family in whatever way she can. Through her family's trials Ruth learns that the most valuable thing that one could lose is hope.

You Can't Count a Billion Dollars and Other Little-Known Facts About Money by Barbara Seuling. Did you know that some medieval doctors gilded pills to make them more acceptable to rich customers and that the life expectancy of a dollar bill is about eighteen months? Learn fascinating things about the use of money through the ages.

Add the titles of books and articles that you find.

- _____
  _____
- _____
  _____
- _____
  _____

Copyright © 1995 Open Court Publishing Company

Name

Reproducible Master 58

BIBLIOGRAPHY

Amos Fortune, Free Man by Elizabeth Yates. An African prince captured into slavery is determined to obtain his freedom and maintain his self-respect.

Buddies by Barbara Park. At Camp Miniwawa, Dinah Feeney struggles with the problems of friendship. Is it more important to be popular than to be kind?

Do People Grow on Family Trees?: Genealogy for Kids & Other Beginners by Ira Wolfman. Learning something about your ancestors' lives means learning something about yourself. This fascinating guidebook shows you the steps to discovering your genealogy.

Gold and Silver, Silver and Gold: Tales of Hidden Treasure by Alvin Schwartz. Here is a collection of legends, true stories, and tall tales all about treasure—hunting it, finding or losing it, and the good and bad luck it can bring.

368

A Place Called Ugly by Avi. The cottage on Grenlow's Island has been Owen Coughlin's summer refuge for the past ten years. Now the woman who owns the cottage wants to tear it down to build a hotel. Can Owen save the summer place that he cherishes so dearly?

Shabanu: Daughter of the Wind by Suzanne Fisher Staples. Shabanu's unhappiness about an arranged marriage causes her to examine her personal happiness and independence against the values of Pakistani custom: obedience, tradition, and loyalty.

Walking Through the Dark by Phyllis Reynolds Naylor. Ruth Wheeler comes to terms with her family's gradual descent into poverty in Depression-era Chicago.

Waterman's Boy by Susan Sharpe. Someone's dumping oil into Chesapeake Bay. Young Ben Warren is determined to find out who—and to help clean up the water pollution that is threatening the lives of flora and fauna in the area.

Recording Questions

Do you have questions about value that you would like to learn more about? If so, write them here.

_____
_____
_____
_____
_____

If not, think about these questions: What does value mean to you? What sorts of things do you value most in your own life?

_____
_____
_____
_____

Compare ideas with your classmates. How are what people value and their ideas and feelings about value different?

_____
_____
_____
_____

Now is there anything about value that you would like to explore? Go back to the first question on this page, and write down ideas and questions that you would like to explore.

_____

Unit 6/Value   EN 109

Copyright © 1995 Open Court Publishing Company

Explorer's Notebook, page 109

Professional Checkpoint: Guided and Independent Exploration

Learning to work collaboratively in groups is an important skill. Advise the students that each member of a group must take responsibility for some aspect of the group's learning. Allow them to choose projects on the basis of shared interests. Give the students within a group time to work out problems before offering advice.

Notes:

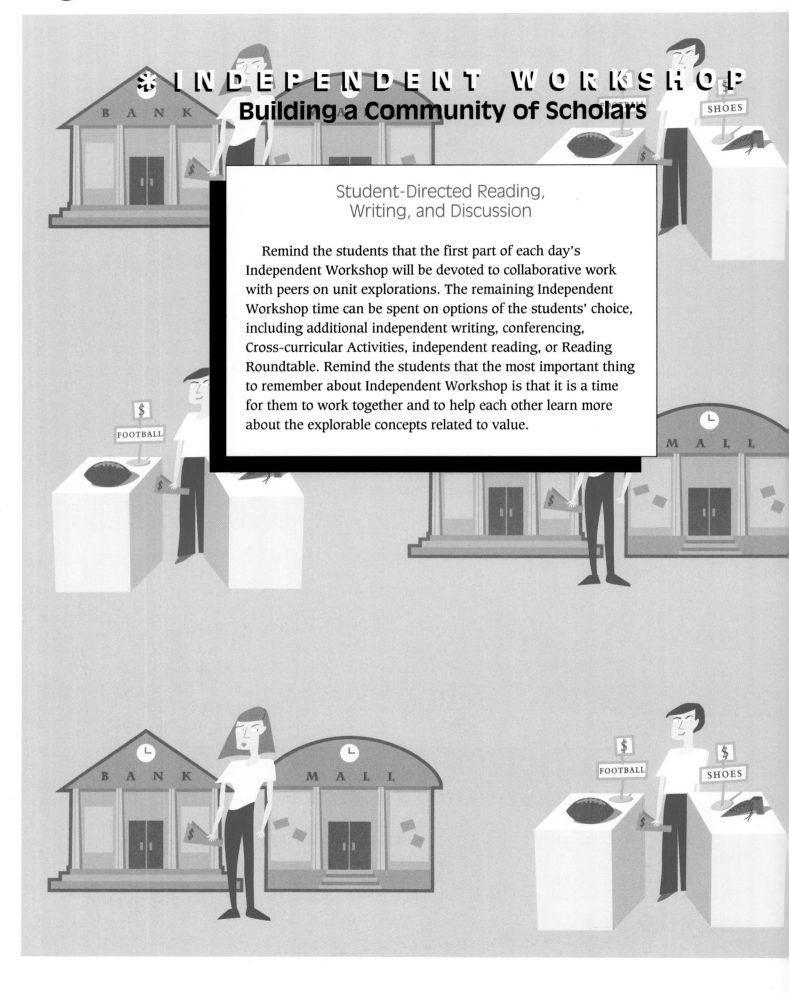

✴ INDEPENDENT WORKSHOP
Building a Community of Scholars

Student-Directed Reading, Writing, and Discussion

Remind the students that the first part of each day's Independent Workshop will be devoted to collaborative work with peers on unit explorations. The remaining Independent Workshop time can be spent on options of the students' choice, including additional independent writing, conferencing, Cross-curricular Activities, independent reading, or Reading Roundtable. Remind the students that the most important thing to remember about Independent Workshop is that it is a time for them to work together and to help each other learn more about the explorable concepts related to value.

Additional Opportunities for Independent Reading, Writing, and Cross-curricular Activities

✻ Reading Roundtable

Hundreds of fables are attributed to Aesop. Many books offer a collection of various Aesop's fables. Many other books focus on a single fable. In addition, there are numerous animal tales told by many different societies (such as the Native-American coyote stories or the African Anansi stories) that have been used for generations to teach lessons. Students may enjoy reading such stories and comparing them to Aesop's fables.

✻ Writing Seminar

Suggest to students who have decided to write a fable that they first consider the lesson that they want to teach and then think of ways in which to present it. Remind them that idea webs are excellent tools to use during the prewriting phase.

Cross-curricular Activity Cards

The following Cross-curricular Activity Card in the Student Toolbox is appropriate for this selection:
- 6 Math—Gold!

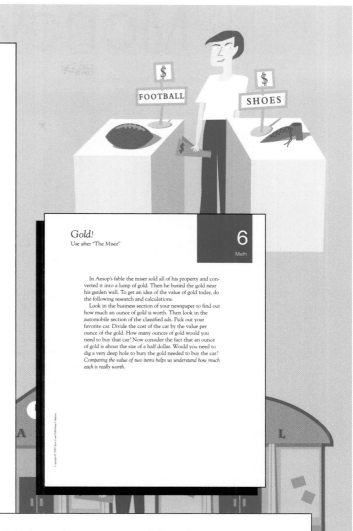

Gold!
Use after "The Miser"

6
Math

In Aesop's fable the miser sold all of his property and converted it into a lump of gold. Then he buried the gold near his garden wall. To get an idea of the value of gold today, do the following research and calculations.

Look in the business section of your newspaper to find out how much an ounce of gold is worth. Then look in the automobile section of the classified ads. Pick out your favorite car. Divide the cost of the car by the value per ounce of the gold. How many ounces of gold would you need to buy that car? Now consider the fact that an ounce of gold is about the size of a half dollar. Would you need to dig a very deep hole to bury the gold needed to buy the car? *Comparing the value of two items helps us understand how much each is really worth.*

Additional Opportunities for Solving Learning Problems

Tutorial

Use this time to assist students who need help in any area. Students should be made to understand that asking for clarification of vaguely understood concepts is a continual and essential part of the learning process. The following teaching aids are available in the Teacher Toolbox for your convenience:
- Writer's Craft/Reading: Choosing Precise and Vivid Verbs, Teacher Tool Card 22
- Writer's Craft/Reading: Genre—Folk Tale and Fable, Teacher Tool Card 1
- Writer's Craft/Reading: Indicators of Time and Order, Teacher Tool Card 29
- Grammar, Mechanics, and Usage: Phrases, Teacher Tool Card 50

Money Matters

1 READING THE SELECTION

About the Selection

In this tender excerpt from Belinda Hurmence's *Tough Tiffany,* young Tiffany worries that her spendthrift mother will never finish paying for the bunk beds that mean so much to Tiffany. Meanwhile, Tiffany's frugal grandmother is frantic with worry, convinced that someone has stolen her secret cache of retirement money. Can Tiffany come up with a solution to both problems?

Link to the Unit Concepts

"Money Matters," pages 240–253, is about Tiffany, a young girl caught between two extreme attitudes toward money. Her mother spends money faster than she earns it. Her grandmother, on the other hand, is afraid to spend money for fear of not having it in the future. By the end of the story, Tiffany decides that her own feelings about money fall somewhere between her mother's and her grandmother's. After reading this selection, the students, like Tiffany, may be wondering about the true value of money.

About the Author

Tough Tiffany was Hurmence's first book for children. It was named a Notable Children's Trade Book in the Field of Social Studies and an American Library Association Notable Children's Book of 1980.

Hurmence was born in Oklahoma. All four of her grandparents had homesteaded in the Oklahoma Territory, and when Hurmence was growing up much of the state still had a frontier flavor. She says that when she read *Slave Narratives,* a collection of oral histories of more than two thousand ex-slaves, she recognized in these people the same strength and spirit of sharing that her own ancestors possessed. She tried to capture that spirit in her second book, *A Girl Called Boy,* a story about a slave child. Her most recent book, *Nightwalker,* is set in South Carolina in modern times.

LESSON OVERVIEW

"Money Matters" by Belinda Hurmence, pages 240–253

READING THE SELECTION

Materials

Student anthology, pp. 240–253
Explorer's Notebook, p. 105
Assessment Master 1

READING WITH A WRITER'S EYE

Minilessons

Writer's Craft: Dialogue—Speaker Tags
Writer's Craft: Describing Characters'
   Thoughts and Feelings

Materials

Reading/Writing Connection, pp. 41–42
Reproducible Master 15

FYI

Teacher Tool Card
• Spelling and Vocabulary: Building
   Vocabulary, 77

Options for Instruction

Writer's Craft: Genre—Realistic Fiction
Spelling and Vocabulary: Compound
   Words
(Use Teacher Tool Cards listed below.)

GUIDED AND INDEPENDENT EXPLORATION

Materials

Home/School Connection 42
Explorer's Notebook, pp. 110–113

Independent Workshop

**Optional Materials from
Student Toolbox**

Tradebook Connection Cards

Cross-curricular Activity Cards
• 25 Social Studies—Paper Money
• 26 Social Studies—Bank Documents

Student Tool Cards
• Writer's Craft/Reading: Using
   Dialogue in a Story, 20
• Writer's Craft/Reading:
   Characterization, 13
• Writer's Craft/Reading: Reading and
   Writing Realistic Fiction, 3
• Spelling and Vocabulary: Compound
   Words, 81

FYI

Learning Framework Card
• Reading Roundtable, 6

Teacher Tool Cards
• Writer's Craft/Reading: Using
   Dialogue in a Story, 20
• Writer's Craft/Reading:
   Characterization, 13
• Writer's Craft/Reading: Genre—
   Realistic Fiction, 3
• Spelling and Vocabulary: Compound
   Words, 81

NOTES

Asterisks (*) throughout the lesson indicate learning frameworks. Learning Framework Cards and Teacher Tool Cards can be found in the Teacher Toolbox.

Tell students that "Money Matters" has been excerpted from Hurmence's book *Tough Tiffany*. The students may notice that the characters' speech is not always grammatically correct. Point out that Hurmence has her characters speak in a regional dialect to add realism and color to the story.

Share with the students any information about the author that you think is appropriate. Suggest that as they read, they may want to think about why Hurmence called her book *Tough Tiffany*.

*

COGNITIVE AND RESPONSIVE READING

Setting Reading
Goals and
Expectations

Have the students **browse** the **first page** of the selection, using the **clues/problems/wondering procedure.** Students will return to these observations after reading the selection.

During browsing, make sure that the students read the background information printed in italics on page 240. Some students may want to make predictions, based on the background information, about what will happen in the selection.

Recommen-
dations for
Reading the
Selection

Allow the students to decide how they want to read the selection. Because it contains some interesting regional dialect, the students may enjoy **reading** the story **aloud.** If they choose to read orally, use and encourage think-alouds. If they choose to read silently, allow discussion as needed. Discuss problems, reactions, and strategies after reading.

This would also be a good selection for **responding** to text **by connecting with the feelings of the main character** while reading aloud. You might want to model this response, and then invite the students to do the same.

About the
Reading
Strategies

Because this selection involves a mystery and its solution, the students may find themselves **predicting** whether and where Tiffany will find her grandmother's nest egg.

Hurmence does a nice job of plotting this story so that, although the outcome is predictable, the way in which it is brought about is unexpected. These unusual plot twists offer additional opportunities for predicting.

Think-Aloud Prompts
for Use in Oral Reading

Notice the think-aloud prompts with the page miniatures. These are merely suggestions for helping the students use the strategies. Remind the students to refer to the **reading strategy posters** and to use any strategy they feel they need to help make sense of what they are reading. Encourage the students to collaborate with classmates when confronted with difficulties while reading.

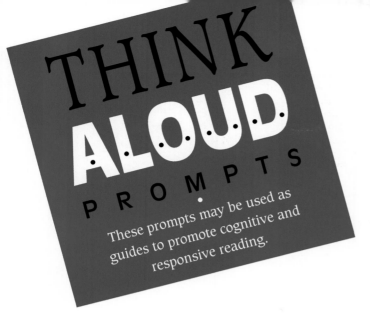

These prompts may be used as guides to promote cognitive and responsive reading.

MONEY MATTERS

from TOUGH TIFFANY
by Belinda Hurmence
illustrated by Marcy Ramsey

Tiffany Cox—known as Tiff—lives with her parents and five <u>siblings</u> in a small, crowded house in North Carolina. Tiff is forced to share a bed with her twin sisters until the day her mother makes a down payment on two sets of bunk beds. Tiff gets a bunk to herself, and it soon becomes her special, private place.

But the Coxes have trouble making payments on the bunk beds, and a man comes to repossess them. Tiff talks him into waiting one more day. She promises him they will have the money then, but Mama uses some of the bunk-bed money to pay other debts. "When he come around tomorrow, I give him this seventeen dollars and he'll take it and be tickled to get it, you'll see," she assures her children. The man does take the money, but he's angry. He leaves only after Mama promises to pay the remaining balance on her next payday.

Tiff worries when payday arrives and Mama spends her check on new clothes for the family instead of the beds. The Coxes return home that evening to find a note: "Final Notice! Balance Due $76." Tiff wishes that her special bed could be paid for; it is more valuable to her than her new dress.

That weekend, Tiff stays with Granny to help out with a big family <u>reunion</u>. Tiff loves her grandmother and tries to treat her with respect even though the old woman is strict, cranky, and as frugal as Tiff's mother is wasteful.

🌀 240 🌀

The next day, Monday, Tiff was to go home. For the time of the reunion, she had postponed thinking about the bunk beds, but on Sunday night when she climbed into the lumpy bed she shared with Granny, she wondered if there would be any bed at all for her to sleep in at home, tomorrow night. She thought about the man she had deceived, coming for his money, and she stirred uncomfortably.

"Settle down there, you girl," Granny said. "Can't nobody get they rest with you threshing around in the bed."

So she lay as still as she could, not moving at all until Granny's snores <u>liberated</u> her; and even then she could not find a smooth place, but kept turning cautiously, lying first on one side and then the other, and thinking longingly of her bunk bed up under the ceiling, her own smooth place, hers alone. When fatigue finally released her into the privacy of sleep, she slept deeply and did not rouse when the old lady arose at dawn, according to her custom.

Sounds from the kitchen mixed in with her dreams, sounds of doors opening and closing and dreams of somebody waiting on the porch; sounds of heavy things being lifted, shifted, quickening sounds of furniture sliding, dreams of her bunk bed sliding down from the ceiling; and a queer little whickering fitted neatly into a dream she managed to shape—Tiny whimpering? herself?—whickering, whispering—what? The dream lost shape as she felt a presence, something, or somebody hovering. She woke with a small jerk to find Granny beside the bed, fumbling under the mattress. Fumbling, whispering to herself, and that queer little whickering.

"Granny?"

"My money," the grandmother quavered. "I can't find my money."

Tiff said drowsily, "Did you look in your pocketbook?"

"Not that money. My other money, that I keep."

Tiff rolled creakily out of bed and stumbled to the bathroom. When she came back, Granny had the mattress turned back on itself and the sheets and pillows jumbled in a pile on the floor.

The old lady said wildly, pathetically, "It's gone. My money's all gone. Somebody's come and took my money away from me." She began to cry, with hacking, gasping little sobs that horrified Tiff. Granny wasn't the kind of woman who ever cried about anything.

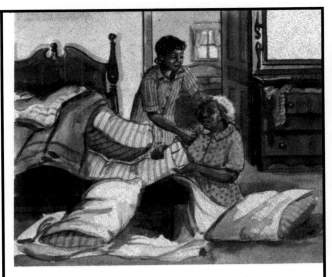

"Don't cry, Granny," she begged. "I'll help you look for your money. Maybe you just forgot where you put it. Where was the last place you saw it?"

The old lady showed her a sort of pocket in the mattress, cleverly sewed, easy to overlook, empty.

Tiff said reasonably, "Did you always keep it there? Maybe you moved it, and forgot." She opened a bureau drawer and searched through an assortment of rolled-up stockings.

"I already looked in there. It's gone, for sure, it's been stole." The old lady showed her a narrow rack, fastened to the back

1 The word *whickering* might confuse the students. Encourage them to **use context clues** to clarify what Granny is doing. Students who want the exact definition of the term might **check the Glossary or a dictionary** to find out that whickering is a soft neighing sound made by horses.

of the bureau drawer, cleverly fashioned out of linoleum scraps, shallow enough that the drawer could be closed, but adequate for holding a sheaf of bills, perhaps; empty.

Tiff moved everything off the shelves of Granny's closet and began searching through boxes.

"I already looked there." The grandmother now wept so uncontrollably that Tiff could not question her further. She searched the house through, moving furniture, groping inside vases, looking under rugs, checking half a dozen or more secret hiding places the grandmother showed her, false floor boards, backs of picture frames, hiding places that would have delighted her if she had not been <u>intent</u> on the more urgent business of soothing the distraught old lady.

"Are you sure you looked in your pocketbook?"

"Yes, but it ain't that money, it's my money that Mr. Honeycutt give for our farm, that was going to last me my days. I never kept it in my pocketbook. It's gone! Oh, help me, Lord, how'm I going to take care of me in my old age?" Tears streamed down her face.

"I'll take care of you, Granny, don't worry. I'll always take care of you. Please don't cry, Granny. Let's look in your pocketbook just to make sure."

The grandmother spread the contents of her pocketbook out on the mattress. There were her handkerchiefs, the lace one for show, the flowered one for blow, her accordion rain bonnet, the door key on a knotted string, her spectacles, her coin purse. Tiff snapped open the coin purse. Inside were some coins and folded bills with a dusty look to them, smelling faintly of country ham. "Here's money, Granny."

"But my other money—my other—" Her voice broke.

᪥ 244 ᪥

Tiff studied the folded bills and figured. Something. What? "Where did this money, this in your coin purse, where did it come from?"

"Why, I take it, little bits at a time, when I need it, from my other money."

Something more, something more! "Well, your other money, you got all those hiding places you keep it in, and I figure you keep moving it around so nobody will see you going to the same place all the time."

The grandmother nodded.

"Did you ever forget where you put it the last time?"

"Yes, but I kept looking, and then when I found it, I remembered when it was I changed the place."

"Do you ever make up new hiding places to keep it in? You could have made up a new place and forgotten, you know."

Hope struggled with irritation in Granny's face. "You think I forget where I keep my own money?"

"Well, you're always complaining you can't remember anything one minute to the next." Tiff rubbed the bills from the coin purse. Dusty. She was almost sure. "Do you keep your other money in a plastic bag, Granny?" **2**

"In four plastic bags. How you know that?"

"Are they plastic bags that country ham comes in?"

"Yes! Yes! Those good heavy bags that they won't nothing punch a hole in. How you know that, girl? I know you never saw my money." Granny was trembling all over.

Tiff wheeled and ran to the kitchen. The grandmother hurried after her. Saturday, making biscuits, Tiff hadn't been allowed to measure flour out of the big lard can where Granny stored it. Now, she lifted the lid and plunged her bare arm

᪥ 245 ᪥

2 This paragraph marks a turning point in the story as Tiffany comes up with an idea about what might have happened to Granny's money. The students may want to pause here to share their ideas about what Tiffany is thinking and to **predict** whether and where she will find the money. Remind the students to base their predictions on what they have already read. Allow volunteers to share their predictions with the class.

inside, feeling, exploring the dusty white until she touched a packet buried there, just the way she had figured. She fished it out, and after it in quick succession, three more flat important packets, <u>dredged</u> with flour. "All ready for the fry pan, Granny," she teased.

Of course! the old lady said disgustedly; now she remembered. But it had given her a bad time. She sat down at the kitchen table to recover, and to fondle her money.

It was all hundred-dollar bills! Millions of them, it looked like! First time Tiff had ever seen a hundred-dollar bill, let alone millions of them, and she said so.

Granny said gratefully, "Well, you going to look all you want, honey, for one of them hunderd dollars is yours, for a reward, finding my money for me."

(§) 246 (§)

"I don't want any reward," said Tiff. "All I did was help you hunt. You'd have found it by yourself, when you used up the flour."

But she might have grieved herself to death, by the time she made that many biscuits, Granny said, smiling now, holding out the reward. "Take it. I want you to have it. You get the look of a hunderd-dollar bill in your mind, and the feel of it in your hand, and you won't never want to break it down, I guarantee you."

Tiff took the bill in her hand for the honor of it, to look at and feel, but not to keep. She could understand how Granny felt, a little. A hundred-dollar bill was an important-looking thing you'd hate to break; but if you didn't break it, what was it good for? She wouldn't say so to Granny, but she'd rather be a spendthrift, like Mama, buying things she couldn't afford and enjoying the spending, than hiding money away for enjoyment. "Granny!" she exclaimed, handing back the bill, "I really truly don't want any reward, but would you lend Mama seventy-six dollars instead?" She explained about the bunk beds and about the man who would almost certainly come to take them back today, and she promised to repay the loan herself, as fast as she could earn the money, or save it from what Mama and Daddy gave her to spend.

Granny snorted. "No, I'll not! Give Flora money for them beds and she'd have it spent on something else before the day's out."

Tiff couldn't argue with that. It had happened too many times before. "Well, anyway, you oughtn't to keep all that money here in your house. It's dangerous. You might get it all stolen."

(§) 247 (§)

---

3 Students may be unfamiliar with this usage of the word *dredge.* Remind them that the **context** in which *dredged* is used should give them clues to the meaning of the word.

4 This is an important point in the story as Tiffany's thoughts return from Granny's problem to her own. The students may want to **predict** whether the bunk beds will ever be paid for, and if so, how. Remind the students to keep their predictions in mind as they continue reading the story, and to check to see how accurate the predictions were.

"I kept it in my house all this time and hasn't nobody stole it off of me."

"That doesn't mean it couldn't happen. You thought it did happen this morning, and look how scared you were. You ought to put your money in a bank."

Granny began telling what was wrong about banks, how your money got mixed up with other people's and the bank people never knew which money was yours and which belonged to somebody else. Tiff didn't know a lot about banks herself, but she knew a whole lot more than Granny did. For an hour she explained the things Ms. Lackey had taught them last year, about checking accounts and deposit slips and passbooks and savings accounts. When she told how the money could earn interest in a savings account, she saw at once that the old lady was <u>intrigued</u>. "Any time you wanted to take your money out, a little bit or all of it, you could just write a check," she urged.

The grandmother fingered her precious hoard and looked sullen. "That's the thing," she admitted. "I don't know how to write but just only my name."

"You can write numbers!" Tiff said. "You're good at numbers. Anybody that can write numbers and their name can write a check." She offered to go with her to the bank and do the talking, and to her satisfaction, the grandmother agreed. When had Granny ever listened to her? It made Tiff feel like she counted for something. Real tough.

"Wait," she said, as Granny put on her hat. "Count your money before you take it to the bank."

"I don't need to count it. I know how much there is of it."

☯ *248* ☯

"Well, count it anyway. Ms. Lackey says you ought to always count your money before you do business, so in case you make a mistake, you don't go blaming the other fellow." Granny made her turn her back so Tiff wouldn't find out how much money was in the plastic bags. Listening to the dry shuffle of the floury bills, Tiff felt a twinge of regret that she hadn't accepted Granny's reward. There were so many of those one-hundred-dollar bills, Granny would never miss one. But she went over her reasoning once more and decided she had been right: she was content with her refusal.

"I'm ready," said Granny. She snapped the packets inside her pocketbook and stood up. "Let's go."

The way it happened, Tiff didn't have to do the talking for Granny after all. They arrived at the bank a few minutes before opening time, but they didn't have to wait. A roly-poly man with a fringe of gray hair and a fringe of gray mustache, unlocked the thick glass front door and let them in. "Miss Effie!" he said, hugging Granny and laughing. "I bet I haven't seen you in twenty years!"

He was Mr. Montgomery Todt, president of the bank. Gold letters spelled out his name on the door of his office, where he led them, but Granny called him Gummy, for she had nursed him as a little chap when he couldn't yet say his own name.

"This here's my grandbaby; she the smart one," Granny said, shoving Tiff forward. "Say something girl. Show Mr. Gummy how smart you are."

Mr. Todt saved her by pronouncing roundly, "She already said her smarts, Miss Effie. A girl that could get an old pack rat like you to put her money in the bank just bound to be smart as they come."

Granny giggled at him calling her a pack rat, but Tiff didn't appreciate it one bit. That was her granny he was making fun of, even if she *was* a pack rat.

Mr. Todt asked one of the bank tellers to open a savings and checking account for Granny while she waited in his office. "Where did you get all that money, Miss Effie?" He seemed surprised when Granny told him the money had come from his own mother's father, years ago. "I didn't realize Honeycutt was your homeplace," he said thoughtfully. "No doubt Grandfather told me, and it slipped my mind. I used to listen to him by the hour, back then. Kids today never listen to old folks the way they ought to. I bet a chap as bright as Tiffany here doesn't either."

Granny signed her name in five different places for the bank, and she watched closely when the teller showed the amount deposited. "Wait a minute," she said, and took Tiff aside for a whispered conference. "She says I give her a hunderd dollars more than I did!"

Tiff said, "Ask her to count it again, in front of you."

🌀 250 🌀

The grandmother did as she was told. Carefully, slowly, the teller counted the money. "Is that correct?" she inquired.

"If you say so," said Granny. With joy she returned to Tiff. "They giving me a hunderd dollars just for putting my money in here."

"No, they aren't, Granny; you must have made some mistake counting it at home."

"I made a hunderd dollars, just for walking downtown here!" she marveled, not listening.

The old lady was so delighted that Tiff gave up trying to convince her of her mistake. At least it got her banking off to a good start.

Back at the house she set about teaching Granny to write checks. She showed her the place to write in the amount and the line for her signature. "When you get those two lines filled in, any store or person you're paying the money to will write in their own name, if you ask them to," she assured the old lady.

"Let me practice it once," said Granny. "I got a place where I want to pay some money to."

Proudly she wrote her signature, in the round, careful letters she used to sign her social security checks: Effie Turner. Laboriously, in her trembling script, she wrote out the numbers and pushed the check across the table. "You write the rest for me," she directed with a smirk.

Nobody could question the legibility of her handwriting. There stood her name, plain and positive as Granny herself: Effie Turner. Her numbers looked like first grade numbers, but they were equally plain: $76.00.

"Write it, The Outlet Furniture Store," Granny ordered.

🌀 251 🌀

5 Students who have been paying close attention to the text may be able to **predict** where Granny's first check will go. Ask volunteers to share their predictions with the class. Remind the students to check the accuracy of their predictions as they continue reading.

"Oh!" was all that Tiff could think to say immediately. She thought of her bunk bed and her private place up at the ceiling, saved. She thought, humbly, that she didn't exactly understand how she felt about money—a little like Mama, a little like Granny, not much like either of them. She would have to figure some more on that one.

She could scarcely see to write the words, but she did write, blinking, as carefully as Granny wrote: Outlet Furniture Store.

"Now you hand that to you mama," said Granny, "and tell her I say she don't have to pay it back, for I already made me a hunderd dollars today."

It was the best reward Granny could have given her, since she still seemed to think Tiff deserved a reward. And it wasn't money loaned that Mama could spend on something else.

"Thank you, Granny," she said meekly.

The old lady clamped her lips tight—her way of showing she was pleased. "Guess you ain't the only one that can figure things." She closed her checkbook importantly. "Now help me find where I'll keep my bank stuff, and after we eat our dinner and clean up around here, I want you to pull that Moody grass out of my flower beds. You done just about half a job last time you was here, and I want you to make it right fore you go home."

Home! Tiff scarcely heard Granny's scolding. She couldn't wait to see their faces at home when she waved that check in front of their noses. What a homecoming it was going to be!

ℰ 253 ℰ

6 Invite volunteers to **sum up** the entire selection. As they review the main events of the story, remind the students to check any predictions they made.

*

EXPLORING THROUGH DISCUSSION

Reflecting on the Selection
Whole-Group Discussion

The whole group discusses the selection and any thoughts or questions that it raises. During this session, the students will **return to the clues, problems, and wonderings** they noted on the chalkboard during browsing.

Assessment

To assess the students' understanding of the text, engage them in a discussion to determine whether they understand the following ideas:
- how Tiffany's grandmother feels about money
- how she feels about Tiffany's mother's attitude toward money
- why Tiffany doesn't agree completely with either woman concerning money

Response Journal

Tiffany's feelings about her mother and grandmother may elicit strong responses in the students. Allow ample time for them to record their personal responses to the selection.

Exploring Concepts Within the Selection
Small-Group Discussion

Remind the students to refer to the Concept Board and the Question Board to keep their discussions focused. Circulate among the groups and encourage the students to consider their original ideas about value as they discuss this selection's relationship to the unit concepts.

Sharing Ideas About Explorable Concepts

Have the groups **report their ideas** and **discuss them** with the rest of the class. It is crucial that the students' ideas determine the direction of the discussion.
- The students may point out some of the very different ways in which money mattered to Tiffany, her mother, and her grandmother.
- Some students may comment on Tiffany's decision to refuse her grandmother's reward money.

As these and other ideas are raised, have the students **add them to the Question Board** or the **Concept Board.**

Exploring Concepts Across Selections

Ask the students whether this selection reminds them of anything else they have read. They may make connections with other selections in the student anthology.
- The students may point out that both Granny and the title character in "The Miser" enjoy having their money more than spending it and that both are deeply disturbed when they cannot find their money.
- Some students may point out that both "Money Matters" and "Broken Bird" from the unit on music and musicians are about family members learning to cope with each others' ideas and attitudes. They may recognize that both Tiffany and Jimmy Jo often behaved more responsibly than did their mothers.

Recording Ideas

As students complete the above discussions, ask them to **sum up what they have learned from their conversations and to tell how**

TEACHING TIP Teachers should be collaborators, not controllers.

ASSESSMENT TIP This may be a good opportunity to observe students working in groups and to mark observations in your Teacher's Observation Log.

Connections Across Units

Explorer's Notebook, page 105

they might use this information in further explorations. Any special information or insights may be recorded on the **Concept Board.** Any further questions that they would like to think about, pursue, or investigate may be recorded on the **Question Board.** They may want to discuss the progress that has been made on their questions. They may also want to cross out any questions that no longer warrant consideration.

❯ After discussion, the students should individually record their ideas on page 105 of their Explorer's Notebook.

Evaluating Discussions

2 READING WITH A WRITER'S EYE

MINILESSONS

Writer's Craft:
Dialogue—
Speaker Tags

Have the students discuss what they know about speaker tags, the **words that indicate which character is speaking** and often **the way or reason that he or she is speaking.** The students should be familiar with the two most common tags, *said* and *asked.* You might make a list on the chalkboard of the different speaker tags that students can think of. Explain that good writers try to use different speaker tags when they are writing dialogue. This variety makes the dialogue more interesting for the reader. Also, speaker tags can reinforce the mood that the writer wants to evoke. For example, "'Don't do that,' Ed *begged*" is very different from "'Don't do that,' Ed *warned.*" Adverbs can also be part of a speaker tag and can help to further indicate the mood of the speaker: "'Don't do that,' Ed *warned angrily.*"

Hurmence does a good job of showing her characters' attitudes through dialogue. For example, on page 242 when Granny is looking for her money Hurmence writes:

> "My money," the grandmother quavered. "I can't find my money."
> Tiff said drowsily, "Did you look in your pocketbook?"

By using the word *quavered,* Hurmence reinforces her readers' understanding that Granny is agitated and upset. By saying that Tiffany answered *drowsily,* Hurmence reminds readers that Tiffany was awakened by Granny's whimpering.

Selective Reading:
Focus on Speaker Tags

Now have the students go back to "Money Matters" to find other interesting speaker tags. Encourage volunteers to read aloud any speaker tags that they find particularly interesting and to explain how each tag adds to or affects the mood of the passage.

Other interesting speaker tags include the following:
- page 242: The old lady said wildly, pathetically, "It's gone."
- page 243: "Don't cry, Granny," she begged. "I'll help you look for your money."
- page 243: Tiff said reasonably, "Did you always keep it there?"
- page 246: "All ready for the fry pan, Granny," she teased.

Independent Practice:
Speaker Tags

▶ To provide further practice with speaker tags, have students work in small groups to complete Reading/Writing Connection, page 41.

Writer's Craft:
Describing
Characters'
Thoughts and
Feelings

Ask the students to discuss characterization. They should understand by now that authors have different ways of revealing their characters to readers. They can simply **describe the characters** in narrative or they can **have the characters say or do things that help readers to understand them.**

Writers show their characters' emotions by showing how characters act in certain situations. For example, on page 242 of "Money Matters," Hurmence shows how panicky Granny is when she can't find her money. On page 248, Tiffany is feeling really proud of herself because she convinced Granny to put her money in the bank. On page 249, Hurmence shows that Mr. Todt is genuinely delighted to see Granny.

Whether writing in first person or in third person, authors often reveal the thoughts of only the main character. For example, on page 241, Tiffany thinks about the man from The Outlet Furniture Store coming to collect money that her family didn't have. On page 245, Tiffany considers why Granny's money is dusty and why it smells of ham. On page 247, Tiffany thinks about how important a one-hundred-dollar bill seems.

Characterization

Speaker Tags

"Money Matters"

In "Money Matters," the author uses a variety of verbs and adverbs in the speaker tags to make dialogue more interesting or to reinforce the mood of a passage. Look at other stories that you have read for more examples of how writers use speaker tags. Record your findings below.

Title: _____ Page: _____
Example: _____
How the tag affects the mood: _____
_____

Title: _____ Page: _____
Example: _____
How the tag affects the mood: _____
_____

Title: _____ Page: _____
Example: _____
How the tag affects the mood: _____
_____

Title: _____ Page: _____
Example: _____
How the tag affects the mood: _____
_____

Refer to this page when you need help in using speaker tags in your own writing.

Name

Copyright © 1995 Open Court Publishing Company

Unit 6/Value

Dialogue
R/WC 41

Reading/Writing Connection, page 41

Granny's thoughts are not revealed to the reader except as they are revealed to Tiffany. For example, on page 251, Tiffany realizes that her Granny isn't paying attention as she tries to explain that Granny must have miscounted her money before going to the bank: "'I made a hunderd dollars, just for walking downtown here!' she marveled, not listening."

Selective Reading: Focus on Describing Characters' Thoughts and Feelings

Have students go back to "Money Matters" and look for other passages that describe Tiffany's or Granny's thoughts or feelings. Invite volunteers to read aloud and explain any examples they find.

Other examples include the following:

- page 246: "It was all hundred-dollar bills! Millions of them, it looked like! First time Tiff had ever seen a hundred-dollar bill, let alone millions of them, and she said so."
- page 246: "Granny said gratefully, 'Well, you going to look all you want, honey, for one of them hunderd dollars is yours'"
- page 250: "Granny giggled at him calling her a pack rat"
- page 251: "The old lady was so delighted that Tiff gave up trying to convince her of her mistake."
- page 252: "She thought, humbly, that she didn't exactly understand how she felt about money—a little like Mama, a little like Granny, not much like either of them. She would have to figure some more on that one."

"Money Matters"

Describing Characters' Thoughts and Feelings

Look at some stories that you have read to find examples
of how writers reveal their characters' thoughts and
feelings. Record and explain your examples below.

Title: _____ Page: _____
Example: _____
_____
What this passage shows about the character: _____
_____

Title: _____ Page: _____
Example: _____
_____
What this passage shows about the character: _____
_____

Title: _____ Page: _____
Example: _____
_____
What this passage shows about the character: _____
_____

Title: _____ Page: _____
Example: _____
_____
What this passage shows about the character: _____
_____

Characterization
42 R/WC   Value/Unit 6

Reading/Writing Connection, page 42

Independent Practice:
Describing Characters'
Thoughts and Feelings

❯ For additional practice in understanding authors' methods of
describing characters' thoughts and feelings, have students work in small
groups to discuss and complete Reading/Writing Connection, page 42.

WRITING

Linking Reading
to Writing

Remind the students that when they write fiction, they should try to
make their characters as interesting as possible. The more readers
understand the characters' actions, the more sympathetic the readers will
be to the characters. By describing a character's thoughts and feelings, a
writer can reveal the character to readers on a more intimate level than
by using other methods of characterization. Suggest that the students
look through their writing folders to see whether they can find pieces in
which the characters could be better defined by revealing their thoughts
and feelings.

✱ Writing Process

If the students have elected to revise existing pieces, encourage them
to focus on ideas and content during this phase of the writing process.
During proofreading, they will be able to focus on correcting mechanical,
grammatical, and spelling errors.

Some students may be working on first drafts or revisions of fables
about value that they began in the previous lesson. Remind them that

fables do not usually include much dialogue or characterization. If your class is using the optional Writer's Handbook, refer the students to it for help with their writing.

VOCABULARY

Concept-related words from the selection that students may wish to remember and use include *privacy, spendthrift,* and *precious.*

Other words from the selection that may come up in discussion include *script, liberated, fatigue,* and *intrigued.* Have copies of Vocabulary Exploration form, Reproducible Master 15, available for students who request them. Remind students to add these or any other words or phrases from the story to the Personal Dictionary section of their Writer's Notebook. Some students may wish to share these additions with the class. For additional opportunities to build vocabulary, see **Teacher Tool Card 77.**

> *Adding to Personal Word Lists*

3 GUIDED AND INDEPENDENT EXPLORATION

EXPLORING CONCEPTS BEYOND THE TEXT

Guided Exploration

The students will select activities that allow them to explore concepts related to value. Refer them to the **Exploration Activities poster** and give them time to discuss what they wish to explore and how they would like to go about it. If students need help, here are some suggestions:

➤ The students have now read two stories dealing with the question of how money can best serve its possessor. Some students may enjoy taking a survey to find out about different attitudes toward and uses for money. Interested students can use Explorer's Notebook, pages 110–111, for assistance in planning and conducting their surveys.

➤ Distribute Home/School Connection 42. Encourage students to discuss with their families the procedures that people must follow in order to maintain a checking account, which is an important tool for managing money.

> ** Exploring Through Reflective Activities*

Generating Questions to Explore

Have the students review the questions on the **Question Board.** Remove any that have been addressed to their satisfaction or that are no longer appropriate.

➤ Have students turn to Explorer's Notebook, pages 112–113, to continue planning their exploration on value. Remind them to add their thoughts about possible ideas to explore.

Planning a Survey

If you wanted to conduct a survey to find out what attitudes your family and friends have about money, what questions would you ask? Do you think the age of the person you ask would make a difference? Write three or four questions you think would help you find out what people think about saving or spending money.

1. _____
   _____
2. _____
   _____
3. _____
   _____
4. _____
   _____

Decide how you will conduct this survey. Will the people you talk to write their answers, or will they speak while you take notes? Will they put their names with their answers, or will the survey be anonymous? What can you do so that you will know which answers are from students and which are from adults? What do you think you will find out? Write your ideas here.

_____
_____
_____
_____
_____
_____
_____
_____

110 EN   Value/Unit 6

Explorer's Notebook, page 110

Now think about how you will record the results of your survey. Here's one idea:
- Put the answers into groups, by age.
- Look at the answers for each group. How many different attitudes toward money do you find?
- Compare the groups to see whether some of the same concerns are important to each.

What did you find out? Write the results of your survey here.

_____
_____
_____
_____
_____
_____
_____
_____

Did you find out what you thought you would find out? Explain.

_____
_____
_____
_____
_____
_____
_____
_____

Unit 6/Value   EN 111

Explorer's Notebook, page 111

A message from _____

The second story from the Value unit in our reading anthology is "Money Matters." In this story Tiffany shows her grandmother how to write checks. The next time that you must write checks to pay bills, invite your child to watch you write the checks and record them in your check register. Explain the reason for each part of this procedure. Show your child the calculations that you must perform to keep your account balanced. Point out that you cannot write a check for more money than you have in your account or else the check will "bounce" (be returned uncashed).

Unit 6/Value   H/SC 42

Home/School Connection 42

Planning Exploration

How can you find out more about value? You probably have already thought about and discussed what some of the characters in the reading selections value. Write down some other ways you can explore value.

Conduct a survey about value.

_____

_____

_____

_____

As you begin your exploration of value, you will want to keep a list of things to do. Here are a few things you might want to remember to do. Add to this list as you become more sure of the route your exploration will take. Check off each item as you complete it.

Things to Do	Completed
Talk to friends.	
Talk to adults.	
Find and use books listed in bibliographies.	

Copyright © 1995 Open Court Publishing Company

Explorer's Notebook, page 112

What ideas do you have for exploring and writing about value? What ideas about value would you like to explore further? Write your thoughts here. Don't worry if you don't have many ideas right now. You will probably think of more ideas as you read the rest of the stories in the unit. Add to this list each time you get a new idea.

_____

_____

_____

_____

_____

_____

Now think about possible ways to present your information to the class. Remember, you don't have to present a written report. If you wish, you can make a poster or a video, give a speech, or present your information in whatever way you think is best. List your ideas for presenting your project to the class. Add to this list as you read, explore, and think of new ideas.

_____

_____

_____

_____

_____

Copyright © 1995 Open Court Publishing Company

Explorer's Notebook, page 113

Some students may choose to work in collaborative groups. Encourage them to use the Concept Board and the Question Board to form groups based on common interests.

Organizing Collaborative Teams

✳ INDEPENDENT WORKSHOP
Building a Community of Scholars

Student-Directed Reading, Writing, and Discussion

The students should spend the first part of Independent Workshop working together in small groups to discuss their ideas and questions about value. They may refer to the Question Board or to the Concept Board for topics, or they may initiate new topics. Encourage the students to add new ideas or questions generated by the discussions to the Question Board or the Concept Board.

WORKSHOP TIP

As the students begin to work in teams, suggest that they divide responsibility by assigning each team member a question to explore using a reference book or a resource from one of the bibliographies.

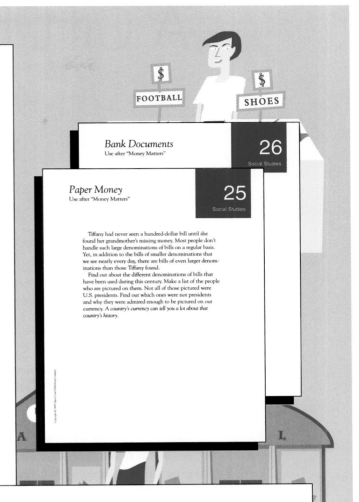

Additional Opportunities for Independent Reading, Writing, and Cross-curricular Activities

✱ Reading Roundtable

Remind the students that the Tradebook Connection Cards in the Student Toolbox contain activities connected with many well-known children's books. Some students may want to read Belinda Hurmence's book *Tough Tiffany* to find out how Tiffany learns to relate to her family. For additional ideas to use during **Reading Roundtable,** see **Learning Framework Card 6.**

✱ Writing Seminar

Some students may want to work on unfinished pieces in their writing folders. Remind them that revising and proofreading are two constantly recurring phases of the writing process.

Cross-curricular Activity Cards

The following Cross-curricular Activity Cards in the Student Toolbox are appropriate for this selection:

- 25 Social Studies—Paper Money
- 26 Social Studies—Bank Documents

Bank Documents
Use after "Money Matters"
26
Social Studies

Paper Money
Use after "Money Matters"
25
Social Studies

Tiffany had never seen a hundred-dollar bill until she found her grandmother's missing money. Most people don't handle such large denominations of bills on a regular basis. Yet, in addition to the bills of smaller denominations that we see nearly every day, there are bills of even larger denominations than those Tiffany found.

Find out about the different denominations of bills that have been used during this century. Make a list of the people who are pictured on them. Not all of those pictured were U.S. presidents. Find out which ones were not presidents and why they were admired enough to be pictured on our currency. *A country's currency can tell you a lot about that country's history.*

Additional Opportunities for Solving Learning Problems

Tutorial

Steps Toward Independence The students should be taking responsibility for their learning by using the Student Toolbox to help them with their work. Remind them of the ways in which this resource can help them.

Provide help for any students who express a need. The following aids are available in the Teacher Toolbox for your convenience:

- Writer's Craft/Reading: Using Dialogue in a Story, Teacher Tool Card 20
- Writer's Craft/Reading: Characterization, Teacher Tool Card 13
- Writer's Craft/Reading: Genre—Realistic Fiction, Teacher Tool Card 3
- Spelling and Vocabulary: Compound Words, Teacher Tool Card 81

A Gift for a Gift

1 READING THE SELECTION

INFORMATION FOR THE TEACHER

About the Selection

When a poor but honest miner brings a bushel of potatoes to a generous king, the king rewards him with a new house and a three-acre farm. But what reward lies in store for the miner's brother, who has decided to present the king with his finest stallion? Readers may be surprised at the conclusion of this folk tale from Saxony, delightfully retold by children's-book author Eric Protter.

Link to the Unit Concepts

The events of "A Gift for a Gift," pages 254–257, bring out the idea that such intangible qualities as honesty, integrity, and generosity may be more valuable than tangible material possessions. Further, the fable demonstrates that a gift is sometimes worth much more—or much less—than its actual monetary value.

About the Author

Eric Protter has written and edited several books for children, including *A Children's Treasury of Folk and Fairy Tales, A Harvest of Horrors, Monster Festival, Explorers and Explorations, Painters on Painting,* and *Story Time with Great Painters.*

About the Illustrator

Krystyna Stasiak was born in Poland and moved to the United States in 1966. Her works have been exhibited in Detroit and Chicago, as well as in Milan, Italy, and Warsaw, Poland. She especially enjoys illustrating children's books that deal with fantastic creatures such as fairies, gnomes, and unicorns.

INFORMATION FOR THE STUDENT

Tell the students that the story they are about to read is a folk tale from Saxony—a country that has become part of the German nation.

LESSON OVERVIEW

"A Gift for a Gift" by Eric Protter, pages 254–257

READING THE SELECTION

Materials

Student anthology, pp. 254–257
Explorer's Notebook, p. 106
Assessment Master 1

READING WITH A WRITER'S EYE

Minilesson

Writer's Craft: Theme in Folk Tales

Materials

Reading/Writing Connection, p. 43
Reproducible Master 15

FYI

Teacher Tool Card
- Spelling and Vocabulary: Building Vocabulary, 77

Options for Instruction

Grammar, Mechanics, and Usage:
  Dependent and Independent Clauses
Grammar, Mechanics, and Usage:
  Punctuating Dialogue
(Use Teacher Tool Cards listed below.)

GUIDED AND INDEPENDENT EXPLORATION

Materials

Explorer's Notebook, pp. 114–115
Home/School Connection 43

Independent Workshop

Optional Materials from Student Toolbox

Tradebook Connection Cards

Cross-curricular Activity Cards
- 27 Social Studies—First Born
- 18 Science—Burning Rocks

Student Tool Cards
- Writer's Craft/Reading: Reading and Writing Folk Tales and Fables, 1
- Grammar, Mechanics, and Usage: Clauses, 51
- Grammar, Mechanics, and Usage: Using and Punctuating Dialogue, 70

FYI

Learning Framework Card
- Independent Workshop, 5

Teacher Tool Cards
- Writer's Craft/Reading: Genre—Folk Tale and Fable, 1
- Grammar, Mechanics, and Usage: Clauses, 51
- Grammar, Mechanics, and Usage: Using and Punctuating Dialogue, 70

NOTES

Asterisks (*) throughout the lesson indicate learning frameworks. Learning Framework Cards and Teacher Tool Cards can be found in the Teacher Toolbox.

Inform them that this tale is about two brothers, one rich, the other poor. Explain that during the Middle Ages, when the tale originated, the eldest son in a family often inherited all of his father's money and property, while the other children received nothing. This custom might account for the disparity in wealth between the two brothers. Share any information about the author and the illustrator that you feel may be useful to your students.

✳   ## COGNITIVE AND RESPONSIVE READING

Activating Prior Knowledge

Ask the students to look at the title of the selection. Invite them to discuss their ideas and opinions about gift giving.

Setting Reading Goals and Expectations

Have the students **browse** the **first page** of the selection, using the **clues/problems/wondering procedure.** Students will return to these observations after reading.

Recommendations for Reading the Selection

Ask the students how they would like to read "A Gift for a Gift." It is a simple, straightforward story that they should be able to **read** easily **on their own.** If the students elect to read orally, use and encourage think-alouds. If they elect to read silently, allow discussion as needed. Discuss problems, strategies, and reactions after reading.

This would also be a good selection for **responding** to text **by visualizing.** Model this response, and then invite the students to do the same.

About the Reading Strategies

Because this story contains a few plot twists, the students may want to pause at certain points to **predict** what will happen next. Also, some students may occasionally find themselves **wondering** about the characters' actions and motivations.

Think-Aloud Prompts for Use in Oral Reading

Notice the think-aloud prompts with the page miniatures. These prompts are only suggestions. Remind the students that what they read should make sense to them. If it doesn't, they should refer to the **reading strategy posters** for help. Invite students to share whatever strategies they use to solve a reading problem. They should also feel free to express any thoughts and reactions they have while reading.

THINK ALOUD PROMPTS

These prompts may be used as guides to promote cognitive and responsive reading.

1 Students may **wonder** about the king's rather curious statement. Invite them to share their thoughts about why the king enjoyed the potatoes more than any beef he had ever eaten.

2 Students may want to pause here to **predict** how the king will respond to the miner's offering. Encourage volunteers to share their predictions with the class, reminding them to form their ideas on the basis of what they have already read.

A GIFT FOR A GIFT

edited and adapted by Eric Protter
illustrated by Krystyna Stasiak

"Honesty is the best policy" is one of the most popular and lasting of all folk tale themes. The original version of this story is attributed to Saxony, and it dates from the 17th century. The author is unknown.

A mighty king once lost his way while hunting alone in a forest, and late at night, when he was cold and weary and hungry, he at last reached the hut of a poor miner. The miner was away digging for coal, and his wife didn't realize that the gentleman who rapped on her door and begged for a night's lodging was the king himself.

"We are very poor," she explained, "but if you will be content, as we are, with a plate of potatoes for dinner and a blanket on the floor for a bed, you will be most welcome." The king's stomach was empty; his bones ached; and he knew that on this dark night he would never find his way back to his castle. And so he gratefully accepted the woman's hospitality.

254

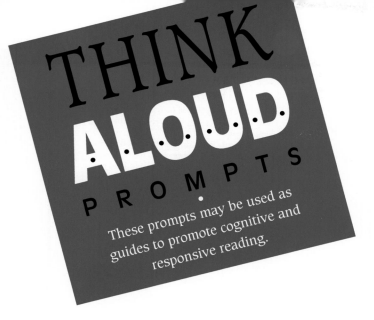

He sat down to dinner with her and greedily ate a generous portion of steaming potatoes baked in an open fire. "These are better than the best beef I've ever eaten," he exclaimed. And still smacking his lips, he stretched out on the floor and quickly fell fast asleep.

1 Early the next morning the king washed in a nearby brook, and then returned to the hut to thank the miner's wife for her kindness. And for her trouble he gave her a gold piece. Then he was on his way to his palace.

When the miner returned home later that day his wife told him about the courteous, kind and distinguished guest who had stayed overnight in their home. Then she showed her husband the gold piece he had given her. The husband realized at once that the king himself must have been their overnight guest. And because he believed that the king had been far too generous in his payment for their humble <u>fare</u> and lodging, he decided to go at once to present his majesty with a bushel of potatoes—fine, round potatoes, the very kind the king had enjoyed so much.

The palace guards refused at first to let the miner enter. But when he explained that he wanted nothing from the king— that in fact, he had come only to give the king a bushel of potatoes—they let him pass. **2**

255

"Kind sire," he said when he finally stood before the king, "last night you paid my wife a gold piece for a hard bed and a plate of potatoes. Even if you are a great and wealthy ruler, you paid much too much for the little offered you. Therefore, I have brought you a bushel of potatoes, which you said you enjoyed as much as the finest beef. Please accept them. And should you ever pass by our house again, we will be happy to have the opportunity to serve you more."

These proud and honest words pleased the king, and to show his appreciation he ordered that the miner be given a fine house and a three-acre farm. Overjoyed by his good luck the honest miner returned home to share the news with his wife.

Now it so happened that the miner had a brother—a wealthy brother who was shrewd, greedy, and jealous of anyone else's good fortune. When he learned of his brother's luck, he decided that he too would present the king with a gift. Not long before, the king had wanted to buy one of the brother's horses. But because he had been asked to pay an outrageously high price, the king had never bought the animal. Now, thought the <u>avaricious</u> brother, he would go to his sovereign and make him a gift of the horse. *After all,* he reasoned, *if the king gave a three-acre farm and a house to my brother in return for a mere bushel of potatoes, I will probably get a mansion and ten acres for my gift.*

③

256

He brushed the horse and polished its harness, and then rode to the palace. Past the <u>sentries</u> he walked, directly into the king's audience chamber.

"Gracious sir," he began, "not long ago you wanted to buy my horse, but I placed a very high price on it. You may have wondered why I did so, great king. Let me explain. I did not want to sell the horse to you. I wanted to *give* it to you, your majesty. And I ask you now to accept it as a gift. If you look out your window you will see the horse in your courtyard. He is, as you know, a magnificent animal, and I am sure that not even you have such a fine stallion in your royal stables."

The king realized at once that this was not an honest gift. He smiled and said, "Thank you, my friend. I accept your kind gift with gratitude. And you shall not go home empty-handed. Do you see that bushel of potatoes there in the corner? Well, those potatoes cost me a three-acre farm and a house. Take them as your reward. I am sure that not even you have a bushel of potatoes in your storeroom with so high a value on them."

④

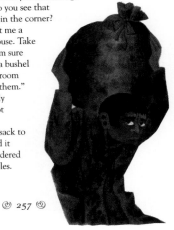

What could the greedy brother do? He dared not argue with the king. He simply raised the heavy sack to his shoulders and carried it home, while the king ordered the horse put in his stables.

257

③ This passage contains several difficult words, including *avaricious* and *sovereign*. If the students have trouble understanding such words, remind them that using **context clues** and **checking the Glossary or a dictionary** are two good ways to clarify meaning.

This is also a good place for students to make their own **predictions** concerning the wealthy brother's plan. Allow volunteers to tell whether they think the king will respond the way the brother thinks he will. Encourage them to explain their reasoning, and remind them to check their predictions when they finish reading the story.

④ Students may **wonder** how the king could tell that the wealthy brother's gift was not honest. Invite them to share their ideas and opinions with the class.

Discussing Strategy Use

Allow time for the students to discuss the strategies they used and the passages in which they used them. Students who **wondered** or who made **predictions** as they read "A Gift for a Gift" might discuss whether these strategies improved their understanding and enjoyment of the story.

EXPLORING THROUGH DISCUSSION

Reflecting on the Selection
Whole-Group Discussion

The whole group discusses the selection and any thoughts or questions that it raises. During this time, students also **return to the clues, problems, and wonderings** they noted on the chalkboard during browsing.

Assessment

To assess the students' understanding of the text, engage in a discussion to determine whether the students understand the following:

- how the miner's reasons for giving a gift to the king differed from those of his brother
- why the king treated each brother as he did

TEACHING TIP Allow students to express their ideas without interruption.

Response Journal

Students' responses and reactions to the selection may vary. Provide time for the students to record their responses in their personal response journals.

Exploring Concepts Within the Selection
Small-Group Discussion

While the small groups discuss the relationship of the selection to value, **circulate and observe the discussions.** Remind the students to refer to the Concept Board and the Question Board to keep their discussions focused.

ASSESSMENT TIP Take your Teacher's Observation Log as you circulate among the groups. As you observe the students' discussions, enter any remarks that you feel will help you to assess their progress.

Sharing Ideas About Explorable Concepts

Have the groups **report their ideas** and **discuss them** with the rest of the class. It is crucial that the students' ideas determine this discussion.

- Students may realize that when the king arrived at the miner's door, he was so hungry that a simple plate of potatoes had more value to him than the gold coin he gave in return.
- Students may recognize that fairness, honesty, and giving full value for the money paid were important to the miner even when he was dealing with someone who could easily afford to be generous.
- Students may point out that the miner's brother acted purely from greed; he was already wealthy and did not need the king's reward.

As these ideas and others are stated, have the students **add them to** the **Question Board** or the **Concept Board.**

Exploring Concepts Across Selections

Ask the students whether this folk tale reminds them of any other selections they have read. Students may make connections with other selections in this unit or in previous units.

- Students might note that Aesop's miser and the miner's brother both valued money for its own sake. Students may point out that neither the miser nor the miner's brother profited from their greedy behavior.
- Some students may compare the miner to Tiffany in "Money Matters." They may point out that both characters were concerned with doing what was right, and that both were eventually rewarded for their fairness and generosity toward others, as was the miner's wife, who had kindly sheltered and fed the stranger.

- Some students might compare the plight of the lost king in this story to that of the Ingalls family in "It Can't Beat Us." Both parties found themselves in a state of desperate hunger, in which even the simplest food seemed delicious and very valuable.

Recording Ideas

As students complete the above discussions, **ask them to sum up what they have learned from their conversations and to tell how they might use this information** in further explorations. Any special information or insights may be recorded on the **Concept Board.** Any further questions that they would like to think about, pursue, or investigate may be recorded on the **Question Board.** They may want to discuss the progress that has been made on previous questions and to cross out any questions that have been addressed to their satisfaction.

❯ After discussion, remind students to record their ideas and opinions about the selection on page 106 of their Explorer's Notebook.

Connections Across Units

Evaluating Discussions

Explorer's Notebook, page 106

Recording Concept Information continued

"A Gift for a Gift" by Eric Protter

_____
_____
_____
_____
_____
_____

"What Money Is" by R. V. Fodor

_____
_____
_____
_____
_____
_____

"The Shoeshine Stand" by Clyde Robert Bulla

_____
_____
_____
_____
_____
_____

106 EN   Value/Unit 6

Professional Checkpoint:
Cognitive and Responsive Reading

A good reader knows when and where to use familiar strategies. Students can become autonomous in their use of strategies only by being given years of encouragement in choosing appropriate strategies. Thus, you should not tell the students when to predict or when to summarize. Rather, you should prompt the students who are not using strategies to check the strategy posters and choose a strategy that helps them make sense of what they are reading.

Notes:

2 READING WITH A WRITER'S EYE

MINILESSON

Writer's Craft: Theme in Folk Tales

Ask for volunteers to tell what "A Gift for a Gift" is about. Allow two or three students to explain the plot in their own words. Then ask if students see any lesson that can be learned from the story. After volunteers have contributed their ideas, guide discussion to the understanding that a story's plot and its theme are two different things. Explain that **plot is what happens in the story,** while **theme is the message that the author wants readers to get from the story.** Use "A Gift for a Gift" as a model to point out the difference between plot and theme. The plot of this selection involves two brothers who bring gifts to the king: One brother gives an honest and generous gift and is rewarded handsomely; the other brother tries to deceive the king and is punished. The message of the story is that honesty and generosity are good while dishonesty and greed are bad.

Tell students that this message is similar to the theme of most folk tales: Sensible and virtuous behavior is rewarded while cruel, dishonest, and foolish behavior is punished. Explain that adults used folk tales to teach children how they should behave in the real world. Point out that even today, writers often create their stories with similar themes in mind.

Selective Reading: Focus on Theme in Folk Tales

Have students review "A Gift for a Gift." Tell them to look for sentences and passages showing that the miner and his wife are honest and generous people, and for sentences and passages that show how these qualities are rewarded. Have them search, also, for sentences that tell what a greedy and dishonest person the miner's brother is, and how he is punished for his dishonest behavior.

Afterward, let volunteers point out these sentences and read them aloud to the rest of the class. Examples the students might point out include the following:

Selection-Based Practice

- page 254, paragraph 2: "'We are very poor,' she explained, 'but if you will be content . . . you will be most welcome.'"
- page 255, paragraph 1: "And for her trouble he gave her a gold piece."
- page 256, paragraph 1: "Even if you are a great and wealthy ruler, you paid too much. . . . Therefore, I have brought you a bushel . . ."
- page 256, paragraph 2: "These proud and honest words pleased the king, and to show his appreciation. . . ."
- page 256, paragraph 3: "a wealthy brother who was shrewd, greedy, and jealous of anyone else's good fortune."
- page 257, paragraph 3: "The king realized at once that this was not an honest gift."

Independent Practice: Theme in Folk Tales

❯ Have the students work alone or in small groups, using Reading/Writing Connection, page 43, to reinforce their understanding of the theme in folk tales. As students work, circulate through the class and make sure that each student understands what he or she is to do.

Reading/Writing Connection, page 43

"A Gift for a Gift"

Theme in Folk Tales

In "A Gift for a Gift," the theme of goodness prevailing over evil is prominent. Look at other folk tales that you have read or heard and describe how this theme is presented. Write the title of the story and then describe how good characters are rewarded and how evil characters are punished.

Title: _____

How a good character is good and how he or she is rewarded: _____
_____
_____

How an evil character is bad and how he or she is punished: _____
_____
_____

Title: _____

How a good character is good and how he or she is rewarded: _____
_____
_____

How an evil character is bad and how he or she is punished: _____
_____
_____

Title: _____

How a good character is good and how he or she is rewarded: _____
_____
_____

How an evil character is bad and how he or she is punished: _____
_____
_____

Theme

Name

Copyright © 1995 Open Court Publishing Company

Unit 6/Value

R/WC 43

WRITING

Linking Reading to Writing

Encourage the students to look through their own writing folders for stories with strong central themes and to add some examples of themes to their Writer's Notebook. If the students locate stories that could be improved by strengthening or clarifying themes, they may want to revise these pieces. Encourage volunteers to share and explain their examples and revisions in class.

＊Writing Process

Remind students that "A Gift for a Gift" is an adaptation of an old folk tale. Ask them if they know what it means to adapt a story. Explain that Eric Protter wrote a new version of a story that had already existed for many years. He may have read or heard several different versions of the story and then decided that he could write a version that would be more interesting or easier to understand. He may simply have liked the story a lot and decided to write a fresh version for young readers to enjoy. When a writer **adapts or retells a folk tale,** he or she usually **makes minor changes in the story but keeps the original theme.** For example, the writer may **describe** the **characters or** the **setting differently,** add or remove minor characters, increase or decrease the number of events leading up to the climax, make certain events or characters from the original more or less important, and so forth. In essence, the writer **tells the story as he or she imagines it,** choosing his or her own words and writing in his or her own way.

Suggest that students write their own adaptation of a folk tale. Ask students to name some folk tales or fairy tales that they have read. After a number of titles have been mentioned, invite the students to rewrite the folk or fairy tale of their personal choice. Remind the students that while they can change and update the setting, the characters, and, to some extent, the plot, they should not alter the theme of the original. To get ideas for their adaptation, the students may want to locate and reread the story they have chosen to adapt. They might also find it helpful to read two or more versions of the same story, noting what has changed and what has stayed the same from one version to the next.

VOCABULARY

Concept-related words from this story that students may want to remember include *avaricious, hospitality,* and *shrewd.* In addition, there are several other words that students may find interesting, including *distinguished, sentries,* and *sovereign.* Have copies of Vocabulary Exploration form, Reproducible Master 15, available for students who request them. Remind the students to insert the words or phrases that they want to remember into the Personal Dictionary section of their Writer's Notebook. Invite volunteers to tell which words they chose and why. For additional opportunities to build vocabulary, see **Teacher Tool Card 77.**

Adding to Personal Word Lists

3 GUIDED AND INDEPENDENT EXPLORATION

EXPLORING CONCEPTS BEYOND THE TEXT

Guided Exploration

Students will select activities through which they can explore concepts related to value. Refer them to the **Exploration Activities poster** listing activities and give them time to choose an activity and to discuss what they wish to explore and how they wish to go about it. If the students need further help, here are some suggestions:

- The miner and his wife both did favors for the king without expecting a reward. Invite students to consider and discuss occasions on which they have done favors for other people. Why did they do the favors? Did they expect rewards? How did they feel after doing the favors? Students might also consider times when others did them favors. How did they feel? Did they want to do something in return for the good deeds? Some students might enjoy writing personal experience narratives telling about a time when they gave or received a favor or reward. Provide time later for the students to share their completed narratives with the class.

- In "A Gift for a Gift," the king is pleased to receive a bushel of potatoes from the miner because he knows that the miner could ill afford to give him anything at all. The miner's brother, however, is not at all pleased with the same bushel of potatoes. Invite the students to discuss favorite—and not-so-favorite—gifts they have received. Encourage them to think about and discuss why they liked or did not like the gifts. How—if at all—did their feelings about their gifts relate to the gifts' material value? This discussion might also form the basis for a personal experience narrative. Students who are not interested in writing about favors and rewards as their topic might want to write about memorable gifts they've received. Again, provide time later for students to share their narratives with the class.

> ❯ Students may want to compare and contrast the values held by some of the characters they encounter in this unit. They can use the Explorer's Notebook, pages 114–115, to examine what is most valuable to each character and to note how the character's values are revealed. Students should frequently return to this page as they proceed through the unit.

> ❯ This would be an appropriate time to distribute Home/School Connection 43. Students and their families are asked to discuss the concept that virtue is its own reward.

Continuing Exploration

Students should continue to discuss and plan their exploration of value. Remind them to return to pages 112–113 in the Explorer's Notebook and record any new plans. As they raise new ideas and concepts relating to value, students should add these to the Concept Board.

✱ *Exploring Through Reflective Activities*

Writing a Personal Experience Story

Exploring Value Through Literature

As you proceed through this unit, you will meet a variety of characters, each with his or her own ideas about what has value. Keep a chart telling about the characters that interest you the most. List each character's name, and then make a note of something that character values highly. It may not be a material good but rather a particular idea, moral characteristic, or personality trait. Then examine the ways you can tell what the character values,

Story and Character	What Is Valued	How I Can Tell	Other Notes
"The Miser" a miser	gold	He buried all his wealth in the ground and never spent any of it. He was distraught when it was stolen.	

114 EN　　　　　　　　　　　　　　　　　　Value/Unit 6

Copyright © 1995 Open Court Publishing Company

Explorer's Notebook, page 114

and make some notes in the third column. In some cases, the character may have discussed what he or she values; in other cases, you will need to infer what he or she values. You may also make note of information from your class and collaborative-group discussion. Use the final column to record anything else that interests you about the character's ideas. For instance, you might note how one character compares with other characters you have encountered.

Story and Character	What Is Valued	How I Can Tell	Other Notes

Copyright © 1995 Open Court Publishing Company

Unit 6/Value　　　　　　　　　　　　　　　　　　EN 115

Explorer's Notebook, page 115

"A Gift for a Gift"

A message from _____

In our unit about value, we have just finished reading and discussing "A Gift for a Gift." In the story, two brothers—a poor miner and his wealthy brother—bring gifts to their king. The miner's gift is a sack of potatoes, but the thought behind the gift is sincere, and the king rewards him with a house and farmlands. The rich brother, seeing how the king rewarded a sack of potatoes, decides that giving the king a fine horse should earn him a much greater reward. The king sees through the rich brother's scheme, however, and repays him with the sack of potatoes. The poor brother expected no reward at all, and his rich brother was hoping for a great reward. Neither got what he expected, and each got what he deserved.

Discuss the story with your child, including ways in which the story could have ended differently. The gift of a house and land, for example, would certainly change the poor brother's life. Such a reward would make anyone happy. But what if the king had merely accepted the potatoes and given nothing in return? Since the poor miner expected nothing, would he have felt cheated? Or was the giving of the gift enough to make the miner happy?

Discuss with your child times when you did something for other people without expecting anything in return. Describe your feelings. Ask your child if he or she has ever felt good about doing something for someone else even when there was no reward involved. On the lines below have your child write an example of virtue being its own reward and bring it to school to share with the class.

_____
_____
_____
_____
_____
_____
_____

Copyright © 1995 Open Court Publishing Company

Unit 6/Value　　　　　　　　　　　　　　　　　　H/SC 43

Home/School Connection 43

* INDEPENDENT WORKSHOP
Building a Community of Scholars

Student-Directed Reading, Writing, and Discussion

Remind students that they will spend the first part of Independent Workshop in small groups, discussing and carrying out their ideas and plans for exploring value. As they pursue their explorations, they should feel free to use one another's suggestions, the library and classroom resources, and any other materials and resources that might prove useful. For a review of how to handle Independent Workshop in your classroom, see **Learning Framework Card 5.**

WORKSHOP TIP

Remind the students that this is a good time to return to the Explorer's Notebook to complete unfinished pages or to discuss ideas with classmates.

Additional Opportunities for Independent Reading, Writing, and Cross-curricular Activities

✱ Reading Roundtable

Remind the students about the Tradebook Connection Cards in the Student Toolbox. Encourage the students to recommend and share other books they have read that have value as their theme.

✱ Writing Seminar

Students who are writing an adaptation of a folk tale may continue their work at this time. Remind the students to follow the appropriate phases in the writing process as they work.

Cross-curricular Activity Cards

The following Cross-curricular Activity Cards in the Student Toolbox are appropriate for this selection:

- 27 Social Studies—First Born
- 18 Science—Burning Rocks

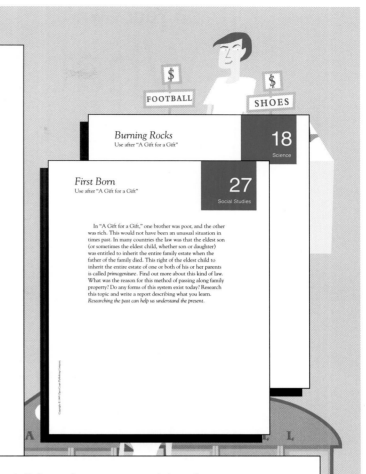

Burning Rocks
Use after "A Gift for a Gift"

18
Science

First Born
Use after "A Gift for a Gift"

27
Social Studies

In "A Gift for a Gift," one brother was poor, and the other was rich. This would not have been an unusual situation in times past. In many countries the law was that the eldest son (or sometimes the eldest child, whether son or daughter) was entitled to inherit the entire family estate when the father of the family died. This right of the eldest child to inherit the entire estate of one or both of his or her parents is called *primogeniture*. Find out more about this kind of law. What was the reason for this method of passing along family property? Do any forms of this system exist today? Research this topic and write a report describing what you learn. *Researching the past can help us understand the present.*

Additional Opportunities for Solving Learning Problems

Tutorial

Use this time to help individuals or small groups of students who have exhibited a need in any area. Encourage the students to request help if they feel that they are having trouble in certain areas. The following teaching aids are available in the Teacher Toolbox for your convenience:

- Writer's Craft/Reading: Genre—Folk Tale and Fable, Teacher Tool Card 1
- Grammar, Mechanics, and Usage: Clauses, Teacher Tool Card 51
- Grammar, Mechanics, and Usage: Using and Punctuating Dialogue, Teacher Tool Card 70

On Your Own

What Money Is

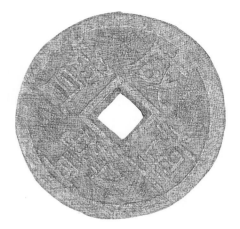

1 READING THE SELECTION

About the Selection

Money is something that we are all familiar with. Rarely does a day go by that we do not handle currency. Money is the fuel that powers our business and the standard by which many people judge success. In R. V. Fodor's "What Money Is," readers will find a fascinating account of the history of currency, as well as a straightforward explanation of how it is manufactured today.

Link to the Unit Concepts

The worth of an object is in the eye of the beholder. In this selection, on pages 258–269, Fodor describes the mostly antiquated practice of bartering one item for another and explains how barter eventually was replaced in most societies by the more familiar practice of exchanging money for goods. Along the way, he poses and then answers a question that may puzzle many young readers: Why is money—which, after all, is just paper and metal—valuable?

After reading this selection, students may find themselves thinking about the concept of supply and demand and the relation between value and need.

About the Author

Ronald V. Fodor, born in Cleveland, Ohio, in 1944, is a "writing" research scientist with a Ph.D. in geology and an interest in a wide variety of subjects. For adults Fodor has written the *Complete Handbook on Auto Repair and Maintenance: With the Repair-O-Matic Guide* and *Competitive Weightlifting.* His books for children range from treatises on geology—*Meteorites: Stones from the Sky* and *What Does a Geologist Do?*— to a primer on currency—*Nickels, Dimes, and Dollars: How Currency Works,* the book from which the selection was excerpted. Fodor's research has taken him to Hawaii, South America, Europe, and Africa.

LESSON OVERVIEW

"What Money Is" by R. V. Fodor, pages 258–269

READING THE SELECTION

Materials

Student anthology, pp. 258–269
Explorer's Notebook, p. 106
Assessment Master 2

READING WITH A WRITER'S EYE

Minilesson

On Your Own

Materials

Reproducible Master 15

FYI

Teacher Tool Card
• Spelling and Vocabulary: Building Vocabulary, 77

Options for Instruction

Writer's Craft: Genre—Expository Text
Writer's Craft: Elaboration Through Providing Specific Facts
(Use Teacher Tool Cards listed below.)

GUIDED AND INDEPENDENT EXPLORATION

Materials

Explorer's Notebook, p. 116
Assessment Master 1

Independent Workshop

Optional Materials from Student Toolbox

Tradebook Connection Cards

Cross-curricular Activity Cards
• 7 Math—From Dollars to Pesos to Francs
• 28 Social Studies—Create Some Cash

Student Tool Cards
• Writer's Craft/Reading: Reading and Writing Expository Text, 9
• Writer's Craft/Reading: Telling Important Facts, 41

FYI

Teacher Tool Cards
• Writer's Craft/Reading: Genre— Expository Text, 9
• Writer's Craft/Reading: Elaboration Through Providing Specific Facts, 41

> N O T E S

Asterisks (*) throughout the lesson indicate learning frameworks. Learning Framework Cards and Teacher Tool Cards can be found in the Teacher Toolbox.

INFORMATION FOR THE STUDENT

Share with the students some information about R. V. Fodor. Explain that this selection is the first chapter in a book about the nature, use, and management of money.

* COGNITIVE AND RESPONSIVE READING

Activating Prior Knowledge

Tell the students that this selection contains information about the practice of bartering. Invite the students to tell what they know about the bartering and the trading of goods.

Setting Reading Goals and Expectations

Have the students **browse the selection using the clues/problems/ wondering procedure.** The students will return to these observations after they complete their reading.

Recommendations for Reading the Selection

This selection has been designated as an On Your Own selection. Tell the students that they will read "What Money Is" silently on their own. Remind them to use any of the reading strategies that they have learned to help them read and understand the selection. Encourage them to check the **reading strategy posters** if they encounter a reading problem or if they are unsure about how to use a strategy.

Remind the students that after they finish reading they will discuss problems, reactions, and strategies. Let them know, however, that they can raise their hands to ask questions or to identify problems for discussion at any time during their silent reading. After they have read the selection, the students will complete the Self-Assessment Questionnaire.

TEACHING TIP To help the students think about what they read, questions, comments, problems, and strategies should be shared openly in the group.

THINK ALOUD PROMPTS

To foster independence, think-aloud prompts are not provided for On Your Own lessons.

WHAT MONEY IS
from NICKELS, DIMES, AND DOLLARS: How CURRENCY WORKS by R. V. Fodor

© Nawrocki Stock Photo

Each week you are involved in activities that require money. Sometimes you spend small amounts, shopping for school supplies, buying lunch, or going to the movies. Other times you spend more, buying a new set of

clothes or flying across the country in an airplane. Whether the amount is small or large, some money is spent for practically everything you do.

Money is a part of everybody's life, and each person handles money in his or her own way. Some save as much of it as they can. Others spend it as fast as they earn it. Still others find ways to spend it faster than they earn it. Money changes hands quickly and constantly, within neighborhoods, across states, and among countries.

Few people, however, stop to think about what money really is. Certainly we recognize it as coins in our pockets or as paper bills in our wallets, but little thought is given to why those coins and bills are special and called "money." After all, coins are made of the same metals used in your home appliances, and paper bills are not much different from magazine paper. Why then is money so valuable?

Money is something that someone will give or take in return for goods and services. It is a medium of exchange. Money is also a standard to determine the fair value of those goods and services.

We use coins and paper for exchange, but actually any article can be called "money" if people agree to it. In the past, cattle, tea, salt, and animal teeth were among the items used as money. Whatever the material, however, money is valuable only because we make it so—and believe that it is so.

Money has not always been around. In many ancient civilizations, exchanges were made without it. Goods and services were obtained by bartering. This method of trading occurs when a person offers a product to someone and asks to receive an item at least as valuable in return.

Bartering probably began in prehistoric times when cavemen swapped the stone tools and weapons that they made or traded them for freshly killed game. Egyptian hieroglyphics illustrate that bartering was part of Egypt's early civilization. Markets served as barter places for farmers who had grains, vegetables, and honey, for craftsmen who made jewelry, pots, and leather goods, and for hunters and fishermen with fresh catches.

Barter was also common practice during the settlement of the New World. When settlers arrived in Colonial America, their European money was of no use in obtaining food, shelter, and clothing. They worked to make or grow what they needed. One man who was skilled in building wagons traded his product to another who made fine plow blades. American Indians also played a role in these early communities. They were excellent trappers, and the European pioneers exchanged weapons and tools for their furs and skins.

There are still moneyless societies today. In the jungles of Africa and South America, some tribal groups survive by trading food, clothing, and hunting weapons with others. Often the swap is a dumb barter, or a silent trade, which means that the tribesmen never actually meet. Instead, one group leaves goods in a clearing and retreats into the jungle. Then a second tribe makes the exchange, perhaps leaving meat and honey for ivory and tools.

Bartering remains a way of life for some Americans. Eskimos, for example, may acquire food and luxuries by bringing animal skins to a store owner. Sometimes homeowners swap household items with one another.

❧ 260 ❧

There were times, however, when bartering did not satisfy the parties involved. For example, a farmer may have had a field of vegetables to barter. But when his crops were ready, he could not find anyone with the tools he needed. Therefore, the farmer exchanged his vegetables for something he knew could be traded for tools later. He exchanged them for money.

Money came into existence at different times in different civilizations. Some ancient people used money as we know it more than 2,500 years ago. Other groups still do not use coins and bills today. The island of Yap has one such society. The natives of this South Pacific island use stones for money. Some Yap money consists of small, fist-sized stones, but other pieces are up to six feet in size. This giant Yap money, called "fei," is certainly not easy to exchange for goods. Sometimes it is left in place when the ownership changes. At other times holes are drilled through the stone, so it can be hung on a pole and carried by two men.

This huge stone was used as money on the island of Yap.
© Nawrocki Stock Photo

The early Chinese used bricks of tea for money.
Chase Manhattan Archives

In Far Eastern countries, such as Tibet and China, bricks of tea were used for money as recently as this century. Tea leaves and twigs were collected, dried, beaten, sifted, steamed, and pressed into flat bundles, or bricks. Each one was stamped with a value that depended on its weight. A typical brick of tea weighed about two and a half pounds.

No matter what was used for money, it was sure to be scarce. If the article ever became too common, it was likely to lose its value. This happened to the tobacco-leaf money used in parts of early America. It worked well until too many people planted the crop. Soon tobacco was so widespread that it became worthless as a means of exchange.

Animals have also been used as money. In early European history, a large herd of cattle meant great wealth for its owner. Camels, sheep, goats, pigs, and even slaves were living money. In Newfoundland, Canada, where fishing is a major industry, codfish was the money of earlier times.

Many other unusual objects have served as money too. Some Roman soldiers were paid partly in salt. This practice is the origin of the English word *salary*, which means payment for one's work. Grains like wheat and corn were money in

❧ 262 ❧

Egypt, and the natives of Fiji offered the teeth of sperm whales for the products they needed.

One object that has appeared as money in practically every corner of the world is the seashell. As recently as the nineteenth century, cowrie shells were accepted as money in several countries, and they are still valuable in parts of Africa. An important kind of shell money in America was wampum, or strings of beads made from the shells of quahog clams.

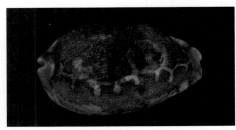

Cowrie shells have been used as money throughout the world.
© George Bernard/Animals Animals

The name *wampum* comes from the Algonquin word *wampumpeag*. The Algonquins used beads made out of white and purple clamshells for money long before Columbus arrived. They cut the shells into pieces, bored holes in them, and threaded them on strings. Throughout the 1600s many early settlers used wampum in their tradings with Indians. The worth of the wampum varied according to its color—the darker, the more valuable.

❧ 263 ❧

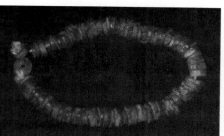

Wampum beads were the money of American Indians.
Numismatic Collection, National Museum of American History, Smithsonian Institution

Wampum served early Americans well until the middle of the eighteenth century when some settlers learned how to make large quantities of the beads rapidly. Factories were actually set up in New York and New Jersey, and the mass production of wampum eventually made it worthless as money.

Metal may have first appeared as money among the Phoenicians and Babylonians, but the first metals that looked like coins were the ancient Chinese disks of about 500 B.C., known as cash. They were made of bronze and had a square hole in their center. Curiously, the English word *cash* is not derived from the name of this Chinese coin. Instead, it comes from the Latin word *capsa*, meaning box or money box.

Gold and silver coins existed before the birth of Christ in the Mediterranean regions of Greece and Lydia (Turkey). Some of these coins had tastefully designed engravings of coats of arms or animals like the lion, bull, or turtle. One of the most famous Greek coins bore the head of Athena, goddess of wisdom, on one side, and an owl on the

A Chinese coin called "cash"
Numismatic Collection, National Museum of American History, Smithsonian Institution

264

reverse side. "Owls," as the coins were called, were the first money to show a human figure. Important gold and silver coins of Lydia were bean-shaped lumps called "electrum."

By the year 330 B.C., coins in Greece were being produced in large numbers under the direction of Alexander the Great. Not long afterward, many early nations were producing copper, gold, or silver money. Some people took advantage of the sudden abundance of coins made from valuable metals. They began to shave off or clip portions of the coin edges in order to collect the precious dust for themselves.

An owl, an early Greek coin
Numismatic Collection, National Museum of American History, Smithsonian Institution

Counterfeiting, or manufacturing fake money, took place, too. Some early Romans and Egyptians coated copper or lead coins with thin layers of silver and then passed them off as silver money. The crime of counterfeiting was serious enough in some societies to merit death.

The penny was introduced as a silver coin in England around A.D. 775. For a long time it was England's only coin and making change required cutting it into half-pennies and quarter pieces known as farthings. English money later evolved into pounds, shillings, and pence, some of which crossed the Atlantic Ocean to the New World with the first settlers.

Spanish money was also found in the American colonies. Best known is the Spanish dollar that bore the number 8. These pieces of eight were commonly cut into smaller portions, or bits, to

Spanish dollars sometimes were cut into bits to make change.
© Nawrocki Stock Photo

make change. That word, *bits*, is still with us as slang: two bits is a quarter and eight bits is a dollar.

Of all the coins brought to America from Europe, the oldest is a Norse penny made about A.D. 1075. This penny has special historic value. It was found buried on the coast of Maine and offers proof that Viking navigators discovered America long before Christopher Columbus arrived in 1492.

The first American coins were minted, or manufactured, in Boston in 1652. They were ordered by the General Court of the Massachusetts Bay Colony. The Court provided a local goldsmith, John Hull, with the proper tools and built a mint on his land. Hull produced shillings, sixpence, and three-penny bits, usually with a pine-tree design, so they became known as pine-tree shillings.

For a long time afterward, this money was used in the settlements along with the coins of foreign countries, such as the French guinea, the Spanish pistole, and the English shilling. Then, in 1785, after the formation of the United States, the Continental Congress established that the official money unit of the new nation would be the dollar. Congress authorized the minting of new gold, silver, and copper money that would include eagles (worth ten dollars), half-dollars, dimes, and the half cent.

The first official United States coin was minted in New Haven, Connecticut. It was the copper Fugio cent, and it bore the inscriptions "United States," "We are one," and "Mind your business." The date on the cent was 1787, and the design included a sun, a sundial, and thirteen linked circles to represent the original colonies.

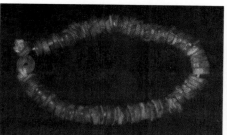

This 1787 Fugio cent was mistakenly struck twice.
Numismatic Collection, National Museum of American History, Smithsonian Institution

In 1793, an official United States Mint began coining money in Philadelphia, Pennsylvania. Still in operation today, along with others in Denver, Colorado, and San Francisco, California, the mint melts and mixes the necessary amounts of copper and nickel to form metal strips from which coins are stamped out. Silver is rarely used in present-day coins.

In the two centuries since the first coinage, money-making has changed significantly. Designs such as the head of Liberty, a symbol of independence, eagles, and thirteen stars stayed in use, but some denominations of coins did not. For example, two-cent, three-cent, five-cent, and twenty-cent coins were introduced in the mid-1800s, but only the five-cent piece, the nickel, has lasted. Gold coins, common in the 1800s, have not been minted since 1933, and true silver dollars were stopped in 1935. Coin sizes change, too. The Susan B. Anthony dollar coin, no longer in circulation, was smaller than other dollars minted this century.

In today's society, paper money is more important than coins. Its origins go back thousands of years, when merchants and traders first agreed to accept promises of payment. These promises to pay later in gold and silver were written on clay tablets.

Not for a long time, however, did paper come into use as notes of promise, or money. Currency, as paper money is called, originated out of the need for convenience. Carrying large amounts of gold and silver was heavy and unwieldy, so paper was used to represent the coins. Some of the earliest paper money appeared in China. The Italian adventurer Marco Polo reported in the 1200s that the Chinese had

267

currency made from mulberry tree bark. The oldest of this Chinese money, the Kwan, was about the size of a sheet of typing paper, and it was stamped with a particular value.

In the United States, the Government first used paper money in the late 1700s. But this early Continental currency was unsuccessful. Too much of it was printed, and by 1790 it had lost its value as money.

The United States Government printed its first official paper money in 1862. The Treasury Department needed currency to pay for the Civil War. These greenbacks, as they were known because of their green ink, lost much of their value shortly after they were issued, however. People doubted that they were as good as gold. By 1864, the greenback dollar had dropped to only thirty-nine cents in gold value, and the Treasury did not acquire enough gold to restore greenbacks to the same buying power until 1879. All the denominations we have today were in use then, although the designs of the bills have changed.

The first currency used in the United States
© Nawrocki Stock Photo

Inspection of new currency at the Bureau of Engraving and
Printing in Washington, D.C.
© Dennis Brack/Black Star

Paper money in the United States is not manufactured in mints, but is made at the Treasury Department's Bureau of Engraving and Printing in Washington, D.C. The Bureau uses secret-formula ink and special rag paper of linen and cotton. Each bill, whether one dollar or a thousand dollars, is printed as part of a large paper sheet of thirty-two bills and has its own serial number. After the sheets are inspected, they are cut into thirty-two parts and put into circulation for our use.

269

Discussing Strategy Use
Since the students have read this selection "on their own," ask for volunteers to share with the group any problems they encountered while reading and any strategies they used to solve those problems.

*

Reflecting on the Selection
Whole-Group Discussion

The whole group discusses the selection and any thoughts or questions that the selection raises. During this time, the students also **return to the clues, problems, and wonderings** that they noted on the chalkboard during browsing.

Assessment

To assess their understanding of the selection, engage the students in a discussion to determine whether they understand the following ideas:
- why bartering was a common practice in ancient societies and why bartering has been rejected as a system of exchange by most societies today
- what forms money has taken and why
- what makes money valuable

Response Journal

The students have learned a lot about a subject that fascinates almost everyone—money. Encourage the students to record their personal responses to the selection.

Exploring Concepts Within the Selection
Small-Group Discussion

Remind the students to refer to the Concept Board and the Question Board to keep their discussions focused. Circulate among the groups and encourage the students to consider their original ideas about value as they discuss the relation of this selection to the unit concepts.

Sharing Ideas About Explorable Concepts

Have the groups **report their ideas** and **discuss them** with the rest of the class. It is crucial that the students' ideas determine this discussion.
- Students may notice that just about any material or item can become a medium of exchange, or money, as long as it is accepted as such by the people who must use it.
- Students may realize that as a medium of exchange becomes abundant, its value decreases.
- Students may observe that for various reasons, societies may replace their medium of exchange or modify it in some way—for example, when it becomes too abundant; when it is no longer convenient to use; when it has to be protected from counterfeiters.

As these ideas and others are stated, have the students **add them to** the **Question Board** or the **Concept Board.**

Ask the students to examine Victor Dubreuil's oil painting, *One Dollar Silver Certificate,* reproduced on page 310 of the student anthology. Encourage the students to share any thoughts or ideas that they have about the painting and its possible connection with the article that they have just read.

Fine Art

Exploring Concepts Across Selections

Ask the students if this selection reminds them of other selections that they have read. Students may make connections with previous selections in the student anthology.

- The students may compare and contrast Fodor's explanation of money and the reason why it has value with the characters' attitudes about money in "The Miser" and "Money Matters."
- Students may remember that in "The Fire Builder," in unit 4, Perseverance, the main character uses a twenty-dollar bill as kindling because it is worthless to him in the woods. They may link his behavior with Fodor's explanation of why money is valuable.

Connections Across Units

Evaluating Discussions

Recording Ideas

As they complete the above discussions, ask the students to **sum up what they have learned from their conversations and to tell how they might use this information** for further explorations. Special information or insights may be recorded on the **Concept Board.** Any further questions that they would like to think about, pursue, or investigate may be recorded on the **Question Board.** They may want to discuss the progress that has been made on their previous questions. They may also want to cross out any questions that no longer warrant consideration.

▶ After their discussion, the students should individually record their ideas and impressions about the selection on page 106 of their Explorer's Notebook.

Self-Assessment Questionnaire

▶ Distribute copies of Assessment Master 2, Self-Assessment Questionnaire, which can be found in the booklet Masters for Continuous Assessment in the Teacher Toolbox. Tell the students to answer the

---

Explorer's Notebook, page 106

Recording Concept Information continued

"A Gift for a Gift" by Eric Protter

"What Money Is" by R. V. Fodor

"The Shoeshine Stand" by Clyde Robert Bulla

106 EN   Value/Unit 6

Copyright © 1995 Open Court Publishing Company

Assessment Master 2

Self-Assessment Questionnaire

1. How would you rate this selection?
   ○ easy   ○ medium   ○ hard

2. If you checked **medium** or **hard**, answer these questions.
   • Which part of the selection did you find especially difficult?
   • What strategy did you use to understand it?

   • Were some of the words hard?
   • What did you do to figure out their meaning?

3. What do you feel you need to work on to make yourself a better reader?

4. Give an example of something you said in the group. Tell why you said it.

5. Give an example of something that people in the group helped you understand about the selection.

Date   Name   INDIVIDUAL   GROUP

Self-Assessment Questionnaire   Assessment Master 2

Copyright © 1995 Open Court Publishing Company

questionnaires after they have completed this lesson. Collect the completed questionnaires so that you can compare the students' current self-assessments with later self-assessments when they again complete the same questionnaire. You might also examine their responses to see whether the students' assessments of themselves are compatible with the assessments that you have noted for them in your Teacher's Observation Log.

2

On Your Own

READING WITH A WRITER'S EYE

MINILESSON

Remind the students that after they completed each previous selection, they discussed something the writer did especially well. For example, after reading "Money Matters" they discussed the way that Belinda Hurmence described the characters' thoughts and feelings.

Tell the students that since they have read "What Money Is" on their own, you would like them to try to identify something they think Fodor did especially well. Does anything about the writing stand out? Suggest that they think back to portions of the selection that they reacted to with great interest or enjoyment. Tell them that such responses may indicate especially good writing.

Allow time, if necessary, for the students to skim the story to refresh their memories. If they have difficulty expressing their feelings about this selection, model a response for them by pointing out aspects of Fodor's writing that you feel are noteworthy. For example, Fodor's clear, concise descriptions make it easy to understand the process of bartering and to visualize the various media of exchange that he discusses.

WRITING

Linking Reading to Writing

Encourage the students to use in their own writing those elements that they particularly appreciated in Fodor's writing. Invite them to go to their writing folders and see what piece of writing they might revise to include something that was done well in this selection.

✱ Writing Process

Although no specific writing assignment is recommended here, the students may concentrate on an appropriate phase of the writing process as they begin new pieces or continue their work on pieces begun earlier in the unit.

VOCABULARY

Standard, bartering, dumb barter, currency, minted, and *counterfeiting* are terms related to value that the students may want to discuss and remember. Other interesting words that they may wish to note are *cowrie shells, wampum,* and *unwieldy.* Provide the students with Vocabulary Exploration forms, Reproducible Master 15, so that they can

VOCABULARY TIP Students need repeated exposure to new vocabulary words. Encourage them to read other books about money and value.

add interesting and important new words and phrases to the Personal Dictionary section of their Writer's Notebook. For additional opportunities to build vocabulary, see **Teacher Tool Card 77.**

3 GUIDED AND INDEPENDENT EXPLORATION

EXPLORING CONCEPTS BEYOND THE TEXT

Guided Exploration

The students will select activities in which they explore value. Refer them to the **Exploration Activities poster,** then give them time to choose an activity and discuss what they wish to explore and how they wish to go about it. If they need further help, here are some suggestions:

- Engage the students in a discussion on the value of money compared with the value of such attributes as good health, kindness, tolerance, honesty, or respect. Have the students formulate several questions that interest them, such as, Is having money more important than being respected among your peers?

▶ Then divide the students into small groups and have each group select a question to discuss. During their discussions the students may record notes, ideas, and observations on page 116 of their Explorer's

* Exploring Through Reflective Activities

Explorer's Notebook, page 116

Discussing Value

My group discussed this question about value:

_____

_____

_____

Here are some of the ideas that came up in our discussion:

_____

_____

_____

_____

_____

_____

_____

_____

Here are some of my personal thoughts and observations:

_____

_____

_____

_____

_____

_____

_____

_____

116 EN   Value/Unit 6

Copyright © 1995 Open Court Publishing Company

Notebook. Following the small-group discussions, the whole class should meet again to share their findings.

- The students might designate a day as "barter day." On this day they could bring in items that they consider valuable but that they no longer want. (You might want to have the students bring in notes from their parents or guardians granting permission for them to barter the items that they have selected.) An area of the classroom should be set aside as the trading post. Several students working in shifts could barter their items with other students. At the end of the day, students who bartered with each other might meet in small groups to discuss the bartering sessions, their way of determining which items to trade for which others, and their assessments of the fairness of their trades.

ASSESSMENT TIP This might be a good time to observe students working in groups. Record your observations in your Teacher's Observation Log.

Continuing Exploration

As the students continue their exploration of value, new questions may arise. Have the students add them to the Question Board. They should also review the questions that are already on the board and remove any that are no longer interesting or appropriate.

Professional Checkpoint: Guided and Independent Exploration

The students' comprehension of a selection is affected by what goes on before, during, and after reading. As they discuss the selection and its relationship to the concepts, notice students who are having difficulty using concept-related terms or making connections among selections. These students may need additional, explicit strategy instruction or modeling in the use of prior knowledge to make sense of new information. Modeling and corrective feedback are powerful tools for improving and refining comprehension skills.

Notes:

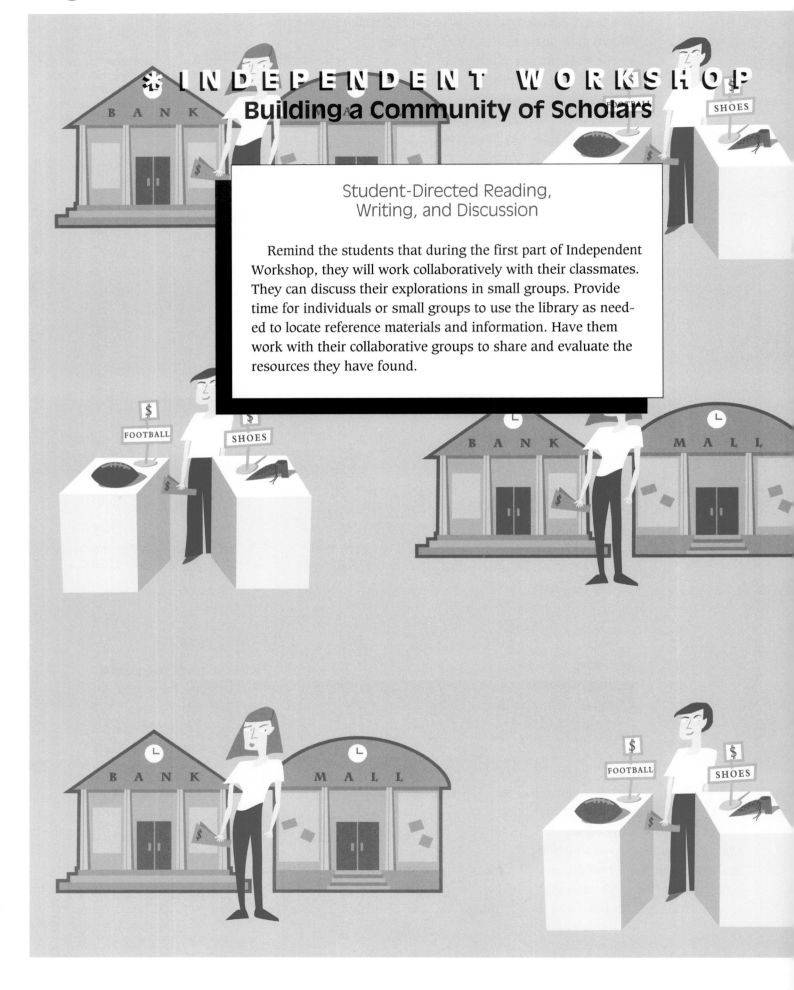

❋ INDEPENDENT WORKSHOP
Building a Community of Scholars

Student-Directed Reading, Writing, and Discussion

Remind the students that during the first part of Independent Workshop, they will work collaboratively with their classmates. They can discuss their explorations in small groups. Provide time for individuals or small groups to use the library as needed to locate reference materials and information. Have them work with their collaborative groups to share and evaluate the resources they have found.

Additional Opportunities for Independent Reading, Writing, and Cross-curricular Activities

✱ Reading Roundtable

If this selection makes them curious about money, the students can get more information by reading the rest of Fodor's *Nickels, Dimes, and Dollars: How Currency Works* or Ruth Cavin's *A Matter of Money: What Do You Do with a Dollar?*

✱ Writing Seminar

Students may use this time to continue revising any of their writing work in progress. Remind them to ask for peer input. Encourage them to refer to the writing strategy posters wherever they need help in their writing.

Portfolio

Remind the students to think about choosing pieces of writing to put in their portfolios.

Cross-curricular Activity Cards

The following Cross-curricular Activity Cards from the Student Toolbox are appropriate for this selection:
- 7 Math—From Dollars to Pesos to Francs
- 28 Social Studies—Create Some Cash

Additional Opportunities for Solving Learning Problems

Tutorial

Use this time to work with individuals or small groups who need help in any area. This is also a good time for peer tutoring. If you have students who would benefit from giving or receiving peer tutoring, match them accordingly and have them refer to the proper Student Tool Cards to guide their work. The following teaching aids are available in the Teacher Toolbox for your convenience:
- Writer's Craft/Reading: Genre—Expository Text, Teacher Tool Card 9
- Writer's Craft/Reading: Elaboration Through Providing Specific Facts, Teacher Tool Card 41

The Shoeshine Stand

1 READING THE SELECTION

INFORMATION FOR THE TEACHER

About the
Selection

Sarah Ida has been getting into trouble at home—money trouble. Before things get out of control, her parents send her to stay with her aunt Claudia for the summer. Aunt Claudia has been instructed not to give her niece any pocket money. Shocked and resentful, Sarah Ida takes a job at the local shoeshine stand, hoping to embarrass Aunt Claudia into giving her some money. Sarah Ida has a few surprises in store for her, however. This excerpt from Clyde Robert Bulla's *Shoeshine Girl* offers well-drawn character studies and an engaging plot. Readers may well be motivated to read the book in its entirety.

Link to the
Unit Concepts

In "The Shoeshine Stand," pages 270–297, the issue of what money is really good for is examined once again. Clyde Robert Bulla, like other authors in this unit, looks at the issue through the eyes of two characters whose differing attitudes toward money bring them into conflict. Aunt Claudia cannot understand why Sarah Ida feels that she must have more money than that required to pay for movies, new clothing, and other specific expenses. Sarah Ida, however, just does not feel right unless she has some spending money in her pocket at all times.

Although she highly values the feeling of money in her pocket, Sarah Ida also enjoys spending money on anything that happens to catch her fancy. She has never had to earn her own money; consequently, she has little concern for saving and budgeting her allowance and little understanding of the relation between money, work, and personal accomplishment. Bulla explores these ideas as he unfolds the tale of Sarah Ida's first job.

Finally, as it has in previous selections, the question of personal value versus monetary value arises. Through her experiences with Al the shoeshine man, Sarah Ida begins to learn that money is not the only

LESSON OVERVIEW

"The Shoeshine Stand" by Clyde Robert Bulla, pages 270–297

READING THE SELECTION

Materials

Student anthology, pp. 270–297
Explorer's Notebook, p. 106

READING WITH A WRITER'S EYE

Minilessons

Writer's Craft: Characterization
Writer's Craft: Dialogue

Materials

Reading/Writing Connection, pp. 44–45
Reproducible Master 15

FYI

Teacher Tool Card
• Spelling and Vocabulary: Building Vocabulary, 77

Options for Instruction

Writer's Craft: Point of View
Spelling and Vocabulary: Contractions
(Use Teacher Tool Cards listed below.)

GUIDED AND INDEPENDENT EXPLORATION

Materials

Home/School Connection 44

Independent Workshop

Optional Materials from Student Toolbox

Tradebook Connection Cards

Cross-curricular Activity Cards
• 29 Social Studies—Snake Oil
• 8 Math—How Much to Tip?

Student Tool Cards
• Writer's Craft/Reading: Characterization, 13
• Writer's Craft/Reading: Using Dialogue in a Story, 20
• Writer's Craft/Reading: Point of View, 12
• Spelling and Vocabulary: Using and Punctuating Contractions, 82

FYI

Teacher Tool Cards
• Writer's Craft/Reading: Characterization, 13
• Writer's Craft/Reading: Using Dialogue in a Story, 20
• Writer's Craft/Reading: Point of View, 12
• Spelling and Vocabulary: Using and Punctuating Contractions, 82

NOTES

Asterisks (*) throughout the lesson indicate learning frameworks. Learning Framework Cards and Teacher Tool Cards can be found in the Teacher Toolbox.

measure of value and to see, in the words of the old adage, that one man's trash is another man's treasure.

As they read "The Shoeshine Stand," the students may find themselves asking questions such as, Does money have more value when you earn it yourself?

About the Author

Clyde Robert Bulla was born in King City, Missouri, on January 19, 1914. He is the author of over sixty books for children, many of which have won awards. Besides writing fiction, Bulla composes music. He has collaborated with lyricist Lois Lensky to write more than a dozen songbooks.

Bulla, largely self-educated, offers to children who want to write the following advice: "Read a lot. Write a lot. Keep looking, listening, and wondering."

More information about Bulla appears on page 297 of the student anthology.

INFORMATION FOR THE STUDENT

Some students may be unfamiliar with shoeshine stands. In earlier decades, these were more commonplace than they are today. Shoeshine stands could be found, for example, on busy city street corners, in barbershops, and in train stations. As hinted at in this selection, shining shoes is not a prestigious job. It is performed, after all, in a servile position, crouched at the feet of the customer. Students need to be aware of this in order to understand why Sarah Ida thinks that taking a job at a shoeshine stand will embarrass her aunt into giving her money.

COGNITIVE AND RESPONSIVE READING

Activating Prior Knowledge

Sarah Ida gets into trouble because she cannot budget her allowance. Invite the students to discuss their own experiences in budgeting and saving money.

Setting Reading Goals and Expectations

Have the students **browse** the **first page** of the selection, using the **clues/problems/wondering procedure.** Students will return to these observations after reading.

Recommendations for Reading the Selection

Ask the students how they would like to read the selection. Bulla's language and style are fairly simple. Students should have no trouble **reading** the selection **silently.** If they choose to read silently, allow discussion as needed. If they choose to read orally, use and encourage think-alouds. Discuss problems, strategies, and reactions after reading.

This would also be a good selection for **responding** to text **by making connections** while reading aloud.

Note: "The Shoeshine Stand" has been divided into two parts in case the students are unable to finish the selection in one class period. The second part of the story begins at the bottom of page 283 and is indicated by a large initial capital letter.

About the
Reading
Strategies

Because of the length of this selection, students may find the **sum-ming up** strategy useful. Remind them to make mental notes of important events in the story as they read. If they have chosen to read the selection aloud, encourage them to pause as needed to sum up aloud what has happened in the selection up to that point.

Think-Aloud Prompts
for Use in Oral Reading

Notice the think-aloud prompts with the page miniatures. These suggestions can prove useful if students encounter passages that are unclear to them. Remind the students to refer to the **reading strategy posters** and to use any appropriate strategy as they read. Invite students to share whatever strategies they use to solve a reading problem. They should also feel free to express any pertinent thoughts about the selection.

THINK ALOUD PROMPTS

These prompts may be used as guides to promote cognitive and responsive reading.

THE SHOESHINE STAND

from SHOESHINE GIRL
by Clyde Robert Bulla
illustrated by Susan David

Yesterday Sarah Ida took the train alone to Palmville, where she is to spend the summer with Aunt Claudia. Her parents have sent her away because she was beginning to get into trouble at home. They hope that a change of scenery, and a summer with Aunt Claudia, will give them and Sarah Ida a fresh start. Sarah Ida, however, feels resentful.

In the morning Sarah Ida put on an old shirt and her oldest blue jeans. She went down into the kitchen.

Aunt Claudia was there, frying bacon and eggs. "Good morning," she said. "Did you sleep well?"

"Yes," said Sarah Ida.

270

"There's apple jelly and plum jam. Which would you like with your toast?"

"Neither one."

They sat down to breakfast. Aunt Claudia said, "You're going to have company."

"Who?" asked Sarah Ida.

"Rossi Wigginhorn."

Sarah Ida frowned. "I don't know any Rossi Wigginhorn."

"She's a neighbor," said Aunt Claudia. "She's been wanting to meet you."

"Why?"

"I told her you were coming. I thought it would be nice if you had a friend your own age."

"Did you ever think," said Sarah Ida, "that I might like to choose my friends?"

"I like to choose my friends, too," said Aunt Claudia. "But when you're in a new place and haven't had a chance to meet anybody—"

"It doesn't matter," said Sarah Ida, "whether I meet anybody or not."

They finished breakfast.

Aunt Claudia asked, "Can you cook?"

"No," said Sarah Ida.

"Would you like to learn?"

"No."

"At least, you'd better learn to make your own breakfast," said Aunt Claudia. "It's something you might need to know. And there are things you can do to help me. I'll teach you to take care of your room, and you can help me with the cleaning and dusting."

271

"How much do you pay?" asked Sarah Ida.

Aunt Claudia stared at her. "Pay?"

"Money," said Sarah Ida. "How much money?"

Aunt Claudia took the dishes to the sink. She came back to the table and sat down. "I don't like to bring this up," she said, "but I suppose I must. I'm not supposed to pay you anything."

"And why not?" asked Sarah Ida.

"Because your mother asked me not to. She told me you had borrowed your allowance for the next two months. She said you had spent it all and had nothing to show for it. She asked me not to give you any money while you're here."

272

"But I've *got* to have money!" said Sarah Ida. "I'm going to *need* it!"

"What for?" asked Aunt Claudia.

"Lots of things. Candy and gum. Movies—and popcorn when I go to the movies. I need it for magazines. And for clothes."

"If you need clothes, I'll buy them," said Aunt Claudia. "We can talk later about movies. If I buy you a ticket once a week—"

"I want money in my pocket!"

Aunt Claudia sighed. "That seems to be what your mother *doesn't* want. I think she's trying to teach you the value of money."

"I *know* the value of money, and if you think you can—!"

"All right, Sarah Ida. That's enough."

Sarah Ida ran up to her room. She could feel herself shaking. They didn't know how she felt about money. They didn't understand, and she didn't know how to tell them. She *needed* money in her pocket. It didn't have to be much. But she just didn't feel *right* with none at all!

Aunt Claudia was calling her.

Sarah Ida didn't answer.

"Sarah Ida!" Aunt Claudia called again. "Rossi is here."

Sarah Ida lay on the bed and looked out the window.

"Rossi has something for you," said Aunt Claudia. "Is it all right if she brings it up?"

"No!" said Sarah Ida. She went downstairs.

Rossi was waiting in the hall. She had pink cheeks and pale yellow hair. She wore a yellow dress without a spot or a wrinkle.

273

"I brought some cupcakes," she said. "I made them myself."

"That was sweet of you, Rossi," said Aunt Claudia.

"Yes, that was sweet of you, Rossi," said Sarah Ida.

Aunt Claudia gave her a sharp look. Then she left them alone.

The girls sat on the porch. They each ate a cupcake.

"I think you're awfully brave, coming here all by yourself," said Rossi.

"It was no big thing," said Sarah Ida. "My father put me on the train, and my aunt was here to meet me."

"Well, it's a long trip. I'd have been scared. Are you having a good time in Palmville?"

"I just got here," said Sarah Ida.

"I think you'll like it. There's a lot to see. Come on down the street. I'll show you where I live."

They walked down to Rossi's house. It was old, like Aunt Claudia's. It was half covered with creepy-looking vines.

Sarah Ida met Rossi's mother. Mrs. Wigginhorn was pretty in the same way Rossi was. She had pale hair and a sweet smile.

She said, "I hope you'll enjoy your visit here."

Rossi showed Sarah Ida her room. "My daddy made this shelf for my library. These are all my books. Any time you want to borrow some—"

"I don't read much," said Sarah Ida. She was looking at something else. She was looking at a blue and white pig on the dresser. "What's this?" she asked.

"That's my bank," said Rossi.

"Is there anything in it?"

"About five dollars."

274

Sarah Ida picked up the pig. It was heavy. She turned it from side to side. She could feel the coins move.

"I need four dollars," she said. "Will you lend it to me?"

"I—I'm saving for a present for my daddy," said Rossi.

"It's just a loan. I'll pay you back."

Rossi looked unhappy. "I'm not supposed to lend money."

"You said I could borrow your books. What's the difference?"

"I just don't think I'd better."

"All right. Forget it." Sarah Ida went to the door.

"No. Wait. You can have it." Rossi was feeling in the top drawer of the dresser. She took out a tiny key on a string. "But don't tell anyone."

"Don't you tell, either," said Sarah Ida.

275

There was a lock on the underside of the pig. Rossi unlocked it. The coins fell out on the dresser. They were mostly quarters and dimes.

Sarah Ida counted out four dollars. "Are you sure you want to do this?"

"Yes," said Rossi.

"Well, then, good-by," said Sarah Ida.

"Don't you want me to walk back with you?" asked Rossi.

"You don't need to." Sarah Ida left her. She walked out of the house and up the street. The coins jingled in her pocket. **1** She was whistling when she got back to Aunt Claudia's.

She awoke late the next morning. There was sunlight in the room. She looked at the pictures on the walls. For the first time she almost liked them. For the first time in weeks she felt almost happy.

The feeling was quickly gone.

The door opened, and Aunt Claudia came in. Her face was like winter.

She said, "You took money from Rossi yesterday—didn't you?"

Sarah Ida sat up in bed. "How—?"

"Mrs. Wigginhorn called me. She said most of the money was gone from Rossi's bank. She said you would know about it."

"I didn't—" began Sarah Ida.

"What happened? I want to know."

✎ *276* ✎

"I borrowed the money. That's what happened. I *borrowed* it."

"You hadn't known poor little Rossi even a day, and already you were borrowing her money."

"Poor little Rossi said I could."

"She's such a friendly child. She didn't know how to say no." Aunt Claudia asked, "Is money so important to you? What do you need it for?"

"I told you. I like to have money in my pocket."

"Do you think that's a good reason?"

"It is to me."

"It isn't to me. Get your clothes on and take that money right back."

Sarah Ida hadn't known Aunt Claudia could sound so fierce. She got up and dressed. The money was in an envelope under her pillow. She stuffed it into her pocket.

She went down the street to the Wigginhorns'. Rossi opened the door. Her eyes and nose were red.

"Sarah Ida—"

"Here." Sarah Ida almost threw the envelope at her. "I might have known I couldn't trust you."

"I couldn't help it," said Rossi. "Mother saw the key on the dresser. She picked up the bank and found out it was almost empty. She kept asking questions till I had to tell her."

"Just forget it," said Sarah Ida coldly. "Forget the whole thing."

She walked away.

Back at Aunt Claudia's, she started up to her room. Aunt Claudia called her. "Your breakfast is ready."

"I don't want any," said Sarah Ida.

✎ *277* ✎

1 Because the story has reached a turning point, the students may want to stop here to **sum up** what has happened so far. Invite a volunteer to share his or her summary with the class. Remind the volunteer to focus on main points, such as the conflict between Sarah Ida and her aunt and Sarah Ida's solution to her money problem.

Then encourage the students to **predict** what will happen next to Sarah Ida and her borrowed money. Allow students to share their predictions with the class. Remind them to follow up on their predictions later.

"Come here, anyway," said Aunt Claudia.

Sarah Ida stood in the kitchen doorway.

"I shouldn't have lost my temper," said Aunt Claudia, "but you don't seem to understand that what you did was wrong."

"I don't see why it was wrong," said Sarah Ida.

"It's wrong to take advantage of someone. And you took advantage of Rossi."

"If you'd let me have some money, I wouldn't have had to borrow."

Aunt Claudia's lips closed tightly for a moment. She said, "This is a game, isn't it?"

"A game?"

"You're trying me out, to see how far you can go."

"I don't know what you mean."

"I think you do. Money really isn't that important to you, is it? You're just using this whole thing to get what you want. At the same time, you're trying to strike back at me, because—"

"The money *is* important!" cried Sarah Ida. "And if you won't give me any, I'll—I'll go out and get some!"

"How?" asked Aunt Claudia.

"I'll get a job."

"Where?"

2 "I don't know, but I'll find one. But if I did, you wouldn't let me keep it. You want to keep me under your thumb."

"Sarah Ida, stop this!" said Aunt Claudia. "If you could find work and earn some money, I wouldn't keep you from it. But ask yourself—what could you do? Who would give you a job? I don't want you under my thumb. All I'm trying to do is—"

"I *know* what you're trying to do. And if you think I'm playing a game, I'll show you!"

278

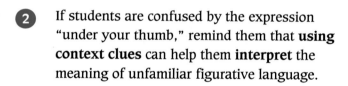

She rushed out of the house. Aunt Claudia's voice followed her. "Come back! Stop!"

Sarah Ida didn't stop. She cut across the yard and ran up the street.

She came to Grand Avenue. She was out of breath, and there was a pounding in her ears.

She stopped in the doorway of a drugstore and looked up and down the street. People were walking by. Cars were passing. Palmville was bigger than she'd thought. In all these stores there must be someone who would give her some work to do.

There was a dress shop across the street, with girls' dresses in the window. She might try there. But she wasn't even wearing a dress, and she didn't look very neat.

She used the drugstore window as a mirror and tried to comb her hair with her fingers. Inside the store a woman was watching her. She looked friendly. Sarah Ida went in.

"Can I help you?" asked the woman.

"I—" Sarah Ida began, and she couldn't go on. How could she say "I want to work for you"? What kind of work could she do in a drugstore?

"I'm just looking," said Sarah Ida. She looked at the candy, but she couldn't say, "I'll have this and this," because she didn't have any money.

279

2 If students are confused by the expression "under your thumb," remind them that **using context clues** can help them **interpret** the meaning of unfamiliar figurative language.

She went outside. She walked past a restaurant, a bank, a hardware store. She came to a pet shop. There were puppies in one window and kittens in the other. She put out her hand to the puppies. One of them came to the window and put his nose against the glass.

She went into the shop. A man and woman were there. All about the shop were animals in cages. There were birds, and in one cage was a green and yellow parrot.

"Do you need help here?" asked Sarah Ida.

The parrot began to squawk. "Polly, Polly! Pretty Polly! My, oh my!"

"What?" asked the woman.

"I said, do you need help!" shouted Sarah Ida.

"Be quiet!" said the woman. "Not you, little girl. I mean that silly bird."

"Silly bird!" said the parrot. "My, oh my!"

The woman threw a cloth over the cage, and the parrot was quiet.

"Now. What was it you wanted?" she asked.

"I wanted to work for you," said Sarah Ida.

"Oh," said the woman.

The man spoke. "What do you know about animals?"

"Not much, but I could learn."

The man said, "Come back when you're a little older."

"How much older?"

"About six years," said the man.

"Do you know where I *could* get work?" she asked.

"What can you do?"

"I—I don't know."

"You might try Al," said the man. "He's got a sign up."

"Yes," said the woman. "He's had it up for a long time."

"He's on the corner." The man pointed. "Why don't you have a look?"

Sarah Ida left the shop. She was sure the man and woman had just been trying to get rid of her. She thought they were probably laughing at her, too.

She went on down the street. And there on the corner she saw the sign. It wasn't very big, and it was stuck to a folding door. It said "Help Wanted."

The folding door was at one end of a shoeshine stand. The stand was a kind of shed with a platform in it. There were four chairs on the platform. Above the chairs was a big sign: "Al's Shoeshine Corner."

A man sat on one of the chairs. His face was hidden behind the newspaper he was reading.

Sarah Ida looked at the "Help Wanted" sign. She looked at the stand. This was the place, she thought. This was just the place!

She would tell Aunt Claudia, "I have a job."

"What kind?" Aunt Claudia would ask.

"Working at a shoeshine stand," Sarah Ida would say. "A shoeshine stand on Grand Avenue."

"Oh, you can't do that!" Aunt Claudia would say.

"You said you wouldn't keep me from earning some money," Sarah Ida would say.

"But you can't be seen working at a shoeshine stand on Grand Avenue," Aunt Claudia would say. "I'll *give* you some money!"

Sarah Ida spoke to the man. "Are you Al?"

He put down the newspaper, and she saw his face. He was not young. His hair was thin and gray. His eyes looked like little pieces of coal set far back in his head.

"Yes, I'm Al." He slid down off the chair. His shoulders were stooped. He wasn't much taller than she was. "You want something?"

"I'm Sarah Ida Becker," she said, "and I want to work for you."

"What do you mean, work for me?"

"Your sign says 'Help Wanted.'"

"I put that up so long ago I forgot about it," he said. "Nobody wants to work for me. People don't like to get their hands dirty. They want to do something easy that pays big money."

"Will you give me a job?" she asked.

"You're not a boy."

"The sign doesn't say you wanted a boy."

A man came by.

"Shine?" asked Al.

The man climbed into a chair. Al shined his shoes. The man went on.

Al looked at Sarah Ida. "You still here?"

"If I worked for you, what would I have to do?" she asked.

"Shine shoes, same as I do. Some days I get more work than I can take care of. Then I need help. But whoever heard of a shoeshine girl?"

"Why couldn't a girl shine shoes?"

282

"Why don't you go on home?"

"You said you needed help. You've got your sign up."

"What do you want to work here for?"

"I need some money."

"You wouldn't get rich here."

"I know that."

He looked her up and down. "I don't think you really want to work."

All at once she was tired of waiting, tired of talking. She started away.

Al said, "What did you say your name was? Sarah what?"

"Sarah Ida Becker."

"You any relation to the lady that used to be in the library? You any relation to Miss Claudia Becker?"

"She's my aunt."

Another man stopped for a shoeshine. When he was gone, Al asked her, "You staying with your aunt?"

"Yes," she said.

"Go tell her you saw Al Winkler. Tell her you want to work for me. Maybe—"

"Maybe what?"

"I don't know yet," he said. "First you see what she says." ❸

Aunt Claudia was waiting on the porch. "Sit down," she said, when Sarah Ida came up the steps. "I want to talk to you." ❹

Sarah Ida sat in the porch swing.

"You must never do this again," said Aunt Claudia. "You must always let me know where you're going. Do you understand?"

283

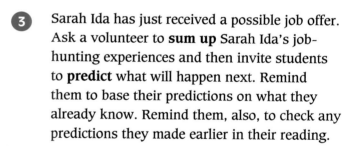

❸ Sarah Ida has just received a possible job offer. Ask a volunteer to **sum up** Sarah Ida's job-hunting experiences and then invite students to **predict** what will happen next. Remind them to base their predictions on what they already know. Remind them, also, to check any predictions they made earlier in their reading.

Note: The first part of the selection ends on page 283. This is a good place to stop reading if the selection cannot be finished during this class period.

❹ If your class stopped reading here during another class period, ask a volunteer to **sum up** the entire first section of the story before the students begin reading again.

If the students have made **predictions** about what will happen to Sarah Ida next, remind them to check those predictions as they read.

"Yes," said Sarah Ida.

"Where have you been?"

"On the avenue."

"What were you doing?"

"Looking for a job. And I found one."

"You found one?"

"Yes, I did."

"Where?"

"On Grand Avenue. Working for the shoeshine man."

"Who?"

"Al Winkler, the shoeshine man."

Aunt Claudia looked dazed. "How did you know him?"

"I didn't know him. He had a 'Help Wanted' sign and I stopped."

"Al Winkler," said Aunt Claudia, as if she were talking to herself. "I remember him so well. He came to the library when I worked there. He hadn't gone to school much, and he wanted to learn more. I helped him choose books." She asked, "Does he want you to work at his stand?"

"He said to talk to you about it."

284

"Do you want to work for him?" asked Aunt Claudia.

"I told you, I want some money of my own."

"This might be a good way to earn some," said Aunt Claudia.

"You *want* me to shine shoes on Grand Avenue?"

"If that's what you want to do."

Sarah Ida was quiet for a while. Things weren't working out the way she'd planned. She'd never thought Aunt Claudia would let her work in the shoeshine stand, and Aunt Claudia didn't seem to care!

Unless—Sarah Ida had another thought. Maybe Aunt Claudia didn't believe she'd go through with it. Maybe she was thinking, *That child is playing another game.*

Sarah Ida said, "You really want me to go tell Al Winkler I'll work for him?"

"If it's what you want to do," said Aunt Claudia.

Sarah Ida started down the steps. Aunt Claudia didn't call her back. There was nothing for her to do but go.

She found Al sitting in one of his chairs.

"What did she say?" he asked.

"She said yes."

"You want to start now?"

"I don't care," she said.

He opened a drawer under the platform and took out an old piece of cloth. "Use this for an apron. Tie it around you."

She tied it around her waist.

A man stopped at the stand. He was a big man with a round face and a black beard. He climbed into a chair and put his feet on the shoe rests.

285

5 This passage marks another turning point in Sarah Ida's summer. Her aunt has unexpectedly granted Sarah Ida permission to work at the shoeshine stand. Invite volunteers to share their **predictions** about Sarah Ida's first day on the job. Remind them to check their predictions later.

"How are you, Mr. Naylor?" said Al.

"Not bad," said the man. "Who's the young lady?"

"She's helping me," said Al. "She needs practice. You mind if she practices on you?"

"I don't mind," said Mr. Naylor.

Al said to Sarah Ida, "I'm going to shine one shoe. You watch what I do. Then you shine the other one."

He took two soft brushes and brushed the man's shoe.

"That takes off the dust," he said. "Always start with a clean shoe."

He picked up a jar of water with an old toothbrush in it. With the toothbrush he sprinkled a few drops of water on the shoe.

"That makes a better shine." He opened a round can of brown polish. With his fingers he spread polish on the shoe.

"Now you lay your cloth over the shoe," he said. "Stretch it tight—like this. Pull it back and forth—like this. Rub it hard and fast. First the toe—then the sides—then the back."

When he put down the cloth, the shoe shone like glass. He untied the man's shoelace. He drew it a little tighter and tied it again.

He asked Sarah Ida, "Did you see everything I did?"

"Yes," she said.

"All right. Let's see you do it."

She picked up the brushes. She dropped one. When she bent to pick it up, she dropped the other one. Her face grew hot.

She brushed the shoe. She sprinkled the water.

"Not so much," Al told her. "You don't need much."

286

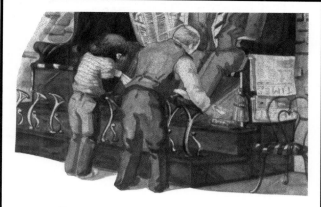

She looked at the brown polish. "Do I have to get this on my fingers?"

"You can put it on with a rag, but it's not the best way. You can rub it in better with your fingers."

"I don't want to get it on my hands."

"Your hands will wash."

She put the polish on with her fingers. She shined Mr. Naylor's shoe. She untied his shoelace, pulled it tight, and tried to tie it again.

Al tied it for her. "It's hard to tie someone else's shoe when you never did it before."

Mr. Naylor looked at his shoes. "Best shine I've had all year," he said. He paid Al. He gave Sarah Ida a dollar bill.

After he had gone, she asked Al, "Why did he give me this?"

287

"That's your tip," said Al. "You didn't earn it. He gave it to you because you're just getting started."

"Will everybody give me a dollar?" she asked.

"No," he said, "and don't be looking for it."

Others stopped at the stand. Sometimes two or three were there at once. Part of the time Sarah Ida put polish on shoes. Part of the time she used the polishing cloth.

Toward the end of the day she grew tired. She tried to hurry. That was when she put black polish on a man's brown shoe.

The man began to shout. "Look what you did!"

"It's not hurt," said Al. "I can take the black polish off. Sarah Ida, hand me the jar of water."

She reached for the jar and knocked it over. All the water ran out.

"Go around the corner to the filling station," Al told her. "There's a drinking fountain outside. Fill the jar and bring it back."

Sarah Ida brought the water. Al washed the man's shoe. All the black polish came off.

"See?" he said. "It's as good as new."

"Well, maybe," said the man, "but I don't want *her* giving me any more shines."

He went away.

Sarah Ida made a face. "He was mean."

"No, he wasn't," said Al. "He just didn't want black polish on his brown shoes."

"Anyone can make a mistake," she said.

"That's right. Just don't make too many." He said, "You can go now." He gave her a dollar. "This is to go with your other dollar."

288

"Is that all the pay I get?"

"You'll get more when you're worth more," he said. "You can come back tomorrow afternoon. That's my busy time. Come about one."

She didn't answer. She turned her back on him and walked away.

In the morning she told Aunt Claudia, "I'm going to the drugstore."

"Aren't you working for Al?" asked Aunt Claudia.

"Maybe I am, and maybe I'm not," said Sarah Ida.

In the drugstore she looked at magazines. She looked at chewing gum and candy bars. None of them seemed to matter much. Her money was the first she had ever worked for. Somehow she wanted to spend it for something important.

She went home with the two dollars still in her pocket.

She and Aunt Claudia had lunch.

"If you aren't working for Al," said Aunt Claudia, "you can help me."

"I'm going to work," said Sarah Ida. Working for Al was certainly better than helping Aunt Claudia.

She went down to the shoeshine stand.

"So you came back," said Al.

"Yes," she said.

"I didn't know if you would or not."

Customers were coming. Al told Sarah Ida what to do. Once she shined a pair of shoes all by herself.

They were busy most of the afternoon. Her hair fell down into her eyes. Her back hurt from bending over.

Late in the day Al told her, "You've had enough for now. You can go. You got some tips, didn't you?"

"Yes," she said. "Do you want me to count them?"

"No. You can keep them. And here's your pay." He gave her two dollars. "And I want to tell you something. When you get through with a customer, you say 'thank you.'"

"All right," she said.

"One more thing. You didn't say yesterday if you were coming back or not. This time I want to know. Are you coming back tomorrow?"

"Yes," she said.

"Come about the same time," he said. "I'm going to bring you something."

What he brought her was a white canvas apron. It had two pockets. It had straps that went over her shoulders and tied in the back. There were black letters across the front.

"Why does it say 'Lane's Lumber Company'?" she asked. "Why doesn't it say 'Al's Shoeshine Corner'?"

"Because it came from Lane's Lumber Company," he said. "Fred Lane is a friend of mine, and he gave it to me."

It was nothing but a canvas apron. She didn't know why she should be so pleased with it. But it was a long time since anything had pleased her as much. She liked the stiff, new feel of the cloth. The pockets were deep. She liked to put her hands into them.

290

That night she thought about the apron. She had left it locked up at the stand. She almost told her mother and father about it in the letter she wrote them. She had promised to write twice a week—to make Aunt Claudia happy. But she didn't think they would care about her apron. All she wrote was:

Dear Mother and Father,
I am all right. Everything is all right here. It was hot today.
Good-by,
SARAH IDA

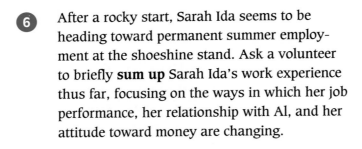

She didn't tell Aunt Claudia about her apron. She didn't feel too friendly toward Aunt Claudia.

There were times when she didn't even feel too friendly toward Al.

There was the time when she shined an old man's shoes. He paid her and went away. Al said, "I didn't hear you say 'thank you.'"

"He didn't give me any tip," she said. "The old stingy-guts."

They were alone at the stand. Al said, "What did you call him?"

"Old stingy-guts," she said. "That's what he is."

"Don't you ever say a thing like that again," said Al in a cold, hard voice. "He didn't have to give you a tip. Nobody has to. If he wants to give you something extra, that's his

291

After a rocky start, Sarah Ida seems to be heading toward permanent summer employment at the shoeshine stand. Ask a volunteer to briefly **sum up** Sarah Ida's work experience thus far, focusing on the ways in which her job performance, her relationship with Al, and her attitude toward money are changing.

business. But if he doesn't, that's his business, too. I want to hear you say 'thank you' whether you get any tip or not."

It scared her a little to see him so angry. She didn't speak to him for quite a while.

But that evening he said, as if nothing had happened, "I could use some help in the morning, too. You want to work here all day?"

"I don't know," she said.

"You can if you want to. Ask your aunt."

She started home. On the way, a boy caught up with her. His arms and legs were long, and he took long steps. He looked ugly, with his lower lip pushed out. He asked, "What are you doing working for Al?"

She walked faster. He kept up with her. "How much is he paying you?"

"I don't see why I should tell you," she said.

"You've got my job, that's why."

The light turned green, and she crossed the street. He didn't follow her.

All evening she thought about what the boy had said. In the morning she asked Al about it.

"Was he a skinny boy?" asked Al. "Did he have light hair?"

"Yes," she said.

"That was Kicker."

"His name is *Kicker?*"

"That's what he called himself when he was little. Now we all call him that. He's my neighbor."

"What did he mean when he said I had his job?"

"I don't know. Once I asked him if he wanted to work for me. He said he did. Then he never came to work. He didn't

292

want the job, but I guess he doesn't want you to have it, either."

"Maybe he changed his mind," she said. "Maybe he wants to work for you now."

"Maybe," said Al. "I'll have a talk with him. I don't think you'll see him anymore."

But later in the week she did see him. He was across the street, watching her.

Every evening, after work, Sarah Ida was tired. But every morning she was ready to go back to Shoeshine Corner. It wasn't that she liked shining shoes, but things *happened* at the shoeshine stand. Every customer was different. Every day she found out something new.

Some things she learned by herself. Like how much polish to use on a shoe. A thin coat gave a better and quicker shine. Some things Al told her. "When a customer comes here, he gets more than a shine," he said. "He gets to rest in a chair. When you rub with the cloth, it feels good on his feet. When you tie his shoelaces a little tighter, it makes his shoes fit better. My customers go away feeling a little better. Anyway, I *hope* they do."

One warm, cloudy afternoon, he said, "We might as well close up."

"Why?" she asked. "It's only three o'clock."

"It's going to rain. Nobody gets a shine on a rainy day."

He began to put away the brushes and shoe polish. She helped him.

"Maybe you can run home before the rain," he said. A few big drops splashed on the sidewalk. "No. Too late now."

293

7 Students may **wonder** about the feelings and actions of some of the characters. They may be curious, for example, about why Kicker is so upset over a job that he did not really want; about why Al sometimes treats Sarah Ida harshly; or about why Sarah Ida's feelings toward Aunt Claudia, Al, and the shoeshine job are so ambivalent. Encourage the students to share their wonderings with the class.

Some students may be able to **make connections** between the characters'—particularly Sarah Ida's and Kicker's—feelings and experiences and their own. If so, encourage those students to discuss with the class the connections they have made.

They sat under the little roof, out of the rain.

"Hear that sound?" he said. "Every time I hear rain on a tin roof, I get to thinking about when I was a boy. We lived in an old truck with a tin roof over the back."

"You *lived* in a truck?"

"Most of the time. We slept under the tin roof, and when it rained, the sound put me to sleep. We went all over the South in that truck."

"You and your mother and father?"

"My dad and I."

"What were you doing, driving all over the South?"

"My dad sold medicine."

"What kind?"

"Something to make you strong and keep you from getting sick."

"Did you take it?"

"No. I guess it wasn't any good."

She had never heard him talk much about himself before. She wanted him to go on.

"Was it fun living in a truck?"

"Fun? I wouldn't say so. Riding along was all right. Sometimes my dad and I stopped close to the woods, and that was all right, too. But I never liked it when we were in town selling medicine. Dad would play the <u>mouth harp</u>, and he made me sing. He wanted me to dance a jig, too, but I never could."

She tried to imagine Al as a little boy. She couldn't at all. "Why did he want you to sing and dance?" she asked.

"To draw a crowd. When there was a crowd, he sold medicine. We didn't stay anywhere very long. Except once.

294

We stayed in one place six months. My dad did farm work, and I went to school."

He told her about the school. It was just outside a town. The teacher was Miss Miller. The schoolhouse had only one room.

"There was this big stove," he said, "and that winter I kept the fire going. Miss Miller never had to carry coal when I was there."

"Did you like her?" asked Sarah Ida. "Was she a good teacher?"

"Best teacher I ever had. Of course, she was just about the *only* one. I hadn't been to school much, but she took time to show me things. Do teachers still give medals in school?"

"Sometimes. Not very often."

"Miss Miller gave medals. They were all alike. Every one had a star on it. At the end of school you got one if you were the best in reading or spelling or writing or whatever it was. Everybody wanted a medal, but I knew I'd never get one because I wasn't the best in anything. And at the end of school, you know what happened?"

"What?"

"She called my name. The others all thought it was a joke. But she wasn't laughing. She said, 'Al wins a medal for building the best fires.'"

"And it *wasn't* a joke?" asked Sarah Ida.

"No. She gave me the medal. One of the big boys said, 'You better keep that, Al, because it's the only one you'll ever get.'"

"And did you keep it?"

He held up his watch chain. Something was hanging from it—something that looked like a worn, old coin.

295

"That's what you won?" asked Sarah Ida.

He nodded.

"That's a medal?" she said. "That little old piece of tin?"

She shouldn't have said it. As soon as the words were out, she was sorry.

Al sat very still. He looked into the street. A moment before, he had been a friend. Now he was a stranger.

He said, "Rain's stopped. For a while, anyway."

He slid out of his chair. She got up, too. "I—" she began.

He dragged the folding door across the stand and locked up.

"Go on. Run," he said. "Maybe you can get home before the rain starts again."

She stood there. "I didn't mean what you think I did," she said. "That medal—it doesn't matter if it's tin or silver or gold. It doesn't matter *what* it's made of, if it's something you like. I said the wrong thing, but it wasn't what I *meant*. I—" He had his back to her. She didn't think he was listening. She said, "*Listen* to me!"

He turned around. "You like ice cream?"

"Yes," she said.

"Come on. I'll buy you a cone."

She went with him, around the corner to Pearl's Ice Cream Shack.

"What kind?" he asked.

"Chocolate," she said.

They sat on a bench inside the Shack and ate their chocolate cones.

"It's raining again," he said.

"Yes," she said.

Then they were quiet, while they listened to the rain. And she was happy because the stranger was gone and Al was back. **8**

MEET CLYDE ROBERT BULLA, AUTHOR

The idea for Shoeshine Girl *came from an experience Clyde Robert Bulla had at a streetside shoeshine stand in Santa Barbara, California. Bulla suspects that he was the first customer of a shoeshine girl who was about nine years old. She shined one of his shoes while a somewhat gruff shoeshine man shined the other.*

"She spilled the water and dropped the shoe polish," Bulla remembers. "Every time she did something wrong, she would hunch her shoulders and look up at the man and say, 'Oh, my! Oh, my!' as if she expected him to scold her."

Later, when Shoeshine Girl *had won the Children's Book Award in three states, Bulla tried to find the real shoeshine girl. He wanted to give her one of the medals that the book had earned. He tried to locate her at the shoeshine stand and then through inquiries at area schools. The local newspaper ran a story urging the little girl, whom they called "Cinderella Shoeshine Girl," to come forward, but she never did.*

"I still have this medal for her," says Bulla.

297

8 Ask a volunteer to **sum up** this final exchange between Al and Sarah Ida. Then have a few students collaborate in summing up the entire story, examining the many ways in which Sarah Ida's attitudes change from beginning to end.

Remind the students to check any predictions they made during the course of reading the story. Some students may like to **predict** what will happen to Sarah Ida when she returns home to her parents at the end of the summer.

Discussing Strategy Use

Encourage the students to share any problems they encountered while reading "The Shoeshine Stand" and to tell which strategies they used to solve those problems.

Reflecting on the Selection
Whole-Group Discussion

The whole group discusses the selection and any personal thoughts, reactions, or questions that it raises. During this time, students also **return to the clues, problems, and wonderings** they noted on the board during browsing.

Assessment

To assess their understanding of the text, engage the students in a discussion to determine whether they have grasped the following idea:
- how Sarah Ida's attitude toward work and her feelings about Al evolve over the course of the story

Response Journal

Sarah Ida is a girl who is about the students' own age and whose experiences, feelings, and relationships with other people may remind the students of events in their own lives. Provide time for the students to record their reactions to the story in their personal response journals.

Exploring Concepts Within the Selection
Small-Group Discussion

Small groups discuss the relation of the selection to the explorable concepts. Circulate among the groups and observe the discussions. Remind the students to refer to the Concept Board and the Question Board to keep them focused on their original ideas about value.

Sharing Ideas About Explorable Concepts

Have the groups **report their ideas** and **discuss them** with the rest of the class. It is crucial that the students' ideas determine this discussion.
- Students may notice that Sarah Ida values her work apron highly even though Al paid no money for it. They may point out that although she is quite self-centered at first, she eventually looks to her own feelings to help her understand Al's, recognizing at last that the worth of an object depends mostly on how much someone cares about it.
- Students may realize that although she does not always articulate such feelings, Sarah Ida grows to value her accomplishments as a shoeshine girl and her relationship with Al and his customers as much as she values the money she earns.

As these ideas and others are stated, have the students **add them to** the **Question Board** or the **Concept Board.**

TEACHING TIP Teach in such a way that you become a collaborator with your students rather than the controller of their learning processes.

Exploring Concepts Across Selections

Ask the students how this story reminds them of others that they have read. Students may make connections with other selections in the unit.
- Students may note that both Sarah Ida and Tiffany, from "Money Matters," are rewarded for their resourcefulness and their responsible behavior.
- Students may compare Sarah Ida's first money-making schemes with the scheme of the miner's brother in "A Gift for a Gift." Both characters use deceitful tactics to try to get what they want, and both see their plans fail.

Recording Ideas

As students complete the above discussions, ask them to **sum up what they have learned from their conversations and to tell how**

Recording Concept Information continued

"A Gift for a Gift" by Eric Protter

_____
_____
_____
_____
_____
_____
_____

"What Money Is" by R. V. Fodor

_____
_____
_____
_____
_____
_____

"The Shoeshine Stand" by Clyde Robert Bulla

_____
_____
_____
_____
_____
_____

106 EN   Value/Unit 6

Copyright © 1995 Open Court Publishing Company

Explorer's Notebook, page 106

they might use this information in further explorations. Any special information or insights may be recorded on the **Concept Board.** Any further questions that they would like to think about, pursue, or investigate may be recorded on the **Question Board.** They may want to discuss the progress that has been made on their questions. They may also want to cross out any questions that no longer warrant consideration.

➤ Following the discussion, students should record their ideas and impressions about the selection and the concepts on page 106 of their Explorer's Notebook.

Evaluating Discussions

Professional Checkpoint: Cognitive and Responsive Reading

By this point in the year, the students themselves should be taking over the complex strategies, such as making connections. They should be commenting spontaneously almost all of the time, relying on teacher intervention only infrequently.

Notes:

2 READING WITH A WRITER'S EYE

MINILESSONS

Writer's Craft: Characterization

Ask students to discuss the ways in which a writer reveals his or her characters to readers. By now, students should know that besides simply describing a character, the writer can **have the character do or say certain things that indicate his or her personality or mood.** Good writers let their readers learn about their characters in a variety of ways.

Clyde Bulla reveals Sarah Ida to his readers in some interesting ways. Her **character** is largely **revealed through** her **relationships with other people and** her **reactions to adverse situations.** Ask students to give their impressions of Sarah Ida. In the early part of the story, she is not a particularly sympathetic character; and most students probably will not like her. In "The Shoeshine Stand," Sarah Ida's very first conversation with her aunt shows that she is impolite. She does not once say please or thank you. In fact, she does not use polite language anywhere in the selection—not when she borrows money from Rossi; not when she asks for and gets a job; and not when she gets a tip.

Selective Reading: Focus on Characterization

Now have students go back to the selection and find other ways in which Bulla reveals Sarah Ida's or any of the other characters' personalities to his readers. Examples include the following:

- page 271, paragraph 12: Sarah Ida interrupts her aunt while she is talking; Aunt Claudia tries to help Sarah Ida find a friend; Sarah Ida is indifferent to everything that her aunt offers.
- page 272, paragraph 1: Sarah Ida wants to be paid for helping Aunt Claudia keep house, even for taking care of her own room.
- page 273, paragraphs 10–14: Sarah Ida does not answer when Aunt Claudia tells her that Rossi has arrived, and she only goes downstairs to stop Rossi from going upstairs.
- page 275, all paragraphs: Sarah Ida browbeats Rossi into lending her money.
- page 290, paragraph 5: Al tells Sarah Ida to start saying thank you to the customers.

Selection-Based Practice

Independent Practice: Characterization

▶ Have the students work individually or in small groups to extend their knowledge of characterization by completing Reading/Writing Connection, page 44.

Writer's Craft: Dialogue

Ask students to discuss why writers use **dialogue** when they write fiction. Students should already understand that dialogue is one way in which a writer **reveals information about the characters** in a story. Explain to the students that dialogue also makes readers feel as though they were witnessing the action of a story as it happens. Dialogue **is often used to move along the plot of a story.**

Now ask the students why **speaker tags** are used when writing dialogue. The most obvious reason, of course, is **to avoid confusion about**

"The Shoeshine Stand"

Characterization

In "The Shoeshine Stand," or in other stories that you have read, look for interesting ways in which authors develop their fictional characters. Write the title of the story, the page number and paragraph in which the character is presented or described, and what the passage shows about the character.

Title: _____

Page and paragraph(s): _____

What the passage shows about the character: _____

_____

Title: _____

Page and paragraph(s): _____

What the passage shows about the character: _____

_____

Title: _____

Page and paragraph(s): _____

What the passage shows about the character: _____

_____

Title: _____

Page and paragraph(s): _____

What the passage shows about the character: _____

_____

Refer to this page when you want to show what a character in your own writing is like.

Characterization
_____
44 R/WC   Value/Unit 6

Name

Copyright © 1995 Open Court Publishing Company

Reading/Writing Connection, page 44

who is saying what. Students should know, however, that speaker tags also serve to **reveal mood as well as character.** The adverbs used in speaker tags to describe *how* something is said also contribute to mood and characterization.

Now point out that as is true for most elements of the writer's craft, **speaker tags can be overdone.** Readers can get bored very quickly with long stretches of dialogue with speaker tags on every line. That is why good writers will often use techniques other than speaker tags to show their readers who is speaking. In "The Shoeshine Stand," Bulla employs several methods to avoid overusing speaker tags. In the first conversation in the story, on pages 270 and 271, Sarah Ida has just come down to breakfast. Point out the reasons for having or not having speaker tags.

Aunt Claudia was there, frying bacon and eggs. "Good morning," she said. "Did you sleep well?" (This is Aunt Claudia's first remark in the story, so the speaker tag is necessary.)

"Yes," said Sarah Ida. (This is her first remark.)

"There's apple jelly and plum jam. Which would you like with your toast?" (No speaker tag is necessary since Aunt Claudia is the one preparing breakfast, and she is the one who would ask the question.)

"Neither one." (Readers expect Sarah Ida to answer, so no speaker tag is necessary here, either.)

Point out that Bulla shapes the dialogue and the narrative so that his readers can easily figure out who is talking even when he uses no speaker tags. It is easier to omit speaker tags when only two persons are talking. Make sure that students understand that a new paragraph indicates a change in speaker.

On page 271, paragraph 6, Bulla employs another method of showing who the speaker is without using a speaker tag:

Sarah Ida frowned. "I don't know any Rossi Wigginhorn." (Because the author begins the paragraph by describing Sarah Ida, readers should be able to tell that she is the speaker.)

Yet another method is used on page 273, paragraph 8:

"All right, Sarah Ida. That's enough." (Because the conversation is between Sarah Ida and Aunt Claudia and because Sarah Ida is addressed in this piece of dialogue, it is easy to tell that Aunt Claudia is the speaker.)

Selective Reading: Focus on Dialogue

Selection-Based Practice

Now have students look for other examples in "The Shoeshine Stand" in which Bulla uses dialogue with or without speaker tags to advance the plot or to reveal character or mood.

This story is full of dialogue. Students should have no difficulty finding passages that contain dialogue with and without speaker tags. Whenever someone cites an example, ask her or him to tell which character is speaking which lines and to explain how she or he determined this.

Other good examples can be found on the following pages:
- page 280, paragraphs 3–20: In this passage Sarah Ida, a parrot, a woman, and a man speak. The dialogue is easy to follow in terms of who is talking until the bottom of the page, where either the man or the woman asks Sarah, "What can you do?" Point out that it makes no difference which of them asks the question, since the question does not affect the plot or any of the characters.
- page 282, all paragraphs: In this passage, Sarah Ida asks Al Winkler for a job at his stand. There are a lot of speaker changes without speaker tags. Students should have no problem explaining how the reader can tell who is speaking which lines.
- pages 294–295, all paragraphs: This passage in which Al describes his childhood to Sarah Ida also has few speaker tags. Readers can easily infer who the speaker is by what is being said.

Independent Practice: Dialogue

▶ For additional practice in analyzing dialogue with speaker tags, have students work independently or in small groups to complete Reading/Writing Connection, page 45.

"The Shoeshine Stand"

Dialogue

Look at "The Shoeshine Stand" or at other stories that you have read for examples of dialogue and speaker tags. Write the title of the story, the page on which the dialogue begins, the reason for using dialogue (to reveal character, etc.), and the speaker tags.

Title: _____ Page: _____
Reason for using dialogue: _____
_____
Interesting speaker tags: _____
_____

Title: _____ Page: _____
Reason for using dialogue: _____
_____
Interesting speaker tags: _____
_____

Title: _____ Page: _____
Reason for using dialogue: _____
_____
Interesting speaker tags: _____
_____

Title: _____ Page: _____
Reason for using dialogue: _____
_____
Interesting speaker tags: _____
_____

Name

Copyright © 1995 Open Court Publishing Company

Unit 6/Value

Dialogue
R/WC 45

Reading/Writing Connection, page 45

WRITING

Linking Reading to Writing

Encourage students to use what they have learned about characterization and about dialogue with and without speaker tags to revise and improve some of their own writing.

* Writing Process

If students have elected to publish any previously written, revised, and proofread pieces, encourage them to place the pieces in the classroom library to share with the rest of the class.

VOCABULARY

The vocabulary in "The Shoeshine Stand" is well within reach of most students at this level. Some words or phrases that may come up during discussion are *pocket money, blackmail,* and *offend.* Encourage the students to fill out Vocabulary Exploration forms, Reproducible Master 15, for any new words and phrases that they want to remember. Remind them to add the forms to the Personal Dictionary section of their Writer's Notebook. For additional opportunities to build vocabulary, see **Teacher Tool Card 77.**

Adding to Personal Word Lists

3 GUIDED AND INDEPENDENT EXPLORATION

EXPLORING CONCEPTS BEYOND THE TEXT

Guided Exploration

Students will select activities in which they explore the concepts related to value. Refer them to the **Exploration Activities poster** and give them time to choose an activity. Allow them to discuss what they wish to explore and how they wish to go about it. If the students need further help, here is one suggestion:

* Engage the students in a discussion of their prized possessions. Invite volunteers to tell the class what their favorite belongings are and why. Encourage the students to examine the various reasons why their prized possessions are so valuable to them. Students may give reasons related to sentimental value, monetary value, usefulness, attractiveness, entertainment value, and value as a status symbol. Following the discussion, some students may enjoy creating illustrations and/or writing brief descriptions of their prized possessions to post on the Concept Board or elsewhere in the classroom.

At this time, students can return to pages 114–115 in their Explorer's Notebook to continue examining, discussing, and recording what the story characters value most.

➤ Distribute Home/School Connection 44, which encourages students to find out about the first jobs held by older members of their families. Allow time later for students to share their findings with the class.

Continuing Exploration

Encourage the students to discuss what they have learned about value from their reading and their discussions. If important concepts or ideas about value are expressed, be sure to have the students add these to the Concept Board.

✳ *Exploring Through Reflective Activities*

TEACHING TIP Encourage students to answer other students' questions or to suggest where answers might be found.

A message from _____

Our class has just finished reading "The Shoeshine Stand." In this excerpt from Clyde Robert Bulla's *Shoeshine Girl*, a money-hungry young girl gets her first job, as an assistant at a shoeshine stand. Ask your child to tell you more about the story.

Then share with your child the story of your own first job. These are some questions that you might want to answer: Where or for whom did you work? What were your responsibilities? What were your wages? How did you feel about having a job? Besides your paycheck, what were the rewards of your job? What were the drawbacks? Did you have to give up anything you enjoyed because of your job? How did you spend the money you earned? If your first job was particularly unusual or if you held a position that is now obsolete, make sure to explain this to your child, too.

If your child has any kind of job of his or her own, compare your thoughts and experiences with your child's. Encourage your child to share his or her findings with the class.

Notes: _____
_____
_____
_____
_____
_____
_____
_____
_____
_____
_____
_____
_____
_____

Unit 6/Value   H/SC 44

Copyright © 1995 Open Court Publishing Company

Home/School Connection 44

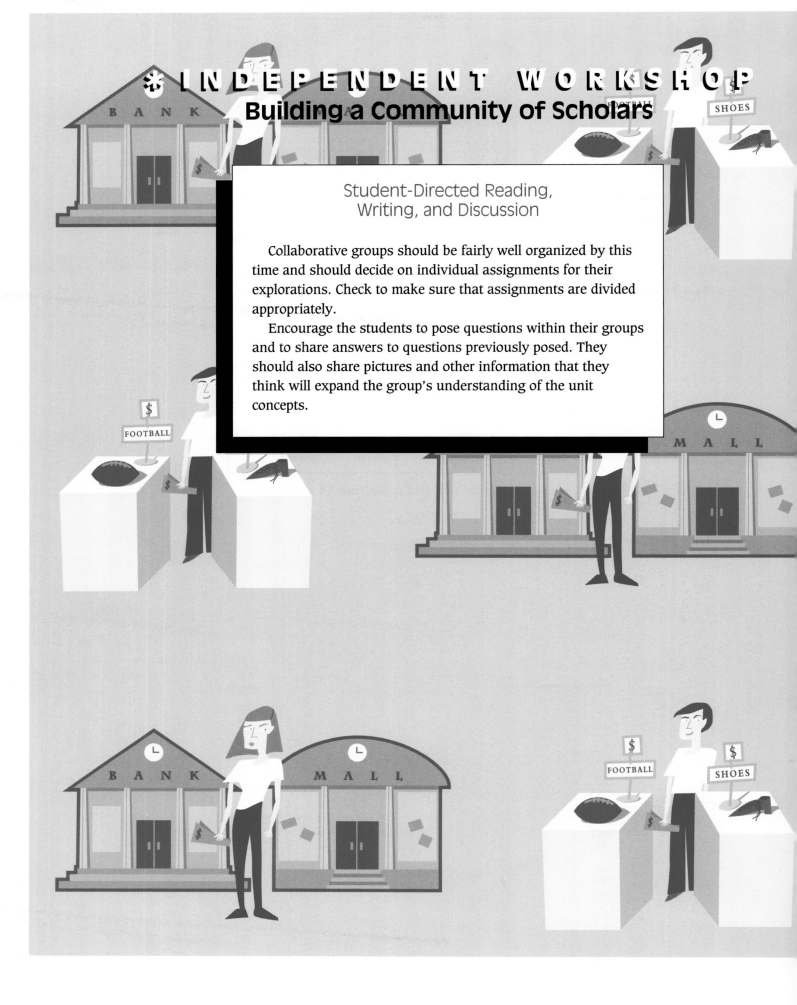

* INDEPENDENT WORKSHOP
Building a Community of Scholars

Student-Directed Reading, Writing, and Discussion

Collaborative groups should be fairly well organized by this time and should decide on individual assignments for their explorations. Check to make sure that assignments are divided appropriately.

Encourage the students to pose questions within their groups and to share answers to questions previously posed. They should also share pictures and other information that they think will expand the group's understanding of the unit concepts.

Additional Opportunities for Independent Reading, Writing, and Cross-curricular Activities

✳ Reading Roundtable

Remind students about the Tradebook Connection Cards in the Student Toolbox. If any of them would like to find out more about Sarah Ida's job at the shoeshine stand, suggest that they read Clyde Robert Bulla's *Shoeshine Girl.* Other books by Bulla that they may also enjoy include *Charlie's House, Ghost of Windy Hill,* and *A Lion to Guard Us.*

✳ Writing Seminar

Some students may still be working on the modern adaptations of a folk tale that they began after reading "A Gift for a Gift." Allow them time to work on those. Others may wish to continue revising pieces from their writing folders by improving characterization or adding speaker tags. Remind them to refer to the writing strategy posters if they need help with their writing. Encourage them to begin new pieces about value or about any topic that interests them whenever they wish.

Portfolio

Remind the students to think about choosing pieces of writing to put into their portfolios.

Cross-curricular Activity Cards

The following Cross-curricular Activity Cards in the Student Toolbox are appropriate for this selection:
- 29 Social Studies—Snake Oil
- 8 Math—How Much to Tip?

Additional Opportunities for Solving Learning Problems

Tutorial

You may want to use this time to work with students who need help in any area. The following aids are available in the Teacher Toolbox for your convenience:
- Writer's Craft/Reading: Characterization, Teacher Tool Card 13
- Writer's Craft/Reading: Using Dialogue in a Story, Teacher Tool Card 20
- Writer's Craft/Reading: Point of View, Teacher Tool Card 12
- Spelling and Vocabulary: Using and Punctuating Contractions, Teacher Tool Card 82

The Gold Coin

1 READING THE SELECTION

INFORMATION FOR THE TEACHER

About the Selection

Juan is a thief. He works at night and has not a friend or a relative in the world. Josefa is the local healer. One night, through the window of her cottage, Juan spots Josefa holding a gold coin in her hand and decides to rob her as soon as possible. Before he can carry out his plan, Doña Josefa and her gold depart on a long journey to help an ailing grandfather. Juan sets out after her, but the industrious old medicine woman always remains one step ahead of him as she visits one sick person after another. Will he ever catch up with her? Readers will enjoy learning what happens to Juan along the way. Delicate watercolor illustrations enhance Alma Flor Ada's poignant and engaging text.

Link to the Unit Concepts

The message of *The Gold Coin,* pages 298–309, is beautifully presented but very simple. As he follows Doña Josefa through the countryside, stopping often to help local farmers with their work, Juan learns that friendship, hard work, and concern for other people are more rewarding than money alone.

About the Author

Alma Flor Ada, born in Camagüey, Cuba, in 1938, is an educator, a poet, and an author of children's books. Ada writes mainly in Spanish. She also translates children's books from English into Spanish.

INFORMATION FOR THE STUDENT

This story is about a folk healer in a rural area. Folk medicine has been practiced for centuries, and today doctors recognize the benefits of many of the remedies that healers use to treat their patients. In fact, many modern medicines have been developed from herbs or plant roots that healers have known about since long before the beginnings of

Background Information

LESSON OVERVIEW

The Gold Coin by Alma Flor Ada, pages 298–309

READING THE SELECTION

Materials

Student anthology, pp. 298–309
Explorer's Notebook, p. 107

READING WITH A WRITER'S EYE

Minilessons

Writer's Craft: Story Structure
Writer's Craft: Using Sensory
  Descriptions

Materials

Reading/Writing Connection, pp. 46–47
Reproducible Masters 15, 40

FYI

Teacher Tool Card
• Spelling and Vocabulary: Building
  Vocabulary, 77

Option for Instruction

Writer's Craft: Indicators of Place and
  Location
(Use Teacher Tool Card listed below.)

GUIDED AND INDEPENDENT EXPLORATION

Materials

Explorer's Notebook, pp. 117–118

Independent Workshop

**Optional Materials from
Student Toolbox**

Tradebook Connection Cards

Cross-curricular Activity Cards
• 30 Social Studies—Folk Medicine
• 19 Science—First Aid

Student Tool Cards
• Writer's Craft/Reading: Plot, 15
• Writer's Craft/Reading: Giving
  Descriptions, 40
• Writer's Craft/Reading: Signal Words
  Showing Place and Location, 30

FYI

Learning Framework Card
• Reading Roundtable, 6

Teacher Tool Cards
• Writer's Craft/Reading: Plot, 15
• Writer's Craft/Reading: Elaboration
  Through Providing Descriptions, 40
• Writer's Craft/Reading: Indicators of
  Place and Location, 30

NOTES

Asterisks (*) throughout the lesson indicate learning frameworks. Learning Framework Cards and Teacher Tool Cards can be found in the Teacher Toolbox.

modern medicine. Students should understand that in nonindustrialized regions folk healers have a legitimate and respected role. You might also point out that typically folk healers receive little financial compensation for their services.

Another thing that you may wish to discuss with students is the value of the gold coin in the story. In times when gold was used as currency, it was extremely rare for peasants to see gold, much less possess a gold coin. Peasants bartered for their needs. The gold coin that Doña Josefa offered and the people refused was truly a small fortune to all of them.

*

COGNITIVE AND RESPONSIVE READING

Activating Prior Knowledge

The ideas presented in this story have been discussed earlier in the unit. It should not be necessary to repeat such a discussion.

Setting Reading Goals and Expectations

Have the students **browse** the **first page** of the selection using the **clues/problems/wondering procedure.** Students will return to these observations after reading.

Recommendations for Reading the Selection

Ask the students how they want to read the selection. Students may enjoy **reading aloud** this simple but delightful folk tale. During **oral reading,** use and encourage think-alouds. During **silent reading,** allow discussion as necessary. Discuss problems, strategies, and reactions after reading.

This would also be a good selection for **responding** to text **by visualizing** while reading aloud. Model this response, and then invite the students to do the same.

About the Reading Strategies

Owing to the episodic nature of *The Gold Coin,* students may follow the entire story line more easily if they employ the strategy of **summing up** after each of Juan's encounters with the families of Doña Josefa's patients. Students may also want to **predict** what will happen to Juan as he reaches each successive destination.

STEPS TOWARD INDEPENDENCE By this time in the year, on the basis of their browsing, the students should be able to suggest strategies to use while reading.

Think-Aloud Prompts for Use in Oral Reading

Notice the think-aloud prompts with the page miniatures. These prompts may prove useful if students encounter passages that are unclear to them; however, the prompts are only suggestions. Remind the students that what they read should make sense to them. If it does not, they should refer to the **reading strategy posters** for help with what to do next. Invite students to share whatever strategies they use to solve reading problems.

THINK ALOUD PROMPTS

These prompts may be used as guides to promote cognitive and responsive reading.

2 Like Juan, some students may **wonder** where Doña Josefa's gold is hidden. The students will likely have many ideas and opinions about the gold and its location. Encourage the students to wonder aloud.

This passage also marks a natural place to **predict** what Juan will do next. Encourage students to share their predictions with the class. Remind them to check those predictions as they continue to read.

1 Juan's appearance reflects his character. In order to understand how unpleasant Juan's appearance is, students may need to **visualize** this description of him. Invite students to share and discuss their visualizations with the class.

THE GOLD COIN
Alma Flor Ada
translated by Bernice Randall
illustrated by Neil Waldman

Juan had been a thief for many years. Because he did his stealing by night, his skin had become pale and sickly. Because he spent his time either hiding or sneaking about, his body had become shriveled and bent. And because he had neither friend nor relative to make him smile, his face was always twisted into an angry frown.

One night, drawn by a light shining through the trees, Juan came upon a hut. He crept up to the door and through a crack saw an old woman sitting at a plain, wooden table.

What was that shining in her hand? Juan wondered. He could not believe his eyes. It was a gold coin. Then he heard the woman say to herself, "I must be the richest person in the world."

Juan decided instantly that all the woman's gold must be his. He thought that the easiest thing to do was to watch until the woman left.

 1

298

Juan hid in the bushes and huddled under his <u>poncho</u>, waiting for the right moment to enter the hut.

Juan was half asleep when he heard knocking at the door and the sound of insistent voices. A few minutes later, he saw the woman, wrapped in a black cloak, leave the hut with two men at her side.

Here's my chance! Juan thought. And, forcing open a window, he climbed into the empty hut.

He looked about eagerly for the gold. He looked under the bed. It wasn't there. He looked in the cupboard. It wasn't there, either. Where could it be? Close to despair, Juan tore away some beams supporting the <u>thatch</u> roof.

Finally, he gave up. There was simply no gold in the hut.

All I can do, he thought, is to find the old woman and make her tell me where she's hidden it.

2

So he set out along the path that she and her two companions had taken.

It was daylight by the time Juan reached the river. The countryside had been deserted, but here, along the riverbank, were two huts. Nearby, a man and his son were hard at work, hoeing potatoes.

It had been a long, long time since Juan had spoken to another human being. Yet his desire to find the woman was so strong that he went up to the farmers and asked, in a hoarse, raspy voice, "Have you seen a short, gray-haired woman, wearing a black cloak?"

"Oh, you must be looking for Doña Josefa," the young boy said. "Yes, we've seen her. We went to fetch her this morning, because my grandfather had another attack of—"

"Where is she now?" Juan broke in.

"She is long gone," said the father with a smile. "Some people from across the river came looking for her, because someone in their family is sick."

"How can I get across the river?" Juan asked anxiously.

"Only by boat," the boy answered. "We'll row you across later, if you'd like." Then turning back to his work, he added, "But first we must finish digging up the potatoes."

The thief muttered, "Thanks." But he quickly grew impatient. He grabbed a hoe and began to help the pair of farmers. The sooner we finish, the sooner we'll get across the river, he thought. And the sooner I'll get to my gold!

It was dusk when they finally laid down their hoes. The soil had been turned, and the wicker baskets were brimming with potatoes.

"Now can you row me across?" Juan asked the father anxiously.

"Certainly," the man said. "But let's eat supper first."

Juan had forgotten the taste of a home-cooked meal and the pleasure that comes from sharing it with others. As he sopped up the last of the stew with a chunk of dark bread, memories of other meals came back to him from far away and long ago.

By the light of the moon, father and son guided their boat across the river.

"What a wonderful healer Doña Josefa is!" the boy told Juan. "All she had to do to make Abuelo better was give him a cup of her special tea."

"Yes, and not only that," his father added, "she brought him a gold coin."

Juan was stunned. It was one thing for Doña Josefa to go around helping people. But how could she go around handing out gold coins—*his gold coins?*

When the threesome finally reached the other side of the river, they saw a young man sitting outside his hut.

301

Doña (dô´ nyä)
Josefa (hô sä´ fä)

Abuelo (ä bwä´ lō)

"This fellow is looking for Doña Josefa," the father said, pointing to Juan.

"Oh, she left some time ago," the young man said.

"Where to?" Juan asked tensely.

"Over to the other side of the mountain," the young man replied, pointing to the vague outline of mountains in the night sky.

"How did she get there?" Juan asked, trying to hide his impatience.

"By horse," the young man answered. "They came on horseback to get her because someone had broken his leg."

"Well, then, I need a horse, too," Juan said urgently.

"Tomorrow," the young man replied softly. "Perhaps I can take you tomorrow, maybe the next day. First I must finish harvesting the corn."

So Juan spent the next day in the fields, bathed in sweat from sunup to sundown.

Yet each ear of corn that he picked seemed to bring him closer to his treasure. And later that evening, when he helped the young man husk several ears so they could boil them for supper, the yellow kernels glittered like gold coins.

302

While they were eating, Juan thought about Doña Josefa. Why, he wondered, would someone who said she was the world's richest woman spend her time taking care of every sick person for miles around?

The following day, the two set off at dawn. Juan could not recall when he last had noticed the beauty of the sunrise. He felt strangely moved by the sight of the mountains, barely lit by the faint rays of the morning sun.

As they neared the foothills, the young man said, "I'm not surprised you're looking for Doña Josefa. The whole countryside needs her. I went for her because my wife had been running a high fever. In no time at all, Doña Josefa had her on the road to recovery. And what's more, my friend, she brought her a gold coin!"

Juan groaned inwardly. To think that someone could hand out gold so freely! What a strange woman Doña Josefa is, Juan thought. Not only is she willing to help one person

303

3 Again, the students, like Juan, may be **wondering.** Encourage them to discuss their ideas about why the mysterious Doña Josefa does what she does.

after another, but she doesn't mind traveling all over the countryside to do it!

"Well, my friend," said the young man finally, "this is where I must leave you. But you don't have far to walk. See that house over there? It belongs to the man who broke his leg."

The young man stretched out his hand to say good-bye. Juan stared at it for a moment. It had been a long, long time since the thief had shaken hands with anyone. Slowly, he pulled out a hand from under his poncho. When his companion grasped it firmly in his own, Juan felt suddenly warmed, as if by the rays of the sun.

But after he thanked the young man, Juan ran down the road. He was still eager to catch up with Doña Josefa. When he reached the house, a woman and a child were stepping down from a wagon.

"Have you seen Doña Josefa?" Juan asked.

"We've just taken her to Don Teodosio's," the woman said. "His wife is sick, you know—"

"How do I get there?" Juan broke in. "I've got to see her."

🐚 304 🐚

"It's too far to walk," the woman said amiably. "If you'd like, I'll take you there tomorrow. But first I must gather my squash and beans."

So Juan spent yet another long day in the fields. Working beneath the summer sun, Juan noticed that his skin had begun to tan. And although he had to stoop down to pick the squash, he found that he could now stretch his body. His back had begun to straighten, too.

Later, when the little girl took him by the hand to show him a family of rabbits burrowed under a fallen tree, Juan's face broke into a smile. It had been a long, long time since Juan had smiled.

Yet his thoughts kept coming back to the gold.

The following day, the wagon carrying Juan and the woman lumbered along a road lined with coffee fields.

The woman said, "I don't know what we would have done without Doña Josefa. I sent my daughter to our neighbor's house, who then brought Doña Josefa on horseback. She set my husband's leg and then showed me how to brew a special tea to lessen the pain."

4 By now, students will want to **predict** what will happen to Juan when he reaches the home of the man with the broken leg. Allow a volunteer to explain his or her prediction to the other students, telling how it is based on the reading thus far.

Remind the students to review earlier predictions and see if they were correct.

Teodosio (tā ō dô′ sē ō)

Getting no reply, she went on. "And, as if that weren't enough, she brought him a gold coin. Can you imagine such a thing?"

Juan could only sigh. No doubt about it, he thought, Doña Josefa is someone special. But Juan didn't know whether to be happy that Doña Josefa had so much gold she could freely hand it out, or angry for her having already given so much of it away.

When they finally reached Don Teodosio's house, Doña Josefa was already gone. But here, too, there was work that needed to be done . . .

Juan stayed to help with the coffee harvest. As he picked the red berries, he gazed up from time to time at the trees that grew, row upon row, along the hillsides. What a calm,

peaceful place this is! he thought.

The next morning, Juan was up at daybreak. Bathed in the soft, dawn light, the mountains seemed to smile at him. When Don Teodosio offered him a lift on horseback, Juan found it difficult to have to say good-bye.

"What a good woman Doña Josefa is!" Don Teodosio said, as they rode down the hill toward the sugarcane fields. "The minute she heard about my wife being sick, she

came with her special herbs. And as if that weren't enough, she brought my wife a gold coin!"

In the stifling heat, the kind that often signals the approach of a storm, Juan simply sighed and mopped his brow. The pair continued riding for several hours in silence.

Juan then realized he was back in familiar territory, for they were now on the stretch of road he had traveled only a week ago—though how much longer it now seemed to him. He jumped off Don Teodosio's horse and broke into a run.

This time the gold would not escape him! But he had to move quickly, so he could find shelter before the storm broke.

Out of breath, Juan finally reached Doña Josefa's hut. She was standing by the door, shaking her head slowly as she surveyed the ransacked house.

"So I've caught up with you at last!" Juan shouted, startling the old woman. "Where's the gold?"

"The gold coin?" Doña Josefa said, surprised and looking at Juan intently. "Have you come for the gold coin? I've been trying hard to give it to someone who might need it," Doña Josefa said. "First to an old man who had just gotten over a bad attack. Then to a young woman

307

5 This paragraph marks another turning point in Juan's story, as he catches up to Doña Josefa at long last. The students may want to stop here to **predict** what Juan will do now. Remind them to consider all the information they already have.

Then, before the students resume reading, ask a volunteer to **sum up** the most important parts of the story so far. A good summary might include brief mention of all the people Juan has met, the work he has done, and the changes his experiences have wrought on his body and mind. If any of the students are puzzled about why Doña Josefa's house appears ransacked, a summary might also serve to remind them of the answer.

who had been running a fever. Then to a man with a broken leg. And finally to Don Teodosio's wife. But none of them would take it. They all said, 'Keep it. There must be someone who needs it more.'"

Juan did not say a word.

"You must be the one who needs it," Doña Josefa said.

She took the coin out of her pocket and handed it to him. Juan stared at the coin, speechless.

At that moment a young girl appeared, her long braid bouncing as she ran. "Hurry, Doña Josefa, please!" she said breathlessly. "My mother is all alone, and the baby is due any minute."

"Of course, dear," Doña Josefa replied. But as she glanced up at the sky, she saw nothing but black clouds. The storm was nearly upon them. Doña Josefa sighed deeply.

"But how can I leave now? Look at my house! I don't know what has happened to the roof. The storm will wash the whole place away!"

And there was a deep sadness in her voice.

Juan took in the child's frightened eyes, Doña Josefa's sad, distressed face, and the ransacked hut.

"Go ahead, Doña Josefa," he said. "Don't worry about your house. I'll see that the roof is back in shape, good as new."

The woman nodded gratefully, drew her cloak about her shoulders, and took the child by the hand. As she turned to leave, Juan held out his hand.

"Here, take this," he said, giving her the gold coin. "I'm sure the newborn will need it more than I."

6

❊ 309 ❊

---

6 Have a volunteer quickly **sum up** the final "chapter" in Juan's saga. Allow time for students to compare their predictions with what really happened: did the ending surprise them or was it just what they predicted?

Discussing Strategy Use
Encourage the students to share with each other any difficulties they may have had while reading the story and the strategies they used to help them solve these problems.

✳

EXPLORING THROUGH DISCUSSION

Reflecting on the Selection
Whole-Group Discussion

The whole group discusses the selection and any **thoughts** or **questions** that it raises. During this time, students also **return** to the **clues, problems, and wonderings** that they have noted on the board during browsing.

TEACHING TIP Students should be working—and thinking—as hard as the teacher is.

Assessment

To assess their understanding of the text, engage the students in a discussion to determine whether they have grasped the following ideas:

- how Juan was affected by his farming experiences
- why Juan returned the gold coin to Doña Josefa
- why Doña Josefa called herself the richest woman in the world

Response Journal

This is a thought-provoking story. Students may wish to record in their response journals any additional reactions that they have to the selection.

Exploring Concepts Within the Selection
Small-Group Discussion

Remind the students to check the Concept Board and the Question Board to determine whether their original perceptions about value have changed as a result of reading this selection. Circulate among the groups to see whether any of them are having difficulty relating this selection to the unit concepts.

Sharing Ideas About the Concepts

Have the groups **report their ideas** and **discuss them** with the rest of the class. It is crucial that the students' ideas determine this discussion.

- Students may point out that at first Doña Josefa's values and Juan's values were completely opposite.
- Students may recognize that when she claimed to be the richest person in the world, Doña Josefa was talking about her personal relationships, not about how much money she made.
- Some students may note that Doña Josefa's way of life brought her few material rewards. However, Juan's life among the people made him happier than his life as a thief had.

As these ideas and others are stated, have the students add them to the **Question Board** or the **Concept Board.**

Ask the class to examine Henry Ossawa Tanner's *The Thankful Poor,* reproduced at the top of page 310 in the student anthology. Invite the students to discuss their thoughts and feelings about the painting. Encourage them to tell whether and how they think Tanner's art piece relates to or reminds them of the reading and exploring they have done so far in this unit. If some students feel that they can extrapolate from this painting information about the artist's or his subjects' values, encourage them to share their ideas with the class.

Fine Art

Exploring Concepts Across Selections

Ask the students whether this story reminds them of others that they have read. Connections may be made with other selections in the unit.

- Juan traded his labor for meals and transportation. Students may point out this demonstrates the barter system described in "What Money Is."
- Students may compare Doña Josefa with the miner and his wife in "A Gift for a Gift." All three characters help others simply because they want to rather than because they expect something in return.
- Students may compare Juan with other greedy and deceitful characters in this unit, all of whom learn that their greed brings few rewards.

Recording Ideas

As they complete the above discussions, ask the students to **sum up what they have learned from their conversations and how they might use this information** in further explorations. Any special information or insights may be recorded on the Concept Board. Any further questions that they would like to think about, pursue, or investigate may be recorded on the Question Board. They may want to discuss the progress that has been made on their questions and to cross out any questions that no longer warrant consideration.

❯ Following the discussion, provide time for the students to record their ideas on page 107 of their Explorer's Notebook.

Evaluating Discussions

Explorer's Notebook, page 107

The Gold Coin by Alma Flor Ada

_____
_____
_____
_____
_____
_____

"President Cleveland, Where Are You?" by Robert Cormier

_____
_____
_____
_____
_____
_____

"The No-Guitar Blues" by Gary Soto

_____
_____
_____
_____
_____
_____

Unit 6/Value   EN 107

Copyright © 1995 Open Court Publishing Company

2 READING WITH A WRITER'S EYE

MINILESSONS

**Writer's Craft:
Story Structure**

Have the students share what they remember about developing the plot of a story. Discuss with them the elements of a good **plot: the introduction of the characters, the setting, and the problem; the development of additional conflicts; a climax or major turning point; a conclusion and resolution of the conflicts.** As you discuss plot development, have students refer to Reproducible Master 40, Elements of Plot, in the Story Elements section of their Writer's Notebook. Provide additional copies if necessary. Point out that there are different ways of presenting these plot elements in a story, ways in which the author moves his or her story along. The most common way, of course, is chronologically, where the author creates a series of events that must necessarily build on each other in order to tell the story. In *The Gold Coin,* Ada uses short episodes to move her story along. In the first episode, Juan learns that Doña Josefa has gold and makes his first attempt to steal it. In the second, Juan takes off after Doña Josefa and spends the day picking potatoes with a father and his son. In the next episode, Juan helps a young man harvest his corn. Point out to students that although the episodes following the first one are presented in chronological order, the author could have switched episodes around without affecting the plot or the clarity of the story. Review with them the stories "Money Matters" and "The Shoeshine Stand." Help them to understand that in these stories, the author could not have switched the episodes around and still maintained a cohesive plot.

**Selective Reading:
Focus on Story
Structure**

Now have students find and read aloud other episodes in *The Gold Coin* that Ada uses to move the plot along. Some examples include the following:

- page 305: Juan helps the mother gather her squash and beans.
- page 306: Juan helps Don Teodosio to harvest his coffee beans.
- pages 307–309: Juan catches up to Doña Josefa and finds that the gold is no longer very important to him.

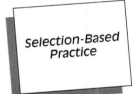

Selection-Based Practice

**Independent Practice:
Story Structure**

➤ To extend their understanding of story structure, have the students work individually or in small groups to complete Reading/Writing Connection, page 46.

**Writer's Craft:
Using Sensory
Descriptions**

Ask students to discuss what they remember about **sensory descriptions.** They should understand that by **describing people and things in a story,** the author makes it easier for his or her readers to visualize the action as it unfolds. Writers should describe not only **how things look,** but also **how they sound or taste or smell or feel.** Point out that in order to provide vivid descriptions, the author, too, must visualize what is happening in the story. Without taking the time to picture his or her characters and settings, the writer cannot possibly describe them to his

The Gold Coin

Story Structure

Look back at *The Gold Coin* or at other selections that you have read for more examples of how the authors structure their stories. Write the title of the story, the page on which it begins, the structure of the story (series of episodes or events related in chronological order or in random order), and a short comment on how the structure works.

Title: _____ Page: _____
Story structure: _____
Comments on the structure: _____
_____
_____
_____

Title: _____ Page: _____
Story structure: _____
Comments on the structure: _____
_____
_____
_____

Title: _____ Page: _____
Story structure: _____
Comments on the structure: _____
_____
_____
_____

Name

Story Structure
46 R/WC   Value/Unit 6

Copyright © 1995 Open Court Publishing Company

Reading/Writing Connection, page 46

The Gold Coin

Using Sensory Descriptions

Alma Flor Ada uses many sensory descriptions to help her readers visualize the settings and the events in the story. Look back at other stories that you have read for examples of how writers use sensory descriptions to make their stories more vivid. Write the title of the story, the page on which the description appears, the descriptive passage, and the sense to which the description appeals.

Title: _____ Page: _____
Description: _____
_____
_____
Sense: _____

Title: _____ Page: _____
Description: _____
_____
_____
Sense: _____

Title: _____ Page: _____
Description: _____
_____
_____
Sense: _____

Look back at this page for examples when you want to use sensory description in your writing.

Name

Copyright © 1995 Open Court Publishing Company

Unit 6/Value   Description
                                      R/WC 47

Reading/Writing Connection, page 47

---

or her readers. In *The Gold Coin,* Ada does a very good job of providing sensory descriptions. For example, on page 298, in the very first paragraph of the story, she describes Juan: "his skin had become pale and sickly," "his body had become shriveled and bent," "his face was always twisted into an angry frown." On page 300, she describes Juan's voice as "hoarse" and "raspy."

Selective Reading: Focus on Sensory Descriptions

Now have the students find and read aloud other examples of sensory descriptions in *The Gold Coin* and then tell to what sense the description appeals.

Examples appear on the following pages:

- page 299, paragraph 1: "Juan was half asleep when he heard knocking at the door and the sound of insistent voices." (hearing)
- page 300, paragraph 1: Doña Josefa is described as "a short, gray-haired woman, wearing a black cloak." (sight)
- page 302, paragraph 10: corn kernels "glittered like gold coins." (sight)
- page 303, paragraph 2: Juan "felt strangely moved by the sight of the mountains, barely lit by the faint rays of the morning sun." (sight)

Independent Practice: Sensory Description

▶ Have the students work individually or in small groups, using Reading/Writing Connection, page 47, to extend their understanding and use of sensory language.

Selection-Based Practice

Linking Reading to Writing

Now have students look through their writing folders for pieces of their writing that might be improved by using a different plot structure. Encourage them to create successive episodes to move the plot along. They might also look for pieces of their own writing that could be improved by providing more sensory descriptions. After a brief period, allow volunteers to read aloud both the original and the revised versions of their writing. Let them explain how the revisions improved the quality of the passages.

＊ Writing Process

Students watched as Juan changed from a greedy thief to a caring person. They may enjoy writing a sequel to *The Gold Coin,* telling more about how Juan's life changes.

If students decide to begin a new piece, encourage them to make brief notes on ideas that they may want to include in their writing. If necessary, have the students meet with their classmates to generate ideas during this prewriting session.

VOCABULARY

Words from the selection that students may want to discuss and remember include *insistent, distressed, ransacked,* and *amiably.* Have Vocabulary Exploration forms, Reproducible Master 15, available for students who request them. Encourage students to add new words and phrases from the selection to the Personal Dictionary section of their Writer's Notebook. For additional opportunities to build vocabulary, see **Teacher Tool Card 77.**

VOCABULARY TIP Have the students choose words from the selections that they may find useful in their speaking and writing about the explorable concepts. Add these words to the Concept Board.

Professional Checkpoint: Reading with a Writer's Eye

Elaborating means to develop more thoroughly or to express in greater detail. For example, a writer elaborates through comparing and contrasting, giving examples, providing descriptions, including specific facts, providing definitions and background information, and so on. It is important that students understand the many ways one can elaborate a text.

Notes:

3 GUIDED AND INDEPENDENT EXPLORATION

EXPLORING CONCEPTS BEYOND THE TEXT

Guided Exploration

Students will select activities in which they explore the concepts related to value. Refer them to the **Exploration Activities poster** and give them time to choose an activity and to discuss what they wish to explore and how they wish to go about it. If the students need further help, here are some suggestions:

* Remind the students that Doña Josefa was probably not paid for the services she provided. She was, for the most part, a volunteer. Have students form small groups to discuss people they know who do volunteer work. Encourage students who are volunteers to share their experiences. Provide interested students with extra library time to explore volunteerism further. Students may enjoy learning about people who have become famous for helping others or about particular volunteer organizations. Doña Josefa felt that by helping other people, she became richer—not in terms of money, but in terms of the way her neighbors regarded her and the way she felt about herself. This is a common attitude among those who help less fortunate people. For many people, helping others is so fulfilling that they make a career of it, accepting salaries that are much lower than they could make in other types of work.

* If possible, arrange for a representative from a local volunteer organization—or a national organization that maintains a chapter in your area—to come to your class and discuss the work of his or her organization. Organizations to consider might include food banks, homeless shelters, animal shelters, the Peace Corps, literacy organizations, Boys and Girls Clubs of America, Habitat for Humanity, legal-aid foundations, and local churches and synagogues. You might want to choose an organization that accepts students as volunteers. Invite the students to decide on some persons or organizations that particularly interest them and, if possible, arrange for an expert of their choice to visit.

Before the class visit, take some time to explain the unit topic and related concepts to the visiting expert and to discuss the information that she or he will present. Tell the class something about the person who will be visiting and provide time for them to generate some questions to ask her or him.

❯ Following the visit, the students may want to form small groups to discuss further what they have learned. Then they can independently complete page 117 of their Explorer's Notebook, recording their ideas about volunteer work.

* Exploring Through Reflective Activities

Questioning a Visiting Expert

Exploring Organizations that Help Others

Many types of organizations have been formed for the purpose of helping people or furthering causes—for example, to help the sick, the aged, the homeless, the physically handicapped, the victims of natural disasters; to protect endangered species; and to preserve wildlife habitats. List some organizations for which you might like to do volunteer work. Tell what these groups do and why their work is important. You might want to explore local, national, or international organizations.

Name of Organization	Kind of Assistance It Provides	Why Its Work Is Important

Copyright © 1995 Open Court Publishing Company

Unit 6/Value   EN 117

Explorer's Notebook, page 117

Exploring the Rewards of Helping Others

For what reasons do people join volunteer organizations?

_____
_____
_____
_____

What rewards might people get from helping others?

_____
_____
_____
_____

What skills or qualities do you have to offer a volunteer organization?

_____
_____
_____
_____

How might working for a volunteer organization help you in a future career?

_____
_____
_____
_____
_____

Copyright © 1995 Open Court Publishing Company

118 EN   Value/Unit 6

Explorer's Notebook, page 118

❯ Have students work in small groups and use page 118 in their Explorer's Notebook to extend their discussion and exploration. Encourage the groups to share their ideas and conclusions with the class. If the discussion suggests ideas for writing, encourage the students to begin with some prewriting or brainstorming activities.

Continuing Exploration

Encourage the students to discuss what they have learned about value through discussions, reading, and exploration activities. Have the students add to the **Concept Board** any important concepts or ideas that come up.

Have students review the questions on the **Question Board** and remove any that have been addressed to their satisfaction or that are no longer appropriate.

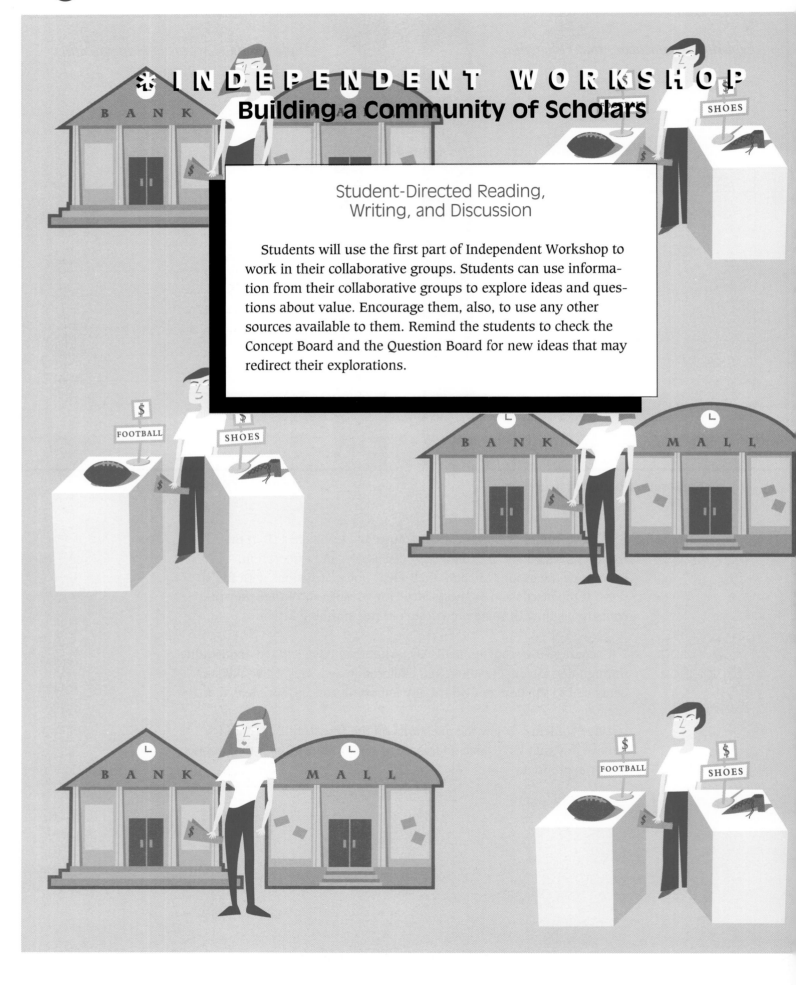

❋ INDEPENDENT WORKSHOP
Building a Community of Scholars

Student-Directed Reading, Writing, and Discussion

Students will use the first part of Independent Workshop to work in their collaborative groups. Students can use information from their collaborative groups to explore ideas and questions about value. Encourage them, also, to use any other sources available to them. Remind the students to check the Concept Board and the Question Board for new ideas that may redirect their explorations.

Additional Opportunities for Independent Reading, Writing, and Cross-curricular Activities

✴ Reading Roundtable

Alma Flor Ada writes primarily in Spanish. One of the best ways for children to learn about other countries and cultures is to read the English translations of books written by authors who live in those countries. Have students share the titles of any such books that they have read and would like to recommend to others. For additional ideas for **Reading Roundtable**, see **Learning Framework Card 6.**

✴ Writing Seminar

Some students may want to work on unfinished pieces in their writing folders. Those who have chosen to write a continuation of Juan's story can continue to brainstorm with other students or begin their first drafts.

Teacher-Conferencing Tip If your class is using the optional Writer's Handbook, remind students to refer to it for help with their writing.

Cross-curricular Activity Cards

The following Cross-curricular Activity Cards in the Student Toolbox are appropriate for this selection:
- 30 Social Studies—Folk Medicine
- 19 Science—First Aid

First Aid
Use after *The Gold Coin*

19
Science

Folk Medicine
Use after *The Gold Coin*

30
Social Studies

In all countries—industrialized and nonindustrialized—alternative medical systems exist. The methods used in some of these predate by centuries those used in modern Western medicine.

In the card catalog in the library, look under such subject headings as Chinese medicine, acupuncture, acupressure, tai chi, and holistic healing. Check out books on topics or methods that interest you. Make notes on what you read and share your information with your classmates. *Researching alternative medical methods will give you a better understanding of medicine.*

Additional Opportunities for Solving Learning Problems

Tutorial

Use this time to work with students who need extra help in any area. The following teacher aids are available in the Teacher Toolbox for your convenience:
- Writer's Craft/Reading: Plot, Teacher Tool Card 15
- Writer's Craft/Reading: Elaboration Through Providing Descriptions, Teacher Tool Card 40
- Writer's Craft/Reading: Indicators of Place and Location, Teacher Tool Card 30

Fine Art

DISCUSSING FINE ART

Included here is some background information about the pieces of fine art shown on pages 310–311. Share with the students whatever you feel is appropriate. Some works may be familiar to them. Encourage them to express their reactions to each piece—for example, what the piece has to do with value, whether they think it is related to this unit, and why.

Encourage them to find out more about artists or artistic styles that interest them. For additional information on discussing fine art, refer to **Teacher Tool Card 125.**

The Thankful Poor. 1894.
Henry Ossawa Tanner. Oil on canvas.

Henry Ossawa Tanner (1859–1937) grew up in Washington, D.C., several cities in Maryland, and Philadelphia. Tanner's middle name, Ossawa, was given to him in honor of the abolitionist John Brown of Osawatomie, Kansas. One day when he was almost thirteen years old, Tanner went walking with his father in the park and saw a painter at work. He watched for an hour and decided then and there to become an artist. The memory stayed with him. With his mother's encouragement and fifteen cents, he bought his first art supplies and began to train himself. Eventually Tanner attended the Pennsylvania Academy of the Fine Arts.

In 1918 Tanner, like many of his contemporaries, went to study in Europe. He decided to remain in Paris; and except for visits to the United States and occasional travel, Tanner spent the rest of his life in France. In 1893 Tanner was invited to speak at the Congress on Africa at the World's Columbian Exposition in Chicago. The symposium addressed African-American as well as African concerns. Tanner delivered a paper entitled "The American Negro in Art."

The Chicago conference had a great impact on Tanner's racial awareness, and he decided to paint scenes of African-American life that would

The Thankful Poor. 1894. Henry Ossawa Tanner.
Oil on canvas. Private collection. Photo: Art Resource

*One Dollar Silver
Certificate.*
c. 1898–1910. Victor
Dubreuil.

Oil on canvas, 9" x 12". Through
prior gift of Charles H. and
Mary F. S. Worcester Collection,
The Art Institute of Chicago.
1987.171. Photo: © 1993 The
Art Institute of Chicago.
All Rights Reserved

Peasant Wedding Feast. c. 1567–1568. Pieter Bruegel the Elder.
Oil on panel. Kunsthistorisches Museum, Vienna.
Photo: Kavaler/Art Resource

311

fight the comical and stereotypical images that were then common. Two works in this vein were *The Banjo Lesson,* probably his most famous work, and *The Thankful Poor,* shown here. The theme in *The Thankful Poor* is one often found in European peasant paintings, in which devotion, humility, and poverty are portrayed. This depiction of an old man and a young boy in prayer is considered by many to be one of the finest images of African Americans in American art.

After 1894 and his return to France, Tanner turned away from African-American subjects and began to paint religious and biblical scenes. Historians have suggested that Tanner decided he could not prosper in France as a painter of African-American scenes and that since he had to earn his living by his work, such practicality on his part was a necessity. Tanner's reputation as an artist grew in the United States and in Europe. In 1897 and again in 1898, he traveled to Palestine and Egypt. He painted the people that he saw there, Jews and Arabs, as figures from the Bible. For Tanner, these people were living representatives of the biblical stories so familiar to him, and the closeness he felt to them is apparent in his work.

After his marriage in 1899, Tanner settled with his wife for a while in Normandy; in 1903 they stayed briefly in Spain and England. Tanner continued to visit the United States and his family, but he believed that as an African American he enjoyed more professional opportunity and freedom in France than in his native country.

In 1923 for exhibiting his work and winning numerous awards since 1894, the French government awarded Tanner the Cross of the Legion of Honor. In 1925 Tanner's wife, Jessie, died; after this blow Tanner virtually retired from an active career. By the mid-1930s, he had fallen into relative obscurity. He died in his sleep on May 25, 1937, and was buried next to his wife in the cemetery at Sceaux.

Without the example of Tanner's work and reputation, many of the artists of the Harlem Renaissance—during which African-American painters, sculptors, poets, and musicians achieved worldwide prominence—might never have dared to follow their dreams into the arts.

One Dollar Silver Certificate. c. 1898–1910.
Victor Dubreuil. Oil on canvas.

Victor Dubreuil was active, primarily as a still-life artist, in the late nineteenth century. Almost nothing is known about him—not the date of his birth or death, nor where he lived. Dubreuil's works are humorous and single-minded; the subject of most of his paintings is money.

Dubreuil painted stacks of coins, barrels filled with cash, even bank robbers at work. One of his paintings of twenty-dollar bills spilling from a barrel was actually confiscated from his studio by the Secret Service. It was kept under lock and key at the Treasury Department in Washington, D.C., where it was eventually destroyed. However, in an odd twist, Dubreuil's name does not appear in any Secret Service files, although there exist files on other artists with whom the Secret Service had a quarrel.

Dubreuil painted during that period of American history from the end of the Civil War (1865) to World War I (which began in Europe in 1914, and which the United States entered in 1917). It was a period of great change in American life. It also seems to have been the period when the glamour of money first attracted the American people. Mark Twain, the writer and acute observer of American society at that time, called it the Gilded Age. Twain recalled that no one during his youth had worshipped money, but that wealth appeared to be an increasing preoccupation.

The United States emerged from the Civil War as a patchwork collection of regions with varied economics, populations, and social attitudes. A few individuals and families grew very wealthy and were labeled Robber Barons because of their disregard for and manipulation of stock and commodity markets, ethics, and law. Making a profit was seen by some as duty. Little consideration was given to the welfare of industrial workers. These values, held by much of the business community and many politicians, prevailed until the late nineteenth century, when the rise of the labor movement and the great labor strikes made labor relations suddenly a matter of business and national self-interest.

The end of World War I in 1918 saw a stronger, richer, more powerful United States. Industry, the labor movement, and the middle class were all growing. Ahead lay Prohibition, the Roaring Twenties, the Great Depression of the 1930s, World War II. Economic, political, and social concerns would be argued over, fought for, sought after. Certainly, so many years later, that has not changed.

Peasant Wedding Feast. c. 1567–1568.
Pieter Bruegel the Elder. Oil on panel.

Pieter Bruegel (1525/30–1569), considered one of the greatest
Flemish painters of the sixteenth century, was born in the Low
Countries, which comprised present-day Belgium and the Netherlands,
or Holland. He spent most of his career in Antwerp and Brussels and
traveled through France and Italy and to the Alps. His lively scenes of
peasant life led to his nicknames "Peasant Bruegel" and "Bruegel the
Jester." However, he was probably a man of some education, with many
friends and patrons in the intellectual and scientific circles of his day.
These friends included the geographer and cartographer (mapmaker)
Abraham Ortelius, the scientific publisher Christophe Plantin, and the
merchant and royal official Niclaes Jonghelinck.

Bruegel's career coincided with the great prosperity of the Low
Countries in the sixteenth century. Antwerp was one of the most important commercial and financial centers in Europe. Merchants and bankers
from many countries crowded her streets and busy exchanges. Ships
sailing under a variety of flags anchored in her harbor. The facade of the
new stock exchange, completed in 1531, bore the inscription For the
Service and Merchants of All Nations and Languages. Antwerp also was
a center of European culture. Her artists were among the greatest in the
world. Her publishers produced books in many languages.

Bruegel's paintings of peasant festivities depict very real, individual-
ized people. Peasants shared in the general prosperity of the sixteenth-
century Low Countries and were known for their generous and high-
spirited wedding celebrations. An imperial decree of 1546 limited to
twenty the number of guests permitted at country weddings. From
Peasant Wedding Feast, shown here, it would seem that the decree was
unsuccessful.

Peasant Wedding Feast has a barn as its setting. In the background,
hay is stacked to the rafters; at the upper right, sheaves of wheat from
the last harvest are hanging. Guests are being entertained by two bag-
pipers, one of whom stares at the food. Sitting with folded hands at the
table, at the center right, is the bride. The serving tray, hefted by two
strong young men in the foreground, has been made from an unhinged
door. Unlike the bride, the groom cannot be identified. He may be one of
the servers. According to a contemporary custom, the groom had to wait
upon the bride's family during the wedding feast. Just behind the servers,
a priest and a bearded man converse. From his costume the bearded man
appears to belong to a higher social class than the people around him;
some scholars believe him to be a self-portrait of Pieter Breugel.

President Cleveland, Where Are You?

1 READING THE SELECTION

INFORMATION FOR THE TEACHER

About the Selection

When the trading-card company stops making cowboy cards and begins featuring the presidents instead, eleven-year-old Jerry and his friends are sorely disappointed. But their disappointment turns to excitement when they learn that the first boy to collect a complete set of president cards will win an autographed baseball mitt. Finally, after weeks of tense competition, Jerry has an opportunity to complete his set first—but a family obligation may stand in his way. Find out what he does in this poignant tale of Depression-era childhood, filled with warm humor, likable characters, and the drama of everyday life.

Link to the Unit Concepts

Given limited resources, is it more important to provide for one's own desires or for those of a loved one? Robert Cormier explores this question in "President Cleveland, Where Are You?" pages 312–329. Cormier's young protagonist, Jerry, must decide between acquiring a coveted baseball mitt or coming to the financial aid of his brother, Armand. Although this story takes place in another era and has as its backdrop the Great Depression, your students will find themselves identifying with young Jerry's dilemma.

About the Author

Born in 1925 to a factory worker's family in Massachusetts, Robert Cormier experienced a childhood affected to a large extent by the Depression. Despite the uncertainties of the time, however, his family offered warmth and support. Cormier was more inclined to reading than to participating in sports. He was influenced by Thomas Wolfe, who inspired him to become a writer, and by Ernest Hemingway, whose books showed him that plain, straightforward prose can be as effective as the

LESSON OVERVIEW

"President Cleveland, Where Are You?" by Robert Cormier, pages 312–329

READING THE SELECTION

Materials
Student anthology, pp. 312–329
Explorer's Notebook, p. 107

FYI
Learning Framework Card
• Setting Reading Goals and Expectations, 1A

READING WITH A WRITER'S EYE

Minilessons
Writer's Craft: Using Adverbs
Writer's Craft: Story Elements—Plot, Setting, Characterization

Materials
Reading/Writing Connection, pp. 48–49
Reproducible Master 15

FYI
Teacher Tool Card
• Spelling and Vocabulary: Building Vocabulary, 77

Option for Instruction
Grammar, Mechanics, and Usage: Using Parentheses, Dashes, and Ellipses (Use Teacher Tool Card listed below.)

GUIDED AND INDEPENDENT EXPLORATION

Materials
Home/School Connection 45

Independent Workshop

Optional Materials from Student Toolbox
Tradebook Connection Cards

Cross-curricular Activity Cards
• 17 Art—Accurate Art
• 31 Social Studies—Uncle Jumbo

Student Tool Cards
• Writer's Craft/Reading: Giving Descriptions, 40
• Grammar, Mechanics, and Usage: Using Adjectives and Adverbs, 68
• Writer's Craft/Reading: Characterization, 13
• Writer's Craft/Reading: Setting, 14
• Writer's Craft/Reading: Plot, 15
• Grammar, Mechanics, and Usage: Using Parentheses, Dashes, and Ellipses, 54

FYI
Teacher Tool Cards
• Writer's Craft/Reading: Elaboration Through Providing Descriptions, 40
• Grammar, Mechanics, and Usage: Using Adjectives and Adverbs, 68
• Writer's Craft/Reading: Characterization, 13
• Writer's Craft/Reading: Setting, 14
• Writer's Craft/Reading: Plot, 15
• Grammar, Mechanics, and Usage: Using Parentheses, Dashes, and Ellipses, 54

NOTES

Asterisks (*) throughout the lesson indicate learning frameworks. Learning Framework Cards and Teacher Tool Cards can be found in the Teacher Toolbox.

vividly descriptive writing of Wolfe. Finally, William Saroyan's writing taught Cormier that stories can be about the drama of everyday life.

Cormier's novels include *I Am the Cheese, The Chocolate War,* and *The Bumblebee Flies Away,* all of which are ALA Notable Books.

<table>
<tr><td>

About the
Illustrators

</td><td>

Mary Beth Schwark and Bob Kuester teamed up to provide the outstanding illustrations for this selection, an easy thing for them to do since they are teamed up as husband and wife away from their easels. They met while they were doing commercial art for an advertising agency, and for a while they both worked out of their home as free-lance illustrators. Although Kuester returned to commercial art, Schwark is still a free-lance artist. Her illustrations appear in *The Kid with the Red Suspenders* and *Your Former Friend, Matthew,* both by Louann Gaeddert, and *Mystery at Camp Triumph* by Mary Blount Christian.

</td></tr>
</table>

INFORMATION FOR THE STUDENT

Many students in the elementary grades today probably haven't even heard of the Great Depression. Tell students that it was a period that began in 1929 and continued during the 1930s. During this time as many as 25 percent of American workers had no jobs and many Americans lost all of their money in bank failures. At the beginning of the Depression, there were no government programs such as social security or unemployment insurance to help people through bad times. You should also point out that prices and wages at the time of the story were much lower than they are today.

COGNITIVE AND RESPONSIVE READING

Activating Prior Knowledge

Trading cards have again become popular in recent years. Very likely some of your students have collections of cards featuring athletes, rock stars, or perhaps even dinosaurs. Ask the students to talk about collecting cards.

Setting Reading Goals and Expectations

Have the students **browse** the **first page** of the selection, using the **clues/problems/wondering procedure.** Students will return to their observations after reading the selection. For a review of browsing, see **Learning Framework Card 1A, Setting Reading Goals and Expectations.**

Recommendations for Reading the Selection

Ask the students how they would like to read the story. Because the selection contains some amusing dialogue and some interesting characters about the students' own age, students may enjoy **reading** the story **aloud.**

During oral reading, use and encourage think-alouds. During silent reading, allow discussion as needed. Discuss problems, strategies, and reactions after reading.

This would be a good selection for **responding** to text **by identifying with characters and situations** while reading aloud. Model this response, and then invite the students to do the same.

Note: "President Cleveland, Where Are You?" has been broken into two parts in case the students are not able to finish reading the selection in one sitting. The second part of the story begins on page 319 and is indicated by a large initial capital letter.

<table>
<tr><td>

About the
Reading
Strategies

</td><td>

This selection is realistic fiction. It contains references to actual people, events, and concepts, though the plot and main characters are purely fictional. As students read the selection, encourage them to respond to the text by **wondering** about the roles that these real people and things played in American society in the 1930s. For example, Cormier mentions that a Ken Maynard serial played every Saturday at the local theater. Students are probably not familiar with Ken Maynard nor with movie serials and may wonder what they were.

</td></tr>
</table>

Think-Aloud Prompts
for Use in Oral Reading

The think-aloud prompts are placed where students may want to use strategies to help them better understand the text. These are merely suggestions. Remind the students to refer to the **reading strategies posters** and to use any strategy they find helpful as they read.

TEACHING TIP Invite students to suggest and model strategies for finding answers.

These prompts may be used as guides to promote cognitive and responsive reading.

1 Rollie Tremaine had about thirty Ken Maynard cards. Obviously, there is nothing practical that he could do with that many cards of the same person. In figuring out what Rollie Tremaine is like, some students might **make a connection** here between Rollie Tremaine and the miser in Aesop's fable whose only use for his gold was to have it.

PRESIDENT CLEVELAND, WHERE ARE YOU?
Robert Cormier
*illustrated by Mary Beth Schwark
and Bob Kuester*

That was the autumn of the cowboy cards—Buck Jones and Tom Tyler and Hoot Gibson and especially Ken Maynard. The cards were available in those five-cent packages of gum: pink sticks, three together, covered with a sweet white powder. You couldn't blow bubbles with that particular gum, but it couldn't have mattered less. The cowboy cards were important—the pictures of those rock-faced men with eyes of blue steel.

On those wind-swept, leaf-tumbling afternoons we gathered after school on the sidewalk in front of Lemire's Drugstore, across from St. Jude's Parochial School, and we swapped and bargained and matched for the cards. Because a Ken Maynard <u>serial</u> was playing at the Globe every Saturday afternoon, he was the most popular cowboy of all, and one of his cards was worth at least ten of any other kind. Rollie Tremaine had a treasure of thirty or so, and he guarded them jealously. He'd match you

☙ 312 ❧

for the other cards, but he risked his Ken Maynards only when the other kids threatened to leave him out of the competition altogether.

You could almost hate Rollie Tremaine. In the first place, he was the only son of Auguste Tremaine, who operated the Uptown Dry Goods Store, and he did not live in a tenement but in a big white birthday cake of a house on Laurel Street. He was too fat to be effective in the football games between the Frenchtown Tigers and the North Side Knights, and he made us constantly aware of the jingle of coins in his pockets. He was able to stroll into Lemire's and casually select a quarter's worth of cowboy cards while the rest of us watched, aching with envy.

☙ 313 ❧

1

Once in a while I earned a nickel or dime by running errands or washing windows for blind old Mrs. Belander, or by finding pieces of copper, brass, and other valuable metals at the dump and selling them to the junkman. The coins clutched in my hand, I would race to Lemire's to buy a cowboy card or two, hoping that Ken Maynard would stare boldly out at me as I opened the pack. At one time, before a disastrous matching session with Roger Lussier (my best friend, except where the cards were involved), I owned five Ken Maynards and considered myself a millionaire, of sorts.

One week I was particularly lucky; I had spent two afternoons washing floors for Mrs. Belander and received a quarter. Because my father had worked a full week at the shop, where a rush order for fancy combs had been received, he allotted my brothers and sisters and me an extra dime along with the usual ten cents for the Saturday-afternoon movie. Setting aside the movie fare, I found myself with a bonus of thirty-five cents, and I then planned to put Rollie Tremaine to shame the following Monday afternoon.

Monday was the best day to buy the cards because the candy man stopped at Lemire's every Monday morning to deliver the new assortments. There was nothing more exciting in the world than a fresh batch of card boxes. I rushed home from school that day and hurriedly changed my clothes, eager to set off for the store. As I burst through the doorway, letting the screen door slam behind me, my brother Armand blocked my way.

He was fourte, three years older than I, and a freshman at Monument High School. He had recently become a stranger to me in many ways—<u>indifferent</u> to such matters as

314

cowboy cards and the Frenchtown Tigers—and he carried himself with a mysterious dignity that was fractured now and then when his voice began shooting off in all directions like some kind of vocal fireworks.

"Wait a minute, Jerry," he said. "I want to talk to you." He motioned me out of earshot of my mother, who was busy supervising the usual after-school <u>skirmish</u> in the kitchen.

I sighed with impatience. In recent months Armand had become a figure of authority, siding with my father and mother occasionally. As the oldest son he sometimes took advantage of his age and experience to issue rules and regulations.

"How much money have you got?" he whispered.

"You in some kind of trouble?" I asked, excitement rising in me as I remembered the <u>blackmail</u> plot of a movie at the Globe a month before.

He shook his head in annoyance. "Look," he said, "it's Pa's birthday tomorrow. I think we ought to chip in and buy him something . . ."

I reached into my pocket and caressed the coins. "Here," I said carefully, pulling out a nickel. "If we all give a nickel we should have enough to buy him something pretty nice."

He regarded me with contempt. "Rita already gave me fifteen cents, and I'm throwing in a quarter. Albert handed over a dime—all that's left of his birthday money. Is that all you can do—a nickel?"

"Aw, come on," I protested. "I haven't got a single Ken Maynard left, and I was going to buy some cards this afternoon."

"Ken Maynard!" he snorted. "Who's more important—him or your father?"

315

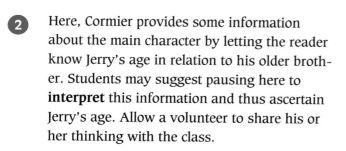

2 Here, Cormier provides some information about the main character by letting the reader know Jerry's age in relation to his older brother. Students may suggest pausing here to **interpret** this information and thus ascertain Jerry's age. Allow a volunteer to share his or her thinking with the class.

3 Students will probably **wonder** how anyone could think that by contributing a nickel apiece, Jerry and his siblings would have enough money to buy any kind of gift at all. If not, model the wondering process yourself. Help students to understand that during the 1930s, a nickel had much greater value than it does today.

His question was unfair because he knew that there was no possible choice—"my father" had to be the only answer. My father was a huge man who believed in the things of the spirit. He had worked at the Monument Comb Shop since the age of fourteen; his booming laugh—or grumble—greeted us each night when he returned from the factory. A steady worker when the shop had enough work, he quickened with gaiety on Friday nights and weekends, and he was fond of making long speeches about the good things in life. In the middle of the <u>Depression</u>, for instance, he paid cash for a piano, of all things, and insisted that my twin sisters, Yolande and Yvette, take lessons once a week.

316

I took a dime from my pocket and handed it to Armand.

"Thanks, Jerry," he said. "I hate to take your last cent."

"That's all right," I replied, turning away and consoling myself with the thought that twenty cents was better than nothing at all.

When I arrived at Lemire's I sensed disaster in the air. Roger Lussier was kicking <u>disconsolately</u> at a tin can in the gutter, and Rollie Tremaine sat sullenly on the steps in front of the store.

"Save your money," Roger said. He had known about my plans to splurge on the cards.

"What's the matter?" I asked.

"There's no more cowboy cards," Rollie Tremaine said. "The company's not making any more."

"They're going to have President cards," Roger said, his face twisting with disgust. He pointed to the store window. "Look!"

A placard in the window announced: "Attention, Boys. Watch for the New Series. Presidents of the United States. Free in Each 5-Cent Package of Caramel Chew."

"President cards?" I asked, dismayed.

I read on: "Collect a Complete Set and Receive an Official Imitation Major League Baseball Glove, <u>Embossed</u> with Lefty Grove's Autograph."

Glove or no glove, who could become excited about Presidents, of all things?

Rollie Tremaine stared at the sign. "Benjamin Harrison, for crying out loud," he said. "Why would I want Benjamin Harrison when I've got twenty-two Ken Maynards?"

317

I felt the warmth of guilt creep over me. I jingled the coins in my pocket, but the sound was hollow. No more Ken Maynards to buy.

"I'm going to buy a Mr. Goodbar," Rollie Tremaine decided.

I was without appetite, indifferent even to a Baby Ruth, which was my favorite. I thought of how I had betrayed Armand and, worst of all, my father.

"I'll see you after supper," I called over my shoulder to Roger as I hurried away toward home. I took the shortcut behind the church, although it involved leaping over a tall wooden fence, and I zigzagged recklessly through Mr. Thibodeau's garden, trying to outrace my guilt. I pounded up the steps and into the house, only to learn that Armand had already taken Yolande and Yvette uptown to shop for the birthday present.

I pedaled my bike furiously through the streets, ignoring the indignant horns of automobiles as I sliced through the traffic. Finally I saw Armand and my sisters emerge from the Monument Men's Shop. My heart sank when I spied the long, slim package that Armand was holding.

"Did you buy the present yet?" I asked, although I knew it was too late.

"Just now. A blue tie," Armand said. "What's the matter?"

"Nothing," I replied, my chest hurting.

He looked at me for a long moment. At first his eyes were hard, but then they softened. He smiled at me, almost sadly, and touched my arm. I turned away from him because I felt naked and exposed.

"It's all right," he said gently. "Maybe you've learned something." The words were gentle, but they held a curious

318

dignity, the dignity remaining even when his voice suddenly cracked on the last syllable.

I wondered what was happening to me, because I did not know whether to laugh or cry.

Sister Angela was amazed when, a week before Christmas vacation, everybody in the class submitted a history essay worthy of a high mark—in some cases as high as A-minus. (Sister Angela did not believe that anyone in the world ever deserved an A.) She never learned—or at least she never let on that she knew—we all had become experts on the Presidents because of the cards we purchased at Lemire's. Each card contained a picture of a President, and on the reverse side, a summary of his career. We looked at those cards so often that the biographies imprinted themselves on our

319

4 Jerry has just expressed some confusion about his feelings, and students may be similarly confused. Students may **wonder** aloud about Jerry's feelings. Invite volunteers to share their **interpretations** of how Jerry feels. If the students are having difficulty expressing their ideas, refer them to the appropriate strategy poster or model an interpretation of your own.

Note: The first part of the selection ends on page 319. This is a good place to stop reading if the selection cannot be finished during this class period.

5 If they read the first part of "President Cleveland, Where Are You?" during another class period, have the students **sum up** the first part of the story before they begin reading the second part.

minds without effort. Even our street-corner conversations were filled with such information as the fact that James Madison was called "The Father of the Constitution," or that John Adams had intended to become a minister.

The President cards were a roaring success and the cowboy cards were quickly forgotten. In the first place we did not receive gum with the cards, but a kind of chewy caramel. The caramel could be tucked into a corner of your mouth, bulging your cheek in much the same manner as wads of tobacco bulged the mouths of baseball stars. In the second place the competition for collecting the cards was fierce and frustrating—fierce because everyone was intent on being the first to send away for a baseball glove and frustrating because although there were only thirty-two Presidents, including Franklin Delano Roosevelt, the variety at Lemire's was at a minimum. When the deliveryman left the boxes of cards at the store each Monday, we often discovered that one entire box was devoted to a single President—two weeks in a row the boxes contained nothing but Abraham Lincolns. One week Roger Lussier and I were the heroes of Frenchtown. We journeyed on our bicycles to the North Side, engaged three boys in a matching bout and returned with five new Presidents, including Chester Alan Arthur, who up to that time had been missing.

Perhaps to sharpen our desire, the card company sent a sample glove to Mr. Lemire, and it dangled, orange and sleek, in the window. I was half sick with longing, thinking of my old glove at home, which I had inherited from Armand. But Rollie Tremaine's desire for the glove outdistanced my own. He even got Mr. Lemire to agree to give the glove in the window to the first person to get a complete set of cards, so that precious time wouldn't be wasted waiting for the postman.

We were delighted at Rollie Tremaine's frustration, especially since he was only a substitute player for the Tigers. Once after spending fifty cents on cards—all of which turned out to be Calvin Coolidge—he threw them to the ground, pulled some dollar bills out of his pocket and said, "The heck with it. I'm going to buy a glove!"

"Not that glove," Roger Lussier said. "Not a glove with Lefty Grove's autograph. Look what it says at the bottom of the sign."

We all looked, although we knew the words by heart: "This Glove Is Not For Sale Anywhere."

Rollie Tremaine scrambled to pick up the cards from the sidewalk, pouting more than ever. After that he was quietly <u>obsessed</u> with the Presidents, hugging the cards close to his chest and refusing to tell us how many more he needed to complete his set.

I too was obsessed with the cards, because they had become things of comfort in a world that had suddenly grown <u>dismal</u>. After Christmas a layoff at the shop had thrown my father out of work. He received no paycheck for four weeks, and the only income we had was from Armand's after-school job at the Blue and White Grocery Store—a job he lost finally when business dwindled as the layoff continued.

Although we had enough food and clothing—my father's <u>credit</u> had always been good, a matter of pride with him—the inactivity made my father restless and irritable. The twins fell sick and went to the hospital to have their tonsils removed. My father was confident that he would return to work eventually and pay off his debts, but he seemed to age before our eyes.

322

When orders again were received at the comb shop and he returned to work, another disaster occurred, although I was the only one aware of it. Armand fell in love.

I discovered his situation by accident, when I happened to pick up a piece of paper that had fallen to the floor in the bedroom he and I shared. I frowned at the paper, puzzled.

"Dear Sally, When I look into your eyes the world stands still . . ."

The letter was snatched from my hands before I finished reading it.

"What's the big idea, snooping around?" Armand asked, his face crimson. "Can't a guy have any privacy?"

He had never mentioned privacy before. "It was on the floor," I said. "I didn't know it was a letter. Who's Sally?"

He flung himself across the bed. "You tell anybody and I'll muckalize you," he threatened. "Sally Knowlton."

Nobody in Frenchtown had a name like Knowlton.

"A girl from the North Side?" I asked, <u>incredulous</u>.

He rolled over and faced me, anger in his eyes, and a kind of despair too.

"What's the matter with that? Think she's too good for me?" he asked. "I'm warning you, Jerry, if you tell anybody . . ."

"Don't worry," I said. Love had no particular place in my life; it seemed an unnecessary waste of time. And a girl from the North Side was so <u>remote</u> that for all practical purposes she did not exist. But I was curious. "What are you writing her a letter for? Did she leave town, or something?"

"She hasn't left town," he answered. "I wasn't going to send it. I just felt like writing to her." I was glad that I had never become involved with love—love that brought desperation to

323

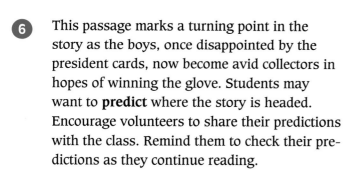

6 This passage marks a turning point in the story as the boys, once disappointed by the president cards, now become avid collectors in hopes of winning the glove. Students may want to **predict** where the story is headed. Encourage volunteers to share their predictions with the class. Remind them to check their predictions as they continue reading.

your eyes, that caused you to write letters you did not plan to send. Shrugging with <u>indifference</u>, I began to search in the closet for the old baseball glove. I found it on the shelf, under some old sneakers. The webbing was torn and the padding gone. I thought of the sting I would feel when a sharp grounder slapped into the glove, and I winced.

"You tell anybody about me and Sally and I'll—"

"I know. You'll muckalize me."

I did not <u>divulge</u> his secret and often shared his agony, particularly when he sat at the supper table and left my mother's special butterscotch pie untouched. I had never realized before how terrible love could be. But my compassion was short-lived because I had other things to worry about: report cards due at Eastertime; the loss of income from old Mrs. Belander, who had gone to live with a daughter in Boston; and, of course, the Presidents.

Because a <u>stalemate</u> had been reached, the President cards were the <u>dominant</u> force in our lives—mine, Roger Lussier's and Rollie Tremaine's. For three weeks, as the baseball season approached, each of us had a complete set—complete except for one President, Grover Cleveland. Each time a box of cards arrived at the store we hurriedly bought them (as hurriedly as our funds allowed) and tore off the wrappers, only to be confronted by James Monroe or Martin Van Buren or someone else. But never Grover Cleveland, never the man who had been the twenty-second and the twenty-fourth President of the United States. We argued about Grover Cleveland. Should he be placed between Chester Alan Arthur and Benjamin Harrison as the twenty-second President or did he belong between Benjamin Harrison and William McKinley

324

as the twenty-fourth President? Was the card company playing fair? Roger Lussier brought up a horrifying possibility— did we need *two* Grover Clevelands to complete the set?

Indignant, we stormed Lemire's and protested to the <u>harassed</u> storeowner, who had long since vowed never to stock a new series. Muttering angrily, he searched his bills and <u>receipts</u> for a list of rules.

"All right," he announced. "Says here you only need one Grover Cleveland to finish the set. Now get out, all of you, unless you've got money to spend."

Outside the store, Rollie Tremaine picked up an empty tobacco tin and <u>scaled</u> it across the street. "Boy," he said. "I'd give five dollars for a Grover Cleveland."

When I returned home I found Armand sitting on the <u>piazza</u> steps, his chin in his hands. His mood of dejection mirrored my own, and I sat down beside him. We did not say anything for a while.

"Want to throw the ball around?" I asked.

He sighed, not bothering to answer.

"You sick?" I asked.

He stood up and hitched up his trousers, pulled at his ear and finally told me what the matter was—there was a big dance next week at the high school, the Spring Promenade, and Sally had asked him to be her <u>escort</u>.

I shook my head at the <u>folly</u> of love. "Well, what's so bad about that?"

"How can I take Sally to a fancy dance?" he asked desperately. "I'd have to buy her a <u>corsage</u> . . . And my shoes are practically falling apart. Pa's got too many worries now to buy me new shoes or give me money for flowers for a girl."

325

I nodded in sympathy. "Yeah," I said. "Look at me. Baseball time is almost here, and all I've got is that old glove. And no Grover Cleveland card yet . . ."

"Grover Cleveland?" he asked. "They've got some of those up on the North Side. Some kid was telling me there's a store that's got them. He says they're looking for Warren G. Harding."

"Holy Smoke!" I said. "I've got an extra Warren G. Harding!" Pure joy sang in my veins. I ran to my bicycle, swung into the seat—and found that the front tire was flat.

"I'll help you fix it," Armand said.

⊛ 326 ⊛

Within half an hour I was at the North Side Drugstore, where several boys were matching cards on the sidewalk. Silently but blissfully I shouted: President Grover Cleveland, here I come!

After Armand had left for the dance, all dressed up as if it were Sunday, the small green box containing the corsage under his arm, I sat on the railing of the piazza, letting my feet dangle. The neighborhood was quiet because the Frenchtown Tigers were at Daggett's Field, practicing for the first baseball game of the season.

I thought of Armand and the ridiculous expression on his face when he'd stood before the mirror in the bedroom. I'd avoided looking at his new black shoes. "Love," I muttered.

Spring had arrived in a sudden stampede of apple blossoms and fragrant breezes. Windows had been thrown open and dust mops had banged on the sills all day long as the women busied themselves with housecleaning. I was puzzled by my lethargy. Wasn't spring supposed to make everything bright and gay?

I turned at the sound of footsteps on the stairs. Roger Lussier greeted me with a sour face.

"I thought you were practicing with the Tigers," I said.

"Rollie Tremaine," he said. "I just couldn't stand him." He slammed his fist against the railing. "Jeez, why did *he* have to be the one to get a Grover Cleveland? You should see him showing off. He won't let anybody even touch that glove . . ."

I felt like Benedict Arnold and knew that I had to confess what I had done.

"Roger," I said, "I got a Grover Cleveland card up on the North Side. I sold it to Rollie Tremaine for five dollars."

⊛ 327 ⊛

7 This paragraph marks another turning point in the story. Armand and Jerry both have problems on their hands, but Armand has offered a solution to Jerry's problem. Students may want to **predict** what Jerry will do now. Allow time for them to share and discuss their predictions. Remind them to carefully consider what they already know before they predict what will happen next.

8 Some students may need to clarify what has happened here. Remind them that **rereading** previous passages, or keeping their questions in mind as they continue reading, will help them figure out where Armand got the money and why Jerry is so unhappy.

"Are you crazy?" he asked.

"I needed that five dollars. It was an—an emergency."

"Boy!" he said, looking down at the ground and shaking his head. "What did you have to do a thing like that for?"

I watched him as he turned away and began walking down the stairs.

"Hey, Roger!" I called.

He squinted up at me as if I were a stranger, someone he'd never seen before.

"What?" he asked, his voice flat.

"I had to do it," I said. "Honest."

He didn't answer. He headed toward the fence, searching for the board we had loosened to give us a secret passage.

🍂 328 🍂

I thought of my father and Armand and Rollie Tremaine and Grover Cleveland and wished that I could go away someplace far away. But there was no place to go.

Roger found the loose slat in the fence and slipped through. I felt betrayed: weren't you supposed to feel good when you did something fine and noble?

A moment later two hands gripped the top of the fence and Roger's face appeared. "Was it a real emergency?" he yelled.

"A real one!" I called. "Something important!"

His face dropped from sight and his voice reached me across the yard: "All right."

"See you tomorrow!" I yelled.

I swung my legs over the railing again. The gathering dusk began to soften the sharp edges of the fence, the rooftops, the distant church steeple. I sat there a long time, waiting for the good feeling to come.

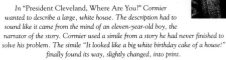

MEET ROBERT CORMIER, AUTHOR

Robert Cormier began his writing career as a reporter and eventually became an author of books. Even though he has been writing for many years there is one aspect of writing that he does not like. "I'm terrible at describing landscapes—trees, buildings. The inanimate things don't interest me. I always think, 'Oh, no, here comes another building I have to describe.' So I usually use a simile or metaphor."

In "President Cleveland, Where Are You?" Cormier wanted to describe a large, white house. The description had to sound like it came from the mind of an eleven-year-old boy, the narrator of the story. Cormier used a simile from a story he had never finished to solve his problem. The simile "It looked like a big white birthday cake of a house!" finally found its way, slightly changed, into print.

🍂 329 🍂

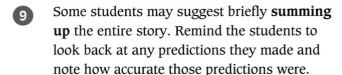

9 Some students may suggest briefly **summing up** the entire story. Remind the students to look back at any predictions they made and note how accurate those predictions were.

Some students may **wonder** why Jerry acted as he did or why Roger felt so betrayed by Jerry's actions. Encourage students to wonder aloud. If some students have **interpreted** Jerry's motives, encourage them to share their thoughts with the class.

Discussing Strategy Use

Encourage the students to share the strategies they used while reading "President Cleveland, Where Are You?" and to discuss how these strategies helped them understand the selection. Students who **wondered** as they read the selection might discuss whether this strategy improved their understanding and enjoyment of the story.

*

EXPLORING THROUGH DISCUSSION

**Reflecting on
the Selection**
*Whole-Group
Discussion*

The whole group discusses the selection and any thoughts or questions that it raises. During this time, students also **return to the clues, problems, and wonderings** they noted on the chalkboard during browsing.

Assessment

To assess the students' understanding of the text, engage them in a discussion to determine whether they have grasped the following ideas:

- what Jerry learned from the experience of contributing to his father's birthday gift
- why Roger was particularly upset that Rollie Tremaine got the autographed mitt

Response Journal

Jerry's story may remind students of experiences in their own lives. Provide time for them to record their thoughts about the story in their personal response journals.

**Exploring the
Concepts Within
the Selection**
Small-Group Discussion

Small groups discuss the selection's relationship to the explorable concepts related to value. Circulate among the groups and remind the students to refer to the Concept Board and the Question Board for discussion ideas.

**Sharing Ideas
About Explorable
Concepts**

Have the **groups report their ideas** and **discuss them** with the rest of the class. It is crucial that the students' ideas determine this discussion.

- Students may comment that unique or unusual items are generally thought more valuable than mass-produced goods. Because the Lefty glove was not sold in stores, even "wealthy" Rollie Tremaine wanted to win it instead of buying an ordinary glove.
- Students may recognize that guilt can be a great motivator in solving value dilemmas. Jerry's sense of guilt over his father's birthday present most likely helped lead him to the later decision to sell his Grover Cleveland card.
- Students may point out that difficult choices can rarely be made with no regrets at all. Both selfishness (the birthday gift incident) and altruism (selling the Cleveland card) make Jerry unhappy in some ways.

As these ideas and others are stated, have the students **add them to** the **Question Board** or the **Concept Board.**

**Exploring
Concepts Across
Selections**

Ask the students whether this selection reminds them of other selections they have read. They might make connections with other selections in the unit.

- Jerry was obsessed with obtaining the President Cleveland card, but when he finally got it, he found that something else was more important. Students may point out that Juan, in the *Gold Coin,* likewise was obsessed with obtaining Doña Josefa's gold, but in the end he also found something that he valued more.

- Students may realize that, like the children in "The Shoeshine Stand" and "Money Matters," Jerry and Armand weren't always able to rely on their parents for money and had to tap their resourcefulness to find ways to earn money and get the things they wanted most.

Recording Ideas

As students complete the above discussions, ask them to **sum up what they have learned from their conversations and to tell how they might use this information** in further explorations. Any special information or insights may be recorded on the **Concept Board.** Any further questions that they would like to think about, pursue, or investigate may be recorded on the **Question Board.** They may want to discuss the progress that has been made on their questions and to remove any questions that no longer warrant consideration.

➤ Have the students record new ideas about value on page 107 of the Explorer's Notebook.

Evaluating Discussions

Explorer's Notebook, page 107

The Gold Coin by Alma Flor Ada

_____
_____
_____
_____
_____
_____

"President Cleveland, Where Are You?" by Robert Cormier

_____
_____
_____
_____
_____

"The No-Guitar Blues" by Gary Soto

_____
_____
_____
_____
_____
_____

Unit 6/Value   EN 107

Copyright © 1995 Open Court Publishing Company

2 READING WITH A WRITER'S EYE

MINILESSONS

Writer's Craft: Using Adverbs

Have students talk about the types of words that make sentences. They should know that sentences must contain at least a noun (subject) and a verb (predicate). They should understand that these two types of words tell that someone or something has done or is doing or will be doing something. Help students to understand that, although a sentence with only a noun and a verb can get an idea across, sentences can be much more informative and interesting if they have adjectives to describe nouns and **adverbs** to **describe verbs.** Tell students that today they will focus on words that describe verbs.

In "President Cleveland, Where Are You?" Robert Cormier **uses**—but does not overuse—**adverbs to describe how his characters perform certain actions.** He strikes a nice balance between not enough and too much description. Although there are examples of adverbs earlier in the story, the best examples begin on page 314. In the third paragraph, Jerry says that he "rushed home . . . and hurriedly changed" his clothes. The adverb *hurriedly* projects the picture of Jerry changing his clothes in a rush. In the fourth paragraph, Jerry says that his brother Armand "had recently become a stranger." The adverb *recently* indicates that the brothers had previously been closer, but lately (perhaps since Armand entered high school) they had grown apart. Explain that, although the adverbs don't cause any drastic change in the meaning of the sentences, *hurriedly* makes the first sentence easier to picture and *recently* makes the second sentence a little more informative.

Selective Reading: Focus on Using Adverbs

Now have students go back to the story and find other adverbs that help to describe action in sentences. Point out that adverbs often end in *-ly.* Let volunteers read aloud sentences containing adverbs. Then have them explain how the adverb enhances the meaning of the sentence.

Examples of sentences with adverbs include (italics added)
- page 315, paragraph 2: "In recent months Armand had become a figure of authority, siding with my father and mother *occasionally.*"
- page 317, paragraph 4: "Roger Lussier was kicking *disconsolately* at a tin can in the gutter, and Rollie Tremaine sat *sullenly* on the steps in front of the store."
- page 318, paragraph 4: "I zigzagged *recklessly* through Mr. Thibodeau's garden, trying to outrace my guilt."
- page 327, paragraph 1: "*Silently* but *blissfully* I shouted: President Grover Cleveland, here I come!"

Selection-Based Practice

Independent Practice: Using Adverbs

➤ Have the students work individually or in small groups to extend their understanding of adverbs by completing Reading/Writing Connection, page 48.

Words that Describe Verbs

Look in "President Cleveland, Where Are You?" and in other selections you have read for more well-chosen, descriptive adverbs. Write the title of the story, the page on which the adverb appears, and the sentence or sentence part that contains the adverb. Then explain how the adverb makes the sentence clearer.

Title: _____ Page: _____

Sentence: _____

_____

How the adverb makes the sentence clearer: _____

_____

Title: _____ Page: _____

Sentence: _____

_____

How the adverb makes the sentence clearer: _____

_____

Title: _____ Page: _____

Sentence: _____

_____

How the adverb makes the sentence clearer: _____

_____

Look back at this page for examples when you want to use adverbs to help your readers visualize an action more easily or to provide your readers with more information.

Adverbs

_____

48 R/WC   Value/Unit 6

Copyright © 1995 Open Court Publishing Company

Name

Reading/Writing Connection, page 48

Writer's Craft: Story Elements— Plot, Setting, Characterization

Have students discuss the story elements of plot, setting, and characterization. They should have a clear idea of what each of these elements entails. **Plot** is the **story line.** It usually involves some sort of a problem and additional conflicts that the characters must resolve. **Setting** is not only the places **where the story occurs,** but also the time **when it occurs. Characterization is the process through which the writer presents the people** in his or her story. Point out that a good writer introduces these elements as the story unfolds instead of simply stating what they are at the beginning.

Cormier does a fine job of introducing these elements in "President Cleveland, Where Are You?" For example, at the very beginning, Jerry and his friends are collecting movie cowboy trading cards. This beginning helps the reader know something about the setting as well as the characters. It doesn't hint at the plot. The plot isn't made clear until the reader finds out that, by collecting the entire set of president cards, a boy can win a free baseball mitt and that the President Cleveland card is the most difficult one to get. That's when the reader understands that Jerry will spend the rest of the story trying to solve the problem of how to find the card. Later on, another conflict is unveiled: how can Armand get enough money to take Sally to the school dance? The third element, characterization, is interrelated with the first two. Characters are revealed not only through description or through their thoughts and feelings, but through their participation in the plot and through the ways they fit into the setting.

Selective Reading:
Focus on Story
Elements

Now have students go back to the story to find other examples in which Cormier introduces plot, setting, or characterization into the story. Other examples of story elements being introduced in "President Cleveland, Where Are You?" include the following:

- page 313, paragraph 1: The entire paragraph describes Rollie Tremaine as the rich, obnoxious kid who can buy almost anything he wants to buy.
- page 314, paragraphs 1–2: These paragraphs reveal elements of Jerry's character and of the story's setting. They show that Jerry is willing to work hard for money to buy the trading cards, and they indicate the levels of wages and prices during the Depression. Jerry spent two afternoons scrubbing floors for a quarter; however, a dime could get him into the movies.
- page 318, all paragraphs; page 319, paragraph 1: The episode involves the father's birthday tie and Jerry's guilt for having contributed so little. Armand's effort to console him shows still more about their personalities.
- page 322, paragraph 5: This paragraph reveals that Armand worked after school and gave the money he earned to the family.

Independent Practice:
Story Elements

❥ To provide practice in recognizing elements of plot, setting, and characterization, have the students work individually or in small groups to complete Reading/Writing Connection, page 49.

WRITING

Linking Reading
to Writing

Have students look through their writing folders for pieces of writing that they could improve by introducing elements of plot, setting, or characterization in a more subtle, integrated, or thorough manner. Students might also use what they've learned about adverbs to improve how they describe their characters' actions. After sufficient time has passed, allow volunteers to read aloud their original versions and their revisions. Ask them to explain how they think they have improved their writing.

✱ Writing Process

Because the students are approaching the end of the final unit, you might want to suggest that they focus on proofreading or publishing any of the pieces on which they have been working.

VOCABULARY

Concept-related words in the story that students may discuss include *swapped* and *bargained.* Another word from the selection which may require some discussion is *muckalize.* Explain to students that this is a slang term that is formed by adding the ending, *-alize,* meaning "to cause to become," to the noun *muck.* Although this particular term is out of fashion now, students may be familiar with similar constructions. Other words the students may want to remember and use are *obsessed, jealously, envy, betrayed, dignity,* and *competition.* Have copies of

Selection-Based Practice

Adding to Personal Word Lists

"President Cleveland, Where Are You?"

Story Elements: Plot, Setting, Characterization

Look at "President Cleveland, Where Are You?" and at other stories that you have read for more examples of ways authors develop plot, setting, and characterization. Write the title of the story and the numbers of the page and the paragraph that contain information about one of these story elements. Then tell what each example reveals about the plot, the setting, or the characters.

Title: _____

Page and paragraph: _____

What the example reveals about either the plot, the setting, or the characters:

_____
_____
_____
_____

Title: _____

Page and paragraph: _____

What the example reveals about either the plot, the setting, or the characters:

_____
_____
_____
_____

Title: _____

Page and paragraph: _____

What the example reveals about either the plot, the setting, or the characters:

_____
_____
_____
_____

Story Elements

Unit 6/Value   R/WC 49

Copyright © 1995 Open Court Publishing Company

Name

Reading/Writing Connection, page 49

Vocabulary Exploration form, Reproducible Master 15, available for students who wish to add these or any other words or phrases from the story to the Personal Dictionary section of their Writer's Notebook. For additional opportunities to build vocabulary, see **Teacher Tool Card 77.**

3 GUIDED AND INDEPENDENT EXPLORATION

EXPLORING CONCEPTS BEYOND THE TEXT

Guided Exploration

Students will select activities in which they explore value. Refer them to the **Exploration Activities poster** and give them time to choose an activity and to discuss what they wish to explore and how they wish to go about it. If the students need further help, here are some suggestions:

- Jerry and his friends had their own reasons for placing a high value on the trading cards they collected. Students may be surprised to learn that serious card collectors today pay hundreds or thousands of dollars for trading cards that seventy years ago came free with bubble gum or candy or even cigarettes. Some students might find books on trading cards in the library. They could report to the class on the various aspects of collecting trading cards. For example, they might find

✱ *Exploring Through Reflective Activities*

out that the value of a card is determined by its condition as well as by its rarity.

- To further explore value as it applies to collecting, students may want to look into the various gimmicks that manufacturers today use to turn their products into collectors' items. For example, makers of porcelain figurines often break their molds after a certain number of the figurines are produced. Lithographers, or printmakers, often do the same thing to make their art prints more valuable. Encourage the students to share their findings with the class.

Students may want to return to pages 114–115 in their Explorer's Notebook. Encourage them to continue exploring and recording ideas about what has value for various characters they encounter in this unit.

❯ Distribute Home/School Connection 45. Encourage the students to collaborate with their families on learning more about the Great Depression of the 1930s.

Continuing Exploration

As the students discuss their ideas and perform their **small-group assignments,** questions may arise that they would like to think more about. Encourage the students to add such questions to the Question Board for later consideration.

Home/School Connection 45

"President Cleveland, Where Are You?"

A message from _____

Our class has just finished reading "President Cleveland, Where Are You?" by Robert Cormier. In this short story, an eleven-year-old boy sacrifices the autographed baseball glove he desperately desires, so that his lovestruck older brother can have new shoes for a school dance. Ask your child to relate the details of the story and explain how it got its title.

One reason behind the brothers' financial troubles is that they are growing up during the Great Depression and their father is frequently laid off from his job. Many children today know little about the Great Depression of the 1930s. You and your child might enjoy learning something about this period in history. Choose an aspect you would like to find out more about and research it together at your local library. Possible issues to investigate include the causes of the Depression, the ways Americans coped with the Depression, some of the phenomena—shanty towns, for instance—that occurred during the Depression, and some of the reasons why the Depression ended—such as the onset of World War II and the many federal programs begun by President Franklin D. Roosevelt during his lengthy tenure in the White House. An alternative way to learn about the Depression is to interview, with your child, an older friend or relative who lived through that time. Find out what your interviewee remembers about how the Depression affected his or her family, community, and the country at large. When your research is complete, help your child prepare a brief report to share with the class.

Notes from the interview: _____

_____

_____

_____

_____

_____

_____

_____

_____

Unit 6/Value   H/SC 45

Copyright © 1995 Open Court Publishing Company

✳ INDEPENDENT WORKSHOP
Building a Community of Scholars

Student-Directed Reading, Writing, and Discussion

The students may need larger blocks of time to complete certain aspects of their exploration of the concepts surrounding value. Some students may be well into the writing stage. Others may need a gentle reminder from you about organizing their time according to an approaching deadline.

WORKSHOP TIP

Have the students meet with the members of their group and list the materials they will need to complete their explorations of value. Remind them to check the writing strategy posters for pointers on writing or revising.

Additional Opportunities for Independent Reading, Writing, and Cross-curricular Activities

✳ Reading Roundtable

Some students may wish to locate and read other stories and novels by Robert Cormier. Encourage them to share their reading with the rest of the class. Be sure to model good reading habits by doing your own outside reading during this time.

Cross-curricular Activity Cards

The following Cross-curricular Activity Cards from the Student Toolbox are appropriate for this selection:

- 17 Art—Accurate Art
- 31 Social Studies—Uncle Jumbo

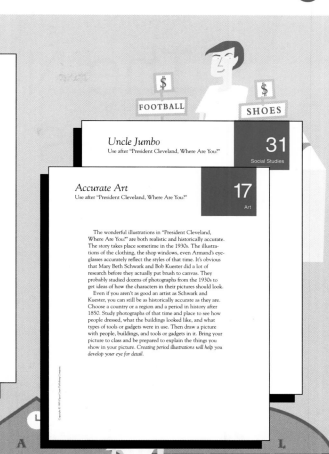

Uncle Jumbo 31
Use after "President Cleveland, Where Are You?"
Social Studies

Accurate Art 17
Use after "President Cleveland, Where Are You?"
Art

The wonderful illustrations in "President Cleveland, Where Are You?" are both realistic and historically accurate. The story takes place sometime in the 1930s. The illustrations of the clothing, the shop windows, even Armand's eyeglasses accurately reflect the styles of that time. It's obvious that Mary Beth Schwark and Bob Kuester did a lot of research before they actually put brush to canvas. They probably studied dozens of photographs from the 1930s to get ideas of how the characters in their pictures should look.
Even if you aren't as good an artist as Schwark and Kuester, you can still be as historically accurate as they are. Choose a country or a region and a period in history after 1850. Study photographs of that time and place to see how people dressed, what the buildings looked like, and what types of tools or gadgets were in use. Then draw a picture with people, buildings, and tools or gadgets in it. Bring your picture to class and be prepared to explain the things you show in your picture. *Creating period illustrations will help you develop your eye for detail.*

Additional Opportunities for Solving Learning Problems

Tutorial

Remember that the group of students who need tutoring may change from one period to another, as well as from one day to another. You may want to use this time to work with those students who need some extra help. The following teaching aids are available in the Teacher Toolbox for your convenience:

- Writer's Craft/Reading: Elaboration Through Providing Descriptions, Teacher Tool Card 40
- Grammar, Mechanics, and Usage: Using Adjectives and Adverbs, Teacher Tool Card 68
- Writer's Craft/Reading: Characterization, Teacher Tool Card 13
- Writer's Craft/Reading: Setting, Teacher Tool Card 14
- Writer's Craft/Reading: Plot, Teacher Tool Card 15
- Grammar, Mechanics, and Usage: Using Parentheses, Dashes, and Ellipses, Teacher Tool Card 54

Assessment

The No-Guitar Blues

1 READING THE SELECTION

INFORMATION FOR THE TEACHER

About the Selection

Fausto dreams of becoming a rock star, but his parents cannot afford to buy him a guitar. He tries to earn some guitar money doing yard work, but nobody seems to be hiring. As he sits dejectedly on a curbside, sharing an orange with a friendly runaway dog, Fausto suddenly has a stroke of genius—but will his conscience let him carry out his deceitful scheme? Gary Soto's perceptive characterization and gentle wit make "The No-Guitar Blues" a thoroughly engaging read. Young readers will also enjoy Andy San Diego's humorous and unusual illustrations.

Link to the Unit Concepts

In "The No-Guitar Blues" pages 330–339, a young boy struggles with the question of whether regaining his integrity is more important than buying the guitar that he desperately wants. Students may find themselves wondering whether it is okay to take money away from those who can easily afford to lose some.

About the Author

Gary Soto is an award-winning poet and writer of prose about working-class Mexican Americans. Born in 1952 to migrant-laborer parents, Soto spent part of his childhood harvesting produce beside his mother and father in Southern California. In his poems and stories, Soto describes the struggle of poor Mexican Americans as they try to survive the street violence of urban barrios or the backbreaking labor of farms, orchards, and vineyards. Besides being a writer, Soto is an associate professor at the University of California at Berkeley.

LESSON OVERVIEW

"The No-Guitar Blues" by Gary Soto, pages 330–339

READING THE SELECTION

Materials

Student anthology, pp. 330–339
Explorer's Notebook, p. 107
Assessment Masters 1–2, 8

READING WITH A WRITER'S EYE

Minilesson

Assessment

Materials

Reproducible Master 15

FYI

Teacher Tool Card
- Spelling and Vocabulary: Building Vocabulary, 77

GUIDED AND INDEPENDENT EXPLORATION

Materials

Explorer's Notebook, p. 119

Independent Workshop

Optional Materials from Student Toolbox

Tradebook Connection Cards

Cross-curricular Activity Cards
- 10 Music—The International Language
- 32 Social Studies—Homemade Tortillas

FYI

Learning Framework Card
- Reading Roundtable, 6

NOTES

Asterisks (*) throughout the lesson indicate learning frameworks. Learning Framework Cards and Teacher Tool Cards can be found in the Teacher Toolbox.

INFORMATION FOR THE STUDENT

Although this selection is fiction, Soto mentions some real people, some real musical groups, and the *American Bandstand* television program, which went off the air before today's elementary students could have viewed it. Soto does so to provide an element of realism to his story. Students do not have to be familiar with the names to understand the plot of "The No-Guitar Blues." However, if they are interested, they can find out more about *conjunto* music, Los Lobos, Ray Comacho and the Teardrops, Lydia Mendoza, Flaco Jimenez, and Little Joe and La Familia. Remind the students to use the Glossary for definitions or pronunciations of unfamiliar words. The following Spanish words may be difficult for some students. The respellings provided here may help. If you have any Spanish-speaking students in class, ask them to help with pronunciations and to translate.

page 330
conjunto (kōn hŏŏn tō)
Flaco Jimenez (flä′ cō hē mä′ nes)
La Familia (lä fä mē′ lē ä)

page 335
empanada (em′ pä nä′ dä)

page 337
chorizo con huevos (chō rē′ sō kōn wä′ vōs)

page 339
Lupe (lōō′ pā)
hijo (ē′ hō′)

COGNITIVE AND RESPONSIVE READING

Activating Prior Knowledge

Ask students whether they have ever wanted something that their parents could not or would not get for them. Encourage students to tell what they did about it.

Setting Reading Goals and Expectations

Have the students **browse the first page** of the selection, using the **clues/problems/wondering procedure.** Students will return to these observations after reading.

Recommendations for Reading the Selection

Explain to the students that they will read this selection to assess what they have learned about value. Place the students in small groups. Tell them that they will decide in their small groups how to read the selection. For example, the groups may choose from among the following options:
• to read silently but stay in groups, stopping to ask each other questions when they need help

- to take turns reading aloud and summarizing one section at a time
- to read silently on their own

Encourage the students to use the strategies that they think will best help them understand and appreciate the story. They should feel free to refer to the **reading strategy posters** whenever necessary. Advise them to collaborate with other students in their groups if they encounter reading difficulties. They should also help other members of their group by offering suggestions.

➤ Distribute copies of Assessment Master 8, Concept Connections for unit 6, Value, which can be found in the booklet Masters for Continuous Assessment in the Teacher Toolbox. Tell the students that after reading the selection in their groups, they will write their responses independently on the Concept Connections page. Afterward, they will regroup and share their findings, changing any ideas they wish.

Assessment Master 8

Concept Connections

1. Explain what this selection is about. Write a short summary.

2. Tell what this selection has to do with value.

3. Tell how this selection is like other selections you have read in this unit.

4. You have read many selections about value. How did *this* selection change your ideas about value?

Date

Name

Unit 6/Value   Assessment Master 8

Copyright © 1995 Open Court Publishing Company

THINK ALOUD PROMPTS

To foster independence, think-aloud prompts are not provided for Assessment lessons.

THE NO-GUITAR BLUES

Gary Soto
illustrated by Andy San Diego

The moment Fausto saw the group Los Lobos on "American Bandstand," he knew exactly what he wanted to do with his life—play guitar. His eyes grew large with excitement as Los Lobos ground out a song while teenagers bounced off each other on the crowded dance floor.

He had watched "American Bandstand" for years and had heard Ray Camacho and the Teardrops at Romain Playground, but it had never occurred to him that he too might become a musician. That afternoon Fausto knew his mission in life: to play guitar in his own band; to sweat out his songs and prance around the stage; to make money and dress weird.

Fausto turned off the television set and walked outside, wondering how he could get enough money to buy a guitar. He couldn't ask his parents because they would just say, "Money doesn't grow on trees" or "What do you think we are, bankers?" And besides, they hated rock music. They were into the *conjunto* music of Lydia Mendoza, Flaco Jimenez, and Little Joe and La Familia. And, as Fausto recalled, the last album they bought was *The Chipmunks Sing Christmas Favorites.*

But what the heck, he'd give it a try. He returned inside and watched his mother make tortillas. He leaned against the

kitchen counter, trying to work up the nerve to ask her for a guitar. Finally, he couldn't hold back any longer.

"Mom," he said, "I want a guitar for Christmas."

She looked up from rolling tortillas. "Honey, a guitar costs a lot of money."

"How 'bout for my birthday next year," he tried again.

"I can't promise," she said, turning back to her tortillas, "but we'll see."

Fausto walked back outside with a buttered tortilla. He knew his mother was right. His father was a <u>warehouseman</u> at Berven Rugs, where he made good money but not enough to buy everything his children wanted. Fausto decided to mow lawns to earn money, and was pushing the mower down the street before he realized it was winter and no one would hire him. He returned the mower and picked up a rake. He hopped onto his sister's bike (his had two flat tires) and rode north to the nicer section of Fresno in search of work. He went door-to-door, but after three hours he managed to get only one job, and not to rake leaves. He was asked to hurry down to the store to buy a loaf of bread, for which he received a grimy, dirt-caked quarter.

He also got an orange, which he ate sitting at the curb. While he was eating, a dog walked up and sniffed his leg. Fausto pushed him away and threw an orange peel skyward. The dog caught it and ate it in one gulp. The dog looked at Fausto and wagged his tail for more. Fausto tossed him a slice of orange, and the dog snapped it up and licked his lips.

"How come you like oranges, dog?"

The dog blinked a pair of sad eyes and whined.

"What's the matter? Cat got your tongue?" Fausto laughed at his joke and offered the dog another slice.

At that moment a dim light came on inside Fausto's head. He saw that it was sort of a fancy dog, a terrier or something, with dog tags and a shiny collar. And it looked well fed and healthy. In his neighborhood, the dogs were never <u>licensed</u>, and if they got sick they were placed near the water heater until they got well.

This dog looked like he belonged to rich people. Fausto cleaned his juice-sticky hands on his pants and got to his feet. The light in his head grew brighter. It just might work. He called the dog, patted its muscular back, and bent down to check the license.

"Great," he said. "There's an address."

The dog's name was Roger, which struck Fausto as weird because he'd never heard of a dog with a human name. Dogs should have names like Bomber, Freckles, Queenie, Killer, and Zero.

332

Fausto planned to take the dog home and collect a reward. He would say he had found Roger near the <u>freeway</u>. That would scare the daylights out of the owners, who would be so happy that they would probably give him a reward. He felt bad about lying, but the dog *was* loose. And it might even really be lost, because the address was six blocks away.

Fausto stashed the rake and his sister's bike behind a bush, and, tossing an orange peel every time Roger became <u>distracted</u>, walked the dog to his house. He hesitated on the porch until Roger began to scratch the door with a muddy paw. Fausto had come this far, so he figured he might as well go through with it. He knocked softly. When no one answered, he rang the doorbell. A man in a silky bathrobe and slippers opened the door and seemed confused by the sight of his dog and the boy.

"Sir," Fausto said, gripping Roger by the collar. "I found your dog by the freeway. His dog license says he lives here." Fausto looked down at the dog, then up to the man. "He does, doesn't he?"

The man stared at Fausto a long time before saying in a pleasant voice, "That's right." He pulled his robe tighter around him because of the cold and asked Fausto to come in. "So he was by the freeway?"

"Uh-huh."

"You bad, snoopy dog," said the man, wagging his finger. "You probably knocked over some trash cans, too, didn't you?"

Fausto didn't say anything. He looked around, amazed by this house with its shiny furniture and a television as large as the front window at home. Warm bread smells filled the air and music full of soft tinkling floated in from another room.

"Helen," the man called to the kitchen. "We have a visitor." His wife came into the living room wiping her hands on a dish towel and smiling. "And who have we here?" she asked in one of the softest voices Fausto had ever heard.

"This young man said he found Roger near the freeway."

Fausto repeated his story to her while staring at a <u>perpetual</u> clock with a bell-shaped glass, the kind his aunt got when she celebrated her twenty-fifth anniversary. The lady frowned and said, wagging a finger at Roger, "Oh, you're a bad boy."

"It was very nice of you to bring Roger home," the man said. "Where do you live?"

"By that vacant lot on Olive," he said. "You know, by Brownie's Flower Place."

The wife looked at her husband, then Fausto. Her eyes twinkled triangles of light as she said, "Well, young man, you're probably hungry. How about a turnover?"

"What do I have to turn over?" Fausto asked, thinking she was talking about yard work or something like turning trays of dried raisins.

334

"No, no, dear, it's a pastry." She took him by the elbow and guided him to a kitchen that sparkled with copper pans and bright yellow wallpaper. She guided him to the kitchen table and gave him a tall glass of milk and something that looked like an *empanada*. Steamy waves of heat escaped when he tore it in two. He ate with both eyes on the man and woman who stood arm-in-arm smiling at him. They were strange, he thought. But nice.

"That was good," he said after he finished the turnover. "Did you make it, ma'am?"

"Yes, I did. Would you like another?"

"No, thank you. I have to go home now."

As Fausto walked to the door, the man opened his wallet and took out a bill. "This is for you," he said. "Roger is special to us, almost like a son."

Fausto looked at the bill and knew he was in trouble. Not with these nice folks or with his parents but with himself. How could he have been so <u>deceitful</u>? The dog wasn't lost. It was just having a fun Saturday walking around.

"I can't take that."

"You have to. You deserve it, believe me," the man said.

"No, I don't."

"Now don't be silly," said the lady. She took the bill from her husband and stuffed it into Fausto's shirt pocket. "You're a lovely child. Your parents are lucky to have you. Be good. And come see us again, please."

Fausto went out, and the lady closed the door. Fausto clutched the bill through his shirt pocket. He felt like ringing the doorbell and begging them to please take the money back, but he knew they would refuse. He hurried away, and at the

335

end of the block, pulled the bill from his shirt pocket: it was a crisp twenty-dollar bill.

"Oh, man, I shouldn't have lied," he said under his breath as he started up the street like a <u>zombie</u>. He wanted to run to church for Saturday confession, but it was past four-thirty, when confession stopped.

He returned to the bush where he had hidden the rake and his sister's bike and rode home slowly, not daring to touch the money in his pocket. At home, in the privacy of his room, he examined the twenty-dollar bill. He had never had so much money. It was probably enough to buy a secondhand guitar. But he felt bad, like the time he stole a dollar from the secret fold inside his older brother's wallet.

Fausto went outside and sat on the fence. "Yeah," he said. "I can probably get a guitar for twenty. Maybe at a yard sale—things are cheaper."

His mother called him to dinner.

The next day he dressed for church without anyone telling him. He was going to go to eight o'clock <u>mass</u>.

"I'm going to church, Mom," he said. His mother was in the kitchen cooking *papas* and *chorizo con huevos*. A pile of tortillas lay warm under a dishtowel.

"Oh, I'm so proud of you, Son." She beamed, turning over the crackling *papas*.

His older brother, Lawrence, who was at the table reading the funnies, mimicked, "Oh, I'm so proud of you, my son," under his breath.

At Saint Theresa's he sat near the front. When Father Jerry began by saying that we are all sinners, Fausto thought he looked right at him. Could he know? Fausto fidgeted with guilt. No, he thought. I only did it yesterday.

Fausto knelt, prayed, and sang. But he couldn't forget the man and the lady, whose names he didn't even know, and the *empanada* they had given him. It had a strange name but tasted really good. He wondered how they got rich. And how that dome clock worked. He had asked his mother once how his aunt's clock worked. She said it just worked, the way the refrigerator works. It just did.

Fausto caught his mind wandering and tried to concentrate on his sins. He said a <u>Hail Mary</u> and sang, and when the wicker basket came his way, he stuck a hand reluctantly in his pocket and pulled out the twenty-dollar bill. He ironed it between his palms, and dropped it into the basket. The grown-ups stared. Here was a kid dropping twenty dollars in the basket while they gave just three or four dollars.

337

There would be a second collection for Saint Vincent de Paul, the <u>lector</u> announced. The wicker baskets again floated in the pews, and this time the adults around him, given a second chance to show their charity, dug deep into their wallets and purses and dropped in fives and tens. This time Fausto tossed in the grimy quarter.

Fausto felt better after church. He went home and played football in the front yard with his brother and some neighbor kids. He felt cleared of wrongdoing and was so happy that he played one of his best games of football ever. On one play, he tore his good pants, which he knew he shouldn't have been wearing. For a second, while he examined the hole, he wished he hadn't given the twenty dollars away.

Man, I coulda bought me some Levi's, he thought. He pictured his twenty dollars being spent to buy church candles. He pictured a priest buying an armful of flowers with *his* money.

Fausto had to forget about getting a guitar. He spent the next day playing soccer in his good pants, which were now his old pants. But that night during dinner, his mother said she remembered seeing an old <u>bass</u> <u>guitarron</u> the last time she cleaned out her father's garage.

"It's a little dusty," his mom said, serving his favorite enchiladas, "but I think it works. Grandpa says it works."

Fausto's ears perked up. That was the same kind the guy in Los Lobos played. Instead of asking for the guitar, he waited for his mother to offer it to him. And she did, while gathering the dishes from the table.

"No, Mom, I'll do it," he said, hugging her. "I'll do the dishes forever if you want."

338

It was the happiest day of his life. No, it was the second-happiest day of his life. The happiest was when his grandfather Lupe placed the guitarron, which was nearly as huge as a washtub, in his arms. Fausto ran a thumb down the strings, which vibrated in his throat and chest. It sounded beautiful, deep and eerie. A pumpkin smile widened on his face.

"OK, *hijo*, now you put your fingers like this," said his grandfather, smelling of tobacco and aftershave. He took Fausto's fingers and placed them on the strings. Fausto strummed a chord on the guitarron, and the bass <u>resounded</u> in their chests.

The guitarron was more complicated than Fausto imagined. But he was confident that after a few more lessons he could start a band that would someday play on "American Bandstand" for the dancing crowds.

339

*

EXPLORING THROUGH DISCUSSION

Reflecting on the Selection

As they read the selection, circulate among the groups to observe the students' understanding of the concepts as well as their collaboration in solving reading difficulties. As you note the students' collaborative group discussions, mark your Teacher's Observation Log for the students in one or two groups. Take a moment to reflect on how each student is changing from unit to unit in his or her ability to use reading strategies effectively. Have the groups break while the students respond independently to Concept Connections, Assessment Master 8.

ASSESSMENT TIP This is an ideal time to mark observations in your Teacher's Observation Log.

Exploring Concepts Within the Selection

When the Concept Connections have been completed, have students rejoin their groups to compare and discuss their responses. Then collect the Concept Connection pages and continue with the lesson as usual.

Sharing Ideas About Explorable Concepts

Have the groups report their ideas and discuss them with the rest of the class. It is crucial that the students' ideas determine this discussion.

- Some students may note that rich versus poor was not really an issue in Fausto's mind. Roger's owners could easily afford to give Fausto twenty dollars; nonetheless, Fausto felt bad simply because he had lied.
- Students may recognize that Fausto's donation was motivated by his conscience alone. He did not have to give away the money—only he knew that he had made it dishonestly—but his conscience troubled him too much to let him keep it.

TEACHING TIP Keep your mind open to new or unexpected student comments.

As these ideas and/or others are stated, have the students add them to the **Concept Board.** If questions arise, add them to the **Question Board.**

Exploring Concepts Across Selections

Ask the students whether this story reminds them of others that they have read. Students may make connections with other selections in the unit.

- Students may compare Fausto with Jerry in "President Cleveland, Where Are You?" Each character wants something that his family cannot afford to buy him, and each sacrifices something that he really wants in order to do what he feels is right. Both boys act to correct previous misdeeds, although Fausto's guilt was more direct than Jerry's.
- Students will probably mention that Fausto, like many other characters in this unit, discovers that deceitful behavior brings no reward.

Recording Ideas

As they complete the above discussions, ask the students to **sum up what they have learned from their conversations and to tell how they might use this information** in further explorations. Any special information or insights may be recorded on the Concept Board. Any further questions that they would like to think about, pursue, or investigate may be recorded on the Question Board. They may want to discuss the

Evaluating Discussions

progress that has been made on their questions and to cross out any questions that no longer warrant consideration.

➤ Remind students to record their findings on page 107 of the Explorer's Notebook.

Self-Assessment Questionnaire

➤ After these parts of the lesson have been completed, you may wish to distribute copies of Assessment Master 2, Self-Assessment Questionnaire, which can be found with the assessment materials in the Teacher Toolbox. Make sure that there is adequate time for the students to complete this important assessment piece.

Explorer's Notebook, page 107

The Gold Coin by Alma Flor Ada

_____
_____
_____
_____
_____
_____

"President Cleveland, Where Are You?" by Robert Cormier

_____
_____
_____
_____
_____

"The No-Guitar Blues" by Gary Soto

_____
_____
_____
_____
_____
_____

Copyright © 1995 Open Court Publishing Company

Unit 6/Value   EN 107

Assessment Master 2

Self-Assessment Questionnaire

1. How would you rate this selection?
   ○ easy   ○ medium   ○ hard

2. If you checked **medium** or **hard**, answer these questions.
   - Which part of the selection did you find especially difficult?
   - What strategy did you use to understand it?

   _____
   _____

   - Were some of the words hard?
   - What did you do to figure out their meaning?

   _____
   _____

3. What do you feel you need to work on to make yourself a better reader?

   _____
   _____

4. Give an example of something you said in the group. Tell why you said it.

   _____
   _____

5. Give an example of something that people in the group helped you understand about the selection.

   _____
   _____

Date _____   Name _____

INDIVIDUAL   GROUP

Self-Assessment Questionnaire   Assessment Master 2

Copyright © 1995 Open Court Publishing Company

2 READING WITH A WRITER'S EYE

MINILESSON

Remind the students that in each selection that they have read so far, they have discussed something that the writer did particularly well. For example, in "President Cleveland, Where Are You?" they discussed Cormier's use of adverbs and his development of plot, characterization, and setting.

Tell the students that they will have the opportunity to decide what Gary Soto did well in "The No-Guitar Blues." To focus their thinking, you might ask them to remember anything in the story that particularly stood out or appealed to them. Encourage them to reread favorite sections. Did the author use any particular writing techniques that made the story interesting, exciting, or unusual?

Allow time for the students to skim the story, if necessary, to refresh their memories. If they have trouble expressing their thoughts about the writing, model a response by pointing out things that you found noteworthy about Soto's writing. For example, you might point out Soto's use of dialogue to create very real characters.

WRITING

Linking Reading to Writing

Encourage students to use in their own writing any techniques that they enjoyed in Gary Soto's story. Suggest that they look through their writing folders for pieces that they could improve by incorporating techniques that Soto used.

＊Writing Process

Although no specific writing assignment is recommended here, remind the students to follow the writing process as they continue their work on pieces begun previously.

VOCABULARY

Words from the selection that are related to value and that students may want to discuss and remember include *deceitful, charity,* and *confession.* Have Vocabulary Exploration forms, Reproducible Master 15, available for students who wish to add these or any other words or phrases from the selection to the Personal Dictionary section of their Writer's Notebook. For additional opportunities to build vocabulary, see **Teacher Tool Card 77.**

STEPS TOWARD INDEPENDENCE By this point in the year, the students should have little trouble identifying and discussing examples of noteworthy writing. Be sure that the students understand that they are to apply to their writing what they learn from their reading.

Professional Checkpoint: Reading with a Writer's Eye

The students should be continually adding to the Writing Ideas section in their Writer's Notebook. Reinforce often that they should put ideas in their Writer's Notebook at any time they occur, not just during writing time. Remind students that they need not use every idea that they record in their notebook, or even most of them. They should not be afraid to jot down ideas that they are not sure about. These ideas may prove helpful later.

Notes:

3 GUIDED AND INDEPENDENT EXPLORATION

EXPLORING CONCEPTS BEYOND THE TEXT

Guided Exploration

Students will select activities in which they explore value. Refer them to the **Exploration Activities poster** and give them time to choose an activity and to discuss what they wish to explore and how they wish to go about it. If the students need further help, here is a suggestion:

Fausto could not keep the twenty dollars because his conscience bothered him, so he gave the money to his church. Some students may feel that he should have returned the money to the couple who gave it to him. Others may feel that because the couple did not really need the money and because Fausto did not benefit from it himself, no harm was done. Still others may feel that Fausto should have spent the twenty dollars on himself. Students may wish to have a debate about what Fausto should have done. If so, suggest that three or four volunteers agree to debate each question or point. The rest of the class can act as the audience, posing pertinent questions to the panel after the participants state their positions and make their rebuttals.

❯ Following the debate, some students may want to meet in small groups to continue discussing and writing about the issues that arose during the debate. Have them complete page 119 in their Explorer's Notebook as they work in their groups.

Continuing Exploration

With only two lessons remaining in the unit, students may want to meet in their collaborative groups to evaluate the progress that they have made in exploring value and to discuss what they must do to wrap up their exploration. Students may also want to begin thinking about whether and how they will present the results of their explorations to the class.

* *Exploring Through Reflective Activities*

Debating an Issue

Doing the "Right Thing"

Did Fausto do the "right thing" by donating the money to the church? How did you feel about it? How did your classmates feel? Record the various ideas that came up about this question during the debate.

_____
_____
_____
_____
_____
_____
_____
_____
_____
_____
_____

If you had been Fausto, what would you have done? Why?

_____
_____
_____
_____
_____
_____
_____
_____
_____
_____
_____

Unit 6/Value   EN 119

Copyright © 1995 Open Court Publishing Company

Explorer's Notebook, page 119

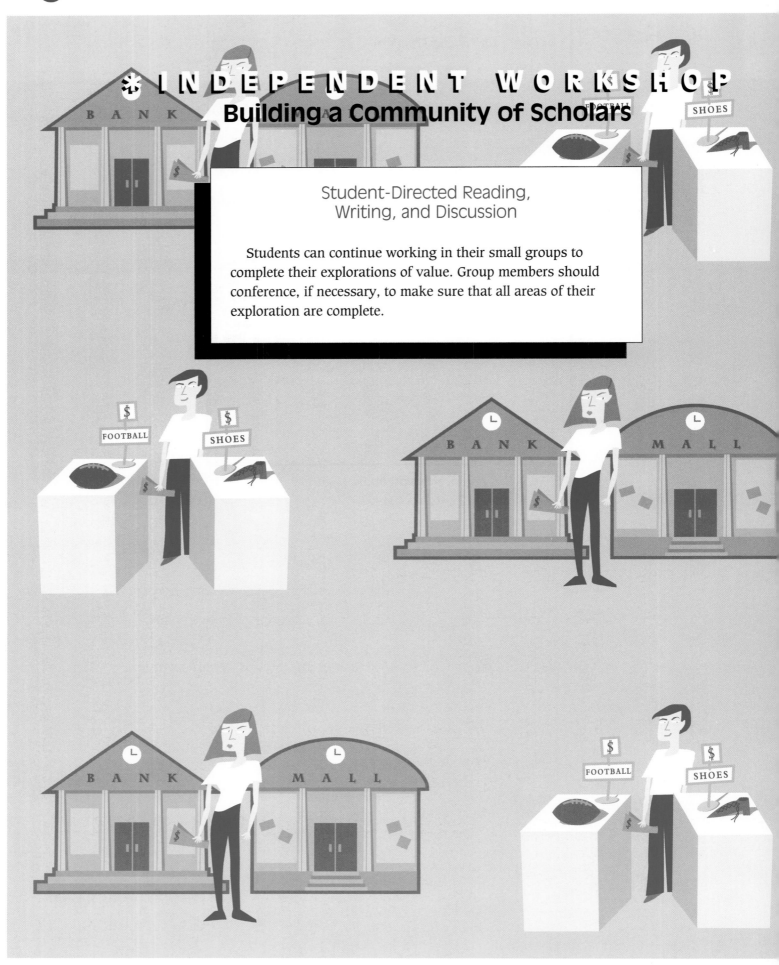

☀ I N D E P E N D E N T   W O R K S H O P

Building a Community of Scholars

Student-Directed Reading, Writing, and Discussion

Students can continue working in their small groups to complete their explorations of value. Group members should conference, if necessary, to make sure that all areas of their exploration are complete.

Additional Opportunities for Independent Reading, Writing, and Cross-curricular Activities

✱ Reading Roundtable

Remind the students that the Tradebook Connection Cards in the Student Toolbox contain activities connected with many well-known children's books. Encourage the students to read other books by Gary Soto and to compare the books for their style, plot, and language. Whenever possible, you should take part in their roundtable discussions. For additional ideas for **Reading Roundtable,** see **Learning Framework Card 6.**

✱ Writing Seminar

As they near the end of this final unit in the reading anthology, students should look through their folders for pieces that they would especially like to publish and share with the rest of the class. Remind them to proofread carefully any piece that they are preparing to publish.

Cross-curricular Activity Cards

The following Cross-curricular Activity Cards from the Student Toolbox are appropriate for this selection:

- 10 Music—The International Language
- 32 Social Studies—Homemade Tortillas

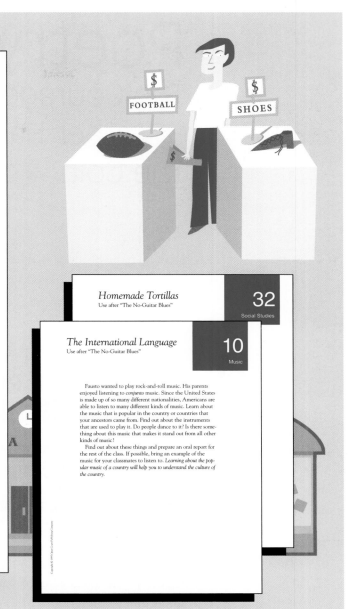

Homemade Tortillas
Use after "The No-Guitar Blues"

32
Social Studies

The International Language
Use after "The No-Guitar Blues"

10
Music

Fausto wanted to play rock-and-roll music. His parents enjoyed listening to *conjunto* music. Since the United States is made up of so many different nationalities, Americans are able to listen to many different kinds of music. Learn about the music that is popular in the country or countries that your ancestors came from. Find out about the instruments that are used to play it. Do people dance to it? Is there something about this music that makes it stand out from all other kinds of music?

Find out about these things and prepare an oral report for the rest of the class. If possible, bring an example of the music for your classmates to listen to. *Learning about the popular music of a country will help you to understand the culture of the country.*

Additional Opportunities for Solving Learning Problems

Use this time to give extra help to individuals or to small groups of students who need it. This is also a good time for peer tutoring. Have students refer to the appropriate Student Tool Cards to guide them as they work. Encourage them to discuss with you any questions that they may have.

Poetry
The Courage That My
Mother Had
The Coin

1 READING THE POEMS

About the
Poems

In "The Courage That My Mother Had," Edna St. Vincent Millay expresses a poignant longing for the courage that her mother could not leave behind in death.

In "The Coin," Sara Teasdale likens a fond memory to a coin that cannot be lost or stolen.

Link to the
Unit Concepts

In the poems on pages 340 and 341, two much-honored poets contribute to the discussion of value by offering their ideas of what is important to them. Both Millay and Teasdale extol, respectively, the value of courage and memories over material objects.

About the Poets

Edna St. Vincent Millay was born in Rockland, Maine, in 1892. In 1917 she published her first book of poems, *Renascence and Other Poems,* after graduating from Vassar College. Millay then went to live in Greenwich Village in New York City, where she enjoyed the bohemian life style so much that she wrote *A Few Figs from Thistles,* a volume of poems celebrating the moral and spiritual climate of the Village during the 1920s. After marrying Eugen Jan Boissevain in 1923, Millay spent most of her time writing at their farm in Austerlitz, New York. Her collection *The Harp Weaver and Other Poems* won the Pulitzer Prize. During this time she also wrote satirical sketches under the pen name Nancy Boyd. In her poetry of the 1930s and 1940s, Millay focused on social and political themes. She died in 1950.

Sara Teasdale was born in St. Louis in 1884, the youngest child of prosperous parents who doted on her. She attended Mary Institute, a girls' school founded by the grandfather of T. S. Eliot, and grew comfortable in its feminist atmosphere, which almost certainly affected her

LESSON OVERVIEW

"The Courage That My Mother Had" by Edna St. Vincent Millay, page 340
"The Coin" by Sara Teasdale, page 341

READING THE SELECTION

Materials

Student anthology, pp. 340–341
Explorer's Notebook, p. 108

READING WITH A WRITER'S EYE

Minilesson

Discussing Poetry

Materials

Reproducible Master 15

FYI

Teacher Tool Cards
- Writer's Craft/Reading: Genre—Poetry, 10
- Writer's Craft/Reading: Figurative Language, 21
- Spelling and Vocabulary: Building Vocabulary, 77

GUIDED AND INDEPENDENT EXPLORATION

Independent Workshop

Optional Materials from Student Toolbox

Tradebook Connection Cards

Cross-curricular Activity Card
- 20 Science—Hard Rock

Student Tool Cards
- Writer's Craft/Reading: Reading and Writing Poetry, 10
- Writer's Craft/Reading: Figurative Language, 21

FYI

Learning Framework Card
- Writing Seminar, 8

Teacher Tool Cards
- Writer's Craft/Reading: Genre—Poetry, 10
- Writer's Craft/Reading: Figurative Language, 21

NOTES

Asterisks (*) throughout the lesson indicate learning frameworks. Learning Framework Cards and Teacher Tool Cards can be found in the Teacher Toolbox.

development as an individual and as a poet. Teasdale's poems are known for their lyrical evocations of personal memories and experiences. Many of them offer poignant glimpses of Teasdale's feelings about love or beauty. She died in 1933.

INFORMATION FOR THE STUDENT

Share with the students any information about the poets that may interest them.

COGNITIVE AND RESPONSIVE READING

Activating Prior Knowledge

Engage the students in a brief discussion of courage. Then explain that "The Coin" is about a memory. Invite the students to talk briefly about memories of pleasant experiences that they have had.

Setting Reading Goals and Expectations

Encourage students to inspect and comment on the forms of the two poems. After browsing, students may notice that "The Courage That My Mother Had" appears to be the more structured of the two. Students may notice that it is written in three four-line stanzas and that every other line rhymes. "The Coin" does not look as structured; however, it has a basic *a a b b* rhyme scheme (*coin, purloin; king, thing*) that you may wish to point out to students.

Recommendations for Reading the Poems

Read the poems aloud to the class so that the students can enjoy the rhyme and the rhythm of each. Then allow the students to read the poems silently. Finally, ask volunteers to read them aloud. Although no think-alouds are provided, students should provide their own think-alouds as they read. Students may be unfamiliar with some of the vocabulary in the poems. They may need to pause to interpret the figurative language in the last two lines of the first stanza of "The Courage That My Mother Had."

Students may benefit from **responding to the poems** by **making connections.** Model this response and invite them to do the same.

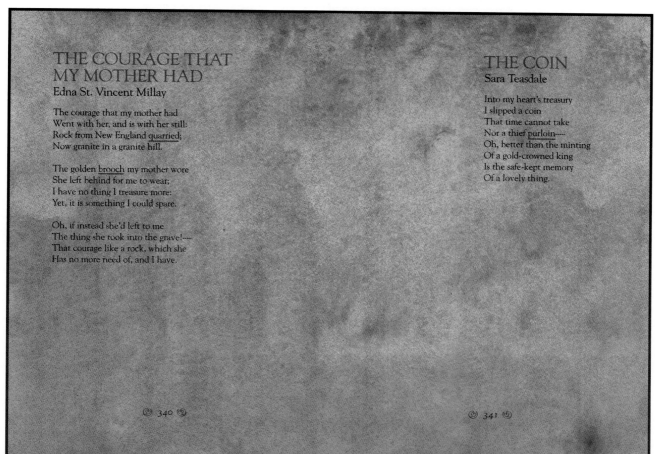

THE COURAGE THAT MY MOTHER HAD
Edna St. Vincent Millay

The courage that my mother had
Went with her, and is with her still:
Rock from New England quarried;
Now granite in a granite hill.

The golden brooch my mother wore
She left behind for me to wear;
I have no thing I treasure more:
Yet, it is something I could spare.

Oh, if instead she'd left to me
The thing she took into the grave!—
That courage like a rock, which she
Has no more need of, and I have.

340

THE COIN
Sara Teasdale

Into my heart's treasury
I slipped a coin
That time cannot take
Nor a thief purloin—
Oh, better than the minting
Of a gold-crowned king
Is the safe-kept memory
Of a lovely thing.

341

---

* **EXPLORING THROUGH DISCUSSION**

Reflecting on the Poems
Whole-Group Discussion

Invite the students to discuss the poems, sharing any **personal thoughts, reactions,** or **questions** that either poem raised. Encourage the students to consider how the mood set in each poem adds to the impact of its message and to think about how studying poems might increase the reader's understanding of value. Students may notice that in the first poem, the mood is sorrowful because the poet laments losing something she values highly, while in the second poem the mood is one of contentment because the poet knows her valued memories cannot be taken from her.

TEACHING TIP Dismiss any preconceived ideas that you may have about what students will say about a selection. Expect the unexpected.

Response Journal

Poetry evokes very personal responses. Provide time for the students to record their thoughts and feelings about these poems.

Recording Ideas

▶ Have the students sum up their discussion and record their ideas and impressions about the poems and the unit concepts on the Concept Board and on page 108 of their Explorer's Notebook.

Evaluating Discussions

Recording Concept Information continued

"The Courage That My Mother Had" by Edna St. Vincent Millay

_____
_____
_____
_____
_____
_____
_____

"The Coin" by Sara Teasdale

_____
_____
_____
_____
_____
_____

The Hundred Penny Box by Sharon Bell Mathis

_____
_____
_____
_____
_____
_____
_____

108 EN   Value/Unit 6

Copyright © 1995 Open Court Publishing Company

Explorer's Notebook, page 108

2

Discussing
Poetry

READING WITH A WRITER'S EYE

MINILESSON

Ask the students if there was anything about the poems that they especially enjoyed. Remind them that in a poem sound and rhythm are important. Poetry is often read aloud so that the listener can hear and enjoy the sounds and the rhythms of the words, phrases, and stanzas. Often these sound patterns increase the impact of the poem on the reader.

Remind the students, also, that poets often use figurative language to express their ideas. Each of the poems in this lesson contains a **metaphor** around which the poet bases her ideas. In the first stanza of "The Courage That My Mother Had," Millay compares her mother's courage to granite and to a rock. She also uses a **simile** to compare her mother's courage to a rock in the third stanza. In "The Coin," Teasdale compares a lovely memory to a coin that cannot be stolen. Explain that **poets like to use metaphors and similes to make their readers stretch their imaginations.** Also, readers who love poetry often enjoy the challenge of interpreting a metaphor or a simile. To review ideas for discussing poetry and for interpreting figurative language, see **Teacher Tool Cards 10 and 21.**

Figurative Language

Linking Reading
to Writing

Encourage students to look through their writing folders for pieces of their writing that they could make more interesting by describing things with metaphors or similes instead of adjectives. Make sure they understand that fresh metaphors and similes are more interesting than overused ones. Invite the students to share examples of how they have used metaphors or similes in their own writing.

* Writing Process

Some students may wish to write poems. Encourage them to brainstorm with their peers. Remind them to follow the writing process as they develop their poetry.

VOCABULARY

One concept-related word from the "The Courage That My Mother Had" is the verb *treasure.* Students may also want to discuss the word *quarried.* In "The Coin" the word *purloin* may interest students. Have copies of Vocabulary Exploration form, Reproducible Master 15, available for students who request them. Remind students to add these or any other words from the poems to the Personal Dictionary section of their Writer's Notebook. For additional opportunities to build vocabulary, see **Teacher Tool Card 77.**

VOCABULARY TIP Encourage students to choose words that they feel are important and to complete Vocabulary Exploration forms. Student choice leads to student ownership of words.

3 GUIDED AND INDEPENDENT EXPLORATION

EXPLORING CONCEPTS BEYOND THE TEXT

Guided
Exploration

Invite the students to discuss some abstract qualities that they value highly. Some students may want to talk about personal qualities such as courage, honesty, and responsibility that they value in themselves or in family and friends. Be sure that the students feel free to mention any character attribute they admire or they wish they possessed, whether or not it is generally considered positive. Students may also wish to discuss the importance of memories and experiences. Allow volunteers to share some of their most valued memories with the class.

* Exploring Through Reflective Activities

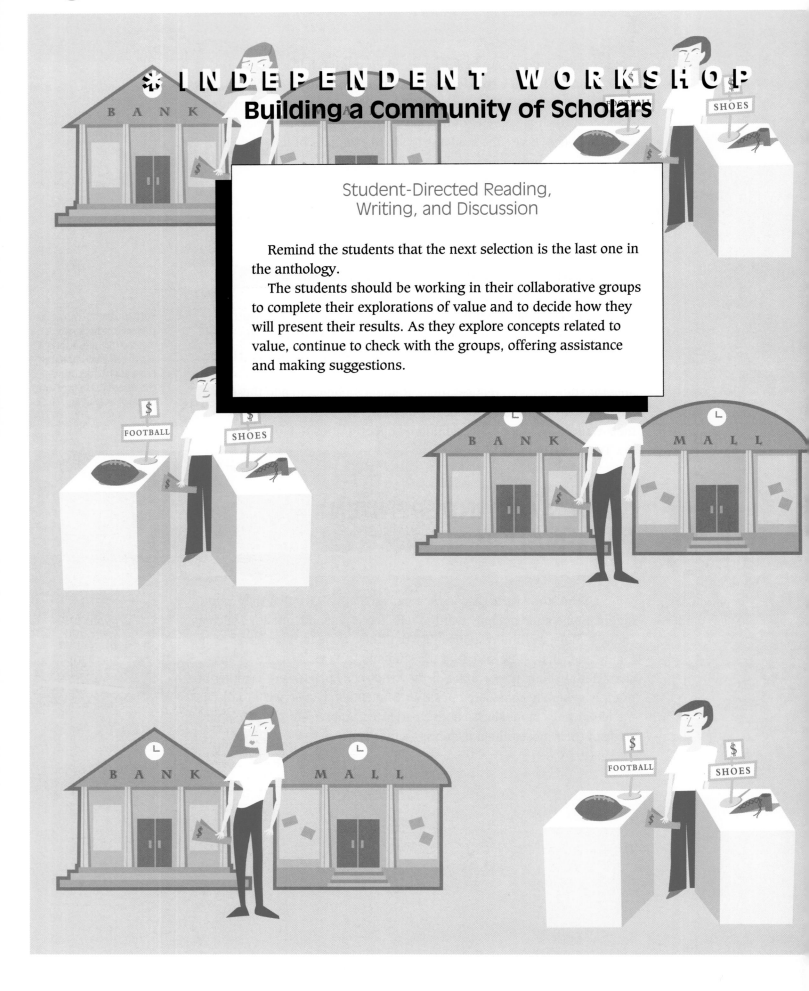

✳ INDEPENDENT WORKSHOP
Building a Community of Scholars

Student-Directed Reading, Writing, and Discussion

Remind the students that the next selection is the last one in the anthology.

The students should be working in their collaborative groups to complete their explorations of value and to decide how they will present their results. As they explore concepts related to value, continue to check with the groups, offering assistance and making suggestions.

Additional Opportunities for Independent Reading, Writing, and Cross-curricular Activities

✻ Reading Roundtable

You might share with the students some of your favorite poetry collections, reading aloud a few of the poems. Discuss the meanings of the poems and the values of the poet that can be inferred from each. Encourage students to share some of their favorite poems with their classmates as well.

✻ Writing Seminar

If they have chosen to write their own poems, encourage the students to consider publishing their poems when these are complete. Remind them that they may need to revise their work several times to achieve satisfaction. For additional ideas for **Writing Seminar,** see **Learning Framework Card 8.**

Cross-curricular Activity Cards

The following Cross-curricular Activity Card in the Student Toolbox is appropriate for this selection:

- 20 Science—Hard Rock

Hard Rock
"The Courage That My Mother Had"

20 Science

Edna St. Vincent Millay used granite as a metaphor to describe her mother's courage. Other writers have used granite to describe things that are hard: a heart of granite cannot be moved; a granite face shows no emotion; a will of granite cannot be swayed from its purpose. The reason that granite is used to describe things that are hard to change is that granite is an extremely hard rock.

Learn more about granite. Of what minerals is it composed? How is it formed? Why is it so hard? How is it taken out of the earth? For what is it used? Find out the answers to these questions at your local library.

Scientists have a way of testing the hardness of minerals. Learn about this method. If you can obtain some granite and some rock composed of other minerals, use this method to compare their hardness. Then write a report describing what you have learned. *Learning about science helps us appreciate the world we live in.*

Additional Opportunities for Solving Learning Problems

Tutorial

Use this time to give extra help to individuals or small groups who need it. Encourage students to discuss with you any areas in which they are having difficulties. The following aids are available in the Teacher Toolbox for your convenience:

- Writer's Craft/Reading: Genre—Poetry, Teacher Tool Card 10
- Writer's Craft/Reading: Figurative Language, Teacher Tool Card 21

The Hundred Penny Box

1 READING THE SELECTION

INFORMATION FOR THE TEACHER

About the Selection

Michael's great-great-aunt, Dewbet Thomas, is one hundred years old and loaded with memories. She has come to live with Michael's family because she is no longer capable of taking care of herself. The problem is that Aunt Dew has brought with her personal mementos of her hundred years. Michael's mother does her best to accommodate the old lady, but some of Aunt Dew's things are so old and raggedy-looking and useless that she cannot stand having them around the house. Secretly, she begins to get rid of Aunt Dew's shabbier possessions. Author Sharon Bell Mathis has drawn wonderful characterizations of people caught in a true-to-life dilemma.

Link to the Unit Concepts

In *The Hundred Penny Box,* pages 342–367, three sets of values are in conflict. With no way to compromise, someone is sure to be disappointed or hurt. Through the eyes of young Michael Jefferson, author Sharon Bell Mathis demonstrates the difficulty of being caught between two of the most important people in one's life. After reading this selection, students should recognize how important objects with sentimental value can be.

About the Author

Sharon Bell Mathis grew up in Brooklyn and taught special-education classes at a junior high school for many years before deciding to focus on her writing. Mathis has written several award-winning books for young people. In 1976 *The Hundred Penny Box* was chosen as a Newbery Honor Book. In 1975 it was designated a Notable Children's Trade Book in the Field of Social Studies, and a *New York Times* Outstanding Book of the Year. Her *Teacup Full of Roses* and *Listen for the Fig Tree* were both designated ALA Notable Books, and *Sidewalk*

LESSON OVERVIEW

The Hundred Penny Box by Sharon Bell Mathis, pages 342–367

READING THE SELECTION

Materials

Student anthology, pp. 342–367
Explorer's Notebook, p. 108

READING WITH A WRITER'S EYE

Minilessons

Point of View
Describing Characters' Thoughts and
   Feelings

Materials

Reading/Writing Connection, pp. 50–51
Reproducible Masters 15, 24

FYI

Teacher Tool Card
• Spelling and Vocabulary: Building
   Vocabulary, 77

Option for Instruction

Writer's Craft: Dialogue
(Use Teacher Tool Card listed below.)

GUIDED AND INDEPENDENT EXPLORATION

Materials

Home/School Connection 46
Assessment Master 1

Independent Workshop

**Optional Materials from
Student Toolbox**

Tradebook Connection Cards

Cross-curricular Activity Cards
• 11 Music—The Gospel Roots
• 33 Social Studies—Living Books
• 34 Social Studies—The Eleven (or
   Twelve) Penny Box

Student Tool Cards
• Writer's Craft/Reading: Point of
   View, 12
• Writer's Craft/Reading:
   Characterization, 13
• Writer's Craft/Reading: Using
   Dialogue in a Story, 20

Teacher Tool Cards
• Writer's Craft/Reading: Point of
   View, 12
• Writer's Craft/Reading:
   Characterization, 13
• Writer's Craft/Reading: Using
   Dialogue in a Story, 20

Asterisks (*) throughout the lesson indicate learning frameworks. Learning Framework Cards and Teacher Tool Cards can be found in the Teacher Toolbox.

Story received an award from the Council on Interracial Books for Children. Mathis currently lives in Washington, D.C., where she coordinates and teaches the writing of children's literature at the D.C. Black Writers' Workshop, and regularly writes a column for *Ebony, Jr!*

About the Illustrators

Leo and Diane Dillon are thus far the only artists to have won the Caldecott Medal in two consecutive years—in 1976 for *Why Do Mosquitoes Buzz in People's Ears: A West African Tale* and in 1977 for *Ashanti to Zulu: African Traditions*. The husband-and-wife team first met while they were students at Parsons School of Design. During an exhibition in which each had a painting on display, they both admired the other's talent; yet, because of their competitive natures, they became instant rivals. The artists eventually united their talents, marrying and freelancing as a team. Diane describes the creative process that has evolved between them:

> On every project we undertake, we hash out ideas together, jointly decide on style and technique, and both work on every illustration, passing the piece back and forth several times. This doesn't always go smoothly. Particularly in the past, we would argue about colors and approach. But after years of collaboration—in spite of competition between us—we have reached a point where our work is done by an agent we call "the third artist." The third artist is a combination of the two of us individually. . . It comes up with things neither of us would have done. In terms of where we come from and how we grew up, we are very different, and we believe that those differences have lent breadth to the third artist.

Together, the Dillons have illustrated a wide range of books, from African folk tales to Scandinavian epics to science fiction and fantasy. They have worked in a variety of media including pastels, watercolor, acrylic, black ink, airbrush, woodcuts, crewel, and plastic and liquid steel (which created a stained-glass effect). "Over the years we've come to accept that trial and error is part of the process," explains Leo. "Technique is to the graphic artist what words are to the writer."

INFORMATION FOR THE STUDENT

Share any information about Sharon Bell Mathis and Leo and Diane Dillon that you feel will interest your students.

*

COGNITIVE AND RESPONSIVE READING

Activating Prior Knowledge

Tell the students that this story is about a young boy who feels a very close friendship toward his elderly aunt. Then ask if any of them have had a similar friendship with an elderly person. Allow time for students to talk about their experiences with their older friends.

Setting Reading
Goals and
Expectations

Have the students **browse** the **first page** of the selection using the **clues/problems/wondering procedure.** The students will return to these observations after reading.

Recommen-
dations for
Reading the
Selection

Ask the students how they want to read the selection. Because the story is long, you might have volunteers take turns **reading** it **aloud.** If it becomes obvious that the class cannot complete the selection in one reading and still have time to discuss the story, stop the reading at the end of the first part on page 356 so that students can discuss the first part while it is fresh in their minds.

During oral reading, use and encourage think-alouds. During silent reading, allow discussion as needed. Discuss problems, strategies, and reactions after reading.

This would also be a good selection for **responding** to text **by expressing feelings** while reading aloud. Model this response, and then invite the students to respond similarly.

Note: Notice that *The Hundred Penny Box* has been divided into two parts should the students be unable to finish reading the selection in one sitting. The second part of the story begins on page 357 and is indicated by a large initial capital letter.

About the
Reading
Strategies

This selection is full of regional dialect. While the dialect works wonderfully well to add realism to the story and is extremely important in the characterization of Aunt Dew, it may challenge readers at this level. Students will probably want to pause occasionally to clarify unfamiliar words and phrases by **determining what is unclear, applying context clues,** and **rereading any passages that do not make sense.** As these strategies become second nature, students will be able to be more adventurous in choosing their personal reading material.

STEPS TOWARD INDEPEND-ENCE By this point in the year, students should be taking over some of the complex strategies, for example interpreting, and commenting spontaneously rather than relying solely on teacher intervention.

Think-Aloud Prompts
for Use in Oral Reading

Notice the think-aloud prompts with the page miniatures. These are merely suggestions for helping students use the strategies. Remind them to refer to the **reading strategy posters** and to use any strategy that will help them make sense of the text. Encourage the students to collaborate with classmates when confronted with reading difficulties.

THINK ALOUD PROMPTS

These prompts may be used as guides to promote cognitive and responsive reading.

THE HUNDRED PENNY BOX

Sharon Bell Mathis
illustrated by Leo and Diane Dillon

Michael sat down on the bed that used to be his and watched his great-great-aunt, Aunt Dew, rocking in the rocking chair.

He wanted to play with the hundred penny box—especially since it was raining outside—but Aunt Dew was singing that long song again. Sometimes when she sang it she would forget who he was for a whole day.

Then she would call him John.

John was his father's name. Then his mother would say, "He's Mike, Aunt Dew. His name is Michael. John's name is John. His name is Michael." But if his father was home, Aunt Dew would just say "Where's my boy?" Then it was hard to tell whether she meant him or his father. And he would have to wait until she said something more before he knew which one she meant.

Aunt Dew didn't call his mother any name at all.

Michael had heard his father and mother talking in bed late one night. It was soon after they had come from going to Atlanta to bring back Aunt Dew. "She won't even look at me—won't call my name, nothing," his mother had said,

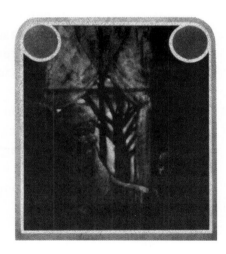

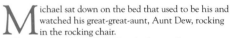

and Michael could tell she had been crying. "She doesn't like me. I know it. I can tell. I do everything I can to make her comfortable—" His mother was crying hard. "I rode half the way across this city—all the way to Mama Dee's—to get some homemade ice cream, some decent ice cream. Mama Dee said, 'The ice cream be melted fore you get home.' So I took a cab back and made her lunch and gave her the ice cream. I sat down at the table and tried to drink my coffee— I mean, I wanted to talk to her, say something. But she sat there and ate that ice cream and looked straight ahead at the wall and never said nothing to me. She talks to Mike and if I come around she even stops talking sometime." His mother didn't say anything for a while and then he heard her say, "I care about her. But she's making me miserable in my own house."

Michael heard his father say the same thing he always said about Aunt Dew. "She's a one-hundred-year-old lady, baby." Sometimes his father would add, "And when I didn't have nobody, she was there. Look here—after Big John and Junie drowned, she gave me a home. I didn't have one. I didn't have nothing. No mother, no father, no nobody. Nobody but her. I've loved her all my life. Like I love you. And that tough beautiful boy we made—standing right outside the door and listening for all he's worth—and he's supposed to be in his room sleep."

Michael remembered he had run back to his room and gotten back into bed and gotten up again and tiptoed over to the bedroom door to close it a little and shut off some of the light shining from the bathroom onto Aunt Dew's face. Then he looked at Aunt Dew and wished she'd wake up and talk to him like she did when she felt like talking and telling him all kinds of stories about people.

"Hold tight, Ruth," he had heard his father say that night. "She knows we want her. She knows it. And baby, baby— sweet woman, you doing fine. Everything you doing is right." Then Michael could hear the covers moving where his mother and father were and he knew his father was putting his arms around his mother because sometimes he saw them **1** still asleep in the morning and that's the way they looked.

344

But he was tired of remembering now and he was tired of Aunt Dew singing and singing and singing.

"Aunt Dew," Michael whispered close to his great-great-aunt's wrinkled face. "Can we play with the hundred penny box?"

2 *"Precious Lord—"*

"Aunt Dew! Let's count the pennies out."

"Take my hand—"

"Aunt Dew!"

"Lead me on—"

Michael thought for a moment. He knew the large scratched wooden box was down beside the dresser, on the floor where he could easily get it.

Except it was no fun to count the pennies alone.

It was better when Aunt Dew whacked him a little and said, "Stop right there, boy. You know what that penny means?" And he'd say, "You tell me," and she would tell him.

But when she started singing it was hard to stop her. At least when she was dancing what she called "moving to the music," she'd get tired after a while. Then she would tell him about the pennies and help count them too.

Michael cupped his large hands—everybody talked about how large his hands were for his age—around his great-great-aunt's ear. "Aunt Dew!" he said loudly.

345

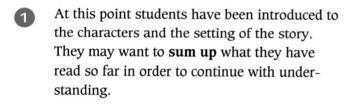

---

1 At this point students have been introduced to the characters and the setting of the story. They may want to **sum up** what they have read so far in order to continue with understanding.

2 Some students may be puzzled by the words in italics. **Rereading** may help, or ask a volunteer to **clarify.** If necessary, explain that the words in italics indicate the words of the song Aunt Dew is singing.

Aunt Dew stopped rocking hard and turned and looked at him. But he didn't say anything and she didn't say anything. Aunt Dew turned her head and began to sing again. Exactly where she had left off. *"Let me stand—"*

Michael moved away from the rocking chair and sat back down on the bed. Then he got up and went to the dresser. He reached down and picked up the heavy, scratched-up hundred penny box from the floor, walked to the bedroom door, and stood there for a moment before he went out.

There was no way to stop Aunt Dew once she started singing that long song.

Michael walked down the hall and held the huge box against his stomach. He could still hear Aunt Dew's high voice.

"I am weak. I am worn."

"What's wrong?" his mother asked when he walked into the kitchen and sat down on a chair and stared at the floor.

He didn't want to answer.

"Oh," his mother said and reached for the hundred penny box in his arms. "Give me that thing," she said. "That goes today! Soon as Aunt Dew's sleep, that goes in the furnace."

Michael almost jumped out of the chair. He wouldn't let go of the big, heavy box. He could hear his great-great-aunt's voice. She was singing louder. *"Lead me through the night, precious Lord. Take my hand."*

"You can't take the hundred penny box," Michael cried. "I'll tell Daddy if you take it and burn it up in the furnace like you burned up all the rest of Aunt Dew's stuff!" Then Michael thought of all the things he and Aunt Dew had hidden in his closet, and almost told his mother.

346

His mother walked closer to him and stood there but he wasn't afraid. Nobody was going to take Aunt Dew's hundred penny box. Nobody. Nobody. Nobody.

"Aunt Dew's like a child," his mother said quietly. "She's like you. Thinks she needs a whole lot of stuff she really doesn't. I'm not taking her pennies—you know I wouldn't take her pennies. I'm just getting rid of that big old ugly wooden box always under foot!"

Michael stood up. "No," he said.

"Mike, did you say no to me?" his mother asked. She put her hands on her hips.

"I mean," Michael said and tried to think fast. "Aunt Dew won't go to sleep if she doesn't see her box in the corner. Can I take it back and then you can let her see it? And when she goes to sleep, you can take it."

"Go put it back in her room then," his mother said. "I'll get it later."

"Okay," Michael said and held the heavy box tighter and walked slowly back down the hall to the small bedroom that used to be his. He opened the door and went in, put the hundred penny box down on the floor and sat down on it, staring at his aunt. She wasn't singing, just sitting. "John-boy," she said.

"Yes, Aunt Dew," Michael answered and didn't care this time that she was calling him John again. He was trying to think.

"Put my music on."

The music wasn't going to help him think because the first thing she was going to do was to make him "move" too.

347

But Michael got off the hundred penny box and reached under his bed and pulled out his blue record player that he had got for his birthday. He had already plugged it in the wall when he heard her say, "Get mine. My own Victrola, the one your father give me."

"Momma threw it out," Michael said and knew he had told her already, a lot of times. "It was broken."

Aunt Dew squeezed her lips real tight together. "Your momma gonna throw me out soon," she said.

Michael stood still and stared at his great-great-aunt. "Momma can't throw *people* out," he said.

"Put my music on, boy," Aunt Dew said again. "And be quick about it."

"Okay," Michael said and turned the record player on and got the record, Aunt Dew's favorite, that they had saved and hidden in the bottom drawer.

The dusty, chipped record was of a lady singing that long song, *"Precious Lord, Take My Hand."* Michael turned it down low.

Aunt Dew started humming and Michael sat down on the bed and tried to think about what he'd do with the hundred penny box.

Aunt Dew got up from her rocking chair and stood up. She kept her arms down by her sides and made her thin hands into fists and clenched her lips tight and moved real slow in one spot. Her small shoulders just went up and down and up and down. "Get up, John-boy," she said, "and move with me. Move with Dewbet Thomas!"

"I don't feel like dancing," Michael said and kept sitting on the bed. But he watched his great-great-aunt move both

348

her thin arms to one side and then to the other and <u>hover</u> her hands about and hold her dress. Then she stopped and started all of a sudden again, just swinging her arms and moving her shoulders up and down and singing some more. Every time the record ended, he'd start it again.

When he was playing it for the third time, he said, "Aunt Dew, where will you put your hundred pennies if you lose your hundred penny box?"

"When I lose my hundred penny box, I lose me," she said and kept moving herself from side to side and humming.

"I mean maybe you need something better than an old cracked-up, wacky-dacky box with the top broken."

"It's *my* old cracked-up, wacky-dacky box with the top broken," Aunt Dew said. And Michael saw her move her shoulders real high that time. "Them's my years in that box," she said. "That's me in that box."

"Can I hide the hundred penny box, Aunt Dew," Michael asked, hoping she'd say yes and not ask him why. He'd hide it like the other stuff she had asked him to and had even told him where to hide it most of the time.

3 "No, don't hide my hundred penny box!" Aunt Dew said out loud. "Leave my hundred penny box right alone. Anybody takes my hundred penny box takes me!"

"Just in case," Michael said impatiently and wished his great-great-aunt would sit back down in her chair so he could talk to her. "Just in case Momma puts it in the furnace when you go to sleep like she puts all your stuff in the furnace in the basement."

"What your momma name?"

"Oh, no," Michael said. "You keep *on* forgetting Momma's name!" That was the only thing bad about being a hundred years old like Aunt Dew—you kept *on* forgetting things that were important.

"Hush, John-boy," Aunt Dew said and stopped dancing and humming and sat back down in the chair and put the quilt back over her legs.

"You keep on forgetting."

"I don't."

"You do, you keep on forgetting!"

"Do I forget to play with you when you worry me to death to play?"

Michael didn't answer.

◕ 350 ◕

"Do I forget to play when you want?"

"No."

"Okay. What your momma name? Who's that in my kitchen?"

"Momma's name is Ruth, but this isn't your house. Your house is in Atlanta. We went to get you and now you live with us."

"Ruth."

Michael saw Aunt Dew staring at him again. Whenever she stared at him like that, he never knew what she'd say next. Sometimes it had nothing to do with what they had been talking about.

"You John's baby," she said, still staring at him. "Look like John just spit you out."

"That's my father."

"My great-nephew," Aunt Dew said. "Only one ever care about me." Aunt Dew rocked hard in her chair then and Michael watched her. He got off the bed and turned off the record player and put the record back into the bottom drawer. Then he sat down on the hundred penny box again.

"See that tree out there?" Aunt Dew said and pointed her finger straight toward the window with the large tree pressed up against it. Michael knew exactly what she'd say.

---

3 Some students may be confused by Aunt Dew's statement about whoever takes her hundred penny box also takes her. They may want to **interpret** her meaning. Allow students to share their interpretations. If necessary, share your own interpretation with them. Some students may be able to **connect** what they have read about Aunt Dew's feelings to their own experiences with losing some prized possession.

"Didn't have no puny-looking trees like that near my house," she said. "Dewbet Thomas—that's me, and Henry Thomas—that was my late husband, had the biggest, tallest, prettiest trees and the widest yard in all Atlanta. And John, that was your daddy, liked it most because he was city and my five sons, Henry, Jr., and Truke and Latt and the twins—Booker and Jay—well, it didn't make them no never mind because it was always there. But when my oldest niece Junie and her husband—we called him Big John—brought your daddy down to visit every summer, they couldn't get the suitcase in the house good before he was climbing up and falling out the trees. We almost had to feed him up them trees!"

"Aunt Dew, we have to hide the box."

"Junie and Big John went out on that water and I was feeling funny all day. Didn't know what. Just feeling funny. I told Big John, I said, 'Big John, that boat old. Nothing but a piece a junk.' But he fooled around and said, 'We taking it out.' I looked and saw him and Junie on that water. Then it wasn't nothing. Both gone. And the boat turned over, going downstream. Your daddy, brand-new little britches on, just standing there looking, wasn't saying nothing. No hollering. I try to give him a big hunk of potato pie. But he just looking at me, just looking and standing. Wouldn't eat none of that pie. Then I said, 'Run get Henry Thomas and the boys.' He looked at me and then he looked at that water. He turned round real slow and walked toward the west field. He never run. All you could see was them stiff little britches—red they was—moving through the corn.

352

Bare-waisted, he was. When we found the boat later, he took it clean apart—what was left of it—every plank, and pushed it back in that water. I watched him. Wasn't a piece left of that boat. Not a splinter."

"Aunt Dew, where can we hide the box!"

"What box?"

"The hundred penny box."

"We can't hide the hundred penny box and if she got to take my hundred penny box—she might as well take me!"

"We have to hide it!"

"No—'we' don't. It's *my* box!"

"It's *my* house. And I said we have to hide it!"

"How you going to hide a house, John?"

"Not the house! Our hundred penny box!"

"It's *my* box!"

Michael was beginning to feel desperate. But he couldn't tell her what his mother had said. "Suppose Momma takes it when you go to sleep?"

Aunt Dew stopped rocking and stared at him again. "Like John just spit you out," she said. "Go on count them pennies, boy. Less you worry me in my grave if you don't. Dewbet Thomas's hundred penny box. Dewbet Thomas a hundred years old and I got a penny to prove it—each year!"

Michael got off the hundred penny box and sat on the floor by his great-great-aunt's skinny feet stuck down inside his father's old slippers. He pulled the big wooden box toward him and lifted the lid and reached in and took out the small cloth roseprint sack filled with pennies. He dumped the pennies out into the box.

353

---

4 Besides speaking in dialect, Aunt Dew rambles somewhat incoherently here. Students may feel the need to clarify this paragraph. They might do this by **rereading** and restating the paragraph in their own words.

5 This is an important memory for Aunt Dew. Students may suggest **summing up** to ensure that they understand it and its importance.

He was about to pick up one penny and put it in the sack, the way they played, and say "One," when his great-great-aunt spoke.

"Why you want to hide my hundred penny box?"

"To play," Michael said, after he thought for a moment.

"Play now," she said. "Don't hide my hundred penny box. I got to keep looking at my box and when I don't see my box I won't see me neither."

"One!" Michael said and dropped the penny back into the old print sack.

6 "18 and 74," Aunt Dew said. "Year I was born. Slavery over! Black men in Congress running things. They was in charge. It was the Reconstruction."

Michael counted twenty-seven pennies back into the old print sack before she stopped talking about Reconstruction.

"19 and 01," Aunt Dew said. "I was twenty-seven years. Birthed my twin boys. Hattie said, 'Dewbet, you got two babies.' I asked Henry Thomas, I said 'Henry Thomas, what them boys look like?'"

By the time Michael had counted fifty-six pennies, his mother was standing at the door.

"19 and 30," Aunt Dew said. "Depression. Henry Thomas, that was my late

husband, died. Died after he put the fifty-six penny in my box. He had the double pneumonia and no decent shoes and he worked too hard. Said he was going to sweat the trouble out his lungs. Couldn't do it. Same year I sewed that fancy dress for Rena Coles. She want a hundred bows all over that dress. I was sewing bows and tieing bows and twisting bows and cursing all the time. Was her *fourth* husband and she want a dress full of bow-ribbons. Henry the one started that box, you know. Put the first thirty-one pennies in it for me and it was my birthday. After fifty-six, I put them all in myself."

"Aunt Dew, time to go to bed," his mother said, standing at the door.

"Now, I'm not sleepy," Aunt Dew said. "John-boy and me just talking. Why you don't call him John? Look like John just spit him out. Why you got to call that boy something different from his daddy?"

Michael watched his mother walk over and open the window wide. "We'll get some fresh air in here," she said. "And then, Aunt Dew, you can take your nap better and feel good when you wake up." Michael wouldn't let his mother take the sack of pennies out of his hand. He held tight and then she let go.

"I'm not sleepy," Aunt Dew said again. "This child and me just talking."

"I know," his mother said, pointing her finger at him a little. "But we're just going to take our nap anyway."

"I got a long time to sleep and I ain't ready now. Just leave me sit here in this little narrow piece a room. I'm not bothering nobody."

6 Students may **wonder** about Aunt Dew's statement here. They may be surprised to learn that four African Americans were elected to serve in the Congress and House of Representatives soon after the Civil War.

"Nobody said you're bothering anyone but as soon as I start making that meat loaf, you're going to go to sleep in your chair and fall out again and hurt yourself and John'll wonder where I was and say I was on the telephone and that'll be something all over again."

"Well, I'll sit on the floor and if I fall, I'll be there already and it won't be nobody's business but my own."

"Michael," his mother said and took the sack of pennies out of his hand and laid it on the dresser. Then she reached down and closed the lid of the hundred penny box and pushed it against the wall. "Go out the room, honey, and let Momma help Aunt Dew into bed."

"I been putting Dewbet Thomas to bed a long time and I can still do it," Aunt Dew said.

"I'll just help you a little," Michael heard his mother say through the closed door.

As soon as his mother left the room, he'd go in and sneak out the hundred penny box.

But where would he hide it?

Michael went into the bathroom to think, but his mother came in to get Aunt Dew's washcloth. "Why are you looking like that?" she asked. "If you want to play go in my room. Play there, or in the living room. And don't go bothering Aunt Dew. She needs her rest."

Michael went into his father's and his mother's room and lay down on the big king bed and tried to think of a place to hide the box.

⊛ 356 ⊛

He had an idea!

He'd hide it down in the furnace room and sneak Aunt Dew downstairs to see it so she'd know where it was. Then maybe they could sit on the basement steps inside and play with it sometimes. His mother would never know. And his father wouldn't care as long as Aunt Dew was happy. He could even show Aunt Dew the big pipes and the little pipes.

Michael heard his mother close his bedroom door and walk down the hall toward the kitchen.

He'd tell Aunt Dew right now that they had a good place to hide the hundred penny box. The best place of all.

Michael got down from the huge bed and walked quietly back down the hall to his door and knocked on it very lightly. Too lightly for his mother to hear.

Aunt Dew didn't answer.

"Aunt Dew," he whispered after he'd opened the door and tiptoed up to the bed. "It's me. Michael."

Aunt Dew was crying.

Michael looked at his great-great-aunt and tried to say something but she just kept crying. She looked extra small in his bed and the covers were too close about her neck. He moved them down a little and then her face didn't look so small. He waited to see if she'd stop crying but she didn't. He went out of the room and

Note: The first part of the story ends on page 356. This is a good place to stop reading if the selection cannot be finished during this class period.

7 If students read the first part of the selection during another class period, ask volunteers to **sum up** what has happened so far before they begin reading the second part.

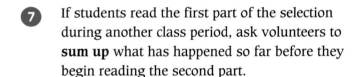

down the hall and stood near his mother. She was chopping up celery. "Aunt Dew's crying," he said.

"That's all right," his mother said. "Aunt Dew's all right."

"She's crying real hard."

"When you live long as Aunt Dew's lived, honey—sometimes you just cry. She'll be all right."

"She's not sleepy. You shouldn't make her go to sleep if she doesn't want to. Daddy never makes her go to sleep."

"You say you're not sleepy either, but you always go to sleep."

"Aunt Dew's bigger than me!"

"She needs her naps."

"Why?"

"Michael, go play please," his mother said. "I'm tired and I'm busy and she'll hear your noise and never go to sleep."

"She doesn't have to if she doesn't want!" Michael yelled and didn't care if he did get smacked. "We were just playing and then you had to come and make her cry!"

"Without a nap, she's irritable and won't eat. She has to eat. She'll get sick if she doesn't eat."

"You made her cry!" Michael yelled.

"Michael John Jefferson," his mother said too quietly. "If you don't get away from me and stop that yelling and stop that screaming and leave me alone—!"

Michael stood there a long time before he walked away.

"Mike," his mother called but he didn't answer. All he did was stop walking.

His mother came down the hall and put her arm about him and hugged him a little and walked him back into the kitchen.

358

Michael walked very stiffly. He didn't feel like any hugging. He wanted to go back to Aunt Dew.

"Mike," his mother said, leaning against the counter and still holding him.

Michael let his mother hold him but he didn't hold her back. All he did was watch the pile of chopped celery.

"Mike, I'm going to give Aunt Dew that tiny mahogany chest your daddy made in a woodshop class when he was a teen-ager. It's really perfect for that little sack of pennies and when she sees it on that pretty dresser scarf she made—the one I keep on her dresser—she'll like it just as well as that big old clumsy box. She won't even miss that big old ugly thing!"

"The hundred penny box isn't even bothering you!"

His mother didn't answer. But Michael heard her sigh. "You don't even care about Aunt Dew's stuff," Michael yelled a little. He even pulled away from his mother. He didn't care at all about her hugging him. Sometimes it seemed to him that grown-ups never cared about anything unless it was theirs and nobody else's. He wasn't going to be like that when he grew up and could work and could do anything he wanted to do.

"Mike," his mother said quietly. "Do you remember that teddy bear you had? The one with the crooked head? We could never sit him up quite right because of the way you kept him bent all the time. You'd bend him up while you slept with him at night and bend him up when you hugged him, played with him. Do you remember that, Mike?"

Why did she have to talk about a dumb old teddy bear!

"You wouldn't let us touch that teddy bear. I mean it was all torn up and losing its stuffing all over the place. And your

359

daddy wanted to get rid of it and I said, 'No. Mike will let us know when he doesn't need that teddy bear anymore.' So you held onto that teddy bear and protected it from all kinds of monsters and people. Then, one day, you didn't play with it anymore. I think it was when little Corky moved next door."

"Corky's not little!"

"I'm sorry. Yes—Corky's big. He's a very big boy. But Corky wasn't around when you and I cleaned up your room a little while back. We got rid of a lot of things so that Aunt Dew could come and be more comfortable. That day, you just tossed that crooked teddy bear on top of the heap and never even thought about it—"

"I did think about it," Michael said.

"But you knew you didn't need it anymore," his mother whispered and rubbed his shoulder softly. "But it's not the same with Aunt Dew. She will hold onto everything that is hers—just to hold onto them! She will hold them tighter and tighter and she will not go forward and try to have a new life. This is a new life for her, Mike. You must help her have this new life and not just let her go backward to something she can never go back to. Aunt Dew does not need that huge, broken, half-rotten wooden box that you stumble all over the house with—just to hold one tiny little sack of pennies!"

360

"I don't stumble around with it!"

His mother reached down then and kissed the top of his head. "You're the one that loves that big old box, Mike. I think that's it."

Michael felt the kiss in his hair and he felt her arms about him and he saw the pile of celery. His mother didn't understand. She didn't understand what a hundred penny box meant. She didn't understand that a new life wasn't very good if you had to have everything old taken away from you—just for a dumb little stupid old funny-looking ugly little red box, a shiny ugly nothing box that didn't even look like it was big enough to hold a sack of one hundred pennies!

Mike put his arms around his mother. Maybe he could make her understand. He hugged her hard. That's what she had done—hugged him. "All Aunt Dew wants is her hundred penny box," Michael said. "That's the only thing—"

"And all you wanted was that teddy bear," his mother answered.

"You can't burn it," Michael said and moved away from his mother. "You can't burn any more of Aunt Dew's stuff. You can't take the hundred penny box. I said you can't take it!"

"Okay," his mother said.

Michael went down the hall and opened the door to his room.

"No, Mike," his mother said and hurried after him. "Don't go in there now."

"I am," Michael said.

His mother snatched him and shut the door and pulled him into the living room and practically threw him into the stuffed velvet chair. "You're as stubborn as your father," she

361

said. "Everything your way or else!" She was really angry. "Just sit there," she said. "And don't move until I tell you!"

As soon as Michael heard his mother chopping celery again, he got up from the chair.

He tiptoed into his room and shut the door without a sound.

Aunt Dew was staring at the ceiling. There was perspiration on her forehead and there was water in the dug-in places around her eyes.

"Aunt Dew?"

"What you want, John-boy?"

"I'm sorry Momma's mean to you."

"Ain't nobody mean to Dewbet Thomas—cause Dewbet Thomas ain't mean to nobody," Aunt Dew said, and reached her hand out from under the cover and patted Michael's face. "Your Momma Ruth. She move around and do what she got to do. First time I see her—I say, 'John, she look frail but she ain't.' He said, 'No, she ain't frail.' I make out like I don't see her all the time." Aunt Dew said, and winked her eye. "But she know I see her. If she think I don't like her that ain't the truth. Dewbet Thomas like everybody. But me and her can't talk like me and John talk—cause she don't know all what me and John know."

"I closed the door," Michael said. "You don't have to sleep if you don't want to."

"I been sleep all day, John," Aunt Dew said.

362

Michael leaned over his bed and looked at his great-great-aunt. "You haven't been sleep all day," he said. "You've been sitting in your chair and talking to me and then you were dancing to your record and then we were counting pennies and we got to fifty-six and then Momma came."

"Where my hundred penny box?"

"I got it," Michael answered.

"Where you got it?"

"Right here by the bed."

"Watch out while I sleep."

He'd tell her about the good hiding place later. "Okay," he said.

Aunt Dew was staring at him. "Look like John just spit you out," she said.

Michael moved away from her. He turned his back and leaned against the bed and stared at the hundred penny box. All of a sudden it looked real *real* old and beat up.

"Turn round. Let me look at you."

Michael turned around slowly and looked at his great-great-aunt.

"John!"

"It's me," Michael said. "Michael."

He went and sat down on the hundred penny box.

"Come here so I can see you," Aunt Dew said.

Michael didn't move.

"Stubborn like your daddy. Don't pay your Aunt Dew no never mind!"

Michael still didn't get up.

"Go on back and do your counting out my pennies. Start with fifty-seven—where you left off. 19 and 31. Latt married

363

that schoolteacher. We roasted three pigs. Just acting the fool, everybody. Latt give her a pair of yellow shoes for her birthday. Walked off down the road one evening just like you please, she did. Had on them yellow shoes. Rode a freight train clean up to Chicago. Left his food on the table and all his clothes ironed. Six times she come back and stay for a while and then go again. Truke used to say, 'Wouldn't be *my* wife.' But Truke never did marry nobody. Only thing he care about was that car. He would covered it with a rain-coat when it rained, if he could."

"First you know me, then you don't," Michael said.

"Michael John Jefferson what your name is," Aunt Dew said. "Should be plain John like your daddy and your daddy's daddy—stead of all this new stuff. Name John and everybody saying 'Michael.'" Aunt Dew was smiling. "Come here, boy," she said. "Come here close. Let me look at you. Got a head full of hair."

Michael got up from the hundred penny box and stood at the foot of the bed.

"Get closer," Aunt Dew said.

Michael did.

"Turn these covers back little more. This little narrow piece a room don't have the air the way my big house did."

"I took a picture of your house," Michael said and turned the covers back some more.

364

"My house bigger than your picture," Aunt Dew said. "Way bigger."

Michael leaned close to her on his bed and propped his elbows up on the large pillow under her small head. "Tell me about the barn again," he said.

"Dewbet and Henry Thomas had the biggest, reddest barn in all Atlanta, G–A!"

"And the swing Daddy broke," Michael asked and put his head down on the covers. Her chest was so thin under the thick quilt that he hardly felt it. He reached up and pushed a few wispy strands of her hair away from her closed eyes.

"Did more pulling it down than he did swinging."

"Tell me about the swimming pool," Michael said. He touched Aunt Dew's chin and covered it up with only three fingers.

It was a long time before Aunt Dew answered. "Wasn't no swimming pool," she said. "I done told you was a creek. Plain old creek. And your daddy like to got bit by a <u>cottonmouth</u>."

"Don't go to sleep, Aunt Dew," Michael said. "Let's talk."

"I'm tired, John."

"I can count the pennies all the way to the end if you want me to."

"Go head and count."

"When your hundred and one birthday comes, I'm going to put in the new penny like you said."

"Yes, John."

Michael reached up and touched Aunt Dew's eyes. "I have a good place for the hundred penny box, Aunt Dew," he said quietly.

"Go way. Let me sleep," she said.

365

"You wish you were back in your own house, Aunt Dew?"

"I'm going back," Aunt Dew said.

"You sad?"

"Hush, boy!"

Michael climbed all the way up on the bed and put his whole self alongside his great-great-aunt. He touched her arms. "Are your arms a hundred years old?" he asked. It was their favorite question game.

"Um-hm," Aunt Dew murmured and turned a little away from him.

Michael touched her face. "Is your face and your eyes and fingers a hundred years old too?"

"John, I'm tired," Aunt Dew said. "Don't talk so."

"How do you get to be a hundred years old?" Michael asked and raised up from the bed on one elbow and waited for his great-great-aunt to answer.

"First you have to have a hundred penny box," his great-great-aunt finally said.

"Where you get it from?" Michael asked.

"Somebody special got to give it to you," Aunt Dew said. "And soon as they give it to you, you got to be careful less it disappear."

"Aunt Dew—"

"*Precious Lord—*"

"Aunt Dew?"

"*Take my hand—*"

Michael put his head down on Aunt Dew's thin chest beneath the heavy quilt and listened to her sing her long song.

MEET SHARON BELL MATHIS, AUTHOR

As a child Sharon Bell Mathis loved to read and write. When she graduated from college she wanted to become a writer, but was advised that African-American writers were not often hired so she became a teacher instead. She could not keep herself from writing, though, and discovered that she had a special talent for depicting children. Eventually her works began to be accepted and published.

Like Dewbet Thomas in The Hundred Penny Box, *Mathis's beloved grandfather kept a small penny collection—although Mathis didn't know this when she wrote the book. After he died, at the age of 92, his small, worn leather pouch was opened to reveal ten pennies covered with green mold.*

MEET LEO AND DIANE DILLON, ILLUSTRATORS

Leo and Diane Dillon work so interdependently when they are illustrating a book that, after the project is finished, they can't be sure who painted what. Illustrating The Hundred Penny Box *presented a special challenge to the artistic team. The story is told through dialogue rather than action scenes. The Dillons were concerned with preserving the sense of intimacy created by the words. "We wanted to . . . give the reader the feeling he was looking through an old family photo album," Diane says.*

Their illustrations were done in brown water color, using water and bleach to lighten tones, thus creating the look and feel of old photographs.

367

Discussing Strategy Use

Encourage the students to share any problems they had while reading *The Hundred Penny Box* and to explain the strategies they used to solve them. Have any students who developed their own problem-solving strategies share them with their classmates.

*   EXPLORING THROUGH DISCUSSION

Reflecting on the Selection
Whole-Group Discussion

The whole group discusses the selection and any personal thoughts, reactions, or questions it raised. At this time, remind students to **review the clues, problems, and wonderings** they noted on the chalkboard during browsing.

TEACHING TIP After reading a selection, encourage open discussion of any difficulties students encountered. What did they learn from these reading problems?

Assessment

Engage the students in a discussion to determine whether they understand the following ideas:
- the ways in which the feelings of both Michael's mother and Aunt Dew are important to him
- the ways in which Michael tries to placate both his mother and Aunt Dew
- why the box means so much to Aunt Dew . . . and to Michael

Response Journal

Encourage students to record their feelings about the story in their response journals.

Exploring Concepts Within the Selection
Small-Group Discussion

Small groups discuss the relationship of the selection to value. Circulate among the groups and observe the discussions. Refer the students to the Question Board and the Concept Board to keep them focused on their original ideas about value.

Sharing Ideas About Explorable Concepts

Have the groups **report their ideas** and **discuss them** with the rest of the class. It is crucial that the students' ideas determine this discussion.
- Students may point out that Aunt Dew cherished her hundred penny box for the same reasons that many other people value worn-out and seemingly useless belongings—the box reminds her of special events and people from her past. It is a memento of her deceased husband (who started the penny collection), and it is one of only four things that she can truly call her own.
- The students may understand that Michael's mother perceived Aunt Dew's stubborn clinging to her belongings as a rejection of the new life Michael's mother was trying to create for her. For this reason, Michael's mother found Aunt Dew's things particularly unnecessary.
- Students should recognize that Michael had to make a choice between two important attitudes—pleasing and obeying his mother or being understanding and caring toward Aunt Dew. Students may point out that Michael chose to do what he felt was really important, rather than what would have been easier and least troublesome for him.

Ask the students to turn to page 311 in the student anthology and examine the fine-art piece *Peasant Wedding.* Encourage them to share their ideas and reactions to the painting. Can they make any connections between the subject of the painting and the selection they just read?

As these ideas and others are stated, have the students **add them to** the **Question Board** or the **Concept Board.**

Fine Art

Exploring Concepts Across Selections

Ask the students how this selection reminds them of others they have read. They may make connections to other selections in the unit.

- Students may notice a strong resemblance between Michael's relationship with Aunt Dew and Tiffany's relationship with Granny in "Money Matters." Both children feel protective toward the elderly women.
- Each penny in Aunt Dew's hundred penny box represents a precious memory of her life and personal history. Some students may remember that in "The People on the Beach," in the unit on ancient civilizations, Sara Bisel told a story about the people's personal histories: their health, social status, and daily existence. Students may recognize Aunt Dew's box as a nonscientific type of artifact.

Connections Across Units

Recording Ideas

As students complete the above discussions, ask them to **sum up what they have learned from their conversations and to tell how they might use this information** in further explorations. Any special information or insights may be recorded on the **Concept Board.** Any further questions that they would like to think about, pursue, or investigate may be recorded on the **Question Board.** They may want to discuss the progress that has been made on their questions. They may also want to cross out any questions that no longer warrant consideration.

➤ Following the discussion, students record their ideas and impressions about the selection and the concept on page 108 of the Explorer's Notebook.

Evaluating Discussions

Explorer's Notebook, page 108

Recording Concept Information continued

"The Courage That My Mother Had" by Edna St. Vincent Millay

_____
_____
_____
_____
_____
_____
_____

"The Coin" by Sara Teasdale

_____
_____
_____
_____
_____
_____

The Hundred Penny Box by Sharon Bell Mathis

_____
_____
_____
_____
_____
_____

108 EN   Value/Unit 6

2 READING WITH A WRITER'S EYE

MINILESSONS

Writer's Craft: Point of View

Ask the students to tell what they know about establishing the point of view in a story. If necessary, remind them that point of view is **the perspective or vantage point from which an author presents the action or information** in a story. Explain that authors sometimes use the perceptions and attitudes of a character to influence a reader's understanding of a story. Ask the students to determine from whose point of view *The Hundred Penny Box* is written, and to explain how they decided this. If necessary, help them to see that although the narrator is an observer and not a character in the story, the narrator tells the story from Michael's point of view. They, the readers, experience what is happening through Michael's eyes, and are told only his thoughts and feelings. Everything they learn about other characters comes from what is said in their conversation or from what Michael notices or thinks about them. Some examples of how the narrator tells what is happening in the story from Michael's point of view include the following:

- page 344, paragraph 1: From Michael's memory of eavesdropping on a conversation between his parents, readers learn about his father's loyalty towards and love for Aunt Dew.
- page 347, paragraph 1: Here, the narrator tells Michael's thoughts: that he was not afraid to stand up to his mother and insist that she could not take the hundred penny box. (Notice that in the following paragraphs, the narrator does not tell how Michael's mother felt or what she thought about his behavior, only what she said and how she acted in response to his actions.)

Invite the students to discuss how telling the story from Michael's point of view influenced the way they, the readers, felt about events or characters in the story. Point out to the students that by telling only Michael's thoughts and feelings, the author brings readers closer to Michael because they see and experience what is going on in the story from inside his mind. Ask them to discuss how the story would be different if it had been told from the point of view of Aunt Dew or of Michael's mother.

Selective Reading: Focus on Point of View

Now have the students go back into the selection and find and read aloud other places where Michael's point of view is apparent. Students might mention the following examples:

- page 357, paragraph 2: The narrator describes Michael's thoughts concerning where he could hide the box and his assumption that his mother would never know. His mother's thoughts are never revealed.
- page 359, paragraphs 1 through 6: In this discussion between Michael and his mother about why Aunt Dew is crying, Michael's feelings are revealed but not Aunt Dew's or his mother's; only their actions are described.

Selection-Based Practice

- page 361, paragraph 3: The narrator reveals Michael's feeling that his mother didn't understand what the hundred penny box meant. (If the narrator had recounted the scene from Michael's mother's point of view, it would have been much different.)

Independent Practice: Point of View

❯ Have the students work in small groups, using Reading/Writing Connection, page 50, to extend their understanding of point of view.

Writer's Craft: Describing Characters' Thoughts and Feelings

Ask the students to discuss what they know about **characterization.** Remind them, if necessary, that authors do not simply state that a character is brave or selfish or caring. Writers reveal what characters are like by **showing how they act,** as well as through the **characters' dialogue.** Another way writers inform readers about characters is by **revealing the characters' thoughts and feelings.** Explain that just as people change, fictional characters may also change. You might point out the following examples from the story of developing characterization by describing characters' thoughts and feelings:

- pages 342, last paragraph–344: Mathis shows readers that Michael's mother is sensitive. She has tried hard to make her husband's great-aunt happy in her new home and feels hurt and frustrated when the elderly woman ignores her efforts.

Reading/Writing Connection, page 50

The Hundred Penny Box

Point of View

The Hundred Penny Box is written from Michael's point of view. You see the characters and the situations in the story the way Michael does. Find passages from this story or others that you have read in which a character's, or a narrator's, point of view is apparent. Record the title of the story, the page and the paragraph of the passage, and the person from whose point of view the story is told. Then explain how the point of view influenced your feelings about the events or characters.

Title: _____

Page and paragraph: _____

From whose point of view is the story told? _____

Explain how the point of view influenced your feelings about events or characters:

_____
_____
_____
_____
_____

Title: _____

Page and paragraph: _____

From whose point of view is the story told? _____

Explain how the point of view influenced your feelings about events or characters:

_____
_____
_____
_____
_____

Name

Point of View
50 R/WC   Value/Unit 6

Copyright © 1995 Open Court Publishing Company

- page 347, paragraph 1: Through Michael's thoughts, the narrator shows that Michael was brave because he was concerned for Aunt Dew; Michael stood up to his mother and insisted that she could not take the hundred penny box.

Selective Reading: Focus on Characters' Thoughts and Feelings

Have the students look again at the story for places where, through Michael's thoughts and feelings, Mathis reveals what various characters are like. Encourage the students to read the examples aloud and explain what each one tells about the characters. Students may cite the following examples:

- page 344, paragraphs 1 and 3: Michael's father is a kind and intelligent man who loves and feels indebted to Aunt Dew yet also loves his wife and understands her frustration.
- page 353, paragraph 11: Michael's desperation reflects his sincere love and respect for Aunt Dew and his concern about how she would react if his mother got rid of the box.
- page 358, paragraph 10: Michael's seeming lack of respect for his mother shows that he is a fiery young boy with a mind of his own.

Independent Practice: Characters' Thoughts and Feelings

❯ Use Reading/Writing Connection, page 51, for additional practice in understanding characterization. Have the students work in small groups to complete this page and discuss their answers. Circulate among the groups and note students who may need help during Independent Workshop.

WRITING

Linking Reading to Writing

Students might want to record good examples of characterization on Reproducible Master 24, Characterization, in the Author's Style section of their Writer's Notebook. Provide additional copies if necessary. Encourage them also to look for pieces in their writing folders that can be improved by adding thoughts and feelings of characters that reveal more closely what they are actually like. Remind students to use *The Hundred Penny Box* as a model for how they might develop characters in future stories.

Have the students also consider whether they used the narrator effectively in their stories. Encourage them to think about how their stories might change if they had told them from a different point of view. Suggest that they try rewriting one or more pieces using a different narrator, either another character in the story or an outside observer.

✱ Writing Process

If students have chosen to publish any previously written, revised, and proofread pieces, encourage them to include the pieces in the classroom library for the rest of the class to enjoy.

The Hundred Penny Box

Characterization

What are the characters in *The Hundred Penny Box* like? What makes you think so? Write down passages from this story or others that you have read in which the author gives you clues to what a character is like by telling you the character's thoughts and feelings.

Story: _____

Character: _____

Things the character thinks or feels: _____

_____

What these things tell you about the character: _____

_____

_____

Story: _____

Character: _____

Things the character thinks or feels: _____

_____

What these things tell you about the character: _____

_____

_____

_____

Story: _____

Character: _____

Things the character thinks or feels: _____

_____

What these things tell you about the character: _____

_____

_____

_____

Characterization

Unit 6/Value   R/WC 51

Name _____

Copyright © 1995 Open Court Publishing Company

Reading/Writing Connection, page 51

VOCABULARY

Concept-related phrases that might come up in discussion include *sentimental value* and *intrinsic value.* Have Vocabulary Exploration forms, Reproducible Master 15, available so that students can use them to make additions to the Personal Dictionary section of their Writer's Notebook. Allow time for students to complete these forms and to share the words and phrases they have chosen with the rest of the class. For additional opportunities to build vocabulary, see **Teacher Tool Card 77.**

Adding to Personal Word Lists

3 GUIDED AND INDEPENDENT EXPLORATION

Guided Exploration

EXPLORING CONCEPTS BEYOND THE TEXT

Students will select activities in which they explore concepts related to value. Refer them to the **Exploration Activities poster** and give them time to choose an activity and to discuss what they wish to explore and how they wish to go about it. If the students need further help, here is a suggestion:

- Students may want to role-play their own ideas of how to handle the situation presented in the selection. Let volunteers play the parts of Michael, his mother, and Aunt Dew. Give the volunteers time to prepare their role plays, encouraging input from the rest of the class. Then provide time for the volunteers to perform their role plays for the class.

Remind students to return to pages 114–115 in the Explorer's Notebook to complete their observations of what various story characters value.

❯ Distribute Home/School Connection 46. Encourage the students to collaborate with their families in recalling and sharing memories of earlier years.

* Exploring Through Reflective Activities

Role-Playing

Home/School Connection 46

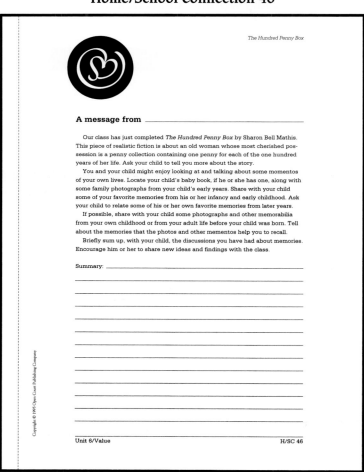

The Hundred Penny Box

A message from _____

Our class has just completed *The Hundred Penny Box* by Sharon Bell Mathis. This piece of realistic fiction is about an old woman whose most cherished possession is a penny collection containing one penny for each of the one hundred years of her life. Ask your child to tell you more about the story.

You and your child might enjoy looking at and talking about some momentos of your own lives. Locate your child's baby book, if he or she has one, along with some family photographs from your child's early years. Share with your child some of your favorite memories from his or her infancy and early childhood. Ask your child to relate some of his or her own favorite memories from later years.

If possible, share with your child some photographs and other memorabilia from your own childhood or from your adult life before your child was born. Tell about the memories that the photos and other mementos help you to recall.

Briefly sum up, with your child, the discussions you have had about memories. Encourage him or her to share new ideas and findings with the class.

Summary: _____
_____
_____
_____
_____
_____
_____
_____
_____
_____
_____
_____
_____
_____

Copyright © 1995 Open Court Publishing Company

Unit 6/Value   H/SC 46

Presenting
Exploration
Results

If any of the collaborative groups have information to present to the rest of the class, allow sufficient time for them to do so. Encourage the students to take their time and make their presentations as interesting to their audience as possible. Be sure that any audiovisual equipment the students need has been provided.

After each presentation, encourage classmates to respond. What did they enjoy most about the presentation? Which ideas were the most interesting? What new facts did they learn? Can they link information from the presentation with something they have learned during the course of the unit? During the course of the year?

ASSESSMENT TIP An ideal time to observe students and mark your Teacher's Observation Log is during the presentation of their exploration results.

Professional Checkpoint: Guided and Independent Exploration

To promote intentional learning, keep the students aware of what they are learning and why, rather than letting them focus on the activities. It means to turn over—gradually, of course—the responsibility of learning to students themselves. It should not forever be the teacher who notices misconceptions and gaps in knowledge, who decides what is learned from an activity, who monitors the learning and thinking of remedial actions. Eventually students must learn to do these things themselves if they are to go out into the world as lifelong learners.

Notes:

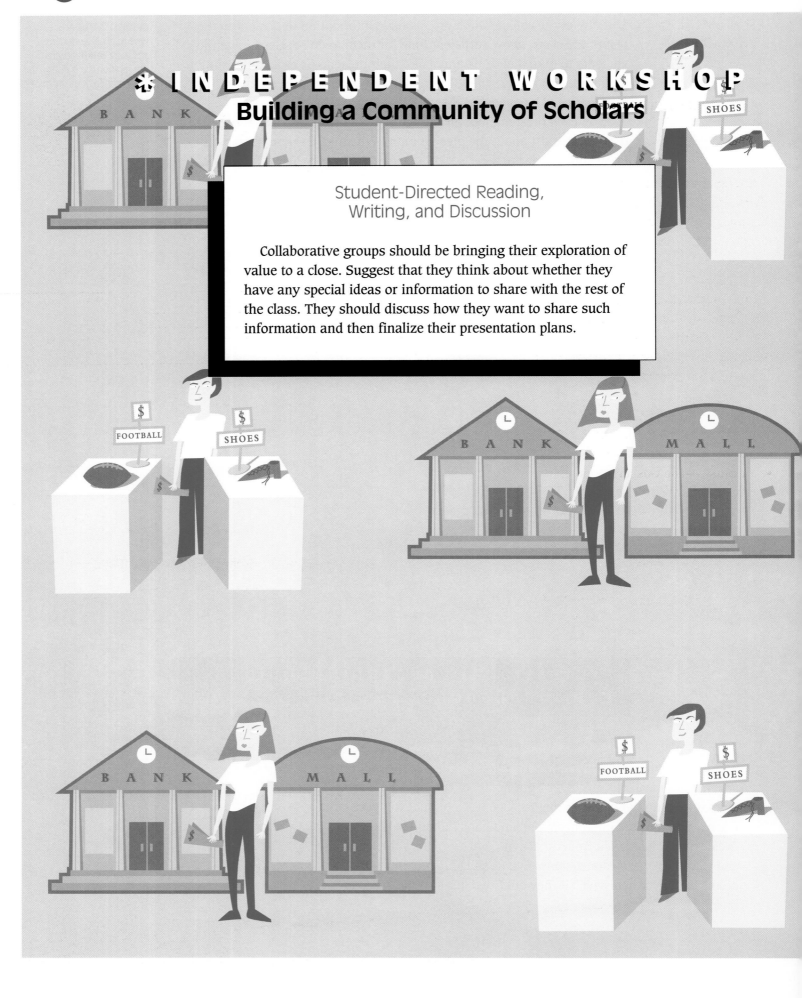

*INDEPENDENT WORKSHOP
Building a Community of Scholars

Student-Directed Reading, Writing, and Discussion

Collaborative groups should be bringing their exploration of value to a close. Suggest that they think about whether they have any special ideas or information to share with the rest of the class. They should discuss how they want to share such information and then finalize their presentation plans.

Additional Opportunities for Independent Reading, Writing, and Cross-curricular Activities

✱ Reading Roundtable

Encourage the students to share and discuss the value-related outside reading they have done during the course of this unit. Students may be interested in drawing up a list of recommended titles to post in the classroom.

✱ Writing Seminar

Remind the students to look through their writing folders to determine whether there are any pieces they would like to prepare for publishing. Remind them to proofread carefully before they publish, making any necessary corrections in grammar, spelling, and punctuation.

Cross-curricular Activity Cards

The following Cross-curricular Activity Cards in the Student Toolbox are appropriate for this selection:

- 11 Music—The Gospel Roots
- 33 Social Studies—Living Books
- 34 Social Studies—The Eleven (or Twelve) Penny Box

The Eleven (or Twelve) Penny Box — **34** Social Studies — Use after *The Hundred Penny Box*

Living Books — **33** Social Studies — Use after *The Hundred Penny Box*

The Gospel Roots — **11** Music — Use after *The Hundred Penny Box*

Aunt Dew liked to sing her favorite spiritual, or gospel song, to comfort herself when she was feeling sad. Gospel music, of course, has its roots in religion, but you may be surprised at the different types of music that have borrowed harmonies, styles, and themes from gospel music. Many famous popular musicians began their careers by singing gospel music in their church choirs.

Research the beginnings of gospel music and the influence of gospel music on the music that came after it. Create a poster on which you trace these connections on a "family tree." Include the names (and, if you wish, drawings) of modern performers who began their careers by singing gospel music. *Learning about the history of one special kind of music helps us to understand music in general.*

Additional Opportunities for Solving Learning Problems

Tutorial

You may want to use this time to work with students who need extra help in any area. The following aids are available in the Teacher Toolbox for your convenience:

- Writer's Craft/Reading: Point of View, Teacher Tool Card 12
- Writer's Craft/Reading: Characterization, Teacher Tool Card 13
- Writer's Craft/Reading: Using Dialogue in a Story, Teacher Tool Card 20

Unit Wrap-up

Initiate a general class discussion on the unit, centering on the explorable concepts relating to value. Remind the students to think about their previous discussions on ideas from the Concept Board. You might encourage them to refer to page 104 of their Explorer's Notebook to remind themselves of what their ideas about value were when the unit began and of what they expected to learn from the unit. Ask them what new ideas they have acquired and what new information they have gained.

The discussion may be extended to include

- an evaluation of the unit selections. Which selections did students find most interesting? Which did they find the least interesting?
- an evaluation of the unit activities. Which activities were the most enjoyable or informative? Which did not seem interesting or valuable?
- an evaluation of the overall unit. How well did the unit cover the explorable concepts related to value? Was value a worthwhile subject to examine? Why?
- suggestions of ideas related to value that are worth further exploration, possibly beginning with any questions left on the Question Board.

Small-Group Discussion

As an alternative, you might have the students work in small groups to discuss the unit. Encourage group participants to refer to the Concept Board, browse the anthology selections, and **review** their **Explorer's Notebook pages** for unit 6 to refresh their memories of important ideas raised in the unit. Then have the groups share with classmates important points and conclusions from their discussions.

Informal Assessment

❯ **Give the students the opportunity to make individual evaluations** of their learning experiences during this unit by completing pages 120–121 in their Explorer's Notebook. You may want to hold **individual conferences** with the students to discuss their evaluations.

End-of-Unit Assessment

At this point, you might wish to carry out end-of-unit assessments for unit 6, Value. You will find the following end-of-unit assessment booklets in the Teacher Toolbox:

Comprehension Assessment

- Understanding the Selection
- Making Connections Across Selections

Unit Wrap-up

How did you feel about this unit?

☐ I enjoyed it very much.   ☐ I liked it.

☐ I liked some of it.   ☐ I didn't like it.

How would you rate the difficulty of the unit?

☐ easy   ☐ medium   ☐ hard

How would you rate your performance during this unit?

☐ I learned a lot about value.

☐ I learned some new things about value.

☐ I didn't learn much about value.

Why did you choose this rating?

_____

_____

_____

_____

_____

_____

_____

What was the most interesting thing that you learned about value?

_____

_____

_____

_____

_____

_____

_____

_____

120 EN   Value/Unit 6

Explorer's Notebook, page 120

What did you learn about value that you didn't know before?

_____

_____

_____

_____

What did you learn about yourself as a learner?

_____

_____

_____

What do you need to work on as a learner?

_____

_____

_____

What resources (books, films, magazines, interviews, tool cards, other) did you use on your own during this unit? Which of these were the most helpful? Why?

_____

_____

_____

_____

_____

_____

_____

Unit 6/Value   EN 121

Explorer's Notebook, page 121

- Checking Skills
- Multiple-Choice Option

Essay and Writing Assessment

You may pick and choose among the various assessment components to find the right mix for assessing areas you want to stress. See *Formative Assessment: A Teacher's Guide* for specific suggestions on how to use these assessment materials.

UNIT CELEBRATION

Have the students suggest how they might celebrate their completion of this unit. They may offer such ideas as these:

- Rank in order of its worth each idea, quality, and belonging valued by the characters they read about in this unit. Students could then create a classroom store or a trading post or invent their own board game, with a focus on swapping "valuables."
- Invite other classes or family members in for a classroom "tour." Some students might pose as fictional characters from the stories in the unit. They would explain to the visitors who they were, what they valued, and why. Other students could act as tour guides, pointing out value-related projects and displays and explaining their significance as well as explaining concepts from the Concept Board.

Appendixes

Appendix 1　Scope and Sequence

STRATEGIES AND SKILLS	LEVEL					
	1	**2**	**3**	**4**	**5**	**6**
Print Awareness						
Capitalization	■					
Constancy of words	■					
End punctuation	■					
Follow left-to-right, top-to-bottom	■					
Letter recognition and formation	■					
Paragraph indention	■					
Relationship between illustrations and print	■					
Relationship between spoken and printed language	■					
Word boundaries in text	■					
READING STRATEGIES						
Setting Reading Goals and Expectations						
Activate prior knowledge.	■	■	■	■	■	■
Browse the text.	■	■	■	■	■	■
Consider why you are reading.	■	■	■	■	■	■
Decide what you expect from the text.	■	■	■	■	■	■
Responding to Text						
Make connections between what you are reading and what you already know.	■	■	■	■	■	■
Visualize, or picture, what is happening in the text.	■	■	■	■	■	■
Wonder freely as you read.	■	■	■	■	■	■
Predict what will happen next.	■	■	■	■	■	■
Think about how the text makes you feel.	■	■	■	■	■	■
Checking Understanding						
Interpret as you read.	■	■	■	■	■	■
Sum up to check your understanding as you read.	■	■	■	■	■	■
Ask questions to check your understanding as you read.		■	■	■	■	■
Clarifying Unfamiliar Words and Passages						
Apply decoding skills if there are unknown words.	■	■	■	■	■	■
Determine what is unclear.		■	■	■	■	■
Apply context clues if there are words whose meanings you don't know.	■	■	■	■	■	■

STRATEGIES AND SKILLS	LEVEL					
	1	2	3	4	5	6
READING STRATEGIES						
Clarifying Unfamiliar Words and Passages *continued*						
Check the dictionary.		▓	▓	▓	▓	▓
Reread the passage that didn't make sense to you.	▓	▓	▓	▓	▓	▓
WRITING STRATEGIES						
Planning and Setting Writing Goals						
Use reading to improve your writing.	▓	▓	▓	▓	▓	▓
Record interesting and important topics to write about.	▓	▓	▓	▓	▓	▓
Note information you will need in order to write.		▓	▓	▓	▓	▓
Decide on the main goals of the writing.		▓	▓	▓	▓	▓
Revise your plans.		▓	▓	▓	▓	▓
Considering Readers						
Make your topic interesting.		▓	▓	▓	▓	▓
Decide what effect you want to have on your readers.		▓	▓	▓	▓	▓
Determine if readers will understand.		▓	▓	▓	▓	▓
Predict your readers' reactions, and then compare their reactions to what you expected.		▓	▓	▓	▓	▓
Summarize audience reactions.		▓	▓	▓	▓	▓
Revising Content						
Reread very carefully.	▓	▓	▓	▓	▓	▓
Pinpoint parts of your writing that can be made clearer.		▓	▓	▓	▓	▓
Identify information confusing to readers.		▓	▓	▓	▓	▓
Reorganize ideas or information.		▓	▓	▓	▓	▓
Use a story frame or plot line.		▓	▓	▓	▓	▓
Consider your own reactions and ideas.		▓	▓	▓	▓	▓
CONVENTIONS/SKILLS						
Writer's Craft/Reading						
Causal indicators	▓	▓	▓	▓	▓	▓
Characterization	▓	▓	▓	▓	▓	▓
Choosing vivid verbs		▓	▓	▓	▓	▓
Dialogue	▓	▓	▓	▓	▓	▓
Elaboration through comparisons and contrasts		▓	▓	▓	▓	▓
Elaboration through forming questions and conjectures		▓	▓	▓	▓	▓
Elaboration through giving opinions		▓	▓	▓	▓	▓
Elaboration through giving reasons or causes	▓	▓	▓	▓	▓	▓

Writer's Craft/Reading *continued*

Strategies and Skills	__1__	2	3	4	5	6
	1	**2**	**3**	**4**	**5**	**6**
Elaboration through including lists and examples		■	■	■	■	■
Elaboration through providing background				■	■	■
Elaboration through providing descriptions	■	■	■	■	■	■
Elaboration through providing explanations or definitions		■	■	■	■	■
Elaboration by providing opposing viewpoints				■	■	■
Elaboration through providing problems and solutions		■		■	■	■
Elaboration through providing specific facts	■	■	■	■	■	■
Exaggeration			■	■	■	■
Figurative language		■	■	■	■	■
Formal versus informal writing				■	■	■
Foreshadowing				■		■
Genre—adventure				■	■	■
Genre—biography and autobiography		■	■	■	■	■
Genre—expository text	■	■	■	■	■	■
Genre—fable	■	■	■	■	■	■
Genre—fairy tale	■	■	■			
Genre—fantasy	■	■	■	■	■	■
Genre—folk tale	■	■	■	■	■	■
Genre—historical fiction		■	■	■	■	■
Genre—legend	■	■	■	■	■	■
Genre—myth, tall tale			■	■	■	■
Genre—play/drama	■	■	■	■	■	■
Genre—poetry	■	■	■	■	■	■
Genre—realistic fiction	■	■	■	■	■	■
Genre—science fiction					■	■
Humor			■	■	■	
Indicators of additional information			■	■	■	
Indicators of differing information			■	■	■	
Indicators of place and location	■	■	■	■	■	■
Indicators of time and order	■	■	■	■	■	■
Irony						■
Persuasive writing		■	■	■	■	■
Plot		■	■	■	■	■
Point of view		■	■	■	■	■
Process description		■	■	■	■	■
Setting	■	■	■	■	■	■
Staying on subject			■	■	■	■
Strong topic sentences		■	■	■	■	■

STRATEGIES AND SKILLS	LEVEL					

Writer's Craft/Reading *continued*	1	2	3	4	5	6
Suspense and surprise		■	■	■	■	
Using headings and captions	■	■	■	■	■	■
Using quotations in writing				■	■	■
Variety in writing		■	■	■	■	■
Writing good beginnings		■	■	■	■	■
Writing paragraphs		■	■	■	■	■
Writing personal experiences		■	■	■	■	■
Grammar, Mechanics, and Usage						
Capitalization	■	■	■	■	■	■
Clauses and phrases			■	■	■	■
Comparing with adjectives and adverbs	■	■	■	■	■	■
Complete and incomplete sentences	■	■	■	■	■	■
Compound sentences		■	■	■	■	■
Compound subject and predicate				■	■	■
End punctuation	■	■	■	■	■	■
Kinds of sentences	■	■	■			
Parts of a sentence		■	■	■	■	■
Parts of speech		■	■	■	■	■
Pronoun/antecedent agreement		■	■	■	■	■
Punctuating titles of works (books, movies etc.)				■	■	■
Subject/verb agreement		■	■	■	■	■
Using adjectives and adverbs		■	■	■	■	■
Using colons and semicolons				■	■	■
Using commas in dates, addresses, and parts of a letter		■	■	■	■	■
Using commas in introductory phrases			■	■		
Using commas in a series		■	■	■	■	■
Using dashes and ellipses			■	■	■	■
Using gerund phrases				■	■	■
Using negatives correctly			■	■	■	■
Using parentheses		■	■	■	■	■
Using possessive nouns	■	■	■	■	■	■
Using possessive pronouns		■	■	■	■	■
Using prepositions and prepositional phrases		■	■	■		■
Using and punctuating dialogue	■	■	■	■	■	■
Using reflexive pronouns				■	■	■
Verb tense		■	■	■	■	■

STRATEGIES AND SKILLS	LEVEL					
	1	2	3	4	5	6
Phonics/Decoding						
Blending sounds into words	▓	*	*			
Consonant clusters	▓	*	*			
Consonant digraphs	▓	*	*			
Consonant sounds and spellings	▓	*	*			
Outlaw words	▓	*	*			
Phonemic awareness	▓	*	*			
Syllables	▓	*	*			
Vowel diphthongs	▓	*	*			
Vowels: long sounds and spellings	▓	*	*			
Vowels: r-controlled	▓	*	*			
Vowels: short sounds and spellings	▓	*	*			
Spelling and Vocabulary						
Adding prefixes and suffixes		▓	▓	▓	▓	▓
Building vocabulary	▓	▓	▓	▓	▓	▓
Compound words	▓	▓	▓	▓	▓	▓
Frequently misspelled words		▓	▓	▓	▓	▓
Homophones	▓	▓	▓	▓	▓	▓
Inflectional endings	▓	▓	▓	▓	▓	▓
Long-vowel spelling patterns		▓	▓	▓	▓	▓
Regular and irregular plurals		▓	▓	▓	▓	▓
Short-vowel spelling patterns	▓	▓	▓	▓	▓	▓
Spelling generalizations		▓	▓	▓	▓	▓
Synonyms and antonyms	▓	▓	▓	▓	▓	▓
Unstressed vowel sounds (schwa)				▓	▓	▓
Using and punctuating contractions	▓	▓	▓	▓	▓	▓
Study and Research						
Alphabetical order	▓	▓	▓			
Choosing sources		▓	▓	▓	▓	▓
Comparing information across sources				▓	▓	▓
Formulating questions and conjectures		▓	▓	▓	▓	▓
Interviewing		▓	▓	▓	▓	▓
Making a bibliography					▓	▓
Making and using a time line		▓	▓	▓	▓	▓
Note taking		▓	▓	▓	▓	▓
Observing and recording details		▓	▓			

* Optional review at this level

STRATEGIES AND SKILLS

Study and Research *continued*

	LEVEL 1	2	3	4	5	6
Organizing information in a chart		■	■	■	■	■
Outlining				■	■	■
Parts of a book	■	■	■	■	■	■
Using a dictionary or glossary	■	■	■	■	■	■
Using a thesaurus				■	■	■
Using an encyclopedia		■	■	■	■	■
Using and understanding diagrams				■	■	■
Using maps, globes, and atlases		■	■	■	■	■
Using primary sources				■	■	■
Using the card catalog (including electronic cc)		■	■	■	■	■
Using the *Reader's Guide*			■	■	■	■

SETTING READING GOALS AND EXPECTATIONS

Reading Strategies	Ask Yourself
ACTIVATE prior knowledge.	What do I already know about this?
BROWSE the text.	What kind of text is this? What seems important? What looks interesting? What might cause problems?
CONSIDER why you are reading.	Am I reading this for fun? Am I reading this to learn something? What do I want to learn?
DECIDE WHAT you expect from the text.	What might this be about? What do I want to find out?

RESPONDING TO TEXT

Reading Strategies	**Ask Yourself**
MAKE CONNECTIONS between what you are reading and what you already know.	What does this text remind me of? Have I read or experienced anything like this before? Does any of this surprise me? Why?
VISUALIZE what is happening in the text.	Can I picture in my mind what is described in the text? How might a picture or diagram help me picture and understand the text?
WONDER freely as you read.	I wonder why this is the way it is? I wonder what else there is to know about this?
PREDICT what will happen next.	What part of the text helped me predict? What did I already know that helped me predict? Which illustrations helped me predict?
THINK ABOUT how the text makes you feel.	How do I feel about what I'm reading?

Copyright © 1995 Open Court Publishing Company

CHECKING UNDERSTANDING

Reading Strategies

INTERPRET as you read.

SUM UP to check your understanding as you read.

ASK QUESTIONS to check your understanding as you read.

Ask Yourself

What does the text mean to me and others?
Does it have more than one meaning? What?
Does the text change my mind about anything? How?

Does this make sense?
What is this section about?
What is the whole selection about?
How would I explain this in my own words?
Can I find out more if I look back?

What might a teacher ask here?
What might be on a test?
What question is answered by the most important idea here?

CLARIFYING UNFAMILIAR WORDS AND PASSAGES

Reading Strategies

APPLY DECODING SKILLS if there are unknown words.

DETERMINE what is unclear.

APPLY CONTEXT CLUES if there are words whose meanings you don't know.

CHECK the dictionary.

REREAD the passage that didn't make sense to you.

Ask Yourself

Have I seen this word before?
What words that I already know are like this word?
Can I sound this out?
How can I break this long word into parts?
What prefixes or suffixes do I recognize?
What small words within the long word will help me read it?

Do I understand the meanings of all the words?
Which parts are unclear? How can I make sense of them?
What, if anything, did the author leave out?

What context clues can I find in the rest of the sentence or in sentences around the word?

Does the passage make sense now?

DISCUSSION STARTERS

I didn't know that…

Does anyone know…

I figured out that…

I liked the part where…

I'm still confused about…

This made me think…

I agree with _____ because…

I disagree with _____ because…

The reason I think…

Copyright © 1995 Open Court Publishing Company

PLANNING AND SETTING WRITING GOALS

Writing Strategies	Ask Yourself
USE READING to improve your writing.	What did this author do that I really liked? How can I do this in my writing?
RECORD interesting and important topics to write about.	What is important or interesting to me and others? Did something happen to me that I'd like to share?
NOTE information you will need in order to write.	What are the important ideas that I want others to know about this? What do I already know? What will I need to know?
DECIDE on the main goals of the writing.	What is my purpose for writing this? What are the important points that I want to get across?
REVISE your plans.	Have my writing ideas changed after thinking about my topic? How? How does new information change what I will write?

CONSIDERING READERS

Writing Strategies	**Ask Yourself**

MAKE your topic interesting.

Will others be interested in this?
What can I do or add to make this topic more interesting to others?

DECIDE what effect you want to have on your readers.

Who am I writing for?
How do I want to make readers feel?
What do I want readers to learn?

DETERMINE if readers will understand.

Will readers understand this?
Is there enough information? If not, what can I add?
Is it clear and well written?

PREDICT your readers' reactions, and then compare their reactions to what you expected.

If readers don't know anything about this topic, will they enjoy reading this?
If they are reading this for the first time, what might they say about the topic?
What will my audience say about the topic?
Was I right?

SUMMARIZE audience reactions.

Did many readers have the same comments? What were they?
What is good about my composition?
What do I need to change?

REVISING CONTENT

Writing Strategies	Ask Yourself
REREAD very carefully.	Have I left out words or put in unnecessary words? Does my writing make sense?
PINPOINT parts of your composition that can be made clearer.	Is this passage descriptive enough for readers to visualize? Should I say more through examples or explanations?
IDENTIFY information confusing to readers.	Were my readers confused? Could this information be wrong? How can I check and correct it?
REORGANIZE IDEAS OR INFORMATION.	What's my purpose for writing this? Am I achieving that purpose? Do I need to include more facts? Do I need to take out any unnecessary information?
USE A STORY FRAME OR PLOT LINE.	Who are the main characters? What is the problem? What are the story events? Are there conflicts or blocks? Does my story build to a high point? Does the story come to a satisfactory conclusion? Would dialogue help to develop my story?
CONSIDER YOUR OWN REACTIONS AND IDEAS.	How do I feel about my writing? Am I pleased with my writing? Did I include all the information I had planned? What would I like to change?

PHASES IN THE WRITING PROCESS

Prewriting

Drafting

Revising

Proofreading

Publishing

Copyright © 1993 Good Year Publishing Company

THE RESEARCH CYCLE

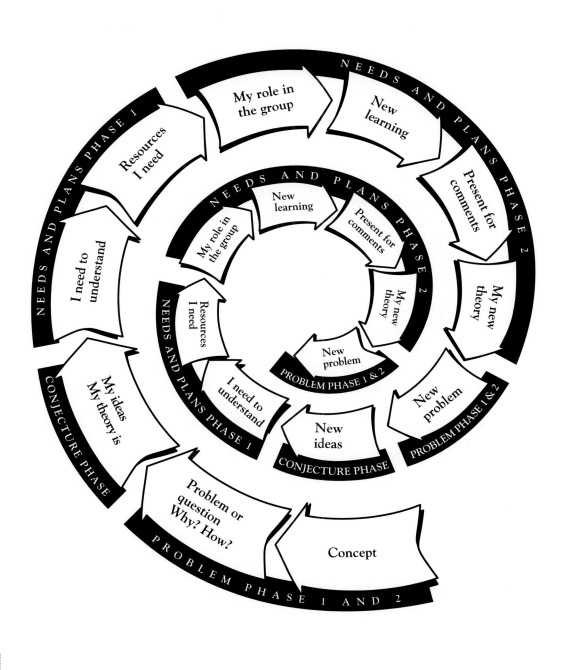

EXPLORATION ACTIVITIES

- A **literature search** to pursue a question or a problem. Discussion or writing may follow.

- An **original playlet** or **puppet show** based on situations related to the explorable concepts.

- A **role-playing game** to work out a problem related to the explorable concepts.

- A **panel discussion** with audience participation on a question or problem. (This discussion would have a leader and may be videotaped.)

- A **debate** on an issue related to the explorable concepts.

- An **advice column** dealing with problems related to the explorable concepts.

- A **personal experience story** related to the explorable concepts.

- The **questioning of visiting experts** about some aspect relating to the explorable concepts.

- An **interview** with someone on a subject related to the explorable concepts.

- A **survey** on an issue or question related to the explorable concepts.

- A **picture** or photo essay about the explorable concepts.

Appendix 3 Audiovisual Sources

AIMS MEDIA
9710 De Soto Avenue
Chattsworth, CA 91311
(800) 526-2467

BFA EDUCATION MEDIA
13-A Jules Lane
New Brunswick, NJ 08901
(800) 221-1274

MCGRAW HILL MEDIA
1221 Avenue of the Americas
New York, NY 10020
(212) 997-1221

PHOENIX FILMS, INC.
468 Park Avenue South
New York, NY 10016
(800) 526-6581

RECORDED BOOKS, INC.
270 Skipjack Road
Prince Frederick, MD 20678
(800) 638-1204

VESTRON VIDEO
c/o Live Home Video
15400 Sherman Way
PO Box 10124
Van Nuys, CA 91419-0124

THE VIDEO PROJECT
Films and Videos for a Safe and
Sustainable World
5332 College Avenue
Suite 101
Oakland, CA 94618
(800) 4 PLANET

Appendix 4 Learning Framework Cards

1. **Cognitive and Responsive Reading**

   1A. Setting Reading Goals and Expectations

   1B. Responding to Text

   1C. Checking Understanding

   1D. Clarifying Unfamiliar Words and Passages

2. **Exploring Through Discussion**

3. **Exploring Through Reflective Activities**

4. **Exploring Through Research**

   4A. Problem Phase 1 and 2

   4B. Conjecture Phase

   4C. Needs and Plans Phase 1 and 2

5. **Independent Workshop**

6. **Reading Roundtable**

7. **Writing Process**

   7A. Prewriting

   7B. Drafting

   7C. Revising

   7D. Proofreading

   7E. Publishing

8. **Writing Seminar**

Appendix 5 Teacher/Student Tool Cards

TEACHER TOOL CARDS

STUDENT TOOL CARDS

Writer's Craft/Reading

1 Genre—Folk Tale and Fable	1 Reading and Writing Folk Tales and Fables
2 Genre—Myth, Legend, and Tall Tale	2 Reading and Writing Myths, Legends, and Tall Tales
3 Genre—Realistic Fiction	3 Reading and Writing Realistic Fiction
4 Genre—Historical Fiction	4 Reading and Writing Historical Fiction
5 Genre—Fantasy	5 Reading and Writing Fantasy
6 Genre—Science Fiction	6 Reading and Writing Science Fiction
7 Genre—Adventure	7 Reading and Writing Adventure Tales
8 Genre—Biography and Autobiography	8 Reading and Writing Biography and Autobiography
9 Genre—Expository Text	9 Reading and Writing Expository Text
10 Genre—Poetry	10 Reading and Writing Poetry
11 Genre—Play/Drama	11 Reading and Writing Plays/Drama
12 Point of View	12 Point of View
13 Characterization	13 Characterization
14 Setting	14 Setting
15 Plot	15 Plot
16 Foreshadowing	16 Foreshadowing
17 Irony	17 Irony
18 Writing from and About Experience	18 Writing About Your Own Experiences
19 Formal versus Informal Writing	19 Differences Between Formal and Informal Writing
20 Using Dialogue in a Story	20 Using Dialogue in a Story
21 Figurative Language	21 Figurative Language
22 Choosing Precise and Vivid Verbs	22 Choosing Precise and Vivid Verbs
23 Using Repetition for Emphasis	23 Using Repetition for Emphasis
24 Writing Paragraphs	24 Writing Paragraphs
25 Strong Topic Sentences	25 Strong Topic Sentences
26 Writing Good Beginnings	26 Writing Good Beginnings
27 Staying on Subject	27 Staying on Subject
28 Variety in Writing	28 Variety in Writing
29 Indicators of Time and Order	29 Signal Words Showing Time and Order
30 Indicators of Place and Location	30 Signal Words Showing Place and Location
31 Causal Indicators	31 Showing Cause and Effect
32 Using Quotations in Writing	32 Using Quotations in Writings

TEACHER TOOL CARDS	STUDENT TOOL CARDS
33 Persuasive Writing	33 Writing to Persuade
34 Process Description	34 Describing a Process
35 Using Headings and Subheads	35 Using Headings and Subheads
36 Using and Understanding Captions	36 Using and Understanding Captions
37 Elaboration Through Providing Comparison and Contrast	37 Comparing and Contrasting
38 Elaboration Through Giving Reasons or Causes	38 Giving Reasons or Causes
39 Elaboration Through Providing Examples	39 Giving Examples
40 Elaboration Through Providing Descriptions	40 Giving Descriptions
41 Elaboration Through Providing Specific Facts	41 Telling Important Facts
42 Elaboration Through Giving Opinions	42 Giving Opinions
43 Elaboration Through Providing Background	43 Giving Background
44 Elaboration Through Providing Definitions in Text	44 Giving Definitions
45 Elaboration Through Providing Problem and Solution	45 Giving Problem and Solution
46 Elaboration Through Forming Questions and Conjectures	46 Writing Questions and Conjectures

Grammar, Mechanics, and Usage

TEACHER TOOL CARDS	STUDENT TOOL CARDS
47 Complete and Incomplete Sentences	47 Complete and Incomplete Sentences
48 Compound Subject and Predicate	48 Compound Subject and Predicate
49 Compound Sentences	49 Compound Sentences
50 Phrases	50 Phrases
51 Clauses	51 Clauses
52 Using Commas in a Series	52 Using Commas in a Series
53 Using Commas in Dates, Addresses, Direct Address, and Parts of a Letter	53 Using Commas in Dates, Addresses, Direct Address, and Parts of a Letter
54 Using Parentheses, Dashes, and Ellipses	54 Using Parentheses, Dashes, and Ellipses
55 Using Colons and Semicolons	55 Using Colons and Semicolons
56 Punctuating Titles of Works	56 Punctuating Titles of Books, Stories, and Movies
57 Capitalization	57 Capitalization
58 Parts of Speech	58 Parts of Speech
59 Using Possessive Nouns	59 Using Possessive Nouns
60 Using Possessive Pronouns	60 Using Possessive Pronouns
61 Pronoun/Antecedent Agreement	61 Using the Right Pronoun for the Right Noun
62 Using Reflexive Pronouns	62 Using Pronouns with *-self*
63 Using Present-Tense Verbs	63 Using Present-Tense Verbs
64 Using Past-Tense Verbs	64 Using Past-Tense Verbs

TEACHER TOOL CARDS	STUDENT TOOL CARDS
65 Using Future-Tense Verbs	65 Using Future-Tense Verbs
66 Using Helping Verbs	66 Using Helping Verbs
67 Subject/Verb Agreement	67 Making Subject and Verb Agree
68 Using Adjectives and Adverbs	68 Using Adjectives and Adverbs
69 Comparing with Adjectives and Adverbs	69 Comparing with Adjectives and Adverbs
70 Using and Punctuating Dialogue	70 Using and Punctuating Dialogue
71 Using Negatives Correctly	71 Using Negatives Correctly
72 Using Gerund Phrases	72 *-ing* Verbs Used As Nouns
73 Using *can* or *may*	73 Using *can* or *may*
74 Using *lie* or *lay*	74 Using *lie* or *lay*
75 Using *sit* or *set*	75 Using *sit* or *set*
76 Using *raise* or *rise*	76 Using *raise* or *rise*

Spelling and Vocabulary

77 Building Vocabulary	77 Building Vocabulary
78 Spelling	78 Spelling
79 Homophones	79 Words That Sound the Same (Homophones)
80 Synonyms and Antonyms	80 Synonyms and Antonyms
81 Compound Words	81 Compound Words
82 Using and Punctuating Contractions	82 Using and Punctuating Contractions
83 Adding Prefixes and Suffixes	83 Adding Prefixes and Suffixes
84 Short-Vowel Spelling Patterns	84 Short-Vowel Spelling Patterns
85 Long-Vowel Spelling Patterns	85 Long-Vowel Spelling Patterns
86 /k/ spelled *c, k, ck,* or *ch*	86 Ways to Spell the *k* Sound
87 /f/ spelled *f* or *ph*	87 Ways to Spell the *f* Sound
88 /j/ spelled *j, g,* or *dge*	88 Ways the Spell the *j* Sound
89 /r/ spelled *r* or *wr*	89 Ways to Spell the *r* Sound
90 /z/ spelled *z* or *s*	90 Ways to Spell the *z* Sound
91 /ch/ spelled *ch, tch,* or *t*	91 Ways to Spell the *ch* Sound
92 /sh/ spelled *sh* or *ti*	92 Ways to Spell the *sh* sound
93 Unstressed Vowel Sounds (Schwa)	93 Ways to Spell the Schwa Sound
94 Spellings for /ər/	94 Ways to Spell the *er* Sound
95 Spellings for the /əl/ Ending	95 Ways to Spell the *əl* Ending Sound
96 *ie* and *ei* Spellings	96 *ie* and *ei* Spellings
97 Regular and Irregular Plurals	97 Forming Plurals
98 Inflectional Endings	98 Spelling Words with Endings
99 Frequently Misspelled Words	99 Words Often Misspelled

TEACHER TOOL CARDS

STUDENT TOOL CARDS

Study and Research

100	Parts of a Book		100	Parts of a Book

Classroom Supports

Classroom Participation

Appendix 6   Cross-curricular Activity Cards

ART

1 Watercolor Painting
2 Painting a Concerto
3 Mythical Beasts
4 Orpheus's Journey
5 Design an Album Cover
6 Cliff Dwelling to Rent: Modern
   Appliances and Canyon View
7 Making a Wall Painting
8 Design an Egyptian Temple
9 Embroidery
10 Illustrating the News
11 Castle Architecture
12 Feelings
13 It Was a "Goodyear"
14 Sketching Habitats
15 Paint a Mural of a Natural
   Habitat
16 Designing an Aviary
17 Accurate Art

DRAMA

1 Become an Opera Performer
2 Make a Music Video
3 Poetry Dance
4 Writing a Play: The Minotaur
5 Writing a Play
6 Famous Speeches
7 Selling Newspapers
8 Role Play

MATH

1 Love Songs
2 How Many Hours?
3 Counting Pigeons
4 Just How Big Is Borneo,
   Anyway?
5 Malaria Mortality
6 Gold!
7 From Dollars to Pesos to Francs
8 How Much to Tip?

MUSIC

1 Great Composers
2 Make Your Own Musical
   Instrument
3 Creating a Song
4 Making a Gourd Shaker
5 Band Without Instruments
6 Rhythm and Blues
7 Singing in Solfège
8 Russian Music
9 The Sounds of Music
10 The International Language
11 The Gospel Roots

SCIENCE

1 Songbirds
2 Making a Birdbath
3 Experimenting with Music and
   Plants
4 Nature Recording
5 Diagram a Piano
6 Understanding Einstein
7 Can You Dig It?
8 Making a Diagram of Vesuvius
9 A Pinch of Salt
10 Wild Food
11 Wolf Behavior
12 Pioneer Foods
13 Airplanes
14 Tracking Wildlife
15 Alligators of the Everglades
16 Plant Rubbings
17 Capturing Prey
18 Burning Rocks
19 First Aid
20 Hard Rock

SOCIAL STUDIES

1 Animals of China
2 Debate an Opera Issue
3 Disabilities Awareness
4 Award a "Notable Prize"
5 Checking It Out at the Library
6 What's in a Name?
7 Journal Entry, August 24, A.D. 79
8 Life in Arkansas
9 The Quakers
10 New York City
11 The British Empire
12 Newspapers
13 Mapping the CIS
14 Heraldry
15 Sign Language
16 Today's Miracles
17 Taming Fire
18 Tools of the Past
19 To Be a Pioneer
20 Discovery
21 Report from Kitty Hawk
22 Making a Map of the World's
   Rain Forests
23 Creating a Time Line
24 The Sport of Falconry
25 Paper Money
26 Bank Documents
27 First Born
28 Create Some Cash
29 Snake Oil
30 Folk Medicine
31 Uncle Jumbo
32 Homemade Tortillas
33 Living Books
34 The Eleven (or Twelve)
   Penny Box

Appendix 7 Tradebook Connection Cards

Call It Courage. Armstrong Sperry. Macmillan, 1940. Mafatu, known as the Boy Was Afraid, set off in a canoe to prove his bravery.

From the Mixed-Up Files of Mrs. Basil E. Frankweiler. E. L. Konigsberg. Atheneum, 1967. Claudia convinces her brother Jamie to accompany her, and they run away to take up residence in the Metropolitan Museum of Art.

Frozen Fire. James Houston. Macmillan, 1977. Matthew and his friend Kayak search for Matt's father, who hasn't returned from a prospecting mission.

A Gathering of Days. Joan Blos. Scribner's, 1979. A New England girl's journal tells of the hardships and joys of pioneer life.

The House of Dies Drear. Virginia Hamilton. Macmillan, 1968. The Small family moves to Ohio and lives in a house that was an important station in the underground railroad. There Thomas and his father discover an age-old secret.

Island of the Blue Dolphins. Scott O'Dell. Houghton Mifflin, 1960. Karana, a young Native-American girl, is left on an island, where she learns to build shelter, find food, and fight the wild dogs.

Journey to Topaz. Yoshiko Uchida. Scribner, 1971. After the bombing of Pearl Harbor, Yuki and her family are evacuated first to a horsetrack and then to a desert camp.

Roll of Thunder Hear My Cry. Mildred D. Taylor. Dial, 1976. Cassie and her brothers wonder why only the white schools have buses and new books, and they watch their friend T. J. get mixed up with the wrong crowd.

The Shark Beneath the Reef. Jean Craighead George. HarperCollins, 1989. Tomas must decide whether to become a fisherman or to go to high school. Meanwhile, he only dreams of capturing the whale shark.

The Sign of the Beaver. Elizabeth George Speare. Houghton Mifflin, 1983. When Matt is left alone in the Maine wilderness, he is befriended by an Indian chief and his grandson, Attean.

The Summer of the Swans. Betsy Byars, Viking, 1970. Sara forgets about her own petty problems to search for her lost brother.

The Whipping Boy. Sid Fleischman. Greenwillow, 1986. Bored with his life, the prince runs away, taking his whipping boy with him.

Acknowledgments

Grateful acknowledgment is given to the following publishers and copyright owners for permission granted to reprint selections from their publications. All possible care has been taken to trace ownership and secure permission for each selection included.

Atheneum Publishers, an imprint of Macmillan, Inc.: *The Gold Coin* by Alma Flor Ada, illustrated by Neil Waldman, text copyright © 1991 by Alma Flor Ada, illustrations copyright © 1991 by Neil Waldman.

Bradbury Press, a division of Macmillan, Inc.: An excerpt entitled "The Fire Builder" from *Hatchet* by Gary Paulsen, copyright © 1987 by Gary Paulsen.

Carolrhoda Books, Inc., Minneapolis, MN: *Saving the Peregrine Falcon* by Caroline Arnold, photographs by Richard R. Hewett, text copyright © 1985 by Caroline Arnold, photographs copyright © 1985 by Richard R. Hewett.

Channel Press, Inc.: "A Gift for a Gift" from *A Children's Treasury of Folk and Fairy Tales,* edited and adapted by Eric Protter, translations copyright © 1961 by Channel Press, Inc.

Doubleday, a division of Bantam Doubleday Dell Publishing Group, Inc.: An excerpt entitled "Money Matters" from *Tough Tiffany* by Belinda Hurmence, copyright © 1980 by Belinda Hurmence.

Harcourt Brace Jovanovich, Inc.: "The No-Guitar Blues" from *Baseball in April and Other Stories* by Gary Soto, copyright © 1990 by Gary Soto.

HarperCollins Publishers: An excerpt entitled "Miracle at the Pump House" from *The Helen Keller Story* by Catherine Owens Peare, copyright © 1959 by Catherine Owens Peare. An excerpt entitled "Amaroq, the Wolf" from *Julie of the Wolves* by Jean Craighead George, text copyright © 1972 by Jean Craighead George. An excerpt entitled "It Can't Beat Us" from *The Long Winter* by Laura Ingalls Wilder, illustrated by Garth Williams, text copyright 1940 by Laura Ingalls Wilder, illustrations copyright 1953 by Garth Williams, copyright renewed © 1968 by Roger L. MacBride. "The Passenger Pigeon" from *I Am Phoenix: Poems for Two Voices* by Paul Fleischman, text copyright © 1985 by Paul Fleischman.

An excerpt entitled "The Shoeshine Stand" from *Shoeshine Girl* by Clyde Robert Bulla, copyright © 1975 by Clyde Robert Bulla. "The Courage That My Mother Had" from *Mine the Harvest: A Collection of New Poems* by Edna St. Vincent Millay, copyright 1945, 1946, 1947, 1952, 1953, 1954 by Norma Millay Ellis, copyright 1941 by Edna St. Vincent Millay, copyright 1949 by Curtis Publishing Co.

Holiday House, Inc.: An excerpt entitled "Back to the Drawing Board" from *The Wright Brothers: How They Invented the Airplane* by Russell Freedman, with original photographs by Wilbur and Orville Wright, copyright © 1991 by Russell Freedman.

Alfred A. Knopf, Inc.: "Mother to Son" from *Selected Poems of Langston Hughes* by Langston Hughes, copyright 1926 by Alfred A. Knopf, Inc., and renewed 1954 by Langston Hughes.

Little, Brown and Co.: *Saint George and the Dragon* retold by Margaret Hodges, illustrated by Trina Schart Hyman, text copyright © 1984 by Margaret Hodges, illustrations copyright © 1984 by Trina Schart Hyman.

Macmillan Publishing Co.: "The Coin" from *Collected Poems of Sara Teasdale,* copyright 1920 by Macmillan Publishing Co., renewed 1948 by Mamie T. Wheless.

Morrow Junior Books, a division of William Morrow & Co., Inc.: An excerpt from *Windows on Wildlife* by Ginny Johnston and Judy Cutchins, copyright © 1990 by Ginny Johnston and Judy Cutchins.

William Morrow & Co., Inc.: "What Money Is" from *Nickels, Dimes, and Dollars: How Currency Works* by R. V. Fodor, copyright © 1980 by Ronald V. Fodor.

Pantheon Books, a division of Random House, Inc.: "President Cleveland, Where Are You?" from *Eight Plus One* by Robert Cormier, copyright © 1965, by Robert Cormier.

Penguin USA: *The Hundred Penny Box* by Sharon Bell Mathis, illustrated by Leo and Diane Dillon, text copyright © 1975 by Sharon Bell Mathis, illustrations copyright © 1975 by Leo and Diane Dillon.

Charlotte Pomerantz, Writers House, Inc., and Jose Aruego: *The Day They Parachuted Cats on Borneo: A Drama of Ecology* by Charlotte Pomerantz, illustrated by Jose Aruego, text copyright © 1971 by Charlotte Pomerantz, illustrations copyright © 1971 by Jose Aruego.

Laurence Pringle: An excerpt entitled "A Natural Force" from *Natural Fire: Its Ecology in Forests* by Laurence Pringle, copyright © 1979 by Laurence Pringle.

G. P. Putnam's Sons: "The Sticky Secret" from *Micromysteries: Stories of Scientific Detection* by Gail Kay Haines, copyright © 1988 by Gail Kay Haines.

Steck-Vaughn Co.: An excerpt from *Protecting Wildlife* by Malcolm Penny, copyright © 1989 Wayland (Publishers) Ltd.

Photographs
25 Bernie Goedhardt
97 Goodyear Tire and Rubber Company
100 Goodyear Tire and Rubber Company
106 Culver Pictures, Inc.
159 Becky Mojica
215 Caroline Arnold, Richard Fish
233 Daniel Pomerantz (top)
297 Katy Peake
329 Beth Bergman
367 Marcia C. Bell, Pat Cummings

Illustration
12F–14F Van Howell
19F–29F Barbara Kelley
340–341 Luis Vasquez

Index